I AM THE MOST INTERESTING BOOK OF ALL
THE DIARY OF MARIE BASHKIRTSEFF VOL. 1

I AM THE MOST INTERESTING BOOK OF ALL
THE DIARY OF MARIE BASHKIRTSEFF VOL. 1

Translated by
Phyllis Howard Kernberger
with Katherine Kernberger

CHRONICLE BOOKS
SAN FRANCISCO

Printed in the United States of America.

Library of Congress Cataloging-in-Publication Data:
Bashkirtseff, Marie, 1858–1884.
    I am the most interesting book of all : the diary of Marie Bashkirtseff /
translated by Phyllis Howard Kernberger with Katherine Kernberger.
        p.   cm.
    Includes index.
    ISBN 0-8118-0224-8 (hc)
    1. Bashkirtseff, Marie, 1858–1884—Diaries. 2. Russians—France—Diaries. 3. Authors,
Russian—19th century—Diaries. I. Kernberger, Phyllis Howard. II. Kernberger, Katherine. III. Title.
DC34.5.R8B3713   1997
944.081'2'092—dc21
    [B]   96-39815
                                                                    CIP

Cover photograph: Marie Bashkirtseff, photographer and date unknown
Spine illustration: *Self-portrait with Palette,* Marie Bashkirtseff, 1883
Book and cover design: Carrie Leeb, Leeb & Sons
Composition: Blue Friday Type & Graphics

Distributed in Canada by
Raincoast Books,
8680 Cambie Street
Vancouver, B.C. V6P 6M9

10 9 8 7 6 5 4 3 2 1

Chronicle Books
85 Second Street
San Francisco, CA 94105

Web Site: www.chronbooks.com

ACKNOWLEDGMENTS

Hearty thanks to all those who worked with my mother over the almost 20 years she spent producing the translation—Edith Gay and Veronica Gregs, Kathryn Charon and Bernyl Sanden, in particular. Thanks also to Eric Bond Hutton, who helped locate notebook 89 in the Bibliothèque Cassole in Nice. I am indebted for financial, academic, and moral support to those who have helped me where I teach at Linfield College. I received a sabbatical for 1994-1995 and a grant for student assistance on the computer. My colleague Dawn Nowacki has helped me with names in Marie's impenetrable Cyrillic. Our research librarians have guided me to the far corners of Marie's intellectual and physical universe. My husband and my friends have fed me well at the end of long days and have patiently listened to talk of Marie.

I am particularly indebted to Annie Barrows's belief in the project and the unflagging help of Karen Silver and my copy editor David Featherstone at Chronicle Books for seeing me through.

I have used my mother's notes and letters in constructing the introduction to this volume, with the intention of staying as close as possible to her views of Marie.

For those interested in reading all 106 notebooks in French, the *édition integrale* is in progress, undertaken by professors Lucile LeRoy and Dominique Rochay. Publication date is as yet unknown.

TABLE OF CONTENTS

INTRODUCTION

Marie Bashkirtseff died in 1884, less than a month before the beginning of her twenty-sixth year. She had been writing in a diary, often daily, for eleven years. She had realized that her readers (sometimes "dear readers" and sometimes "damned readers") would be "posterity," since what she was writing was not only secret, but too intimate and revealing for her own time. As she wrote very early, "I have the idea that I may die."

In the more than one hundred years since it first appeared in print, Marie's journal has attracted numerous admirers and some detractors. What is the key to its continued appeal?

This edition of the journal is timely in certain ways and beyond the limits of time in others. The fact that Marie was known as a "new woman" in her time is of primary importance. In her century, Marie's flutterings toward freedom were rather successfully repressed by her family and by society, but they reveal her to us as a modern woman striving for liberation. The stream-of-consciousness mode of the diary gives us a glimpse of more than the diarist knew of her own intentions—certainly more than the filtered light of a lapsed century has exposed about her life.

Early in the diary, Marie remarks on the disadvantages of being a woman. Although she acquiesced in many conventions governing female behavior and, admittedly, hypocritically used other conventions to her own benefit, she energetically denounced many restrictions placed on girls and women. She complained bitterly about the educational and economic limitations imposed on women, even on those of the upper classes. As an ambitious woman, Marie looked for various avenues to attain fame; becoming a great singer or a great artist both appealed to her. Marriage was one way of rising in the world open to women. But the double standard of sexual conduct, ever-present in the gossip and example of associates of her family circle, gave all the freedom and privilege to men—before and after marriage.

Though her expectation of a large dowry might have attracted the sort of titled aristocrat she favored, the men (or boys) who actually fell in love with her were themselves too conventional, too dependent, or not wild and extravagant enough to satisfy her inflated notions of operatic or novelistic romance. She regretted that she could not herself propose to the men she wanted, but instead had to wait for them to notice her.

By 1880, at the age of twenty-one, she was losing her hearing and suffering increasingly from the signs of tuberculosis. She had changed many of her adolescent attitudes during the three years she had studied art at the Académie Julian. There, in association with other young women, most of them dependent on their art for their economic survival, she escaped the flattery and adulation paid her by her family and became more independent of them.

She dropped her earlier monarchist views and declared herself in favor of a republic; she joined the French women's rights movement, publishing articles under a pseudonym. Much of this growth in Marie's thought has been missing in previous versions of the journal.

Thus, one appeal of Marie's journal is that it shows us a woman—almost our contemporary—struggling to assert herself in a world uncomfortable with such female assertiveness. But Marie's story is also timeless in its appeal. The strivings of this ambitious, gifted, and tenacious spirit, clinging to its purpose in spite of diminishing expectations, failed hopes, and waning strength, impress the reader with an acute sense of loss for a stoic heroism which is at once tragic and ironic. Indeed, the Pyrrhic victory of Marie Bashkirtseff's achievement points to another loss as well: her death left the world one brilliant painter the fewer, removed from the French galaxy of end-of-the-century stars.

The fame Marie dreamed of has long been hers, in a way, but the real diary remains unknown and her image is still unclear. Yet we have always had the means of providing a better focus.

The publication history of the journal is complex, and I can only touch on a few points here. After Marie's death in 1884, her mother provided copies (not originals) of extracts of the journal to its first editor, André Theuriet. Her selection omitted much that seemed to her unsuitable in the opinions and actions of her daughter. His French edition (1887) and all subsequent English translations until Doris Langley Moore's *Marie and the Duke of H* (1966) were based on this biased selection.

Although it has been shelved at the Bibliothèque Nationale in Paris for more than half a century, the journal has been seen by only a few, since Madame Bashkirtseff donated it to the library upon her death in 1920. After 1925, a few editors (Borel, Ulmès) used the manuscript to expand the excerpts available, but never considered publishing the whole journal or correcting the inaccurate portrait given by Theuriet's two volumes. The diary was released for public viewing in the 1930s.

In 1966, Moore published *Marie and the Duke of H*, concerning the beginning of the diary and Marie's first "crush," the Duke of Hamilton. Moore's treatment of the first few books of the journal showed how much had been excised in the first French edition and subsequent translations. But Moore herself made many mistakes; the worst one was assuming that the man referred to as "Papa" was Marie's father and that he lived with her mother, her aunt, her cousin Dina, her brother Paul, and herself in Nice. "Papa" was Marie's grandfather, called so by his two daughters—Marie's mother and aunt—and therefore by Marie, Dina, and Paul. Much of Marie's grief comes from the ambiguous situation of these two Russian women living on the margin of good society, with their father and children but no husbands.

Moore is editorially critical of Marie in her assessment of the diarist's views concerning her family, greatly contrasting with Colette Cosnier's *Marie Bashkirtseff: Un Portrait sans Retouches* (1985). Cosnier incorporates unedited and unpublished excerpts from the journal itself into her French biography, speculating freely when interpreting events in the journal, pointing out inconsistencies in earlier works (including Moore's), and whetting appetites for more on Marie.

When my mother, Phyllis Kernberger, retired from teaching English at Pierce Junior College in 1973, she became interested in the journal of Marie Bashkirtseff. Years before, in a graduate class at the University of Southern California, she had come across the diarist in a chapter of George Bernard Shaw's *The Quintessence of Ibsenism*. Shaw identified Marie as an "unwomanly" woman, a *new* woman like some of Ibsen's heroines, who aspired to fame just as men did.

My mother began with a 1919 reprint of Mary J. Serrano's 1889 translation: *Marie Bashkirtseff: Journal of a Young Artist: 1860 [1858]-1884*. She then learned from reading Moore's *Marie and the Duke of H* that the original manuscript was in the Bibliothèque Nationale and wrote asking for microfilms of the 105 extant notebooks. She appealed to friends to help in translating (especially involved were Edith Gay, a native French speaker, and Veronica Gregs, a native Russian speaker) and typing of the manuscript (Kathryn Charon and Bernyl Sanden).

As my mother acquired various versions of the diary, she realized how completely Marie's true voice had been suppressed. Although she saw the true Marie, uncut and unvarnished, in the real journal, she never lost her commitment to let Marie's life appear with all its difficulties, many seemingly of her own making. She saw the vitality, honesty, and despair in Marie and wanted to alter the false picture given by the earlier editions.

In 1990, an article by Gwyneth Cravens deploring the lack of a modern and true translation of Marie's journal appeared in *The Nation*. When my mother wrote to Ms. Cravens, she suggested we contact Chronicle Books. Although we had not yet received a contract at the time of my mother's death in 1991, we were both convinced that her work would finally appear in print—and Marie's voice would speak out loud and bold. At last, it will.

GENEALOGY
OF THE BABANINES

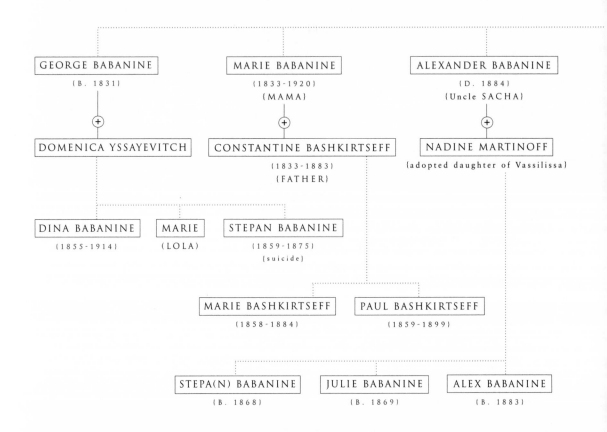

GEORGE BABANINE
(B. 1831)

MARIE BABANINE
(1833-1920)
(MAMA)

ALEXANDER BABANINE
(D. 1884)
(Uncle SACHA)

DOMENICA YSSAYEVITCH

CONSTANTINE BASHKIRTSEFF
(1833-1883)
(FATHER)

NADINE MARTINOFF
(adopted daughter of Vassilissa)

DINA BABANINE
(1855-1914)

MARIE
(LOLA)

STEPAN BABANINE
(1859-1875)
(suicide)

MARIE BASHKIRTSEFF
(1858-1884)

PAUL BASHKIRTSEFF
(1859-1899)

STEPA(N) BABANINE
(B. 1868)

JULIE BABANINE
(B. 1869)

ALEX BABANINE
(B. 1883)

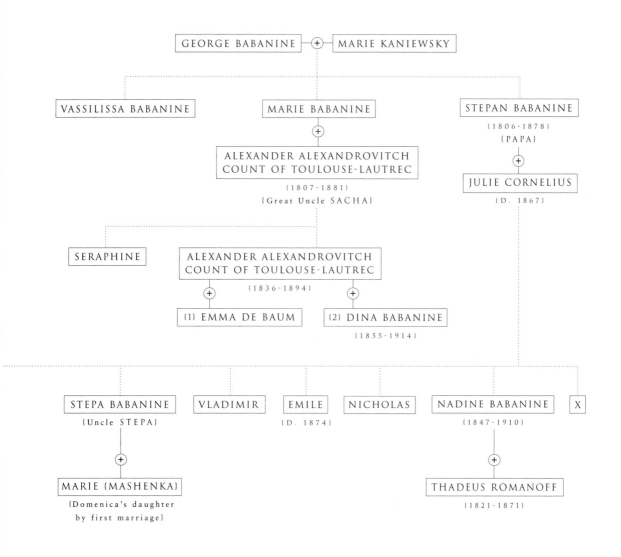

GEORGE BABANINE ⊕ MARIE KANIEWSKY

VASSILISSA BABANINE

MARIE BABANINE
⊕
ALEXANDER ALEXANDROVITCH
COUNT OF TOULOUSE-LAUTREC
(1807-1881)
{Great Uncle SACHA}

STEPAN BABANINE
(1806-1878)
{PAPA}
⊕
JULIE CORNELIUS
(D. 1867)

SERAPHINE

ALEXANDER ALEXANDROVITCH
COUNT OF TOULOUSE-LAUTREC
(1836-1894)
⊕   ⊕
(1) EMMA DE BAUM   (2) DINA BABANINE
(1855-1914)

STEPA BABANINE
{Uncle STEPA}
⊕
MARIE {MASHENKA}
{Domenica's daughter
by first marriage}

VLADIMIR

EMILE
(D. 1874)

NICHOLAS

NADINE BABANINE
(1847-1910)
⊕
THADEUS ROMANOFF
(1821-1871)

X

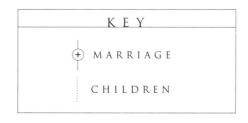

KEY

⊕ MARRIAGE

CHILDREN

CHRONOLOGY

Chronology of Marie Bashkirtseff (1858-1884)

1858   Born November 12, at Gavronzi near Poltava in the Ukraine: Marie Bashkirtseff, daughter of Constantine Bashkirtseff and Marie Babanine.

1859   Born at Gavronzi, Marie's brother, Paul Bashkirtseff.
Mrs. Bashkirtseff leaves her husband and returns to her parents, taking her children.

1870   Babanines leave Russia for Europe. Visits to Vienna, Baden-Baden, Geneva, Munich, and Italy.

1871   Family settles in Nice. Beginning of the Romanoff lawsuit.
Babanines / Bashkirtseffs are excluded from high society.

1872   Crush on Borreel, then on the Duke of Hamilton.

1873   Journal begun in Nice in January.
Marriage of the Duke of Hamilton.

1874   Studies.
Begins to notice Audiffret.
Trips to Paris, Spa, Ostend, London.
At Spa, flirts with Baron Gericke d'Herwynen and is courted by Count Mirzisky.
First signs of tuberculosis.

1875   Audiffret seems to court her.
Trips to Paris, Schlangenbad, Florence.

1876   Stay in Rome. Meets Pietro Antonelli, nephew of the Cardinal Antonelli, discussion of marriage.
Trip to Naples where Marie sees Larderel.
Return to Nice with Antonelli situation undecided.

Volume I ends here.

Stay in Paris where she meets the Deputy Paul de Cassagnac.
Visits her father in the Ukraine and brings him back.
Return to Nice.

1877   Trip to Naples.
        Various cures.
        Moves to Paris.
        Enrolls at the Académie Julian.

1878   Flirts with Cassagnac and interests herself in politics.
        Cassagnac marries.
        Cure in Soden.

1879   Trip to Nice for the Carnival.
        Cure at Dieppe.

1880   Prince Soutzo asks Marie to marry him.
        Exhibits at the Salon: "The Divorce Question"
        Cure at Mont-Dore. Open air studies.
        Becomes a republican and feminist.

1881   Contributes to *La Citoyenne* as "Pauline Orell."
        Exhibits at the Salon: "L'Atelier de jeunes filles."
        Gabriel Gery asks her to marry him.
        Trip to Russia. Romanoff lawsuit settled.
        Trip to Biarritz and Spain.

1882   Trip to Nice.
        Paintings: "Dina," "Fillette au parapluie," "Autoportrait."
        Illness gets worse.

1883   Exhibits at the Salon: "Jean et Jacques" and the "Tête au pastel" that receives
            an honorable mention.
        Sculpture "Nausicaa" and painting "Les Saintes Femmes."
        Goes almost deaf.
        Her father dies at Gavronzi.

1884   Exhibits at the Salon: "Le Meeting."
        Invited to the Russian Embassy.
        Coughs blood.
        Visits sick friend Bastien-Lepage.
        Stops keeping her journal on October 20th.
        Dies October 31 in Paris, aged 25.

MARIE BASHKIRTSEFF, 1884

MARIE'S "PREFACE"

[This is the preface she wrote in the 104th notebook of her journal, May 1, 1884, at the age of twenty-five in Paris.]

What is the use of lying or pretending? Yes, it is clear that I have the desire, if not the hope, of staying on this earth by whatever means possible. If I don't die young, I hope to become a great artist. If I do, I want my journal to be published. It cannot fail to be interesting. Does my anticipation of its being read spoil or destroy the merit of such a book? Not at all. I wrote for a long time without dreaming of being read. And now it is just because I hope that I will be read that I am absolutely sincere. If this book is not the exact, absolute, strict truth, it has no reason to be. Not only do I always say what I think, but never have I dreamed for one moment of hiding what could seem ridiculous or unfavorable about me. Anyhow, I look upon myself as too admirable for censure, even by me.

You can be sure, kind readers, that I show myself whole and entire. Perhaps I have only a slight interest for you; then don't think it's I you are reading about, but a human being who tells you all her impressions from childhood onwards. It is very interesting as a human document.

My journal begins with my thirteenth year but doesn't signify very much until my fifteenth or sixteenth; so to fill in the gap, I'm going to write a kind of preface that will afford some understanding of this human and literary document.

There! Let's suppose that I am famous, and begin!

I was born the 11th [elsewhere given as the 12th] of November, 1859. [Actually born November 12, *1858*, by the Russian calendar; November 24, 1858, by the Gregorian calendar, which is twelve days ahead of the Russian. The family celebrated her birthday each year on the day they *claimed* she would have been born if she had been a full-term baby—January 12 by the Russian calendar, January 24 by the western calendar. She learns later—in Book 83, December 29, 1878—from her father (but does not apparently accept his statement, as she ignores it here in her preface) that she *was* a full-term baby, suggesting that she was conceived before her parents had married and that all the mystification about her date of birth was intended to cover up that embarrassment.] It's horrifying just to write it, but I console myself by thinking that I certainly will not have any age when you read me.

General Paul Grigorievitch Bashkirtseff, my father's father, was of the minor nobility, but brave, tenacious, hard, even ferocious. He received his rank of general after the Crimean

War. Early in life he had married a young girl who was said to be the natural daughter of a very great lord. I don't know who he was. And I never saw her, because after she had borne the General four daughters (two of them hunchbacks) and a son, she died at the age of thirty-eight. The son was my father, Constantine. After leaving military service, the General proceeded to acquire a magnificent property, Gavronzi, near Poltava in the Ukraine. He was said to have bought it very cheap from some young people—minors—who were ruined. They also say he showed much avarice and little generosity in the matter. I suppose that's only human! My father gave up a mistress and two children by her to marry my mother, the beautiful Miss Marie Babanine. That was when Mama was twenty-two; she had refused several eligible suitors before she married my father, I've been told. Her family claims to be of the old provincial nobility, and Grandpapa Babanine boasted of being of Tartar origin from the first invasion, saying that Baba and Nina were Tartar words. I always laughed at that, taking a lot of his talk as probably mere bragging. He had been a contemporary of Lermontov, Pushkin, and that generation. I always thought of him as Byronic, a soldier, but literary, a poet. And he had had adventures, spending some time in the Caucasus.

When he married Grandmama, Julie Cornelius, she was only fifteen and charmingly sweet and pretty. That was what the family said, but I knew her only after she had had his nine children, grown old, and become enormous and coarse. Everybody agrees that she had been absolutely sacrificed to Grandpapa, a good-looking despot who boasted about the number of his children (forgive so few!). Mama and Nadianka were the only girls. Of the seven sons, George was the nightmare of us all. I'll get back to him.

But even by the time Mama had grown into a young girl, Grandpapa was already living an uncivilized life—as if to prepare for my torture. He went around the country dressed like a French peasant in a grey linen blouse, velvet trousers, and a panama hat, with an enormous diamond on his finger. And he pronounced the words *blouse* and *panama* with an affectation of gallicism. His was a nature that had failed; his success was terrible and null. He had wanted to be someone, but being nothing, he set about writing verses, which he didn't even publish, and took to liberalism.

Grandmama had always told me that I absolutely belonged in the great world of *society*, but I was realizing more and more how far short of my dreams our way of life was. Other people seemed to live such free, social, happy, orderly lives. But our family—Oh!

When my parents were married, my father passed for a very rich man because the General had made an immense fortune, according to the standards of Poltava. But Papa took Mama to Gavronzi, where his four sisters still lived at home. I was the first child, and then Paul was born.

By that time Mama had had all she could stand of the four sisters and her father-in-law, and she fled back to her own home, Tcherniakovka, without taking thought for anything. And after that nobody expected Constantine Bashkirtseff to provide his family with money or anything else.

I have spoken of George, who, I claim, assassinated us all. At nineteen that abominable and unhappy man had given himself up to every folly. Nevertheless, the family regarded him as a genius and adored him, whereas he trampled on the heads of everyone and made his debut with scandals. An encounter with the police would send him scurrying to hide behind his mother's petticoats in spite of the fact that he often beat her. He was very often drunk, but then he would stop drinking for a short time and become a charming cavalier, well-informed, witty, and seductive (being tall and handsome), drawing caricatures, making up delightful burlesque verses, and then—the brandy again and the horrors.

And everyone was there to wait on him.

At twenty he married Domenica, a beautiful thirty-six-year-old widow with some children of her own. Dina was the first child in her marriage with George. When Dina came into the world, Grandmama went and unceremoniously took her from her mother, keeping her for good. That was four or five years before I was born. As Mama adored her, and since Dina's real mother wasn't too attached to her, she remained with us. George's wife was a practical woman, full of fun, they say; and while adoring George, who abandoned her, she allowed herself some distractions. She and George had two more children, Lola and Stepan. The girl is married. The boy died at sixteen, as you will see.

After their separation, George spent a wasted life. Although he had all the instincts for grandeur and elegance (and financial juggling, too!), he and the other brothers performed some nice follies at Poltava, as elsewhere. They thrashed town officials and played tricks on everyone in a way that put up the backs of the whole province. The police interfered, and hence the affairs and proceedings that are still going on. Finally the governor was obliged to interfere, until my grandfather found that impertinent and began to rebel against all the governors of Poltava successively. In 1865 George was at last seized and shipped off to Viatka between two policemen. He had not committed any classified crime—not anything you could put your finger on—but only a thousand little dirty tricks that angered everyone.

And there began the foolish and terrible drama whose repercussions still follow us. My mother's family broke with all society, and all the strength, all the intelligence of the whole family had only one object—to save George. They went to the authorities; they wrote to ministers of the government; they spent their lives coming between George and the police.

As I said, after the first two years of her marriage, Mama took me and Paul and went to live with her own family. Young, ravishing, and intelligent, but ignorant of the world, she, like all the others, was employed in serving George. She made visits to governors, who received the beautiful provincial and then persecuted her with their unwelcome attentions.

Mama went to the Crimea to bathe in the sea. She was courted there, too, but she was good; yet all the while she was compromising herself, just by being there without her family. Actually, my readers, she had no idea of such things. You see, Mama was brought up in the country away from society. She never understood that it was imperative to keep up a certain dignity. Oh, never! And yet with all that she was very vain.

Beyond the small circle of Poltava she knew nothing. Whether she found herself at Petersburg or at the seaside, her beauty was sensational. Being courted, she was satisfied with that and never dreamed of going into society. Here in France, a well-born woman who doesn't go into society but is the center of gossip becomes déclassé. It was not so at all in Russia. There a lovely young woman coming from the depths of her province into a city was often in such a situation, and no one was shocked. Further on you'll see I'm not defending Mama; I'm just trying to tell things as they are. In 1862 she made a special journey to St. Petersburg with my aunt and George. Well, this tells something about my uncle: even when his sisters were supposed to be under his protection, he had to escape from St. Petersburg disguised as a woman! And Mama came home practically dying.

Of course I was left back there in the country with Dina and Grandmama, who idolized me. Along with her there was always my Aunt Nadianka to adore me whenever Mama didn't take her away. My aunt was younger than Mama, but not so pretty. She was sacrificed by everyone and sacrificed herself for everyone.

My father and my grandfather, the General, made attempts to see Mama again. One time when Paul and I had been brought to see our father, he carried us off and hid us in the country to force Mama to come back. But Grandmama and Mama's brothers hurried there and took us back by force.

I vividly remember the scene in the yellow pavilion at Gavronzi. Paul and I were in one room, Grandmama in another, and my father in a third, separated from the others by a corridor that divided the pavilion in two. Grandmama, furious, like a woman who spends her life shouting at servants, was vociferating insults. And my father, intimidated, was answering her without letting himself be seen. I remember he even remained comparatively respectful all the time. Since then I have thought that this was from a repugnance for vulgar scenes, because my nature has a good deal of his in it.

Then they took us away to Tcherniakovka.

In the meantime George's adventures were running their course. I don't remember whether it was in 1866, before we met Romanoff, or 1869, just before we left for Vienna, that Domenica obtained a change of the town of that miserable creature's exile. Of course! It had to be 1866. They transported the dear treasure from Viatka to Akhtirka, a terrible hole where there are holy relics and where people go on pilgrimages.

And there this monster reigned and commanded and sometimes amused himself by coming to read horrid books to Mrs. Brenne, my French teacher. I listened to all that and understood, but without its making me think of anything as to myself.

It was there that they caught my Uncle Romanoff, later to be my Aunt Nadya's husband, a rich bachelor of forty. Actually, it was Uncle George's idea. (He had already tried to get the fortune of Grandpapa's sister, Vassilissa, but after a lot of chicaneries he got only twelve or fifteen thousand rubles of her money.)

Well, it was at Akhtirka that all of the family except Grandpapa installed themselves when they got George away from Viatka. And it was there they found Romanoff. (He had a sister he hadn't seen in twenty years who was still richer than he.) Then the family set themselves to entangle him; it was Mama who was brought to the fore, very flirtatious. And he fell in love with her. Then they moved on to Kharkoff. Well, Romanoff followed them.

Absolutely unversed in the ways of the world and egged on by George, they led a life there that was unbecoming. Romanoff would send tickets every evening for boxes at the theater, where we all paraded ourselves; and between the acts he had trays with fruits and candies sent to us. George fell in love with one of the actresses and had the family receive her at the house.

We went to Yalta in the Crimea to bathe in the sea, and again Romanoff followed. Here it was that Mama met the emperor. She knew that he used to pass a post-station several versts from where we were living. Mama went there, taking me with her; and the emperor, noticing this pretty woman, spoke to her for about a quarter of an hour. Amusing himself with this very enthusiastic subject, he promised he would see her at Yalta. Mama always had had much attention paid to her, and three or four times the emperor spoke to her briefly in public places there in Yalta. But soon he'd had enough of it, as she was constantly in his way. But the interest he had shown in her had brought a number of generals of the Court to the house; they wanted to make sure of being seen by one who might become a favorite.

The family talked a lot about Romanoff, and when we returned from Odessa he came to stay at the same hotel we were living in. Then, one fine morning, everyone said that it must be finished off, that my aunt would never find a better match. All that was necessary was Monsieur's consent. Since he was a big silly accustomed to us all and not the least in the world Mama's lover—no matter what anyone may have said, that was not true—even I employed my nine-year-old's eloquence toward the match.

We got them married, and they went back to Tcherniakovka ahead of us. But it seems that although we had got them married, they were not really married at all! (It was like Mama's leaving Poltava.) My aunt protested so strongly that the rest of us returned within a few days, and three days after our arrival Grandmama suddenly died.

Romanoff became ill with fits of delirium and madness. (Madness ran in the Romanoff family.) We took care of him very well. That was in 1867, I remember.

For a long time after that I was still under the impression of Grandmama's death. I had loved her very, very much, and she had spent hours telling me I was divine. She called me by the tenderest, craziest names! Poor Grandmama. If only I had been her only care! But there was that awful George whom she insisted upon regarding as "an unhappy child" and whom she finally bequeathed to Mama on her deathbed. Mama believed from that time forth that she must obey the wishes of her dying mother. She sacrificed her reputation, her children, and her own personal life to the monstrosities of that ignoble wretch. And as always at Tcherniakovka the family was united for George. It was nothing for the other brothers to drop everything and go four or five hundred leagues in a post chaise for George. And they even wined and dined policemen in the hope that those men would be kinder to him. Bah!

I mentioned Grandpapa's sister Vassilissa and George's attempt to get her fortune. When she was beautiful, rich, young, elegant, charming, and witty and could have married, she didn't. Then, when she adopted a little orphan, people thought her ridiculous, even a bit crazy. The orphan was Nadine Martinoff, who, when she was fourteen, made haste to leave her protectress to come and live at Grandpapa's, where there were more distractions than at home.

Furthermore, as the little one had some twenty thousand rubles, my Uncle Alexander, being very practical (and she likewise) indoctrinated her. They were married when she was fifteen-and-a-half years old. They made an excessively rapacious, covetous, and happy couple. Grandpapa was furious, but then all his sons had married without telling him. However, Grandpapa didn't worry too much, being very self-absorbed and inclined to pose, as I have said.

When Vassilissa used to come on a visit to Tcherniakovka, the house was all dressed up for her arrival. The first time she stayed, the terrace was trimmed with plants, and an air of festivity reigned in the house. Spoiled by her own father, she had in the past dominated everyone; and her brother, Grandpapa, still paid her the respect and admiration he always had. Then, one time she came as usual for a few weeks; and later, while she stayed on, they took away the plants from the terrace. She still stayed. She stayed forever, forever venerated, but less and less until Grandpapa's departure, after which her adoptive daughter and Alexander secluded her in a miserable room of an old pavilion where she remained until she died, abandoned by everyone.

In 1870 Romanoff was much better and no longer out of his mind, and free with his big fortune. We all left—all except Alexander and Nadine—to go abroad, a dream long cherished by George and also by Mama. (Of Mama I must say I believe she was really good. Hers is a nature that scattered itself about in inconsequences, but would never go as far as—the deed.)

First we went to Vienna, where we stayed a month, intoxicated with the novelties, the beautiful stores, and the theaters. There George found a streetwalker and took her along with him. Grandpapa also was eager to sample this Europe he had known only from books. Alexander and his wife, on the other hand, remained in the country, masters of everything and making their fortune by stealing from Grandpapa on all sides. From that time on they sent him only the most insignificant sums and kept all the rest for themselves.

We got to Baden-Baden in June, at the height of the season. The city was full of luxury, full of Paris. Here is how many we were: Grandpapa, Mama, Mr. and Mrs. Romanoff, Dina, Paul, and I, and the angelic and incomparable Lucien Walitsky.

Walitsky was a Russian Pole without any exaggerated patriotism, a good-natured, very winning man who drew caricatures in the studio in Akhtirka, where he was the district doctor. He had been at the university with Mama's brothers and was frequently at our house, coming three or four times a day when we were in the country at Tcherniakovka. Each of his visits was a pure joy for everybody. He had an admirable brotherly and sacred worship for Mama, who treated him like a dear child.

As we were going abroad, it was necessary to have a doctor for Romanoff and even for Mama, who liked to think of herself as ill and sometimes really was. They brought Walitsky along, promising him the fixed salary usual in such cases. I really believe that he received almost nothing of it, too delicate to ask and contenting himself with a few sous now and then to pay his tailor, to whom he owed several hundred francs when he died. This admirable man was always for each of us a second self.

Naturally it was at Baden that I first understood society and elegance and that I was tortured by vanity. Near the Casino there were several groups of children, and right away I found out which was the fashionable one and longed to become part of it. Those children, who imitated the grownups, noticed Dina and Paul and me, and a little girl, Bertha Boyd, came to talk to me. I was so happy about that that I talked too much and said so many silly things that the children made outrageous fun of me.

Bertha, twelve, was English. She had several charming older sisters who had a fine social position in Baden; they enjoyed pride of place. She was linked with all the children of the aristocratic families, who, of course, knew her family. Mine didn't know anybody and devoted themselves to roulette and thirty-forty.

Bertha had a boyfriend of thirteen named Remy de Gonzales-Moreno. The father, Mr. Gonzales, fell in love with Mama, and Remy would slip away from Bertha from time to time to make eyes at me. Mama's free manners had inspired confidence in the Argentinian republican, and that made his wife jealous. And here one sees an almost incredible naïveté in Mama: she simply made the acquaintance of Mrs. Gonzales, who behaved very coolly toward her. But Mama redoubled her friendliness, thinking that the wife could not feel differently toward her than the husband who had been so charming. When they were leaving Baden, Mama went to the station to see them off. The lady told her in a very frigid way, which I saw very clearly, that it embarrassed her to deprive Mama of her outing on such a beautiful day. But Mama answered that it gave her a great pleasure to see such charming people off. When I remember what she said and the way she said it, I am still amazed. Mr. Gonzales was astonished and proud about it all because he believed he had had some kind of success. And later, after some rude surprises, this man ended by understanding Mama and becoming our friend.

But the Franco-Prussian War broke out on July 28 [1870] and chased us from Baden to Geneva. However, I have not yet told enough about Russia or about me, and this is my story. According to the custom of families like ours living in the country, two governesses were engaged, one Russian, to teach us music and dancing, the other French, to teach us French. The first of these Russians I remember was a Mrs. Melnikoff, a society woman, educated, romantic, and separated from her husband. She had decided to become a governess after reading a number of novels about women who had done that. She was a friend of the family and was treated as an equal. All the men paid court to her, and she eloped one fine morning after hearing some romantic story. (We are very romantic in Russia.) She could have said goodbye and left naturally, but the Slavic character, tied in with French civilization and novels, is a funny thing.

My gullible and sentimental family was sure that her departure made me ill. They looked at me with sympathy, and I think Grandmama even made me a special soup always served to invalids. I felt that I was getting rather pale before this show of sensibility.

Though I was rather puny, thin, and not pretty, that fact did not prevent everybody's considering me a being who must fatally, absolutely become someday the most beautiful, the most brilliant, and the most magnificent. It was about that time that Mama went to a Jew who told fortunes. He said, "You have two children. The boy will be like everybody else, but the girl will be a star." Again, one evening at the theater a gentleman laughingly said to me, "Show me your hands, Miss," and turned to Mama saying, "Oh, the way she is gloved she will undoubtedly be a terrific flirt." That made me very proud.

I think that from the age of three (I was nursed until I was three and a half) my poor head was filled with aspirations toward greatness. My dolls were always queens or kings. Everything I thought about and everything people said around Mama always seemed to refer to these grandeurs, which inevitably would be mine.

At five I would dress myself in Mama's laces, and with flowers in my hair I would dance on the balcony. I was the great danseuse Maria Petipa, and everyone in the house was there to look at me. Paul was almost of no importance, and Dina didn't resent me, although she was older and the daughter of their beloved George.

After Mrs. Melnikoff went, I had Miss Sophie Dolgikoff, aged sixteen, as a governess. Holy Russia! And there was one more French woman, Mrs. Brenne, who wore her hair in an old-fashioned Restoration style, had pale blue eyes, and seemed very sad with her fifty years and her consumption. I loved her very much. She made me draw, but I made only one drawing for her, a little church in outline! Anyway, while the grownups were playing cards, I often drew on the green tablecloth. Mrs. Brenne died in 1868 in the Crimea.

The little Russian, Dolgikoff, treated just like any other child of the house, was about to marry a young man whom Walitsky had brought there, a young man known for the number of times he had been jilted. Everything seemed to be going very well when one evening, upon entering her room, I saw Miss Sophie crying like a lost soul with her nose in the cushion. Everyone came in to ask what was wrong. Finally, after many tears and sobs, the poor child ended by whimpering, "I can never. No, never!" And then more tears flowed. And everybody kept on asking, "Why?" and offering kind advice. "Because . . . because I can never get used to his face!" Her fiancé heard all that from the drawing room, and an hour afterwards he had locked his trunk, soaking it with tears as he did so, and left. It was the seventeenth marriage he had missed. Sophie's lament had come so much from the heart that I understood it very well even then. Why, it would have been truly horrible to marry a man whose face you couldn't get used to!

When the Franco-Prussian War brought us to Geneva in 1870, I vowed to pay Bertha Boyd back for slighting me. Every night before going to bed, I said this prayer in a very low voice: "My God, make me friends with Bertha and let me have cavaliers to pay court to me." The whole prayer began with the our Father. Then I said the Hail Mary and then, "My God, let me never have the smallpox, let me be pretty, let me have a beautiful voice, let me be happy in marriage, and let Mama live a long time."

At Geneva we stayed at the Hotel de la Couronne, on the lake shore. It was charming. I was given a drawing teacher who brought me models to copy—little houses in which the windows were made like trunks of trees, unlike anything I had seen in real chalets. I refused to use the models, so the nice old man told me to copy the view from the window.

By that time we were moving to the family pension Überkoller, opposite Mont Blanc. Then I scrupulously copied what I saw of Geneva and the lake, but that all stopped there, why I don't remember. In Baden we had had time to have our portraits made from some photographs, and these paintings seemed to me ugly and overworked in their effort to be pretty.

I started writing this diary during January of 1873 at Nice, when I'd just turned fourteen. That was when I used to see the Duke of Hamilton taking his way past our house on the Promenade des Anglais toward No. 77, where Amelia Gioja lived. He would be driving at breakneck speed in a low-slung carriage pulled by four white horses and usually lighting a cigar when I saw him. My family said Gioja was his mistress. Three years before that I had seen him in Baden-Baden, in 1870, the year we left Russia. But at that time I was too young to appreciate him the way I did when I was a little older.

Actually, I thought I was in love with young Borreel, who lived near us on the Promenade; and it was a considerable time before I could bring myself to reject all thoughts of him and fill my mind with Hamilton, to wait for the time when I could marry him. But it was no idle girlish crush that led to my decision. My age had little to do with it. I knew I would have to wait until I was sixteen or maybe even eighteen. But the Duke's position, his title, his magnificent person, and what I regarded as his achievements decided me to give up all earlier ideas regarding Borreel. Not that I had the slightest acquaintance with either man, but a girl can dream. And the more I dreamed, the more I fell in love with the unknown Duke, so prestigious, so rich—the most romantic of all the young lords of England.

And I should say, too, that although we were all delighted to be traveling abroad, our leaving Russia was connected with Uncle Romanoff in two different ways. We could not have left without him, as he was the only rich one among us; it was also because of him that our departure from Russia had become a necessity. As soon as he and my Aunt Nadya were married, Romanoff's family began to make trouble. His sister's husband, before that time safe and secure, suddenly realized that almost half of the enormous wealth of his wife's family had slipped into other hands. He and she started a lot of gossip about my family, charging entrapment and other outrageous things against the Babanines. They told terrible lies about us. Romanoff fell very ill almost at once after the wedding and was a long time recovering. It was not until after we had come to Nice that Uncle Romanoff fell ill again, and after another long sickness the poor man died. Immediately the sister and her husband filed a lawsuit to prevent my aunt from getting her husband's money although the sister was even richer than Romanoff.

The second disaster of our life in Nice was that one of my father's sisters, Mrs. Tutcheff, already lived there. She gossiped about us everywhere, spreading the news of the lawsuit and other stories about Mama and accusing her of such frightful behavior that almost nobody in society received us in spite of the fact that she lied at every turn.

My many problems connected with the family show how important it was for me to try to find a way to be rich and famous in my own right—to be independent of them. It looked as if a good marriage should be the way out.

I began my first notebook on August 6, 1872, and I alone can read it because I used a secret sign-writing to protect it from inquisitive eyes. I used circles, crosses, dashes, and dots, a code language no one else knows. It helped me recall my past impressions and emotions and protected the book from "eavesdroppers" in case I got careless with it. I always put such writings in a safe place, such as behind a painting or under a stack of clothes in the bottom of a dresser drawer. I find great pleasure in reading and rereading what I've written when I can be alone. Sometimes it's fun, of course, to read certain passages aloud to others.

May 1st, 1884, Paris

MRS. BASHKIRTSEFF (HOLDING DOG)
AND MARIE AS A CHILD

B O O K   O N E

Notebook No. 1
[These pages are translated from Pierre Borel's *Le Visage Inconnu*, published in 1925 after Mrs. Bashkirtseff's will had given her daughter's diary to the Bibliothèque Nationale. Notebook number 1 of the diary has since disappeared from the library's holdings and exists only in the reduced extracts offered by Borel.]

January 11, 1873. This evening we attended the [Verdi] opera *Un Ballo in Maschera.* There were many people in the theater, but in spite of that I was sad.

January 12, 1873. We went to the Public Gardens in the afternoon for the music. Sitting in the carriage as we listened, we talked a lot about the Duke of Hamilton. In the evening we went to the Français. The program was *The Joy of the House* and *The Italian Straw Hat*, by Ravel. It was a full house. My pretty blue dress was very much noticed.

January 13, 1873 (Our Russian New Year). We went to church and paid visits. Tomorrow, the Floreal Ball.

Last night, putting a mirror under my pillow after the Russian custom, I dreamed among other things that we were looking for a man through whom we could meet the Duke of Hamilton, and that we absolutely wanted to make his acquaintance because we wanted to show ourselves at the races with someone from high society.

January 14, 1873. This Floreal Ball brought out a lot of people, but there weren't many pretty dresses. I wore pink. A good many people came to our loge. Borreel doesn't attract me any more. And to think how much interested I was in him! Actually I believe it's the way he walks that displeases me. I had always seen him in a carriage or on horseback until last night.

January 15, 1873. A good horseback ride. In the evening the opera. On our way to the theater I saw the Duke of Hamilton's carriage. Oh, if only he would come to our house, I would be beautiful that day!

January 18, 1873. The Club Méditerranée. A crowd of people. Mama danced. In the evening at the Français for *The Martyrs of the Inquisition*, by Meran. Borreel came close to me but I felt nothing. Strange!

January 19, 1873. From the carriage all at once I saw the Duke of Hamilton for the first time in weeks. His carriage passed ours on his way to Gioja's. I began beating time with my foot. I was blushing, but less than usual, thank God. It was close to raining, and the carriage was half closed. Miss Collignon [Marie and Dina's current governess in Nice] said, almost severely, "Don't do that, Marie. It annoys me so much!" She saw that I was blushing, too. He passed quickly looking straight ahead.

January 20, 1873. On the Promenade (green dress, grey jacket). It rained, but still there were a lot of people. I was going toward the Public Gardens, as was the Duke of Hamilton. I saw him all at once. He was with someone. I couldn't look at him. I turned around and stayed behind Miss Collignon to hide my blushing. He wore a brown hat and a white rain cape. I saw him only for a minute, but he is beautiful and I love him.

The other has paled before him. He is nothing anymore. But the Duke of Hamilton is everything. I asked God to let me see him more often, and He has granted it. What if He could grant me now the other indulgence I have asked so that I wouldn't blush when I see him?

January 24, 1873. Today is my birthday. [See note in Preface.] I just turned fourteen [actually fifteen]. We went with Mama to the Howards'. I stayed with the children in the garden. On returning, I went to the terrace. What a beautiful view you get from there! But Miss Collignon was calling, "Come, Marie!" just at the moment the Duke of Hamilton was passing on the Promenade. He looked the way he did the other day. He was very beautiful, but he was out of sight without seeing me, pretty as I was with my green skirt and my grey jacket. It's a shame! How many times have I come here alone on this terrace hoping to see him! One day it was dark, the sky was sad, a deep fog covered the sea and a part of the city, and it was very humid. It was just at the moment I was leaning on the railing of the terrace. He was sitting low in the carriage to light a cigar and didn't see me.

It was then that I reflected, "A man of thirty years, a man who knows nothing except races, horses, shooting, and hunting, and who adores good wine and bad women, goes to his mistress, lights a cigar with a quiet and satisfied air; and I, fool that I am, look at him and imagine that he can see only me!" I thought about all that and also that in spite of everything I had been very happy since the day I'd seen him last. Deep down, that was the thing I desired most, seeing him.

I still had my vision of the Duke when I buried my head against Miss Collignon, whom I kissed several times because I was so happy inside.

January 26, 1873. Today we saw an enormous number of people at the music. As we were returning to the villa by the Promenade, we saw a yacht with a huge British flag. Right away I guessed it was the Duke's. Behind it there was another that belongs to his cousin. At the moment when the Duke's ship passed near the Promenade, I recognized some ladies on the bridge and the red umbrella of Mrs. Witgenstein. The two yachts were sailing toward Monte Carlo.

On the terrace I was reading the program for the first two days of the races. The horses of the Duke were not listed.

January 29, 1873. I had a spendid horseback ride. Then I did my music assignment and in the evening studied English.

January 30, 1873. Mama and Dina went to an afternoon concert at the Hotel Chauvain for the benefit of a poor Russian. As they were leaving the house, I saw Gioja in a closed carriage with a man, and it was not the Duke.

The other one, Borreel, continues to turn around to look at me when our carriage goes by. I am grateful to him because he teaches me how to make myself interesting and to make myself loved, whether I notice him or not.

February 1, 1873. I have been thinking very clearly about my feelings; nothing is mixed up in them for Borreel; I'm not in love with him. Here is how I explain all that, I love them both—Borreel and the Duke—the same way. So I can give my preference now only to the richer and to the one who will love me the best, since in a way they are equal for me.

However, I know that I love the Duke better, not because he is a duke, but for all his qualities. I am sure that if I prefer him, well, all that gives me as great a pleasure as when I see Borreel. I cannot endure it without seeing one or the other. If, when I see Borreel, I am joyous, then equally, when I see the Duke, a ray penetrates my heart.

It's funny, such a state!

All things considered, I still prefer the Duke. I would so much like to know his age; I believe he is twenty-eight. Oh, if he would only leave that woman! She doesn't love him. Tomorrow she will love someone else who will give her money. She will ruin the Duke. My God, help me!

February 2, 1873. Tomorrow the races! What a joy! Yesterday he passed on the Promenade in front of my terrace. He certainly did not see me. He was in a closed carriage. But I saw him. And isn't that the joy I prayed to God for?

February 5, 1873. The day of the races at the Var was the biggest day of the season for me. This morning, ten horses led by jockeys passed in front of the villa. My God, is there anything more beautiful than a racehorse?

Although the Duke is commissioner of the races, I didn't see him. I was in the tribune with the highest society of Nice! I saw Borreel. He was dressed well, but he never dresses as well as the Duke. He is decidedly too fat. However, the Duke is fatter than he is, but I love him. So there it is. . . .

Oh! If he would abandon that woman! I saw her in black in a closed carriage, alone. She didn't come to the races. Where is she? And I haven't seen the Duke today. Oh, I hope I'll see him at the pigeon shoot tomorrow!

February 6, 1873. At noon we were at Monaco. A big day for me, bigger than that at the races, because the Duke should be there. If he were, he'd be in the shoot, whereas he doesn't take part in the races even though he is a commissioner. Make it happen, God, that he will make my acquaintance.

Of all that I write I try to correct everything I can. Not the spelling. That would be too difficult. I don't correct myself. I make mistakes, I tell my feelings, and I hardly correct the errors of places and persons. Today my style is not sublime, but a few months ago it was simply abominable. My little tricks and explanations are funny, and I blush at them, but I leave everything. This is an important document for literature and posterity. [Added later: When I was writing the first notebooks, it seemed to me that they would be cited as literary models. What a mistake, I know now!]

At the pigeon shoot I learned that the Duke was ineligible for competition—because of his superiority. Good. I won't see him again. I don't have any luck.

How sad that I didn't see the Duke as I wanted to so much! I started the day deliciously, but what sadness in the evening! His yacht was sailing in front of the terrace all the time the shoot was going on.

The grandstand reminded me of the tribunes in Baden and Nice. My God, make me see the Duke tomorrow at the races, I ask you by supreme grace.

February 7, 1873. Now I know why the Duke doesn't want to see me. He is too occupied with Gioja. I had believed that he would leave her. But that was only a dream. She knows him too well. He is too used to her; she has so many ways of holding him, and she knows so many tricks. However, a while back he looked at me, and I blushed. Perhaps he felt that I love him. How funny that is!

This evening at the Club Méditerranée there was a concert given by the Countess Vigier of songs from *La Sonnambula*, by Bellini. I wore pink, and my hair was dressed high in a very becoming style. The Vigier voice is a little worn, a little shrill, but magnificent. All of Nice was there except Borreel. But I was so happy to have seen the Duke that I didn't even care about seeing Borreel for myself! I wished, however, that he could have seen me for himself because I was truly very pretty.

February 8, 1873. Today, all at once I heard someone whistling behind me. It was the Duke. He whistled the way he did when I first saw him in Baden. (Even in writing that my heart beats fast.) I turned around and he saw me. Then I blushed and my heart started beating like a hammer.

He wore a suit made in the style of my jacket, a blue shirt, and a brown hat. He remained a moment near me. Never had I imagined a happiness so great! My God, make him always stop like that, very close to me.

I made a mistake when I said I thought he was fat. Nearby he looks very nice, and how sweet his voice is, especially when he talks French, and—how majestic his face is! I also believed he had red hair (a color I detest). But he doesn't; his hair is the color of mine and gracefully waved.

What I want now is for him to know that I love him. He spoke to some beautiful ladies. When he came back on my side of the garden, our eyes met again. What happiness!

One day, perhaps, if God wishes, I shall be his wife. I'll be reading all that I can't see now behind that impressive forehead. I'll remember my feelings, and I'll probably make fun of myself about them.

Oh, but no. It's too great a happiness. However, if that happened, my prayers of all the days would be granted! I am so happy to have seen him and so happy that he looked at me that, in spite of myself, I hope. And yet, it is sad to say, I am not and never shall be his wife! Besides, how can I have hoped for such a thing? But what a deep happiness for me to write today's joy on pages for myself alone. My God, again once more, hear me: let him know what I wish! Hear my voice and grant my prayer. (It's tender and nice, what I say there.)

February 9, 1873. It's curious how I have pleasure in reading only what I write about him. All the pages composing this notebook are perhaps stupid; but for me, the evening when I read them again alone in my room will be a great, a delicious pleasure. And I thank myself for having noted all these impressions; these lines talk to me of him. I love them also for that.

Oh! How wrong I have been to imagine (never having wanted to look at Gioja because of jealousy) that she was ugly! I saw her just now, that abominable woman; she is beautiful, more beautiful than I am. I shall never be completely beautiful. I'll be nice sometimes. That's all. This woman, I detest her, but the day when she will no longer be my rival I'll not have any more hate for her. On the contrary, I love the Duke. And to think that my love is condemned to remain unknown to him! Tomorrow, my God, it's the pigeon shoot. I'll see him, won't I?

February 10, 1873. I didn't go to the pigeon shoot. That gave me a lot of sorrow. I cried like an animal at the piano, in the afternoon, at dinner, and even in the evening. I regretted the shoot, but above all it was the missed opportunity to see the Duke that hurt me.

February 11, 1873. For the Promenade I wore a black velvet dress and a hat with roses. There was a regatta of more than sixty little boats and an immense crowd watching. Later on I went alone for a drive with my dog Prater beside me. I was looked at a lot. I saw Gioja walking, and then Borreel looked at me. I pretended not to see him, which must have annoyed him. And I looked very good. It seems to me that I'll be very pretty when I grow up. But how satisfying it would be if *he* fell in love with me. That would amuse me. What a shame that he doesn't see me when all the others admire me. We came back at 3:30 in the morning. I was very tired, but tomorrow I have to get up at eight. Yet I wanted absolutely to write my impressions before going to bed.

Borreel was at this ball. Again he seemed indifferent. Yet I would have been furious if he had danced with anyone. I was annoyed to see him courting a pretty Scottish girl. He wasn't gay, but only tender and faithfully in love. Oh! How I would like him to fall in love with me to punish him!

February 12, 1873. As I was walking in the Public Gardens, I suddenly found myself face to face with the Duke. He looked at me and I looked at him. In my mind I was saying to him, "Now that nobody sees me, I speak to you. I would like to make you understand through my look all that I feel inside for you." He looked at me again with a lot of curiosity and went on with slow steps. I could have seen him again by turning around. But I was satisfied already. When he passed us again, Hélène, who was with me said, "Look, there's the Duke of Hamilton. He looks like a butcher!"

She can say what she wants; I think she likes him too! I know from myself that we talk like that about men who please us.

I am satisfied with my English lessons, which I started on January 12, 1872, here in Nice with Miss Collignon, and with my Italian, which I began on March 17 last year with Miss Micheletti.

B O O K   T W O

Book 2 of my Journal
Begun Sunday, February 16, 1873
Ended Thursday, March 12, 1873
Concerning Marie Bashkirtseff
Promenade des Anglais, No. 51, Villa d'Aquaviva, Nice
I pray the Editor to suppress the repetitions about the Duke of Hamilton.

Sunday, February 16, 1873. At the church while we were stopped at the music, Borreel passed us in a two-horse carriage. He tipped his hat, greeting Mama as he drove by. I blushed and asked, "Why did he salute you, Mama?"

"He was showing respect," she told me.

Well, I reflected, if he greets her, that means he doesn't want to avoid me. If he wanted to he could very well have done nothing, not having been introduced. Or maybe he wanted to see the reaction on my face. Later he drove past us slowly several times. He was really handsome today! He pleased me a lot, but I must not show it.

That moustache of his makes him look like my dog Prater. I said so once, and ever afterwards they teased me about it, and because of that I blush when I see him. I hoped he would find a way to be introduced. And then if some day he suggested that I loved him, I could say no, but that I had found a certain resemblance between him and my dog. Then maybe he would like to be loved by me, and maybe he would love me. I wonder whether the Duke is at Gioja's house, because she didn't go out today.

Monday, February 17, 1873. Today in the Public Gardens Borreel drove his carriage around us and in front of us several times, and because I was blushing, the others concluded I was in love with him. How nice! That way, I told myself, their suspicions about my feeling for the Duke will disappear! And so for that reason I am satisfied with my blushing for the Dutchman. If I could always see them both at the same time, it occurred to me, everyone would believe I was blushing for Borreel. The Duke would notice and believe it was for him, as it really would be; and Borreel would be delighted because when I blush I'm very pretty. But when I think of Hamilton, his height, his look, his wide chest, his voice, I love only him. I am praying to God to let me see him once a week. But *love*? Really, I am abusing the most charming word in the world! However, I was very glad to see Borreel today because, as I have already put him out of my mind, I was able to put on some superb and independent airs.

If you think I don't know what I want, you're mistaken. I was praying for Hamilton, yes. But if Borreel had been the Baron Finot, as I thought he was when I first saw him, and if I had got interested in him before I saw Hamilton, I would have been the happiest of mortals. But his having no title or fortune made me realize that as a husband he could not satisfy my caprices, and without that I would be unhappy and I would make him unhappy.

While I was out, I discovered where the Duke of Hamilton lives in Nice: I saw Gioja with the little boy going to the Grande Bretagne Hotel to see him. During our promenade we saw Borreel many times. He bowed, stayed at the side of our carriage, looked at us, and (almost) followed our carriage. How happy I am, and how good God is! Oh! I thought, if He will just give me Hamilton! (even while telling myself that the Duke is too much attached to Gioja). She was superb today—not so much with beauty as with her ways and her thousand artifices. I know he is hers, and it is a cruel conviction. How funny it is! I see Borreel: I like him, I admire him, I love him; and that suffices until the Duke appears, only to destroy all that and make me think only about him.

I have a big worry on my mind: ever since I erased the name of Hamilton from the map of Scotland, I've been afraid of the day (which must come) when we reach Scotland in our study of geography. What will Miss Collignon say? I know I'll blush.

Friday, February 21, 1873. I'm very unhappy today—in an awful state, in fact. If it continues, I don't know what I'm going to do. I'm afraid all the time that the journal will be discovered and my secret about the Duke will be known. Then I think about the city of Hamilton I scratched from the map in my book, and I dread the day when we'll study Scotland. How happy are those who have no secrets! If they knew what I have to endure for it! I foolishly erased the name. I don't know why. It would have been better to leave it underlined. It was less conspicuous that way. But Miss Collignon knows about it. I am expecting the terrible day when I'll be obliged to mark the cities of Scotland! Oh, my God, save me! Make me calm!

Sunday, February 23, 1873. Going downstairs to take my bath this morning, I lost *this book*. When I finally missed it, I became terribly afraid. I was ready to cry like an insane person when I found it on the floor.

Ricardo Barnola (from the theater) called on us after lunch. He told us that Borreel wore a bandit costume to Mrs. Sabatier's ball.

When the cavalcade of young men rode along in costume, we saw Borreel in his bandit outfit. To do him justice, I must say he was the handsomest man there. It was an enormous, brilliant, and magnificent procession. One beautiful float, covered with violets, carried the society ladies, masked.

Monday, February 24, 1873. We went for a few errands with Patton (our Russian consul) in the carriage. Young Abramovitch came to our house. Today I was bored because I didn't see Borreel. So, my gaiety comes from him. How miserable I am! We cannot live independent: we always depend on someone. For example, I depend on Borreel and the Duke of

Hamilton because I love them—two at once! However, it's like that. I've already said that it seems I can't go one day without seeing one or the other. As long as I had only Borreel, I had fun thinking of him. But now I cannot be serious about him and also must hope that I'll have the Duke—because he is rich, has a title, comes from an almost royal family, and likes entertainments the way I do. He's a perfection. I love him. (But Gioja—how I hate her!) On the other hand, Borreel has exactly the same character as I. (He looks like me— same face.) He loves all the parties, the receptions, the fashion, the promenades. He likes to be seen. That's just like me. We are made for each other. It's the pure truth. If he only loved me!

Mardi Gras, Tuesday, February 25, 1873. We went in the carriage today with iron masks and our white lace dresses. We had an enormous number of bouquets and made the rounds five or six times, following the line of carriages, which seemed endless. Today there were more people, and we received a lot of small and big bouquets. Most of the lovely people were on the platform of the square next to the Prefecture. They threw us big bouquets. All of the people we knew by sight were smiling at us and covered us with flowers.

I had a lot of fun throwing flowers to all the society people in the stands, too. It seemed they almost talked to me.

In the evening in spite of all the reasons I offered saying it was improper for Dina to see Offenbach's *La Belle Hélène*, she went. Mama and my aunt went to Monte Carlo.

Inwardly and in the journal I continued my debate over the Duke and Borreel, concluding finally that I could marry only the Duke, and that I would like Borreel to love me only to humiliate him since he probably thinks I love him because of my blushing and the flowers. Positively I love the Duke of Hamilton, and for fun I like Borreel.

Thursday, February 27, 1873. Early this morning, in the study, I heard a special kind of noise, and looking out I saw the Duke's carriage on its way to Gioja's. I was trembling. Feeling how much I loved him, I hurried to finish the translation I was doing and went out on the terrace to learn the sentences there. But of course it was really to see the Duke. Thinking he would come out of her place, I waited. Then I looked toward her house and saw the empty carriage passing it. I continued to wait. Nothing. Nothing. Nothing. Oh, if he knew all that—how I go running only to have a glimpse of his carriage and not daring any more to hope to see him! I said nothing to anyone, but at each instant I thought about him. I trembled at the sound of each carriage, trying to recognize the sound of his. At 8:10 I came back in and sat down, getting ready to play the piano, when Mama told me, "It's all finished with the Howards as far as we're concerned."

"Why?" I asked.

"They had a dinner party; they asked the Tutcheffs to come and not us."

Walking with Collignon at the Promenade, we saw a big crowd and met the Howards with their mother. They came up to me as nicely as ever and held my arms on both sides and walked with us.

Then I began to wonder what it meant that I was not seeing either the Duke or Gioja. Although I have kept my eyes peeled for two days, I've seen neither one of them, and I'm so sad! There was an afternoon dance scheduled for the Club, and I suggested that we drop in there. Around six we entered together, walked once around the room, and left. We were overwhelmed by the greetings; our appearance was sensational. I think we stayed two minutes, but everyone was looking at us. I think that's because we just went in, glanced at the people, and got out. The impression we made was good, and I am very happy. As our day is Monday, I told those we talked with to come. I am happy; that way we'll be able to have some acquaintances. Really I was very satisfied. I am writing more sensibly. Oh, how happy I am! I have almost everything I have asked for. Oh, my God, thank you! Lord, make things go so that the Duke is introduced to us, I beg you.

Saturday, March 1, 1873. The others went to Monaco, and Dina and I went to church and to the music; but after a few moments of music the rain started, the music stopped, and the carriages scattered. We strolled a little in town. My God, how sad the weather is! Furthermore, it is depriving me of seeing Borreel; I haven't seen him for three days. And also it prevents my being seen by others. I don't hope or ask to see Hamilton any more, and if I were seeing him, it would be like a dream, a happiness too big to be true.

Sunday, March 2, 1873. This morning Mama told us she saw Borreel at Monaco. My aunt added, "With the cocottes. He is repulsive."

"He behaves very badly," Mama told me. "I wanted to scold him." But she added, "I didn't see him with the cocottes, and he did bow to me and talk. I told him I had seen him dancing with a Russian lady, a small brunette, and he blushed."

This day we had our At Home reception. I was so happy! Everyone who knew about it came. It was a good number, including Mrs. Markevitch, who stayed on for supper. There was a crowd on the Promenade, but I didn't see Borreel; and I am dead when I don't see him. I can't get those cocottes out of my mind! I had thought him a model, good, well-mannered, one who loves his family. Now I ask, how worthy is he? In the past I thought he looked dignified and distinguished.

Walitsky says that Miss Collignon is as ill as Kykyev, who just died. He says she might live five years more, or that she could die in three weeks. So many misfortunes at once!

Even if I married Borreel what kind of life would mine be staying all alone, or maybe surrounded by common men who would like to court me, giving parties (if, at least, I had the means) and letting myself be carried away on a whirlwind of pleasures? All this is what I dream about; it's what I wish, but only with the man I love near me, loving me, too. Under those circumstances the compliments of those silly and stupid men would seem amusing, and all the pleasures would be heaven. Yes! But without him? And to be envied by so many who would say, "How happy she is! The husband different, the wife different; there is a happy woman!"

But for me to know in the middle of each good time that maybe at that moment he was pinching a cocotte: oh, it would be abominable! It makes me cry. I don't say he'd do it in the first year of marriage. Maybe not the second, but after! Being used to a dissipated life as a bachelor, he'd continue it when married. At the beginning the novelty of marriage would distract him. But later? My God, what am I saying? I don't even know him, and I've married myself to him! How silly. And he might not even want me.

After my spontaneous stream of imagination calmed down, I realized that I'd never marry him even if he asked me on his knees. And besides, even if he couldn't live without me, I have set another goal. On the other hand, I believe I could forgive the Duke his dissipated life.

We went with guests to the Français to hear *Héloïse and Abélard*.

Finally, all those things I've been writing seem awfully silly now, but what I wrote was really what I felt.

A while ago at the piano, Sophie [Marie's cousin, Sophie Grigorievna, not an aunt, as various editions indicate] was playing some little Russian songs that took me back to Tcherniakovka. Memories of the old women of the village reminded me of Grandmama, and tears came to my eyes and overflowed. I was too young then to love her as she deserved. The sounds of Sophie's playing are still coming to my ears in bits and pieces and penetrating my soul. I can revel in memories and in writing, because tomorrow will be Sophie's name day and we won't have any lessons.

Oh, my God, give me the Duke of Hamilton and I'll love him and make him happy; I'll be happy, too, and do good to the poor. (I know it's a sin to believe that one can buy the grace of God with charity, but I don't know how to express myself!)

All those things I wrote regarding Borreel, all those feelings—I cannot even understand them now. But they are what I really felt at the time.

Tuesday, March 4, 1873. We had a party this evening. Mrs. Howard came with Hélène and Lise. Mrs. de Daillens came, Count de Markoff, and Mrs. Markevitch, Mr. Barnola, Count Gabrielli, Mr. Patton, and Mr. Abramovitch. We served a tea, and Dina dressed up as a Chinese and later as a nun. Markoff asked to see my paintings. I am happy; I had a lot of fun. I wore my violet dress, with the blouse open in front, and left my hair loose. I looked very nice, but my face looked a little tired.

Coming back from the Reserve after lunch with Gabrielli, we passed the port. Gabrielli talked about the Duke of Hamilton and his yacht. We stopped to ask whose yacht was there in front of us and were told that this was not the Duke's, that his and Witgenstein's had both left Nice eight days ago.

So, he is gone! And she, too, because I don't see her any more. Oh, rage! So I'll not see him until next winter. But who knows where he'll be then? And to be ignored like that! But then, he left without having known that I existed. And even if he knew. . . . Oh, he has a woman he loves. Oh, I think he doesn't really love her, that he prefers to be free. But it's necessary for him to have a woman and horses and all that because these are the attributes of a great young English lord fallen from grace in a bad society. And I can do nothing!

And the other, the poor child, engulfed in that abyss! The poor dear, to be perverted by that awful Monaco! I would like to see him again.

Wednesday, March 5, 1873. Because Dina had a headache, I took two hours for my piano lesson. While I was having the lesson, a vision of the Duke came to my mind—I don't know why: He stood on the deck of his yacht commanding, giving orders to his men, and taking care of everything. He presented himself to my imagination as young, handsome, rich, free, noble. What a happy man with such enormous revenues! He was distributing them wisely (something I think he does not do, but I don't know). Now that he is gone, it seems to me he's dead. He was what I wanted as a husband in every respect, and he is gone. If I didn't love him, what would I care for his money and position? I could always find somebody else.

Today we were walking on the Promenade, and I saw Borreel coming from a long way off in a one-horse carriage. As he passed us, I didn't look at him. I think I did right. When we got back in the carriage, we saw him again. I was really satisfied to see him. I am interested in him because he doesn't run after me nor make any effort to be introduced to us. And I can see by myself that when one seems indifferent one gains more, and people pay more attention to one. Why don't I follow this method?

Friday, March 7, 1873. I went riding on the Promenade; I had a very pretty, lively, even fiery black horse. On leaving the house, I turned toward the Var with the idea of taking a riding lesson, but at that moment I met Borreel in a one-horse carriage. He looked at me a lot. At the end of the Promenade I met Mama and the others coming back from Mrs. Howard's, and she followed me with the carriage. There was a crowd, and I was enormously looked at. It seemed that all Nice was on the Promenade. I galloped a lot and spoke with several gentlemen we know. Mama stopped to talk with the Count; I, too. At that moment Borreel's sister and her husband passed, and they looked at us a lot. I think they are going to say something at the house because they saw me galloping too hard.

Then Dina said directly, "It's because he saw you riding the horse. And how he turned around! Simply awful. . . ."

Never before have I been admired as I was today. And when I came back home and looked at myself in the mirror, I found myself pretty—white and pink. His look surprised me. On the Promenade I looked at him and . . . I did not find an iron gate any more. He looked at me the way I had looked at him that time. I must say I'm satisfied.

Saturday, March 8, 1873. Mama told me, "Today is confession and tomorrow you will take communion."

This evening at the Italiens I heard Verdi's *La Forza del Destino* for the first time. I liked it very much.

Sunday, March 9, 1873. Dina, Miss Collignon, and I went to the Howards' where we had been invited to spend Sunday with the children. We walked in the garden and then went into the house. Because the children are so nice and kind, it's a pleasure to go there. When we were ready to leave around 5:00, Mrs. Howard came back to say she had got permission to keep us until evening; so we stayed for supper (Patton, our consul, was there) and afterwards went to the big living room, which was dark. The girls begged me to sing, and the other children did the same. We laughed a lot. I sang "Santa Lucia," "The Sun Is Risen," "I am Only a Herd Girl," and some arpeggios. They were so ecstatic that they all kissed me—awe-fully!—yes, that's the word! I sang not too badly. The grownups were in the other room listening, too. I didn't know it at first, but when I realized it I continued singing. The children were looking at me and talking with emotion. They were full of surprise and respect for my voice. They predicted a glorious future for me and were in such ecstasies that Lise kissed my shoulder and then my hand. I cannot describe the excitement I inspired in the girls, and the boys imitated them.

If I could have the same success with the public, I would go on the stage right away! It feels so wonderful to be admired for something other than your clothes. Truly, this admiration from the children entranced me. I wondered what would happen to me if I were admired by others! I had not expected to please them so much. Lise was jealous of Hélène. Each wanted to have me to herself alone. I had a lot of fun because I was admired. What does it mean to have talent? To be admired, loved, respected, honored! One is even looked upon with superstitious reverence. I enjoyed it very much. And the girls kissed me endlessly. Hélène, Lise, and Jean played very well on the piano.

I am made for triumphs and emotions; so the best thing for me to do is to become a singer (*if the good God wishes to conserve, strengthen, and develop my voice*).

In singing I can have the triumph I long for and the satisfaction of being known, admired, and famous. And through this I can have the one I love. Staying as I am, I have very little hope of being loved by him; he is ignorant of my existence. Oh, he has seen me. But that's not what I'm looking for. I want him to see me surrounded by glory and triumph. Men are ambitious. He'll leave Gioja for me. I am sure—(if God wants it).

I would be received in society because I'll not be a celebrity coming from a low class or a dirty street. I am noble and don't have to work, so it will be easier to rise. Through this my life will be perfect. I dream of celebrity, of fame. To appear on the stage and see thousands of people waiting with beating hearts for the moment when I start to sing, to know when looking at them that one note of my voice will put them all at my feet, to look at them with pride as if saying, "I can do everything!"—this is what I am dreaming; here is my life, my happiness, my desire. And then, being surrounded by all that, I'll see Monseigneur the Duke come like the others to prostrate himself at my feet. But he will have a different reception from the others. My dear, I love you so much! You will be dazzled by my splendor, and you'll love me. You'll see the triumph that will surround me. And it is true that you, only, are worthy of the woman I hope to be.

I'm not ugly, but rather pretty; and I'm liked. I have the body of a statue and beautiful hair. I have coquettish manners, and I know how to behave with men. I know very well how to pose. I can't practise it now, but later I will. And finally, I'll be a celebrity of the world.

All these things must put him at my feet. He must not marry another woman! I'll be worthy of him, of his rank, of his riches, of himself. I don't pay any attention to the Pattis, because they belong to everybody and because they are taken by royalty. But I'm not like that. I am honest; I wouldn't even kiss any man except my husband, and I can boast about what other girls of fourteen cannot—that I've never been kissed by a man or kissed one. I'll be able to tell my husband that, and it will be true.

So he'll see a young girl at the height of the fame a woman can win, loving him since her youth, honest and pure. That will attract him. He'll want to have me at any price and will marry me through pride. But what am I saying? Why put myself in such a low rank as a woman? Why can't I admit that he can love me *as I am*? I'll be better than Gioja! If he were paying attention to me now, he would think he was honoring me. Come on! I'll show him that it is *I* who honor him by marrying him because I give all my fame for him!

Of course, if I am able to become his wife without being a singer, I'll be equally satisfied; but I think I'll never be able to attract anyone if I'm not a singer. God, you have made me understand that by the use of my voice I can obtain what I am asking; so it's on my voice I must concentrate all my thoughts and take care of it and keep it. I give you my word, Lord, I'm not going to use my voice any more, or rather, I'm not going to shout any more the way I've been doing.

Monday, March 10, 1873. This was our day to receive. We had quite a few guests. I went in only for a few minutes to ask something of Mama, acting like a little girl. Among others, I saw Markoff and Abramovitch. I am very happy about my poise; before entering the room, I went upstairs to look at myself in the mirror and found I was white and pink.

Tuesday, March 11, 1873. While I was having my lessons, Papa [this is Marie's grandfather; all the family call him Papa, as his two daughters, Marie's mother, Mrs. Bashkirtseff, and Marie's aunt, Mrs. Nadya Romanoff, do] came to tell us in a frightened voice that Mama had fainted. We ran to her right away; I was scared. She was really sick—Walitsky said it was a nervous spell, but for a moment we feared for her life. I was shouting and crying; then looking out through the doors I saw the Prince of Witgenstein. Then I was angry because the others saw me watching him.

Miss Collignon did all she could, running everywhere. That pleased me, coming from her. But everywhere in the house was a terrible confusion. We sent for all the doctors we knew. Oh! What an awful thought—to lose Mama! I was trembling. It was the strongest emotion I have ever felt. Around three o'clock, thanks to God and Walitsky, she was feeling better, but stayed in bed. When there is something really terrible, I can't describe it.

All during the day our acquaintances came to ask about Mama's health. I can't believe how fast everything is known! This was a day of big troubles, and I'll remember it.

Wednesday, March 12, 1873. Today when I saw Borreel, Mrs. Markevitch was with us. He had been wrinkling his hat the way the Duke does. She asked who he was, and I didn't blush. He acts absolutely like Hamilton and even dresses a little like him. He even copies his attitudes; he has the same kind of life, except for Gioja; he doesn't have the means for that! The way he carries on must be very painful for his mother.

BOOK THREE

Book 3 of my Journal
Begun Thursday, March 13, 1873
Ended Monday, April 14, 1873
Concerning Marie Bashkirtseff
Promenade des Anglais, No. 51, Villa d'Aquaviva

Thursday, March 13, 1873. My life is turned upside down by this awful, dark, rainy weather! It's so rainy and windy I don't go out any more and I don't see people. Everybody here either goes to Monaco or stays at home. When the weather was good it was as if everything went on schedule; I would go out for an hour in the carriage and then for an hour of walking. That way I could see everybody and—the dresses, everything. I was looking at others and being looked at. All those people whom I see all the time seem acquaintances or friends, and I am lonely without them.

Friday, March 14, 1873. In my study this morning I heard the noise of a carriage in the Rue de France and looked out to see the Duke's carriage with four horses going to Gioja's. "Oh, my God, is he back? Lord, have pity! Help me!" I prayed, "because if he is there, she is, too." I was trembling. If he is here, I reasoned, he'll go to the other contests and the shooting next month in Monaco. I vowed absolutely to go, too.

And I saw Mrs. Paskevitch, the "good friend" of Carlos Hamilton [Lord Charles Hamilton, the Duke's brother]. I was very happy to see her—not for herself, but because she, like most of these other people, reminds me of Baden.

There I could see the Duke almost every day where he stayed on the Promenade. If only I had loved him then! But no, it would have been of no use because I was a child; but if I could have a summer in Baden now! When I think that Grandpapa met him in a store! They even talked together. If I could have foreseen the present, I would have continued that acquaintance; I would have spoken to him myself, and under any and all pretexts whatever I would have been with Papa. By now he would know me and would speak when he met me.

But why dream about things of the past that cannot come back?

Mama is still sick in bed.

Sunday, March 16, 1873. After Mass we talked to acquaintances who wanted to know how Mama is.

Monday, March 17, 1873. Dina says Gioja was at the theater yesterday with her old lady and a gentleman. I wondered whether it could be that the Duke is out of money and that she has abandoned him? People have been saying he is ruined. I thought about all that and knew it was probably not true. After all, she is not his wife, but a high-class cocotte; and he probably doesn't expect her to be true to him. But then, if he considers her that way, why would she travel with him and why would he go every day to see her? I don't know what to think about all that, but I pray God to help me.

Miss Collignon was quite disagreeable yesterday at dinner. We were talking about drawing rooms, and I was expressing my taste and disagreed with her. "Marie," she said in an impertinent tone, "you have never been in a beautiful salon," and I answered her with the same tone and she left the table.

Today during my lesson she started the same conversation again, and I told her I dislike having people talk to me impertinently. She answered, "We said harsh things, but my conscience is clear."

I told her, "You were impolite toward all of us, because if I have never seen a beautiful salon, then neither have any of the others!"

A few months ago she had talked that way, like a sovereign. I think she'll be leaving, and I'm not sorry about it. Before, when she was not like that, I missed her; but now I won't. I'll even be pleased because I'll get an English teacher and learn English conversation.

All these last few days they have been talking about the Hamilton name, and this gives me an enormous pleasure when I don't blush.

Wednesday, March 19, 1873. At last we have beautiful weather! I saw everybody on the Promenade, and I'm happy about it. We were one hour in a carriage and then we walked, but the rain surprised us. "He who has not been thirsty does not appreciate water," they say in Russia. That's true. Before the storms our going out was an ordinary thing. But now going out is a great pleasure for me (I don't go to see anybody, but just for what being out means) because I was deprived of it for a few days.

Now I understand what the word *rival* means—but can I be her rival? I saw her all dressed in black. She has in her expression something that can belong only to a woman who has everything. With her head slightly leaning on the side, she looks at everybody as if she were saying, "I am happy. I have everything I want, and I am surprised that there are any unfortunate people who do not. I worry very little about them. I am powerful; none resist me." It is only such a conviction that can give her the expression she has. Oh, she is beautiful! And what a miserable creature I am next to her! I am so excited when I see her; she provokes in me as strong an emotion as he does, but one of another kind. It is painful. All of which shows me how far away from her I am. I almost blushed when I saw her! And of course she has no idea of all that. When I saw her going to her house, I thought she would be followed by him; I was afraid to see him while I was in front of the others in the carriage, because where was I to hide my confusion? I prayed God not to let me see him, because even though I always want to, I didn't want it then. What could I possibly do not to betray myself?

Friday, March 21, 1873. Mama is feeling no better. Dear God, help us!

He came to my mind again in all his royal majesty. Nobody sits like him; he has the attitude of a king when he is in his carriage. Oh, God, let me see him riding on his horse; that's the only place I could meet him alone—on the bridle path—where it wouldn't be noticed by others.

Saturday, March 22, 1873. This morning, reading in the Swiss *Times*, I looked at the list of foreign visitors, not just in Nice, but everywhere under the *H*'s and I found *Hamilton, the Duke of*, in Naples. It was a list from the tenth of March. When I first read it, I thought it must be impossible, but sure enough, there it was. It was as if I had been hit by thunder. I was trembling and couldn't take my eyes from it. He was staying there at the Hotel du Louvre. And I began to pray to God for the Duke.

We could see from the carriages that there was a party at the Club Masséna. And I saw Gioja in her carriage, wearing black. She was beautiful, perfect—hair, dress, surroundings. It's always that way; nothing is missing; everything is elegant, rich, distinguished, magnificent. Really, one would think she was a society lady!

I was thinking that it's natural that all these things contribute enormously to her beauty—her house with the salons, the little corners with a soft light coming through beautiful curtains and some greenery. And herself, dressed and cared for always in the best ways, sitting in a magnificent room like a queen where everything is planned to enhance her beauty. It is natural that she should please him and he love her. If I had all that help, I'd be better too!

I'll be happy with my husband because I'll not neglect myself. I'll always try to please him the way I shall the first time I meet him. Besides, if a man and a woman can love each other always as long as they are not married, why shouldn't they try to please each other all the time? Why, being married, wouldn't they continue in the same way? Why should all that stop with marriage? Why would a woman profane her marriage by showing herself in curlers and robe, with cold cream on her nose, trying to get money from her husband for dresses? It's natural for her to try to please him and for him to love her. Why not stay always coquettish with a husband and treat him as a stranger who pleases you, with the difference, of course, that we must not permit too much with a stranger? Is it that they don't because a man and his wife can love each other openly because it is not a crime, and because a marriage is blessed by God? Is it because everything that is not forbidden has little interest? Or because one finds pleasures only in forbidden and hidden things? I understand it differently. Why does Gioja keep the affection of the Duke? It's because they have a relationship—not just as friends, and not dirty either, but correct. That doesn't mean they are playacting.

But can we be naturally good? Yes, we can. With the help of God I'll live happily.

Monday, March 24, 1873. Mama called me at 7:00 this morning to show me a letter from Miss Collignon addressed to my aunt. It said, "I cannot stand Marie's vain character and impertinence any longer." She wants to leave. Before this I wanted her to leave and thought it wouldn't make me feel sad. Suddenly I remembered when she was good. But as soon as I saw her my regrets disappeared because she is no longer what she was. Before this, Mama also wanted her to leave, but now she puts all the blame on me and regrets her, enlarging all her qualities. It's always like that: the worst thing seems very beautiful when lost.

In the painting class, we talked with Mr. Bensa about the Duke. And Bensa told us, speaking about the fortune of Audiffret, that the Niçois must be rich if he can give gifts of 20,000 francs. We asked him, "To whom?"

"The Duchess of Hamilton," was the answer.

"But how can she accept a gift of 20,000 francs from anyone but her husband?"

"She's not his wife. She's a high-class cocotte who follows him. It started here in Nice."

"But the Duke of Hamilton is rich. She needs nobody else."

"This kind of person always needs more."

"But how can he put up with it?"

"Oh, he doesn't pay too much attention to it. He's indifferent to it."

That last statement characterizes the Duke perfectly! He's unlike others; a good man, insouciant, who lives as he pleases and doesn't torment himself. Still he's a bad boy, a spoiled child. I like his character, and what Bensa said made me happy. We talked a lot all day about him with Bensa and everyone—even Mrs. Markevitch—about his villa, his liaison with *her*, and his fortune. How happy I am when someone will talk about him! At such times I feel I really love him.

During dinner I spoke to Papa about Baden. I got him to talk about Hamilton, prolonging the conversation as much as possible. He answered certain questions I put to him, saying, "No, he's no fool," and "He is proud, but sometimes very cordial" or "gay and lively" or something like that. He said, "I wasn't even drinking, but he drank glass after glass." And I liked that too!

Friday, March 28, 1873. I must not lose a minute but use every moment and study. Sometimes (I am ashamed to admit it) I hurry my lessons without understanding them so I can finish faster. And I'm happy when I have to do them again because for the following day I'll have less to do! I must reform. I want to finish all I'm studying now as soon as possible so I can start serious studies like the men. I must study music more, start the harp, begin singing, and read a lot. These are my goals.

I have been forcing my voice and hurting it, and that's why I swore not to sing any more until I have lessons. I have asked God to make it stronger, more developed, purer, and to let me keep it. To prevent myself from singing now I made a terrible condition: if I sing before I have lessons, I'll lose it. It's an awful condition, but I'll do everything to keep my promise.

Hamilton, dear, she is not worthy of you.

Sunday, March 30, 1873. I dreamed about the Duke. He was wearing three kinds of jackets—the most extravagant. He was in our house and looking at our paintings, appreciating them. I was talking to him. I was very much moved and could barely hide it. He was talking very kindly to me about Bertha, and said, "Oh, yes, Bertha. I was talking with her and asked her to sit and talk to me about you."

I was telling myself, Oh, my God! So he talked about me with her, and it was because of me that he was speaking with her. . . . How happy I am! At last my prayers are granted.

Today I painted in an oval space a beautiful woman in natural size from a very small lithograph. It turned out very well.

Monday, March 31, 1873. This was our day to receive. We had many more guests from society, but I think that by buying this villa we'd improve our acquaintance even more. But would they sell this dear Aquaviva?

Tuesday, April 1, 1873. I would like to know why people look at me—whether it is because I am funny looking or pretty. I would give big money to the one who would tell me the truth. I have the urge to ask a young man naively if I am pretty or funny. I might make a mistake. But if it is an illusion that I'm pretty, I prefer to keep it because it's flattering. Life is so beautiful and so short!

I keep wondering what Paul will do when he grows up. What profession will he have? He must not pass his life like so many others who have lives of leisure and throw themselves into the world of gamblers and cocottes. Anyway, he wouldn't have the money for that! He *must* be a man!

Wednesday, April 2, 1873. At Mortier's we chose a hat for Dina, and the Countess Vigier came in wearing a lot of makeup. She was grotesque. I blushed because I thought she hadn't returned Mama's visit; I didn't say hello but turned my back. Then I heard her asking if Mama had come to her house. She had looked for us in vain at the Villa Meynadier, not knowing where we live. She said other kind things. We talked about hats, and finally she said she hoped Mama would consider this conversation a visit, and that next year they'd get together. I was very satisfied because I had thought she didn't want to visit with us. She is charming even though ridiculously dressed and made up. So at last we have an acquaintance from society and not one of those dirty old prehistoric Russians who come to Nice. Here is another one of my prayers answered!

Tomorrow is the pigeon shoot!

Thursday, April 3, 1873. I started to dress before lunch, but my aunt and the others brought up obstacles to my going to Monaco. That's a habit of theirs; they try to find objections to everything just as they do to my bathing at the beach—and they always end by finding nothing to object about. I put on the black taffeta dress from Dina (since she is wearing long dresses now, I have all her short ones) and the hat with roses.

The crowd at the railway station included the Galvis with Miss Galvi in a simple and pretty grey linen. Our party included Miss Collignon, my aunt, Mama, Mrs. Markevitch, Count Gabrielli, and Miss Kolokoltsoff. My heart began beating fast. We stayed a minute in the game room, and then I went to the shooting with my mentor, Walitsky.

There wasn't much of a crowd, and there were no extravagantly dressed Englishmen, no broken and dirty hats, no more plaid jackets, and no wildly gesticulating and shouting bettors. Everything was quiet. I was waiting for *him*, but he didn't come. I think he doesn't like to mix with such scoundrels when they're shooting. Besides, he's too rich and fashionable to stay in Nice in April. I don't even know who won; the newspaper will tell.

All of a sudden I saw Gioja entering with another woman. I looked at her. She passed very close to us, stopped without looking at us, and then went downstairs. She is much uglier than I thought! Yet in a carriage, at the theater, at a distance she's charming and beautiful. But she walks badly and seems conceited and has coarse features painted in that powdery white way. At the same time she has self-assurance and *such* audacity! But she has nothing extraordinary—no eyes, no mouth—she's a pretty woman. That's all. I had been thinking she was not a cocotte after all; but today I'm sure she is.

Looking at the names of the members of the shooting committee, I asked Gabrielli, "Where did they find so many dukes?" I'd found several on the program.

"None of them is present." He told me where the others were and then said, "Hamilton is on his yacht traveling to the Orient. He's in Cairo, I think."

My heart sank into the ground. I'll not see him any more; we plan to leave for Russia this summer. Can it be that the Duke is traveling because he has broken with her? A crazy idea. She holds him tight! God help me!

Friday, April 4, 1873. Mrs. Markevitch seems to have become a member of the family. She's good natured, friendly.

Saturday, April 5, 1873. Before 7:00 I was on the terrace reading. The sea, the sky, the magnificent air! No one can deny God!

Monday, April 7, 1873. I got up at 9:00 A.M. for the 10:00 Italian lesson. Bensa came at 11:00. But at 11:30 I went to dress because this time I didn't want to miss the shooting. I went with just my aunt to Monaco. We were on the train with the Howards. I talked with them in English, and Mrs. Howard complimented me on my fluency. My aunt played roulette for about a half hour, and at last we went to the shooting. The same crowd was there as before. We went over to the left side, where we found Mrs. Durand and her daughter with Mr. Lewin, who is courting her.

We sat next to the box where the dead pigeons were thrown. This seemed to absorb my aunt. She was taking a great interest in everything, although she wouldn't admit it, but I was pleased, because there is nothing more disagreeable than to be with somebody who is bored, like Walitsky. I found a program and kept the score.

I was as excited as the others. I'd like Paul to take up shooting. What am I saying? I myself would like to shoot! This was the first time I ever came with anyone who wasn't bored. I saw how much I adored the sport, and I tied it all together in my mind to my feeling for the Duke. But that doesn't explain the good time I had. I had fun such as I'd never had before because always before I went to the contest to see the Duke, and the shooting didn't interest me. But now (although it would have been heaven if I could have seen him), not having hoped he would be there, I enjoyed what was going on; and now I understand everything. The marksmen interested me because at last I understood what was easy and what was difficult. I was so involved in what was going on I almost forgot the Duke of Hamilton. What a shame!

But then it seems to me that an abyss separates me from him since I don't exist for him. At such thoughts I feel a slow, calm, awful pain. Strange! Not long ago I was thinking about the gaiety at the shooting, and now I have the saddest ideas imaginable!

Wednesday, April 9, 1873. Miss Collignon and I walked for about an hour. We saw almost nobody except Audiffret on our way back. Generally, he doesn't look at anyone and passes with his eyes fixed in front of him in an affected manner. Here is my idea about such an attitude: if the person passing looks at you, that means you are like everyone else for him; but if he passes without looking at you at all, but only straight ahead in a strained or affected way, that means you are something to this person and that he or she, having seen you from a distance, wants to show you that you are *not* being looked at, that no attention is paid to you, which, of course, is not true.

Thursday, April 10, 1873. All our days are the same: we often go to Monaco or to the theater. At dinner Grandpapa is always looking for a quarrel and unfortunately I don't have the patience to remain silent. Vulgar words come to my mouth. Today we separated sulking, but before he went to bed I told him good night and everything was forgotten. Poor man, he's old. Even when he attacks the family and my name, what he says has no importance.

With the others I gossip about the Souvaroffs and the Prodgerses. I talk about my secrets with no one. It's much better. I could be sorry about it later. So I am secretive about all my decisions for the future. Most of the quarrels between me and Mama come from the fact that, at the place where she ought to listen until the end, she thinks she foresees all my words and says, "Don't shout, don't scold, don't swear," when I have no intention of doing any of those things. But when I come to kiss her good night, I really get irritated and tell her disagreeable things. It's her fault. And that's the way I have to live! As for Dina—she does nothing but sleep. I can't imagine what her thoughts are, or even try to guess. She is apathetic, but I'm sure she must have a few secrets, too!

Friday, April 11, 1873. Today Mama said she would be leaving at 2:00 for Geneva to settle a business matter with Krumling. I think he wants to charge more than we owe him for the pawned diamonds. I asked to go, too, and everything was arranged for me to accompany her. My clothes were packed, I dressed in the green woollen dress with the grey jacket, and it was drawing near the time to leave.

We planned to see Paul and the Sapogenikoffs, as well as the city of Geneva. Then I don't know what happened. Someone said, "You can't go yet," and everything was postponed until tomorrow. That made me angry. I'm always angry when things are postponed, and that is what is always happening.

Saturday, April 12, 1873. The trip to Geneva? I don't know anything about it!

Audiffret is now really cock-of-the-walk. Although he doesn't go anywhere, he creates interest in himself by imitating the Duke, poor lost boy! It's too bad; he's handsome and rich, but already in the hands of this woman. He's cock-of-the-walk because Borreel is gone, Lewin is leaving, and the others have been gone a long time. It's too bad. He's the best of them all here. What a shame that he is already dedicated to the vagabond life, out of all society except that of cocottes and gamblers, determined to spend everything, ruin himself, and become a wastrel! He has already put horns on the Duke, and he's as carefree as a spoiled child.

Maybe the Duke has broken altogether with her! But she cannot stay where she is without income, and here is a poor child she'll reduce to poverty and then repudiate. Horrors! I must forget it. It's unworthy of me to speculate like this.

At the Français we saw Molière's *The Doctor in Spite of Himself*. The play was quite amusing. I said silly things and laughed a lot.

Sunday, April 13, 1873. I'd like to know what it signifies that Gioja is not going out. Her house is open, but the gate is closed. Often men can be seen coming to ask something. The door is not opened for them, but the servant speaks through the gate. I can only suppose she is sick. If that's so, then *he* has left her, because otherwise wouldn't he be there? But maybe she hasn't told him about her illness because men don't like women like her to be ill. She would be right not to tell him. But maybe *she's* not in Nice; maybe the house is open because her children are there. How could I know anything about all that? Only, I would like to see *him*. I'm in such a sad mood when I don't see him. But I have no hope that one day he'll love me.

Monday, April 14, 1873. This is the first day of our Holy Week, and I went to church tonight to do my devotion. I dislike many things in our religion. We have several blind and meaningless customs I cannot believe in. But I believe in God, in Christ, in the Holy Virgin, and in good faith. I pray every night, but I don't want to be bothered by trifles that aren't doing a thing for true religion. Dear God, I'd be so happy if I could have him! I *have* to write that I love him. Otherwise I'd explode, word of honor! It's a relief and diminishes the pain.

BOOK FOUR

Book 4
Begun Tuesday, April 15, 1873
Ended Saturday, May 17, 1873
Concerning Marie Bashkirtseff
Promenade des Anglais, No. 51, Villa d'Aquaviva

Tuesday, April 15, 1873. At dinner Miss Collignon said something which struck me profoundly: "When a woman wants a man, she always gets him." Oh, for that it would be necessary for me to be a woman, not a child! When somebody mentioned Hamilton, I blushed as red as a beet.

Wednesday, April 16, 1873. From the church we went to the Promenade; and on the bridge, while we stopped our carriage to speak to Mr. Anitchkoff, we saw another carriage with a tall, dark, thin young man I thought I recognized. I did! It was Lord Hamilton, the Duke's brother; and without thinking I shouted: "It's Carlos Hamilton!"

The others asked me who he was, and I only said, "Miss Collignon stepped on my foot."

He doesn't look at all like his brother. Anyway, I was more than happy to see him. Oh, if we could at least meet him—because through him we could meet the Duke! I love this one like my own brother because he is *his* brother. If I knew him I could find out where the other one is, and I could talk about the Duke with him.

When we got back from church in the evening, we found the Consul, Mr. Patton, waiting for us. I didn't know why. I can't pray in church; I can only pray at home, alone. In church I think about other things.

Thursday, April 17, 1873. Later, at the de Mouzays' we discussed religion and talked about the Duke of Edinburgh. I said I thought he was ugly, but Miss Collignon said, "At least he looks like a nobleman! Look at the Duke of Hamilton, a fat butcher," et cetera.

"I didn't say that. Bertha said it," I told her. I behaved very well and didn't blush.

They talked a lot about him; what a pleasure for me! Then Miss Collignon exclaimed, "What society he keeps! In Cairo he was always with the donkey-drivers, sitting in one of their carriages joking with them." At the mention of his name I shivered.

And Mrs. de Daillens spoke up for him: "He's a good man—good to everyone."

Oh, I know that! That's why I love him. I defended him, saying he is very nice, has beautiful features, and is not too fat; but I suddenly saw I was going too far, because they were looking at me in such a way. . . . I recovered myself, telling them that Bertha had told me these things.

After I got to know her in Baden, she told me that he must be seen closer for one to see how beautiful he is and that he improves on acquaintance. (How strange it is! She and I have the same desire. Who is going to have him? That's the question.) She told me that he is not vulgar; on the contrary, he is charming, and finally she described him as he is now for me. She has hopes, poor insane one! But then, I, too, am crazy. I am sure of it.

Here is a strange thing: I got my education about society in Baden. The children imitated the adults; they loved each other and courted each other. I saw Bertha Boyd and Remy de Gonzales; and I don't know why, but I wanted Remy to love me.

However, at the end of the summer season when Remy left, Bertha and I met. It was then that she told me about the Duke. She wanted absolutely to make me understand that he was in love with her, but I was too stupid then and didn't understand her until six months later in Nice! She believes she has the Duke.

Friday, April 18, 1873. This was Good Friday. During our Holy Week we go to church every day. Today we went at 2:00 for the procession of the Bier of Christ. The church was full. When everybody went to pay homage to the Bier, or bow down and kiss, I looked at all their faces and all of a sudden *his* face, vivid, alive, appeared to me as if he were there, and handsome! Never before have I had so distinct a vision of him. My heart was beating violently, and I started to pray. I tried afterward to call up the vision, but in vain. My love for the Duke is not like the love I had for Borreel; it is an adoration. Oh, this apparition! Then an idea struck me: there were a lot of flowers near the Bier, and I took a daisy, telling myself, "This flower is holy. It was near our Savior." By its intervention with our Lord, I hoped it would tell me if my desires would be fulfilled; with my heart beating fast, I plucked the petals off: yes, no, . . . yes! Oh, my God, thank you! Everything foretells my happiness. I believe in this last prediction. It is holy.

Now back to earth. They say Gioja has left for Russia to settle her inheritance from Simonoff. Should I still fear her? No.

Saturday, April 19, 1873. Today at confession the priest told me that I like people to notice me, that I am vain, et cetera. Then after a day at home and all kinds of errands in town, we left at 11:00 for midnight Mass. Miss Collignon was with us and behaved very well. Miss Galvi entered with an English couple. Coming into our strange church not accompanied by a Russian could be very embarrassing.

We're not going to Russia after all, and I'm happy about that because I may have more opportunity to meet him here. What a situation! I love a shadow that I can't run after. He doesn't know me and could never imagine that I love him, and yet I use all my time to anticipate his desires!

It's 4:00 A.M. I'm going to bed.

Sunday, April 20, 1873. Easter is our "Bright Holiday," and very important in the Russian Church. I got up at 11:00.

The Howards came and Lise was like a bliss; she stayed with me in the bedroom, I being still in my nightgown. Then other visitors came. One brought me my new Italian straw hat. I was very pleased with it—it's so pretty. I put on the black dress with the ecru tunic from Dina and went out on the terrace after reading the prayers I wrote last night. My hope was so great that it seemed they would be answered, especially as I had put so much warmth into them.

After church we went to the music. All the handsome men of Nice were there. But how I would like to go away! I am so bored! I don't know whether it's because I was so tired yesterday or because I'm really lonely. But there is *nobody* here now, and Nice is impossible. And I'm so unhappy today! I'm always lonely and bored during holidays.

Monday, April 21, 1873. But I am so extraordinarily sad! It's not due to the lack of people. I don't know what it is, but I can't find a place for myself. I am unhappy without a reason. Could this be a forewarning? Oh, my God, save me! Spare me the misfortunes! Give me back my gaiety.

Even Mrs. Prodgers is gone, and I don't want to stay in Nice. Now it's only a place for gamblers and bad women. And it's not good for me ever to go into such society as there is here. Even though I'm not ready yet, time passes fast; and we won't have time to back up when I'm a young lady of sixteen. Nice, Baden, and such places are where I wouldn't want to live. Who are the young ladies here? They come and stay many seasons, have some little affairs with the young men, and then go away, older and without their freshness. On the other hand, what I have not said is that these places are fine for married women. For example, if I were married, I would come to Nice. But this city for young girls? The answer is no.

Tuesday, April 22, 1873. In the evening we went to the Français and saw a comic opera, *The Queen's Musketeers.* There was a crowd, but nobody from society. I keep thinking of how I would like to move to Italy.

Thursday, April 24, 1873. First, I must say that we broke relations with the Russian Tolstoy family next door about a month ago because our monkey bit their little boy, and there have been scenes. Mrs. Tolstoy has an extraordinary hatred for us and spreads the most awful calumnies about us, the darkest that a human mind can imagine. I don't think that the monkey is the cause of it. There is some hidden reason that we don't know about. Since then we have had very bad relations, or rather, no relationship at all, except that they make faces at us or stick out their tongues, et cetera. For this time, I can affirm that we are fair and that we did not deserve the actions they took.

So it is very natural that as we got into the carriage today—Mama, Dina, Markevitch, and I—and saw Mrs. Tolstoy coming onto our property under the pretense of showing the apartment to some of her friends, we were revolted. Mama ordered the servants not to let her enter. "Don't let Mrs. Tolstoy come in," she said. "The others can visit, but people who slander us, who hurt us, who even put notices about us in the newspapers cannot enter our home."

In spite of this Mrs. Tolstoy came up the steps with her husband and the others and tried to enter against the servants' opposition. They succeeded in preventing her. Mama had spoken very well, with meaning and dignity.

"We've been thrown out!" the ladies exclaimed.

"You are mistaken, ladies," Mama answered. "You can come to see the apartment, but this woman may not enter. She is liable to do anything. She could steal some letters or other papers from us. This woman who wrote those letters is herself the mother of a family. Yet she sent anonymous letters to us and to many other people saying the most horrible things about us. She is a nasty woman who sends a letter to a child, insulting that child's mother."

They didn't say anything, but with their cowardly faces went away. I really cannot get over the woman's audacity. It amazed us all.

Tomorrow at 11:00 we are going to a picnic with the Howards.

The family is all seated in the dining room and talking quietly. They assume I am studying. They don't know all the turmoil going on within me; they don't know what my thoughts are. They don't know that I must be either the Duchess of Hamilton—sought-after, known, esteemed, spoken of, who will live in the middle of parties of the highest society—or a famous singer on the stage. But the career doesn't seem so desirable as being the Duchess.

Saturday, April 26, 1873. The weather was uncertain; when the Howards came at 10:00 it was raining. The older people left in one carriage—Mr. and Mrs. Howard, my aunt, and Mr. Copland. We girls—Hélène, Lise, Aggie, and I—left in the second, and Miss Collignon, Miss Gaspard, and the two boys in the third. Dina still has a pain in her foot, and Mama was sick because of that scoundrel of a Tolstoy woman.

When we arrived at our objective on Mount Vinagrier, the rain started up again and then poured. After wandering in the neighborhood, we found an empty villa and decided to go in and have our lunch there. The servants opened the rooms downstairs for us and we set the table in a kind of winter garden. We ate, drank, laughed, and were happy. Everything was good, and there were all kinds of food imaginable.

Then the sun came out, and we returned with the carriages opened. The children were charming. Hélène has a little of my personality; she said she doesn't like flowers, beautiful views, and so on, but society. Lise is more romantic. And Aggie is witty. The boys are kind, extremely nice and considerate. It was a happy day.

Sunday, April 27, 1873. In the evening we went to *La Favorita,* by Donizetti—my first time. The theater was full of people from Nice; the visitors are almost all gone. Disgusting! It was the same at the music today, lots of Niçois, but hardly anybody else. On the other hand, when we went to the theater last night we saw Princess Souvaroff. She had two boxes—one for her daughter and a gentleman, and the other for her *bataclan* [caboodle, entourage] and her son. Souvaroff is not so beautiful; there are many women more beautiful than she who are not so much admired. It's that her wealth, her name, her position, her extravagance, her gambling, and her habits are more attractive than her beauty. For people like her, everything goes well; she has all she desires. Her face has a pleasant expression that says she is satisfied with everything, and that adds enormously to her natural charm.

In the evening I spoke my thoughts on marriage to Mama, telling her I don't hope for anything in Nice. But she said yes, there are possibilities, and told how the old Hamilton once wanted to abandon his family to marry a Russian lady. We talked a lot about him. Mrs. Markevitch was there, too. They said I'll have a title. I expressed myself openly about life, about a husband and wife. I was understood and approved. We talked about the Hamiltons, and I said that this one, too, will be found dead in some café the way his father was in the Maison d'Or in Paris. Mama said, "There is nothing wrong with that. It happens to men," and added that Mrs. Markevitch's father died like that.

"If your husband is a duke," Markevitch said, "he won't appreciate your being able to cook potatoes!" She said that because Mama was preaching the virtues of a domestic life. One could say I'm silly to be excited about all these suppositions about the Duke, but after they almost said I may very possibly marry him, it seems to me that that might be true.

Tuesday, April 29, 1873. Dear God, make me see the Duke in Vienna!

Wednesday, April 30, 1873. Now I am getting up at 5:30, and I'm in bed by 10:00. But Miss Collignon is neglecting the lessons. She postpones; she is often tardy or absent. And this makes me unhappy; I can't describe how I feel. I'm losing time I'll never be able to recover.

After lunch I went into Mama's room. She's not up yet, but she feels better. What frightens me is her great sadness. I want to cry because she's been sick so long. We talked about where we'll go this summer, about my education, about foreign languages and things like that. Dina and I are right to complain about Miss Collignon. Although I know the English language, I don't speak it with ease; she gives lessons like a professor, but never *speaks* English. And she neglects even the lessons she does give. I can't say this to her face, and that's why I'm irritated. I can't have anything without asking for it, but I'm sure she herself doesn't see it. I'm so upset that I'm always speaking with irritation. Today when talking with Mama and the others, I fumed, shouted, and almost cried. I was even laughing at myself. I was pleading to go to Vienna. I wish we could leave Nice, but unfortunately we can't just now; we must wait. Oh, my God, make the lawsuit end! We are nailed in Nice, but I would like to go to Florence, Naples, Rome and study painting, singing, and music. In Nice these things are as impossible as going into Nice society is for us.

Thursday, May 1, 1873. We went to the Promenade. Miss Collignon and I took a fiacre with one horse and two seats, and after remaining a while at the music she said to me all of a sudden, "Let's go to the Port!"

"Quick! Quick!" she told the driver. "Here's a one-franc tip."

"What's going on?" I asked her. She didn't answer. She just kept looking ahead and seemed very excited.

When we arrived at the quai, I saw in front of us a fiacre like ours with a man and a woman in it. For one instant I thought it was Borreel, married, and that she wanted to show him to me, not knowing that he was unimportant to me. But as we got closer, I saw a very skinny gentleman—the man she was in love with a long time ago. We knew vaguely that he existed, but she disliked talking about him. We had teased her about him, but here he was with a woman!

Miss Collignon still seemed calm. There was no expression on her face; all her agitation was in her eyes. Her calm surprised me and I told her so, but she answered, "However, I am *not* calm!" Her speech seemed broken with exclamations of surprise. I think she seemed tranquil because when extraordinary things happen and we are grief-stricken, we are less demonstrative than for little things.

On our way back I asked her all kinds of questions about him, but she didn't seem to be listening. Sometimes she answered me.

"Oh, I would like to follow them!" she said when we first saw them. I offered to leave her there and go home by myself, but she didn't want that. When we finally got home, she asked me not to mention the man, but I didn't know whether she meant it seriously. I came into the house laughing.

"What are you laughing about?" they asked.

"Nothing," I said.

Then Mama got angry and said, "You've done something silly! I won't let you go alone with Miss Collignon any more. I don't trust her. Your reputation—" et cetera.

I felt obliged to tell what I could, if it was necessary, to Mama alone, but scatter-brained as I am, I told it in front of everybody. At lunch, Walitsky mentioned it to her hoping to make her laugh, but she cried and went to her room. If I had been in her place, I would have blushed when I saw that man, but she didn't blush. Was it too much for her? Why did I tell? If he has abandoned her. . . . Oh, the poor thing! I'm so sorry for her!

Then she went out—I don't know where.

Today the family talked a lot about Prince Miloradovitch, a boy I knew as a child in Poltava. Mama hopes I'll marry him. I can't see it. Seeing a light in Miss Collignon's room, I went in to light the candle. She was writing some letters, her eyes full of tears. I don't understand anything about it and don't dare to ask.

Friday, May 2, 1873. We went to choose gifts for Mama, as tomorrow is her saint's day. Dina got her a beautiful fan for fifty francs. I bought her a bouquet. While we were out, we saw Miss Collignon's man again. He didn't see her, but she almost fainted. I can't see how it's worth that for a skeleton like him.

Saturday, May 3, 1873. I gave Mama my bouquet, but she's in bed.

After dinner Markevitch and I talked. We sat in the little dark salon and analyzed the misery of our world. She is quite nice, intelligent. Then we talked about our tastes. Later, when I went to my room, I saw her lying on Dina's bed. I sat down near her and she asked me if I really write my journal. In Russian, Walitsky calls it a *night diary* instead of a *day diary* because I write it at night.

"It's very interesting," she said, "to read a diary years and years *afterwards*. There are moments in life which we forget, and if you write them down, one day years later you may again live in the past and have all your life before you. Your feelings may change; you can compare what you have been with what you have become!"

Sunday, May 4, 1873. Mr. Howard and Hélène came with some others. We showed Hélène our paintings, my studio, and my study, where we talked almost all the time she was here about friends. She has had only one, a very peculiar girl who never said what she thought, but always the opposite. I said I had had none and that there was only one I should like to have—Bertha Boyd. "I love her," I said, "but we were acquainted for only three or four weeks, and then we parted. God knows when we shall meet again." I told her my tastes and she told me hers. We look a little like each other. We spoke of the society in Nice and of the Boutonsky girls. "They always have secrets," she said, "secrets in corners, letters, boys. Each has a so-called lover. . . ."

"Such funny little people," I said. "My wish is to go to Florence, where I can study singing, piano, and painting."

"Why can't you do that here?" she asked, surprised.

"In Nice? Impossible! Here we have no galleries, no musicians, no conservatory."

She hopes I'll stay here next winter.

Inwardly wondering if I can ever leave here, I said, "I'll come for the horse races. You will see a complete change in my outfits: instead of richer fabrics and styles you will see utter simplicity as becomes a young lady." She didn't believe me.

Miss Collignon has lost her voice and can barely talk. I don't know if it is a cold or because of her Indian. I call him that because he went to India to make his fortune, always promising to marry her when he got rich enough. It's as if he couldn't work, being married! (I didn't say that to her, of course.) She believed him, and now he's married and has dropped her.

Monday, May 5, 1873. We drove out with Mrs. Markevitch, who is now living downstairs at our house. We went to the Port, as I very much wanted to know whose yacht it was we saw yesterday. We passed it twice, the first time without Dina or Markevitch noticing; I diverted their attention to the spot where there was a landslide a few months ago. I was afraid on the trip back that I would blush. Dina shouted, "Oh, there's a yacht! How lovely! Whose is it?" I was waiting for that and immediately offered to ask someone. The carriage stopped and Dominique, our coachman, said, "It's the Duke of Hamilton's." But then for Dominique every ship is the Duke's. We asked another man, but he said he didn't know. Dominique asked if it wasn't the Duke's, but the man answered in the patois of Nice, "Don't you know *him* perfectly like everyone else?"

Then I muttered something against the Duke in Russian like, "Oh, he's well known here and was probably rolling around while drunk. All the common people recognize a 'scarecrow' very well." I was saying that for the others, but in my mind I was delighted that the people know him. He must be very kind and popular. He likes to joke with common people; Miss Collignon said that about him in Cairo. He must be a jolly fellow, not a rigid, frigid

Englishman. He's a *polisson*, a scamp, and I adore him for his character and everything. I am sure he is a charming man, a splendid fellow! I don't know how to express what I think of him, but I will try: charming, spiritual, gay, beautiful, joking, prideless with low people, majestic, noble. Even though he drinks too much—I'd not forget it in another—in him it is charming. I would talk to him, soothe his fury when he was drunk, and endure all his bad behavior.

Tuesday, May 6, 1873. I must tell in what continuous trouble I find myself: I am always afraid to hear the word *duke*, or even a name that bears that title because I blush. If he only knew how troubled I am for his sake! I never sit down without being ready to go out if his name is said or if something is mentioned about his family because I am instantly red and trembling, and I say quite the contrary of what I'd like to say. This is why Mama scolds me. It's natural that I appear to have bad manners; I am always suspended, not knowing what to do, unquiet, always afraid I'll blush and also afraid that if I do they'll guess what I'm thinking.

I must confess that I am pretty satisfied with my face—not always, but sometimes. I think I really am pretty, but I'd like to hear some competent man express his opinion on the subject. I often pass my time before the looking-glass. It's not right, but it's so. I particularly like to look at myself at twilight with candles behind me so as to have a somewhat blue reflection on the face and the ears transparent, and I am very often occupied so. I will not conceal that I am frequently annoyed in a society of women and that I prefer the company of men.

But for a woman with a good position the society of women is indispensable, like bread. Because if a woman neglects other women and old people, they will be so angry with her she'll be talked about. There are rules; a woman must often be in the society of other women and old people. This is obligatory for her well-being, and when she has met this requirement, she may do what she pleases; she may even flirt with the men. But if she has the hatred of women, she has only to die, as they have a rather long tongue, especially if she is pretty. Even though she may be the most innocent in the world, they will charge her with all sorts of crimes, being jealous and ugly. I will follow these rules. They are mine.

Wednesday, May 7, 1873. At 7:00 this morning, after yesterday's rain, it was beautiful—so cool! The trees lighted by the sun were so green that I could not study. Furthermore, I had time. I went to the garden, and placing my chair near the fountain, I had a splendid scene because from this fountain surrounded by trees you cannot see the sky or the earth; you see a kind of stream with a fountain and some rocks covered with ivy and moss, and all around are trees of different species, lighted here and there by the sun. The green lawn was soft-looking, and I longed to lie on it and turn over and over. The grass was like a clump of trees, cool, neat, velvety soft, and so beautiful that it is in vain I try to give any idea of it.

Yesterday, when I prayed on my knees, I felt that God heard me, and I cried. Three times already He has heard me and granted what I asked. The first time I asked for a croquet set. That time I prayed more than I ever had in my life before, and a few days later my aunt brought me a croquet set from Geneva. The second time when I asked Him to help me learn English, I screamed and cried so much that my imagination became excited, and it seemed

I saw the face of the Virgin in my bedroom promising me what I was asking. I could even recognize which picture of the Virgin I saw there. The third time, it was to have Remy court me and tell me he loved me. But there have been many more times He has given me what I asked—my amazone [riding habit], my riding lessons, my acquaintance with Bertha in Baden, and even the dresses I wanted. Blessed be His name!

We wanted to tell the Howards goodbye as Mr. and Mrs. Howard and Hélène leave tomorrow for Russia, but we didn't find them home. Later we met them on the Promenade on their way to our house. We took Hélène to the garden. She has a great friendship for me, which makes me very happy. Mrs. Howard told Mama that she likes my reasoning on the education of children.

Thursday, May 8, 1873. We saw the Howards off at 2:30. Lots of people came to tell them goodbye, and ours was a big group. Dina and I strolled in the railroad station with Hélène. She's a spoiled child, but I love her because she doesn't pretend to admire the views nor to adore flowers. She doesn't say she is sensible or sentimental and doesn't compare herself to a flower like Miss Collignon. She certainly admires the scenery and flowers more than those people who say they do but are so busy showing it to others they don't have time to do it sincerely.

We went as far as Monte Carlo with the Howards. I was next to Hélène. We agree on a lot of things, and she showed me some affection without saying anything. She says it with her eyes and in brief words—sometimes brutal. When talking casually about different things, I asked her to write to me. They are going to Italy first. The family was very friendly to us. How Hélène's mother adores her!

Friday, May 9, 1873. I waited for Miss Collignon thirty minutes for my lesson. Every day it's the same thing, but Mama reproaches me and doesn't realize that I also am upset about it, that I am boiling inside with impatience, anger, indignation. Miss Collignon skips the lessons and makes me lose my time. I'm already fourteen. What's going to happen to me? Sometimes I'm pale, and sometimes my cheeks burn, my heart beats fast, and I can't remain quiet in one place. Then tears fill my heart, but I manage to hold them, which only makes me more unhappy! All these things are ruining my health. They damage my character, making me irritable and impatient. People who lead quiet lives show it in their faces; and I, who am at each instant irritated by trifles, show all that in my face. Miss Collignon is stealing from me by taking away my studies. When I am sixteen or seventeen I will have other interests, but now is the time for me to learn.

If this infamous young woman without conscience makes me lose my time now, I can still catch up by studying an extra year; but it will be a year deprived of pleasure because of her. I wouldn't want people to believe that when I'm through studying I'm only going to dress and dance. No. Being finished with elementary studies, I'll be busy seriously with painting, music, and singing, since I have a lot of talent for all of these.

Well, it made me feel much better to write all this! I feel calmer. But this constant agitation is bad for my character and my health, and also for my face. This blushing makes my cheeks burn like fire, and then when I calm down they're not cool and pink. In place of the one color they should have, I am sometimes red and sometimes pale—and at other times

I'm tired. It's her fault because of the agitation she provokes. Sometimes I even have light headaches after burning that way. Mama accuses me, saying it is my fault that I don't speak English. That outrages me.

Well, Miss Collignon has arrived.

Maybe I've accused her unjustly. She's ill, and because of that she misses classes; but when she's not sick she still misses. However, the fact is that she takes my hours away—on wings— and as this happens every day, the time I lose is enormous.

Saturday, May 10, 1873. I went to the baths at 11:00 and had a good swim, but there were a lot of the handsome Niçois men in the water and that bothered me considerably.

When Mama and I left the house, we went down near the sea where some poor old fishermen were pulling out their nets. We waited to see what they'd caught. Only six fishes! What misery! Mama bought all of them and gave the men some extra money. While she went back to the house to get the money, I waited for her on the Promenade, leaning against a tree.

On the Promenade, our carriage was headed for the Howards' (as we were going to see the children) when we met them in their carriage. We all got out and walked. Lise considers me superior to her and would like to become my friend; but I already belong to Hélène, even though I am not completely her confidante yet. But this will come. As for myself, I would never say *everything* to a friend, and I don't consider the friendship between two girls strong. But I have never had any girl friend, and I really can't know what friendship is. I can't believe in it as I've never experienced it. I know it can happen between two men, two "bon vivants" who don't go deeply into anything, who live without the trouble of unnecessary torments, and who are friends especially for a hunting trip or for a dinner, for example.

Generally it is this light, frivolous friendship that is the most sincere and the most devoted in case of need. Between women this will to be friends without looking too deeply into things can exist on the same terms, friends for good times, parties, clothes, and that sort of thing. But it's very difficult to be friends seriously and positively. It's useless to look for that; it will come naturally for me and Hélène or we'll not want it.

Sunday, May 11, 1873. After church we took Nathalie Patton back with us, and at 1:00 we went to their home. Mrs. Savelieff, Mrs. Patton's mother, is dying. For the last two days she has been in a coma and doesn't talk any more. She had been sick for days. When we went into her room we saw the old woman, but at first when I looked for the patient in the bed, I didn't see anything. Then, going closer, I saw her head. She had lost so much weight that from a strong, tall, enormous woman she was reduced to almost nothing. Her mouth was open; her eyes were closed, or a little open sometimes, but veiled and dead-looking. Her breathing was loud and difficult. Everyone talked in a low voice, but she didn't move at all.

Although the doctor said she doesn't feel anything, I think she can hear and understand everything around her but cannot scream or talk. When Mama touched her, she was moaning.

We met old Savelieff on the stairway. He took Mama's hand and burst into tears, sobbing, "You don't take care of yourself! You yourself are sick! You must take care of yourself." The poor man! My heart ached for him.

Then the daughter arrived silently, going close to the bed. She called to her mother with loving words and cried. Poor thing! She's been like that for days. It must be horrible to see your mother dying slowly day after day. I went with the old man into another room. He asked me to stay with him there. How he has aged in the last few days! Everyone else has a consolation; her daughter has her children and her husband, but he is alone. Living with his wife for thirty years is something. Has he lived with her well or badly? Maybe the habit alone is a lot!

I returned to the patient several times. Their maid was so desperate! It was good to see so much affection for her mistress in a servant. The old man has become almost like a child. But, after all, I believe the most awful thing about it was for the old woman's daughter, because you can have many brothers and sisters; you can even have another husband. But a mother is unique, and no other love in the world can be compared to hers.

Monday, May 12, 1873. I think I may soon go to Vienna. God gives!

Tuesday, May 13, 1873. I want to go to Vienna for a *double reason*—first, because I think the Duke of Hamilton will be there since he is everywhere things happen, and second, because the Exposition is there this summer and I want to see it.

Wednesday, May 14, 1873. Today I really set out to get them to approve the Vienna trip. I talked to the end of my endurance, giving a thousand reasons why we should go (except my secret reason). Finally I said I didn't want to spend the entire summer in Nice. I cried, I asked, I was in a sad mood. I am disturbed, without a desire to do anything or speak to anybody.

Mrs. Savelieff died last night and today at 11:00 Mama and Dina went to attend the church service for the dead, and this evening Mama and I went to the house. There was a crush of people. There was sorrow on the right, sorrow on the left, sorrow on the ceiling, sorrow on the floor, pain expressed on each chair, in the light of the candles, even in the air.

Mrs. Patton became hysterical after the service. The baby was crying, too—all of them. I took the little one away with me and kissed her hands and set her down next to me. I wanted to say something consoling to her, but I could not. (What consolation is there?) "Time only can—something." What I have said before today has seemed good, but today I found it unseemly, stupid. What is there to do? Everything has an end. Yet if someone in our family were dying, I couldn't think that way!

Thursday, May 15, 1873. Except for my aunt, who has a very high fever, we all went to the funeral at 8:30. First there was a service at the home, and then the casket was brought to the church where we all had gone in the meantime for a Mass and a funeral service. Many people there were unknown to me, but I recognized the two Grand Dukes. At the end Mrs. Patton fainted and the old man fell into a chair, where he was no longer crying, but screaming. We took care of him and gave him some water. The scenes of their sorrow were so awful that I cried and am still shaken. All around me were tears, cries, sobbing—all the horror of distress and despair.

Friday, May 16, 1873. Of what I saw and heard yesterday I can say, remembering the lines from the *Inferno*:

> Here sighs, weeping, and high griefs
> sounded through the starless air,
> so that at the beginning, I cried for them.

> *[Quivi sospiri, pianti e alti guai*
> *risonavan per l'aere sanza stelle,*
> *per ch'io al cominciar ne lagrimai.]*

> *Inferno* III, 22-24

I asked Mama to come with me to order my dress made, but she answered, "What do you take me for? Nadianka is ill. I cannot leave her!"

There is no answer to that; she is ill. I left with Dina and Markevitch. I took the dress they're to copy, but not being completely satisfied with its style, I wanted Mama to be there to help me. I came back only to find that Mama had gone to Monaco with those horrible Anitchkoffs. She couldn't give a half hour to me, because it would mean *leaving her sick sister*; but she left to go for the whole day with those people! It was too much. I was indignant. If anyone else had betrayed me like that I wouldn't have cared. But my own mother!

I called to Markevitch to come down; we got a carriage, and I ordered Dominique to take us to the railroad station in the hope of catching her in time to shame her. In the carriage I behaved like a crazy girl, laughing and talking, but nobody else saw me, thank goodness! I was not in my normal state of mind.

When we arrived, the train had already left. No longer angry about Mama, I had another idea: we returned home, I took five francs, and with Markevitch I went to Rumpelmayer's, where we had hot chocolate and pastries. We laughed like happy people, and I rewarded myself for Mama's betrayal.

At present it is understood that Dina, Walitsky, and I will be going to Vienna. What a joy! When we mentioned our plans at lunch, Miss Collignon looked very disappointed, even mortified; and trying to hide her feelings as much as possible, she said, "It's not possible! How beautiful it is; Dina and Walitsky going away together, and a little girl will be their 'screen.'"

People really are mean! She said that so disagreeably that it hurt me terribly and I said, "You are the first person to think of such a thing! I can see all your meanness." That was the end of it.

But I understand her discontent very well. Only a few days ago she was heartbroken about her Indian, and she was hoping to go with us to Vienna for a vacation in spite of the fact that everything has been falling apart in her job. I am very sorry for her, but what can we do? She isn't angry any more, and that's why I am more sorry for her.

In Vienna I'll see him. Oh, God, let it happen!

Saturday, May 17, 1873. George is with us. He starts drinking in the mornings. Toward the end of the dinner he was not at the table, and Miss Collignon, who had been out for a short time, came rushing in, shouting, "What a screaming in the garden! Will someone go and see? I don't know what it is!" We all got up; I had just left the room when someone told me, "George has slapped the Tolstoy woman. Stay quiet. I'll tell you afterwards what happened, but just now don't show that you know."

I asked questions; ran here and there; didn't know what I was doing. All the house was upset, and just then George appeared, saying, as he flexed his right arm, "My arm is strong and I gave it to her. She will know now!"

And somebody else said, "She certainly took a fall!"

How unfortunate! My aunt has been very sick for a week—seriously ill. What a horror! And to crown all this disgrace and its embarrassment, Miss Kolokoltsoff, Mrs. Daniloff, and Mrs. Teplakoff dropped in to visit us at that moment. They were taken into the yellow room. I was in the dining room with Mama, who was almost fainting; and George, the hero of the catastrophe, also arrived just then in the yellow room to tell his story to the ladies. We tried to lead him into the dining room, but he didn't want to go because he was drunk.

Mrs. Teplakoff offered her carriage, saying that he would have to leave at once or be arrested. "Quick! Quick!"

We thanked her. Everybody was afraid for George. He, on the other hand, wanting to show his courage, would not leave. I was trembling. Oh, if he could only escape! I ran to my study and fell on my knees asking the One-Who-Can-Do-Anything to protect George. Miss Collignon had stopped a carriage in the Rue de France (behind the house), and she offered to take him, if not so far as Eze or Monaco, somewhere away from the railroad station. The carriage was waiting for him downstairs. My aunt, sick as she was, got up. We calmed her down when the "Lion's Heart" entered, drunk, screaming, scolding, striding with huge steps in the room. He wanted to get away, but he didn't want to show he was afraid.

Then Adam came in, saying, "The police are here!" That meant the Tolstoys had called them. We were frantic. I ran to George and I spoke to him forcefully, magnificently, like an actress at the end of an act, even though I didn't believe myself capable of it.

"Get out, George! Leave!" We begged him.

I ran to Miss Collignon's room and put a hat on her head. She ran, George with her, down the back stairs. I returned to the window and looked out, but the carriage had not moved. I was afraid they'd catch up with him. I devoured the carriage with my eyes, and the moments seemed centuries. I went to another window and then ran from one to the other, ending by missing their departure.

Then I thought, He heard our prayer! and I thanked God.

But there is nothing reassuring about George's predicament. If he comes back to Nice, he won't escape, that's sure. But as God had let him get away, certainly George won't come back—will he? He is the cause of all our troubles. All our misfortunes come from this vagabond! All that is bad for us is the work of his hands, and we could live quite differently without this scoundrel!

He disappeared for a year, and then in a few days he made up for all the time he had left us in peace. Now he's gone away again.

But what acquaintances are possible for us after this? Nobody will want to mix in such scandals as ours. And yet other people do ten times more mischief than we, but without any noise!

When the bell rang, nobody wanted to open the door, but finally we did. It was two dress-makers with Mama's dress. They said two policemen were outside asking very politely for Mr. Babanine. Good! After talking with Grandpapa they saw that any charges made against him couldn't be true; so they went away to look for another man. Everybody was relieved except Dina, who was having a tragic crying fit. After all, George *is* her father!

BOOK FIVE

Book 5 of my Journal
Begun Sunday, May 18, 1873
Ended Wednesday, June 4, 1873
Concerning Marie Bashkirtseff
Promenade des Anglais, No. 51, Villa d'Aquaviva

Sunday, May 18, 1873. In his capacity as Prefect, Mr. Patton paid Mama a call to talk about George.

"But my brother doesn't want to appear in court here in Nice," Mama was telling him, "even though my lawyer says that if he did, Mrs. Tolstoy's charges could be presented and refuted."

"Your lawyer is right," Patton told her. "Your brother cannot have an attorney represent him if he himself doesn't appear. But the Tolstoys will have one who will be able to accuse your family of anything, and there will be no one to stop him."

I am broken up about it. The Tolstoys are slandering us everywhere, and now after this they will be able to say anything! My name is tarnished, and that's killing me. I cried like an animal, dismayed, humiliated.

Thursday, May 22, 1873. Without any preparation at all, here we are on our way to Geneva! Dina offered me her grey dress, and she, Walitsky, and Markevitch saw us off at the depot. (My aunt is still sick in bed.)

[The next few pages are in English, alternating with passages in French, given without specific changes in day or date.]

[In English:] I knew we were in Geneva when I saw the cathedral I drew last year. From the railway station we took a coach and drove directly to Paul's school. I was waiting in the parlor when I heard a rude voice in the antechamber. I saw a boy of about seventeen spring into the carriage where Mama was waiting out in front. When he came into the room with her, he was quite different from the boy we left here a year ago. He's really only thirteen and a half. His voice was disagreeable and so altered that I couldn't recognize it at all; just as if somebody else's voice is now in Paul and his is gone!

We breakfasted at our hotel, I dressed myself ([in French:] *ecru dress, musketeer hat, tired but very good*), and we went on foot to Mrs. Sapogenikoff's, Mama, Paul, and I. She was not at home; the children were alone. Mary is as little as she was, but Olga is a little taller than last year. I don't like that sort of girls [sic], secrets, little letters, signs, sighs, glances with the boys. There's a boy, Stephen, who lives with them. We played at croquet. I enjoyed it. Then came Mrs. Sapogenikoff and Mr. Yourkoff. I had a bad headache and was almost unable to speak and answer to the jokes.

Then at home [the hotel], the goldsmith Krumling, came for this affair. They [Mama and Mr. Krumling] counted, [in French] *subtracted, divided and multiplied*. They have done nothing for Mama was very impatient and would not listen to what he said. Then very happily came Yourkoff for the relief. He also after lossing [sic] his patience several times, at last made them understand. I am very glad indeed that it is ended!

Saturday, May 24, 1873. [In French:] We dined with the Sapogenikoffs, saw a circus with them, took a horseback ride into the forest, and bought a beautiful croquet game like the one the Boyds had in Baden. I found the children to be like the ones I'd seen in Baden; the boys courted the girls, and all of them imitated the grownups. I thought I might like to live in Geneva, but if I did I would have to know everybody or it would be like living in a tomb, because people here don't gather in the streets as in Baden and Nice.

Sunday, May 25, 1873. After church Abramovitch came to the hotel to talk to us. He paid me a lot of compliments and said some silly things, but I found him likable because he's so sympathetic. And then he went with us to the Sapogenikoffs' house.

Somehow, I did not feel at ease in their home. I thought the girls were too free, blunt, and intimate with the boys. Mary asked me to speak English with her. But then after a while she turned to Mama and said something like, "She's not speaking badly at all! She still lacks. . . ." Her patronizing manner made me furious.

Monday, May 26, 1873. When we were all packed to leave, the bellboy came at 11:00 to announce Paul's friend Abramovitch; but as Mama wasn't ready, we talked for a few minutes and then I invited him to come with us to lunch.

We talked about Nice, our acquaintance, and our friends. Abramovitch was very attentive to me again. "I always take your side when you are accused of anything," he told me.

"Accused?" I couldn't believe my ears.

"The other day at the Pattons' they were talking about you, and I vigorously defended you," he explained.

I didn't ask him *from what*, but I was glad he had championed me. To be the subject of drawing-room conversations in Nice makes me sad. I have done nothing wrong!

Mrs. Sapogenikoff and Yourkoff took us to the railway station, and Paul stayed with us until the train finally pulled away. He will stay in Geneva for his examinations before returning to Nice. He is planning to prepare himself at the lycée for the university.

At Lyon I asked Mama if we could take a sleeping car. She agreed, and how comfortable we were, being able to undress while traveling! We were perfectly at ease, but I slept badly because we would have to leave the train at 5:00 in the morning at Marseille to change trains and I was afraid the conductor might open the door and see us in our nightclothes. So although the train was an hour late, we were still tired when we hurried to dress, drank a few drops of bad coffee, and got off to wait in the station for an hour.

As we drew closer to Nice the greenery changed, becoming pale. The ground was no longer black, but reddish, and the trees, covered with dust, looked faded. How different it was from beautiful Switzerland! Arriving at 3:00, we were met by Walitsky and Solominka [Mrs. Markevitch]. Aunt Nadya was still in bed.

"I think Marie liked Geneva more than any other place we've been," Mama told the family.

"There were more boys!" I elucidated.

Our own apartment appeared beautiful after the hotel. Still, Nice was unbearable now, and I was literally burning to get away.

However, as we were committed to leave the Aquaviva, our hunting for apartments went on. But nothing seemed to suit us. If the house was large enough, the garden was too small. I wanted to set up the croquet game in the garden, and this presented a new difficulty. There were several places we could have used if it had not been for that.

I agreed to teach our maid Polashka the Russian alphabet.

Thursday, May 29, 1873. We spent all day looking for an apartment. We saw the Villa Durand, which was really magnificent but a little too far. If we were going to buy it, that would be a different matter. But then I don't want to buy anything in Nice.

I returned to my studies today, and I also began teaching Polashka.

Friday, May 30, 1873. Today after the painting lesson I had an important discussion with Mr. Bensa. I told him I wanted to study seriously—to start at the beginning, because what I'm doing doesn't teach me anything. It's true. The present course is only time lost. On Monday I want to start drawing again. It's not his fault if he doesn't make me study right. He said before I had lessons with him he thought I had studied with someone else because of some mouths, eyes, and noses I'd drawn. That flattered me because the drawings I showed him were the first ones I had ever done by *myself*.

Saturday, May 31, 1873. Today when I asked Miss Collignon for an explanation of the math problem she assigned me, she said, "You must understand it by yourself."

"But what I don't know must be explained to me," I protested.

"There is no *must be* here," she answered. "Let's continue."

"But I would like to try to understand this first problem before I start the others," I said in an extra-calm tone. I think she was enraged not to find anything impolite in my answer.

She steals my time. Four months already lost! She is ruining my life and my future happiness. When I ask her for an explanation of something, she answers me in a vulgar voice, "I don't want to be spoken to that way," or something like that. I think she is a little mad, as she is naturally so mean, and her illness makes her impossible. When I said again [that I wanted to learn the first problem before moving on], she looked at me with the eyes of a she-devil and shouted with all her strength: "Do what I tell you! How dare you speak to me like that? You are impolite with everybody, but I won't stand for it."

I asked, "Why are you screaming?" in such a calm tone that I surprised myself. In situations where I am irritated, moved, or angry, I become unusually calm. My tone irritated her still more, as she was expecting me to explode.

"You are fourteen years old. How dare you talk to me that way?"

"Exactly, Miss. You say I am fourteen. I will not permit anyone to talk to me like that. Please don't shout."

She left, furious, still shouting all kinds of impolite things, while all the time I continued peacefully, which put her in a rage. "That's the last lesson I'll give you!"

"Good!" I said as she left the room. I really was much relieved. I sighed, feeling freed of a hundred-pound load hung round my neck. As I left to go to Mama's room, she ran into the hall and started again. I continued my tactics, paying almost no attention to her. We walked along the hall to Mama's room together, she like a Fury and I with the most imperturbable air imaginable. In Mama's room I found my aunt, Dina, and Markevitch already gathered; and then Walitsky entered, saying, "I understand you've had an argument with Collignon."

"It's not that," I said. "I do not quarrel. She is leaving."

Markevitch rushed toward me, kissed me, and said in Russian, *Very good! How happy I am for you. Glory to God!* Naturally I told them what had happened. Mama had a short explanation, speaking to this "dearie" and telling her all the duties she had been missing and some other things.

But Collignon's conscience, her honor—where are they? What audacity! She insisted that she was doing her duty, that she was constantly with us, that she was speaking English. Oh, that is too much! Such a lie!! I have early known human perfidy. Anyway, for my happiness, at last, she is leaving next week.

As I was dressing to go out I received a letter from Princess Galitzine, saying that the Tolstoys are about to publish an *awful* article about us in *The Lighthouse of the Coastline*. I took it to Mama at once. George's case came before the court today; and as he was not present, he received a sentence of a month in jail, a fifty-franc fine, and a 2,000-franc charge for damages and interest. People who don't appear for their trials always get the maximum. But that's George! Instead of appearing and telling the truth, he hides and lets himself be accused of what he hasn't even done. Not to appear at your own trial! The Tolstoy attorney can say what he likes, whereas if George had come he could have exposed that woman, showing what she is and what she has done! But because of one person, all the family is tarnished.

Mama got the prosecutor to do what was necessary to stop publication of the article. Then she went to Lefèvre, and he, too, rushed and pushed to have it stopped. Although George has been sentenced, Lefèvre says the case is far from lost; if my uncle would come here . . . but that stupid animal, that donkey, that horror doesn't want to. He doesn't care! He came here for a week, made a scandal for us, soiled us for a year, and left for a place where he is not known. As for us, we remain and have to endure these insults. What can we do? We went to the Howards', visited with the de Mouzays and Lefèvre, and yet all the time, even as I am writing now, I was and am thinking of *him!*

Sunday, June 1, 1873. Mama and I went with Lefèvre to Monaco to persuade George to come to Nice. We took a carriage from the station and drove directly to the house where

George lives. We entered a poor little room which has another next to it where the servant lives and a dining room, used when it's necessary as a salon. Anna was there. We sat and started to discuss, but in vain. George wouldn't listen. His reason, like a baby's, is no reason at all. After we talked, screamed, and offered our arguments for two hours, I proposed going to the Casino. On leaving, I held out my hand to Anna, and she kissed it. I was very confused, and not knowing what to do, I kissed her.

We went to the Casino where now one must have a personal card to get in. We found the salons *clean*, rid of all those low-class people—the cocottes, et cetera. It was more like a refined drawing room, but a little monotonous. I realized that when those other people were there it was more animated, and I prefer Monaco as it was then.

Mama won 300 francs and I won thirty. Solominka and Walitsky were there. He had gone at 10:00 to persuade George, but he didn't have any luck either.

My aunt is feeling better, and I hope we'll soon go to Vienna. I'm praying for that.

Monday, June 2, 1873. As Miss Collignon is leaving Thursday, I was free all evening. We were all together, the family playing cards or talking and I playing the piano. I played quite well. After we talked quietly (a rare event in our house), I sang a song from Dante. We joked and the time was passing agreeably when Mr. and Mrs. Patton came and started to talk about the Tolstoy affair, urging that we must not let things go this way—that George has been attacked and must come to defend himself, and so on. We can't force him, but I know how to succeed; I'll pray to God to give him reason.

I have decided that until I get a new teacher and some professors I'll resume my studies, but only for review. I'll take up everything I've learned, in order, following my plan of study.

Wednesday, June 4, 1873. It is 6:40 A.M., and I'm writing because I had a horrible dream. We were in an unknown house when all of a sudden I or somebody else—I don't remember who—looked out the window and saw the sun, which became bigger and bigger, filling almost half the sky. It was not shining or hot. Then it divided. A fourth of it disappeared, and the rest started to spin, changing colors. We were horrified! Then a cloud covered almost half of it. Then it stopped and we were horror-struck. Everyone screamed, "The sun stopped!" as if its natural appearance were that of spinning. It stayed like that a few minutes, motionless and enormous, but pale. Then the whole earth became strange. It was not that it tipped over; I can't express what it was. It was something unknown to us in everyday life. Words do not exist to express what we don't understand. Then it started to turn again like two wheels, one inside the other. I mean the sun at times was covered by a cloud as round as itself. The tumult was general. I was asking myself if this was the end of the world. I wanted to believe this was only for a moment, but at that moment everything started again. It's the end of the world for sure! I thought. But then I asked myself, Why didn't God tell me about it? Am I not worthy alive to witness this day? Now I'm wondering if the dream was sent by God to inform me of some great event. Or is it simply "nerves"? I can recall it all.

Miss Collignon will leave soon, and I am a little sad about it. Even a dog with which you lived for a month makes you sad when leaving. In spite of our relationship, good or bad, I have "a worm in my heart."

As we were leaving for a bath at the beach (the sea was *so* good!), we learned that George is accepting what he must do about the Tolstoy case. Our friends have been going to Monaco every day to persuade him to come here, and Mama and my aunt have been going to Monaco for the same reason. When I went with them last time to the railway station, I declared positively that I do not want to wait any more—that I want to go to Vienna. I spoke warmly and even cried. The result: we are going on the twentieth of this month.

I don't do anything in the evenings, but time flies like an arrow. I study in the mornings and I spend two and a half hours at the piano. When we took Miss Collignon to the train—Mama, Dina, and I—she said farewell to everyone quite tenderly, and we kissed her good-bye. I was very composed, giving her practical advice for her trip, but not without a certain—well, not a regret, but with a habit of feeling close to her. I was surprised to find that her departure touched me. On her part she was not at all upset, and no special word was exchanged between us. Let's hope we'll be able to find a good substitute!

Manotte was very pleased with me this morning as I played part of Mendelssohn's *Concerto in G Minor* without making one mistake.

I have no energy and cannot work. Summer in Nice kills me. Not only is the heat enervating, but there is nobody interesting here and I am bored. I am irritated, sad, and ready to cry at any moment. I feel that this is ruining my character, my health, and finally, my looks. In the name of all I hold dearest in the world, I pray God to give me peace of mind.

I feel guilty. Maybe I am being punished for my fancies and for the things I say to my mother and other people. It's as if a voice were telling me to change before it's too late and that I'll be punished if I don't change. Oh, dear God, I'll be good and sweet if you'll only help me!

Do you know, I woke up feeling almost gay? Could it have been my prayers? And after a fitting for a beautiful dress, I felt almost light!

And today I worked well; I was proud and happy. The heat was not excessive and a little rain made the day delicious.

Yesterday a Russian man accosted Mama in the train, and both she and my aunt talked to him. He came today, followed by a boy carrying some pastries and something else. I think he's rather low class. He was bragging, saying bizarre things. He certainly must be one of the secret police.

Mama hasn't enough character to teach such a person to know his place, and she accepted his gifts laughingly. It's a weakness; she doesn't see too much difference between talking on trains and at roulette. I will never start a conversation with a stranger. I'm like the English. But one doesn't have to be English to have good judgment. The man stayed far too long, and that irritated me. I take everything seriously, and it's bad for me. To crown my happiness (really, it was too much!), we took him back in our carriage!!—a man we had seen for the first time—and so strange. They suspected that he might even be a traitor and didn't have the strength to get rid of him. I predict that we'll be sorry; I think he's a dangerous man. Oh, my God, how much I suffer because of the kindness, the weakness, and the trust of Mama!

We've been looking everywhere for a new apartment, as time is running out here at the Aquaviva.

At dinner we talked about marriage, affection, et cetera. I insisted that an honest girl *cannot* love a married man. "Oh, I could *like* him, yes. But *love* him? Never!"

Mrs. Markevitch argued that that was without importance. "Love makes no distinctions," she argued.

I think she is a woman without principles, a silly jade.

I asked her, "If the coachman pleased you, you would love him?"

"Yes, probably, if he pleased me."

I was a little embarrassed for her. As for myself, men of a lower position than mine do not exist for me. I tell myself that they are not men, but machines who are serving us.

Then Markevitch came back with, "For you no man is important if he is not a duke."

At those words, afraid I'd blush, I got up to beat her with my napkin, saying, "Be quiet, straw head! What a dummy, stupid fool!"

Mama and my aunt were looking on and smiling indulgently. They have their own ideas.

Vienna! Oh, make me go there, my God. Do that!

We have finally settled for the Villa Baquis. It seems to me noble, beautiful, a big house with a fine garden. There are many rooms. Only one thing bothers me: I'll be deprived of the happiness of seeing *him*, as this villa is not on the Promenade des Anglais. But Dina and my aunt also like the house. Tomorrow we are signing the lease for 5,500 francs for the year. Then there will be no more delay, and we'll be able to go to Vienna. And there I'll see. . . . Oh, I am silly!

And then that horrible Molchapov, the one we think is a spy, came again. I wanted to have the servant say nobody was home, but Papa wanted to receive him. Mama and the others went downstairs to receive him in the garden. He disgusts me, and I still suspect that he is a secret agent. Oh, but they are imprudent! It's that there have been so many people who have misled us. I don't understand how they can receive a suspect, unknown person in their home, and I'm afraid they will regret it.

Papa [Grandpapa] and I had another quarrel when he spoke badly about my family name; he even mentioned my father. I asked him to moderate his language and explained that I owe nothing to Constantine Bashkirtseff. I told Papa, "He does not give me anything; I owe him nothing; I live on my own money."

And then I discovered that while we were arguing, those ladies had taken the spy in their own carriage and gone to Monaco! Oh, rage! Oh, horror!!

Poor Solominka Markevitch! She has to return to Russia. Our group went to see her off, and when the train started to move, she called to Mama, "Goodbye, Maria Stepanovna. You have given me some really good memories!" We all said goodbye and after a few minutes we could see only some smoke and a little black dot far away. That was all that was left of poor Solominka.

The Howards have returned, and I have to confess that Hélène has become so pretty I am a little envious of her! But for only one reason: I have a fear that, because she is travelling a lot—the summer in England, the spring in Russia, the winter in Nice—she will please *him*. Yes, it's crazy of me, but anything can happen.

Oh, I am ugly. I recognize it now. I'm sure he'll love her! And I'll detest her. No. I'll be calm. Humiliated, I'll recognize that I can't compare with her beauty, that I was crazy to hope. And I'll love her, too. I'll be humble. But her presence will be insupportable. I'll not love her nor detest her; I'll feel only envy. Oh, what a rage when one feels one's own impotence!

Why is it that one is beautiful and the other is not? Why this injustice? Oh, there are things that are loved more than beauty. Do I have them—grace, sweetness, intelligence, knowledge? This last one I'll have. And the others? Yet not one of these things can replace beauty. One can even say that they are the virtues of ugly persons.

But now I am so afraid of her! I know some day she could be a rival. I am not a fool, my God. Deliver me from these horrible fantasies, which make me unhappy and restless, and which make me weep!

BOOK SIX

Book 6 of my Journal
Begun Monday, June 16, 1873
Ended Saturday, July 12, 1873
Concerning Marie Bashkirtseff
Promenade des Anglais, No. 51, Villa d'Aquaviva
Villa Baquis, the Buffa Quarter

Monday, June 16, 1873. "Moussia, why don't you go to Sacco's and make the arrangements for the lease?" my aunt proposed. "You talk to them. Plan and arrange everything right." I wondered if grownups had ever before depended upon their children like this. Mrs. Sacco, the landlady of the Baquis, was very sympathetic; but she wouldn't let us have the three-months' lease we were asking for, and I knew her argument was fair. The family accepted the one-year's arrangement she required and we signed, ready to take possession immediately.

Walitsky came in, telling us that Nina Sapogenikoff was in town on business; and so we went at once to find her at the Grand Hotel. She confided to us that she was in debt and had come to borrow from Daouis, but he was gone and she was very annoyed. She didn't want her husband to know about her debts. She told Mama a lot of things that we learned later: her arrangement with her husband, unusual to say the least, was that she live in Geneva with the children and Mr. Yourkoff, a friend who never leaves them, like one of the family.

The husband comes to see them twice a year, and the two spouses have the most agreeable relationship. When one leaves to go to town, they kiss each other. Maybe it's very nice, but . . . this gentleman, their friend? It's not very clear.

Tuesday, June 17, 1873. I slept until 9:00 when I learned that Nina Sapogenikoff, Mama, and my aunt had come in at 11:00 P.M. and that our friend had spent the night at our house. She told them about the troubles she's been having caused by a sort of Mrs. Tolstoy, a malicious woman who has been sending letters to all the Geneva merchants warning them that they will not be paid if they sell to Nina. She was forced to pawn her diamonds and felt threatened with the possibility of not recovering them. She came here looking for a source of money to pay the pawnbroker. Well, at lunch time Walitsky came in with the money for her, and he saw her off on the afternoon train.

I am pale. I have been for a long time, and it seems to me I've become ugly. After a visit from the Howards, Mama scolded me for my pallor and the bags under my eyes. It's not my fault and I feel abused. I would give anything to be pink and pretty! Maybe I'm pale because I keep worrying about the time I've been losing, the lessons I've missed, and the fact that I'm not learning anything now. And of course I keep wondering whether I'll ever see the Duke again, and if I do whether he'll love me.

We went, among many other people, to see the Howards off on the train, taking several boxes of candy for them. We're very good friends, and I love them all. I thought Mrs. Howard showed the most affection for our family.

Mama and my aunt cherish the plan of my marrying Oritza Miloradovitch. (We call him "Gritz" or "Grisyo.") It would be a splendid match. He's young, handsome, extremely rich, and, above all, has no brothers or sisters, which would be a great happiness. And my two mothers cannot imagine anything better! All their wishes would be fulfilled if I married him, just the way the degrees of the globe meet at the poles!

I am the only one who is not unhappy about the new apartment. At the moment when I was finishing my third hour at the piano, the carriage arrived with Mama's order to carry the paintings away. I was very happy to have something to do because for the last week I was held in suspension, like those poor souls Dante wrote about:

I was among those who are suspended
And a woman, blessed and beautiful, called to me,
Such that I asked her to command me.

[Io ero tra color che son sospesi,
e donna mi chiam beata e bella,
tal che di comandare io la richiesi.]

    Inferno II, 49-51

The thing that bothers me most is that I'm losing my time. It's awful! I cry about it and grow pale and ugly because of my distress.

Well, we're going to be settled. The Lord must have heard my prayer! I began gathering all the paintings and the landau came twice to fetch them. What a splendid thing it is to take an active part in things! My self-esteem was fully gratified when I saw that all were indebted to me for the quick transport of all the little things which, each apart, seem nothing, but when put all together, fill the largest trunks. My pride received another boost when Polashka said, "If it had not been for Maria Constantinovna, nothing would have been moved. She did it all." All my ambition is to be useful. Far from wishing to be a man, I'm very glad to be what I am. In my understanding a woman can be just as useful to her country and to humanity as a man, and there *was* (not *is*) only a difference in education. I cannot live ignored and lost in the crowd; I must distinguish myself. It's a pity that people are still a little stupid and don't yet look at women as they ought to. Their attitude will prevent me from doing some brilliant deed or occupying a notable place in the government, or even becoming the president of a republic—France, for instance. But no, that's too easy. In France each worthless talker counts for something and can be the president. But I want to become something in reward for my services, not for a fine speech.

I regret very much leaving this apartment, not because it was so comfortable but because it is an old friend. When I think that I'll never see my dear study any more, or the table over which I bent every day as I wrote everything—the sweetest, most hidden thoughts in my soul—it seems to me that there is not one thing in the world I did not think of when I was in this little room, from the simplest to the most bizarre, nor one circumstance in which I did not include Hamilton—rich, poor, dead, living, angry, good, etc.

Friday, June 20, 1873. This morning, after going downstairs at 10:00 for my usual bath, when Polashka was going to pour the water on me, I felt dizzy. "Wait," I told her and sat on the edge of the tub, my eyes closed. When I opened them later, I realized I had fallen into the empty tub. Polashka was holding me with one hand and pouring water over my face with the other. At first I didn't know what that meant; then I realized I had fainted. What a strange feeling! I was very much afraid. The silly girl told me she tried calling for Adam but he hadn't heard. Imagine if he had entered! I was completely naked. Thank heaven she doesn't have a stronger voice! I had to lie down on Mary's bed for a few minutes I was so dizzy.

George came and talked with Malaussena about the Tolstoy business. At last everything's going all right; he's no longer acting like a fool.

As for the new villa, everybody is screaming about it, and I must admit I, too, would rather stay here. I can't bear to leave the Promenade! But there's nothing else to do now, and who knows? Maybe I'll be happier over there. "Whatever happens is for the best," they say.

Saturday, June 21, 1873. At six this morning I found everybody up, preparing to attend George's hearing. He was to appear at 8:00. I sat at the piano, and until Mama returned, I was hopeful; but it seemed there was trouble with the witnesses. When Lefèvre arrived [in court], George insulted him (without consequences, fortunately) and then Mr. Patton, Mr. and Mrs. Anitchkoff, George, and Walitsky all came to have lunch at our place in order to return by 2:00.

As for the lawsuit, no news has come from Russia, so we assume it's bad over there. Oh, if we should lose that suit! As I sat at the piano, some terrible ideas came into my mind. It isn't surprising I look tired; I wouldn't want my enemies to suffer as much as I do! All the horrors of our position are very real to me. The carelessness of my mother and my aunt is simply killing me! I lack words strong enough to express my pain, but I show my feelings differently from others. While my friends are lamenting, I am calm as if made of wood and seem to feel nothing. My irritation finally expresses itself in the anger I feel against everybody and everything. Others think I'm mean and have a bad temper, whereas it is the sorrow, the awful, unbearable anxiety that causes me to behave this way.

I am silently tortured. If I could only take a hand in everything!!!! It's not this miserable Tolstoy suit that worries me. I don't even think about it. It's there in Russia that the important thing is happening. I am not partial; our suit is just, and we should win. God is merciful; He'll not abandon me. Oh, Holy Virgin, protect us!

I know that freshness, beauty, and youth all depend on the tranquillity of the soul. Who am I at fourteen? An aged woman, nothing more. Two months ago I was white, rosy, fresh, gay. Now my complexion is faded, my skin wrinkled, pale, and yellowish. (Partly I blame Miss Collignon.) Dear God, inspire the others with some energy as you inspired George with the desire and courage to appear in court! I have prayed a long time for some relief from this trouble.

Around 5:00 they returned. It seems not even one independent witness would swear he had *not* seen George hitting Mrs. Tolstoy. All these friends are enemies! All who had asked for the appeal stepped aside or said unworthy things. Patton simply spoke against it, and he was the one who shouted the most.

George is condemned to six days in jail and must pay a 500-franc fine. That sentence diminishes nothing! Two months or six days are the same! He is very irritated and has again insulted Lefèvre, poor fat one, who did what he could but talked too much and said things he shouldn't have. Well, it's annoying, but really nothing to me. It's Russia that Mama is almost sick about: she's in tears about it. We seem to live in a kind of general confusion. George's case will be appealed in Aix, I think.

Sunday, June 22, 1873. My books are packed in boxes at the other house, and until we move I can't do anything. I bathed at the beach and then started to read some English—a witty novel by Oliver Goldsmith.

Monday, June 23, 1873. I cried. Mama cried, and the scene lasted for two and a half hours, only to be interrupted by a fire in the Rue de France behind our house. In a courtyard surrounded by four buildings full of hay, the flames were getting stronger, but those stupid Niçois were running around without knowing where they were going and were doing nothing to put out the fire. In fact, when they got far enough away from it, they seemed to stop and enjoy the show!

In Nice each neighborhood has a fire-engine with twenty horses. The firemen wear gold helmets and the harness is hung with a lot of little bells (like Hamilton's horse). The noise they made could be heard long before they arrived, and finally—it seemed a half hour later—here came a barrel of water pulled by ten men who looked triumphant! Add to all that four soldiers with guns. Were they going to use those on the fire? Fortunately, by that time the fire had been put out. And I returned to all the things I'd said. "It's my farewell, farewell to all the rude, nasty, mean, impertinent things I've been saying to you. I am completely changed; my character is reformed," I told Mama and my aunt. "I have become good, nice, kind. If anyone looks for an argument, I will leave." I really plan to be the good spirit of the house and do everything possible to avoid quarrels. I'll try to conciliate, arrange everything for the best, and anticipate the wishes of everyone—Papa, Mama, and my aunt. And I hope to be loved by all from the last beggar to the Duke and the King. It is the promise I have made to God. Since I want such great happiness, I must be worthy of it.

For the first time I have a bedroom to myself! The new house is not so beautiful as the last, but it's large and practical. My bedroom is the most beautiful room in the house. When all the furniture was finally in, I had the others help hang the paintings. At first it seemed we'd never be able to put everything in place. I had to climb on tables, raise my arms, measure the distances. The soles of my feet were burning, but I kept on. I was afraid that if we left it to the servants, the job would be badly done. In spite of the Anitchkoff children (they live next door), we finished by 11:30. I'm going to bed exhausted.

Wednesday, June 25, 1873. Paul is a good boy, but he's a worry to me, especially as Papa and George have so much influence over him. They cancel out everything Mama and the rest of us do for him. They preach such awful things, enough to poison him! Most especially, they destroy his respect for Mama by contradicting her advice. Even at dinner when Mama made a remark to him, Papa said she was wrong. She reproached him and left the table.

Thursday, June 26, 1873. I've already had an Italian lesson in the new house, and I've started, little by little, to organize the lessons.

Friday, June 27, 1873. Today, for the first time in the new house, I got up at 5:30. I worked well. How happy we are when we are satisfied with ourselves! And when I think that my happiness just depends on me! I have, then, only to study well, and that means *do what I must.* A secret voice tells me what I must do; I listen to it always. Once or twice I silenced it, but how much I paid for that! Never again! If you let go, you're lost.

We went again to the beach to swim. A lot of the nice Niçois people were there. I even got my hair wet on this great occasion, and there is no doubt that I was the heroine among the bathers. The Durands were there, and I introduced Paul to them.

We had company at dinner, including Princess Galitzine and Mrs. Anitchkoff. Everybody was nice to me, and I am very happy to please them—especially the women. We stayed in the garden all evening; it's nice here because we're never alone. But Dina and I took the carriage for a drive to see our dear Aquaviva. Dina shouted, "There's Gioja! I'm not joking." She was in a fiacre with a little girl. We turned around to see her. It had been such a long time . . . but our dear Dominique was driving so slowly that we couldn't catch up with her. Has she dispatched the Duke? It's hard to understand anything about it. Maybe she found too many adorers in Russia, richer. . . . People have said she was like a sovereign over there. And the Duke of Hamilton—I am sorry for him, poor fool. He'll no doubt crawl back to her like Simonoff, in the last row. But she'll probably be generous and grant him some kind of place in her friendship.

I envy her because he loves her, and I also envy her for her beauty (or, rather, her way of being in fashion and pleasing people).

Saturday, June 28, 1873. This morning while I was taking my piano lesson, Walitsky came in and gave Manotte a watch for his daughter from Mama. Manotte is leaving us, and he asked me for a photograph of me with my signature.

Then Paul and I went for a horseback ride, with Mama and Dina, and young Khalkiopoff, who lives next door, following us in the carriage. I trotted quite well, but the horse wanted to gallop all the time; and as I had to hold him in, I came back with my hand quite numb. But once I had a splendid full-speed gallop!

As I write the journal, Dina is playing some very sad pieces. She puts feeling in her playing, and each note hits my heart. I find it teasing and at the same time charming.

Sunday, June 29, 1873. At 3:00 we went to the beach. Nobody else was there. I threw myself from the bridge into the water and then took a little boat out. When I was far enough, I jumped and swam back. It was thrilling! It's almost two years since I'd jumped from the bridge. This was the first time I ever took a boat out.

Mrs. Teplakoff and Princess Galitzine came to dinner. The Princess is nice but crazy. (To myself I call her Bête.) Then we all went to the music, and when the Durands passed by us with Audiffret in their carriage I blushed! Mama saw it. We left the Princess at her house and Teplakoff at hers. Mama was telling her that the doorman calls Walitsky "Baron," and on our way back home she asked me, "If he were a baron and rich, would you marry him?"

"No, never!"

"You don't like him?"

"He's a very good man, but no, I don't like him."

"Wait! Who, then? Khalkiopoff?"

"Oh, Mama, you're pulling out the most awful ones!"

"Well, if Audiffret . . . Would you . . . ?"

"Oh, no, no! I don't like him at all!"

"Yes, I think you do—a little."

"Not at all."

"Yes, a little!"

"Really, I assure you no! I know why you think so; it's because I blushed a while ago when he was passing!"

"No, it's not for that. One blushes sometimes without reason."

"Besides, you don't know the one I like."

"Who, then?"

"You don't know him. No one does."

Then Dina shouted, "I know who it is! Honest."

"Well, if you know, tell me. But say it only if you're not guessing, in which case I'll tell you the truth."

"It's Hamilton."

I had known for five minutes she would say that. "But you're making it up," I told her. "He's nothing at all—ugly, fat . . ."

"Well, that's so, I know."

"Who?" Mama asked. "The one with red hair?"

"Yes," said Dina.

"Well, see here," I said, "I know he's your ideal. You liked Borreel, too."

"Well, both are good-looking, and Hamilton is better-looking than many others," Dina conceded, unconvinced.

Mama was looking at me tenderly, smiling. But in spite of myself, Dina knows. When Mama had left for Monaco with the others and we were alone, I started to chat under the influence of our conversation. I told her how unhappy I was to blush all the time everywhere. "I blush when I see anyone!" I recalled all the times I could remember at the moment, without hiding anything. Then I told her, "You behave badly, Dina."

"How is that?"

"I don't mean that exactly, but you know how susceptible I am; you add to it with your teasing."

I had to admit to myself. Great God, she notices everything! And the more I tried to be cautious, the more I gave myself away against my will. I'm a silly, stupid girl. I can't think of anything without the others knowing it. I've been very frank with her, and then she heard me talking in my sleep about Hamilton. On our drive back from the station I told her all my wishes except a few. But it was a mistake; she teases me about him openly, and once she screamed his name very loud, breaking the silence. I'm sad now about what I told her. Tomorrow his name will be profaned I'm sure. Tomorrow the first thing I hear from Walitsky will be "Duchess of Hamilton" and jokes like that. But this is not like the Borreel story; I love him; I don't like having it known. . . . I just like to hear people talking about him, but without any reference to me. I'm very angry about what happened. Mama knows about it, too!

I have to think about our Russian proverb: "Whatever is done is for the best." Well, the others don't know yet, and maybe the thing will die down. I hope so.

Dina's at the piano again playing those sentimental pieces, and now she irritates me.

At dinner the Princess Galitzine was telling us about her husband. She is in love with him, and he, the scoundrel, told her, "Madame, love whom you wish; I don't stop you. I want to be free and you bother me!" How can she stand it? I would be terribly unhappy because I'll always love my husband; if he said such a thing to me, I'd die! I'll probably be unhappy because I love, and I'll love all my life, whereas there is no husband who will love always; two years, perhaps, and then a cold friendship—maybe not even that. It's awful!

Tuesday, July 1, 1873. Grandpapa has been talking for several days about his will. At first I didn't think he was serious about it, but I felt he ought to take care of it because one never knows what can happen. Yesterday he told me to plan to be free today to help him and to buy some paper, and so after lunch today I told him I was free and that everything was ready. We went to his room, and he dictated the will to me. I felt it was a great honor for me and wondered whether anyone else had ever asked a fourteen-year-old girl to do such a thing before. So it's not just my silly imagination, but true that I'm not like everybody else. My heart was racing a little when I started because it is such a serious and important matter involving the destiny of all his children. From the sound of his voice and the way he started to pace the room very fast, I could see that he was agitated, too.

He is giving part of the land, the house with his library and the paintings (which he had already given to me ten times, as well as the library, but what importance is that?) to George.

To Mama he also gives a little piece of land—200 hectares, I think, and a forest next to the land. The rest will be shared according to the law, which means equally between all the brothers. Married daughters, according to the law, get nothing unless it is specified in the will. He has disposed of everything he acquired himself, but the lands he received as inheritance cannot be given in a will; they are shared according to the law. But Papa is going to sign over some banknotes to Mama, and this way everything will be settled. There is always a way to give away the inherited estate; we always find ways!

To my aunt he is giving nothing now. He says she doesn't need anything with all the fortune left to her by her husband. However, if the lawsuit turns against her, he will give her some 30,000-ruble drafts, the same as to Mama. That is very little, since the fortune, I believe, is many millions of francs. But one must never be a spendthrift (I repent of being that), and besides, God could punish the one who is never satisfied. This evening we played croquet as we do every day.

George is staying with us. After taking him to the railway station at 8:00, Dina, Paul, and I went to eat some ice cream. Then back at home they came to my room. I mean Dina and Paul; the others are in Monaco. We heard a guitar under the windows. "A serenade!" I screamed, and all three of us flew to the terrace. But it was only the boy from the kitchen playing for the gardener, who began to scrape away on an out-of-tune violin. So we fled back to my room where they stayed with me until 10:30, when I was obliged to send them away. I like to have people in my room, and they like to gather there. I hope it will increase with time. There is no order in the other rooms, which are clogged with unpacked boxes and furniture not yet arranged. Mine is always neat, light, clean, and coquettishly arranged. It offers an agreeable spectacle for the eyes.

Naturally they prefer to stay in my room. Besides, I make them feel at home; but I never let them pass beyond certain limits of etiquette, and that pleases. I hope that in my home it will be the same. I don't ask better than to have company from morning to night, especially since people enjoy coming.

Wednesday, July 2, 1873. If my days continue as they are now, I'll have nothing to write in my poor Journal, which has been so empty for a month!

Paul is a nice boy, very pleasant. But I wish he were more serious and had more precision. He still doesn't understand that he must work. If I were a boy, I'd start to work now; and I'd stop only on the day when I got rich. Because, to get married, the husband or the wife must have some income. You can't make a dinner out of love alone.

Thursday, July 3, 1873. Around 9:00 almost all the Russian people we know here came to visit us. It was like a children's reunion. They sang and played in the garden.

Friday, July 4, 1873. As I predicted, my bedroom is the center of everything. Again this morning everybody met in my room. And tonight, after they all had left, the moon was lighting the room so that I didn't light the candles. I went out on the balcony and heard from far away the sounds of violins, guitars, harmonicas, and flutes. I moved my chair to the window, where I could listen better. It was charming! It's been a long time since I listened to music with such pleasure. When we go to the concert in the Public Gardens, I always spend more time watching than listening; but tonight in the moonlight I was devouring this serenade, because it *was* one! The young men of Nice intended it for us. Could anything be more gallant? Unfortunately, the fashionable young men don't do such innocent and charming things anymore. They prefer to pass their time drinking in the company of bad women. . . . But what is more beautiful in the world than music, especially singing a Spanish serenade? It stirs up in me all kinds of romantic ideas. I think God made me a woman to prevent my committing all the follies I would like to! Before the serenade was finished, Dina and Paul came in and listened with me.

Around 4:00 we went to the beach. I jumped from the bridge and from the boat to show Mama how I do it; but I promised myself and the others not to wet my hair anymore as the water makes it darker, and I'm sorry I've been doing that. I gave my word of honor not to, except, of course, in some extraordinary case when I might be with special people and want to show off for them. But in summer in Nice I'll not jump anymore from the bridge.

After dinner Mama, Dina, Maria Bagdanovna, and Papa went to see the procession. I stayed because Paul was to come in a fiacre to pick me up. It was a nice carriage and the horse traveled very fast.

The procession was beautiful, but I'm no judge because I detest all these comedies. For me, it is a sacrilege. They carry an effigy of the Holy Virgin all over the city. For me even the pictures and the statues of the saints are sins. It's against my religion to think this way, but I see many mistakes in what we do. God forgive me, but my belief is real, honest, and pure.

Monday, July 7, 1873. Today I took my first English lesson with a Miss Elder, who will be coming to the house. Although she teaches quite well, she's really too young and lacks experience. That's not a fault, and she improves with acquaintance. I have two hours with her three times a week.

Tuesday, July 8, 1873. This morning we had a letter from Alexander. "Affairs are not going badly," he says, but he won't leave Russia until July 20—Russian style. It's horrible! That will be August 2, here, and when he arrives here it will be September already, because he'll stop in Vienna. I couldn't help bursting into tears. How many tears this expedition has cost me! How are we ever to get to Vienna this summer?

Papa received 3,000 rubles from Alexander, although he expected 7,000. But dear Alexander always pockets something, taking advantage of our absence. I do *not* want to wait anymore. I'll die if we don't leave soon. I didn't say so, but they knew how I felt when I cried.

Now they tell me we are leaving in a week and that there'll be no more waiting for anybody. But I know this trip still depends on me. I think this happiness comes from God. He deigned to listen to my prayer.

Mrs. Tolstoy is telling in town that I am seventeen, and everybody believes it. And Paul, my own brother—the imbecile—said the same thing! So at dinner Mama pulled out my birth certificate, together with Paul's and her wedding certificate, and read them aloud, proving that I am fourteen and Paul thirteen. I hope they are convinced. The others went out, but I stayed home and listened to the frogs. I was both awakened and put to sleep by them. The heat has been impossible to describe.

Wednesday, July 9, 1873. We are leaving for Vienna on Saturday, but Mama will be staying here, which is annoying. It's true that there is no pleasure without pain!

Thursday, July 10, 1873. We went to Monaco at 5:00 with the eternal Anitchkoffs. It is Paul's saint's day, and we had dinner in Monaco. But as always happens in our family, all of them lost their tempers and none of them took the responsibility of ordering the dinner. Instead, they went into the gaming rooms on arriving; they lost and then were angry about it. Everything that needed to be done fell back on me. People of good sense would have ordered the dinner when we arrived, since we had invited the Anitchkoffs. But they all went in to play roulette first. They lost, they fought. No, such amusements are not for us! Instead of taking everything in hand, neither Mama nor my aunt tried to maintain order and gaiety. Instead, they took pleasure in quarreling and scolding each other! I feel like a martyr; I can't endure such disorder!

I had thought it was my fault that we were like this, but since I promised to be good and not to say one word too much, I can see that it is not my fault. But this atmosphere of strife is a curse on all the family. We love each other deeply and are incapable of doing the least harm to each other; we would cut our heads off for each other, but there is not one hour of tranquillity with us. We eat each other! We scold, stick needles in each other, then at table, if someone says, "The soup's not good," and I have the misfortune to answer, "But it's always like this," they'll ask me, "Why are you angry?" and follow it up with "Oh, my God, my God, what is she going to do? What an awful temper!" I used to go away from the table screaming and crying and plugging my ears. Now, to keep my promise, I get hold of myself. I'm calm. I don't say another word, but in me there is an awful anger suffocating, an uncertainty.

Well, tonight at Monaco, after a lot of trouble we went to eat, and it started again. "Why order so much? Nobody's hungry," etc. And I can't say a word without being stared at and having them say, "What's she doing? How she's screaming!" I feel like running away! And this is the kind of parties we have.

Toward the middle of the evening there was a little gaiety. I can say without bragging that I animated the dinner, and at the end everything was almost fine. Back at the roulette table, I played rather well, guessing a lot of numbers, especially at the beginning. Finally, with nothing I won forty francs, but I didn't want to take the money. I wanted to play some more because I won it there and there I wanted to leave it. I took back with me only twenty francs, and that's fine with me.

At last we are going to Vienna—Dina, my aunt, Paul, and I. Mama wants me to go for several different reasons: to see the exposition, to have some distraction, to have a shift of scenery, to run away from the heat, but *especially*, I think, because I may see Mrs. Miloradovitch and her *son*. With this trip she wants to arrange an interview so that by mere chance we may see each other there. She very much hopes I'll marry Oritz. That's all she wants for me. She believes that if she could be reassured of that, she could be at peace on my account. It has nothing to do with what I want. It's true he is rich and young. If I wanted only riches, I'd marry him. I'll probably never marry a poor man; it would be his misfortune *and* mine. Because when we lack everything. . . . And then, I love the Duke. I am capricious; I have big ideas—I want parties, society; I care a lot about clothes. Being poor or only moderately well-off, I'd be miserable. I could stand it for one or two years, but later on when love cooled off. . . . Being rich, that wouldn't happen. I mean, I'll always love. Busy as we'd be, we'd have less time; and seeing each other less often we'd only have time for love. I wouldn't quarrel, and I'll love my husband all my life. It would not change with circumstances or with age. But to keep a husband, all that care is necessary. Men don't like simple women, and they like well-dressed women. They may not know it, but even a woman who is not very pretty can seem so if she is surrounded by luxury. But prettiness is not all: through proper means she pleases and attracts. Of course she must have good manners because clothes are not everything.

No. I don't want Miloradovitch. I don't love him, and I'd never be able to pretend. So I must choose a husband I love, because I'll be faithful.

I know another one might marry a man she didn't love because she would be able to take lovers. I'd never be able to. How could you possibly live with a man whom you would betray? But I'll probably be blushing every minute all my life. With this Miloradovitch, I'd probably become the greatest coquette in the whole world. He'd become infatuated with me. I know how to flirt, and I'd pretend to be modest and simple and not thinking about him (which would be true). I mean I would show him I was indifferent toward him, and then from time to time I'd blush. It's easy to do that; I just have to talk about Hamilton. Well, I'd make him fall in love with me and then martyrize him to have my revenge on Hamilton.

Friday, July 11, 1873. I got up at 9:00; Mama and my aunt came into my room, and we made plans for the Vienna trip. This is the second time that Mama mentioned Oritz. At that instant the little mirror fell on the floor, and I was mortally afraid. I didn't dare to pick it up for fear it was broken. A broken mirror is an awful omen. But, thank God, it was all right.

Mama tried to drop her subject into the conversation in a casual way. "If you should see Oritz and Elizabeth Ivanovna, give them our regards. Be kind and gentle with Grisyo." She used the plural pronouns, but I could see very well it was for me. Now I must confess that, when leaving Russia when I was eleven, Miloradovitch courted me, but we were children. I didn't like him for one minute. Almost everything is packed.

In the evening we went to pick up my new white dress, and while out we met Mr. Howard, just back from Vienna, where, he said, "the cholera is raging." This news upset all my plans. We are going to wait, and the government is to discuss the question in a big session.

Today I practised for four and a half hours and finished learning the *Concerto in G Minor,* by Mendelssohn. I'll continue to work on the rhythm.

I'm reading *The Last Days of Pompeii,* as well as several other books, but I'm not doing all I should. We've put off the trip for another two weeks.

B O O K   S E V E N

Book 7
Begun Sunday, July 13, 1873
Ended Sunday, August 10, 1873
Nice
[Vienna]

Sunday, July 13, 1873. I slept until eleven this morning because I reviewed my diary last night. I didn't get it all read, but I spent two hours on it. I found some absurdities in it of which I am ashamed. Mama and the others went to Monaco, leaving Dina and me with Princess Galitzine to go to the music. I am at ease with her because I can say what I think to her, whereas with others I am embarrassed. I told her I don't like the bourgeois; that I prefer the aristocracy; that the society of Nice is too mixed because one finds salesmen and secretaries all mixed in with the others; that I like to shop in the best stores for my dresses. I criticize at will, whereas in front of others I cannot express my ideas or opinions because everyone in Nice, more or less, has the faults I'm irritated with.

We even touched upon the question of marriage. "Marry a baker as long as he's rich, but don't look for titles. God preserve us from them!" she exclaimed. I think she probably looked for a title and found that scoundrel of a husband she has. Well, my opinion is different: I detest peasants. I proposed that we eat some ice cream—in our carriage, of course— at the Victoire, and then we left Madame at her house.

Wednesday, July 16, 1873. Mr. and Mrs. Howard say the cholera in Vienna is not too bad and that the city is full of visitors. In the meantime I am being painted by a miniaturist, and Mama reads aloud from that very silly novel, *The Precipice*. How could the heroine fall in love with that man?

It's been a whole week since I could pray. I say the words, but without feeling. I have even (oh, horror!) even dared to deny God. I was not able to make myself believe in divinity. It was awful! I was most unhappy and wondered to whom I could pray after this, if there were no supreme being. But then I concluded that God, to test me, abandoned me and sent these horrible doubts. I decided I must hold firmly to my faith and not let it go. The burden seemed too heavy, and I begged God to stop his punishment and let me pray. I cried, and all of a sudden my doubts vanished and I prayed as I never had before. It seemed I understood, but I was shivering and afraid. It was as if I had received what I was asking in one instant!

That the scientists who have discovered the rotation of the earth and the planets, their positions, and the truth about the sun have no religious beliefs surprises me. It seems to me that because they know more about the mysteries of the world, they should have the greatest faith. When I look at the sky, the trees, the houses, everything, I am astonished; and it seems there just must be a creator behind it directing it. I am joyful to be able to pray again!

We went on another picnic with the Howards. We sat on the grass, and the dishes were laid out for us. Mr. Howard made a drink of one bottle of champagne, two bottles of red wine, some sugar, two lemons, some ice, cucumber peelings, and a siphon of water. All of those ingredients mixed together were not at all bad! I began to have a good time, and to my very great pleasure, some of us went fishing—Paul, Walitsky, Mr. Howard, and I. Not that I had a fishing-pole, but I watched theirs with interest. It was my first experience on a fishing trip, and I enjoyed it. The three hours we stayed there fishing seemed like three minutes. Then Dina and Mama arrived where we were and started to talk. Mr. Howard was too polite to tell them their talking was disturbing, and they paid no attention to what I tried to tell them. Then Mrs. Howard and her maid (what a frump!) came to join us, and that was our worst misfortune.

We had caught four miserable little fishes. The eel was about to get away, and nobody could catch it; I finally got it under my foot and cut its head off. Back at the house they all were commenting on my "cruelty," but I told them that feelings should be put aside and that I preferred to give relief to an unfortunate animal instead of just making faces, for an eel *or* a pigeon!

Mr. Howard is funny. With his sports tweeds, his pipe, and a stupid expression (like that of an Englishman of second rank at the shooting), it seems he's playing the philosopher. He says he is tired of everything. But what pleased me was that he talked about horses.

I miss our old house on the Promenade, and it annoys me that we are no longer there. But what annoys me most is that we lose time in Nice in the summer—not seeing anyone, getting up, having lunch, talking and arguing, dining in Monaco, and going to bed again. It's an existence that revolts me. When I think that we live only once! To lose all this time and not enjoy life, either! When I ask them, "Why don't we have any acquaintance?" they answer, "There's nobody in Nice in summer."

"But who is keeping you here? If you would go into society you would prepare a place for me when I'm sixteen. I know you don't like society, but a little sacrifice is necessary. Do it for me! Will no one do anything for me?" I ended by crying, "Living as we do is unforgivable! I'll end by getting ugly and old because of this way of life! It doesn't have to be Nice. It could be London or St. Petersburg, or Paris. . . ." I don't want to have to marry to live as I like. If only Mama and my aunt would shake themselves out of their laziness!

Monday, July 21, 1873. This morning I did a terrible thing. A book that Mama bought more than a year ago, *Courtesans of the World,* has been forbidden to me, and all that time I avoided it; but yesterday afternoon I found it on a table in the room where the miniature-painter disfigures me. I took it up, afraid that he would see this awful book. I don't know how I happened to open it, but standing there I read a few pages; and it interested me so much that I decided to read it the next day. At 2:00 this morning I began to read it. It is very well written, and I completely share the opinion of the author that it is not immoral and further that "every woman who will read it will be saved." The author's name is Houssaye. I was reading and my thoughts were deep in what I was learning—I was entranced—when suddenly I came upon this: "All the stables of the Duke of Parisis have been sold to the Duke of Hamilton." It was so unexpected that I stood there literally stupefied. I stopped breathing; my heart beat faster, and it was as if my eyes were covered with a veil. I read it again to be sure it was true, but the words were dancing. I read it again ten times. He, too, has been in so many adventures! And this is his society described by the author. . . .

Well, they really have a good time—the men. The woman is always the victim. I would like to be a man. I would surpass every one of those gentlemen!

Tuesday, July 22, 1873. I posed again, and the portrait has a pretty face. But it's not me. I'm disappointed. I was expecting to have something beautiful.

I had another talk with Paul, and I tried to be serious without seeming to be. He's a good boy and likes children. I was telling him I want to go around the world.

"You'll need a lot of money!"

"A hundred thousand francs will be enough for me alone."

"But you'll go with your husband and your children. . . ."

"How? I'll have no children." We laughed. "I'll leave them with Mama," I said.

"Oh, no! I'll always be with mine," Paul said. "I'll watch their lives; I'll see them ten times a day!"

The portrait arrived and it's awful. And Mama says it's my fault. That is too much! The Princess went to speak with the painter and suggested that when we return from Vienna he should start another. I'll not sit for him again. He had the nerve to say that I ordered him to make the hair dark, the liar!

One more catastrophe has delayed our trip, and now we'll not leave before next Tuesday. Yesterday at the beach George had lunch with a Monaco guard and some other man. After they had eaten and drunk they went swimming at about 1:30. Anna was on the beach. Noticing some blackbirds flying above the swimmers, she concluded that it was a bad omen and started to scream with all her strength. Hearing her, George came back, but the guard had sunstroke and died! Because George had been drinking heavily, he was in an awful condition and we feared for his life. I cried because of this new delay. I am the most unfortunate creature!!

These postponements will kill me.

After dinner I went out with the Princess. We went to the London House and ate peaches and grapes and then went to the Promenade. Then suddenly she said, "You'll marry the Duke of Hamilton."

"What makes you say that, Madame?"

"Nothing in particular. It just suits you; that's all."

"But why? Do you know him?"

"No."

"But you have seen him? The fat, the red. . . ."

"Oh, yes. I've often seen him."

"But how funny! Who has made you think. . . ."

"Oh, it would be very nice. You'll be Duchess and rich. Never marry a poor man. All husbands become mean with time, so it's better to shade trees with a golden fleece than a doormat."

And that was the way we talked for at least two hours. I again inquired where she'd heard all that. To tell the truth, I was enchanted. It was like a beautiful dream, hearing someone talk of him to me that way!

At home we found the Howards, and they were still going on about the cholera in Vienna. I resolved that if Mama and my aunt dared to delay us beyond Tuesday, I would lie down on the bed and scream until I drove them crazy with fear until they let us go. I was so sad that I was afraid of breaking into tears at any moment.

Sunday, July 27, 1873. When I awoke and reread those ten pages, nothing surprised me; it all seemed very normal, except for one thing: what could have given the Princess all those strange ideas?

I love to go to the beach, not only to swim, but also to flirt. Today when I was getting ready to go, my aunt and the Princess entered my room and the latter said, "Just look at her! Isn't she a picture?"

My aunt agreed, but Papa has dared to say that I am badly built! However, everyone else defended me.

Monday, July 28, 1873. They went to the bank and came away hopeful; our last planned departure was delayed because of lack of money, but we shall have some at ten tomorrow. But all the time we were at the baths I was begging my aunt to pack for the trip; she refused just to tease me!

Tuesday, July 29, 1873. At 10:00 Paul and Walitsky went to the banker and came back successful at last! After many suppositions, some oppositions against Vienna, and all kinds of alarming fears, we left!!

In a way, the departure was very gay (although I didn't fail to cry when they talked against the trip). Mr. and Mrs. Anitchkoff went with us as far as Monte Carlo. But here is another adventure—instead of continuing, we stayed in Monte Carlo to gamble and have dinner, and shall leave only tomorrow at 8:00. We gambled, and the dinner was very gay. Here is the menu: soup, salmon and shrimps, filet steak with mushrooms, peas, duck, dessert, grapes, brioche, fresh hazelnuts, and some wines.

As usual, I was the soul of the party, and I think everyone was amused. But after a while my aunt said, "Well, now, we are going to Vienna. But if I die, not one of you will get anything. What will you do then? There is no will!"

"So make one!" we shouted. Mr. Anitchkoff also approved, and we all went from the dining room to our bedroom.

I said, "My dear aunt, everything for me!" I was infected with a gaiety that started when we left Nice. But Mr. Anitchkoff is a serious man, and when he dictated the will for me to write down, I couldn't remain serious and kept making remarks about each sentence he gave me, turning everything into a ridiculous comment. Finally he was forced to tell me, "Well, now, if you tell all your foolish thoughts in this room, there will not be enough space. . . ."

I didn't get angry. He is a nice man, and if he is more free with me than the others it's because he is a true friend.

He corrected what I had written, and my aunt started to copy. She ruined several sheets of paper, but finally everything was over. She has given everything to me under the condition that I pay 25,000 rubles to Dina, the same to Mama, and 6,000 to Walitsky. (Paul will inherit from our father.) Outside of all these payments, I'll still have a pretty fortune.

At 11:00 we returned to the roulette table.

Mama had given me 500 francs for the trip and Papa only twenty-five rubles (the miser!). Our bedrooms were Nos. twelve, eleven, and seventeen. Mama lost so much money that Paul was sent to Nice to bring some more.

When we went to meet Paul's train from Nice at 8:00, he wasn't on it; and we knew we would have to wait six more hours.

We gambled again after breakfast, and it was with great pain that I drove them from the table after three more hours. When we finally left, I was very sorry to part from Mama, and I cried. It was such a pity she couldn't go with us!

Finally we were on our way. In spite of the beautiful views from the train, I began to long for the green trees of forests and would have liked to arrive quickly in Vienna.

We got off at Genoa for the night and went to a hotel. Without expecting to get it, we asked for a bath—and they brought a funny tub that you sit in like a chair. With lots of laughing and joking, I sat in it, without the water, of course. And I had to ask the hostess to send me a shoe man. (I had wanted to show off my feet in my new boots at Monaco, and by the time we got off the train I had to have help taking them off because my feet were swollen.)

On our way through northern Italy and into Switzerland, there was no time to do anything but look at the scenery! And with two places arranged for a bed for each of us, we slept perfectly.

Friday, August 1, 1873. We were wakened at 5:00 A.M. at the Austrian frontier, and while we were dressing, a doctor and his assistant came to dust us with a perfumed powder against the disease which I don't dare name. The powder produced a bad effect on me, and I fell asleep again, not waking until 11:00. After that I couldn't close my eyes, it seemed, because of the extraordinary beauty of the countryside. What greenery! What trees! What pretty, clean houses! What lovely, cultivated fields! Everything was charming, delicious, superb. Even the girls were pretty. It was such a change—relief—from our customary rocks and pale olive trees of the Mediterranean landscape. Oh, I admire our grave and dry land by the sea, but the tree-covered mountains and the velvet-green fields, the pretty cottages and the farmers working with their cows and horses provided such a contrast with our usual sameness! They flew by us all day. Everything turned, passed, and ran away as we watched, and it was all enchanting. I stood at the window all day not to miss a thing and only at 6:00, when the dinner was served, did I sit down. I even talked English and Italian with some young German girls who were shouting in our ears from a station platform, "Fresh water! Fresh water!"

When the German conductor came, I spoke English to him, but all he could say was, "*Was? Was?*"

Arriving around 10:00 at night in Vienna, we had to endure another dusting. Our aunt took us to the Grand Hotel. Everything there was superb except that it was too late for a bath. We had to be satisified with scrubbing in our rooms after those four days on the train with smoke pouring into the windows, but even in the train we had washed twice a day.

Because she was so afraid of the cholera, our poor aunt's face had looked like a hangman's during the whole trip. "Are you ill? Do you feel well? Have you a pain somewhere?" she would ask us every now and then. But at last we were reassured: there was not a case of the disease in Vienna, and how her face changed!

Saturday, August 2, 1873. We made a general tour of the Exposition today, went to the races, and drove through the Prater. The first was promising, but the races were a disappointment—rather lacking in spirit (no Englishmen in the stands, let alone the Duke)—and during our drive through the park we met none of those wonderful carriages like the ones you encounter any day in the Bois in Paris.

Added to these disappointments was the fact that my aunt scolded constantly for no reason I could see, and I seemed to be the target of her naggings. I got so depressed it seemed my heart had never been so heavy. On the other hand, Dina's little airs of vivacity irritated me. She acted like a charming little child posing with a certain amount of self-satisfaction. For someone pretty that's bad enough, but when you're ugly it's unbearable!

For two days I was in a kind of trance-like lethargy, but by Monday I began to enjoy myself. In the Russian restaurant, which was neither Russian nor a restaurant, we enjoyed the bouillon and the caviar, both of which were superb. The Italian exhibit had some beautiful statues. I recognized two of them—Dante's lovers in Hell, Francesca da Rimini and Paolo—and I thought of that line, "He kissed my mouth, all trembling" *[la bocca mi basciò tutto tremante, Inferno, V 136].*

One thing is clear: Russians can always say that the motherland is still that! Every single thing in the Russian pavilion was beautiful. I examined each piece with ardor, and seeing names and inscriptions written in our language moved me to tears. I admired the sterling silver most.

But Vienna itself is beautiful, and I particularly delighted in a Viennese salon done in pale pinks and blues. By 7:00 in the evening, we were "as tired as horses delivering mail" when it was time to leave.

Paul went to the country to visit with his friend Gutman, and we walked into a hall where we heard music playing, strictly Viennese. As soon as that orchestra stopped playing another started up in the pavilion across from it, and we went in there. We found all kinds of people streaming in—members of the Imperial family, society ladies, young dandies, all in a swirl of gaiety—and I became very excited, wanting to see everything and go everywhere. And in Vienna the climate is delicious compared to the burning summers of Nice. What a pleasure and relief!

Tuesday, August 5, 1873. Although I finally feel at home here, I keep looking for the one person who is not in the crowd. This evening we went to see the ballet *Fantasia,* and seated in the Imperial box with the Emperor and Empress was the handsome Shah of Persia. Although more of a pantomime than a dance, the ballet was beautiful. However, I was looking again for the Duke unsuccessfully, and at last I decided to forget the ungrateful beast. I've humiliated myself enough for him. I should let him look for me instead of looking always for him. I want to be proud, and I'd like to say, "Let him go to the Devil!" but I can't. I want God to protect him. Yet how can I love him when I never see him? Especially when I'm not loved in return. Go, animal! Fat barrel, I hate you!

Paul invited his friend to the hotel to meet us, and we all went shopping. I bought a riding-whip for fifteen florins, some silver buttons, and a bird-shaped paper-weight. And I decided to order an English saddle.

Taking a glass of champagne when we lunched at the Provenceaux, I got a little tipsy for the second time. (The first time was yesterday at the hotel; my aunt won't let me drink the water.)

All of us went to hear Offenbach's *La Belle Hélène* at the Vienna theater. It was well played, but they sang it in German and all the French jokes were lost. And because it was performed in modern dress, it wasn't nearly so much fun as when we saw it in France. Hélène was all covered up!

Because I still get up early, the way I do at home, I'm reading *Gulliver's Travels* until the others are ready for breakfast.

Friday, August 8, 1873. On our way to the Oscar Carré circus, our carriage met that of the Emperor and Empress, and our coachman was so delighted to see them that he turned around toward us, showing a radiant, fat face. It was a good show, but I "woke up" excited, charmed, and moved by the Great Steeplechase of twenty horses with their men and women riders. They jumped magnificently and then climbed a kind of mountain on the stage, galloping in a superb manner. I want to learn to ride like that—jump gates and ditches and everything on my horse.

Saturday, August 9, 1873. We ate at the hotel. Decidedly, to eat is the prime thing! But oh! To be corseted and dressed as we are in such weather, where there seems to be no air but a driving, burning wind is very disagreeable. Besides, there is no crowd now, and we see only Germans of the third quality. I am bored. There is not one of our acquaintances anywhere, and I feel absolutely alone. So I'm bored, bored, bored. And it's so hot I'm suffocating. We spend one hour near the fountain, take a walk through the galleries, and then go to the music. Today they played an atrocious piece and left us with a long intermission, after which we heard that Fantasy from *Oberon* which I learned and which is played everywhere so that I consequently detest it.

But when Johann Strauss appeared, in an unexpected way he gave another character entirely to the orchestra! Each musician began to smile and look excited. Strauss was called back once, twice, three times after they had finished and taken their bows.

At dinner under a tent at the Provenceaux, we heard some voices: it was the notorious cocotte Saxe quarrelling with the restaurant owner, who was shouting, "Don't touch me or I'll hit you!" Then her voice went *crescendo* as she struck him with her fan. He said such things to her as I don't want to write, and ended bellowing, "I don't want prostitutes in my café. Leave, you filthy tart, or I'll pull off your skirt and spank your. . . ." What a horror! We were acting as if we heard nothing, but I wanted to hear everything.

This woman pleases me very much. You can tell she is amusing because it shows in her face. Such women of fourth quality, kept hidden like a great mystery, interest me. I would like to take the shape of a monster and follow them in their excursions, or even get inside their skins to know what they feel. Poor Saxe has trouble everywhere; she was thrown out of the casino at Monte Carlo. Here in Vienna, she wears beautiful dresses. And I must say, her face reminds me of Gioja's.

But let's forget this. I lower myself by talking about these creatures, and I'm ashamed to have tarnished my journal with this stupid, improper story. However, I have to add that I am very sympathetic toward her, and I would very much like (incognito, of course) to become her friend. Oh, what horror! Horror!

Gutman left loge tickets for us to hear *Lucrezia Borgia,* and without changing and only washing and fixing our hats, we left for the theater, arriving just before the second act. Miss Wilt's singing was admirable. It has been a long time since I have had such a beautiful evening. Her voice is magnificent—possibly a little too deep—and she is a little fat. But really, I was charmed! I am very difficult to please, but she is good. How much I would like to be able to sing like her! Yet the audience applauded very little. . . . For my part, I cannot accept opera without such voices.

Sunday, August 10, 1873. Wonderful! The weather turned cold and I am awake. It even rained.

At the Exposition I wanted to take the elevator to the top, but at the half-way point, my aunt wanted to come back down. She said she was going back to the hotel, but I knew very well that she would wait for me so I continued. The stairs were flooded, and we barely touched them without wetting our feet. From the top we saw a marvellous view—all the buildings of the Exposition, the pavilions, and the fountains.

After dinner we heard the opera *Hamlet* (my first time). Ophelia was good and drowned admirably. However, I found the funeral scene stupid. Still, the women were beautiful and the costumes gorgeous. But it's the theater itself that is faultless. Everything was perfect. Three years ago, when I was here first, I was less difficult to please; but now I know it's good.

BOOK EIGHT

Book 8 of my Journal
Begun Monday, August 11, 1873
Ended Sunday, September 1, 1873 [sic, August 31]
Concerning Marie Bashkirtseff
Returning (from Vienna)
From August 18, Grand Hotel, Paris
Thursday, August 28, to Nice

Monday, August 11, 1873. I want to go to Paris before we return to Nice, but my aunt is opposed to it. Yet I know that if I insist, she'll give up. So I'm not buying anything here because the Paris styles are so much more chic. How happy I am! All that I want is happening, thank God!

We went to hear an all-women's orchestra—except that the trumpeters were young boys. It was curious to see, and we stayed for three numbers and then walked back to the hotel through the delicious weather, which started to sprinkle. How my aunt adores me! I just have to say one word and everything is done. When we asked to go to the circus, she didn't answer yes or no until I had stopped talking. She never does anything without hearing from me, and she does all I want; I am really very happy. She even stays up while I am writing in the diary until I go to bed. Definitely, she adores me. When Paul was teasing me just for a laugh, she came to my aid. When she does things like that, I often have to laugh in spite of myself.

When a lady from a dress shop came and Dina and my aunt ordered some things, I told her, "I am waiting for Paris." Yesterday, having finished my journal, I asked, "Well, are we going to Paris?" When she told me *no* in a very decisive tone and I still insisted, with her still refusing, I began to despair and to be ashamed of my assurance of my power. But remembering that I had promised not to make any scenes, I resolved to conduct my siege slowly, and pray. But my aunt was simply enraged. I didn't know what had happened to her. "We don't have enough money!" she said.

"But that's not true," I said reasonably. "We still have a few thousand francs, enough to stay in Paris and to buy two or three dresses."

After a half hour of chaos because I couldn't say anything else than, "Please give me the pleasure!" and "Let's go!" etc., I succeeded with her by calculating the cost of the hotel, the carriages, and so on, proving to her that we had plenty. But then she took another tack—because of the lawsuit and a lot of other things, she could not. Finally she declared very loudly, "I don't *want* to!"

In a very humble voice I continued to beg her. I really wanted to explode, but my promise held me back. She talked about the money again, and I showed her again that we had enough. Then I begged and almost cried, and I triumphed!! First she said she would let me know tomorrow and that I must go to bed. I realized I had won.

Thursday, August 14, 1873. I have decided to take the courses at the lycée in Nice. In all I'll have nine and a half hours with tutors a day. I plan to work like an ox. I don't want to be inferior to my husband and my children. Women *must* receive the same education as men! And I *want* to work—with God's help.

We have been packing since morning. My bag is packed, and the rest does not concern me. But what an annoyance; I've been sick (with the "curse") since morning. I'm generally laid up for three or four hours with this disagreeable visitation. I couldn't eat lunch and came back upstairs, undressed, and went to bed. And my aunt was in a terrible state of fear. She followed me upstairs with the dire statement, "It's the cholera!" I told her what it was, but nothing seemed to reassure her. How she loves me! After a two-hour nap I felt fine, and we all went to dinner and then to a circus, even though the rain was pouring.

The Saxe woman was sitting near us. She has a very good profile, but her face up close looks haggard; and we know it's because she gets tipsy. But I very much like this type of face. I like the nose, flat at the tip.

Saturday, August 16, 1873. Paul failed to get exact information about the departure of our train, and we waited an extra two hours. It was a lost day, as we could have gone to the Exposition and had lunch there. Finally we left. As if in a dream, we passed the city, the villas. Then everything passed and we were in the woods, and then in the meadows. It was strange! Yesterday we were at the Grand Hotel. And now we were being taken away past cities, villages, forests, huts, men. . . . In each little house people were living, loving, quarreling. Yet from our train, the view of each human being showed him to be less than a fly on the wall. Those people we just saw from our coach looked like dolls, but if you could look into their hearts they would seem a world apart and all different from each other. Each has his joys and sorrows.

Sunday, August 17, 1873. "Wake up, Mousinka! Munich!" I suppose my aunt wanted to stay there a few hours, but I was asleep. And later I wanted to read, but the train was shaking so badly that I gave up.

In the evening we got down from the train to find something to eat. (I can't stand the meats that have been [carried] in the train five minutes.) We found some ham and champagne. Paul brought the foods into the car, and we had a feast! I laughed all the time, and my aunt was angry. Then, to cap all my sillinesses I smoked a cigarette. When I got to the end, my aunt grabbed it imperiously from my hand and threw it out the window. I didn't pay any attention to that. I like fun and partying, and when I start I go all the way.

Monday, August 18, 1873. At 5:00 A.M. they woke us. It was Paris. And although we dressed quickly, it was still fifty minutes before we got to the station.

It was cool—cold. We took a carriage first to the Hotel de Hongrie et Espagne, but there was no vacancy. So to my great pleasure we went to the Grand and found rooms there.

In the mornings Paris is strange; one sees only butchers, bakers, shoemakers, business proprietors, etc., opening and cleaning their stores and cafés. I noticed some maids, apparently in a hurry, running with their eyes lowered. They seemed not to see anything except the tips of their feet, and yet they passed with such skill that it is surprising. Two years ago we arrived in Paris in October at the same time. I feel at home in Paris; here I live, I breathe. Everything interests me. Far from being lazy, I am, on the contrary, too much in a hurry. Walking is not fast enough! I want to fly. And how I appreciate this city now after that slow German city!

We went out and found the streets animated, charming. We went to Ferry's, Rue Scribe No. 11, which address I had got at the Exposition. I bought two pairs of button boots—one in black and the other in grey chamois leather with steel heels. They are closed on the sides with hooks in the same metal. These are the second boots of this style appearing on the market; one was at the Exposition and the other on me.

Tuesday, August 19, 1873. After a lunch at the hotel, we wandered on the boulevards. At Jouvin's I ordered a dozen and a half pairs of gloves. (I pay for my own clothes. Out of my 2500 francs a year I have already received 1000.) Then we took a carriage and went to Laferrière's. I ordered a dark brown wool costume trimmed with faille. The 300-franc price surprised me; I was expecting to pay 400, at least. From there we went to the Rue de la Paix, and all of a sudden my aunt said, "Here are the Boyds!"

"Where?"

"In this store."

"And Bertha also?"

"No, the two oldest ones."

I went into the shop under the pretense of asking the price of something. Yes! It was the Boyd sisters. Blanche has gained weight, and she is as dark as my aunt. A smell of powder and much more exhaled from them.

We doubt everything. Well, tonight I permit myself to doubt. I ask myself, Do I really love the Duke of Hamilton? And I have to answer, No, I don't. It's just imagination. I've thought of him so much that I've imagined things that aren't true. I could marry someone else or love someone else—even kiss another. I imagine myself the wife of another man; he speaks to me, he touches me—oh! no, no, no, never in my life! I'd die of fear!!! All men disgust me—except him. In the street, at the theater, in the drawing room I can stand them. And without them, I am bored; men are necessary. But as for loving one of them or imagining one of them kissing my hand with love puts me beside myself. I can't explain it, but I understand. Very often I've tried to know exactly what it is hidden deep inside me. The truth—what is this me, my soul? I think all that I feel, all that I say is only superficial. I don't know for sure, but it seems to me that there is nothing—or too much. For example, when I see the Duke I cannot know whether I hate him or adore him. Sometimes I even become enraged; I want to enter into my soul and I cannot. When I have to resolve a difficult problem, I start to think, and it seems that I get it; but at that moment when I want to gather everything in order to verify and understand, all is lost, all is gone, and I understand nothing. At that same moment my mind goes so far away—so far that I am astonished and understand nothing. All I have said does not get to the *bottom of my heart*. I don't have any. I live only in appearance. To stay or to go, to have or not to have—it's all one with me—has no importance. My sorrows, my joys, my pleasures, my pains, do not exist. I am nothing! If I imagine my mother dead or the love of Hamilton, only then do I enter into myself. And yet this latter seems to me so unbelievable, impossible, unnatural that I can only think of it superficially, in the clouds where I understand nothing. It's this that drives me mad!

And this is Paris, of which everyone talks and the authors write. I can't really believe I'm here. I know now that I want to leave Nice and live in Paris. All the beauty, all the virtue, all the vice—it's Paris. The world is Paris, and Paris is the world. At last I have found what I wanted without knowing it! I want to take an apartment in Paris, have a carriage with horses as in Nice, and enter into society with the aid of the Russian Embassy.

Wednesday, August 20, 1873. Awaking at 11:00, I started to count my money and realized that 2,500 francs is nothing when we want to spend it. Even 3,000 is modest. I can't manage with less than that. I bought stationery stamped with my initials, had my umbrella recovered, and ordered a pair of high-topped grey shoes, gloves, and a dress at Worth's. Now I need hats. I haven't the money to pay for the blue dress at Worth's and am short 350 francs. They will send it to Nice.

Thursday, August 21, 1873. I subscribed to the *Derby* for twenty-eight francs per year.

At the Russian restaurant Dina insisted on ordering a salad with onions for her lunch, and I was in such a rage about it that I went over to the piano and began playing. I find onions revolting.

Friday, August 22, 1873. We went back to Worth's, where Paris has the most expensive and the most beautiful dresses in the world. At first I feel uneasy when I go into a fashion house, but now I'm getting used to Worth's. They think I'm just a little girl, but I showed them how I'm made; and I want to show them my fantasy for dress in all its splendor. They'll see that my taste surpasses everybody else's. I can't use all my genius for myself now, but later on I'll be the queen of the establishment as a customer. I'll dress only at Worth's because, beside him, all the others are peasants! But I'll need at least an additional 1,100 rubles a year to dress there (the interest on the little Orel property, which is mine). I am going to try to obtain that sum because no one can be dressed for less than 3,300 francs; that's a modest sum.

Saturday, August 23, 1873. I had barely awakened when the gloves and shoes arrived. More and more I see that I need 3,500 francs. Worth will send my order COD. I can't do otherwise because I have left from my paid orders only three francs, ten sous, and an Austrian crown. As my aunt hasn't enough to pay for the dress, Mama will pay for it in Nice. It's not right; I should be able to manage on my 2,500, but then—sometimes a son has debts and sends them to his mother, who pays. Why shouldn't I, a girl, a weaker and inexperienced creature, make mistakes, too?

We went to the races. What a contrast with those in Vienna! There we didn't hear any shouting or excitement, and we saw no gestures of enthusiasm. The ladies were surrounded by the gentlemen, and people were talking about everything but the races. Here in Paris every face was full of excitement, life! When I see horses coming up to the finish line neck-and-neck I go crazy, and it takes a lot of character not to scream. If I could have, I would have roared loud enough to frighten the entire population. Besides, weren't they all shouting, too? What thrills me is that everybody is inflamed like me. They all run, scream, gesticulate.

When the Duke's horse was racing today, I was very moved. It's silly to say it, but it's true! It's the first time I've had a favorite horse. All the horses are the same for me; so my love for the races, the jockeys, the betting, the horses, etc., is a result of my interest in *him*. This time there was a difference, and it cannot be otherwise from now on.

Monday, August 25, 1873. I went straight to Laferrière's to try my dress and have them change the front. Last night I couldn't sleep until midnight for thinking about the black velvet one advertised by Worth in the program. I'm dying to have that dress. The one from Laferrière is ugly. I had ordered a Reubens hat in brown at Montel, but I'd much rather have the black velvet dress with a hat to match that! And the Reubens cost me 100 francs. . . .

I've been feeling the way I did when we first got to Vienna—all dead, sad, and sleepy. Dina has a taste for the kind of things you get at the Bon Marché, so we went there and then into the old part of Paris. After we'd gone back to the hotel and I changed my dress, I began to feel alert; and we went out on the boulevards as we do every day. Near Klein's, Dina said to me, "Look on your right—the framed picture!"

It was a photograph of a beautiful woman—Gioja. I called my aunt's attention to it, and Paul said, "Oh, it's Gioja!"

"It's not proper to say her name aloud," I reproached him.

But I couldn't take my eyes from the picture. When I saw her at the Shooting Club the other day, I thought she looked disagreeable, but I was stupid. She is beautiful, beautiful, beautiful! Her features, the expression of her eyes, the oval of her face, her bust—everything is superb. She is complete perfection. And she has a lively, intelligent expression, at once very feminine and without malice. And there is a simplicity about her that adds to her perfection. I'm sure he must love her, and the portrait says she is worthy of him.

We found ourselves surrounded by three French ladies, who arrived first, and then a cocotte with a man, and then a couple. We were in society, but I ate well. I started at the end and finished at the beginning, imagining what those ladies thought about my meal—four cups of tea, two crawfishes, three cucumbers, some beef, more crawfishes, and some fruit! With all that I took a small glass of brandy, but here it is diluted. I swallowed that at one gulp. We were, as usual, very happy at dinner.

After dinner we strolled again, and I wanted to pass once more by Klein's; I wanted to be sure that she really was that beautiful. But we didn't go that way. I bought a big straw hat for two francs twenty-five and then tried to turn them the other way, but I did not succeed and could not insist as I had no reason to give. So we returned home.

Before now I had not really accepted the fact that Gioja was there. I simply thought it would be a question of time, and that if I could get to know him he would love me. Now I realize all my folly—a man loves a beautiful woman, and here comes a little gypsy who imagines that he will forget the woman for her and love a little girl. Well, . . . I was crazy!

Tuesday, August 26, 1873. Between packing and finishing last-minute errands, I managed to pass again in front of Klein's, and I stopped again to look at Gioja. But she cannot be so beautiful in reality! First, she wears a lot of makeup and then she is not—gracious. I mentioned my impression of the photograph to Dina and asked whether the photographer might have touched it up a lot. She said, "It's an excellent photograph, made by Walery of the Rue de Londres."

Wednesday, August 27, 1873. We left the city I adore so much by 10:15 in the morning—without having seen that miserable man. Too bad; I had taken the trip with the hope of seeing him somewhere, somehow! If someone had told me he was in China, I would have gone there immediately to see him. Not to speak to him, just to see him passing by would have been enough. I found that decision, distinct and without doubt, at the bottom of my heart. I cannot imagine what I would feel if he died, but I can clearly see my situation if he should get married! That would be so terrible that it is better not to think about it!

As for Gioja, those things that make her terribly beautiful to me are what give her poise and that air of triumph—that assurance in her eyes.

On our way to Nice, we went through a terrible storm. The lightning would flash straight, like a Roman candle, a long way off, and then leave a silvery line in the sky for several seconds.

Thursday, August 28, 1873. I was trying to read Dumas's *Impressions of a Russian Voyage* but fell asleep. They woke me near Marseille. We ate very well in Toulon; and then, as we drew near to Nice, I was under a great pain. All places are the same for me except Paris (which I adore) and Nice (which I hate as the heat is so oppressive). But the good things about Nice, like those four times I went swimming by myself, and seeing the Duke and many other things, endear it to me. Walitsky and the Princess met us at the train. "Where is Mama?" we asked, and they said she was tired from Monaco, and then that she was a little bit sick. The truth is she had fallen out of bed and had hit herself against the nightstand.

But she was at the door when we arrived. I made her sit down in the dining room. Arrivals at our house are always impossible. Everybody spoke at once; we asked, we answered. We talked about everything. The lawyer Abrial came to tell us that George has been arrested at the Austrian border; his Anna has run away, stealing his passport, and without that, he is being detained. And we have engaged a little black boy who will accompany us in the carriage. His name is Said, but we'll call him Fortuné, although I like Chocolat better. And Prater met us in the street.

As long as I don't look out the window I'm happy, but I can't stand this pale greenery and this burning sky! So Mama said that we'll live in Paris. Oh, my God, how much I would like that!

I showed my hats, and we talked about the dresses. Mama doesn't like the velvet. I see I must rely on myself only.

So here I am in Nice. There was yesterday in Paris, and now today! I feel strange each time I arrive; there is no ceremony, no importance. I look upon my stay in Nice as an exile.

I am setting up my schedule of the hours and the days for my professors, and on Monday I'll start my review of those studies so infamously interrupted by Collignon.

And with winter will come the season; it will not be Nice any more, but a little of Paris for four months. There will be the races, and the pigeon shoot, and the Duke of Hamilton, who will be coming back. I'd like Nice then because it is the only city where I have the joy of seeing him. It's a happiness I've forgotten and no longer understand.

Friday, August 29, 1873. Mama was in bed, and all of us were around her when Walitsky returned from Patton's to tell us that Abramovitch is dead! It is terrifying, unbelievable—strange! And Walitsky thinks he probably died of cholera. Our "dear Consul" is dead. . . . It seems to me he'll always be back here in winter with his yellow wheels, his famous fur coat, and his plaid lap-robe. Death is awful, especially for a man so kind and well-mannered, . . . a boy like Abramovitch. I am very, very upset by his death! So, there are people like Gros and Saëtone who live, and a young man like Abramovitch dies! We are all saddened, even Dina. It was being said that Hélène and he were going to be married. I started a letter to her, mentioning Paris, etc., and then in the middle I put the death of this poor man and finished by telling about the races.

The Princess has reassured me about Gioja's beauty—it's the photography. That's all. Besides, I'll see for myself. Winter will be coming soon. I saw Bensa at Delbecchi's, where I went for paper and pencils. I told him to get me some professors, and with God's help I'm going to settle myself properly at work, and study!

I wish the Princess wouldn't exaggerate so much! She's always saying how beautiful I am, and I know it's not true. But I wish the men thought the way she does. She really embarrasses me when we go to the market. She haggles. I give them the money they ask, and why not? I go only once in a while. Today I gave a few extra pennies to the women and children who were around us. My God, what a pleasure! They were looking at me as if I were Providence. One woman said, "How nice you are! May the good God go with you!" Oh, if God only would give me a look once in a while!

I've started to fix the hours of my lessons and the days, and tomorrow I want to start my studies, nine hours a day. I am praying for the extra energy and courage I need to study, and I hope that this time nothing will interrupt, since there will be no more scoundrels like Collignon in the house. I am making a beautiful centerpiece for the table designed like a jockey cap.

Poor Abramovitch! How much I regret him. . . .

Sunday, September 1, 1873 [sic, for August 31]. Mama was well enough to go to Monte Carlo with my aunt, so Dina and the Princess and I went to the Var to a country ball.

We didn't stay very long as it was boring. Dina saw Gioja, and when we drove back by her house I saw the famous creature seated on the balcony surrounded by her foxes, which bark like mad. As we passed, she lifted her head and then lowered her eyes. She likes to lower her eyes. Maybe she's a witch. . . . But she is far from being as beautiful as she is in her portrait. True, she wasn't all dressed up and didn't have a straw hat on her forehead. She has a spot on her left cheek that gives her a cute, charming little air. All I mean to say is: today she was not pretty. Silly! I'm really stupid. What does it matter? She pleases; that's all that matters. I make myself ridiculous with all these remarks, and contemptible as well. I shouldn't even know anything about her—who she is, what she is, or whose she is. She is really fortunate, but I don't envy her. I don't completely envy anybody, because I find no one worthy of that.

Today the Princess offered me an ice cream. I mention it because I have paid for her for two months. Mama came to pick us up in the carriage on the Promenade. It was there that the conversation started about poor me. They started by saying I must have a rich house-hold, house, servants, and everything, and in that tone Mama talked of Miloradovitch, saying that I'll marry him. Her mouth pulls, like mine when I talk about Hamilton, when she says things about my marrying Gritz. But I reminded her that I don't care for the short ones, the skinny ones, or the dark ones. Then they mentioned Walitsky, again, who is so blond he's almost white. Such talk I find very displeasing. I always think of Walitsky as a brother.

Then Dina said, "I know Borreel pleases you as well as Hamilton." In the family in gen-eral we don't say "Sir" or "the Duke of," but always "Borreel," "Audiffret," "Hamilton."

"Hamilton is scandalous," Mama said.

"Miloradovitch is too poor," I answered. "He has only 75,000 rubles of income a year."

"That's enormous!" Mama countered, "whereas Hamilton has only 20,000 pounds sterling."

"Well," I answered, "that's 500,000 francs.

"No! That's only 10,000," she said.

"No, Mama, only five and three-tenths, if you wish!" I laughed.

The Princess told her, "I have said that Marie should marry the Duke of Hamilton."

I didn't have enough tongue to protest on every side, but I was vexed. I didn't want the Duke to become a public subject on my part . . . because what humiliation I would suffer if nothing should succeed! I am very, very angry. During our whole drive the stupid Princess called me "Duchess," and at no time when she did it could I prevent a smile, which encour-aged her in spite of anything else I did.

At home I found that my copy of the *Derby* had arrived, and I had the pleasure of reading the name of the Duke several times. Outside of that, I'll learn a lot from this newspaper; it is very instructive, especially for anyone who wants to own horses.

I wonder whose hands my journal will fall into? Until now it's of interest only to my family. If I become a beautiful person, it will be interesting to everyone. Now it's for me, and I love to read it!

BOOK NINE

Book 9 of my Journal
Begun Monday, September 1, 1873
Ended Monday, September 22, 1873 at 9:15
Concerning Marie Bashkirtseff
at the Buffa Villa Baquis, Nice

Monday, September 1, 1873. Hamilton is in fashion, and they're going to tease me like stupid fools. The next time the Princess said he was "red-hair ugly," I told her, "He is ten thousand times better than your husband!" And when Mama brought up the subject that Bertha expects to marry him, the Princess asked, "Who is this Bertha? An unworthy rival? That's all right. We'll kill her!" And looking into my face she asked again, "Are you devoured with jealousy?"

I told Mama more about Bertha, and she said to me, "But you are as far from Hamilton as I am from the Emperor of Russia." I made her a gesture of silence. I was afraid she would say something about that encounter with the Czar in the Crimea when I was little. She dropped the subject, but continued with what she has said so many times before about how she would refuse if the Duke should ever ask for me, and mentioned his mistress again. Then she said, "Just before my being married to your father, a very simple young girl, Maria Ivanovna Perlich, came to our house, closed the door, and told me, "Miss Babanine, I know you and like you; do not marry Bashkirtseff. He has a mistress and she has children. Do not count on your youth and your beauty. Two weeks after you are married, he will go to see his mistress. . . ." Mama said so much that I got really scared. I wanted to answer with things like I've written in the journal, but I stayed silent not to look ridiculous. I could see that Mama is truly afraid I might marry the Duke!

I got myself a jumprope, and I've been learning how to jump.

Wednesday, September 3, 1873. When Bensa came to give me the drawing lesson, he reported on my request for professors. He talked with the principal, who, looking at the note I'd given to Bensa, asked, "How old is this young lady who wants to learn so much? And how did she know how to prepare such a program?" That stupid Bensa told him I'm sixteen!

"I'm furious!" I told him. "Why lie about my age?"

He apologized, and then tried to flatter me. "In intelligence you are twenty, and if I'd said fourteen he would never have believed it." I exacted a promise from him that he would tell them my true age.

A terrible wind blew today, and to make matters worse, Mama was doing housework, which makes me furious. I would like to see her elegant and beautiful instead of looking like a cleaning-woman in an old dress and with Dina's dirty monkey on her shoulder, hanging on to a cucumber. Most of the time I try not to say anything to avoid scenes. After a shopping trip, on the way home I begged Mama not to be a housewife any more, but in vain! She was offended and started a long speech, saying that I detest her, that I think she is unworthy the way she always does.

Tomorrow my Italian professor is coming.

Thursday, September 4, 1873. And today my French teacher came, too. I'll be having lessons on Tuesdays and Saturdays. I went horseback riding with Paul in the evening, and finally I can seem at ease when trotting. But Paul's horse was absolutely unruly; he wanted to walk or gallop—nothing else, and that was terribly enervating for me.

Saturday, September 6, 1873. My print of a Negro head arrived from Worth. And today Mr. Brunet gave me my first lessons in literature, grammar, rhetoric, history, and mythology. It was a kind of test.

It's been raining for the last two days, and I am happy—I breathe, I live, I am reborn. And Mama is giving me her sleeveless blouses from Paris; she doesn't like them and I adore them.

I'm writing by the light of the moon—or rather the clouds, as the moon is behind them. I've good eyes and I'm ruining them. It's the last time I'll do anything so silly. It's getting very dark and I can barely see.

Sunday, September 7, 1873. I proposed going to Monte Carlo, and we went; I won. Then when it was time to come downstairs to catch the 5:00 train, Mama detained us. When we did leave it was too late; we had missed our train. Back upstairs we met my aunt. She, too, wanted to leave. I was very angry, and Mama was sorry for me. She proposed that we go and have supper, but the dining room wasn't open yet; so we played again.

Again it was the same story with Mama. "It's time," I said.

"Not yet."

I would have missed the train again if Walitsky hadn't come down with me. We had only four minutes. We ran, and I regret it. Just at the corner of the casino, I saw Gioja on the arm of a handsome young man. I wanted to return, but I was already down and there was just time to get to the train. Walitsky came with me.

George is at our house. Walitsky told me secretly that during our absence George dared (oh, I blush!) to bring Anna to the house for dinner. He does it every time Mama is away. But how does he dare? I can't understand his audacity. What a dirty man! But Papa is also a dirty pig! He is crazy, depraved! It's a sacrilege to encourage George that way! Just the idea makes me shiver. My brother will never dare to tell me that such a person exists; he'd rather die! And so I have to admit that George's presence in the house is a disagreeable fact for me.

At dinner when I said that woman is equal to man, they all answered me that this is not true; that a woman has her work and a man his. For example, a man is a professor, but his wife must be a housewife. Then Walitsky said, "Then Hamilton will go racing and Marie will have to curry the horses in the stables." After that there were other remarks about Hamilton. I don't blush any more, but I couldn't avoid smiling at the beginning; and the more I tried, the brighter my smile became.

Monday, September 8, 1873. My teacher of math and cosmography came; and while we talked with him, Paul came and brought my hat from Paris. Mama wanted to see it before paying; so we went downstairs, and in looking at the hat we forgot the professor. At 7:00 P.M. we received a letter from him saying that he had been badly received, et cetera. It is really true, and I am very sorry about it.

Tuesday, September 9, 1873. My first lesson in German. For a long time I didn't like this language; but recently it has attracted me, and I like it! I study it with ardor.

I told Bête (my secret name for the Princess) that I would like to go to my father's place in Poltava "to spray dust in their eyes" as we say in Russia—to draw attention to myself, to dazzle them!

"And to pursue Oritza Miloradovitch," she said, smiling.

"What nonsense!" I retorted. But I would like to go for two weeks. It was not at all my idea to look up Gritz. I wouldn't go for such a dirty thing.

"Oh, he's a superb possibility for you, my dear. So rich!"

"I'm not interested. He's ugly."

"How old is he?"

"Eighteen. He's too young to pursue the way you pursue your 'dear' Leo. Besides, he hasn't done anything silly yet." (I didn't want to say "he hasn't experienced life," but she understood. If he does stupid things after he's married, well—thanks, just the same!) It's better to take a husband of thirty, a man who has already lived and not some greenhorn. When I'm thirty, he will be thirty-four, and so on. And besides, a truly Russian young man like Gritz is a mama's boy. He's never done anything yet with his life, and he could not make me happy. He wouldn't understand that one can be his wife's lover. But seven years after the wedding, he'd probably start fooling around with some actresses and French women. And I, abandoned—by whom? A know-nothing Russian kid! No, it would be too humiliating! But I think I humiliate myself; with a youngster like that nothing would be easier than to hold him on a leash. Am I a poor innocent who can be dropped at will?

Wednesday, September 10, 1873. I tried to draw a smiling face and succeeded partially, only missing the teeth. It's only a sketch, but I'll finish it tomorrow.

In the evening we stayed in the dining room. I burned some sugar. Papa sat in his armchair, and I was next to Paul in another corner of the room. We were all talking quietly for almost the first time in my life. My aunt sat pensively in her chair, and Mama next to her. Then the Anitchkoffs came with the children. Ouf! Mrs. A. sat near Papa, and Mr. A played cards with Walitsky. Khalkiopoff and Paul watched the players. The room was full of people; we felt good; we talked. We had company, and I was happy. Here is how we should live!

Once or twice my aunt tried to start one of her scenes, but I stayed mute and the tranquillity returned.

Thursday, September 11, 1973. Mrs. Patton came to talk to Mama, very upset and anxious. There is a rumor that her husband will lose his job as Consul. It would really be too bad; the Tolstoy woman and her friends would triumph. Mrs. Patton even sent a telegram to the Grand Duchess and another to the Countess Keller. Add to that worry the fact that her little boy, whom she is nursing, is sick.

Paul and I drove out in the evening to order 100 personal cards for Mama, and then we paid the teachers. I also took my buttons that had been broken, and I bought an alarm-clock for twenty francs. Mama scolded me because I had gone out without telling her. But they had the calèche, and it was understood they would follow! Mama had been to Monaco; and when she was returning, Mr. Clausade was in the coupé with them. He talked about me and thought I was sixteen. He said my arms are superb. She asked him where he had seen me, and he said at the theater. Everybody is talking about me and thinks I am sixteen. What an insult! How do they dare talk about my arms and my bust? When people say these things, I am vexed, uneasy. It gives me a funny feeling. I want them to know I'm not older than I am.

Friday, September 12, 1873. Today I worked well, and I am pleased with myself. The English teacher says I'm speaking very well: "Indeed, hearing you I would never say you are a foreigner." Somehow, I can't believe I'm speaking well, I've wanted to for so long! I believe the people who say that, but within myself I cannot credit it. I'm studying English, French, Italian, Latin, and German, as well as the piano and drawing. I'll also be taking science—geography and cosmography—and arithmetic, grammar, literature, history, and natural science, among other subjects. Today I worked exactly nine hours. Manotte, the piano teacher, comes tomorrow.

Saturday, September 13, 1873. Good work again today. However, Manotte came and made me lose an hour. What he had me doing was very tiresome, but—bah!

Dominique came with the landau, and I am very pleased about it. We have been shaken for the last three months in those ugly calèches. Mama is still sick.

Sunday, September 14, 1873. It is raining and windy. Mama and my aunt are at the Anitchkoffs'. I am going there too (rain coat, not bad). I took them to the railroad station and returned to take the Princess to the London House for some hot chocolate.

Monday, September 15, 1873. Although I got up late and was lazy all day, I had a good English conversation with the Scottish lady. For the first time I spoke Italian. Poor Micheletti looked as if she would faint and went to the window. I am satisfied with myself; I can say that I am *speaking* Russian, French, English, and Italian. And I am seriously studying Latin and German. The day before yesterday I had my first chemistry lesson. Oh, how pleased I am with myself; I'm very happy.

In the new issue of the *Derby*, I discovered that the Duke has a lot of horses racing at Baden. How much I would like to be there! But I must study, although after reading about all that I have to make a great effort to calm myself. I went to bed repeating, "Let's study! Let's study. Our turn will come . . . (if God wants it)."

Tuesday, September 16, 1873. My only free time is the lunch hour, and that is when everything happens. There seems to be no day any more when they don't mention Hamilton. I blush, but I'm no longer afraid of it. I justify myself by saying that I blush for everything and nothing. Mama takes my part: "Why do you tease her with this Hamilton? He has his Gioja and some children."

Mama was so nice today that I'll certainly end by becoming her friend. She was telling us about when she was sixteen and repeated some poetry, laughing. She was gay and teasing and didn't seem to mind the Hamilton subject any more. It's rare when she, herself, does the teasing! Most of the time she scolds me with something like, "Silly girl! What have you made up now?"

Dina is in an inspired mood again, but there's a reason: she's going horseback riding.

The weather is turing colder and the season is on its way. I can hardly wait for winter! The houses open their shutters, people start to show on the Promenade, and it's getting cold. In short, life starts again. In the evening, Dina, Bête, Paul and I went to Walitsky's room and played cards—Kings—with a lot of noise and gaiety. Khalkiopoff came in. He didn't play, but stayed next to Walitsky and mixed in the game. As we played we shouted, laughed, and whistled. "It's like a jockey club!" Walitsky told us.

I have no rest, and I don't know why. My heart is in despair. *He* is on my mind all the time. Winter is coming and he will come. When I tell myself that, if I am seated, I stand up. If I'm at the piano, I stop and cannot go on for several minutes. If I'm talking, I suddenly fall silent. In fact, the thought completely overthrows me. I get agitated, I can't think, and my breathing sounds excited, cutting off my voice. Then I get a chill down my back, and I kick the rug like an impatient horse! The longing to see him, the hope, the fear, the incertitude, the desire to be loved by him, and the impossibility of such happiness all gnaw at me. And then I tell myself the truth: "You're a crazy little girl!"

I finally talked them into going to the beach, but Mama, Auntie, and Papa were all opposed to it. As ever and always I listened to them all. But I'm not joking; these people spoil all my pleasures. Before conceding anything to me, they sing a funeral mass. Mama didn't go, and finally I went only with Bête. In the water I showed everything I know. I swam on my back very simply; I dived; I did everything, in short. And then, to finish with honor, I had them pull the diving board and jumped into the sea. After that, not to spoil the effect, I got out of the water. But I did come out of the cabin once more in my bathing suit and took Prater, throwing him into the water from the bridge.

There were a few nice people on the beach. We are starting to see some action and some life; the season is approaching! Mama came looking for us, and we walked back.

Well, some people started to look at me! I can see now that they do it, not because I'm wearing anything ridiculous, but simply because—they look at *me*. Why shouldn't it be possible that I might attract people's interest? It is true; I am noticed everywhere and always.

Mama said, "When you left the cabin, everybody looked at your feet." But my mind keeps going back to him. Am I asking him to change his life? To live like a good husband? No, I just want to take Gioja's place—with his wife's title. He can do what he wants and just give me a few hours—one hour a day—and assure me that he loves me. To be what Gioja is for him here is what I want, but before the world I want to be his wife. The thing is, I don't want him to treat me as a wife and then go looking for pleasure with another Gioja!

As the activity comes back to the Promenade, I know more and more that I have to live in society. I can't live without seeing people. We saw Gioja. She was wearing her hair loose and short. It was mixed with some false hair, certainly, and her face was painted very white; but she looked nice—beautiful, even, if you didn't see her too close. But how can she be kissed with a mask like that? A young man would become an old one with a white moustache! And then all that false hair. . . . Bensa called it beautiful. But mine is ten times more beautiful—natural in color and everything!

Saturday, September 20, 1873. In my French lesson, I read the Holy Story and the Ten Commandments of God. The professor said we must not fantasize about what is in the heavens, and that the Catholics and the Greeks are wrong, being idolaters who worship statues and paintings. I am far from following such ideas. I believe in God, our Savior, and the Virgin. And I honor a few of the Saints—not all of them, only a few—because some of them are made the way we make plum cakes. God will forgive me this reasoning if it is wrong. . . . Can I believe that He has ordered a tabernacle built for His oracle? He is too great, sublime, for these pagan sillinesses. I adore God in everything; He is present everywhere; one can pray everywhere.

I had an argument with Khalkiopoff; he said that men are degenerated monkeys.

"You don't believe in God?" I asked him.

"I can only believe in what I understand," he said.

Oh, the ugly little animal! All these boys who start growing moustaches have these ideas. They are little greenhorns who think that women cannot reason and understand. They look on us as dolls who speak without knowing what we are saying and listen to us with the air of protectors. I told him all these things, except for the ugly animal part. I think he has read some book he didn't understand, but repeats passages from it anyway. As proof that God could not have created the earth, he noted that they have found bones and frozen plants at the poles; once long ago these things lived and now there is nothing but the frozen remains. I said nothing against this, but I did say, "Wasn't our earth overthrown by several different revolutions before the creation of man? We don't believe to the letter that God created the world in six days. The elements have been formed through centuries and centuries. But God *is*. Can we deny that when we see the sky, the trees, the men? Can't we say that there is a hand directing, punishing, and rewarding? Surely it is absurd to imagine God in a burning bush or in Noah's ark or in a column of fire. It's absurd to represent Him in statues or paintings. I can understand drawing Jesus, who has been on earth with a human body."

"I have a much greater conception of God. But didn't the pagans or even the pantheists recognize a supreme power? The ones who called it Nature? But isn't that the same thing? What is Nature? Another name for God."

Just now as I set all this down, a vain thought came to my mind. I thought what I was saying must be agreeable to God, but at the same moment I recognized my misery; and the most insignificant worth is erased by such a presumptuous idea. Even the humiliating words expressing it are a sin because, involuntarily, I want to deserve something for this humility.

Gioja is now the goal of my promenades, to see if she is beautiful. I would like to see her for a long time and be close enough to speak to her. But I would be numb and speechless. . . .

Monday, September 22, 1873. I went down to the dining room in my famous "conspirator" coat. Everybody was still there. I recited some of *Phaedra* from Racine, threw myself on the floor, took some tragic poses, and left.

I have asked Bête *not* to mention Miloradovitch; that subject vexes me more than I can say.

I spoke about Hamilton with my English teacher and asked if she had ever seen him. I invented an atrocious description, saying, "If you see a very fat man, very red, with red hair, little grey eyes, a Scottish jacket, a dirty tie, a pink or blue shirt, a dirty grey or brown hat with the ribbon hanging from one side, driving in a very small, low vehicle, and a very little horse running extremely fast, then you are sure it is the Duke of Hamilton, of the best family in England, the noblest, of royal blood, as you have just told me!"

Then she told me this extraordinary thing: The Duke rented the entire theater where the *La Belle Hélène* was playing in London and attended the performance with only one or two friends. She said he is nicknamed "Alcibiades." However, I see no resemblance. She also told me that whatever is the most extraordinary, the funniest, the strangest, the most extravagant—that is what the Duke is doing. I told her that he always whistles and that that is a way she can recognize him. And I told her the story of Carlos and the pig. (It was not the Duke who tied it to his foot, but his brother.) We laughed like two crazy girls, but the tips of my fingers were cold.

In the carriage during our drive, we seemed to be pursuing Gioja. How I despise her! But I can't look at her with calm because I envy her so much! Oh, misery! I'm jealous. May God forgive me for being so low.

I had another theological discussion, this time with Bensa. Like Tony [Khalkiopoff], he denied God and I told him, "You are less than an eggshell." But after a lot more things like this, I told him, "God will forgive you."

BOOK TEN

Book 10 of my Journal
Begun Tuesday, September 23, 1873
Ended Monday, October 13, 1873
Concerning the day of greatest unhappiness up to now and always of
Marie Bashkirtseff
Rue de Temple, Villa Baquis, Nice
On this day my hopes are smashed, and for me to be happy, only God can do this for me—render me happy.

Tuesday, September 23, 1873. I had my first math lesson with this detestable new teacher, another Bensa. Oh! I still had another hour of lessons started, French with Mr. Brunet, when I was told the dresses from Paris had arrived. I was dying to rush out and see them, but I finished the lesson. They were really very pretty.

At dinner I had another argument with Papa—about beauty. I insisted that I had a greater right to speak on the subject, and then Papa said, "So people have told you so much that you think you are a beauty?"

"Oh, no, Papa, not at all. But I am nice. I don't pretend to be beautiful. There is no doubt I'm better looking than Collignon, but that doesn't prove anything. Miss Collignon was always imagining that it was she people looked at when they stared at our carriage, but it was *me*. I could prove that if I could ask the people on the Promenade. . . ."

Dina was nodding agreement, but Papa was furious that I had dared to speak in such a manner of his goddess.

"Well," he said, "if anyone asked me, I'd choose Dina." These words seemed so crazy that for a minute I didn't know what to answer; but then I thought, he can see very little; he's a blind old man.

Pitou, Dina's monkey, was making a nuisance of himself and Papa wanted him locked up, but nobody could catch him until I tricked him. He was pleased about that, and we were reconciled for a bit; but I was in hot water again with him for caricaturing Collignon. Poor old men! How they can be fooled! Imagine, if he should ask her to marry him!

Wednesday, September 24, 1873. Miss Elder, our English teacher, told me today that she heard an American boy saying he admires me.

My aunt pretends that the Duke has thrown Gioja out. Everybody was talking about it at lunch. Stupidity! She could throw him out, but he her? Some say she is married to him. "That's not possible," my aunt argued. "Would she be refused entry to the Casino in Monaco if she were his wife?" Besides, I don't believe she'd be going around with that Soubise woman if she were. The more I see of Gioja the more I detest her, because I have to confess that she is beautiful. I adore her, I envy her, I admire her, and I hate her. Maybe it's that victorious air that embellishes her, or maybe it's her superb tallness. I try not to let her see me looking at her when we pass her in the carriage, but I've seen her even turn around and look at us when she has passed us. What wouldn't I give to talk with her! If she were shorter, she would lose one quarter of her beauty, but this majestic, divine tallness—oh!

George is with us, and he's a little drunk.

Thursday, September 25, 1873. My professor of Latin is enchanted with my progress. At 4:00, when I was finished, we went to the Public Gardens to hear the music. While we were there, Mrs. Daniloff's chambermaid came to find us, asking for Walitsky.

"Who is sick?" Mama asked.

"Mr. Khalkiopoff," she said. "He's sick in bed."

At that Dina started to blush terribly, and to pretend indifference she began to arrange her hair. But alas! I had seen, and my aunt, too. I saw her throw two or three looks in Dina's direction, full of astonishment and then anger. Indeed, if this little peasant has succeeded in pleasing her . . . But it's impossible—such a villain! In any case, it's the first time I've ever seen her blush. Mama went out with us on our second drive, and Dina stayed home. If it's for that scoundrel she is inspired . . . !

When we saw Gioja again, Mama said she was beautiful, and my heart jumped. "But why does she look so miserable?" Mama asked. "Where is her elegance? She is really run down."

I wanted to answer, "It's time! She's thirty-five or more"; but I only thought that, I didn't say it.

"Yes," Mama continued, "she's been reduced to the point of taking on Audiffret. He goes to her house every day."

"She'll get all his fortune, which is considerable," my aunt said.

"Well, then the Durands won't want him," Mama observed.

I asked, "Why not?"

"Because Lucy's mother will not have it! She will forbid Lucy to consider him."

"Why?" I persisted.

"Because Audiffret goes to Gioja. So why marry? For tears and unhappiness? Because this man will return to this old friend after his marriage, and at his own home he'll find everything wrong, ugly. He'll rob his wife of her jewels, her dresses—to her last one—and he'll give all he has to the other woman, with whom he'll pass all his time."

"But still—if he finally gets married, doesn't that mean he no longer loves the other one?"

"Oh, no! Even though he forgets her for a while, he'll start again."

I am not deceived; this is a message for me. Really, it seems Mama and the others think that people get married to tyrannize over each other!

Friday, September 26, 1873. The town is filling up. Mrs. Skariatine is back and the Corinthianne is open. The curtains are at the windows, and in the drawing room the candles are lighted. I saw the Borreels arriving, and the Witgenstein Villa gardens are being watered. The house is open and is being repaired.

Dina is still blushing at the name of Khalkiopoff! What a horror! Thank you, God, for having preserved me from such a scandal!

Saturday, September 27, 1873. I started lighting the candle yesterday morning when I got up, and I'll be doing it from now on. It's so dark at 5:30.

We went to the Français to hear *The Baroness.* I intended to stay for only a half hour, but the play interested me and I remained seated behind Dina, where nobody could see me. Some say the play is immoral. Well, I think the contrary. At each intermission Mama was trying to point out the horrible things about it and gave me some moral talk in a roundabout way. That's the way parents destroy the confidence of their children. It was over at 11:00, thank God, which is early for Nice, where they sometimes martyr us until 2:00.

Monday, September 29, 1873. Today is my aunt's saint's day, and also that of Bête, of her daughter, and of little Vera Anitchkoff. Paul and I went out in a fiacre, and at the fruit market we met Mama, Dina, and Walitsky! I think we impressed the poor people of Nice. I ate some very good grapes. Paul and I went on to Gamel's, where we bought a handkerchief of Valenciennes lace for our aunt and some candies for the children. While we were out we passed a Jewish wedding party.

We are getting ready to have a dinner for certain people we feel obliged to; however, why waste our time and money? It would have been better to pick up six dinners at Gala's and ten bottles of Medoc and set a table in the kitchen for them. Holy God, as the Niçois say, what people! But Mama is so good that she does the honors of the house to everybody but me. I'm no angel, and I admit that the scoundrels who dine here displease me enormously. Who? Manotte, Lefèvre, and Abrial!!!

Oh, my God, for which of my sins am I living in the filth of the Buffa? Every day I lament our darling, beloved, adored Aquaviva. How much I would like to exchange this apartment for that!

At last the honorable scoundrels came. They didn't even know how to eat! I didn't dress up for them, and thank Heaven I sat between Papa and Bête. All these people scream, talk, chew, and swallow! Impossible manners! I was ready to sob. Mama wasn't looking at them, but true to the laws of hospitality she played the part of a good hostess. How happy she is! She can endure everything and doesn't tire others by talking about her troubles or her illnesses. I'm sure she felt as I did, but she concealed it first not to upset anyone, and second for me. But for me in vain. I don't need an assistant; I see all too well! Sometimes I would like to be wrong. Toward the end of the dinner they smoked and screamed—enough to make you go and drown yourself in the first stream. I did better than that. I drank some wine and got a little dizzy.

Bête drew me a picture and said, "When society comes to your house, they'll find Hamilton on a couch drunk and snoring, and your Ladyship on another in the same condition." An unceremonious dinner is really nice with people of your own kind, but these peasants! Manotte is as vulgar as a herd of beef cattle. Imagine—a musician! Among real peasants and country people I feel free and gay, but with these neutral beings I cannot. When they asked me to play the piano, I gave them the Andante movement of Mendelssohn's *A Minor Concerto*. Although I played it well, it did not please them. But they adored the things from *Madame Angot's Daughter* that Manotte played for them. Then they politely asked me for another étude, which I banged out any old way. Pigs! Lefèvre sang a little song I had heard some time ago. Poor man! He was ridiculous. At each verse everybody clapped frantically, the dogs barked, and the cats meowed. (It reminded me of the famous *Assembly of Peter the Great*.) And the children were banging and screaming. Out of fear the monkey climbed up the drapes. It was quite funny! We lived quite well until we came to this accursed Villa Baquis. Now we are transformed into bourgeois! And I can't say anything for fear of a scene.

Tuesday, September 30, 1873. I went to Mama's room to tell her nicely about my feelings of yesterday. There was no scene, for once. On the contrary, I was right. I was slowly crying, with my head bowed in such a way that the tears wet the floor. I thought, if we were living in mythologic times a spring should start from there! Mama told me that we cannot go into society very much because of my dear aunts and that Tolstoy woman—that we are not acknowledged, or recognized by Mrs. Skariatine, who is the leader of our Russian society in Nice. The Consul was supposed to have introduced us at the Prefecture, but Patton and the Prefect are not on good terms.

While we talked I was crying, desperate, and unhappy. I'll die of this misery! Mama is sorry for me, and as she pities me, she offered to send me back to my father. Nonsense! But they'll always be stupid in our family. Because we were lied about by a good-for-nothing, must we believe we are guilty? Because we cannot meet Mrs. Skariatine because of her friendship with my aunts, must we see nobody? A thousand thunders! We'll see! I'll work at this.

Wednesday, October 1, 1873. When Mama and my aunt went to the Anitchkoffs, the rest of us, including Papa, drove out for a promenade.

Later we walked from the end of the Promenade to the London House, where we ate some fruits and then brought home some suckling pig in a jar, some asparagus, and a cucumber. Meanwhile Mrs. Anitchkoff had sent some salted cucumbers, a bouillon with little flaky, filled pastries, and a delightful little chicken. We ate all those delicacies, followed by grapes. I haven't eaten like that for a long time!

We finally had a chance to see the Parisian hit *Madame Angot's Daughter*! The house was full, but there was nobody there of importance. How people are corrupted! Everywhere they try to find something scandalous. For example, my aunt and Bête were looking at each other and smiling, saying there were some questionable parts in the play. I didn't find anything dirty in the play—absolutely nothing. On the contrary, it is very decent. True, there were times when everybody but me was laughing.

At the intermission, Walitsky, Paul, and Khalkiopoff came up from the orchestra and paid a crowded visit to our little box.

Friday, October 3, 1873. Paul passed his tests and has been accepted as a day student in the fourth class, to my great satisfaction. However, at home he'll never be able to work regularly.

Back from a drive with Bête and Papa, I found all that muddy company playing croquet. Walitsky had invented an especially diabolical game: Triphon [Grandpapa's valet] had to kill a bat for each good stroke he received from Walitsky. Paul and Khalkiopoff each had to pay a franc if they missed. If Triphon missed he had to put his head in the stream circling the lawn. Twice the poor beast had to plunge his head in, but he had won six francs. In the stream were frogs and other frightful things, so I offered more. I bet three francs, and multiplied by four for all of us was twelve, that if Triphon should fail he would have to lie down entirely in the stream. Too bad! Just before we got started on my plan, we were called to dinner. It was so funny to hear Triphon before each stroke saying a prayer aloud!

At dinner Dina announced, "January seventh is Walitsky's saint's day, the eighth is mine, and the twelfth is Marie's." And then she whispered to me, "I know what I'm going to give you!"

I guessed it was Gioja's photo, and she nodded, "Two, you know—*one*, and the *other*."

I guessed that the other would be the Duke's, and then I bet with her that neither would be forthcoming.

Would Dina really have the courage to ask Gioja for her picture? I would have such courage, but would she? "Are we going to bet for both photos?" I asked her as we went upstairs.

"Do *you* want to bet?" Dina asked.

"Well, one louis only. But where will you get both? I know who one is, but I'm not sure of the other."

"Oh, you know, all right. And I'll give it to you in a frame trimmed in cherry red and gray."

"You'll not be able to get it," I predicted.

"Yes, I'll have both," and she added, "except, of course, if he doesn't come to Nice."

I was so exhausted I drank a pitcher of water and fell asleep in an armchair. When I woke up I heard Mama speaking in Russian: "I was at Monaco from 3:00 to 5:00 today, and they let Gioja come in with the Soubise girl. You know, they are famous people. Not everyone is allowed there. But I think Hamilton has completely left Gioja. She looks so pitiful! Formerly she behaved so proudly. She entered the game room like a goddess, and everything she wore and did was fine. When she sat next to a window or walked to a table, everyone's eyes were on her. Now everything is Soubise. And Gioja seems to have none of her former pride. Even her clothes look pitiful; things don't become her. The hat is awful, and the shoes. And her face is haggard, pale. In a word, she looks dreadful!"

Mama's whole speech was addressed to Mrs. Anitchkoff, but I knew it was really for me.

Next Tuesday is Paul's birthday—October seventh [fourteenth by western calendar]. For two months we'll both be fourteen.

Sunday, October 5, 1873. Mr. Brunet came, and we set the hours for my lessons with him. Then Paul and I went to the English church. (Poor Childers preached miserably!)

When Mama drove out with the Princess, the Prince of Witgenstein stopped short to look at Mama, who is really very beautiful.

Bête asked Mama at dinner, "Isn't he charming?"

"Very handsome," Mama agreed.

"Adorable?"

"Yes."

"Better looking than Hamilton?"

"No."

Bête turned to me. "When we saw him today, how he looked at your mother!" And then abruptly she said, "I've changed my mind. You should have Witgenstein."

"Princess, you're crazy!" I said. "Always men with abandoned women."

"But who has no women?" Bête chattered on. "Witgenstein is superb—not better looking than my husband, of course, but good-looking. Tell me, don't you find my husband handsome?"

"Not at all," I said. "Hamilton is good-looking, and so is Witgenstein. But your husband—no."

I was hoping we could go to Monaco so we could shoot, but we missed the train; now we have to wait until Paul's birthday on Tuesday.

But now since Witgenstein had become the hero of the day, I was blushing when they talked about him. Dina noticed and mentioned it to me. "Yes, my dear. Twice already! That's my misfortune. Tell us, Princess, what can a person do to avoid blushing?"

"Pinch the lobe of your ear," was her advice.

When we saw Gioja at the music, I teased Mama, "You're not so beautiful as Gioja. You're not the tenth of her. Dye your hair, paint your face and your eyes, take care of yourself, and you'll be good-looking."

"If Witgenstein would like to be my beau," Mama laughed, "I'll dye my hair!"

Monday, October 6, 1873. Driving on the Promenade, we saw Gioja, beautiful as a star, walking with Witgenstein's friend, Rosalie, who looked awful. Mama and Bête began again, wondering how Prince W. could have lived with her for twenty years. They have children, but of course he's never married her. Then they got on the subject of Miloradovitch, and I could see clearly that it's Mama's most precious dream that I marry that young man.

Misery of miseries! I tried as best I could to prove that one can be happy in marriage. I explained the "woman" side, saying, "A husband won't go running after other women if he loves his wife."

"All the husbands in the world run after women. There is no other kind," the Princess said.

"I assure you of it!" I argued. "For example, you said that Audiffret is already going around to see Gioja? So! He's not running away from her. . . ."

They both started at once! "Yes, but—" Mama finished, "It's only for a month or two, and then it will be over."

"Sometimes it's forever," I said. "Witgenstein doesn't run around, and his affair with Rosalie has lasted over twenty years." They didn't answer me, and I finished, "If I were a man I wouldn't get married!"

"My brother, now, has picked up such a piece of trash—" Mama said, referring to George's Anna.

"For a man," I told them, "it would be better to live alone, because a man who doesn't get married is not an old maid."

Tuesday, October 7, 1873. For Paul's birthday, I had canceled all my lessons because I hoped to go to Monaco. But the family had not yet received the money they were waiting for, and to my great disappointment we stayed home. At 11:00 I went to the window to see what was happening in the garden. There were Paul and Triphon with the gun. I jumped from the window into the garden, and we went down into the corner to shoot. My hands were trembling a little when, for the first time in my life, I took up a loaded gun, especially because Mama is so afraid of all firearms.

My first target was a pumpkin about twenty steps away. I hit it perfectly, but I wouldn't have believed it if I had not found all the contents of the cartridge in the pumpkin. My second target was a piece of paper about a foot square. This time, too, I hit my mark. The third time I aimed at a leaf and hit it; I got very excited. All my fear disappeared, and I took the pumpkin, the paper, and the leaf in to show Mama what I had done.

She was very proud of me although a little uneasy. But my aunt and Papa started one of their horrible scenes. Papa sang a funeral mass, and my aunt began to gesticulate and quack, her voice rising the way it does when she's excited: "Murder! Horror! Terror! Misfortune! Death! Earthquake!"

Needless to say, Mama was swayed in spite of herself; she didn't want to take sides with me against her own sister. Their voices rose to the sound of a desert hurricane, a thundering fortissimo. They screamed and lamented, describing a thousand terrible accidents. All the time I just stood smiling and calm. But finally, to quiet their din, I shouted, "Why is it so terrible for me to shoot? I'm not going to be one of those disgusting women-men with glasses and a cane. Will shooting a gun prevent me from being sweet, nice, gracious, thin, vaporous (if I may use the word), and beautiful?"

By that time they were listening to me, so I told them, "To shoot I push down my hat and pull up my collar. I spread out this leg to keep my balance, but as soon as I fire the shot I turn around as nice, as elegant, and as feminine as if I were picking bachelor-buttons and singing a pastorale. And when I know more about shooting, I won't need to push down my hat and do all those other things, even to aim."

After that I dashed up the stairs and set down a catalog of all my excellence in the diary: "I am everything. At the shooting I'm a man; in the water a fish; on a horse a jockey; in a carriage a young girl; at an evening party a charming woman; at a ball a dancer; singing at a concert a mockingbird with low and high notes that penetrate the soul and make the heart jump. In my bedroom I am Venus. (I'd be perfection if I had pretty hands and feet, but they're not remarkable.) Seeing me with a shotgun, one cannot imagine that I can be nonchalant and soft at home. Sometimes when I undress in the evening, I put on a long black coat that half covers me; and as I sit in an armchair, my word of honor, I look so sweet and gracious (which I truly am) that no one would remember I can shoot.

After more of the same kind of thing, I suddenly put down my pen and went back to the garden, this time to shoot from a thirty to thirty-five-foot distance. My last shot was "capital," as the English boys say, and I was happy.

Paul's birthday dinner was a success. There was good conversation, and I felt that I sustained the equality, or even the superiority of women. The others were not indulgent; they talked with me as if I were an adult or a man.

After dinner we danced and sang, going out on the terrace in the moonlight. I played a Cossack piece, and Dina and Walitsky danced. Walitsky crouched and kicked out his legs in the best Russian fashion, to everyone's delight. Then we all danced. Not knowing how to dance formally, I danced by inspiration.

Sunday, October 12, 1873. We've been seeing Audiffret on the Promenade more and more with his bataclan, including Saëtone and another imbecile; and the Princess today insisted they were talking about me, especially as they were looking at me. "Let them," I answered. "It's nothing new." I was sure they were not making fun of me. I also noticed that Gioja's house is now completely closed.

Monday, October 13, 1873. I was starting my English lesson with Miss Elder and had just picked up my speller when she said, "You know the Duke of Hamilton is going to marry the daughter of the Duke of Manchester very soon . . ."

"Indeed?" I mumbled. I held the book closer to my face because I knew I was red as fire. It was as if a sharp knife had been plunged into my heart. I started to shake so hard I could barely hold the book, and my breathing was heavy and trembling the way it was recently when only my breathing bothered me. I thought I would faint, but the book saved me. To calm myself, I pretended for a while that I was looking for something. I was by now reading my lesson in a drowned voice, interrupted by my trembling breathing. I gathered all my strength the way I did once when I jumped from the bridge at the baths. I *must* get hold of myself! I took five pages of dictation so as not to have time to speak. Then I got up, delighted not to have given myself away. I stretched and went to the piano to play, but my fingers were stiff and cold. I don't know what I'd have done if the Princess had not come just then.

"Marie," she asked, "will you teach me how to play croquet?"

"With pleasure!" I said, but I could still feel the tremble in my voice.

Just then Dina called that the carriage was coming, and I rushed upstairs to change. As the Princess and I drove off, we saw Gioja's house open and some workers, ladders, and other evidences of repairs. Clearly Gioja was gone! Where? To Russia to make her fortune?

And all the time I was trying to find a way to announce to the Princess that *he* was getting married, but I didn't have the strength. It's an unhappiness unlike any other I've ever had, such as over the wallpaper for a bedroom or furniture, or anything like that.

"Let's go to the London House," I suggested. I didn't know how to tell the news, but Bête would soon hear it; so it was better for me to tell it myself. When we came back, I chose a moment when we were about to sit on the sofa. The light was behind me, and my face was not very visible. In Russian I said, "Do you know the news, Princess? The Duke of Hamilton is getting married?" I did not blush. Outwardly I seemed calm.

"Who said so? When? How? But it's impossible! Why did you wait until now to tell me?"

"I forgot it," I said.

"You didn't have the courage!"

"I'm not in a state to discuss it," I told her.

It was the same when I told Dina later, and when I told Paul he protested that I was trying to give him my cold!

Much later the Princess confided, "Oh, Marie, I'm sick about it. All my plans are upset. I thought he would come this winter, fall in love with you, and throw Gioja out."

I was surprised at my own courage. I told her "Goodnight" in a comic way, and she said, "Goodnight, lost Duchess!" As I went up to bed, I thought of her nickname for me and how she had told me, "He gives her jewels which should be yours, Bebelle." Her name for me was a kind of stuttering over "Beauty."

All day I felt stunned. I didn't have one minute of peace, and from moment to moment I kept trying to push away the horrible thoughts that keep crowding into my mind. Finally, here in the bedroom, I abandoned myself to despair. I knelt where I've been praying every day for the Duke and wept. It was a flood of tears. When I got up and looked into the mirror, I saw I was pretty. Why doesn't he love me? I prayed to the Virgin for help. It was as if I were suffocating and as if several knives were cutting into my chest. Would I suffer even so much for Mama if she died?

Oh, if I could be unhappy for only an hour and cry it all out. But I can't even cry any more. I'm condemned to a slow martyrdom. I don't even have the consolation of being able to think of him. I'm haunted, enervated, tortured. I'm on burning charcoals. I'm crazy!

I love him and I don't want to stop, but now I feel jealous of the new woman and that makes the pain worse! I'd prefer that he stayed forever with Gioja.

Finally I could feel nothing at all, and I prayed God to give me back my despair.

Maybe the situation will change! Maybe it is not true? On my knees again I swore not to go to the theater for two months if . . . if . . . Oh, I was in a painful fog, and prayed, "Yes, God, give me back my despair."

If I could have done so, I would even have run to Gioja and confided my misery! But not even this consolation is mine; I have no one with whom to pour out my soul, and I'm alone, alone, alone.

All the house is calm as it is every day. The others are more or less happy. They don't know that I, who will appear to them gay and smiling tomorrow, am alone locked in my room with misfortune. I am a woman in my feelings and even when I'm thirty I'll not make fun of myself over this. My imagination has been my misfortune. I've lost him and he's dead to me, but I still want to doubt it.

I have a slight headache. It's already 10:00 P.M., and I have to prepare my lessons for tomorrow.

It's my first misfortune. It seems I am too calm, but that someone has smashed something of mine and that that something was Hope. Now I have nothing left, no goal in life. It was that hope that nourished me—made me live. Where shall I go? Toward what? How? I'm wrapped in a fog. I don't know what's happened to me. But I'm being eaten! Maybe I'm really a sinner to be punished in this way; I'm driven to think that maybe I don't have enough respect for my elders. Ever since I promised to change I've continued to be hard. I'll renew my promise to God and let Him strike me down with all the possible calamities if I should fail again. Oh, if I could only hope! What *shall* I do? I should have been worthy of what I was asking. These thoughts ran through my mind for some time.

Then I realized how silly all this is. He'll probably be getting married in a few days—maybe even tomorrow. He is escaping from me forever. He is in love this time seriously, and I myself have said he knows what love is because he's had experience.

Oh, happy she. Unhappy me!

My jealousy of the new woman led me to beg God for forgiveness even at the moment I realized I was unworthy, because when I humiliate myself I think I'm doing a lot and hope to be rewarded for that. So I'm also guilty of hypocrisy!

The Princess told me she would draw a caricature of the Duke rejecting a pearl—myself. Ruefully, I tell him goodbye.

BOOK ELEVEN

Book 11 of my Journal
Unhappiness!
Begun Wednesday, October 15, 1873
Ended Friday, October 31, 1873
Concerning Marie Bashkirtseff
Rue de Temple, Villa Baquis, Nice

Wednesday, October 15, 1873. When I woke up, I remembered that this was another of Miss Elder's days, and then everything came back to my mind.

For a crutch I took my atlas into the school room, planning to ask how she had learned about the Duke's marriage. But I could not say a word. My fingers got cold and stiff, my heart seemed to stop, and finally I felt even more out of breath than usual. When I tried to name a river, my voice trembled. Finally I made a supreme effort, trying to be casual. "Oh, by the way, where did you read that the Duke of Hamilton is to be married? We had such a long dictation I didn't take time to ask."

"In the *Morning Post*," she answered, bright and cheery. Privately then I resolved to subscribe to that paper so I could read about the wedding. I put down the atlas and took dictation, but my hand was trembling. My jealousy ate into me, but I smiled, breathed irregularly, and discovered I was hoarse.

Later, at the piano, I played furiously for a while; but in the middle of the fugue my fingers weakened, and I left the keyboard to fling myself into a chair and lean back exhausted. In five minutes I recovered my breath, but it was the same thing again. Something happened in my throat, preventing my breathing normally. Ten times I jumped up to go out on the balcony. I gave up and went in to dress myself. But for what? I asked bitterly.

All along I had imagined it *had* to happen *my* way. Gioja's reign would end and all for *me*. I *thought* I was hoping, but now with terror I realized I had been *sure*! It seems I was just waiting for the moment to come. Was what happened punishment for that assurance?

Thursday, October 16, 1873. I woke this morning in the midst of a terrible rainstorm, and I decided to read the *Iliad*.

I promised myself I'd not say one disagreeable word. I swore it to God, sure that a violation of my sacred oath would be sacrilege. But maybe I swore to do an impossible thing;

I've asked a miracle which I probably can't obtain because I dared to ask it, and in exchange I gave my miserable promise.

It seemed the news of the wedding had evaporated, and I was tempted not to believe it. Such a misfortune was impossible! Besides, the Princess began her jokes, and everything went on as before.

Friday, October 17, 1873. I was playing the piano when the newspapers came. I took up *Galignani's Messenger*, and the first lines I read were: "The *Berlin Journal* states that the betrothal of the Duke of Hamilton to Lady Mary Montagu, daughter of the Duke of Manchester, was celebrated at the Court of Baden on the ninth inst." The newspaper did not fall from my hands but stuck as if glued. Not having the strength to stand up, I stayed there and read those lines ten more times to be sure I wasn't dreaming.

Why was I so unhappy? Back in my room I could not write. I fell on my knees and cried; but when Mama entered, in order not to be seen like that, I got up and went out saying, "I'll see if the tea is ready." And then, oh torture! I had to take a Latin lesson. I was on the rack. I could do nothing, but I couldn't stay quiet. No word can explain what I felt. But what dominated me, made me crazy, and enraged me was envy, jealousy. If only I could show it, express it! But no, I had to pretend, be calm, and that made me more miserable still.

When Bensa came, however, I told him and Dina that the Duke was to be married; I joked very calmly and simply. Still, I felt sure I had the face of a hanged man because when we picked up Mama at the station she told me my face looked drawn. "You really are too thin!" she told me. My aunt agreed, but I explained it by reminding them of all those classes I have on Saturdays and that I study most of the time.

Later when I got the courage to tell Mama he was getting married, it seemed to be the first she'd heard of it: "Is he already engaged? Well, well, well! So what about it?"

Sunday, October 19, 1873. In my nightgown I went to my aunt's room, where they all were recalling the events at Monaco yesterday. They had seen Prince Witgenstein with his cocotte, and everybody agreed that she is old and ugly.

"He was holding her arm," my aunt said.

"So perhaps she's his wife," Papa added. (I knew that no gentleman would take any other woman's arm than his wife's, although he might offer *his* arm to any lady.) "And I don't believe that Hamilton has dropped Gioja," he insisted.

"But he is *marrying* Lady Montagu!" we all said in chorus.

"What a fool!" Papa muttered sadly. "Life could have passed like a beautiful dream."

"No, Papa. How could that be? Who would inherit the Dukedom?" I realized that they would all be glad if we did!

When someone remarked that Gioja must be stupid not knowing how to keep Hamilton, my aunt said the Witgenstein woman knows how to keep her man, offering as proof, "She's been with him twenty years."

"No, Auntie, she keeps him because he doesn't love anybody else. But some day, if he meets a woman he really likes, Rosalie will be sent to the devil like Gioja," I said.

Monday, October 20, 1873. Today I read in the *Galignani* that the Duchess of Manchester and Lady Mary Montagu arrived in London on Thursday from Germany. I got the impression that the wedding will take place in London. That doesn't make me feel any better.

I was playing the piano when I heard gunshots. From the window I saw Paul with the beautiful new gun he has bought. I went outside and found that a photo of the Marksmen's Club came with the gun. In it I discovered the Duke! True, only his ear and his back showed, but I recognized his neck and ear. I took the picture, put it away in my room, and went back to shoot with Paul.

I shot from the first sixty-eight steps, and then from the second 100. Finally I began to hit from a distance. And now I must learn to hit flying objects.

Friday, October 24, 1873. Walitsky continued to irritate me with his quips and jokes about the Duke; each word was a stinging needle in the wound. And Bête, too. She was saying, "I used to know the Duchess of Manchester when her daughter was two or three. She must be twenty-two or twenty-three now. Oh, he'll run away from her the day his mother, the old Duchess, dies."

"*Why* will he run away? He adores his fiancée."

"Yes, she must be beautiful, and he adores her without doubt!"

"So they adore each other!" I affirmed. Oh, these *he adores, she adores, they adore*'s! As if I didn't have enough torments, already!

Saturday, October 25, 1873. I was almost asleep when I heard Paul and Dina at my door. "Marie, wake up!"

"Go to the devil!" I shouted, pulling the covers over my head.

"It's Mama!" came Paul's voice. "She's sick."

"Hurry!" Dina insisted. I leaped up, pulled on my coat, and ran with them to the dining room, where Mama sat upright on a chair—wretched, moaning and wringing her hands. Around her I saw the worried faces of the rest of the household, including George, who had come earlier. Mama said to me, "I wanted to see you again before I die."

Seized with horror, I tried not to show how I felt, but everybody else seemed to be in despair. Walitsky had sent for Dr. Rehberg and Dr. Macario, and the servants were dispatched for various remedies here and there. I kept thinking, looking at George, that he has the eyes of a madman. Poor George!

Never before has Mama had such an attack of nerves. But when I saw so many others around her, I sat in the armchair by the window and finally fell asleep, only to be awakened again at midnight when she called out, insisting that she was dying. By that time the Anitchkoffs had been called, and they rushed in. I was grateful that all those people were there and could do what was required. I, myself, have an extraordinary aversion and disgust for taking care of sick people. Never before have I been so frightfully unhappy or suffered so much. Yes! On October 13 I did when I heard the news of the Duke's coming marriage, but that's another kind of suffering. When I thought Mama was about to die, I was shouting to Walitsky. It was awful! Then I prayed. The doctors were going back and forth constantly. Finally, with the help of mustard plasters and other horrors, they managed to do something for Mama and put her to bed in her room, where everybody immediately crowded around her. Finally she calmed down, but I was shuddering at the doctors' warning that frequent recurrences of such attacks could be "very dangerous."

The crisis passed, and they all relaxed, staying for a time in Mama's room. As the ocean after a great tempest becomes tranquil and seems frozen, all of them sat there calmly together after their trouble—so calmly that I could not quite understand what had happened. Beyond the calm exterior, within the soul of each reigned such comfort and perfect, sweet peace that it seemed we had never been so happy. George was the first to say that— poor George, who had been so afraid that he had not dared to enter, but remained near the door, haggard, asking the news of each one who went out.

I finally got to bed at three. But what was strange was that during almost all that time of suffering, my unhappiness about Hamilton was added to the anxiety for Mama, and never had I more vividly or more profoundly regretted him. When at last I threw myself on the bed, it was with the words, "O, Hamilton! O, Hamilton!" Then I reprimanded myself and on my knees thanked God for saving Mama.

Solominka Markevitch has returned to Nice, bringing news of Oritza Miloradovitch. "He asked me for your picture; and when I showed him the one you gave me, he said you were sweet and appealing and always well dressed," she informed me.

"You don't say!" I said. "For a Russian pig like him I am 'nice'! Is that it?" I feel only pity and contempt for him.

But the really unpleasant news she brought back from Russia was the doings of Constantine Bashkirtseff. I told Bête what Solominka had said to Mama: "My very dear father has a French actress of forty-two named Durocher. She lives with him and his sisters, and he's in love with her!"

"How do you know that?"

"He buys diamonds for her. And he's planning to give us the pleasure of coming to Nice with her!"

She was so sympathetic that I told her the rest. "You know how swinish they are in Russia? Well, my father doesn't make any attempt at keeping up appearances. After the theater, they dine together and then get into the carriage in front of *everybody* and drive home— my father and the actress. But society doesn't seem at all shocked! Solominka says that in a garden restaurant two tables were set, one for this Durocher and the other for some society ladies. In the middle of the supper, my father got up and went from one table to the other without any shame."

"Maybe if you would go to see your father . . ." the Princess started to suggest.

"No. I wouldn't like to stay in Russia. I want to be English," I said, very near to tears.

Bête proposed that we take Papa and go to Rumpelmayer's for some ice cream. "I'm rich," she said. "My mother-in-law sent me 2,000 francs."

More and more Grandpapa seems to talk like a madman, especially since Solominka returned. He said the most awful things at dinner, attacking the Bashkirtseff name and behaving not only like a silly old man, but like an unfeeling rock. I told Mama, "He's morally rotten to soil my young ears with his talk, and he makes me enraged, crazy. He doesn't appreciate the honor I do him to be his granddaughter, and I just can't stand it any more!" As Mama has no way to oppose his ravings, being still confined to her room, I've decided to get up and leave the table the next time he decides to wage war. It's one thing for me to criticize my father, but quite another for my grandfather to do it!

After Dr. Rehberg said Mama is much better, I felt a little less miserable, especially when I went up to my room and lifted the blotter on my desk to look again at my treasured photo of the Duke's neck and ear!

Friday, October 31, 1873. Our new English teacher, Miss Hitchcock, is to arrive on Saturday. So the unpleasant business of dismissing Miss Elder has to be got out of the way. I went to where Mama was in bed to discuss it with her. Then Paul's laziness depresses me so that, what with my own disappointments, I am beginning to wonder if my heart has not moved over to the other side of my body—it seems so far from where it belongs!

BOOK TWELVE

Book 12
My unfortunate Journal
Begun Saturday, November 1, 1873
Ended Thursday, November 20, 1873
Concerning me
Unfortunate journal! These three last books of the journal are full of misery!

Saturday, November 1, 1873. When Miss Hitchcock had been brought from the train and installed at our house, I realized that I was annoyed to have to make a change, to start again. She is English, skinny, dark, and dry. After sitting next to her at dinner I found her very dull. I took her to her room, we said something about the train trip and her fatigue, and we bade each other goodnight. I told myself, You *would* do it! You will *have* to learn now, my girl! Then I went to my room, took the geography book from the shelf, opened it to the map of Scotland, and tore out the map and burned it.

Sunday, November 2, 1873. Miss Hitchcock took tea with us this morning, and I'm glad to say I found her very nice. I've settled into taking the usual lessons, and it's all right. But Paul worries me because he's doing nothing. He spends his time with Antonio Khalkiopoff, imitating his manners and driving me out of my mind. How can a boy of fourteen fail to understand that he must work?

Another unsettling thing: the Howards saw Miss Collignon at the train with her brother. They say she may be coming back to Nice to stay. I sincerely hope she won't. Papa, poor old man, has been made deaf by her flattery, and it wouldn't bother him to leave his children penniless. Well, God protect us from that!

Friday, November 7, 1873. My dear father is coming to Nice!

Saturday, November 8, 1873. We met the Howard family at the train and went with them to their villa, where tea was waiting. I believe I have some real friends here. I prefer Hélène and so Lise is jealous, poor child!

I fell asleep thinking how beautiful Hélène is. And the terrible thing is, I'm beginning to be jealous of her. I had hardly sat down to the piano the next morning when the Howard girls came wearing new felt hats—modish, tasteful, elegant. Hélène has got slender—almost skinny. And though she doesn't seem very well-built, she is charming, dainty, and delicate. And she has a naive expression. Her pink and white complexion is delicious! Then I realized that next to her I am ugly. All at once I became shy, confused, and silent beside her and felt I looked most miserable. On the other hand she seemed so sure of herself that she was animated, quick, and talkative. Unhappy the one who recognizes her own inferiority!

Hélène told me she loves me very much, and I believe her. She can be my friend without any danger; she's prettier. Finally I recovered and got dressed up to go out. Lise, Hélène, Dina, and I all got into the carriage. We had little Said, whom we call *Fortuné*, riding in the coachman's box. How nice it was not to have an annoying governess with tight lips with us! Paul followed us in a fiacre, and we drove on the Promenade. We stopped to pick up the candies I had ordered at the London House—some glazed oranges and grapes. When I offered the girls the confections back in my room, they refused, saying, "Mama doesn't permit us to have sweets before supper." But I told them this was really fruit, and it was amusing to see them all swallowing bunches of glazed grapes and slices of sugary oranges.

I am very angry to be so ugly. I am envious. I detest seeing anyone better looking than myself. And how many there are! What an unfortunate personality I have. It's really stupid! As I think about it, I become furious, excited, angry, enraged. I am no more at peace; everything within me seems upside down. All I need to be completely happy is to be as pretty as Hélène! And I know I love her.

I both said and did silly things this evening, especially when I played "Chopsticks" and told Miss Hitchcock it was the Russian anthem. And my grandfather, too. He told the teacher the story of his dog Reynard! When I came in, I heard him talking about Hamilton and saying the things he had repeated so often before. My attention was caught when I heard him use the word *mistress*.

Oh, he must be stupid not to know there are things one doesn't say in front of children— above all when there are strangers! But then, Mama mentioned Gioja, too.

When we walked out with Miss Hitchcock, the teacher was advising Mama: "She is so innocent; she must not go every day to the Promenade." My look of incredulity brought a quick explanation: "Everybody will know you!" I laughed so hard that it was Miss Hitchcock's turn to be puzzled.

I thought it was very good of her to come and kiss me goodnight.

Sunday, November 9, 1873. We went to the Howards' today. As we drove up we saw radiant faces at the windows. Aggie kissed me a lot and thanked me for the little box. I spoke English before everybody, and I'm beginning to have a little confidence. At lunch we talked about the theater, dresses, and so on, and I realized that Hélène and I were maybe getting to be friends.

Hélène told us about Adelina Patti's triumph in London, about the beautiful gowns in the theater, Patti's dresses, her bouquets, and her jewels; and all at once I was inflamed by what she said and longed to be able to sing on the stage like her.

Monday, November 10, 1873. The horses had been brought, and I was to go riding with the Howard girls—and Paul, of course. (It would be unthinkable for us to go without a man in attendance, or a boy, at least, if there were no adults in the riding party.) But today my horse seemed to be skating and making mistakes. He was not surefooted and didn't seem to want to go ahead. He kept trying to turn around and even tried to climb the sidewalks. At first I held him to a walk with difficulty, but toward the end he went so well that I was delighted.

At dinner to surprise Miss Hitchcock, I drank a glass of red wine with water and a quarter of a glass of brandy—all at once. Then I became very happy, and it would be impossible for me to repeat all I said. I only remember that I laughed, the teacher laughed, we all laughed. Later in the drawing room, Walitsky played some music, and as he plays well, it was truly delightful. The talking, the playing, the singing—how much I would have liked to stay with them all downstairs. But the lessons had to be prepared. "What a plague!" I said, and told them all goodnight, taking myself upstairs amid a flood of eulogies. I liked the praise, but I lowered my face when I also heard that I was looking "so white, so pale." Most of them think I am doing too much studying. "Why should you be studying?" they ask me. I'm sure they are trying to influence me to give it all up.

Tuesday, November 11, 1873. My breakfast in the early mornings is a great pleasure. I look forward to it every day but didn't have time for it today, and after my lesson everything had been put away. Only with difficulty was I able to get some bad tea, cooked cream, and unsalted bread, which I detest. Miss Hitchcock walked with me to buy a compass box for the metric system lessons. We walked more and more, until my feet were tired; but Hitchcock can hold out better than anyone else! Finally we got into the carriage, which always follows us. I got the chemistry book by Troost and a book of German readings. On the way back we stopped at the Sainte Réparate fruit market. Fortuné follows after us and carries what we buy. I bought cucumbers and fruit. But what a difference between this fruit and what we get at the London House! I bought only a few "crumbs" and lightheartedly let fall 1.50 francs as I clowned with the merchants. I abandoned the fallen money and returned to the carriage triumphantly. Tomorrow I will get a world globe and a pair of scales.

Friday, November 14, 1873. You must never let yourself be seen too much, even by the ones who love you. You must go away in the middle of a good time and leave some regrets for your going—some illusions. If you do this you will seem better—more beautiful. People always regret what is gone, and they will have the desire to see you again; do not satisfy that desire immediately. Let them suffer—not too much, however. (Something Hitchcock said to me suggested the idea.) But if they have to suffer for you (even if you're ugly), they'll think, "She must be something extraordinary to have everyone looking for her and still make herself so scarce!" Without more deliberation they will decide that you are something special. Then you will be queen.

Brunet is always telling me how Paul does nothing at school and behaves stupidly. He seems incapable of achieving anything and looks dissipated. Added to all that, he often misses class without a reason. Yet no one saying such things could be more polite than Brunet.

How awful it is to hear such things! I'm convinced Paul will never come to any good. I'm not angry, but it's no use keeping secrets from oneself. I have to admit the truth; I've been right all along. I have to be objective and realize that he is a vain, empty, ignorant boy. Alas! It's the truth I've so much wanted to deny!

Monday, November 17, 1873. In the *Galignani* there are some more horrors. The Duke of Hamilton is getting married on the tenth or eleventh of next month. The Duchess and the Princess of Monaco will go to London to assist with the wedding. It is still killing me. I cannot become accustomed to this idea. I still consider that his name and position are an irreparable loss for me, and I do not think I'll meet another who will please me so completely. He unites all the qualities I admire, and besides that, I love him.

It's not just that I loved him; I think even more about the name, the money, and the luxury. Love in poverty doesn't last long—only until the . . . no, I'm too young to say such things! But love with riches is *sometimes* lasting, and the cooling which seems to be necessary is— warmer—no, not that: more noble, more delicate, more suitable. Anyway, considering my tastes, I've lost the chance at perfection. I couldn't have chosen better if I'd ordered a husband made for me!

Well, I've become cold now. I'll marry the first man who wants me who is rich enough and from a good family. Oh, of course, I'll love my husband, but if I should see the Duke again I'd start to sing a *Miserere* with variations. And seeing that I can't be completely happy married, I'll have no scruples . . . I'll take the most acceptable one and then—oh, I don't dare say that! What a horror! God, please don't punish me for these atrocious fancies; forgive them! I'll have a good time, but I'll be honest all my life. I know that in spite of my foolishness, if I had one blemish on my soul I would die!

My problem has been, alas! that I was too sure. Now I am punished for that. But it seems to me that I've been robbed of something that was mine.

Tuesday, November 18, 1873. George has been acquitted at Aix. He was required only to pay a fine of 500 francs for the two slaps he gave Mrs. Tolstoy. I pray every night that God will let us go to Russia and settle that stupid affair which keeps us all unsettled, especially me. It eats at my heart and poisons my life. Then I would like to return to France and settle in Paris decently. The way we live now, with no place in society and no part in it, is awful. We remain alone among this dirty aristocracy, where even our own relatives gossip about us. Our situation torments me so much that every pleasure, even, is still an annoyance. When we go out, it is alone; we go to the races alone, to the theater alone. We have no bataclan [entourage, clique]. We are complete strangers who know nobody. We have only the charm of novelty. Everyone wants to know who we are, yes. But we are *nobody*! We are worse than nothing, and for me it is a shame, a pity. And then they talk about buying a villa here— in Nice!

Wednesday, November 19, 1873. Several days ago we went riding a second time with the Howard girls, and what happened to me is still bothering me. I had asked for the grey trotting horse, Kitty, and can't understand by what chance that filly was given to Hélène instead. So I took Paul's "dancing horse," the one he trained for the steeple-chase. He was doing rather well, but didn't trot. Dina came, too, and the man had to hold her horse by the reins. It was awful. Dina is miserable on horseback because she's afraid. Here is what happened to me: Right in front of No. 57 on the Promenade (I still can't figure out how it happened), my horse fell and I found myself on the ground. But in a second I jumped, and there I was, safe and sound on the sidewalk! At that moment young Barber's father caught the horse by the bridle and asked, "Are you badly hurt?"

"I'm not hurt at all, Sir," I said, "but thank you very much!" Had I answered gaily? Dina was almost scared to death. I got up again calmly enough, but I saw that the fetlock of my horse was bleeding. And I rode in the carriage with the others back to the Howards'. Now as I look back on it, I am only surprised at how easily I'd been able to hold myself in the sidesaddle wearing a riding habit! I can't understand why I was not hurt. Yes, I do understand: I owe it to God. He saved me.

And it was all right for me to admit my fall from this horse because he had knelt on all four of his legs, and that was why I was able to get down. But I regret it because of the Howards; I don't like riding with them. In fact, it was disagreeable. When Hélène had finished her ride, I took Kitty and returned to my house at a good, easy trot. What a delight!

Mrs. Howard came over a little while before dinner and talked about my fall from the horse. I told her I was only trotting, but she tried to convince me I had been galloping. Actually, I've not galloped since summer, but I have observed, on the other hand, that both Hélène and Lise gallop—awfully! The truth is, I have been practising trotting for some time, and I prefer it, as I consider it to be more learned and beautiful. I was trying to get the horse to do it.

Walitsky, who knows I've just read the *Iliad*, addressed me with a twinkle in his eye, "Miss Marie, the side of the flank was powdery where you used your riding-whip. In this extraordinary occurrence I suggest that a god was pricking your horse with a goad!"

BOOK THIRTEEN

Book 13
My miserable journal
Begun Friday, November 21, 1873
Ended Tuesday, December 9, 1873
Relating to me, a silly girl of fourteen
Rue de Temple, Villa Baquis, Nice
The vigil of his wedding is over in this wretched book.
After his wedding a new era begins.

Friday, November 21, 1873. Mama's Uncle Alexander, Count of Toulouse-Lautrec, has asked us to help him find a proper hotel. "He's as hard to please as I was when we were looking for an apartment!" I told Mama, with Bête and Solominka in mind. "Anyway, I'm glad he doesn't expect to settle in our house the way some others have done!" No one commented on what I'd been saying; so I explained: "Everyone is nice as long as we are friends without being too intimate. But friendship, as I understand it, doesn't exist. Nor the truth. Money is everything!"

I am trying hard to like the new English teacher, but by Saturday I had to admit that as the days go by it's more and more clear that Hitchcock is ignorant and stupid. She knows nothing—absolutely nothing!

One of my great problems, I am realizing, is the small value the rest of the family places on my attempts to get an education. When the others all visit together, more often than not I excuse myself and go to my room, sometimes to study, sometimes to write in the diary, and sometimes to sleep.

This evening the fact that I went up to go to bed set them all talking about how hard I am working. "You really are studying much too hard!" my aunt said, and to deny all these charges I felt that I had to say again, "I really study very little." By that time I was in my room and talking through the door.

Mama has bought a hat that makes her look adorable, and it's only now that, regarding her as a stranger, I discover how ravishing she is—beautiful as the dawn. Yes, that's it, even though she is tired from all her sorrows and serious illnesses. When Mama talks, her voice is very sweet, feminine, without being shrill or whimpering. Her skin is tanned and soft, and her manners are as pretty and natural as my own. In my whole life I have never known a person less selfish than Mama. Hers is that completely natural grace that is beyond all artifice. If she would only give a little more attention to her looks, everyone would admire her! Of course, dresses make a great difference. A woman ought to be a little under-dressed or else very well-dressed, but my mother has lately been wearing "rags"! However, today she had on the brown dress they brought her from Spitzer's in Vienna and the new blue hat and the blue coat with feathers. "Word of honor, she is adorable and today she's my passion!" I told Dina.

Dina and I went with Mama and our aunt to the Howards'. Mrs. Howard had invited us "on the spot" at church, whereas it looks as if the Boutonskys and the Pattons were invited earlier. It looks as if they were expected, too, and still they were not at church. Why are we never invited ahead of time? Thinking of all this, I was in a bad humor. I felt I had to find a way to tell Mrs. Howard tactfully.

And finally, as always, when we returned home in the carriage, I started to comment upon how awful it is that in Nice we do not know anybody and nobody wants to know us, and that the Howards almost always invite us separately when they have no other guests.

Then Mama said, "Mrs. Howard told me she didn't invite you children today because the others were coming. I was very surprised and I asked, 'What *enemies* can children have?' and she told me, 'They are the Boutonskys. They are jealous of us, and they look disapprovingly on your children.' I told her, 'That's because you and your family came to see us first when you arrived in Nice.'"

I have felt the ill will of those people. Also, I know that Mrs. Howard scolded Hélène because she said in front of everybody that she loves Marie Bashkirtseff above everyone else and that the others don't count.

I see all of this society as filthy, but ourselves as *apart* from it. And yet they look at us as if *we* were dirt! Oh, if God would permit us to win our lawsuit!

Tuesday, November 25, 1873. I looked into Dina's room [in the morning], found her awake, and announced, "My venerable father has arrived! Walitzky saw him last night at Monte Carlo with that actress, Miss Durocher. How awful! It's shameful! Arrival indeed! It's a scandal! Dina, do you think he has come for Mama? That wretched, poisonous reptile?"

"With Durocher along?" Dina asked. "Not likely!"

We were to have gone riding; but as Dina doesn't ride well, her presence on horseback is always a bother to me. Because she doesn't trot, she can't keep up with me; so I have to ride ahead alone. Many riders were out, as well as carriages, and there were numbers of people just walking. My "dear" father was strolling with Solominka and Paul—that contemptible boy who is the despair of the whole family.

"When you ride up to the carriage, I want you to stop and talk with your Papa," Mama had earlier told me. Now I had already passed him twice without seeing him; but finally, yielding to Mama, I stopped the horse, which Paul held for me, and got off. As I kissed my father I thought, "How unhandsome he is! And how stupid! He's too full of Poltava's pitiful thoughts and phrases; in short, a small-town boy." I talked with him about horses and the new saddle.

"Has your temper softened any?" he asked.

"I am always gentle with the gentle and stern with the hard," I replied in Russian. As we stood there for quite a long time, with everybody who was riding or driving by looking at us, I felt sure they all knew he was Constantine Bashkirtseff. Farther off from the carriage, I saw Mama walking with Uncle Sacha, and I wondered whether she had seen her husband.

When Dina finally joined me on the riding path, I confided, "Just to know that Paul is in our father's company reminds me again that my brother has been behaving like a crazy fool. It's a pity to witness the perdition of a young man!"

I had to return home for my piano lesson.

Wednesday, November 26, 1873. [The next morning they are again on the Promenade.]

"There's my famous father!" I said. Constantine Bashkirtseff was sitting on one of the many benches that line the Promenade des Anglais, at a point halfway between one end and the other. Mama asked the driver to stop, and I was suddenly conscious of the crowd of strangers around us. Mama and I got out, and Papa stood up all very naturally, shaking hands with his wife as he did so. Then he was equally "natural" or at ease with me, but I felt that he was really play-acting; I didn't believe that he was truly himself with us and thought his easy behavior was a studied kind of grace, all of it learned in society.

My parents uttered a few more banal phrases; Mama spoke of the weather and finally of me. Earlier Papa had told Paul, "Marie seems cold—even impertinent. You remember how two years ago when we all got into the carriage she sat by her mother and didn't talk to me?"

Today that wild hippopotamus asked Mama to come to his hotel. Mama refused.

"If you want to talk, you can come to us; but Mama will not go to your hotel," I told him. "You have to come to her and not she to you."

"If Mama lived alone, I would always come to her," he replied, "but . . ."

Unimportant excuses, I reflected.

"No matter what kind of a father one is—a criminal, a cad—one is still a father—a necessary fact of anyone's life," he said, a little more heatedly.

"I cannot judge what kind of father you are, but if you treat us as strangers, you have to be respectful," I retorted.

"I don't behave differently toward strangers than to people I know; I always treat people with the same respect," Constantine said in a mollifying voice.

The carriage was approaching and I started toward it, saying, "Well, Mama, I have no time to stay. . . ."

"Yes, it's always the same thing. No time," he scolded. "Mary, he said, addressing himself to Mama, "stay here a while with me, and then go . . ."

Mama remained, and I was angry, feeling that that was a stupid thing for her to do. In my fury I had to admit that I do not understand this woman. She seemed all excited, and, I thought, acted without dignity.

"She should have come with *us*," I complained to Dina. Oh, how vexing it is to see people so wanting in tact and judgment!

However, in the evening the whole family went to Monaco—Constantine, too. Mama accepted a thousand francs from him and lost it on the spot.

"Good for him!" I whispered to Dina. Everyone was surprised to see Mama taking money from a man—without even counting it!

Thursday, November 27, 1873. Today Mama had a headache and didn't get up at all. My adorable Papa left. He gave some money to Paul and asked Mama to give me five hundred francs, but she wisely refused, and I am delighted. I am proud. I'll not take money from this miserable family deserter. Paul told me that Papa had taken him to the actress's place and had advised him about what he ought and ought not to say to the family about the visit.

I am even more disillusioned with Miss Hitchcock: we need an Oedipus to deliver us from this Sphinx! She's a disgusting, detestable ignoramus. She knows nothing. I finally know enough English to start the literature and study seriously, but she's as incapable, stupid, and boring as the eldest daughter of the Anitchkoffs!

At the Howards' a balloon is to be launched and there will be fireworks. And although five big boys from fourteen to seventeen have been invited, I tell myself: "O bother! I prefer mature men." But I've decided to wear my beautiful old blue cashmere dress with a half-open sailor collar of spotted lace pinned with a beautiful brooch of assorted turquoise and diamond settings (my aunt's) and the heavy gold bracelet. With that I contrived a modest hairdo. Dina, Paul, and Miss Hitchcock went with us.

The Howards were waiting for us when we arrived. The boys were introduced with great ceremony. Then we all ran to the garden and tried to launch the balloon, but the wind was so strong that we gave up and started to light the firecrackers instead. We remained on the croquet lawn until someone started chasing the others with sparklers, and then everybody started throwing them. Everyone was running, shouting, screaming, and laughing. Even Mr. Howard got excited to the extent that he was chasing the youngsters with the sparklers and behaving like a child. I found him really very nice. For a while nothing could be heard but screaming and laughter in all those comings and goings, and we were even running up and down the hill. Finally our fun was interrupted by an unexpected visitor—the rain. I was all disheveled and pink from the wind. We went into the house to the blue room where we had coffee.

The upshot of this wonderful day was that my family invited all the Howards and those young boys to come to our house next Thursday at two to play croquet, have dinner, shoot off fireworks, and dance. I thanked God I am not ugly. It was funny! These boys all shook hands when they were introduced! Truly, I began to think, if *boys* can be so much fun, then what must men be like?

Friday, November 28, 1873. I read at teatime that the great wedding [the Duke's] is set for twelve days from now—December tenth. I tore the page from the paper and read it. In the social world this will be the most important event—the wedding of the biggest "bad boy" in society. Everyone is interested, and I would have loved to be able to tell how I felt, whereas all I could do was hurl my pen through the air and shut my mouth with my hand.

Saturday, November 29, 1873. When I looked into the mirror this morning, I was dismayed at what I saw. My face is covered with spots; my eyes are small, and my nose is longer! I look pitiful!

I told myself, She has everything and I nothing. She has riches, the world, parties and balls, beauty—probably—and him. Whereas I am locked in Nice in the Buffa, in miserable Nice, not even surrounded by unimportant people, but ignored by the world. Don't make fun of me. I am not dying of hunger; I have pretty dresses, and I ride in a landau for my outings. That's all true! But oh, how I envy her! It seems that if I should see the future Duchess of Hamilton, my eyes would start out of their sockets, and that I could only look at that fortunate woman with hate and rage. Again I read those lines I have read a hundred times:

THE DUKE OF HAMILTON
The marriage of the Duke of Hamilton to Lady Mary Louise Montagu, eldest daughter of the Duke and Duchess of Manchester, is definitely fixed and will be solemnized on the tenth of December.

My hands shook a little, and my eyes stared at an unknown point in the distance. I tried to read something else, but didn't understand a thing.

When the others returned, someone read aloud from a Russian newspaper about the singer Adelina Patti, who has had a great triumph at Maslon. On the stage she was given thirty enormous bouquets, and some 500 more were thrown to her until the stage was covered with flowers! The paper says she was "sublime" in the uncharacteristic role of Marguerite in *Faust*, and that she has been given a magnificent brooch. She was called back by the audience a hundred times and finally burst into tears.

For me this story was even more enervating than the Hamilton report, since I have dreamed of capturing the love of the Duke by singing divinely on the stage.

One thing particularly torments me even more than the cause of the torment: that I might read all this again in a few years and laugh at myself because I would have forgotten, alas! All these pains would then seem to me childish and affected. But I want not to forget. I beg you, do not forget. When you return to these lines, think that you are fourteen [actually fifteen] years old, that you are in Nice, and finally, that it is happening *now*.

At *last* we are to meet that long-ago Seraphine of Mama's childhood, Sacha's daughter. I was expecting to meet a gracious, elegant, well-built woman with exquisite manners. But when she entered, she appeared with an enormous head like a package of hay topped by a black hat with many white plumes. She wore a long, badly made black velvet dress. The yellow chiffon blouse was embroidered on the shoulders and trimmed with lace, pearls, and diamonds. Her powdered face has a conceited expression, and her manner seems affected. But her most serious drawback is a body that is not well made. Her appearance produces the opposite effect of what I expected. To the eye, Seraphine is a "detestation"!

She paid us a very short visit. Dina's monkey unfortunately frightened her and made her scream. Then the door of the study blew open in a sudden gust of wind, and Seraphine screamed again, making a big jump backward. It was a bad first impression, but I decided to withhold judgment. Apparently Seraphine looks at Mama the way I look at Hélène. How beautiful Mama was! How simple, harmonious, round, regular next to this little monkey! They talked and called the Princess, and we all went to Rumpelmayer's. Never have I been more bored! Still, I can't forget that it is Seraphine's little boy who has just become a marquis with twelve millions! I can't help but consider my own unpromising prospects;

nothing has changed in our family life since the first day in Nice—except to get worse. Now we are living in the Buffa!

[Later, at night:]

At the top of the next page I wrote, "In six days." Then I put away the book and started to dress for the party. But when the Barber boys arrived at two, I was not quite ready.

Then Tibbett arrived, Allen, Ashton; I am not sure of who came, followed by the Howards. We had planned to play one game of croquet and then cricket. When the two Striker boys arrived, there were eleven boys and six girls.

I have to confess I have been waiting for this day with impatience. Every day I asked myself, Why is Thursday so slow in coming? But here it is, at last!

All the boys were amusing. Barber number one was very nice to me, but I didn't want him; I preferred Tibbett, the one who seems to be courting Lise—a tall, serious well-mannered eighteen-year-old. I could see that Lise likes him too, the way she talked to him. How awful it is, coveting what others have! I had to admit to myself that I was a little irritated that such a commonplace boy as Tibbett *dared not* bend before me.

At four we returned to the house. We had played cricket enough for me to become crazy about it. In the apartment our guests were free to do what they wished. I didn't want to do what that French Countess, our neighbor on the third floor, does to her unhappy guests—oblige them to perform, sing, and play little games constantly. "In my house—liberty and brotherhood," I announced. And I went to my room to change from the brown dress to the blue. I made myself agreeable, showing them through the albums. Nobody was bored. They laughed, ran about, chatted.

But I was embarrassed for Paul. He behaved like an unfortunate fool, talking only about Marie Petit, the actress. Lately he was passing all his free time at her house, I knew, and I found this behavior for a fourteen-year-old disgraceful. "He acts like a ninny!" I whispered to Dina. "He jumps around, makes faces, and doesn't end his words. He acts like a simpleton!"

Dinner was served for twenty-one. I had arranged the seating and sat between Hélène and Tibbett, whom I had placed next to Lise. The after-dinner fireworks didn't turn out well.

"What's going wrong?" Dina asked.

Under my breath I told her, "It's that damned Walitsky. He's always putting up obstacles because of his frights and fears of danger." But in spite of the Doctor's precautions, Adam damaged four rockets in one minute by holding all of them under his arm and somehow letting them catch fire, scorching his arm and hand. This mishap, as far as I was concerned, seriously spoiled the fireworks display.

Everybody returned upstairs to the salon, the Howard girls first changing into dresses their mother had brought for the dancing.

I was satisfied with myself even when I looked at Hélène. What if I had been *really* well dressed? When we all had danced a lot, we organized the "blue" dance for which the girls could ask the boys. I also discovered the pleasure of being asked to dance when I was seated among the ladies, and at one time found myself harum-scarum and harebrained as one boy fanned me, another stood near me looking on, and a third stood behind me talking—Striker, Tibbett, and Barber No. 1. How adorable it is, I realized, to be surrounded! Yes, it was above all other pleasures in the world—and furthermore, by these *youngsters*! No, there is nothing to be compared with it! The two Strikers were delightful, and the elder is not even sixteen yet! They look so nice—so clean!

Uncle Sacha and Tornosoff dined with the party and remained for the evening.

I decided that the Princess might be right, after all. She has said, "Everything done by a woman is for the man—all, all, all."

I have begun to love to dance, especially to waltz. Striker, I decided, is my charming little boy—so clean, so white, so noble. By contrast Paul's face is drowned-looking, stretched out, haggard! It's a result of all those days he's been spending at Miss Petit's house and all those nights at the theater. Added to that, his manners are common and he has no conversation. What a misfortune to have such a brother! Still, I pity him. He is not a child, but a wastrel, a "rotter"—yet pitiful! Beside the others, who are certainly far from "uncut diamonds," he is a slob!

But I had fun because there was no reason to be bored—nothing else to do but enjoy myself and be amused. Finishing a waltz in a whirl, I flung myself dizzily into a chair, and Striker—or Paul or Barber—I can no longer be sure, came up and fanned me. And I began to think: If it were the Duke who invited me to dance, I couldn't dance because I wouldn't have the courage to give him my hand and endure his arm around my waist. I couldn't be close to him! And the blue dance—I wouldn't have the courage to invite him for that! . . . I would have been shaking and unable to speak; in fact, I am sure I would have fainted! How courageous men are! They love; they speak and say they're in love!

At ten the ball was over.

Well, it's nice to know a lot of boys, because that's the way one can learn how to hold the men.

Uncle Sacha was charming at dinner; and when the other guests had gone, he made all of us laugh by imitating Dina's way of making eyes, and added in Russian, "Well, the lad is a fool, not understanding! Another wouldn't have eaten for three days, but right away this one stuffed a pear into his fat cheeks!"

Dina's eyes were shining as he finished.

Tuesday, December 9, 1873. This morning I seized my pen and wrote on the next blank page, "Tomorrow." Then I found Dina, telling her, "I want to read you THE MAR-RIAGE OF THE DUKE OF HAMILTON. It's in the *Galignani.*" I thought I could read it quite calmly.

"Are they going to sacrifice some pigs?" Dina asked, "or kill some pigeons for the occasion?"

"On the contrary," I was able to answer her lightly, "it's truly magnificent!" Then I read aloud the article I had agonized over last night. Regarding the gifts and the rejoicings, Dina commented, "They certainly are very nice over there in England!"

No one else could be as angry, jealous, and disappointed as I. I am not talking about my love. I am too proud to do that. It's *all my life* that I'd hoped for in general! And then to have to look like a dog driven off with its tail between its legs!

This is the first real denial I have faced. But even worse, I can never be Duchess of Hamilton! Now, even if I were to marry a Russian prince or a French marquis, the marriage could never be extraordinary. It would never be like that marriage in England—the luxury, the great pomp, the solid wealth of my dreams. Such magnificence! Such aristocracy! Those ruined nobles in Scotland, their ancient legendary towers, their family seats brooding over the land for centuries! Those antiquities—unlike those even in Italy, which sometimes nauseated me with their worn-out splendor. The noble British castles—rich, luxurious, imposing—make my heart beat faster and my hands almost freeze just to think about them.

BOOK FOURTEEN

Book 14
My Journal
Begun Wednesday, December 10, 1873
Ended Wednesday, December 31, 1873
Concerning me.
Rue de Temple, Villa Baquis, Nice.

Wednesday, December 10, 1873. This is the first day of my new era! It marks my great unhappiness and my first failure, as well as the realization that God is . . . not always good and great. I am miserable this morning as if in a dream. At 10:00, I don't know by what foolishness, I imagined that it was at that moment they were being married, and I sat down at the piano and began to play Beethoven's celebrated funeral march. Truly I have plunged myself into the depths of suffering for nothing. I have become ugly and often have red spots on one of my burning cheeks.

Thursday, December 11, 1873. Well, there are moments when I am pretty! While combing my hair in front of the glass, my robe half-open at the throat and one curl falling on my neck, I saw my reflected image as a portrait, the neck leaning a little—long and graceful—and the hands crossed somehow near the right cheek. I had the air of a dream, of a caprice, a little languishing air. And the costume was so poetic! I would have given everything in the world to have such a portrait.

Well, it's hard, but now it's necessary to let nothing interrupt me, to live as if nothing has happened, to go on studying and playing the piano, and to look ahead to cultivating my voice.

Friday, December 12, 1873. My mirror is broken. If I were superstitious, I would take it for a sign that I must die. When I first broke it I did think of that, and I resolved to burn my journal. I wasn't afraid until I began to wonder what would become of Mama.

Saturday, December 13, 1873. [From *Galignani's Messenger:*]

THE MARRIAGE OF THE DUKE OF HAMILTON Kimbolton, Tuesday.

The ducal castle at Kimbolton, which has a grand history of its own, is today the scene of <u>unwonted</u> gaiety, incidental to the wedding festivities of the Duke of Hamilton and Lady Mary Montagu—

The lawn meet of the Oakley Hounds, under the mastership of Captain Arkwright, this <u>morning was a most animating sight, the weather being gloriously fine, and both sexes vying with each other to render the spectacle as brilliant as possible. Aristocracy and yeomanry mustered in great force, attracted by the fact that Lady Mary Montagu was to take part in the hunt. Her Ladyship, who looked remarkably well, as [she went (ink blot)] with the Duke of Hamilton and a large party of Royal and noble friends to the place of the meeting.</u> Shortly after the company from the castle arrived, the work of the hunt commenced in earnest. [Marie's underlinings.]

This evening the Duke and Duchess of Manchester give a ball in a spacious tent erected within the precincts of the castle. Messrs. Coote and Tinney supply the music, and invitations have been sent out to all the principal families in Huntingdonshire, Cambridgeshire, Bedfordshire, and Northamptonshire. The usual custom of giving the dance is departed from on this occasion, in order that the bride and bridegroom may mix among their friends, which they could not do tomorrow night, as after the wedding they will go to spend their honeymoon at the Duke of Hamilton's Suffolk estate, Easton Park.

I don't say anything. There's nothing to say. I'm so unhappy that during the lessons I can hardly hold back the tears. When I went horseback-riding I kept thinking of the way they dress in those magnificent red coats for the English hunt. Oh, if I could just die!

I keep trying to imagine what he says to her. I can't imagine him as a husband. It's like death: I can believe in the death of Mrs. Savelieff because I saw her dead, but I can't believe in the death of Abramovitch; it seems he is not dead and must return.

Sunday, December 14, 1873. [Clipping from *Galignani's Messenger:*]

MARRIAGE OF THE DUKE OF HAMILTON

The marriage of the Duke of Hamilton and Brandon, premier Peer of Scotland, with Lady Mary Montagu, eldest daughter of the Duke of Manchester, was celebrated on Wednesday at the parish church of Kimbolton. The building was beautifully decorated, and a large company were present.

At twenty-five minutes past 11:00 the bridegroom, who had walked from the castle, entered the church, accompanied by his groomsman, Baron de Tuyll, Prince Edward of Saxe-Weimar, Viscount Mandeville, Prince Louis Esterhazy, the Duke of Beaufort, the Earl of Sandwich, the Earl of Gosford, Lord Ossulston, the Hon. G. Fitzwilliam, the Hon. A. Bourke, Colonel Steele, Mr. Chaplin, Mr. Cal-Craft, and Sir Seymour Blane. <u>The bridegroom</u> and his best man took their place by the altar, <u>and awaited</u> the arrival of the bride. The gentlemen ranged themselves along the south side of the chancel, the Duke of Manchester's pew, on the north side, being occupied by the Princess Monaco, Princess Edward of Saxe-Weimar, the Countess of Sandwich, the Hon. Mrs. George Fitzwilliam, the Duchess of Beaufort, Miss Eyrich, etc. Shortly after the Duchess of Manchester and *the Duchess of Hamilton arrived, and took up their positions on the north of the altar. Immediately after half-past 11:00 a carriage and four brought to the gates of the church-yard the Duke of Manchester and the bride, who proceeded through a large crowd of spectators along the carpeted path to the church. The bridesmaids were Lady Louisa Montagu, sister to the bride, Lady Blanche Somerset, daughter of the Duke of Beaufort, Lady Florence Montagu, daughter of the Earl of Sandwich, and Lady Alice Montagu, youngest daughter of the Duke of Manchester. The bridesmaids wore white silk dresses, and white bonnets trimmed with rosebuds. Immediately on the arrival of the bride and her father the wedding ceremony proceeded, being conducted by the Rev. F. Hope Grant, M. A., vicar of Kimbolton, assisted by the Rev. N. B. Young, vicar of Tillbrook. After the ceremony was completed the attesting party entered the vestry and witnessed the registration, the signataries being the Duke of Manchester, the Duchess of Manchester, the Duchess of Hamilton, Prince Edward of Saxe-Weimar, etc. <u>On the completion of this formal duty the Duke of Hamilton conducted his bride down the aisle and along the churchyard path to the gate, where they entered a carriage,</u> and were conveyed to the Castle; the town, which consists mainly of one street, being by this time densely crowded. The wedding breakfast was given in the large marquee in which the ball was given on the previous night. The principal toast was, of course, "The Health of the Bride and Bridegroom," which was very briefly responded to by the Duke of Hamilton. About a quarter-past 2:00 the bride and bridegroom left the Castle in a carriage and four, and proceeded to the Kimbolton station, a distance of three miles or thereabouts, amid the hearty good wishes of all. At the Kimbolton station of the Midland Railway they entered a saloon carriage attached to a special train, which proceeded to Wickhambrook, where they arrived about half-past six, and were received by a guard of honour consisting of the local volunteer corps. <u>The noble bridegroom</u> and bride proceeded thence to Easton Park to spend the honeymoon, being received by the Suffolk tenantry with a hearty welcome. [Marie's underlinings.]*

When I read this, each line seemed to me a slap in the face. I wondered whether during the wedding ceremony he looked as if he were frozen and felt his soul oppressed? Did he want to get out of there fast? Were his boots covered with dust? How stupid I am! It's December and in England it's cold. Are they bored? It must be a delicate situation. . . .

Grandpapa has been very sick, and he's been talking about making his will. Well, I hope he does, because we need something in writing. If he died suddenly, Mama and my aunt would have nothing, being married women. God help me to manage the business matters— and prolong my grandfather's life!

Monday, December 15, 1873. At Momby's Dina and I looked at all sorts of adorable things including Scottish plaids and some raincoats we call Conspirator coats because they look like the conspirators' costumes in that wonderful light-opera by Offenbach, *Ba-Ta-Clan.* I ordered one in dark blue because I was afraid a plaid one would remind me too much of the Hamilton tartans.

As we were returning to the carriage to take Bête to the London House, Dina was telling me about that poor sick boy Walitsky has been treating. She has seen him walking for the first time since his illness. As she told me about him, she got so red she pretended to be hunting for something in her handbag in order to cover her confusion. Can there be something between them? I find it very disagreeable.

It is Hitchcock who has been disagreeable. She wants Dina to go with her to Mrs. Teplakoff's, but Dina doesn't want to. And when Mama leaves the table at dinner, she has the nerve not to leave with Mama. She told us that wherever she has formerly worked she always went into society with the family. She argues and is sometimes very rude. Today she got up and threw her napkin on the chair and left. I would have been furious if she were not such a mean, contemptible creature. But all of the unpleasantness of my life, including this last, is like a drop of wine that falls into a glass of water. The water is darkened, but as time goes on one notices it less and the mixture seems to become the true color of pure water. Its color has changed, but so completely that one finally asks if it has ever been anything else!

Friday, December 19, 1873. Tonight when Mama and my aunt went to the Howards' for dinner, we had the two Strikers to dine with us. They are charming, but of course they are Americans. I don't care for their manners. Paul, the silly, offered them cigarettes so that they smoked in the drawing room. With intimate friends it's different, but with two big boys— fie! I was very nice to them in spite of their manners, but I kept thinking of our Russian saying, "When you live with wolves you learn to howl like wolves." The younger one kept making eyes at me, and I was dying to laugh. At dinner I laughed all the time. The older one taught me the song, "Shoo, Fly, Don't Bother Me." I learned it, but I couldn't help thinking how very unaristocratic these Americans are. Besides, they're so young. For me, a man is not perfect until he's at least twenty-five. But all men are amusing, and without them it's death!

Saturday, December 20, 1873. This was an adorable day. There wasn't that "sun that gives light and life," but a sweet, fresh, grey sky. I went out with Hitchcock and Walitsky. And I saw that Gioja is back! Actually, Dina had seen her at the theater, beautiful in black velvet, gold lace, and diamonds. I think she loved the Duke very much. It wasn't what you'd call a pure love, but it was a love; I think she must have loved him as much as anyone in her position could love anyone. Well, I feel a sort of tenderness for her. I wish I could talk with her. Still—how *could* he leave her? Is the Duchess a goddess?

Every time I think about the possibility of the Duke's coming to Nice I go cold with fright. But after that long numbness—to have had this beautiful day! I was flooded with feeling again, and that reminded me that I am alive, if suffering. And I'm happy even to be unhappy!

Thursday, December 25, 1873. It looks as if Seraphine doesn't want to know us, although Uncle Sacha comes every day and is very amiable. We know everything the scoundrelly Tutcheffs have said about us (lies, all of it), and we know that it was their saying these things that started all the talk about us. Well, Uncle Sacha has given the press information about the "opposite party"—us. It hurt to read what he wrote, but so many lies have been spread—calumnies!

Saturday, December 27, 1873. I've just read the *Apocalypse,* and I don't understand any more of it than any of the others do!

It rained a lot this morning, but around noon there was a charming sun. (This is like me): There were drops of water falling through the sunbeams that were shining through the rain. This year there was no autumn. When it rained for six weeks everybody went out in water-proofs with umbrellas, the carriages constantly splashing unfortunate pedestrians. The winter regulars were arriving in the city by ones and twos. They made their appearance on the Prom, glancing to the left and the right with a surprised look and a pleased air, which seemed to say they recognized everything and everybody. Strangers who had come for the first time would make a tour of the town with a superb air, pass the quays, and stop with the crowds to watch the waves, which were washing up on the Promenade, bringing peb-bles and bathing everything else with seawater. Sometimes the too-curious English or other foreigners who wanted to take the fresh air would stand on the beaches and talk in loud voices, pointing at things in the sea with the ends of their umbrellas. Finally these crowds all arrived together and seemed glued like flies at the side of this terrible river Var, which was rolling with the impetuosity of the Styx and hurling itself furiously into the sea, fight-ing with the waves, which were colored by its waters. The whole thing looked like a mass of coffee with cream. The bathhouses were moved onto the Prom, and the bathers changed their clothes to become again drivers, liveried servants, etc. Then everyone started to com-plain about the bad weather, and when the sun appeared for an hour, it was news for the paper! Mrs. Prodgers would appear majestically, lying in her victoria with her nose in the air and her hat way up on her head, her feet covered with a fur of doubtful origin. The Countess Vigier would also pass, pulled by two impetuous, dragon-like horses in an ante-diluvian shell of a carriage, looking at the people with the expression of a fairy who had just conquered her domain.

One day I saw Borreel all in blue in a bus with his well-groomed poodle, and then I saw the "great" Audiffret, who, I'm sure, was not able to leave town after the season and had been hiding during the summer in order to put on the attraction of a stranger. Finally the Faulkners came, and Lady Howard and her husband with the fat Merck, an indivisible trin-ity. By that time Nice was already glutted with cocottes of all sorts. At this same time last year the Duke of Hamilton had appeared on foot. He always had the air of flying over the earth, hardly staying anywhere, even for a few minutes. He would stand talking to some-one briefly and then throw himself into his carriage, to be hurried away by the trotting horses. Sometimes he was seen before the England Hotel, his cane resting on the toe of his foot, or with Lady Howard and her friends, but always passing like an arrow on the Promenade. After that people could see his splendid horse-and-carriage, his head leaning toward the door of No. 77, or around five o'clock with Merck. The two would be carried together toward a mysterious palace. Or he might be seen during the rain in a white rain-coat but without umbrella, lighting a cigarette, and going toward a house, or sometimes driving with the little Italian Marquis. Seeing the contrast of their two backs next to each other was amusing. And there at last on the terrace seated with his Lois, since he himself was Alcibiades—he could be seen eating, sitting and looking as if he were in a cloud, flying as on a beam of light. But that was *last* year.

But this is no longer autumn. It's mid-winter. This unfortunate year there is nothing like that at all, and the rosy light I've been looking through is all in the past.

Monday, December 29, 1873. I didn't want to go to Monaco, but not having done my lessons for Hitchcock, I went with the others. Dina, Paul, and I went to the shooting contest; afterwards, just as we got upstairs, we met my aunt at the top. She was very pale.

"What's the matter? What happened?" we asked all at once.

"A man just shot himself with a pistol in the roulette room."

We all ran into the casino. There was a turmoil. Some people were leaving and others coming in; some were running and others talking in loud voices. There were groups talking together, gesticulating. In order to pass, we had to push as if we were in a crowded church.

The man who had shot himself was lying on a sofa at the end of the Turkish room. I saw blood on the floor and someone pouring water on him. Then he was lifted up and carried out.

Paul asked, "Where are they taking him?"

"To the Paris Hotel." That's because he wasn't dead.

He kept saying, "Oh, how badly I've done it!" We could hear him still lamenting as they took him away.

Nobody knew where he was from. Some said he was English.

"Who is he?" "Why did he do it?" Those who didn't know anyone else were suddenly talking with others, and then they all seemed to know everybody else. And they all seemed in a state of shock. I decided then and there to avoid traveling in any other conveyance than a coupé or a compartment on the train to avoid such a horribly public agony if anything terrible should ever happen to me.

Wednesday, December 31, 1873. Just before midnight and the end of this dying year, I tried to write down my wish in the last half-minute: "*To marry a very rich English Duke and to live. . . .*" My time was up, but I had wanted to write, "*to live as I like.*" *NOW: Greetings to the new year, 1874!*

B O O K   F I F T E E N

Book 15 of my Journal
Begun Friday, January 2, 1874
Ended Sunday, January 25, 1874
Concerning Me
Rue du Temple, Villa Baquis, Nice
I have already written 2,700 pages!!!!

Friday, January 2, 1874. How strange it is: one day is gone and the year is gone! I can't believe it. It is the same for the rest.

On New Year's Day I received all the cards from those who pour their sciences into my head.

Is it what I would like? No, it is not such a New Year as I desire! Well! "Let's wait; let's wait for the first day of happiness."

Saturday, January 3, 1874. The Duke of Hamilton is already listed in the Monte Carlo Casino among the members of the shooting club. Soon we shall see him, and his wife, too, probably.

I am curious to see her. She must not be blonde, chestnut, red-haired, or grey. She is a different person on her own. But we shall see.

Monday, January 5, 1874. I decided not to go to the shooting in Monaco. It is not proper for me to be seen there all the time. I was taking my piano lesson when Walitsky said that Uncle Stepa had come. I ran, and embraced him, and we went to Mama's room, where Mashenka had already arrived.

Tomorrow is Noël [Russian Christmas, English Twelfth Night]. They said we must play a fortune-telling game: If we put a dish full of water under the bed, we'll dream about our future. I want to do it.

Tuesday, January 6, 1874. First I went to church. What bad taste! Then I walked with Hitchcock.

I have a very pretty waist. Also, I tightened my clothes a little more because usually I am loosely fitted. My chest is free.

Wednesday, January 7, 1874. The Howards have invited us to a children's party next Thursday at their home. I will not wear my blue dress: I fear the boys without my gloves!

Thursday, January 8, 1874. It was Grandpapa's nameday and everybody gave him gifts. Walitsky gave him a cane that seemed to be like one of Hamilton's.

Friday, January 9, 1874. The Strikers were here at 2:00, and we sent them to the Howards' with Paul and Nadia, who is proud of her dress (white and green)—the one she wore to the second ball in Baden. This girl is full of promise: she loves only men!! Everybody was in my room . . . it was annoying!

Mrs. Howard received us. Yesterday I was engaged for the cotillion by Striker No. 2. And it was the cotillion which they were dancing when we arrived! I was very much surrounded. At 6:00 the little ones left, and we stayed with the young men. The young Ajax gave me a rose, which I kept. It will be a talisman.

How nice it is to have some followers! We order, we command, and they obey with delight, whereas I am always the same. I am now becoming very cold, cold like an English girl. My boots are too tight.

I compare myself to frozen water in its depth; like frozen water I am moving only on the surface, because nothing interests me deeply.

Saturday, January 10, 1874. At the Witgensteins' everything is open; we no longer see the Centifolia [Gioja] there. Her protector, Audiffret, tries miserably to copy his predecessor. In the morning he passes quickly in a carriage almost like the one Hamilton used to drive, with two horses. He thinks that he can imitate him, he a peasant and the other such a great lord! . . .

Sunday, January 11, 1874. We were talking about [Russian] New Year's and how we will spend it, how Mashenka proposed telling fortunes. We were in accord on the choice of a mirror, and with it Mashenka told us surprising things, among them many things which are not yet accomplished. She also saw horrible and frightening things. I was so excited I could not eat. I wanted to ask her again the next day to do it, but I was afraid and did not. I also asked how to arrange the mirrors, and now I know how to do it.

I am burning with impatience; tomorrow the fortune-teller is coming. I will tell my fortune but under the protection of God.

Monday, January 12, 1874. I am starting to have a thin and pretty waist.

[Marie tries to have a "séance" for herself in front of her mirror.] For a long time I saw nothing. Then I started to see little faces, but no more than four inches tall. I saw many heads, only with the most bizarre coiffures: toques, wigs, bonnets of all sizes, all turning around. Then I perceived a woman in white who looks like me, a scarf on her head leaning on her elbows on a table, her chin in her hands, but the eyes slightly raised. Then it disappeared. I saw a church floor in white and black marble and out in the middle of it a costumed group; one person was lying down, the others were seated, and some were standing. I did not understand very well. There seemed to be a few men on the left. In the middle, standing, wrapped in a long coat, with a hat and her head leaning (like Gioja in the photo), was the Countess Galvi. I saw her more than the others. Then afterward it seemed to me as if they were in a fog—a man in a tuxedo and a woman, but the faces were invisible.

I saw Mrs. Vigier, who dominated all heads; then I saw myself, I believe, but only the bust, in all kinds of costumes, changing all the time, the poses and necklines, too. The scene was very brilliant.

At the beginning, the frame of the mirror seemed reflected endlessly, looking like a coffin. You must understand that I was afraid of seeing something awful. But the women's hairstyles brought back my calm.

I got up, tired; I might have been able to see something else, but I stopped.

I went to Mama's room and told her everything; but she was asleep, and it produced very little effect on her. Tomorrow I'll tell everybody what happened, because it is strange! I would have seen better, but I was changing the mirrors and the eyes.

Hurrah for the Year 1874 in Russia!!

Farewell 1873!!! [See note on the Russian calendar in Marie's preface, page 1.] Hurrah for 1874!!!

Wednesday, January 14, 1874. Everybody went to Monaco. At the station we took a carriage and went straight to the hotel for breakfast. The shooters eat there, too. I would like more than anything to be with this "Group" blessed by God! I understand life only with men; skirts make me sick.

I have never before been there at the beginning of the tir [pigeon shoot]. Today is the first time. I stood behind a column because of the sun; looking into the sky I saw something like a horse, but it was a balloon in the shape of a cow. Then we moved, but stayed in the first row.

Thursday, January 15, 1874. One can criticize this society, but anyway, it is a society, and a good one. It has many great names, good dresses, and pretty women. They all know each other, talk to each other. Only we miserable ones know nobody. We are well-dressed. I would prefer not to be in order to be able to tell what I feel, to describe my indignation, my envy. The lowering of one's self is too difficult a thing and cannot be expressed by my pen . . . the more the others have fun, the more my soul and my heart are torn. It is not for myself, I am only fourteen, but I will be sixteen, one day!! My aunt was as miserable as I was—more, possibly—but she was hiding it. There is much good society here, people of good manners; and I, unfortunate that I am, look with envy at what is owed to me. Paul was with us, this ill-mannered boy who was running everywhere. The monster carriage left with all the ladies, but I could not see who was in front. We were the last ones to leave because we had to wait for my brother, who conducts himself like a peevish, badly brought-up peasant.

At dinner I did not talk. Then Mama said: "You do not know yourself what you really want; you are spoiled or too pampered." Then, *"She wants a man, but it is too soon for her"* [in Russian]. That put me out of myself, I would have liked to weep or shout. This is how my feelings are interpreted! Here is how I am understood! I am dissatisfied, as they are; but they want to conceal it from me. My God, forgive all this moaning! Let us live a moment as I would like. Remove this curse from over our heads! Save me! Oh, if at least we could live like all these other people—in Nice at least!

Friday, January 16, 1874. It is raining. I am going to bring my white mousseline dress to Simon to have it refreshed for Monday. I do not want to wear the blue dress because there will be some pigs without gloves. With Hitchcock we walked under this heavy rain.

In the evening we went to see Hélène dressed for her first ball. I rushed upstairs and found her ready; she was not well-dressed. The coiffure was bad and possibly the dress, too. In a word, it was not as I would like. She is not badly formed, and for her standing and her youth it is all right. She is radiant and inspired. We covered her with a white wool wrap, borrowed from us. Lise kissed me a thousand times; what a charming soul, open and pure! I don't know if it is through envy, but I do not any longer find Hélène pretty. I forgot to tell yesterday that Centifolia was the most beautiful, as usual (in grey and violet). She is a true beauty, Venus!

Saturday, January 17, 1874. We went to the theater. I wanted to see *The Reveillon* by Ravel. I liked it. Gioja was in her box. She wore the same bronze colors as in Monaco. She was so beautiful, so beautiful that I was breathless. We turned around to see this beauty. Mama said in Russian, "I am glad that Hamilton did not see her today!" Mama thinks she is superb, and I am pleased. Why did Hamilton abandon her? She is as beautiful as a goddess, and he is as handsome as a god. My two ideals—my two perfections!

The Saxe woman was in a box on the street floor, on the left. This woman is also beautiful. Tonight she looked magnificent—especially her face. I liked her languid and merry attitude. Tonight she was a Phryne or a Lois. I am still speaking of her face. Gioja is more modern but dazzling, outstanding—especially in her poise, her manners, her height. We left at the end of the last act.

Sunday, January 18, 1874. After church I went to pick up my white dress. Later we went with the Strikers for a ride. The weather is cool, the way I like it. I feel free, gay . . .

At the tir there were many people; the crowd was about the same as last time. Centifolia was in black and wore a Directoire hat. She was pretty, and all the men were around her carriage. Poor Audiffret! He was "melting" near her. He is always smiling, looking inspired. She is so beautiful! It is not banal beauty. You have to be a connoisseur to realize that.

When I passed in front of Gioja, who was on her little terrace with the Soubise, I remembered the other year when I saw Him with her at the same place. I do not walk one step without having a reminiscence.

Friday, January 23, 1874. One day will come when all over the world my name, like thunder, will be heard, the men trembling in front of my laws; my salons will become the ambition of Kings.

Sunday, January 25, 1874. We went to church late. Afterwards we went to the Promenade and later to visit Mrs. Teplokoff, who is still ill. There is no sun, but the air is sweet.

We received a telegram from Domenica Pavlovna [George's wife]; she is asking the Consul to tell George that his son is dying. We did not say it to Dina or George. In the Russian newspaper we read that the student army-dodger, Stepan Babanine, has stabbed himself with a dagger in his mother's house. It is awful! Dina knows nothing about it. I came out of the carriage with Mama while someone was looking for Grandpapa.

I walked again with the Howards. We passed through the middle of the "vile crowd." Tomorrow we shall go horseback riding.

I am washing my hair.

MARIE AT AROUND TEN YEARS OF AGE

BOOK SIXTEEN

Book 16 of my Journal
Begun Monday, January 26, 1874
Ended Saturday, February 21, 1874
Concerning Me
Rue du Temple, Villa Baquis, Nice

Wednesday, January 28, 1874. There was a crowd on the Promenade. The Princess Souvaroff was with her daughter in a carriage—white dresses with blue velvet, the same hats. They dress the same and look very much alike. The mother seems as young as the girl, but more beautiful. The carriage is low, like the Duke's, charming and small, with two grey horses. Miss de Galvi, who wore a dark red dress, followed in the landau. Audiffret is with them. This group is the only one in Nice. I hope that with time I'll have one also like this one. With the help of God. . . .

Thursday, January 29, 1874. We went to the Filimonoffs'. All the family was there. I talked about the Carnival.

Friday, January 30, 1874. I have begun to speak of the trip to England which I would like to take this spring. I am already fifteen! How much that is, and how little! It's a century and it's a day.

Sunday, February 1, 1874. For the last few days I have been very hoarse and speak in a very low tone, and they do not hear me because one has to shout so much in this house.

Mama asked the Princess to tell Hitchcock that we do not need her any more, and this adorable star (Hitchcock) said that Mama should tell her, herself. Then Bête said that she was telling her in the name of Mrs. Bashkirtseff. Then the star said that she will stay three more weeks, that she does not have any intention of leaving before March. Here is adoration!!

My project of travel to Russia seems out, and all my hopes are gone. I am again in the dark. I was thinking that by going to Russia to conquer our enemies we would purify ourselves and then come to live in Paris, as I would love to. Again I am going to repeat an old proverb: Man proposes and God disposes. I am punished for my sins.

I thank God for having curbed my ambition and for having given me some good lessons. Almost nothing I wished for is done. At fifteen I am broken.

Monday, February 2, 1874. At last Mama said to Miss H. that she can leave because we are going to travel.

Everybody is at Monaco today. I went out with Dina. I was remarkably white and pink today. At the moment of our leaving, George arrived, and we took him with us. I took the chemistry list to Devaux. There was a big wind, and it was a grey day. Unfortunately, we also had to take Papa. Then, with George there, both men started to shout, laughing so loudly that the horses were neighing. The men started to say terrible things. We picked up Paul from Nash's. Ordinarily, I like having many men with us. Even though it is only Papa, Paul, and George, that looks good. But they did so much harm by shouting that I came back home miserable. My God! Nothing revolts me like these natures deprived of any feeling of delicacy, of any respect for our age. I am only fifteen!! Wornout leftovers! Better that they never existed! Such coarseness and rudeness to the highest degree! I go crazy over it.

George was all embarrassed to come to ask Mama in an undertone for advice as to how he could dress Anna in a better manner for the ball today at Monaco. Mama gave him her pearl-grey satin dress to take to Anna. It is generous, and I am touched by it.

Mama bought some books for me again. I am reading *Louis XIV and His Century*. The book is open before me, and I am looking at Buckingham. He is so beautiful! Only an Englishman can be so handsome. There is nothing like a Parisian-English Duke. In a few years these readings will make me yawn.

Tuesday, February 3, 1874. I can't sleep; the Carnival occupies my mind. I am going downstairs to see Dina, who is reading with Josephine's lamp. For a long time we talked . . . about how we shall go. We are sorry about our lives. Cold weather—grey. But we have beautiful complexions with such weather!

I think we'll have a hard time getting rid of Hitchcock. She said, "I think you won't go before March," this unworthy creature!

Wednesday, February 4, 1874. I met Mr. Filimonoff, and when he was leaving he said again not to forget to come next Wednesday at 2:00 to dress the bride. Paul will put her shoes on her, as she has no brother.

Thursday, February 5, 1874. Allard is fixing my hair; half of the hair is up, and the other part is left hanging. Dina has the same hairdo, and with her magnificent hair she has success. Simon made her a dress that is a copy from Worth. Tonight is the concert. I wore a grey and pink dress. We had our seats in the second row. Almost all the Russians were there. I was calm because I knew almost all in the room. Hélène was badly dressed. And she was ugly; she has no eyebrows.

The concert was charming. Mrs. Conneu sang with rapture, but her Russian was not good. Nagarnoff, on the other hand, played admirably, and I very much liked the violin.

The crowd was very refined, and we had a number of acquaintances there, among them the most important. And there were many men, also. I think that one day I'll go insane;

I always feel that people make fun of me, and it is an awful feeling. I would like to get rid of it.

Saturday, February 7, 1874. Tonight they are playing *Hernani*, which I have been waiting for for a long time.

I wore my beautiful blue dress, and Mama and Dina and my aunt also had pretty dresses. We had to wait in line, as there was a crowd; there were torches in the street and guards and policemen, and finally the parade was complete. I could not have done better if it had been for myself. There were servants, posted like statues all along the stairs, in great liveries, majestic and beautiful. We were in the fifth row, one of the best places in the house. The room was as brilliant as possible, and everything rich, beautiful, and elegant was there.

Mrs. Vigier has remarkable costumes, beautiful and rich, and they look ravishing on her. And the other artists were excellent. She was given a monstrous bouquet carried on straps by four men, and followed by Lewin, Prodgers, etc. Then another huge bouquet which seemed a child next to the first one, which was unbelievable! There were more bouquets thrown or given, by six little poor girls with flowers. The first one gave a little speech to Mrs. Vigier, who held out her hand to the girl, who kissed it. All the words and effects were splendid, but the applause was not warm enough.

Her voice failed more this year than last. During intermission I went out. I felt better; my blouse was not too tight any more. It was cool and nice outside. All the men were going out, too.

We left with Mama at the second intermission. I was very much looked at—too much.

This evening is one of the ravishing, brilliant evenings that I love. Only my aunt, instead of going to the antechamber to wait for the carriage—I love to stay there—pulled us, running after the carriage, which we caught at the Hotel des Anglais. This, of course, spoiled our last impression.

Monday, February 9, 1874. It is beautiful! In the carriage with Dina, in the Rue Masséna, we met Patton, who came to our door and stopped a half hour to talk. In spite of some uncouthness, he is very gallant. We passed by the Promenade. Mrs. Witgenstein was in an armchair. She is ill. . . . No one sees her majestic husband any more.

In the evening, right after dinner, I undressed and came downstairs to talk with Mama and my aunt about a grave and serious thing. I started, "Well, I have come to talk to you. How old am I?" Then I asked, "Where shall I live when I am sixteen? In which society? And how? It will not be in Nice, among the 'dust' who exasperate and kill me!!"

But they did not answer seriously. It would be marvelous to get an answer on a first attack. I hope to renew the talk again and to obtain something—with God's help. Since my fifteenth birthday the thought has not left me. In fact, I cry miserably at the thought of living or dying—I pray to God. Perhaps He will have pity on a miserable, ambitious one.

Tuesday, February 10, 1874. Mama was bothering me with reproaches about my face, saying that I must go to bed earlier, etc. . . . Is it my fault if there are other girls more beautiful than I? I am annoyed because of our life; it causes me many worries.

Wednesday, February 11, 1874. They awoke me for Allard. Very fast I took a cold bath, and downstairs I found him working furiously on the heads of Dina, Mama, and my aunt, doing a fantastic improvisation with fury. Really, that man does a good job. Simon is bringing the dresses, which are superb. I wore my blue dress, which is charming. Mama and my aunt were in dresses of purple velvet and yellow faille with lace.

We went to the house of the bride to dress her, but she was already dressed. However, I gave her a last "touching up." She is very pretty, this little one. Mrs. Fedaroff was there. The matron of Honor, Mrs. Berr, arrived, and then Mrs. Woerman and Mama, as well as Mrs. Howard with Hélène and Lise, both in white dresses of chiffon. The young girls and the bride stayed in a room together. I was asked to attach a sprig of orange blossoms to the lapel of the Baron [Woerman], and I was trembling putting it into the buttonhole. This was the first time that I have touched the lapel of a man.

The moment arrived. The couple was blessed, and everybody went to the church. There we found an important crowd. Those who belong to the wedding party of the groom's family were in the first row on the right, and on the left were my aunt, Mrs. Howard, and we young girls—on the bride's side. Poor little Dinette was very emotional. I am sure I would love to marry her if I were a man.

But the Baron is a weak man; he could not hold the crown for five minutes. Paul was constantly helping him, and Mr. Berr was holding it steady. It was laughable when the priest put the crown on Potemkin's head! The religious ceremony lasted rather a long time.

From the church we went to Mr. and Mrs. Potemkin's brother-in-law's house. Champagne was served after a hundred toasts! Mrs. Potemkin, as well as the ushers, retired to the next drawing room; and they took us to the buffet. I went with the Baron, who is very gallant and who condescended even to bring me a pear and to hold the dish all the time I was eating! Today he was as nice as I like. That is all I ask. I would like to be able to describe the hustle and bustle, the gossiping and chattering, the felicitations, and especially Potemkin I. This man is really charming. A good, happy, frank person—all one asks for in a man.

It was about four-thirty when we undressed the bride and helped her put on her costume for the voyage. (They are going to Antibes in a carriage.) In a jiffy we dressed her. There were five of us to do it. I did most of the work. I went with Masur (the bride), and she showed me her dresses. She was as friendly as a bride can be.

It was very amusing for me, it being the first time. But a wedding has always something dirty; young girls should not be taken there. To hear what the priest said leaves a funny impression. Everybody came out to see the couple leaving.

Friday, February 13, 1874. A beautiful and cold day! Hitchcock is leaving Wednesday. What a joy! The son of the King of Hanover is in Nice. I am curious to know what he is like.

I bought forty-five kilos of confetti, as a beginning. Then we passed by all the places where there are preparations for the Carnival.

I went down for supper, but an onion smell suffocated me. As onion is eaten here every day, I am more in a rage about the smell than about the audacity of these people, who know my disgust for this vegetable and dare to eat it. . . . I am upset by it. I had supper upstairs.

I bought some black gloves, secretly, and also a fan. How unhappy I am today!

Sunday, February 15, 1874. At the end of my lesson, Brunet told me that tonight, at the Club Méditerranée, the Viennese ladies are giving a concert. I would like very much to go to that Club for any reason, because there always are refined people there. I let Brunet leave early and decided to tell the family that I wanted to go to the concert. So I went to dress. It took me an hour to fix my hair. (Blue dress. The back fits well.)

My aunt went with me. When we entered, the room was full. I cast an eye on the grandstand, occupied by Princess Souvaroff, who had rented it all.

Then I withdrew into myself, and I was miserable. We were literally alone, alone, alone. There was not a soul we knew—nobody! I wanted to get under my chair. Why look for happiness in this society, which is an assembly of monkeys? Dresses, actors, heartless people—false, and I don't know what more. Have they never felt what I am feeling? I am well-dressed, but for what purpose? Why do I have nice manners? Why do I have good taste?!!!!!

With all the love I have for society, to be as I was was awful! At last, at the door when we were leaving, there was another humiliation. My aunt took our coats at the cloakroom, and we left alone, humiliated. Fortunately, our carriage was the second one.

At home I went directly to Mama's room, but did not say anything. What's the use? She can't do anything about it. But my aunt, who was as furious as I, did not control herself. She was reproachful (as if it were my fault)! She was reproaching Mama, and that was unjust!

Permit me to write an expression—a terrible Russian expression. I am blushing as I write it: "To piss in the spouts." These people are not sinful; they are simply a society. But this is what is extraordinary: it seems that everybody would say that it is I who reproach, who am angry. Primarily they are used to hearing me talk, but yesterday (I do not hide anything) I did not scold, I did not say anything that could offend the most cynical person. Mama started to cry, saying that she cannot do anything about it, that we would do better to live with the Tutcheffs, that she is ashamed, etc. Walitsky was looking at me as the cause of these tears, and a surprising thing—my aunt, too! But I don't think she did this out of malice.

I have a good remedy for my sorrows: I cry. I kneel in my alcove, I sob, and then I am fine. I went down to Mama's and sat near her bed. She was crying slowly with her eyes closed.

Then suddenly I undressed except for the stockings, and I snuggled near Mama. I forgot my griefs. She fondled me. I fell asleep with Mama, without praying.

Monday, February 16, 1874. Auguste arrived all in costume. We left. It was raining a little, and I put on my black raincoat, which was quite good-looking. Dina wore white, Mama blue, and Walitsky was in ordinary clothes. The Carnival was under way, but the stands were not filled up. The carriages were numerous and elegant, and the floats were numerous and beautiful. The cavalcades and the people in the parade also were very original and beautiful. If the weather turns nice, the Carnival will be superb. There were five orchestras. The society people were at the Prefecture, and there the battle was the most furious; but as it was raining, I saw nobody. Mrs. de Galvi, the English girl, and Shoopinsky—they all threw us many bouquets, principally the good old one, who must be very amusing, and Mr. de Galvi. He pleases me very much. I would like to have him as a friend.

My aunt, Mashenka, and Stepa were in the grandstand, too. They told us afterwards that they were throwing flowers at each other furiously, more than others elsewhere, and it must have been beautiful! Souvaroff threw many bouquets to my aunt. Everybody had fun and was excited.

"*Semel licet in anno insanire.*" [Latin: Once in a year may one go insane.] I was the craziest one. I had a lot of fun, although I did not know many people.

When Mama was already in bed, I went into her room. We talked about men, and Mama praised Doria's beauty. I was on her bed when someone mentioned Hamilton. I cannot express the joy that his name gives me. I never grow tired of hearing the story that Papa used to tell and still does, in a monotonous voice—about Lady Hamilton, Peter the Great's mistress.

It was a long time ago, when I had not yet seen him, that Hamilton always made my heart beat faster and appeared to me like someone dear and near. From the races at Baden (an inexhaustible source of memories) I recall when Remy told me: "I just talked with the Duke of Hamilton." Something strange happened then. Then I remembered his back when he was standing on the lawn in front of the grandstand—the silky cord of his eyeglasses—and I remember also that in his jacket he seemed fat. I was twelve years old and did not know anything about these things. Then I remember him at Kazan's . . . one morning at 9:00 his tucking his trousers into his boots—Oh, I remember so well! The shops had not opened, and his horses were stopped but still pawing the ground, shaking their heads and ringing their bells—all of this while he himself was perched up high. And why do I remember all that so well? All in one word that surrounded that carriage that morning. I did not think of anything then, however. I never thought that I could become a woman. I was living the life of a child, and I do not know why he and all that surrounded him should be impressed on my mind. Why don't I also remember as well anybody else I know? Because the Duke of Hamilton was, is, and always will be for me an extraordinary person . . . apart, divine and will never cease to be.

Tuesday, February 17, 1874. I am going with Mama to buy two pink dominos for Dina and me. The sun is shining, and I must say that there are more carriages and people to be seen out than yesterday. I have received several bouquets and many boxes of candy! At the corner, in front of Visconti's, the four windows were occupied by some Russian gentlemen with whom we furiously battled yesterday. Today, and as if by accident, I threw them a bouquet; from that moment they stopped throwing flowers to me. Yet it seems that I received more bouquets than anybody else. When the carriages were very crowded, we were stopped at each step. It was enough to make us stop near the Hotel Grande Bretagne. We did not have any more confetti.

The most elegant float was Gioja's, with its violets and camellias. In her carriage no one wore dominos, but magnificent white costumes and headdresses of white crepe de chine and violets. I was very gay, but I did not really have a good time. I do not know how to have a good time without many people around me. I do not understand life in the street.

After dinner we went to Rumpelmayer's; we went to the illuminations and then to the "burning of the martyr" Carnival.

Let's return to the unfortunate fancy-dress ball. Dina cried, I cried, and Mama suffered. This was all at the beginning. Afterwards, we finally went, but by then I no longer wanted to. They begged me to; and so to avoid more long discussions, I went—all in black, like Dina, without the domino. Paul and Walitsky went in the pink dominos. We were not elegant. (I? Yes, but the others, No.) But we were unrecognizable, and that was what was necessary. It was midnight; the Tutcheffs were there, without masks or else with the white masks like those on Gioja's float. Their costumes were exquisite. The ball had not yet started.

We saw two dances like the ones at country balls in summer. I was all mixed up by all our pesterings, and I could hardly see or understand anything. At 12:45 we left. It is stupid. With our unhappiness we cannot appreciate any pleasure.

Wednesday, February 18, 1874. Poor Hitchcock is leaving today; and now that she is going, it seems that I was wrong, that she was not so silly or unbearable, and that it is my fault. I regret her principally because, when leaving and saying her farewells, she was crying. It makes me remember the brashness of Collignon who, after two years, did not shed a tear, especially as her tears came easily. I miss that poor, silly thing. . . . That troubles me very much.

Thursday, February 19, 1874. In the evening we played roulette. I bet heavily; when I forgot to play, somebody else had taken my place. They know my favorite number. I like the game.

Saturday, February 21, 1874. I was unhappy with my dress, my face, with everything. This blue dress never really pleased me. Furthermore, now that it is no more in the first flush of its youth, I am very dissatisfied with it.

We went to the Masséna Gardens. We entered and there was a big crowd. The Princess Souvaroff and her daughter and Miss de Galvi had the most beautiful booth. It was the one-franc raffle. All three ladies wore fire-red dresses with assorted hats, and the dresses were simply poetic!

In an hour, the Princess sold 7,000 tickets and could have sold double that if she had had them. I do not know why she is so nice with all of us . . . the crowd was dense. Hélène took my arm. It was very hot.

Everybody admired the Princess, who is known as a divinity. How beautiful she is! How tall and superb!

Around four o'clock the sun had pity on us. This Souvaroff is really admirable. She is so simple, so good, so sweet! What embellishes her more than anything else in the world is the assurance, the triumph she wears; it wins the admiration of everybody. She is satisfied, sure and proud, and brilliant. Add to that some divine dresses.

I am nothing more than an insensible dreamer, without a future and yet full of ambitions . . . etc. . . . .

Before closing this book, I still look at the old ones. How pleasant it is! The clippings from the newspapers, my ecstasies, my opinions, my ideas. The time when I was thinking of the Duke of Hamilton seems to me unbelievable. I think that he never existed.

BOOK SEVENTEEN

Book 17
My Journal
Begun Sunday, February 22, 1874
Ended Friday, March 27, 1874
Concerning Me
Rue du Temple, Villa Baquis, Nice

Sunday, February 22, 1874. I went to church. Afterwards I went to town alone. Wrong—
I went in the company of Prater, who gravely occupied the place of honor beside me. There
was a wind-and-dust storm. Very disagreeable.

We went to the London House—Mama, my aunt, Dina, and I—and from there we went
to Countess de Mouzay's. She is very ill.

Monday, February 23, 1874. A part of the Carlone Villa has been bought by my aunt. There
is a house and a pavilion, which I'll live in alone. Everybody is very satisfied.

At six when I went downstairs, the Princess told me that they want to sell one of the lots
on the Promenade. For us to have only one seemed terrible to me; in fear that they might do
something wrong, I called Mashenka. I put on a hat. We ran past the church; I called a carriage, and we flew to the Carlone Villa. I found that the lot can be sold. The construction
man, Biasini, was there. "For the constructions," I told him, "you need to consult with me."

"At your service, Miss." He made us visit everything, and we considered how best to
build a big dining room and a drawing room on the second floor. The house is not furnished,
but the ceilings, tapestries, doors, fireplaces, and windows are very new, very rich, and very
good. From there we went to the [attorney] Deforges's, where my aunt paid the first 18,000
francs. The whole is to cost 218,000.

Wednesday, February 25, 1874. This morning they opened a letter from Domenica. It told
about the death of her son, Stepan. We knew from the newspapers that he died from a
dagger-wound, but she didn't mention that. We are dismayed. How are we to tell Dina that
her brother is dead? The letter ended with these disagreeable and surprising lines: "Before
he died, he begged for someone to send his photograph to Moussia (me), whom he had loved

since childhood." He had, she said, my photograph near him. I don't wish to know about it. I understand nothing.

They decided to tell Dina that he is dying. . . . Mama and my aunt went to Monaco, and Mashenka and I to the villa at No. 55 on the Promenade. It is truly beautiful and charming, and when we add the two large rooms it will be magnificent.

We visited and examined the kitchen, the pavilion, the stable, the garden—everything. I'm afraid that in the coming week there will be higher bids. Well, that will be our fate. . . . I don't know whether I should laugh or cry about this purchase. Our position in Nice is miserable; I've been hoping for an improvement, a change with the villa. But we'll not change ourselves.

I wish that Dina had not needed to learn of this death until after the concert at the Von Derwieses'. I'd so much like to attend!

Thursday, February 26, 1874. Mama came into the salon all in tears; now Dina knows. I am not going to see her tonight; it's stupid to impose on a person when she is grieving. There is no other consolation but time.

We are not wearing mourning although I would have liked to; I've already imagined a simple mourning for the family—charming. Pardon my lightness; I am crazy and silly.

I don't see anyone. I have nothing to say. I am bored. Poor Dina ate a little today for the first time in two days.

Saturday, February 28, 1874. I had a very disagreeable scene with Manotte this morning. It was a matter of playing an overture for two hands at a morning recital at his house. I consented to play, but he brought me the hardest and ugliest score I have seen. I told him the score was not pretty. Then he said it was.

We argued. Then he began to shout. I told him not to shout, that I'm not used to it. I told him that he could shout with Tolstoy, but not with me. Then he became impertinent and shouted so loudly that I didn't know what to do. I should have gone away at once, but I was so astonished that I stayed seated and heard all his expressions of bad temper. I don't know where this fury comes from; I think a little of it must be because he was refused lessons with Dina. It goes without saying, I'll take no more lessons from him. My aunt was in the next room and did nothing about it. Nobody will have any respect here because people can do and say anything—the elders don't care and won't lift a finger.

God, among what ruffians and rogues I live! I believe it. I've felt it for a long time, and today has given me the opportunity to write it down. Indeed, I don't hate my mother; I love her very much. I adore her. If I lost her I'd go crazy. But I'm always fair, and I say she doesn't know her duty; she doesn't know what it means to be the mother of a fifteen-year-old daughter. She gives me dresses and thinks that's enough and that she's the best of mothers. What a mistake! She is good only to love me, but she loves me in the wrong way.

Paul went to Princess Souvaroff's, as she had begged Mama yesterday to send him to get the tickets for the benefit concert of the Samaritans at Valrose.

"If at least," Mama said, "we were accepted in society at Nice! But then—" And big, silent tears ran from my eyes. Mama feels that I am right, and my aunt also.

[At Valrose] This was the second time I have seen this immense house, one that transports and inspires you involuntarily to a feeling of its greatness and its richness (and of its bad taste!). Its false ruins, cascades, grottoes, statues, fountains, valleys, hills—all are found there in profusion. The architecture of the mansion is atrocious. It's a pity to realize all the money it took to build such an obelisk. Besides the house, there are a great many outbuildings, the courtyard with cut stones, terraces, banks, and earthworks, and finally the new concert room, walled with white satin and soft blue velvet. There is a loge in the shape of a shell for Mr. and Mrs. Von Derwies. I thought of them here in the middle of all these splendors, seated like princes, and how he was only a poor clerk twenty years ago. Then Mrs. Derwies had only two percale dresses, wearing one while the other was bleaching; she went herself to market without a hat, her basket under her arm. It is surprising and incredible.

The trustees, among others, are the Baron and the true Prince. It is written that the Prince, wherever he is commissioner, must show the guests to their seats. The Baron mumbled some stupidities as he put us in the second row. Mrs. Souvaroff and all those people were near the entrance. Then, as she is patroness besides, she walked past everyone in the whole room. . . . I don't envy Derwies. The place is too big and too beautiful to be envied. . . . The Russians were all present. Only my aunt and I went. On the way home, by way of the Promenade, we saw only Audiffret. He seems to me an excellent boy. I never noticed him before, but since Paris and Gioja, I have. I would like to know him, as he pleases me very much. My aunt stayed at the Baquis, but I went with Bête to the London House.

Wednesday, March 4, 1874. Just now, at 8:00, I read what I wrote yesterday. It doesn't give the slightest idea of what I was feeling. It's a caricature. Oh, what I wouldn't give to know how to write! I went twice to the notary's to find out if there has been someone with a higher bid; the second time I met him in the street, where he told me that all is finished: the house is ours!

I am happy not because we have a villa in Nice, not because it is the first business that I personally had a hand in seeing finished, but because nothing prevented the purchase and that it happened as we planned.

Papa and Mashenka took a fiacre and went to tell the good news.

For three Wednesdays Mama has not been to Mrs. Howard's. I go there, not for a visit, but to see the children. The reception was over when I got there. It was nearly six when I went up to the drawing room. At the gate I encountered my very dear uncle, my very dear aunt, and my very dear cousin, the Prince [the Tutcheffs]. These are the three scoundrels who have caused all the trouble that has happened to us at Nice. They are the ones who have spoiled my life—the ones who make me cry. Vampires, serpents, scoundrels.

This evening many people talked to me about them. Mrs. Howard invited me to stay to dine, and I was foolish enough to consent. She sent a little note to Mama. Was it intentional or by accident that the Tutcheffs were mentioned before me at dinner and this evening? If it was intentional, that is horrible. Apparently my inestimable relations will always have the preference! I think our property will be only a new source of troubles and tears for the poor head that makes this journal.

We stayed in the Grand Salon—I, Hélène, and Lise—to speak sweetly, calmly, and seriously . . . of friendship; apropos of this I told Hélène that I don't care at all for her friendship because it does not exist, or that if it does, it will end shortly. We had some tea, and I went at 9:00.

Everybody was very friendly, as always. But the Tutcheffs bother me. Why do the Howards talk so much about them before me?

If God will have pity on my folly, He will give me what I ask; if not . . . if not, I don't know what will happen. Only I wish very much that He pity me without my having to be so unhappy. With the villa will come more than ever the desire to live as I want to—to entertain and not to be "dust"—and I'll torment myself a hundred times more than before.

Thursday, March 12, 1874. There are many arguments about the cypress trees by our villa. It's my opinion that they must be cut down; they're not beautiful or regular, but crooked and twisted and give the whole property a bad appearance.

The idea of my dowry diverted me. The villa at No. 55 belongs to me. With the furniture it will be worth 300,000 francs. Out of that Mama will receive one of these days 20,000 rubles or 70,000 francs. Twenty thousand francs will be spent and 50,000 put in the bank for me. So what I possess now is mine alone, without counting the estate that I hope to receive from my aunt. And there is the estate from Mama, etc., etc. You will remember that my aunt made a will almost all of which is in my favor. But that's for later. So let's count 300,000 francs from the Villa and 50,000 put in the bank—in all, 350,000 francs, which is quite a pretty dowry. That gives me 19,500 francs in interest: It's not enough even for my dresses when I get married. But my aunt has at least 30,000 rubles of income and that makes an additional 117,500. That's enough for my dresses even when I'm married!

Friday, March 20, 1874. The reception began with the visit of the gracious Souvaroff. She has shown a lot of warmth for Mama during all the winter season in Monte Carlo, and finally she called on her. She left her photograph and obliged Mama to come to her house in Paris, which she just bought. She reproached Mama for not having invited her to come to visit the Villa. In a word she is a most charming and agreeable woman.

Today there were quite a few guests, so I hope things will be better soon.

I showed Miss Collignon the Villa. After repeated showings to all our acquaintances, I have become like the guides in Switzerland who show the points of interest to foreigners. I know by heart what I'm going to say.

Horseback riding with Paul, I went up to all the terraces, into the alley with the cypresses, and everywhere. Many times I wished to meet that dear Émile, who copies the Duke; but I met him only once when I was not expecting him at all. Poor little one, he thinks he has become completely like Hamilton—fat-with-red-hair Hamilton. The carriage, the horses, the attitude, the least little gestures—everything comes from this sublime model. And that's not bad, really. He even goes to Gioja's at the same time the Duke went—and he walks near the Public Gardens in front of the hotels. It's true I'd like to see Lady Montagu. I am very curious and hope to have the chance to see her next winter.

Saturday, March 21, 1874. I just indulged myself in a crazy dance in my nightgown in front of the mirror. And then the ribbon of the gown broke and the gown fell away, but I continued, uninterrupted, my bosom bare. I'd make a good dancer, especially for a lively, spirited dance.

It's hot, and I'm not the same any more. I like the weather when it's cold. Now my complexion is dark, and my cheeks are burning. When it's cold I am pale, and in the evening I breathe better, tonight in particular. I went out on the terrace and walked around admiring the new moon, the coolness of the night, and the stars. I thought nothing could be more beautiful than the night, but the morning at sunrise makes me think the same thing. The afternoon in summers tires me, of course. I remember with enthusiasm the mornings in Baden—the magnificent trees, the boys, the brooks, the little bridges. It's impossible to give an idea of all those romantic beauties, so elegant and well-tended. Those who know the morning in Baden don't need a description of it. As for me, I am incapable of giving the least idea of it. I know only how to admire it, to understand it, and to feel about it.

BOOK EIGHTEEN

Book 18 of my silliness
Begun Saturday, March 28, 1874
Ended Thursday, April 23, 1874
Concerning Me
Rue du Temple, Villa Baquis, Nice.

Saturday, March 28, 1874. We were waiting on the train at the station, headed for Monaco—Mama, my aunt, Mashenka, Dina, Walitsky, Stepa, Paul, and I. All the marksmen were assembled at the end of the platform, but little by little they came closer; and finally Galvi, Lambertye, Furstenberg, and a few no-goods came to sit in the compartment next to ours. What have I done to see myself mistreated in this way? That Lambertye, that good-for-nothing, Fedus, that oily, wrinkled, and ridiculous little man dares to stare at me, laughing. They stayed near their compartment next to us, and Fedus—no, this unworthy being does not deserve a nickname, but let him be Fedus—stared straight into my face! The foxy one! He placed himself in such a way that none of us except me could see him. This Lambertye matter is not funny any more; it is simply insulting, a vulgarity that has no equal.

What does he think about me? Or am I laughable? My God! Now I have the idea that I am absurd and that this idea will make me really ridiculous. And it's his fault.

Sunday, March 29, 1874. When going into my room, I almost fainted. I had no strength to undress. I could breathe only with great difficulty. I thought I was going to die because I was feeling so bad, but when I opened the window it was almost evening and the air revived me.

Monday, March 30, 1874. I didn't want to go out at eleven, but Mama wanted to and we left. Dina, Paul, and I lunched at the Paris Hotel. I didn't find it very suitable, but then it's not possible to prevent what happens. All the worse for them and us! To pass the immoderately long time, I went to the reading room with Dina.

In the Casino, Mama made me angry many times when she said to the croupier, "What time is it? The little one is afraid she'll miss the train." She said it innocently, but that "little one" revolted me so much that even now I must get up and walk around my room just thinking about it. . . . I wasn't at ease in the rooms after the concert.

147

Only the cocottes were left, but we had to wait an hour and I was forced to stay there. . . . Each man stayed with his lady. It was not really very suitable for me to be there. But what was most unfortunate was their departure. Those gentlemen taken away by those women—what shouting, what songs! The train was already moving, and we could still hear the songs. How little in harmony were those songs and that laughter with the beautiful sky, the moon, and the sea, standing out against the somber mass of mountains!

The charming scene continued and lasted a long time—all the way home. Oh, misery, is it true that all men live the way those we saw tonight do? All of that produced in me a very disagreeable impression. Those men—and those women—each taking with her "trophy"!

Thursday, April 2, 1874. O Night! It is only you that I love. You are beautiful; you are great, mysterious, deep, sweet and calm. I just closed the window. The moon shines, the frogs are chanting, and their song is what I prefer. Why doesn't night last forever?

Domenica has written, and finally she gives the cause of death, but very vaguely. She had said (or someone had said) in front of Stepan that it was a lost cause, that they would be left without a name. [George Babanine, Stepan's father, had arranged for the annulment of his marriage to Domenica, Stepan and Dina's mother.] Then he struck himself [with the dagger]. But all that is very vague and to be kept quiet. . . . Together we all rambled in the streets. George is with us. Again he is bareheaded. . . .

Friday, April 3, 1874. What a horrible fright! My heart still beats fast. I was going to take my journal from behind the painting, but when I felt around for it, oh, terror! My fingers touched nothing! My blood froze, and I was going to ask out loud if anyone had found it. Then I looked on the table, and there it was. How did it get there? Mystery. Who could have taken it? Why wasn't it behind the picture? That's what I cannot account for.

Sunday, April 5, 1874. Lise is always the same; Hélène has changed a little because she is a teenager and because she is envious. And Mrs. Howard is also changed—I don't know why. I excite Hélène's envy by telling her which salons we'll have, what furniture, that we'll entertain a great many people. She envies my clothes, my taste in dressing, and the way I fix myself up. But who knows? Maybe I'm wrong about all that.

It was raining, but around 3:00 P.M. the weather became the way I like it. The furious sea rolled its yellow waves. The sky was blue-grey and the air pure and cool. Pedestrians were wearing raincoats and carrying umbrellas.

Tuesday, April 7, 1874. I return elated by a sweet joy which is almost unknown to me and new. Even in this miserable climate, spring makes itself felt. When one thinks about it, each season has its own charms. Winter, with the bright, clear, but not burning sun, and the pure heavens. Even summer is pleasant, both morning and evening, and even the afternoon pleases me because then after that I feel better. Its beauty, calm, and charm are as incomprehensible as the evening and the night. Autumn with its rains is a season that I love. And I don't know of anything more agreeable than to go out after it has rained. In vain I try to choose, but all the seasons are beautiful, all the year is beautiful, and all life is beautiful, too. Society and balls are not enough; we must have Nature, too. To be beautiful at a ball, one needs to take a stroll in the woods, to breathe the fragrance of the grass, and to listen to the chant of the frogs; and to understand these charms, one needs to have felt the burning atmosphere and to have suffocated at a ball. The one and the other are inseparable for me.

How rustic I have become! That will pass, I hope. Just now I am crazy about the music of *La Belle Hélène.* I sing it and I play it—"At the Cabaret of the Labyrinth."

Wednesday, April 8, 1874. At 11:00 we went to church to begin the fast. (Blue dress, good, hair down.) I begin to have a remarkable waist.

All day was passed in waiting, for what or for whom nobody knows, but everybody was waiting. We were waiting until the whole Allen family came with the Tibbetts. Mama was with Mrs. Tibbett, who speaks French, and I was obliged to take the three men and try to entertain them. They left soon, and Tibbett took one of the medical wafers of the professors. Will he die like that poor Abramovitch, who took the grey sample from me and promised to remind me the next year of I don't know what? Mama was too late for the five o'clock train and was very upset about it. She was sure she would have won 20,000 francs playing twenty-one.

Saturday, April 11, 1874. After Mass we went to confession. It is embarrassing and useless, principally when you are asked if you aren't rather "choosy." That was what the priest asked me.

Sunday, April 12, 1874. I slept until noon. It's too bad that we do not observe any of the customs. Today it is Easter; yet nothing is changed. There are no gifts, no amusements, nothing. In order not to celebrate, the family separates, and this makes us selfish, hard. In some other families they exchange surprises, gifts, with each other, and that fosters friendship. What moves a person makes that person feel good. Here nothing of that kind goes on.

As soon as tomorrow comes, with the help and under the protection of God, I am starting to plead for our departure before the eighteenth of this month. I would like to be in Geneva by the twenty-first [to bid at an auction of diamonds]. I do not want to wear Mama's jewels. I have the idea that they will give me bad luck. I don't want my life to look like hers in anything.

We went out. It was pouring, but the sea was admirably furious. Taking off our hats to see it better, we went on the trail where the waves and the foam pass over the road ten yards from the carriage. The water is transparent green, clear and misty. At that moment when the sea almost reached me, I was reconciled with Nice. All this furious sea seemed beautiful and stupefying to me.

Monday, April 13, 1874. After dinner Papa talked about the past greatness of Tcherniakovka and explained that there are no more questions about it—it's all finished as far as we're concerned. How I would have loved it! My guessings at each moment made me embarrassed and miserable; I defended them, or I would have been derelict. As it is, I am at peace because I did defend them.

Tuesday, April 14, 1874. Stepa made a scene with his wife, a vulgar scene—barbaric, impossible, furious, savage—because she bought a few trifles in marble, which would add weight to the trunks! He very nearly hit the poor little woman, who was crying. It was revolting and comic at the same time to hear the big voice of this savage monster and then the little voice of Mamoushka, plaintive and weeping. One could see very well that he felt obeyed and feared.

May God and the Angels of Paradise guard me against having a Russian landowner-husband. What vulgarity! What rudeness! What boorishness! Before everything else, dear God, good behavior—good breeding—comes first. Right away Miloradovitch came to my mind when I listened to Stepa's screaming and his stamping feet. My God, keep me from such a husband. I want only an English Duke. That nationality and that adored title seem to me a complete guarantee against all the horrors I fear.

Yesterday, when coming back from Monte Carlo, Mama had a very disagreeable adventure at the railway station in Nice. At the exit, a young German man, perfectly dressed, with the appearance of a gentleman but a little tipsy, came toward Mama, his arms outstretched, saying, "My dear." She had just enough time to throw herself backward out of his reach. I believe he may have touched her, because she did not say anything to me about the incident and when I asked if he had touched her she didn't give me a straight answer.

Then, as Stepa and Mr. Anitchkoff were there close to her, they grabbed him and dragged him outside of the station into the air. Mr. Anitchkoff, this good-natured man of seventy, became as inflamed as if he were seventeen and pushed the man all the time, hitting him with his fists in the neck. Stepa screamed, calling, "Walitsky!" to send him to Mama. Walitsky came running. Then, forgetting all about Mama, Stepa told him, "Get the rascal!" And W., without an instant's hesitation, hit the man in the face and all over. All three men flogged him until one of them drew blood. Stepa assured everybody that if the man lived a hundred years more he would never address another lady without knowing her.

He deserved to be treated that way; but if he is a gentleman, I'm sorry for him, because he's half dead, poor man!

Wednesday, April 15, 1874. What a day of wrangling, annoyances, scoldings!

I begged Mama not to go to Genoa, but to wait until Saturday and go with me. We could stay there a week and a half and then go to Paris, where we could stay a month, and then go on to the place we would choose for the summer; she and I could go and prepare an apartment and have the family and the dogs come there. That could be about June.

It's necessary to have someone stay in Nice to pay for No. 55. My project is magnificent and practical; Mama didn't say yes or no, but she had all her twitchings and annoying tics. Even at the station I begged her to stay. We decided to go as far as Ventimiglia. She lamented and scolded, and then several different little annoyances occurred: they had forgotten Mama's cushions, without which she cannot sleep; they forgot to give Stepa the black silk for Aunt Sophie in Genoa, etc., etc. But toward the end, as usual, I became the central point of the conversation and the cause of the discontent. I had to defend myself vigorously, tooth and nail, and ended by, yes, me, too—crying!

Having arrived in Ventimiglia, they did not know what they wanted to do. To avoid a delay of two weeks, I begged Mama to go; this time it was she who didn't want to. Uncle Stepa and Mashenka were determined to go. The train was waiting for Mama and Dina, who were still undecided, not wanting to leave. Even when the others had left, I was still begging them to go.

At last we returned—I, Mama, Dina, and George. The most important sadness for Mama has been Paul. He was supposed to go with her to Genoa because two women cannot travel alone in Italy, but instead he ran away; and as we were leaving the station at Monte Carlo, we saw him going up the mountain toward the Casino in a fiacre. I am sad to say that this unfortunate boy is completely lost. He disappeared recently for four entire days, coming home at last at 5:00 in the morning. He passes his time with men of thirty, with actresses, and even cocottes. At fourteen! Misery!

Thursday, April 16, 1874. Everyone rushed to the exhibit, and I came alone. A little later Paul and Walitsky came to meet me. Most of all I admired a pig of prodigious size, so fat that she could not move. She and her litter of piglets are of a cream and white coloring. And the rooster Mephistopheles charmed me very much. I looked all over with my aunt, who was amiable today. I asked her for five francs, and she gave it to me. Oh, prodigious!

My pavilion will be covered with greenery and attached to a rustic kiosk set on a rock by a rustic bridge. Starting from my terrace there will be a little pond . . . this belvedere will be near the Promenade. This enchanting project makes my heart jump.

Saturday, April 18, 1874. They brought me my dress, which, happily, is wearable. It is light with a straw hat. Altogether, it is well made and rather original. And young, simple.

We went into the suburbs that these good Niçois made around the Public Gardens in order to hear these bands of music from Mentone, Cannes, etc. It was nice, but only a few people came. Tea things were brought from the London House to the carriage. Mr. Azarevitch and Walitsky came and remained by us.

Sunday, April 19, 1874. At church the Howards invited us for tomorrow evening to a dancing party for children.

Several times I asked Mama to go to Geneva. There is no time to lose as Tuesday is the day. [An auction of jewels where Marie hopes to buy some diamonds.] Perhaps if we go even tomorrow it will be too late. They have consented to go tomorrow.

Yesterday Tcherniakoff was introduced to Mama; today he came to call. There is a very bad story about him. His first wife poisoned herself. Some say that she was poisoned and that afterwards he married the lady who caused his wife to kill herself because she had lost him. In despair she died.

They say no woman can resist him. Nonsense!! He's an old dog with almost rude manners—a man rather like Stepan Lautrec. That is the best description of his person.

We went with him to the exhibit, but there were too many people; no one had to pay today. Then we had ice cream at the London House.

He used "poussière" [dust] in the same sense that I do. He knows what it means. I was astounded and I blushed. When we talked together, he expressed exactly the same ideas as

I do about the cypresses and all that. Here it was already the second time we agreed with each other. He thinks altogether as I do and takes the words right out of my mouth. I am amazed.

It's agreed that we'll go to the concert of the male choirs.

Here is a matter I can't forget: Walitsky will fight a duel with another man who slapped his hand.

I was angry this evening. In a few words it was like this: It was understood that we would go at 8:00 to the competition of the Orpheons in the Public Gardens; with the illuminations at night it is beautiful. Before we went into the Musette we found Viviani there. He invited us to go tomorrow to Beaulieu. Sometimes Mama acts contrarily—goes on escapades like Olga Anitchkoff. Well, without saying a word, she went away and we stayed until ten o'clock. At the end, especially when I found myself again in the street, I became furious. Auguste [the carriage driver] told us that she was at the London House. In fact, we found her there with Walitsky, George, and Tcherniakoff. Angry, I said a few words to show her how I felt. I wouldn't have said anything if she had gone to the L. H. for supper or dinner. I didn't ask to go there. I didn't want to go there. What made me so angry was that she behaved like Olga—like someone who is wild, crazy. Again, it's the lack of acquaintances that causes such behavior. If we saw men more often, we would be used to this behavior; we'd always know how to act properly, not by fits and starts.

This man is a true Lautrec. He's very witty, like me, but he speaks bad French. I was furious, not because I didn't go to the Public Gardens, but because of this irregular behavior and my stupid irritation. Those who feel as I do understand me. "Mr. Lautrec" accompanied me and Dina to the carriage. He stayed a few more minutes, speaking with an affected frankness but very friendly . . . he gave me his hand several times, forcing me to acknowledge that I was capricious when I refused his orangeade; we separated all good friends. Every time he gave me his hand I gave him the fifth, fourth, and third fingers of my left hand. He's completely like me. It's too bad he is a man. Otherwise I would be his friend. But while he's very nice, he's old and married and not at all to my taste. He dyes his hair and looks like an old Émile Audiffret. (Émile is the nice boy who pleases me so very much.) He doesn't seem to be around any more.

I'm not surprised that women like Lautrec No. two. Even Mama is caught by his charm. Shall I please men, since I am like him? He's a good friend, and I would like him if I didn't realize that he is making a play for my mother. However, he's a big bluffer and has an affected simplicity, but I'm the only one who has noticed this pretense. The others take him "for real." But I know myself and I know Mama. I'm better than he is.

Monday, April 20, 1874. There was a scene about the trip to Geneva. They annoyed me, and I was furious, irritated, unhappy.

In the evening at the Howards'. (White dress, hair high and simple . . .)

It was quite amusing. We danced a lot and well; the last quadrille was danced with marvelous spirit.

But the change of mood is visible—the Boutonskys are the gods of the day (the center of attention).

Hélène had the stupidity to say that I do what I like. On that I seriously and rudely reprimanded her. Then I gave her some advice and told her almost all of what I had on my mind. She understood, but no matter.

Hélène and Lise were dressed like rag-pickers. We have started to be more friendly with the Boutonskys. Marie-Hélène, above all, made friendly overtures to me.

The supper was excellent.

It was very funny when Patton waltzed with Mrs. Boutonsky and then Mr. Boutonsky with his daughters. Mr. and Mrs. Boutonsky acted like lovers.

[*Tuesday, April 21, 1874.*] Today is the Tuesday that I wrote for yesterday, Monday. I've forgotten a lot and I'm writing in a hurry.

I went to bed at 3:30 A.M.

The entire evening was very enjoyable.

We had another scene about Geneva.

Oh, how they bother me! And how happy I'll be when I can live as I like without all these pesterings, which make one embittered and disgusted with everything!

I went out with my aunt and Dina, but I was bored. There is no one. No one. No one. It's sad. I fall asleep in summer, as the snakes do in winter. It's too late for Geneva. Saturday I'm going to Paris (with the grace of God) with Mama, and in a month we'll be rejoined by the others and pass the summer there. The furniture is being made in Paris for my villa.

Wednesday, April 22, 1874. I forgot to say that they made me sing in a dark room. I can't sing otherwise. Mr. and Mrs. Filimonoff also wanted to hear me, because the first time only the Howards and Masur were there. They were satisfied, but I didn't sing very well. I had horrible stage fright.

BOOK NINETEEN

Book 19 of my thoughts
Begun Friday, April 24, 1874
Ended Tuesday, May 26, 1874
Concerning me
Rue de Temple, Villa Baquis, Nice
Hotel Scribe, Apartment 22, on the first floor, Paris

Saturday, April 25, 1874. Again to No. 55: Mama, I, Dina, and Walitsky. Together we demolished a meter of the terrace wall. Almost every day we go there. I like to stroll there because I know that this ground is mine—these trees, the buildings—all are mine, and I feel at ease and admire the least little things. I returned for lessons, but at 6:30 I went for a turn on the promenade with Dina.

Sunday, April 26, 1874. I have a headache.

This evening I went to the theater to hear the *Barber of Seville.*

I wanted to prepare a picnic before going to Paris, but there are always obstacles, difficulties; and I give up, that's all! The Duke and the Duchess of Hamilton arrived in Constantinople on the eighteenth directly from Alexandria; the Princess of Monaco accompanied them, according to the *Derby.* Why can't I say how much I envy them? . . . My plans for the future were stolen—my dearest and most secret wishes. And these things now tease and torture me!

When we came up in front of the villa, an awful spectacle met our astonished eyes: the terrace was collapsing where the cement workers plied their task. My aunt was bewildered by what they were doing, and a thousand doubts disturbed her upset mind. Sometimes it seems to her that her celestial trees are the rampart of the citadel and that they are her protectors against the fatal stares of pedestrians. [Here Marie attempts to write two Homeric similes.] Sometimes she fears the dryads who make these trees their palace. As a she-wolf, attacked from every side by the hunters and feeling the sword thrust into her throat, casts her blood-filled eyes about in an attempt to save her little ones, such is my aunt at the look of these lugubrious trees, her heart filled with sadness as she casts frightened looks around, her voice muffled in her throat.

But, on another side, as a lion from the fields of Libya, leaping in rage and courage, hurls himself with a noble ardor on a ewe separated from her flock, while the shepherd, at the sound of flutes, gives himself to the dance (innocent pleasure of the countryside) and forgets to count his flock, not fearing, O Misery! the ferocious lions and panthers, [such am I].

This lion is me. It's no doubt sadly moving when things like these trees are destroyed. It leaves a disagreeable impression that even I have barely overcome by reassuring myself that it is only for a while.

Wednesday, April 29, 1874. I bought some milk, cream, butter, cheese, strawberries, and fresh cucumbers. I eat only small amounts of anything except milk, which I drink in place of water and wine. I was coming back home in a very agreeable frame of mind, and the sight of Prince Witgenstein was part of the reason, like the song of the frogs, the fresh air, and the smell of grass, which all make me dream and feel fantastically well.

Thursday, April 30, 1874. How beautiful the night is! I just closed the door of the terrace. The sky was blue, and the moon, almost full, illuminated this beautiful sky, setting off the city, the mountains, and our tall palm trees in black. As I looked at the sky, the moon, and the black mass, I thought of absolutely nothing, as one is happy this way.

[The page ends with the simple cartoon of a moon face.]

At the Place Masséna, I saw a gentleman signalling to another who was going into the Café Victoire. He was tall, perfectly built, dark, with a noble neck and chin. "Dina, it's Carlo, you know. Oh, Dina!" I couldn't say "Carlo Hamilton" because there were strangers around. But indeed it was Carlo. He alone has this figure of Apollo, this height, and this small, beautiful head, this divine figure that make me recognize him anywhere. He has more grace than his divine brother because he is taller and more slender. I vaguely remember the Grand Dukes Valdemar and Alexis, but I remember enough to know that they are two men of the same type as the Hamiltons. They are made differently from others . . . their gait, their eyes, their gestures—everything is great and sublime—incomparable.

Friday, May 1, 1874. When shall we leave? My God, make Mama well so we can leave!!!

I took some money and went touring all the food shops looking for good things. I am very fond of sweets around 7:00.

Sunday, May 3, 1874. The air is deliciously pure since the rain stopped. During my walk this idea crossed my mind: I'm fifteen, but I've not written one love-letter or exchanged one kiss. As for kissing, it's useless and bad, but almost all the girls of my age have done it. Three years ago it was a kind of silliness with Remy de Gonzales. But that was three years ago! It's three centuries or three days.

Since then—absolutely nothing. It's distressing and stupid, because here are three years lost all because we don't know anyone.

I am going to write instead of reading because I am the most interesting book of all. In Baden, I remember when I had invited all my friends and we played hide-and-seek and the candle was out. It was what I was expecting, having taken care to be the one who does the seeking. Then I held my hand out to Remy, who squeezed it, but afterward the dare-devil wanted to kiss me. By a skillful and surprising maneuver, I disentangled myself quickly so that my cheek, which he intended to kiss, was protected by my hand, which he grabbed in his two and kissed me there. That same evening, as we were supposed to go out into the garden to give the others time to hide, he put his face so close to mine that I had to draw myself back. I am satisfied to be able to say that an impious mouth has never touched my face and that I have never kissed anybody. The hand doesn't count. When Remy left from the railway station, I was holding a flower. He said to me, "Give me that flower, Marie, so that I can remember you." I handed it to him, saying, "How silly."

After he had gone, his father came every day to take me near the gaming table, and we walked together. This man claimed that he could talk with me as he could to a mature person—a grown-up, and that I was astonishing for my eleven years.

When he came back from school one day, it was raining. I stayed in the embrasure of a window in the grand salon of the Casino. Remy came to sit down near us just at the moment I saw Bertha crossing the court. As she entered the room, I purposely said to Remy, so that she would be able to hear, "You may say it until you are blue in the face, but I'll not change my opinion." (I had heard that sentence at the theater, and it pleased me a lot.)

I just read my pages from yesterday. Why can't we write as we think? Who will invent the art of reflection as in a mirror for us to be able to see what we think and what we feel? I had thought I'd find again my memories from yesterday, and the heartbeats and finally a picture of what was happening in myself, but I found only some paper with ink marks on it!

George is drunk.

Mama has seen No. 55 cypress-less. She cried about it, but that will pass. I am especially well—white and pink and transparent. Everybody has noticed it.

Wednesday, May 6, 1874. At 9:00 A.M. we went to see the Howards leave. . . . The Boutonskys were probably there. These little mice prick up their noses everywhere I am comfortable. I wasn't completely satisfied, since the Boutonskys were taking half of everything.

It's not friendship, but self-love. I never have friends and I believe I never will. I don't believe that friendship as I understand it exists in anyone other than myself. I am good, stable, and loving; and I give what I can, although often they prevent me by looks or indirect words which make me ashamed of my kindness and my amiability. They make me cold and suspicious. In a way that's good because there is so much sadness. Every time I praise freedom to my heart and mind, I am stopped by a mean word which freezes and hurts me. . . . Hélène and Lise and Aggie will write to me as soon as they arrive. The farewell was tender.

Friday, May 8, 1874. Again I cried and scolded. They irritate me terribly. Can I never obtain anything without cries and complaints?

There is the beginning of all our trips! Must each pleasure be poisoned?

My miserable Latin professor explains everything the wrong way. The teacher mixed me up and made me write some mistakes, the triple fool!

Saturday, May 9, 1874. What troubles before leaving! It's easy to say: so many newspapers marked. I have the bad habit of writing on everything and of writing everywhere. So I had a lot of trouble gathering my scribblings together in a box, and I locked up my diaries . . . I hope we'll leave tomorrow at 9:00. I'm praying that the trip will not be postponed.

And now that it's time to leave, I'm regretting my books, my lessons, and Prater, principally. He looked at me today so sadly, poor animal. His sadness tugs at my heart. I very much regret leaving my aunt and Papa—even Walitsky. Everybody and everything, in a word. Why do I have such a deplorable nature? I would like to have no regrets and love nothing. I want to stay, and I want to run away. How will it end?

Monday, May 11, 1874. After a terrible scene, we left. The trip itself passed without incident. That is to say that Mama was very red and wanted to quarrel, but stayed quiet.

We were stopped at Marseille from 3:00 to 9:00. I would like to have the Chateau d'Eau.

Tuesday, May 12, 1874. Here we are in Paris. How happy I am! So happy! I've found what I was looking for—Paris! Paris! That's what I like.

We spent two hours looking for rooms, from the Grand Hotel, where there is nothing, to the Hotel Scribe, where we took a little apartment. Again Mama tried to quarrel, but I told her, "Mama, I'm in such a good mood that no matter what you can say, I won't fight; I'll just walk away." In fact, I'm so happy that it's strange.

The idea came into my mind that I'll have a cancer of the left breast because I feel some pains there from time to time. I've been seriously warned, but Mama says that's silly. I don't know what kind of self-esteem dictates to them that they shouldn't believe this, as if I were immortal. I've told them that if I die, then too bad for them. They'll do the crying. Since our baggage is at the railroad station, I was obliged to wrap myself in a sheet when I got out of the tub. That's too bad, because I'm breathing, I'm alive. I'm no more in Nice.

Wednesday, May 13, 1874. Everybody at Laferrière's is in an awful mood. I ordered a dress, but I would have thrown myself from the window if we hadn't been on the street floor. Everything exasperated me! No one will ever replace Worth's for me. I was ready to cry. What was eating on Mama? She made me furious, crazy by saying humiliating, odious things! That's the way to martyrize me, and I'm afraid it was well-calculated. This is poisoning all my happiness at being in Paris! It puts me in a rage and drives me insane. Oh, my God, my God! But the worst thing is that she bellows when bewailing. At such times I think she's crazy. Yet in spite of all these howlings, all these furious words, I'm happy. Life can be found only in Paris.

I must have a house in Paris; some horses, carriages, diamonds, clothes, receptions. I must be looked at, be a part of society, and occupy one of the important places. I must shine in society and be adored, if not for my beauty (which does not exist), then for my name, my money, the parties I give, and—what do I know?!!!

But it isn't Paris that gives me these ideas; I've *always* had them. Must I justify myself for being vain, ambitious? But those who have all these things I long for—are they vain and ambitious, possessing them? . . . If I were rich I'd probably be happy. All these exclamation marks will never be able to give the feeling that these words should express of rage, despair, and passion!

Blanche Boyd has married Lord Paget. We saw her with her sister in a charming carriage with postillions. My God, what carriages! What harnesses! What outfits the ladies were wearing! *I'm breathless* [in Russian]. But there's nothing that I see that is close to the look of the Duke. All the rest is miserable, dirty, in comparison.

Near the Arc de Triomphe we met the Princess Souvaroff. She recognized Mama and greeted her so kindly that Mama thought she was at her house, since the Princess has so often begged her to come there in Paris. She has even loaned Mama 100 francs to oblige Mama to visit.

I am dazzled, dizzy, ravished, and I made Mama admit that to live anywhere else than Paris is to lose one's time, one's face, everything! I had earlier thought that there was only Baden. But now I see that there is Paris *and* Baden. How happy I'd be to live in Paris except for three months of travel.

Friday, May 15, 1874. We went to the Porte Saint Martin to see *The Two Orphans*, a very moving drama—bloody, telling, compelling. On our way home, we saw Paul in a café. The others called to him. He came out, tipsy, but he didn't want to come home with us. Lost soul!

Saturday, May 16, 1874. I started the day laughing, and that's the way I finished it.

Dina is a model of patience and modesty, but she is impossible in her love for variety in stores.

My brother did not come home to sleep, and we don't see him during the day either.

Back home, we all climbed together into the same bed, and I had a lot of fun laughing. . . . Silliness, Mama, silliness.

Every time I'm in bed with Mama, she looks at me and then says, "What will happen to you, dolly? Who will get you?"

Monday, May 18, 1874. We went to the Gaité to see *Orpheus in Hell* which has been made into a comic opera. Its staging was fairy-like. The theater by itself is very beautiful. The loges are comfortable and pretty, which is rare here. But alas, no loges for us! We were in the balcony. The setting, the costumes, the stage effects (except Cupidan) left nothing to be desired. The costumes pleased me *so* much! . . . Unfortunately they are too low-cut (but that's what makes them adorable). Detractors—particularly the old—will cry "scandal," and most of them will be women, the witches! If I could give balls, this would be the way to do it. (With such costumes.)

Wednesday, May 20, 1874. I love Paris so much! . . . I see that one can love a city for itself. Paris is the most beautiful thing I have seen—the most gracious. I'd like to live in Paris *as I like*. But this constant going into the streets and the shops bores me. It's not my style.

Sunday, May 24, 1874. I am ashamed [in Russian] that all the times I thought or wrote about the Duke of Hamilton I felt the same way I would have if I were speaking about a ball to which I had hoped to go but where I had not been invited. There is nothing more to say.

At 2:00 we went to Versailles; we stayed there about two hours. I didn't see much, but I saw enough to want to live there, to have it as mine. I want Versailles for myself. It's dangerous for me to go there, because the next time I'll probably want to be a Louis XIV.

Tuesday, May 26, 1874. This morning I was very annoyed; there were to be races at Auteuil. The weather was magnificent. My feet danced like a cat's on hot bricks, thinking of these races . . . society people, beautiful clothes. . . .

Mama got dressed; I wore my straw hat. But at the entrance of the Bois, oh, terror! Huge drops fell from the angry sky and all these beautiful carriages were closed and made to disappear. The divine costumes, the lips as red as cactus flowers, the hair as yellow as wheat straws, the eyes as brilliant as glowing coals—each heart sank. People pressed close to each other. One turned up her skirts. Beautiful coiffures became messes of wet hair. Complete defeat.

We stayed in the carriage and saw nothing; it was raining.

I saw Bertha Boyd in a carriage with her sisters. She is fat but pretty, and has a satisfied and happy air. She didn't recognize me, or didn't want to. Bah! I came home in an atrocious mood. I suffer from my illness, vanity. The carriages, the beautiful dresses, the social world— vanity, vanity, vanity. But I am good and loving, basically. I'll never be a bad woman; I'll be honest and pure.

We went to visit a house on the Avenue of the Empress. It was very pretty and little, but suitable.

When shall I live as I like?

BOOK TWENTY

H. G. T. D. O. H. [His Grace the Duke of Hamilton]
Book 20 of this which
Begun Saturday, May 30, 1874
Ended Saturday, July 4, 1874
Concerning Me
Hotel Scribe, Rue Scribe 39, Paris!
After June 3, Hotel des Îles Britanniques, apartment 32
Rue de la Paix
After June 24, Hotel de l'Europe, Spa, Belgium

Saturday, May 30, 1874. The weather was very hot, as if this were not Paris.

How shall I begin? The day was interesting. I saw Bertha.

Bertha! We stopped our carriages, got out, and embraced each other. My heart was racing and my voice trembled. But I put on an air of indifference, which annoys me. I got into her carriage, and we drove to her errand at the Bon Marché. Mama followed us in her carriage. B's governess was with her, but I paid no attention to her. Besides, I didn't have any secrets to tell; I never will have with anyone, especially with Bertha. She is sneaky and not frank. I talked with her so much that I don't know where to start. I was excited, but I knew that I would not say what I wanted to. I forgot Bertha.

She began, "It seems that we detested each other in Baden."

"No. I wouldn't say that. There were some little children's villainies, but I remember them always with an enormous pleasure. Isn't that funny?"

"Yes. Have you been in Baden since then?"

"No, we passed the summer in Nice. It was awfully hot. We've bought a villa there where we'll pass the winters. It's boring for me because I don't like Nice. I understand that you don't like Paris, but you like Rome."

"No, I detest Paris. I don't like Rome, either; but we're going to England, and I'm enchanted with it. It's the country I like most."

"I've never been in England, but I think I'd like it very much."

"Everything there pleases me," she said.

"Did you go to the races Monday?"

"Yes, in all that rain! Did you?"

"We, too."

All this time I was wishing to get to the point. We asked each other all the questions imaginable, while I was wanting to say, "So Hamilton is married?" But I was afraid I was blushing and that she would hear those annoying poundings of my heart. Finally, after blushing and then turning pale, I got the courage to ask the question.

"Yes, I know." She didn't turn, and left me free. She was afraid that I would turn and see her face, but I was having the same uneasiness. So we didn't look at each other. We both blushed, our voices were emotional, and we pretended indifference. We were feeling the same thing. We two were one person at that moment. She could have struck me dead by looking into my face, but fortunately she didn't do it; she was afraid for herself.

The moment passed; she recovered. "The Duke is in Baden at this moment. My father saw him. He has become like a stick."

"Really? I'd be curious to see him like that. It seems impossible to me."

"Yes, my father saw him. He's just come back from Egypt. He goes there every winter. . . ."

"Did you see his wife? Is she beautiful? Tall? Little? Brunette? Blonde?"

"She's ugly" (at this word my heart leaped with joy), "brunette, tall."

"Aha!"

"She has German shoulders, square, and she shows them like Gioja." Bertha made a shrugging gesture. "But she has a very pretty waist. Her mother is a beautiful woman with golden hair, and she is tall. You saw her in Baden."

"The Duchess of Manchester? No, I never saw her. The daughter is dark and ugly, did you say?"

"She is not ugly; she isn't beautiful, either. People find her distinguished. Some don't even find her that. Well, she does have a very small waist."

"If she's not pretty, so much better for the Duke, because the Duke, himself," I said with hesitation, "is not . . ."

"They find her distinguished," she said again.

"Yes, but—she's not pretty. How extraordinary! I had heard she was beautiful."

I've forgotten what was said after that, but I was happy to find someone who talks the language I understand, who likes what I like, who thinks as I think, who looks for what I look for, who is interested in what interests me, and who will tell me nothing, just as I will no doubt tell her nothing at all.

Suddenly she said that she had said all she could, with a little, indifferent air. Poor Bertha! Like me, you have dreamed!

I stayed with Bertha when her governess went into the store. Mama's carriage came up beside us and we three talked for a bit before Mama suddenly asked, "Hamilton is married?"

"Yes."

"His wife is beautiful?"

"No. She is ugly. But she has a pretty waist."

"Is she brunette or blonde?"

"Brunette. She has German shoulders. Square, you know."

I said, "But I think . . . that it's the sloping shoulders that are fashionable."

I blushed when Mama asked the next question.

"Then is she just pretty?" Mama persisted.

"No."

"But then who obliged her to . . ."

"I don't know anything about it. He did not wish it. It was the mothers who arranged it. . . . The Duchess of Hamilton and the Duchess of Manchester."

"Is she—what is she? Anything?"

"No. You know the girls in England are not rich."

"Then why did he marry her?"

"They say that he didn't want to, but that it was fixed that way. . . . One evening he was . . . drunk" (there was a little approving gesture from all of us) "and the Duchess of Manchester came and said to him, 'Do you want to do something for me?' 'Certainly, Madame, I'll do whatever you want.' 'Well—Marry my daughter.' He did not understand; he knew nothing, and yet people came up to congratulate him. That's how this happened."

I think Bertha invented this story. If it's true, I'm sorry and I love him more than ever . . . except for this marriage. His being caught in a trap pleases me, but it also upsets and bothers me.

This visit with Bertha is a big event. I've been troubled all day since I saw her.

Thursday, June 4, 1874. We went into several stores to choose a lot of things and to order two vases with our portraits. I've finished the *Three Musketeers*, and I started *Twenty Years After*. The death of Buckingham always makes me sad. We passed our evening reading—Mama the newspaper and interrupting my reading. Dina was devouring the *Three Musketeers*.

Saturday, June 6, 1874. I am in a bad mood. At 5:00 we went out, but I hate going out as we do, step by step on the boulevard, not knowing where we are going or what we will do. And then I feel humiliated to be within the reach of the often impertinent eyes of all those men sitting in the sidewalk cafés. I often would like to give them a sound thrashing, the cads!

Sunday, June 7, 1874. Because we are extremely hard up—it's awful to have to say it—but I am saddened to have to refuse myself some dresses. It's a humiliating privation. Mama dresses up very little. It's loathsome. If the transaction in Russia were settled, we could, with our income, live perfectly well, more than well. But since at this moment, with possibly 1,000 francs in the common till, we need pay only sixty francs each time we drive out in a landau, we can still keep up a good appearance. So why complain? I think God takes care of us, because without a head of the family, without guidance, we are still not reduced to unpleasantness. On the contrary, we live well here, and we are buying a 200,000 franc property without money! But I must add that that bill is not paid yet.

The business in Russia is not going well, but in my ambitious and extravagant head I conceived the project of buying a mansion in Paris. I don't like mediocrity, and as in Nice, on the Promenade des Anglais, here in Paris I hope we'll always be, with the indulgence and extreme kindness of God, well located, well housed, and well furnished. What is missing, alas, what troubles me and makes me despair, is that we do not live in society. The people who can go everywhere, welcomed and feeling at home, can probably spit on the rest of mankind. But the rest of us who cannot—! But I have the folly and the happiness always to hope.

Monday, June 8, 1874. Mama took a loge for 120 francs for us to hear Verdi's Requiem Mass for Manzoni.

The *Three Musketeers* and *Twenty Years After* make me stay up, and my mother irritates me like a dog. The pleasure I have in reading these books is absolutely ruined. It's the same with my poor Races. It's mean! I want to believe that one can be mean *un*intentionally.

We were not late for the concert. The crowd was very mixed. What can I, poor little ignoramus, say about the Requiem Mass? I don't have the strength to criticize. It is very beautiful. . . . I would like to hear it again. A piece of music as serious as this one cannot be understood and judged the first time. There are several parts which escaped me and which come to my mind only now as I write.

Verdi's entrance on stage was frantically welcomed. This excites me like the Races. I was listening, deeply attentive because of Mrs. Waldman and Mrs. Stoltz, because formerly I had a few hopes of singing until my voice began taking those long trips away from me like the Three Musketeers. But I think at this moment it has begun to come back! Stoltz has to make too much of an effort to sing; she looks as if she's ploughing the land and not singing at all.

It was a memorable afternoon. Maybe I'll be able to boast about it one day. . . . to have heard for the first time in Paris the Muse of Verdi singing.

It was excessively hot, and as soon as we got home we undressed.

A telegram came.

"What is it?"

One thousand francs sent by my aunt. All the same, it's something when you don't have very much.

Requiem . . . requiem . . .

Requiem eterno.

[Peace . . . Peace . . .

Peace eternal.]

Mama stood looking out the window. Then she turned toward me and said, "Let's go to the Bois."

So we went.

These days I am pretty. I wore Mama's white mousseline crepe. It fits me well, and in the carriage the length doesn't show. I wore my straw hat, the hair halfway up with a few short natural curls on the neck. I was satisfied with myself and very pleased with my aunt. But in the Bois I behaved like a fool as soon as we arrived at the light cavalry post.

I have finished the book, *Twenty Years After*. I don't want to read more books of this kind. After all, there's nothing left of it. So I'll come back to Herodotus, Homer, and Virgil. It's wiser.

Saturday, June 13, 1874. Twice I have seen that nice boy who pleases me so much—Girofla [Audiffret].

Sunday, June 14, 1874. Grand Prix of Paris

This is the first Grand Prix race I have seen. Although we left at 12:30, we were not the first ones there. The lines of carriages were already long, but soon so many others kept arriving that it seemed that we were at the beginning! The paddock was full. It was like an ocean of flies; all the colors blended, and the horses and the carriages all moving together made a liquid and grey mass.

When I sat on the top seat during the first race and my eyes took in the humming multitude, I didn't feel small and miserable the way some do in a crowd. On the contrary, I felt not only immense, but also as various as the crowd.

Because I was in an elevated spot, I imagined I was . . . reigning over this crowd, which extended from the grandstands to the Bois and was invading the fields from all directions like water under pressure.

Here is this great waited-for day, the Grand Prix. But alone in a carriage, seeing nobody, knowing nobody, for me it is not a Grand Prix. I don't complain. I only say what it is.

Here is that great day waited for by so many. And here is the beautiful resumé: I did not see anybody! I saw only the stands filled up with people, but who they were or what—was impossible to see.

I was there and thinking of nothing. The black hat was pressing on my forehead and gave me a headache. At last the prize—100,000 francs! All the crowd started to move, screaming, waving their arms. The winner was Trent. This year the English had their turn. Yet today was like the others for me.

When it came time to leave, there were more people than ever. A riot must be frightening. From the lakes to the Place de la Concorde, our horses could go but a few steps at a time, starting and stopping every instant. Coming down the Champs-Élysées we saw Witgenstein. How beautiful! . . . Then Mama, upon seeing the Black Prince [Marie's nickname for him], chimed in with her usual observation: "Here is Witgenstein. Such a good catch. Only he's such a rake, fooling around with a cocotte. I would never allow my daughter to marry him."

Tuesday, June 16, 1874. I chased away the deacon and the roulette from the salon.

And although I wanted to write, I read the first book of my journal. What an innocent autobiography! What style! The one I have now is as bad. As I read, I was laughing and I was blushing. [Volume one of the diary is the only one missing.]

Everywhere I spoke of the Duke, always too excited with endless "oh's" and "ah's." There are some things so ridiculous and absurd that I'm obliged to erase them. I marked many places. I must try in the future to write more clearly. My first book is atrocious, but it contains more than I thought. It contains everything, but I must not judge seriously.

When this memory all falls to pieces . . . I am moved just now. I stopped writing to hide my face in my hands. I can't see well because my eyes are full of tears. I stopped again—it's so good to have moments like this one. I tried to draw the outline of a tear that just fell, but it became mixed with ink from the pen, to express the sorrow of mourning. I would like to know how to express myself well to be sure that what I feel would not be ridiculous when transcribed on paper. Only Pindar possessed the secret of how to speak of one subject all the time.

Sunday, June 21, 1874. I slept in church, but the dog market was waiting for me. I took Walitsky and we left. I came back later with Mama to buy a young bulldog they had to offer. The young bull—a bitch—is baptized Bagatelle.

Thursday, June 25, 1874. This is a little difficult. I have not written in the journal since Monday the twenty-second. Many things have happened. The most important is that we are no longer in Paris, as on Wednesday, June 24, we arrived in Spa.

Mama is sick and suffering a lot, another of her nerve spells. I was shivering a lot at each of her moanings, each stronger than the others. Thanks to God and Walitsky, the crisis passed. Mama is against Spa. What are we going to do? Let's first explore the place.

What a strange city! Around the Source there was nobody, in the garden nobody, at the baths a few Russian hippopotamuses yelling their heads off. Nothing elegant, nothing cute. It is not a watering place; it is an ugly hole.

Following an urgent invitation, we went to the Marquise Viviani's. She has a big villa, garden, penthouse, etc. She says that in about ten or twelve days, people will begin arriving. Let's hope so since there is nothing else to do here.

Friday, June 26, 1874. In the evening we went to the music with the Vivianis. We met Mrs. Basilovitch [Bas], and we all went to the Casino.

Sunday, June 28, 1874. At the concert we made a bataclan with Walitsky, Paul, and Mr. Kirsch, a man of wit and good education, who is the director of the Casino and a useful man to know.

Wednesday, July 1, 1874. Arriving at the casino door, Bas at my side, we entered the rooms. As always, I did not dance. We changed seats and rooms many times. I noticed a very young boy following us. He was listening and seemed to understand, smiling also because we were laughing all the time. Bas, eager for escorts, and I not so much as she, went to Paul and begged him many times to try to learn if the boy following us was Russian, but Paul was playing the unfortunate one because Bas was not flirting with him as with a man.

Finally, Mama, passing by, asked the boy, "Are you Russian?"

It seems that he is not Russian after all but that he understands the language. A few minutes later Kirsch was called away, but he returned immediately.

"Madame, here is the Count Mirzisky" (I don't know the name) "who asks to be introduced officially."

In fact, he introduced the Count whom we took for a Russian but who is a Pole. He has finished his studies and is to receive his doctorate, not in medicine but something else. He has a pale complexion and ash-blond hair. He knows how to speak, a rare ability for so young a dog. He is a musician and not stupid, judging by his conversation. After ten minutes, we were talking about Sophocles, Virgil, Homer, about ancient societies, old truths, philosophy, et cetera.

In the cloakroom I took my raincoat off and gave it to the Count M. at his gesture. Then it was my coat that I needed to put on. Pull out the hair, thank you. I am satisfied with myself.

Thursday, July 2, 1874. In the evening, Walitsky took me to the Alley where I stayed with Bas and the Princess Eristoff [one of Marie's paternal aunts].

For a time after the little Pole arrived, he stayed next to me, and we talked about music. I never looked him in the face, to make people appreciate when I do look. I speak, my eyes lowered or fixed on some place. I refused all the dances, and the Count was not dancing. He told me that he adores dancing, making me understand that he wants to dance only with me.

It is very nice, and I think that this young man will amuse me, only he is so young; I don't like puppies.

Then the conversation took a fine turn.

"However, Pygmalion brought the statue to life," I said.

"Yes, but I don't like the beauty of statues; I like living beauty which thinks, which feels; I like spiritual beauty, singular."

He said this leaning toward me and looking at me. I smiled.

BOOK TWENTY-ONE

H. G. T. D. O. H.
Book 21
My Journal
Maison Willem Lausberg, Spa
Begun Sunday, July 5, 1874
Ended Thursday, July 23, 1874

Sunday, July 5, 1874. We climbed the mountain—Paul and I, Eristoff, Body, and the Count, leaving Dina with Bas below. While we were climbing, Princess Eristoff gossiped to me about Bas, speaking of her as *the Basilovitch.*

On the mountain we drank some goat milk. We went on the swings, and that reminded me that we need some at home. We also went on the Giants' Steps. To go there in a white dress should give a charming effect; we flew like butterflies.

Suddenly we saw Bas, her husband, her children, and Dina. We stayed for a while before we descended, I with Bas, who gossiped about Princess Eristoff just as the Princess had about her.

Nothing, probably, of any importance, was said.

At the Pouhon Fountain, Dina and I walked together.

Oh, if I were a *married Lady*, what fun we would have! Today a promenade, tomorrow a picnic, and then a reunion at my house. Then we would dance in a circle surrounded by the trees. At the top of the avenue, they go horseback riding, etc.

We need to find fun in these poor things since we're in such a miserable place.

After dinner I drove the two-horse carriage, taking Mama, Dina, and Paul, (grey dress), and we went to say goodbye to Lambart, without getting out of the carriage. He came to meet us at the music. Tonight is the opening of the theatrical season.

On seeing the comet, I made a wish. I don't know exactly which one: to see the Duke again, as I want to, or to be rich. Aloud, Mama wished me happiness.

We dined at the Tourinière. I, Mama, and Paul went in the carriage, and Dina and the *little young man* [Count Mirzisky] on horseback.

The *little young man* is delicate and pale, and disgusting to me. I can barely stand him. He is a well-brought-up child, but of what importance is that since he disgusts me? But it appears that he doesn't think of me what I think of him. He is courting me as much as a young little man—a mama's boy—can. At twenty, with straight, dirty-blond hair, he rides. He can do that. He bores me so much that I'm afraid of being interrupted at each instant; I say as little as possible.

Paul introduced a Miss Row to us, a charming little American.

Wednesday, July 8, 1874. We went to the casino with Mama and Baron de Bauche, a gentleman who at Monte Carlo had made *advances* toward Mama before he knew who she was. At the present he is very charming and the only *gentleman* here.

He paid for the chairs, gave [us] roses, and talked. In fact, he acts like a gentleman and not like the cads from here. Bas was walking with her husband. I pretended that I was pouting with the Pole, but he bores me. Absolution was given him toward evening. His mother came to sit near us, the cousin with her father, Bas, the Count, Paul, Walitsky, and de Bauche. We were a beautiful circle on the Promenade.

I danced tonight. Two American girls were introduced to me. Miss Row has been so nice to me that I kissed her on the cheek. She invited me, and we danced together. What a charming child—easygoing, simple, and gay. She said to me, "Oh, you dear little thing!"

But there's not one single man, and I'm bored without men.

I'd like to develop a friendship with these Americans. The Americans are very nice with young ladies. I'll tell Paul to bring them when he comes home.

Thursday, July 9, 1874. The same children's ball as last Thursday.

I was happy to see Bas again. She introduced the Baron Charles Gericke de Hermines (a difficult name), a former sweetheart of hers and also a present admirer. Only (she says), he pretends indifference at the beginning. She affects a melancholic, dreamy air, which charms him. He is a Hollander from The Hague. He is an only child, of good family—well-bred, average height, brown hair, and good—admirable profile, rather ugly grey eyes; he wears only a moustache. Twenty-five years old. Well-dressed. He has free, childish manners and is very spoiled by the ladies, a handsome and sympathetic young man. There was a slight drizzle, but we went to the Source with Bas and Gericke. I always go on my mother's arm.

This Baron has very strange manners. He doesn't mind taking your hand or even touching your hat. Bas says he'll even touch your ears. She pretends that this is without intention, like a child. Well, that's all right up to a certain point; after that it becomes a flirtation. After stopping at the Pouhon, we went to the alley. Bas left us to make a visit; so meanwhile we sat under a tree. Gericke (I don't know how to write his name) brought us news of Borreel!—good, fat Borreel, the one I had a crush on in my early teens. He's not married yet, but he has been courting a very pretty girl at The Hague. He, too, is descended from a good family. At the evening music, arm in arm, we passed in front of the chairs. Bibi [Marie's nickname initially for Gericke] came up to us and strolled with us in the Avenue until we sat with Dina and the loathsome Pole.

There's a tall, strong, white-skinned gentleman here with black eyes who wears a soft, bandit-like hat like the one worn by the Black Prince. There is an elderly lady walking with him. He is so handsome that the first time I saw him, when I was driving two horses, I looked back at him involuntarily. He is very good-looking—much too good-looking for a man. His villainous hat engulfs him; he wouldn't be too handsome with another hat. He was sitting on a bench along the alley. Yes, he is handsome, but not my type.

Tonight I waltzed and danced with Bibi, who danced like Borreel and even reminds me of him a little. After each waltz with him, the little Count came to ask me to dance. He is a wretched young man—ugly, yellow, and tasteless. Besides these two, I danced with some Americans, that nice Winslow and another one. Bibi told me, "Wear your hat farther back."

"Why?"

"One moment . . ."

"But why?"

"One minute."

I pushed my yellow hat back from my face.

"Yes, that's fine. I see that without your hat you are much better looking. Wear it on the back. It's prettier." And he tried to push it. What manners!

Friday, July 10, 1874. When Mama and I went out in the evening, we found Bas, Bibi, and the husband—a charming trio. But no joking, Bas is an honest woman—and she is gay and easygoing in appearance, but her admirers complain of her virtue.

At 9:30 we went to the reading room, which was full—Bas, Dina, the young Polish lady! Bibi and I sat around a game of dominos, and I gave him a lesson in Russian. He knows how to say, "I understand," "Good morning," "Good night," "Goodbye," "Fool," "My dear one," "Leave me alone," "You bore me," "You stupid fool," and "Pig." We laughed so much that the ones who wanted to read couldn't have done very much of that. I laughed with all my heart. The Baron is funny, and when he sat down to write I could see his well-set, pretty hair. It's been a long time since I've seen such a nice, pretty, clean head, such as one would want to kiss.

I'm preparing myself for a big scandal which, I tremble to say, must come one day: the one when my journal is read.

Today my journal was in Dina's room. She found it, but assured me that she was not curious. It's really very silly to write what I think, but that's what helps me to verify that I change. Well, (I find) that the principal, the fundamental ideas have not changed. I am satisfied about that.

I forgot to tell what Gericke did in a candy shop where we stopped before going to the Casino. I threw away the core of a pear after I had eaten the fruit, and he took it and bit into it! He did even better than that; with his hand he took the edge of my hat and pushed it back. Then I stopped his hand, seriously.

He is crazy!

Back home I said to Mama [in Russian], *"Do you know what Gericke did? I threw away my pear, and he ate it."* A satisfied smile passed on Mama's lips. *"This is what a young man does when he is interested in a young woman,"* she said. But it's not that. He did it out of nonchalance, forgetfulness, silliness.

It's raining. Bas shouted from her window to say that she'll come to join us at the music. As she didn't come, I went to her house; I was really embarrassed to find Gericke with her. Well, I went with them. Mama said she would be coming right away. Bas gave her and her husband's cards to the Countess Mirzisky. This lady was at home, and I was obliged to wait for Bas in the company of Gericke. We stayed under a window in Hospital Street, saying very ordinary things very quietly. Gericke is a child of good family; he says silly things in society, but alone with me he has been perfect, and that pleases me.

But on leaving Bas's house he did a terrible thing; when crossing the square he was tapping with his cane on her iron bustle as if it were a wall or a chair. I told this with a lot of noise at home. Bas's visit ended, and we went to sit at the music, where first the Marquise Viviani and then Mama came to meet us. We talked about next Tuesday's picnic. The little Pole played it cool as an answer to my impertinences.

Before the ball, a very disagreeable scene took place. My brother put me out of my mind because he doesn't want to give me a certain book, and I wanted to punish him with a chair. Mama was afraid and had an attack of nerves. An hour later, as if by a miracle, Mama was at the ball in the grey dress by Worth. I wore my white one, hair loose on my back (good). The room was full, but Bas and I were the only ones without hats. Bas was with her Count de Toulé, who looks like an opera tenor. I like him. He is well-bred, has good manners, is a proper gentleman—calm and good. He was introduced at once.

De Toulé dances well, especially fast. Everybody was watching when we were dancing. I danced with a lot of men. Then someone introduced the one who dared to ask me. He is an awful Dutch man; after the handsome young man, I liked this one for his huge size, but he has ugly eyes and common manners and seemed to be of no type at all. He didn't know what to do with his hands. Mama introduced him to me. I was expecting a name like Esterhazy, but I heard Paparigapoulo. But that's crazy! Papa, riga, poulo. He is Greek! He's not good-looking; he has small, scared eyes and looks embarrassed.

No, no, no, you're no longer a warbler. Don't use this name! I never liked him, but since he has this name I've become indifferent to him. That's too bad; I was hoping he'd be "somebody"!

Gericke is the most charming one here. He doesn't know how to talk. But in Russian he says very nicely, *"My dear one,"* so that I am in love with these words. When talking to me he calls me (again in Russian) *"My dear sweet one"* and I call him *"stupid fool."* I can talk in this tone with him because he is a nobleman, well-mannered and well-bred. He laughs, he jokes, and so do I, but there is never a word or a gesture that could hurt me. But not always: look at Tuesday.

Then the Dutchman, Papariga, de Toulé, and more and more came around us. It is most agreeable!

I have not been left alone one second. They pretended that I waltz admirably; they compared my head to a Greek sculptured one because of my golden headband. I heard everything, and if I were silly enough, I could have lost my head! Papariga-etc. is very proper.

We came down to the café to have some ice cream, and Gericke disappeared with Paul. They'll eat their sorrows together. De Toulé is triumphant, dressed in white—with dying eyes. First he accompanied us, and then Bas. *The more I see of other men, the more I love Hamilton.*

Sunday, August 12, 1874. Tonight there was a night fiesta in the Alley—a kind of competition by the choral society for music and the musicians. We dined at Flanders Hotel. Later in the evening, Paul and the Baron came with us, finding chairs for us in this enormous crowd, and stayed all evening with us.

Bas and de Toulé were three rows ahead of our seats.

At the beginning we laughed. Gericke was calling me *"dear one"* in Russian, and I called him *"stupid fool"* and *"dear one,"* also in Russian, saying in Dutch, "And you are stupid." It seems to me now that "Dynamenaka" [dear one] is really my name. We didn't lose one word of the conversation going on between the Baron and Mama. I heard everything he was relating about Bas, who let herself be kissed as much as one wanted. Then Gericke begged Mama not to repeat this to anyone, saying that it was a very easy thing (the kissing) to do with each woman: "You clasp her to your heart strongly, you take her by the waist, and you kiss her. There it is; it's done in a jiffy." I heard him ask Mama if she had ever experienced that. He laughed at her negative answer and said he didn't want to believe that, coming from a Russian lady! He said he was not in love with Bas any more, on his word of honor. He told her how he would act the same way with her (Mama) if she were alone. (It was awful, but it was said so nicely, so nobly, that the most scrupulous could not be offended. He said that it was so easy.) Then, for an instant, I wished I might be Mama, and alone with him. No, since he does it as if he were swallowing a candy—that's what he said. I heard Mama tell him that he sees us very wrongly—that never either I or Dina . . . I would confirm that by acknowledging that the only silliness I have done in my life was to give a lock of my hair to Remy. This is the first time I've ever told it to anyone. The music interested me once in a while.

Gericke said he was going to court Miss Row to make Bas jealous, since, he said, she dislikes his not liking her without any reason; and now, having another lover, she wants to keep him. Then Mama said that no one should play with the heart of a young girl. Then he said that American girls have no heart, and besides, for just a courtship young girls don't get stirred up. "I'm going to ask these girls, 'Are the hearts of young girls like you capable of getting excited over an ugly young man like me?'" (I don't recall the exact words he used, only the meaning.)

Then we reassured him that it was absolutely impossible.

And we talked about everything. I thought completely the opposite of what he thought. For a while, I was afraid that this crazy man might become my infatuation until I thought about the Duke; *he* appeared to me so great and so adorable that I have not been embarrassed for one moment. I had been thinking that Gericke might become, as I was saying, an infatuation—for a month—I was saying that as a caprice. But that could not have been, even for one second—even at this moment. A railroad makes many detours, but it is considered to be straight and is so marked in its totality. It's the same for me; the Duke is my straight line, but on the journey my train climbs or descends.

Monday, July 13, 1874. By the time I finished writing yesterday, it was already morning.

Today, after dinner at six we went for a ride to the Four Fountains—I, Dina, Eristoff, Gericke, the Polish Count, Winslow, and Ladd. The rest of the society went in pony carriages by twos—Paul and Row, Bas and de Toulé, Mama and Paparigalo [nickname for Paparigapoulo] (to make a pair with Bas, who had begged her so much). At 8:30 the place of the Pouhon Fountain appeared to be extremely animated; three carriages and seven saddle horses are not seen every day in one place at the same time.

My riding habit was terribly tight on my chest. I left my hair floating under my black velvet cap and got down. Everybody, ready at last, started off at a gallop. Our departure made such a ringing sound on the cobblestones that my heart was jumping with happiness.

Mama was irritated to see the Pole courting Bas. She doesn't know, or doesn't wish to understand, that it is on purpose, that he really is in love with me. Later on I'll give the proof. By the time we got to the top of the mountain, I was suffocating. I cannot stand to have the blouse tight on my chest, especially when it is pulled down. It's awful! I stayed behind with Eristoff and the Count after another hill; I could not breathe any more. Then Paparigalo advised me to unbutton the blouse, which I did while he was holding the bridle. But this was not helpful; I was still suffocating. The Count guided my horse, and I could barely hold myself on the saddle. The Princess, annoyed to see her escort near me, galloped away. I stayed alone with the little one.

I didn't smile or look at him. I said just what was necessary about the horse; we went at a walking pace until we reached the Geroustère, where we found everybody else seated around a table. My two Americans came toward me and sat at my sides. Although they are ugly, I flirted with the two rascals. I don't remember about what subject. Gericke knelt in front of me—"Oh, Queen of my love. . . ." (General laughter.) He is crazy and amusing, but I thought that to have to return the same way as I came would be awful; so I went into a room by myself and arranged my blouse in such a way as to be perfectly comfortable. Gericke put me back on my saddle, put on my gloves, arranged my skirt, and then took my foot in his hand and said, on every tone, "It's very pretty."

The Count came running, as he always does when the Baron is near me. He thinks Bibi is courting me and is worried, but Bibi is not among those who are doing that. He is courting everybody; he goes on without stopping.

"Have you ever seen such a foot? It is marvellous!" Indeed, under the riding pants my foot looked like a child's. He kissed it so well that I could feel the kiss under the leather. The poor little Pole turned his eyes away, but he didn't leave. "Why didn't you wear your boots, Miss?" he asked.

"I prefer these high shoes. The boots make my feet look larger."

"No, that's not possible for a foot like yours," Gericke said. "Let's go, then. But what a foot!" and he kissed it again three times. Smiling, I permitted it, since he was doing it without any bad thoughts; and that makes me very happy. It's too bad that I'm not married; I'd let him court me. I'd teach him some manners. He's too free and too childish.

At that moment de Toulé arrived, and he buttoned up the gloves. I passed with the Baron, and soon Dina took him away from me. The Pole came up, saying, "Miss Marie, let's go for a walk."

He looked me straight in the eye, and his eyes were shining.

"If you were to look at me for an hour, I would not understand you," I said rudely.

"I leave tomorrow," he said in a pleading voice. "Tell me, so that I'll pass my examinations."

I told the Count, "I wish you success in your examination."

"I'd prefer that you wished me something else."

"What?"

"Must I say it?"

"One must always say . . ." (I knew what he was going to say)

"Well?"

"Well?"

"And well?" I was exasperated to wait for the declaration of such an unattractive fellow. Fie!

"I shall leave for four days. You, who forget so quickly . . ."

"Well, I'll forget, that's all . . ."

In front of our house there was another frightful tumult. The Pole helped me jump off my horse—very badly. Then Gericke and the others arrived. "What did you do to your hat?"

"It was Monsieur's fault. He didn't know how to help me. And you didn't come. But you had helped me so well to get up, didn't you?"

His mother pretends that he's been getting thin in the last two days. These detestable Poles! This is not a conquest. I soil myself by discussing this. The lizard has said something against Gericke; what he said means that I've forgotten him for Gericke. Is he crazy? Have I ever thought of him? In order for me to forget him, it would have been necessary for me to remember him! If Gericke were courting me like the Pole, I would give him my hand to kiss. But the Pole repels me. Ugh!

Tuesday, July 14, 1874. I just reread my journal from the first appearance of Gericke. I have been wrong several times: first, in saying that Bas is an honest woman, and second that Gericke has ideas on what is correct, and on our customs in general. It's not true, as Row says.

He has some ideas, but at the same time he has many . . . others . . . and furthermore, he is a very enterprising boy—one who doesn't miss even half a chance, and certainly not a whole one. It is necessary to be on one's guard.

The Marquise with her husband, their protégés, Mrs. and Miss Davignon, and four servants brought the dishes, the table and linens, and a large part of the provisions, and they went at once to prepare everything. All the others agreed to meet at our house.

We arrived at Barisart first. Gericke drives at a gallop.

He had the salad tied in a scarf under his arm.

The Marquise dresses like a cook. The Marquis and the Davignons met us. I understand the poor Marquis well; he doesn't like to go out with his Marquise because she dresses so badly. And she complains that he complains about it!

Bas, with her Count, got there last and would arrange to leave last, managing to have a twosome or some sort of arrangement made for them.

A lot of good things were brought, but the tablecloth was spread on the grass and we had to sit on the grass. It was very rustic, especially for the legs—I don't know how the others did it, but for my part, all the time I was tipping the glasses and the plates over. I preferred not to eat. In haste I swallowed only two sardines, a morsel of ham, the wing of a chicken, a peach, and some glasses of wine. That was all the dinner I had, and I hadn't had any breakfast. Truly, a table well served and some good chairs would have been better. One might say that I'm not a child, but an old lady. I would very much like to put anyone who says this on the floor sitting like a Turk for two hours while dying of hunger. And when reaching out to take something, let that person turn something over or even fall over himself. I wasn't too bad, but everyone complained of all this, and I did like the others. Doubtless with a table we would have been less free; we would have regretted that.

After eating, everybody relaxed. De Toulé stayed near Bas. Row and I seated ourselves on a tree trunk in front of the fellows Walitsky was putting at our feet. Stretched out there were Gericke and Paul, and Winslow next to me. From a distance Ladd was looking, smiling, and taking off his hat each time he talked to me. Row seated herself poetically, also. Dina looked picturesque where she sat under a tree. Mama didn't take any kind of a special pose, and all the others sat without grace and (you could say) disappeared. Ida wanted to smoke, but her sister forbade it. Then we went into the woods with Paul, Winslow, and Ladd.

Suddenly, in the midst of our solitude, Walitsky rushed up and announced the arrival of Kirsch with a barbaric organ and two violins. We ran like mad, and all of that to find out that it was not true! Someone proposed that we go to a restaurant where there was a piano; so we went. The tables were set outside, and we danced.

We arrived before anyone else got there and waited on the balcony.

Wednesday, July 15, 1874. Mama and I dined between Paparigalo and Gericke. Gericke talked with Mama and Paparigalo with me. The conversation was simple and good. He is young—too young. In the evening we went to the fancy-dress ball. (I took off the yellow hat because it didn't stay in place.)

I remember nothing.

Thursday, July 16, 1874. Mama, Dina, and Walitsky are leaving for Liège. Mrs. Bas is taking me with her. There is to be a children's ball.

She has scolded Gericke too much; at least, I think so. I think he's jealous and in love with the bearded beauty. Since yesterday he has been sad and looks unhappy and inattentive, and today he was sullen with Bas and went away with Paul. De Toulé is with us. Bas also seems melancholy, but she said that she was in a bad mood—that she was bored. I went to see if my family had returned. Then I dined with Bas at the Foreigners' Hotel, alone in a separate room. We ate well. Mr. Bas is a good man, and he is witty. But he looks like a Menelaus. Madame plays the coquette with him, makes eyes at him. She told him, *"My dear John, you are the sweetest of all my admirers,"* and told him a hundred times that she was in a bad mood [in Russian]. De Toulé is a charming conversationalist. When he is talking, one feels attracted to him. He seems so good that I think he is bad. He said, "I must have inherited one of the most beautiful castles in France." (I cannot refrain from laughing when I reread these lines.) He is full of nice feelings and kindnesses, and sees Mama as a heroine.

Mama found us still seated under the trees. We went to the Casino, but Bas arranged for a little tête-à-tête with de Toulé before we left. Is it possible that he loves her?

If he is as good as he seems, he cannot love this woman. However, he didn't stop to look at her. Sometimes, when he does look at her, he seems to be in a trance—doesn't seem to hear or understand anything. He is the husband's friend and is often with him, but he seems to adore this woman.

It is too bad.

The poor Baron, I saw, was sad, and I told him so. He answered with a joke, "Give me your hand so that I can kiss it, and I'll be happy." This proves that he is unhappy. Then he claimed, "I am melancholy; I'm very unhappy; I force myself to be jolly." Is it that Bas makes him feel this way? Can a person love so much as that? The poor man is jealous, and I am sorry for him. I wonder why this woman is loved. It is certainly not for her beauty. She looks like any person reflected in a dog's eyes or in a spoon in such a way that the nose protrudes (in the reflected image). Furthermore, she is hairy, like the Boutonskys. She wears makeup, and she destroys the hair that grows under her chin. She is badly built; her chest is (I'll use the Princess Galitzine's expression) like an empty purse that contains only a small coin. She has no hair (to speak of), but it is true that she is elegant and very well-dressed. Her greatest charm is that she is a lady who acts like a flashy woman of doubtful reputation— a demimondaine. That's it.

Friday, July 17, 1874. At last I arrive at this Friday! (Because these last three days have been recorded at once.) One must never [in Russian] *fall behind.* (Linen dress, Massa hat, yellow shoes, which make my feet look adorable and everybody looks at them.)

We went to an evening party at the Marquise's. Gericke is not amusing, but I like him. Gericke is handsome. Gericke doesn't pay attention to me, and I am furious about that. There were about forty there. He danced. I danced. He dares unbelievable things. At the end of a waltz he didn't let me go; instead, he squeezed my waist tightly. I wanted to sit down, but he tripped and Mrs. Malezieux's dog started to bark furiously. (I was about to sit next to her.) He acts like a pig; the ladies of doubtful reputation have given him these impossible manners. What is he thinking?

I almost forgot to say that Bas believes me to be a genius. She consults me and asks me as "the one who has the talent to recognize people." She asks me what I think of so-and-so and whether de Toulé is in love with her. She treats me like an adult and finds me very shrewd. I put on very mysterious airs with her, and sometimes I'm ready to crack up laughing. Often I stay silent, looking as if I have too much to say; and I shake my head with a smile, as if I were saying everything.

Our villa will be called *Dynamika.*

Saturday, July 18, 1874. We got up late, and we seemed to move in an air of confusion [in Russian]. Dina came back from the Pouhon and said that she had seen Bas there with Lambart, and then with de Toulé. Gericke and the Greek were coming from far away. Mama is angry about Lambart, and I am furious about everybody! As soon as you open your eyes you hear this kind of good news. I am jealous of this woman. She captures everyone. It's distressing—so distressing that I almost cry.

It was more animated than usual at Lambart's. Angela Godefroy and Body sang. Malezieux sang a few comic songs with patter in a very amusing style. I spoke Italian with a Count from Venice who looked like a shoemaker, just as his Countess did. During one song, the ladies remained seated at the tables while the gentlemen stood. I decided that Lambart was the best looking. A Count de Jabal was introduced to us all, a man who has settled in St. Petersburg.

We left only at 11:00 P.M.

I am ruining my health; I never go to bed before 2:00, or often 3:00 A.M. I must stop it; I'm hurting myself. I'll change all this tomorrow.

Each evening as we're coming home, I think of him, and sometimes I see him and compare him. What I'm trying to say is so vague that I can hardly understand it. It's that. . . . No. I mean that what I feel for him is something extraordinary. *When I think of him for a minute or two* [in Russian]. When I *see* him. . . . No, it's better not to say anything. I'll never be able to write what I feel, since I can barely gather my thoughts to unravel them, and since I am always afraid I'll lose the thread of my ideas—the thread I don't hold. It's all inside me, and it's not finished! I don't remember anything more.

Sunday, July 19, 1874. At the music there was a crowd of dirty people from the surrounding towns. (White and silver dress. Good.) We hadn't been seated ten minutes when Gericke and the Greek came. Gericke was in a dreamy state. He stayed near me without thinking anything of it. He made some conversation like a machine. Since he was in such a state, he was nice; but I could not utter my beautiful sentences. At 4:30 we all went to the Pouhon, where we met Mr. Jabal, a charming man. Bas appeared at her window, and Gericke ran. She disappeared, and he stopped in the middle of the street. We ate at the Flanders Hotel. Gericke came with us, but as soon as she saw him with us, she came and took him away.

We had the time to visit with Row and sit at the table before Bas let him go. She is going to take him for good; de Toulé is leaving, so she'll take Gericke. If Gericke is not there, she'll take the little Pole, or even Body. What surprises me is Gericke's patience. He knows about de Toulé and waits patiently for his turn! He doesn't want to be the only one to have her; that's all.

We went to the music in the evening with Jabal, de Bauche, Mirzisky (who has passed his examinations very well and is back and is wearing a tube hat).

Eristoff and Body honored us by sitting with us. Mama went to find the Baron, dreaming under a tree. Then he continued to dream with us, but toward the end he started a conversation—very insignificant, like everything else he says. He said, however, one incomparable thing: "When will you allow me to kiss your hand?"

"But never, Sir."

"Come on! That's impossible."

"Then in twenty years."

"I won't want to then."

"No. In ten years."

"All right. I accept in ten years."

In fact, I had thought of giving him my hand to kiss—in time. That's why I said such silly things.

Monday, July 20, 1874. Bas is pale and her eyes are red. Mr. de Toulé left at noon yesterday. She probably *wept all night because of his departure.*

This evening ended badly. I had the silly idea of taking everybody to Bas's to have some lemonade. When we came back, none of these gentlemen got up to accompany us. Mama came home furious, and I felt humiliated and more than furious.

Tuesday, July 21, 1874. We made ourselves beautiful for the theater. Mama was beautiful—magnificent—in her red dress. I had a very nice hairdo, and I wore my pink dress without gloves. We occupied three loges, one next to the other. We saw the plays *Bisette* and *The Coquette*, which were much appreciated here. I could hear very little because I was listening to the Greek and Bas. They were saying the most tender and passionate things. As for her eyes and her face—I can say no more! The Duke came close to her and looked at her as if she were nothing. He made eyes at her as if she were a . . .

Mama launched this woman here, and she [Bas] has monopolized everybody. Yesterday again, in a vulgar way, Body said what I've often told Mama, that the young ladies should band together to oust this woman because she has monopolized all the young men.

Poor Gericke! How patiently he has been waiting. Tomorrow he is supposedly leaving to go to his aunt, but he is leaving with Bas. It's his turn—the Greek will also go to Ostend. I was looking at Mama, who is so beautiful, and at this other woman, who is not beautiful at all.

Gericke pleases me, but his manners are unfortunate.

I ate half a rose and then gave it to the Count. I regretted it after I saw it on his lapel. I would not say that Gericke was jealous; no. I am not for him, but still he felt that I had given a rose to someone else than him.

Bas introduced the Spanish Duke to me. This pure dove could not go back alone with the Greek; she begged us to accompany her, which we did.

After telling her goodbye, we left in a hurry; the Greek came on the run to join us. Then Mama said to Dina, "You see, Dina, how kind we ladies are; we have accompanied a lady and a gentleman, but yesterday they let us leave all alone—three ladies alone!" The Greek didn't say one word. We stayed in Mama's room and talked about the events of the day.

Wednesday, July 22, 1874. Departure of the Diva—the eater of hearts.

Gericke asked Mama whether de Toulé was Mrs. Toutlafait's [Bas's] lover. Mama said that might very well be so.

She is gone, and we are the masters of the situation.

Among other things, we talked about costumes. "But Madame, why do you ask the local dressmakers?" asked Paparigalo.

"Oh, Sir, it's necessary. The cobblestones of Spa demand that the skirts have constant repairs," Mama answered.

"But Dynamika doesn't need that," Gericke said, touching the edge of my skirt with his cane and pulling it up a little with this gesture.

"Baron! Baron!" Mama shouted with anger. "What you just did is incorrect. I saw you doing the same thing to ladies who wanted that; but with young ladies, such behavior is impossible! Impossible!" She took me by the arm and marched away with me, furious, pale, and then red. I think it is too bad for him. He has forgotten himself too much. He needed something to put him back into respectability. When Mama said that, I was afraid. The gentlemen followed us with heads lowered, and we walked next to Dina with the Marquis and were calmly talking of all sorts of things, as if nothing unsettling had happened. Gericke very timidly came back to walk next to me and join in the conversation, still timid. I have such a good heart that I was sorry for him. We all went together to the music, leaving the Marquis with his wife and the Count with his mother. (He is jealous of Gericke.) We went on up the hill.

We climbed quietly. Mama controlled the conversation very simply. Gericke walked up straight, and so did I. I climbed like a monkey, clinging to the branches and grasses, and leaning on the Baron's arm. It was so steep that at the end I was dizzy and I felt my heart beating like a hammer in the middle of my back. The Baron was correct, like de Toulé. We sat on a bench to wait for the others. He asked permission to clean my shoes, which I gave; but at one of my gestures he answered with another that said, "Oh, Miss, be reassured! How could you think such a thing!"

We talked about Nice and Nice society, but as they didn't come, we got up and several paces further on we found them waiting for us on another bench.

At the top of the mountain, we drank some milk. The conversation was very simple and rustic. The gentlemen looked as red as fires in winter. We talked about my aunt, and Mama said she was sure that Aunt Nadya would like the Baron and that he would like her.

Dina wanted to climb and slipped away like a young deer; when I went up, I did so with dignity. But she, excited, was feeling like a butterfly. Gericke took us back as far as the Pouhon.

He behaved perfectly, but he felt constrained. I'm afraid we offended him. I am so silly—always sorry for the others.

I, Dina, and Paparigalo went on horseback, leaving between eight and nine o'clock. Mama invited several, including Gericke, but with his eyes lowered he said it would be impossible; he couldn't go because he had to see his aunt. All the men were saddened by the departure of Bas.

The fact is, there are lots of men here. [In Russian] *In Baden, I would never have known Hamilton if he hadn't been pointed out to me. Once, in the morning, I was strolling with Dina, and we dropped into a restaurant. We saw an ugly beast in white boots with beautiful cuffs, a soiled hat, and a sporty trench-coat, and this ugly beast started shouting to be served shrimps, pâté de foie gras, etc. Then I thought to myself, he must be some peasant stuffing himself. Then I asked and was told who he was. "A total peasant. Ugly,"* I said in a timid voice. But I was very much moved.

After dinner we went to visit the Marquise for an hour. We drew lots for those who were to go in the break or in another carriage. As we were leaving the Casino, Mr. Lausberg put a box and a visiting card into Mama's hands. At the top of the stairs I heard [in Russian], *"Here, Moussia, Gericke brought you a present!"*

I thought they were joking, but downstairs I clearly saw a fan and this visiting card. I couldn't believe my eyes or ears. I blushed and expressed my astonishment in every tone of my voice. It's a very pretty fan, made in light wood and flowers mounted on linen. On the lower part, painted with forget-me-nots, were my initials, M. B. It is charming, but I can't make out why and how Gericke had the idea of giving me a fan! Now I have five—this big one almost as big as the others.

I went to the Casino in my grey dress and hat, and carried the fan. It's my first gift. [In Russian] *Here are the gifts and the evenings you sigh about.* Mama said to me, "Everybody is surprised to see us in afternoon dresses." Only Dina was suitably dressed; she wore her long, black dress from Worth. (Laferrière dresses look miserable next to those of Worth. Only theirs exist.)

Dina is wearing this dress for the Baron, Bas being away. It wasn't I who made the remark; it was Mama.

I danced three or four times. Gericke is hiding and didn't come near us. I was holding the fan and walking with my hand on Walitsky's arm. We found Gericke sitting with another gentleman near a table. This charming Baron, really so charming! So friendly!! What's wrong? It's nothing, really. I don't know—Just a lot of words, jerky, senseless, as always. I don't know why he didn't come to greet us. Mama said that [in Russian] *it must be the first time he paid court to a young lady, and that he became frightened of his own forwardness.*

I said [in Russian], *"He's not paying court."*

Mama said, *"How is that? Of course he is!"*

But it's not that. I'm delighted with the gift; it's my first. The Greek, who went to buy it, probably with Gericke, said when he saw it, "What a beautiful fan! May I see it?"

"It's from the Baron. You know that," I said, holding it out.

The Pole is jealous of Gericke. What a bad temper! Cunning, discontented, enigmatic. . . .

On our leaving at 10:30, Mama was saying to the Greek, "Poor boy, you are sad, etc."

I said, "I am going to console you, Sir, and decorate you," and I fixed a boutonnière in his left lapel. Mama had brought it from Kirsch's office.

Thursday, July 23, 1874. [Ramanche Grotto.] The alarm clock rang when I was already awake.

Everybody was in a bad mood. There was some difficulty regarding the horses. The Marquise was in a bad mood, too. She spoke of Lambart with bitterness.

I had a bad horse that didn't know how to trot. I rode miserably.

The horse martyrized me, and I was delighted to arrive. I was sorry for the people in the break. There were almost no gentlemen—generally only dusty ladies. We reached the inn, and the landlord had difficulties about the kinds of things the party was really lacking. What they lacked was especially a leader (a head). We put on the proper clothes to visit the cave, and each of us was given a light to carry in his hand. The entry was very impressive. Some of the group wore loose, white-hooded clothes; they carried lights and followed each other. The daylight disappeared quickly, and we advanced on slippery ground, uneven stones. Above our heads were huge, terrible black rocks. The echo is very good. Each of us started to yell, producing a roaring of extraordinary volume.

A guide took us, and at each second it seemed that we were at the end of the road. We thought it must be endless, but the guide showed us a tremendous cave, humid, majestic, terrible.

But having reached a ladder, all the group hesitated. In fact, this almost vertical ladder descended through a small and narrow opening; it was not very inviting. I insisted that we must go, and after my harangue I declared that I'd go alone even if nobody else came. All those people raised their arms to the sky and, excited, started to shout, "It's impossible! Your mother won't permit it. It would be death. Nobody will go." They started to beg, to howl, to moan, to cry, being exasperated and in despair, when I stopped in the middle of my descent, leaning calmly on the redoubtable ladder and laughing about their terrors. I was laughing because they looked like the chorus of Druids from *Norma* when they ask for her burning. Paparigalo dared to continue rolling his eyes almost out of their sockets. His mantle opened, his hooked nose rose (which never before had seemed so immense). I took pity on them, not wanting to have an argument, and returned to the Druids, swearing to myself that I'd never go again with this kind of hippopotamus. It would be better to go with the family than in such company!

The impassable passages are marvels where one hangs on with all four paws, closed in on both sides, or else there is a wall of rock on one side and a river on the other, narrow, swift, black, and slippery. But I also saw some deep caverns where the stalactites make bizarre faces—sometimes the virgin and child, or even an old man with a long beard, or even a repentant Magdalene; the organ pipes of a church; sometimes a palm tree or an enormous flower with extraordinary leaves like laundry hung out to dry. Its leaves and curtains were transparent, and I stopped.

I went to see the light of the guide in order to see these marvels. Some stairs, some rocks, seem to fall from the ceiling in stalactites, shining like diamonds. A little time ago I was on top of the mountain; then I was deep in the canyon that I was looking at from the top so recently. The people behind me were saying "Oh!" and "Ah!" endlessly.

I walked that way until the end, admiring, surprised, and slipping. Once I found myself sliding, and I was about to fall. There was nothing to hold on to. To scream would have been silly. Then, with great self-control, I just sat down. This way I was able to keep from falling into the water. At another time my umbrella almost jumped into the river. The grotto ends with a lake—not very large, but deep. We threw stones into it. And is that the end? Taking a boat, we could have continued, but we didn't dare to do that. We returned. I was very surprised to find myself again above the famous ladder, without having to climb it. That was because we went down and then came up by another way, without realizing it.

Unfortunately, I cannot describe this grotto. It would be such a pleasure to write a description of it—a full description of what I have seen. I admired everything a lot, but I know there must be more marvelous caves around here, without mentioning those in other countries where there are marvelous things that make our cave look like nothing. Besides, "We humiliate the masterpieces of Nature by imposing our approbation upon them."

I walked with Lambart in spite of a little rain. I was wet and muddy, climbing and then descending a mountain. Lambart drove; Body was in front, and behind us was the singer. Our return was admirable. In a village, Lambart pulled from a bed a white blanket and from the floor a rug. The rug was given to the others; they wrapped the blanket around Lambart and me, and they secured it with safety pins. My hat was not protected, and in the rain it began to take all kinds of shapes. I came back looking awful—wet, muddy—and I'd barely had time to undress when someone knocked at the door. There was the Greek. I ran away and came back in one of Mama's dresses. But then, instead of going to bed, I changed clothes. I put on the boots with satin straps, the grey dress, and the black hat, and I went to the Redoute with Mama and Dina. We told about the marvellous things I had done, and I began to look at myself with surprise. I danced.

The Baron did not approach us to invite me to dance, and I am vexed, as anyone would be. In fact, my mother, Dina, and I have nothing. My mother is an intelligent woman with experience; she is also very beautiful, but in a society conversation she is zero. She understands nothing of what men say to her, and very often she doesn't hear. Dina is not at all stupid, and as for me, I am too young. In fact, we are three people who think about nothing.

Gericke has changed a lot in the last week, since the departure of Bas. Or maybe it's since Mama's scolding. He avoids us. Walitsky says he behaves like a [in Russian] *fool*. He runs away, his eyes lowered. He almost never looked at me before this, but now it's worse. Tonight he came near us, or, rather, we called him; but he stayed with the ladies at the table d'hôte. Mama is sure she offended him, but really it was necessary. Yet I'm sorry we've lost him.

BOOK TWENTY-TWO

H. G. T. D. O. H.
Book 22
Begun Friday, July 24, 1874
Ended Friday, August 7, 1874
Maison Willem Lausberg, Spa

Friday, July 24, 1874. Since the Baron's change of attitude, Mama runs after him, calls him. It's annoying because he himself runs away. We went to the Square and met the Rows there. Then Mama called the Baron, and as the girls were coming to our house, by force Mama obliged Gericke to come in.

I think that the Count is in love with me, but in a sentimental and serious way. It's unfortunate for him because I feel nothing for him. Yesterday I was cruel, flirting with all the men except him and at the end giving him a flower, saying, "Count, do you want me to decorate you? The gentleman for whom the flower was prepared is gone."

"In that case I do not accept it; I don't like being a substitute. It's all or nothing," he answered.

"I'm sorry. Do you know 'all or nothing'? Well, you'll have nothing," and I turned away seriously.

I forgot to say that my poor [bulldog] Bagatelle died yesterday morning and that yesterday evening her death was my conversation piece and my laughing piece, too. All the men knew about it the day before yesterday and did not dare to let me know. I announced it to them myself, laughing. . . . I've not had a moment to regret this poor little animal. I'm afraid that tonight I'm going to cry about her.

Gericke has disappeared. We do not see him any more. I wonder why? The change started a few days before Bas left, and since then it went crescendo. Some said it was because of de Toulé. Mama scared me when she said that perhaps Gericke changed because he thinks that I am in love with him and that he did not want to encourage a useless love. This unfortunate idea had already occurred to me before she said anything about it. If it is that, I am desperate and tormented.

In the evening Mama sang an elegy, saying that the Count loves me but that at his age such a love is dangerous. She gave a deadly example. She said that this young poet told her that one of these days he is going to have a terrible sorrow, which he will probably not be able to endure; that one must have a lot of strength and courage to etc. They pretended that I became pale and blushed.

It is always agreeable to hear that someone loves you. I don't know why I said that. Probably it would be agreeable even if he died; pleasant for me because it would give me value. They can say what they want to, but I'll never believe that I've been able to inspire anything with my miserable little being. You could say that I think a lot of myself, but I don't have the courage to believe that a man loves me. I don't dare to believe it; I'm afraid to make a mistake and be ashamed afterwards.

Monday, July 27, 1874. But I must tell you about Bagatelle!

Bagatelle is not dead! She was run over by the coach on the day of the Promenade at Remouchamps. Paul got out of the carriage with her, and two of the wheels passed over the body of the poor unfortunate. Paul threw himself on the ground crying and almost passed out. Mama was crying. They threw the dog away into the forest, covering it with a paper so that I couldn't see it. All of this happened right in front of me. All of them were upset, and I, alone, was blind and deaf. I didn't see anything and didn't understand anything. . . . But I console myself. Three days later the coachman, passing by the same road, went to look, out of curiosity, and found Bagatelle perfectly alive. She had dragged herself to the road and was yelling for help. The man took her home with him and cared for her, and in a few days she will be as she was before. Walitsky had invented a story that Bagatelle had become ill, that he sent her to the vet, and that she died there.

Dina is in love, and she had an emotional outburst. Sometimes she is dreamy, and at other times ferocious, which makes her unpleasant. I talked with her about this and then talked with Mama, who told me that nothing is surprising, and that it was, at last, time. I answered that it is better when it happens early, that it is like a necessary illness, that the later it happens the more it is noticed and the more you suffer. It was yesterday that I said this to Dina in front of Mama. Then Dina started to say that I am also in love, but simply and naturally I told them the truth—that no one pleases me and that, when teasing me, they know very well that what they are saying is not the truth; that a man who could please me would be very different from all these people here. At last I told them everything but one; Dina, with a burst of delicacy this time, looked at me straight, asking, "Nobody?"

"Nobody. I absolutely don't know what you are implying."

"I know that the people here please you only a little because you are still in love with the same . . ."

"With whom?"

"Always the same one."

While I was riding, Lambart came to our house and talked in a strange way. He said Dina and I were badly brought up, that we don't know how to enter a drawing room, nor how to talk, nor how to leave, etc., etc., etc. Finally, he said so much that I would have thrown him out the door. But after his departure Mama agreed with him.

But this idea is solely this man's! What an impertinent fool! However, I would like to understand why he said these things.

Tuesday, July 28, 1874. I am solemn. It seems that my manners are awful, that I'm common, fast, etc. Since Lambart said what he did, Mama commented all day long on what he said.

For the last four months I have lived a very irregular life. I've stayed up late and got up late and made myself look very ugly—pale and feeble. I am at fault and should be severely punished.

Today I fainted several times, but in spite of that I dined at Orange.

Thursday, July 30, 1874. I've become so weak that the least movement tires me. Climbing the stairs is too much. I have some buzzings in the ears, and in short, I'm in a miserable state.

I'm going to try to recover. It's insupportable to be reconciled to such a condition.

It's beautiful—no sun, no rain—dream weather for horseback riding. I looked for Paul but couldn't find him, so I couldn't go riding. Around 8:00 the little Count came. I entered the salon wearing my hat and saying I was going to choose a carriage. He proposed to Walitsky that they accompany me. We all three came back to pick up Mama.

Mama and everybody else is on the side of this ugly Count. People think he is handsome, but that's not true. He's not bad-looking and not good-looking, either. That's all.

We entered the Casino and stayed there forty-five minutes. Father Mirzisky was introduced to me.

Reading the *Derby*, I saw Hamilton's name three times. I was red and biting my lips. Although the Count was talking to me, I was barely answering.

"And if we speak of things past?"

"Oh, yes, if those things were agreeable, we can talk about them with pleasure."

"But how can one know if it will be agreeable to you?"

"I don't know."

"Actually I want to talk with you about something I have already discussed with you. When may I?"

"When you wish to."

"Ah, then. The sooner the better."

"Well, I'll talk with you about it the next time we go riding."

"That's good."

It should be amusing, but because of that I hesitate to go with him. This courtship does not please me. He loves me. That's all right; I accept him as an adorer. He can be in the list of suitors. He is the first. He gave me a bouquet, and in exchange I gave him my rose. It did not have a stem. That's why I gave it; I couldn't hold it any more.

Later on I found that having given him a half-eaten rose was too much, and partially to obliterate this favor, I gave the bouquet to Mama.

I am in good health, although my eyes still have dark circles and I am still pale.

For a long time before today, we had not gone to the Promenade. Today it was for a distraction. We met the Countess Mirzisky alone under a tree. On the other side of the tree was Princess Margherita and her court.

I do not like the way the Count looks at me.

But what has happened to me? Every morning I wake up with a headache. To get up and walk from the table to the piano exhausts me. I have no grief, I desire nothing, I am as always. So where does this illness come from? Because it is illness. God, I beg you as before—help me, cure me, have pity on me! Let me be again as I was. I am weak, pale, ugly! My God, heal me, forgive me, have pity on me!

At the Casino, they said Gericke was there. I am delighted that I did not see him, although I was dying to. But maybe he thinks I am pale because of him. It's revolting!

Saturday, August 1, 1874. I am ugly as I have never been before. And I'm ashamed to appear with such a face.

At 3:00 we went out. Mama wore black velvet with white mousseline, trimmed with lavender point lace and silk, and a matching flowered hat. Dina was in black, very nice, and I in my silver-and-white, with a black hat. I am pale and ugly. The commissaries of the party were Messrs. Kean, Clark, Winslow, Body, Mirzisky, Angelle, and Paparigapoulo, who, vexed, did not come.

When crossing the street, we met Gericke, who bowed. Mama returned his greeting. I pretended I didn't see him. I am very well—white and pink. Later, at the ball, we were sitting in chairs next to those prepared for the Princess, and there were no other seats available. She arrived dressed as a Medici princess. The ball was animated by de Jabal, Mirzisky, and Paparigalo. They were our escorts. Gericke was in his corner with the English girls and seemed interesting to me. The Polish Count announced his departure to me.

"When?"

"Tomorrow."

"Where?"

"A two-day excursion."

"Why the day of the races?"

"That's true."

"And I was thinking of going to the races on horseback."

"I am sorry about it. Desperately."

"Why do you do something that makes you unhappy?"

"Often one must. . . . Let me tell you a little story. One day a young girl arrived in Spa with her family. On that same day a young man also arrived with his family. Since the young girl attracted the general attention from the first moment she arrived, the young man saw that this young girl was intelligent and educated and that she . . . I can't say this . . . ," he said.

I insisted on hearing the whole story.

"Oh, you insist. Well, she liked to turn and did turn the heads of everyone."

"How does one turn heads?" (I had not really understood; I was thinking of something else.)

"I mean just that."

"Oh, yes," I said. I finally understood.

"They met again and saw each other every day. The young man was more and more in love with the young girl. He had not yet finished his studies and didn't have the courage to return to school to finish them. But the young girl told him to leave. He did so and came back very happy to have finished, naturally, but when he came back he realized that the situation had changed.

"He decided to forget the young girl. He loved her, and because of that was acting cold and reserved—icy, glacial." (It is true.) "He decided to forget her and avoid her. How can I say what hours of melancholy and sadness he has passed! Of despair! I don't know. It would have to be in a language more flowery than mine to give you any idea of it. Now he thinks he may take a long journey to forget the young girl. I saw that unfortunate young man. Are you sorry for him, Miss?" His voice had become more and more emotional, and toward the end, he made some efforts to avoid trembling.

"If he is unhappy, I am sorry for him. I am sorry for all who are really unhappy."

"Do you pity him?"

"Yes," I said, in a light tone. "If he is unhappy."

"I saw him," the poor Count continued. "He told me he is leaving. What do you advise him to do? To leave or stay?"

At that moment Mama called me to go with her.

"Tell the young man to consult his heart," I told him, quietly shaking his hand. "Goodbye," and, without looking at him, I went out.

He was excited and had made great efforts to remain calm when speaking. I was sitting next to him, quiet and indifferent, without looking at him, but listening with an innocent expression.

I told Mama the story the Count had told me, and she said that we must not go to Ostend since he is going, too. But what silliness! I must oblige him to say directly that he loves me, that I am not yet convinced. I even said that, as a proof, I'd ask him to dance at the casino. Mama became indignant and said that that was mean, but I paid no attention to it; she said that, but thinks like me. . . . But he'll not do it. Why should I endure him if he doesn't do anything?

Tuesday, August 4, 1874. The two Mirziskys and Mama danced the Polish Mazurka, which I saw for the first time and which I found too wild. The woman and the man throw themselves against each other, and that gives me the desire to throw a bucket of cold water at them. I couldn't dance it even with a man I liked. You are in his arms all the time.

It's past 2:00 A.M. I'm like a locomotive; I am satisfied with myself. Hurrah for Worth! Laferrière is a cad. . . .

I am pale again. The color that brightened my face flew away. We went to the children's ball. I didn't have any supper; I don't feel well. I have a pain in the left side of the chest, but then it was only for a few moments. Since yesterday this pain has never stopped. If I die, I'll burn my journal. I would be very sorry to die, but if I cannot live as I wish, I will die. One or the other. My God, I'm only fifteen!

I dressed with difficulty. Paul the scapegrace, played and won 400 francs, and took a loge for us. I felt so uncomfortable this time that I unfastened my blouse. My sickness returned, and I cried behind the curtain. (We were in a stage box.)

Friday, August 7, 1874. Every day I wake up with blue bags under my eyes, and my eyes and skin are dry, crepey. I'm very ugly. Walitsky says that my trouble is some trouble with a nerve; that it's not heart disease or cancer.

Anyway, I'm ugly.

I've been able to prolong our stay in my dear, dear Spa until Tuesday. I'm having trouble parting with my dear and second Baden.

BOOK TWENTY-THREE

H. G. T. D. O. H.
Book 23
Begun Saturday, August 8, 1874
Ended Wednesday, September 16, 1874
At London Court, Spa
Friday, August 14, 1874
Hotel de France, Apartments 8-9, Ostend

Saturday, August 8, 1874. [Spa] I've always had the idea that I'd never be loved.

He [the Count] stays awake, he doesn't eat, he writes at night, he has nervous spells, and his mother complains about it every day to Mama. I always treated him worse than a dog. It's also true that sometimes I looked at him, but it seems that my looks didn't do anything. He loves me. Walitsky has said that I am at fault—that I made eyes at him. But that's not true. It is because it is. [He loves because he loves.] And besides, I feel no remorse of any kind.

He no longer has the bad manners for which I reproached him; he has improved. He is quiet, even beseeching.

Poor boy! I say that the way it's found in books and at the theater. But I've not once been sorry for him, and I still am not.

Sunday, August 9, 1874. Day after day I'm feeling better. Walitsky gave me some quinine pills. They said that I had a fever.

The Count was supposed to leave this morning, but he stayed because yesterday I said to him, "I'm not inviting you to come riding because you always find some *if's* and *but's*."

At 3:00 he was at our house, but Walitsky forbade him to ride because this morning he again had a hysterical fit. He didn't dare to refuse, saying that Miss Marie would be angry. I sent him a very gracious message, saying that he didn't have to ride and that I'd not be angry.

At 4:00 I got on my horse to ride with Paul to pay my farewells to my dear Spa for which I feel a particular tenderness. Mama and Dina were in the carriage to drive the Count to the Vivianis' home. I followed them. On the hillside near the Villa, I stopped the horse, called the Count to come back and gave him the bridle to hold; holding my riding-whip between my teeth, I fixed my hat. This made him happy and did not cost me anything. He squeezed my hand harder than usual, and I raised my eyes to him, which I do not always do.

I was going all the time without saying anything. I was thinking, even dreaming. I would have received a declaration of love with pleasure. I was saying goodbye to this second Baden. I even thought about Gericke and all our excursions when we were with the bataclan. I regretted, I galloped.

Tonight the two princesses and members of the two courts were at the theater. Not a loge was available in the balcony. I was obliged to take four places in the center loge. And I was very uncomfortable placed there. All the Plobsters [men who remind Marie of the Duke of Hamilton: wealthy, titled, worldly, a bit overweight] were at the theater. We saw *The Voyage of M. Perrichon*, a charming play very well performed. Each time Doria [Doria Pamphilii, Marie's current exemplary "Plobster"] made his way to his seat, Mama and I, and even Dina would say, "Good Plobster." I was not too furious about our bad seats, but it was a lost evening with so many society people present while we were buried in the center there.

Thursday, August 13, 1874. I haven't written anything since Monday, but I believe I can remember everything:

On Monday we packed at 6:15. We took the horses with bells, and in spite of the rain, Dina and I said farewell to darling Spa, wearing our "conspirator" raincoats.

If people wanted to gossip about us, they could: two young girls going to a stable, taking a two-horse carriage with bells and driving away without a coachman or servant, stopping at a candy shop [for] some jam and at a café for bread and cheese, and in a heavy rain going into the countryside. As the horses were running, the bells jingled noisily.

However, nothing whatever was wrong. I took all the paths that cross between the meadows, the woods, and the fields. I said that if Mama or Walitsky were with us they would be dead of fear or screaming and yelling to see how I took the curbs of the roads I passed by. I made our brave horses climb the most difficult hills at a fast trot. The rain finally stopped, and we were back home by 9:00 in the evening. I drove everywhere it was possible to pass, and even where it was difficult to do so. I looked at and said farewell to all the trees, all the paths, and all the hills. I like this Spa so much—this so-called "hole"!

On Tuesday, it was raining the way it was when we arrived in Spa. And we are again at the Hotel Europe as we were at the beginning in Spa. They wakened me and told me that Mirzisky is here. I thought it was a joke, but when I went to breakfast, I saw him in the lobby. He had brought me two live crawfishes in a green candy jar. Poor Count! If another man had done what he did I would have been delighted, but I don't like him.

At 2:00 the omnibus that brought us was taking us away. I looked right and left not to miss one instant of Spa.

Mirzisky brought us bouquets and stayed in the rain until the train left. Well, in Spa I made my first conquest! Spa will be my best memory except Baden. I am struck by the truth of the saying, "Our sweetest pleasures are in our memories."

Friday, August 14, 1874. [Ostend—after a stop in Brussels] My aunt is coming because Mama wrote to her that I was dying.

There are a good many people here from Nice . . . and I think I am going to have to endure Bas. We saw her yesterday after the bath. I stayed home. I feel almost well.

I'm glad my aunt is here. I think this is the first time we have been apart three-and-a-half months. At the time she should have kissed me, she stood and stared. I said, "Look at me; I am dead!"

Saturday, August 15, 1874. I am alive again and in the best of health, thank God. What a joy! And I have the beginnings of a pink complexion. My aunt is a woman with poise; she is elegant, the way I like.

No one can reproach her for stinginess or for a lack of dignity. For anything.

Mama tells us that the Plobster who looked so much at us in Spa in the theater is the Count Doenhoff, the chief at the court in Prussia. He has been introduced to her, as have some others, including the Princess Karageorgevitch (of Serbia), who has two little princes of twelve and thirteen years old. She and I hope he will introduce Margherita's Plobsters. She [Princess Margherita] will arrive the day after tomorrow.

Tuesday, August 18, 1874. Here in Ostend I get up earlier and feel fine. But I am in a rage that everybody has conspired to tell me that I am pale, and I cry thinking about it!!!!!

My God! Am I already so pale? And to add to that, Mama was telling her worries and said that I am pale and that when anyone tells me so I become angry! It's enough to die of rage.

They exasperate me talking about this Count. Walitsky talks about him all the time, and his barbarities drive me to tears. And he also mentions Doria Pamphilii, but I laugh at that. They asked me how it happens Doria is a Plobster, not being fat nor red, and being an Italian. Mama finds him handsome.

Wednesday, August 19, 1874. Once I was talking vaguely of octopuses and the Pole asked me if I wanted some. Yes, I answered and forgot about it. This morning the bellboy entered and brought me a beautiful big shell full of them. We told the boy to tell the Count to come upstairs. I was writing and did not get up nor turn my head until I was finished, even to sealing the letter and writing the address. He was expecting a reaction, and there was none. I am like everybody else; I take advantage where I can. But to thank him I gave him several letters to mail.

Bas is running after the Count and wants to grab him at any price. She knows whom he loves and she wants him. It's funny; she's thirty and I'm a puppy of fifteen. She won't get him.

Tuesday, August 25, 1874. As we were leaving, I started to be sad again, the way I was a year ago. I remained preoccupied for hours, alone, as long as they left me alone. All my intimate thoughts consisted of doubts and reassurances. Often it seems to me that I love no one, and then I feel the opposite, like today. I cry and laugh all at the same time, and I have that inexplicable feeling, extraordinary and strange. Could it be true love? I don't know. But I feel it only when I see, think about, or talk about the Duke.

Thursday, August 27, 1874. Florence [Foster] and I went bathing in the ocean. She told me some things about the royal family, and that the Duke's wife is very jealous. While I was swimming in the Atlantic, I saw Mirzisky and the new Plobster looking at me; I floated because of that. I got out of the water, sat on the steps, and had three buckets of water thrown on my feet. All our friends now use the term "Plobster."

At home I was scolded with all kinds of humiliating words. I may some time forget, but I'll never forgive.

Friday, August 28, 1874. All of us went to the beach for dinner, but I ate nothing. I must be sick. I am weak and sometimes fainting.

Monday, August 31, 1874. Today I was tricked: I was fixing my hair when someone knocked on the door. I saw an elderly man and guessed who he was. I rushed to the door, which was closed. I hid under the sofa. It was the king's doctor, whom they wanted me to see against my will. Finally I came out and he examined me. He declared me anemic, not having found anything. He is an imbecile; I know my illness better than he. I've been tired for four months. I need a month to recover, that's all.

Only I'm in a rage because they dare to think I'm ill. I treat them like dogs. I would have hit him with a cane in cold blood.

Tuesday, September 1, 1874. [Marie prepares to leave, and she treats Count M. more kindly, dancing with him and allowing him to buy some cakes for Mama.] He is so happy that he gives himself airs like a butterfly.

Wednesday, September 2, 1874. I am homesick. I want to return to Nice. I am tired of this life. I feel so good in Nice. I want to see the promenade again, our villa, the October rains, Place Masséna, the quays, the Public Gardens, the London House—everything, in a way. I feel an extreme pleasure imagining I am there, but just now I am going to London in order not to melt in Nice. The Count comes and goes. I went to the pier with my aunt. I am very much bored in Ostend, but the concert at the Kursaal was magnificent.

Thursday, September 3, 1874. I weep for Ostend as I wept for Spa. I regret leaving it enormously.

I walked with Mirzisky, telling him that my aunt, Dina, and I were inviting him to come with us to London, and he had the nerve to refuse. . . .

Sunday, September 6, 1874. As we departed, I was gay from sadness. I told Mama goodbye and, when kissing Paul, I said to him, "Don't do anything evil." Mama was trying to hear what I was saying. He is a lost boy. I pity him and sometimes wish I were wrong. The boat was heaving and little by little the faces of Mama, Paul, Walitsky, and the little Count (who never stopped looking, poor soul!) faded away. As a farewell, I simply held his hand and said goodbye.

We passed the Kursaal, the hotels, the sand. Then, bored, I went downstairs to look for a book; but as soon as I was in the cabin, I felt sick and was obliged to go to bed until we arrived at Dover, which seemed to me very beautiful. My aunt was furious, but I don't know what about.

We wanted to go to Canterbury, but my aunt argued that the Howards wouldn't want us, that they had almost mistreated us in Nice last winter, and other things like that; I had to ask myself why all my pleasures, all my trips are ruined. They do what I want, go where I want, give me what I desire, but first they embitter me about everything, making it sad so that I almost never enjoy anything.

Ordinarily I don't look out the windows, but in England I watched all the time, admiring the well-kept land and the beautiful trees. It seemed to me that I was coming home instead of going to a foreign country for the first time. Finally I saw a number of little houses, all alike and far away—a huge city. It was London—the realization of all my wishes in travel!

Arriving at Charing Cross, I was perfectly happy; while being driven to the Hotel Alexandria, I looked right and left with the growing satisfaction one feels when seeing again what belongs to one and what one knows and likes. I recognized all the places without asking anyone. I entered the hotel as if I were entering my own home. Everything was entrancing—the service and, above all, the foods. Never have I been served so well; everything was excellent, and I was surprised to find the things I've missed, not knowing that they existed.

Monday, September 7, 1874. We had lunch absolutely as I like. Then, taking a four-wheeled carriage, we went to the Tower of London; we saw everything there, but it's unnecessary to talk about that. However, I must say that I found everything better than I had expected. I am so enthusiastic that I don't know where to start!

Even the overcast weather pleases me. I had expected to find Paris admirable, and I did; but something is missing there. I did not find it sufficient, feeling it should be better; I was not satisfied.

But London is the way I dreamed it would be. It is the best. It has everything. It is completely my ideal—all the houses, the squares, the monuments, the churches are perfect. They come together in me the way an empty space in a jewel case receives the jewel for which it has been specially made. I am absolutely satisfied and do not wish or imagine anything more beautiful, more great, more magnificent, rich or superb, more grandiose or surprising, imposing, extraordinary, sympathetic or ravishing, more astonishing than London.

I live, I desire, I breathe! I feel I have blood in my veins, a brain in my head, and ambition, pride, and willpower in my soul. I'll hope and pray. If God wants. . . .

When I was in Ostend, Nice appealed to me; but now, from London, it repulses me. I understand that Miss Collignon adores the English people and England and that she was almost impertinent, but that her good breeding prevented her from being very impertinent with the donkeys who talk badly about this country. From now on there is only England for me. My only desire and my constant prayer will be to become as English-like as possible.

Wednesday, September 9, 1874. We visited Westminster Abbey and St. Paul's and all kinds of monuments. What antiquity! What majesty! Among other things I admire the architecture—so solid, massive, gracious, and rich. In the palaces of the continent I missed this beautiful ancient architecture.

I would like to see some London men. There is not another nation in the world that carries the stamp of distinction peculiar to the English people, their manners and their features. Nothing pleases me so much as to see handsome men, especially Englishmen.

Unfortunately, I have become very ugly.

I have such strong heartbeats that I am afraid they can be heard. They sound in my back, but principally in my right ear so that they keep me from falling asleep and bother me when I'm writing. I think I'm going to take some iron. My condition is annoying, and it frightens me. I've slept very little since I've been studying—no more than seven hours, and often only six at the beginning. But what has definitely hurt me is that during all my trip, since the sixth or seventh of May I never went to bed before 1:00 or 2:00, and very often it was not until 3:00 in the morning. And in fact I am picking the fruit of this beautiful life: I am weak; I don't climb ten stairs without being breathless and finding my heart beating the way it was when I found the Duke of Hamilton behind me at the pigeon shoot. I am pale, ugly, rumpled, unattractive. Now I am starting to go to bed at a better time, especially in London, but what can three days of good do against four months of bad!

We went to Brown's and then visited the Crystal Palace, in spite of my aunt's screaming.

It is only in England that there is anything to see. I had a hard time detaching myself from these statues and busts that represent the ancient Romans, which I like very much. I am crazy about the ancient world and romance and history when I find myself in a museum, because there everything represents the subjects of mythology or history.

Saturday, September 12, 1874. We left London at 4:20, I with all the regrets imaginable, arriving at Canterbury by 6:00. Mrs. Howard recognized us, and we jumped from the carriage, already in front of the house. She ran toward us and then all the children. Lise has become prettier than Hélène, who loses a lot in her presence.

Wednesday, September 16, 1874. We stayed with the Howards Sunday, Monday, and Tuesday until 4:00. I did not write anything at their house, and here today I am in Paris; I am going to write about these days all together.

On Sunday, we saw the Cathedral with Hélène and Lise. I read with a great satisfaction and a stronger and firmer belief the prayers, so wise, so just, so suitable to each circumstance of life, to each desire of the human heart, to most ordinary things for which very often I don't dare to pray. I want such a book to read each evening. I'll ask Lise or Hélène what it is called and have it sent to me. I find many beautiful and good things in it, so natural that they do not seem impossible.

I think that having such services and such books—in a word being a Protestant—one cannot be mean unless one is stupid or criminal, by order of God born that way. . . .

Monday went like Sunday. They showed us their factory. . . . On Tuesday at 4:00 we left. Everybody came to the station to see us off, and Hélène and Lise came with us as far as Dover. They have been very kind.

Only, at their house my eyes were swollen, and I had a headache. I really do not know what is happening to me, I'm in such a bad state.

We stayed all night at Dover and took the boat the next day.

Not to find France so ugly after England I am reading the *Odyssey* and have found a part which makes me laugh. It's where Vulcan catches Mars and Venus in a net and all the gods come running and laughing to see them. We are staying at the Hotel des Îles Britanniques. I am eating a soup and writing.

Mama left us a letter in which she says that Uncle Émile is dead. I think I'll wear mourning for six weeks. Mama and my aunt are in mourning, and I, alone, would be in color.

PROMENADE DES ANGLAIS, 55 BIS, NICE

BOOK TWENTY-FOUR

Book 24
Begun Thursday, September 17, 1874
Finished Monday, October 26, 1874
Hotel des Îles Britanniques, Paris
After October 1, Promenade des Anglais, 55 bis, Nice

Thursday, September 17, 1874. [Paris] On the boulevards we met Mrs. Sapogenikoff with the deacon. After talking with them, we continued our errands. To see all of the known faces is a tremendous pleasure for me.

We went to the opera this evening. . . . I can do nothing but praise my aunt; she does everything I ask her to and even anticipates my wishes.

Friday, September 18, 1874. In the Bois we saw that boy I like from Nice, Émile Audiffret.

Tuesday, September 22, 1874. Mama writes that my request for the pavilion has been ignored, that my maid has been lodged upstairs, and that my study is a dining room! But I shall return. . . .

Sunday, September 27, 1874. All of our acquaintances talk to me only about my paleness. I do everything I can about it. My God, make me pink and fresh again! I am already better, but what was done during four months cannot be undone in one week!

I have no wish to go to Nice; I like Paris *so* much! As for London—I couldn't endure the smoke. Everything was smoky, and here I see Paris clear and bright.

This dress by Worth, so young, so simple, so elegant, so noble and absolutely right, tells me I like Worth best. Laferrière lacks the loftiness and the completely right touch. I've never been able to imagine a cocotte dressed by Worth, whereas the dresses by Laferrière have a certain cocotte elegance about them. I wept upon wearing my grey dress for the first time when it had a black train because I looked so much like one of those women. Since that first day the train is gone, but the dress keeps enough of this air that when I wear it people stare at me in a way that I dislike. So I prefer Worth; their dresses are impressive in spite of their simplicity, which I want.

Saturday, October 3, 1874. [Nice] [Upon returning to Nice, Marie learns that her grandfather has been duly installed in what she had assumed would be her house, the pavilion.] I am crying, not for the pavilion, because now I don't care about it, but because they made me dislike it. . . . From the first day it pleased me, and in my mind I was making a thousand projects to furnish it. I planned my study for downstairs and my bedroom for the room with a balcony, looking out over two terraces and a view on the Promenade and the sea from its five windows—all these were pleasing and amusing to me. Now everything is spoiled, destroyed!

I know very well that I can do what I want, *if* I want to; but I don't want to do what I had planned anymore. I cry because they destroyed all my projects . . . turned me from all that by a few things they said . . . made me dislike it in spite of all the great desire I had for it. I don't want it, or the horse; I don't want the rooms. Besides, Grandpa would be sad about it. Now the only thing that pleases me is the annex we planned to build.

But when? There is no money and there is no annex. There is no horse. The furniture has cost 50,000 francs, and the annex will cost as much to be furnished.

Everything is upside down, poisoned.

My aunt alone is good. She doesn't spoil anything for me; she truly cares for me, and not with words alone. She makes me take iron. She has just hung some tulle to prevent the mosquitoes from biting me. In Paris, she ordered a bathtub when the others only talked about it, declaring that I was sick, fainting, dying! My God forgive me if I am unjust. I say *if* because I am so sad that I can't see what is right.

I feel most miserable, and at the same time I think of how many unfortunate people there are, really unhappy, next to whom I and my annoyances are foolish. Then I pray God to forgive me because I am capricious and guilty.

Sunday, October 4, 1874. Mrs. Sapogenikoff and Mr. Yourkoff arrived. He has been coming here since Mama got back, but she came for the first time. Consequently, we showed her the houses. They stayed all day with us until it was time to return to Monaco, where they are living. It is one of my greatest pleasures to entertain at home, to dine in intimacy here. I am perfectly happy when a guest eats and is comfortable in our home. Above all, I like to receive those who are in need. It's important to show an extreme delicacy to the people you oblige, to help them forget their sad state and treat them as if it is we who are honored. Rarely can we expect gratitude; many do not forgive the kindness of others. I don't understand that. If you are proud and obliged to receive help, you should try to return the kindness without hating your benefactor. If you return meanness for kindness, you are not proud, but cowardly.

Tomorrow I'll organize my room before I receive the furniture, and I'll arrange my study somewhere, and I'll look for my teachers. Since I came back I have felt guilty not to have done anything, and I'll not feel comfortable until I establish the schedule of my interrupted occupations again.

I haven't spoken about my dogs, the divine Prater and the good Bagatelle. They follow me everywhere. I was so happy to see them again, especially Prater, my good, old, faithful, beautiful, intelligent, unique dog. I protect and pet Bagatelle because nobody caresses her. She must have been really unhappy during my absence.

Monday, October 5, 1874. How spoiled I am! How unappreciative I am, and I dare to complain! How mean I am! And how good and loving are those around me! I really don't deserve so much.

Grandpapa is often quite irritating with his complaints. He prevents me from playing the piano when he says things like, "What's she playing now? How awful!"

All my books are unpacked and set in a room on the third floor. I'll use that as a classroom until a better time. In spite of my despair the other day, I hope I'll have what I wanted and don't want anymore. Dining in the pavilion is really uncomfortable and ugly, and when winter comes, during the rainy season, it will be easy to see the inconvenience of these trips back and forth between the houses to transport the meals.

Tired of putting my books in order, I went out in the carriage to do some errands. I went into the Ferrara music shop to buy the Verdi *Requiem* score when I saw Audiffret and his friend, Saëtone. Both of these "heroes" stayed for a while to look at us. As for the music, Grandpapa finds it very gloomy, and his feeling about it prevents my working on it.

Wednesday, October 7, 1874. With the books and my chemistry materials put away in three closets, I covered the four walls of my room with my sketches of Dina and myself.

Mama had a very strange headache, which forced her to go to bed, suffering terribly, screaming, and crying; and my face, in spite of my efforts not to let it express my pity, fears, and anxiety, revealed my terror as she rolled on the floor with pain. I pulled myself together immediately and, when anyone else was there in the room or when Mama was looking at me, nothing could be read in my face. Because of that, I am accused of insensitivity and selfishness. This hurts my feelings, but I prefer these wounds made by ignorant people to the expressions on the faces of my aunt and Dina. Dina even exaggerates: she lets her lower lip hang, frowns, has her eyes bulging more than necessary, yells, and runs eagerly to the nurse. . . . It irritates me. So when they ask me, "How's your mother?" I say, "She's fine. It's only a headache."

After Fortuné went with his big eyes to tell George, and George went to tell Papa, they were both shouting and bawling. Then I went downstairs calmly, majestically, and asked, "What's the matter? What's all the shouting about?"

Seeing me so calm, George accused me of insensibility and went out, saying that we will kill Mama. I came back with him and stayed a little while with her. She feels better.

Friday, October 9, 1874. I dressed (grey dress, my hair braided and fixed with a little comb and hat from Ostend), and I roamed around Nice in a carriage with my aunt. I bought *The Women of the Bible* and *Don Quixote* and the works of Byron and Shakespeare. Afterwards we went to Laussel, who gave me the same music schedule as last year.

Tomorrow I am going to make my schedule for my studies, and on Monday I'll call on all these teachers to fix their days and times.

My aunt joins me every evening when I go to my room, stays seated on a box (there's no furniture in my room), and watches me while I write. Then she fixes the mosquito netting to prevent my being bitten, blows out the candle, and [says] goodnight.

Saturday, October 10, 1874. Grandpapa irritates me by talking all the time about Monaco and having a certain tone of voice that I think unsuitable concerning the "pilgrimages" Mama and my aunt make to that place. I withdraw to my room and finish my supper there.

Papa told Mrs. Daniloff that my aunt is losing a lot of money.

"So what?" I asked. "It's her money."

Papa said that part of this money was his. I was revolted that he could say such a thing in front of Mrs. Daniloff, that we are living on his money! It's a lie. It would also be a lie to say that he lives on our money. I returned to my room.

My bedroom is being finished with blue satin, and I'm afraid that we'll be talked about because all the other bedrooms are so simple. Mrs. Howard will hate me and will not fail to gossip about me with a tone of kindness and condolence for the family. Really! When I was thirteen, people were already talking about me. I had enemies.

As soon as I arrived in Nice, I was noticed and spoken of in different ways. Mrs. Patton, that good, kind, teasing, gossiping woman, that blabbermouth, was busy after me.

Poor Patton! Because of his lack of character, he damages himself, and others, too. If he hadn't been Consul, nobody would have known about our lawsuit. After all, there are many families who are suing for money.

He made our lawsuit a public affair. . . . But I have been *somebody* since I was thirteen. I *so much* wish that I could become someone in particular.

We went to the music. There's nobody yet in town except the little Audiffret, who was, as usual, walking in front of the carriages, looking and making himself seen. One has to admit that he is very handsome. I am the first to agree to that. But he walks with a slouch, imitating Hamilton. This morning he had the audacity to dress in grey, with yellow boots, and to walk like Hamilton. He has his clothes made larger than he needs to, to look bigger, or else he's gained weight. I blushed, but he doesn't please me.

From time to time I sing the Verdi *Requiem*, which I am crazy about.

The day before yesterday Lambart stopped here for an hour. He is witty, and in spite of his age is absolutely like a young man, energetic and healthy. Oh, if Dina could become Mrs. Lambart—for me he is too old and unimportant, but for her such a marriage would be magnificent, as Foster said.

Dear Dina is nineteen. She is without beauty and has no chic and only a mediocre body. I'm wrong, she has a beautiful body, and her hair is light ash blond and falls to her knees.

Mrs. Sapogenikoff and Yourkoff stayed for the day with us and went to the theater with Mama and Mrs. Angel, who dined with us. She is a Russian lady of thirty-three. She is beautiful, elegant, and witty, and has magnificent hair. Mrs. Angel is a painter and a musician. During dinner, Mr. Yourkoff and she discussed the effects of Love, the power of Woman over men, and also the power of the mind, of beauty, etc.

I was listening with attention for two reasons. First, their conversation could be instructive, and second, if it should be silly and empty, I could learn from the talk of ignorant people what not to say. What she said was more instructive than otherwise.

When they left for the theater, I went to look for George, who was drunk. He had slapped Mrs. Prodgers' face at Monte Carlo. I am the only one who can stay with this drunkard; with me he is calm and proper.

When they returned, Mama and my aunt and Mrs. Sap. and Yourkoff found us sitting face to face at a well-served table and singing, which amused them enormously. When he gets irritated, I give him something to drink and talk with him, as his condition requires. By refusing him any drink, they make him furious and don't sober him up at all, and he gets violent and creates a scandal. At midnight I succeeded in putting him to bed. To come here in all his drunkenness—why shouldn't he go to his mistress instead?

All this irritates and makes me sad; I like so much to have things correct and right, and this man changes our home into a cabaret.

With Sapogenikoff, we were five women, all in our white robes. Yourkoff said simple white is best for a woman. Because he and Walitsky were there, it was like a family; besides, Yourkoff is a man who can be looked at as a woman because of his engagements and his friendship with Mrs. Sapogenikoff.

Tuesday, October 20, 1874. Mama said that she was disgusted to see me blush when I saw Audiffret. *So was I* [in Russian].

But is it my fault?

George is still drinking and I am indignant. And the lessons are bothering me. They are not yet scheduled, and my conscience is hurting.

Wednesday, October 21, 1874. Another day toward old age. What a villainy!

All five of us drove around in the carriage until 11:30. I will say nothing of the beauties of Nature in Nice because "We humiliate Nature's masterpieces by imposing our approval upon them."

Thursday, October 22, 1874. Today I took my first lessons in Italian and Latin. I was wearing my white robe, and my mother did a nasty thing to me! It's a thing I'll never forget the distaste of and the disgust and horror of. I scolded her. I was rightfully indignant and would have loved to crush her with the words she said to me: [In Russian:] "Get dressed. It's shameful! You can seduce a 100-year-old teacher. Just recently a seventy-year-old man seduced a young girl. Someone may insult you." That's what she said to me! I'll not tell you what I felt when I heard this. . . .

I fixed my hair in such a poetic manner that I would like to have someone to show it to. I am beautiful tonight, and that conviction makes me happy and gives a special radiance to my joyous and fresh face. Is it Nice or the iron I'm taking? Anyway, be blessed, Nice, because in Nice I'm in good health and beautiful.

Saturday, October 24, 1874. Winter is coming and my troubles are starting again. It is painful to write this. For a moment I had forgotten our life, our miserable life! My God, let me beg you as I did years ago; let me ask you not what I did then, but now simply to live in this society. I don't ask anything extra; I only ask to be like everybody else.

Miss Collignon has arrived. She will be staying in Cannes this winter. She wants—she wants many things. Papa is all upset by this visit. His old feelings come back, and I predict all kinds of scenes we may have later on due to the sudden appearance of this belle with the long hair.

I find her very agreeable, intelligent, and sympathetic. If it were not for this unfortunate history of Grandpapa's interest in her, I wouldn't ask for any other teacher. She may have been the ornament of each house where she has taught, but there is always some unfortunate gossip about others.

There has been an argument between Mrs. Sapogenikoff and Yourkoff because of a letter from her daughter, in which she told her mother that Yourkoff is betraying her and that he is ungrateful for such love as he has received. Mary Sap. despises Yourkoff because he threw Stephen out of the house. (I mentioned him in my diary in Geneva.) She is in love with Stephen, and when things started to go too far, Yourkoff expelled him. From these facts, Mary hates Yourkoff and uncovered or invented his unfaithfulness to her mother, who does not hide the feeling she has for this gentleman.

Collignon is staying at our house.

Monday, October 26, 1874. We have started to see some new faces; it's the beginning of the season.

Nina and Yourkoff [nicknamed "Paris" by Nina's daughters, recalling the Trojan who carried off Helen] are to stay here tonight together. Ange (Mrs. Angel) took tea with us and played.

Papa was saying that the playing was not well done; and when Paris sang, Papa remarked that without a voice a song is worthless. I was trying to say something under my breath, and he told me to go to the devil and sent everything to the dogs. I don't know whether he has ever had any intelligence.

BOOK TWENTY-FIVE

H. G. T. D. O. H.
Book 25
Begun Tuesday, October 27, 1874
Finished Wednesday, November 18, 1874
Promenade des Anglais, 55 bis, in my villa, Nice.

Tuesday, October 27, 1874. I'm taking all the classes I need, and I am satisfied.

At dinner Papa was complaining and yelling, "See here, I don't cost you too much. Once a month my shirt is washed. . . ."

When I heard that lie I had the impudence to say, "How strange it is, Papa, that when no one is here you say that we pay for you, whereas when there is the least stranger here you say that we live on your money!"

When he should have stayed silent before this truth, he started to scream with all his strength that I'm a liar. And he began to call me all kinds of dirty names—vulgar and impertinent.

I went pale with rage, but forcing myself to smile, I went on to say, "I'm not lying"; and I repeated his own words in front of Daniloff [Book 24, *Saturday, October 10*]. How astonished I was at such cowardice and audacity! He shouted louder and insulted me, my family, my birth, my grandfather, and my father; he said every possible cruel, hurtful, insulting thing to destroy my self-esteem and my pride, especially about my name and my birth. A person can stand anything except that.

Finally I said, "I know why you dare to mistreat me this way: I talked badly about Collignon. Please know that I have no interest in favoring or preventing your marriage. I am foreign to you, and I have no inheritance rights. You don't need to persecute me for that." Then he changed his tone, after having called me a slut and some other names worse than that.

Then he cried, screaming that he was an unhappy man. "What have I come to, and who is it that insults me? A slut of Bashkirtseff's."

I didn't call him names as he had done to me because my tongue would have been ashamed to pronounce such words, even as my pen is ashamed to write them; but I called him a rake and told him he was drunk and said I didn't want to talk with him.

Mama's headache got worse and Ange and Daniloff came to console her. Ange [Mrs. Angel: from Wednesday, November 4: "I call her Ange not because she looks like one, but because her name is Angel and Ange is shorter and can be written without Mrs. Then Ange has the voice and the character rather of a hussar than of an angel."] showed a lot of compassion for Mama, caressing her and caring for her.

Sunday, November 1, 1874. I didn't go to church, but this religious Dina went with her hair curled in front, being sure to show the most golden locks at the back of her head. Here is a woman who will pass her life in Church and in bed.

Monday, November 2, 1874. I didn't miss my lessons, and I am satisfied. Appetite comes while we are eating, and the love for study when we are studying. I had begun to despair, thinking it would be difficult for me to resume; but I see with pleasure that that is not the case and that with the help of God everything will be as before, or maybe better.

Tuesday, November 3, 1874. Why the devil am I not so good-looking in the day as in the evening? When I looked at myself a while ago in the mirror as I fixed my hair, took my tea, and read and wrote, I was, I dare to say it, quite beautiful. My ears were very pink, the cheeks, too; my mouth was bright red and moist, my teeth little, white, and shiny. And my eyes were brighter than ever, my eyebrows well-marked, contrasting with the forehead, which is whiter than usual tonight. My hair is in disorder, but not untied; owing to this disorder I had two curls around my face, giving me a poetic look. Yes, except for the nose (which is very tolerable, in fact), I would not wish to have another face than the one I have tonight.

Actually, I am satisfied with everything, or at least I have the most brilliant hopes about the villa, the arrangements, everything. In fact, it seems to me that the world is mine when I am pretty. With a kind of satisfaction I saw a double row of carriages in front of the Public Gardens and realized that many of the habitués are here for the season. We even saw Audiffret again—once in a carriage and once on foot. This time I did not blush. He was wearing his tube hat. . . .

He stared at me again, right into my eyes. When he sees us, he seems not to want to lose one minute and looks with a furious happiness to see all that he can, giving the impression that he wants to examine one to the least detail. But God forgive me, I think I am talking about it entirely too often! Well, if his friend Saëtone were staring as this one does, I would talk about it, too. I am always flattered when looked at by anyone.

Wednesday, November 4, 1874. At Monaco we found a celebration for Monaco's Charles III's saint's day. There were fireworks, and the illumination was pretty. When we returned to the tables, Mama played with me, and we lost. I had two louis left. Then Walitsky played for me at 30-40, and I won 300 francs. Now I can get a beautiful gift for Dina and give each of the servants five francs fifty-one.

I must be writing badly tonight; I'm not at all in the mood, and it is with difficulty that I force myself to write. My hand is not steady. And now it's 3:00 and I'm tired.

Thursday, November 12, 1874. At dinner we were surprised by the sound of falling hail. I rushed downstairs to pick up the pearls of this darling hail and sent the servants out to look for more, and in two minutes I had two dishes full. I devoured them! With what love I looked at this snow! It made me feel so good, but who knows? Maybe by now some poor gardener is worried about his destroyed plants; his family cries about the lost crop of olives, and they are cursing this same hail!

One feels a certain joy in looking at the snow. It's not because I haven't seen any snow for a long time, but with the first snow in Russia there was always a certain feeling of lightness of the soul and also a gaiety of the heart. There we felt the need to jump, to move, to run in the sleigh and we came back with cheeks and nose stinging from the cold.

On the other hand, the first green grass produces a different effect—one is happy to see this greenery again after months of snow and cold, and grateful to see this white carpet disappear from the black soil. Then we'd like to run in the woods and do a thousand foolish things, running without touching the ground, but seeming to glide. . . . And at last, in this new greenery, there is a melancholy feeling that squeezes the heart and oppresses the soul. And we feel the need to love. How simple! I don't pretend to have understood that when I was in Russia, but now I affirm that I have felt it and now I understand it. Then, in Russia, what I felt was not the need to love but the need to roll in the new grass and to run to look for snowdrops.

But back to the hail in Nice: To cross the yard I had to put on my boots, as the ground was all white; and as it started to melt immediately, it was half ice, half water. In my joy, I took Porthos [her new mastiff] with me and Bagatelle, too. We dined together and then I lay down with Porthos-Carlos-Victor [other names for the mastiff] and, in that position, I slept until 10 P.M. Then I awoke and wrote these pages.

BOOK TWENTY-SIX

H. G. T. D. O. H.
Book 26
Begun Thursday, November 19, 1874
Finished Monday, November 23, 1874

Thursday, November 19, 1874. If you could know how I am boiling with anger inside! How tight my heart is! How many times tears come to my throat and suffocate me! Can anyone imagine a position like ours? It's this damned lawsuit—nothing else. But a lawsuit is not a crime. Why does everyone seem to avoid us? Today when we passed by the Masséna Quay, I felt one of the cruelest pains of my life: the two Teignettes, silly and newly rich, snubbed Mama even though she had seen them many times at the Howards'. She had looked at them, smiling, to bow to them, but they kept staring in front of themselves and did not look at us. Then Mama, fearing me, wanted to hide her salute and continued her smile, forced and pitiable, making believe she was looking into the boutique windows. I stared at her and saw, painfully, that she was afraid of what I'd say at this humiliation, because I've often told her how unhappy I am at the way we are treated. She suffers more than I because she knows how I feel, and my suffering burns her like fire. That smile tore my soul, and my heart was filled with all the atrocious things of this world. I breathed a sigh that was a roar. Oh, miserable me! Now I understand the anger that they describe in books. I understand all that I saw of various and puffed-up words. I understand, and I weep, O God.

Friday, November 20, 1874. The Countess Mirzisky was at our house today. I am so cold toward the Count that he understands and will leave next Sunday, I think. I never talk to him here. I can't explain these strange gentlemen to myself. Sometimes I detest a person at first sight, with no reason, but only because I cannot stand to see his face. There are few persons for whom I feel this aversion. I felt this for the Count four days after I met him in Spa. That is to say, that from the day I wrote, "The little Pole disgusts me" (and that to the highest degree), when anyone even spoke of him, I lost my appetite. I became excited and cried and would have liked to pull his hair in spite or anger. Since his arrival here, Walitsky has invited him often, especially for dinner. Then I become furious, covering my face with my two hands. I'd like to crush it. Then he says to Triphon, "When the man comes, throw him out." Then I smile, but I hide the smile in order not to lose my dignity.

There are even some moments when I don't want to read or write or play or eat because I am thinking that this man is doing the same thing, too; he is so odious to me. I would not breathe the same air as he if I could help it. I would like it if he would go away to live on the moon so that I wouldn't have to live on the same planet with him.

Saturday, November 21, 1874. We were going to see *The Brigands*, but due to my indisposition, I stayed home and started to write. The horrible and innocent Count passed the evening here, poor devil! I regretted not giving him the joy of seeing me. I restricted myself to some regrets, which is something for a wretch of that kind. Poor soul! It seems to me that human beings cannot have a soul, or rather, must not have one, because I would like to talk about this shell—no, this mollusk—in a special language in order not to soil the one I'm using.

I was so cold toward the Count that he decided to leave on Sunday.

Sunday, November 22, 1874. I have calculated badly, and here I am without anything to wear. The white wool from Laferrière has arrived, but the blouse is ruined. I am in a state of despair and beg my aunt to take me to Paris. It's not that she is opposed to going; it's the money . . . always the money! You can say what you like, but money plays a great part in our happiness. It's better to cry through gold than through iron. That's what Princess Nadine Galitzine used to say. She said that it's better to be unhappy with gold than without it, and there are those who don't have any who talk badly about it!

It is grey and cold, and I am cold and pink. I am comfortable in cold weather.

BOOK TWENTY-SEVEN

H. G. T. D. O. H.
Book 27
Begun Tuesday, November 24, 1874
Finished Thursday, December 24, 1874

Tuesday, November 24, 1874. I just read from my old journal, and I feared that my atrocious expression from that time would have slipped in here. I am far from being satisfied with my present style, but at least it is more French, more Christian. The other one is unbelievably bad.

Mama is sick in bed.

I finished reading Dumas, which was taking all my free time and even my busy time, it was so exciting. Now I'll be able to start some serious reading. I want it and need it.

I went to the music with my aunt. I have nothing to wear.

Wednesday, November 25, 1874. It is cold, with a few drops of rain—the kind of weather I like. But these are not the the kind of people I like. I went out alone. Everybody else stayed at home because Count Mirzisky is here. I left early before the music lesson to avoid him. He is uglier than ever, if that's possible. He looks so miserable, unhappy, confused—crushed—that I cannot stand him. Mama detained me about fifteen minutes, during which time I did not speak to him and turned my back toward him as much as politeness permitted.

There was a crowd. I bought a box of cigarettes because for quite a while I've been smoking, but not openly. I don't hide it either. I pretend it's a whim when I see some cigarettes; but to smoke I hide, although the smoke can surely be smelled sometimes. As Mama is against smoking, I take a few cigarettes from my aunt when she isn't looking. Then I show them to her and run away. Smoking is a bad habit, and I hope it's not a need for me yet; I'll do it only for a while.

There was a terrible scene at dinner. Papa insulted everybody, said unjust things to me, and told some enormous lies. Finally he started to cry, evoking the memory of my grandmother, the woman he had outraged and mistreated all her life; and now he was saying that after her death he had been mistreated, that when she was alive he was respected, that he is the world's most unfortunate man. He told so many lies that even Mama spoke to him about it. We've endured this kind of thing for the last ten days. I lose my mind when I try to understand such imbecility, such folly, such cowardice as Papa is showing. The worst thing is he doesn't hear what we say to him and doesn't want to hear. He continues what he has started for an indefinite time like a hammer, without stopping, without answering the reasons of others. Though I'm a strong girl of fifteen, he even gets on my nerves.

Everyone else has gone to the theater. Victor is sleeping here beside me. He is becoming a dog without equal—kind, intelligent. He follows me everywhere, lies down at my feet, and stays with me during my lessons.

Monday, November 30, 1874. In spite of Mama's asserted dislike for Audiffret, she went on talking about him, insisting that he blushed for me. But when he covered his face with his hand, as if he thought we would notice, I don't think he was blushing. He just has a red face. They started to talk about "Audi" and asked me, "Would you marry him?"

"Yes, at twenty-seven, if I have no other hopes."

When we saw him with Mrs. Prodgers, I was secretly furious. I think Dina has a yen for him, too. (In my diary I began spelling his name backward—Terffidua—and I kept wondering why, if he thought me beautiful, he didn't ask to be introduced.)

Tuesday, December 1, 1874. My honorable Uncle George became furious and impossible yesterday. He screamed at Grandpapa, Mama, and my aunt, saying horrible things that make my hair stand on end and fill me with indignation and rage. There is not a crime in the world that he hasn't made them responsible for. He finished his speeches by saying that he is tired of hiding their horrors and doesn't want to be mixed in their dirty deals. When I hear such things I am lost, and I understand what crimes one can commit when exasperated so much.

Wednesday, December 2, 1874. What a day of vexation and deep humiliation!

The exclamations and the complaints make the pain trivial. I will complain less. Markevitch came this morning to tell my mother that all the colony, tired of all of George's scandals, especially this last (he slapped Mrs. Prodgers's face), want to ask the Prefect to send him away from the Maritimes Alps. And Mama was told that one of these days she must expect to receive an official remonstrance about Paul's case. Mama told us that at dinner and then sobbed. I didn't cry, but I felt such anger and shame that I became very pale. Numbed, and with my eyes fixed and my lips white, I left the dining room, walking like an automaton. My aunt found me halfway up the stairs, and I asked her what Markevitch said.

"Because of George and Paul and all in general," she said, "including Patton's gossipings, they will ask all the family to leave Nice. Patton is one of the complainants," she added.

Absurd as the story is, I believed it completely and thought I was going to die of shame and despair. Mama came and reproached my aunt for having reported to me. Then, to correct it, she assured me that it's not true; but I was so angry that I retired into myself, sitting motionless, my chin in my hand, alone. I fell on the floor on a mattress, stretched out, and started to cry. It was then that I got the idea of poisoning myself with some of the acids in my chemistry set, because there are some things that are more valuable to me than my life. Losing the consideration of one's community—well, the shame and the affront for me are worse than any imaginable torture. I took my diary, opened it, and dipped the pen in the ink, but I couldn't move to write. I was petrified. I asked for some tea. And then I begged my aunt to wash my head, which she did. Calmer, but still bewildered, I wrote.

It's already twenty-four hours since that happened, and I'm still not recovered from it.

Now, our expulsion from Nice—is it true? In fact, why would my aunt invent a thing like that? But it's impossible, absurd. What have we done? And the scandals of George Babanine—are Mrs. Bashkirtseff and Mrs. Romanoff responsible for a brother who lives independently? Maybe Patton has talked so much because he has political reasons? I don't know what to believe, but I know that I am really unhappy. I've barely started my life, and already I'm splashed by the mud from others!! But what have I done to suffer this shame? At this moment I'd give everything in this world to occupy a reputable place. Hear me, God; and if I have sinned, forgive me.

Thursday, December 3, 1874. George has had the unheard of audacity to bring his Anna to this house! We were out, but my aunt stayed. And imagine our grandfather taking her in our carriage with George and my aunt! It seems to me that there have been these horrors all along, but that I've discovered them only now.

But what I long to know is *whether it is true* . . . George has been drunk since Saturday, and we are obliged to stand these horrors! There is no money to take him away from here.

Saturday, December 12, 1874. At the opera again (*Il Trovatore*), we had Florence Foster with us. The house was full and the loges were generally occupied by the young people of Nice. Audiffret, with Saëtone, was in evening clothes. He laughed, moved a lot, and seemed to be posing, all of which seemed to say that he had had a good dinner or that he was particularly happy. As for the other, he had more than ever the air of a man who is having a lot of fun.

I also had a good time. Miss Foster is interesting and amusing. If Audiffret was looking at me, he found me beautiful. My aunt laughed a lot during the intermissions; she said at home later that he was looking at me through his binoculars almost constantly, although I didn't notice that, as his hand shaded his face. If he does find me beautiful, why doesn't he ask to be introduced? Arçon has, I think, said that he asked to be introduced, but I can't be sure of that.

This afternoon I met Lise and Aggie (Howard) in a shop. We talked in a quite friendly way; and at the afternoon gathering, Mrs. Howard was the first to come to greet Mama. This white dress is very nice on me.

Tuesday, December 15, 1874. The weather was magnificent, cold and almost clear.

Wednesday, December 16, 1874. Coming back home from my drive, I was informed that Markevitch had just returned from Mrs. Howard's, who invited her to the party she's giving this very afternoon.

To Mama and my aunt I said, "You see, you didn't go to visit her, and you'll not be invited," adding, "It will be a happy day for Markevitch and for Patton, although I don't believe the visit would have changed anything." Mama and my aunt could have gone today, because Mrs. Howard visited here a week ago last Tuesday; they made her wait as long as they had waited. We are quits. And my family has nothing to reproach itself for; we've seen the coldness of these people. Good heavens, do we have to worry about mean, ordinary pouters? If we were guilty, it would be different; with time and the help of God we'll triumph, and then I'll breathe freely. It's unbelievable, but I swear there's hardly a minute in the day when I'm not sighing! When I wake up, when I'm at my lessons, or practising the piano—especially at the piano—at the table, in the street, at the theater, going to bed, and sometimes when dreaming—everywhere I am tormented! I want to go to Mama and my aunt and beg them to leave Nice because I am suffering too much. I'm afraid it will destroy my body as it has my mind.

Mama and my aunt don't discuss anyone from society before me, because when I hear talk about my torment I explode, I go away, or I cry. Oh, if only this lawsuit would end!

We are going away from Nice soon and will return in two years—I mean for the winters in 1876 and 1877. Perhaps by that time the lawsuit will be ended. Who knows? Maybe I'll not need these happy Niçois anymore. Maybe someone will deliver me and provide me with a social standing. Misery of miseries! What a miserable person I am!

Thursday, December 17, 1874. It is bitterly cold. We went for a promenade by carriage, covered by a beautiful fur of blue fox. Florence was with us. Audiffret and Saëtone have returned. Then Lewin and Clementine passed us like a flash of lightning. Let's hope nothing upsets that happy couple! We had some chocolate at Rumpelmayer's.

Paul, this unfortunate lost boy, almost never is here. He spends his life among the most vile and low people in the servants' clubs and in the cabarets. He borrows money everywhere, has debts. After the things that happened in November, what else could be expected? My mother tried everything—anger, tolerance, tenderness, strictness—but she forgot one thing, the only thing that can save him—to act with firmness. She has none, but it's not her fault. This boy is so corrupted and vicious that the only thing which could save him and save us is his death. She sent him to a famous school in Geneva, but has been obliged to take him back. They didn't want him. At the lycée, a state school both serious and classical, the same thing happened. Finally she decided to keep him at home to prepare him to enter the university. She called him, talked to him with kindness, and begged him to mend his ways. She cried. He cried, too—the hypocrite!—but did not listen to the excellent reasons she gave him.

Today a policeman came to look for him, but we don't know where he is. Do we ever know? What can he have done? Oh, how painful it is for me to know this creature is my brother!

Friday, December 18, 1874. This morning, as I was teaching Victor to jump, my mother gave me a letter and told me to go to my room to read it and then to give it back to her. Here it is [in Russian]:

Honorable Madam Nadezhda Stepanovna:
After long contemplation I have resolved—No, I don't remember enough to write it word for word, but the letter says that after reflection the writer thinks that not for

anything in the world does she want to take her children into a house where the young girls are constantly going to the gambling tables and that, as to the question of good education, she'll never agree with Mrs. Romanoff (to whom the letter is sent) and that it is better to part, because nothing is more disagreeable than forced relations. She regrets all this deeply because my mother is a charming woman, sympathetic and kind. But, alas! Why should she have such a weak brother? It was signed, "Julie Howard."

Outraged and red with anger, I didn't want anyone to see me; when I had calmed down and got my face in order, I returned the letter.

My aunt sent this letter to Mrs. Howard [also in Russian]:

Most Honorable "My Lady" Madam Julia Stepanovna:

Surely you yourself have noticed that the quality of our relationship has changed from what it was before, in the light of certain rumors that have reached me.

It is unjust that you falsely accuse our girls because they go to Monaco, when your own young ladies go just as often. As for the upbringing of our girls, of course we shall never agree upon that. But for me, as for any other truly good woman, the reputation of a young girl is holy. However, as you so easily, so lightly have decided to condemn ours, indeed, let us finish!

Ready to be of service to you,
Nadezhda Stepanovna

It's a letter that I admire and respect.

Well, I was almost expecting it, sad about our status as I am, and anticipating only affronts. But what revolts me is the infamy of the calumny! For God's sake, when do I go to Monte Carlo? I go on the day of a shoot or a firecracker party, and those are once a year. All of the young girls from Nice go there. Is it necessary for me to lower myself by justifying myself when I am not guilty? How vile it is! How cowardly for a mother to use a child as a pretext and to lie about her without even really knowing her! She cannot seriously believe what she is saying.

This action of Mrs. Howard is a result of my Aunt Tutcheff's conduct and the gossipings of that Boutonsky, a depraved woman if ever there was one, and especially of Hélène Howard. Since last year, Hélène has been jealous of me openly about everything and hasn't tried to prevent my seeing that she was. Today she is ambitious and sneaky, whereas when we first met the family, neither she nor Lise had any ideas about good manners or elegance. When they copied me, they had many silk dresses made, feathered hats, etc. When Hélène's admiration of me changed to envy, she continued to copy me and believed she looked better than I.

At last she is satisfied, because at their next Tuesday party she'll probably be the best-looking one there because of the miserable quality of the people they'll have.

Saturday, December 19, 1874. To the drop of ink in the glass of water, a teaspoon of ink has been added. It is a pity that a beautiful girl like me, fresh and pink, should be troubled with such annoyances! If I were only twelve I'd be patient. But I'm sixteen. I have no time, and I find myself crying ten times a day. If I'm not crying, I'm sighing; if I'm not sighing, horrible thoughts come to my mind. When I can't hold my tears before my mother or my aunt, they tell me, "Don't feel unhappy because of trifles. It harms your eyes and your complexion."

But they don't understand that it is all my life! Trifles? If I had to live the rest of my life like this, with joy I'd die now. Why can't I invent words to give an idea of my ceaseless torments?

Wednesday, December 23, 1874. The Howards, when they saw us at Laussel's, kept their eyes lowered before going to the [piano] lesson. We had a unique discussion—to bow or not to bow to the Howards? I told the others, "I'll not bow; if you do without admitting the impropriety of such an action, they will invent some new stupidities about us."

It was no trouble for me not to greet them because they kept their eyes lowered. They wore a confused expression that told me they had had their orders not to speak to us. But I knew that if we had been mixed with society, none of these scoundrels could have done anything. If anyone tries to uproot Mrs. Prodgers or Mrs. Sabatier, etc.—but *basta!* [Italian: enough!] We know the circumstances very well. Our story is necessary to my diary. I will end it where my journal becomes reasonable.

Galula, the notary's clerk, stopped us on the Promenade and talked with my aunt about some papers I hadn't heard of. I asked what it was about, and he answered me, "Oh, Miss, can you know about these things? Why should you have to worry about *papers and notaries?* You mustn't know about such things!" He said all that with the most noble air, smiling in a superior way.

This evening I learned that the papers were the gift from my aunt by which I became proprietor of the villa at No. 55, Promenade des Anglais. The property has two houses and [unclear] meters of land, stables, a barn, and water and gas. Well, here I am, a proprietor! Isn't it amusing? And all this without adding that my aunt bequeathes me all her wealth of more than a million and a half francs, her sterling silver, and her jewels. She gives Mama a place near Tcherniakovka, which can be worth a little more than 100,000 francs, and also her silver and diamonds.

I am rich, am I not? Rich as a young lady, yes, as a married woman, no. [A married woman's property became her husband's.]

Ah, but I forget the lawsuit, this pretty little lawsuit which, without mentioning the defamation, can make me lose my fortune!

Have mercy, powerful God. I have a lot of sins. Forgive them! Make this lawsuit end in our favor and I promise you. . . . I was going to promise not to pursue and punish our enemies. Can I? That's the job of the lawyer. I'll do everything to prevent the pursuit of the people who have hurt us so much. Only, God, make me remember this promise even if I have to be a perjurer and sacrilegious to do my duty.

BOOK TWENTY-EIGHT

H. G. T. D. O. H.
Book 28
Begun Friday, December 25, 1874
Finished Sunday, January 17, 1875
Promenade des Anglais, 55 bis, in my villa, Nice
[From Wednesday, January 13, Paris, Grand Hotel]

Friday, January 1, 1875. I sent two letters to Russia, one to Uncle Stepa and the other to Uncle Alexander. The first is about my trip planned for Russia to get all the books, because Uncle Alexander doesn't send the interest; the second has the goal of softening Uncle Alexander (because earlier I wrote a quite frank request, asking him to send my silverware) to win his good will and to seem good and lovable toward him. Sometimes he is mean, and he could hurt me.

Sunday, January 3, 1875. Tonight again, at the Italien, the same opera, almost the same public. Audiffret, in his box, seemed melancholy, dreaming. My aunt thinks he looks like a twin of her dead husband's—not when she married him, but in a photo we have of him taken in his thirtieth year. Romanoff was called *Beauty* or *Beau* (stronger than good-looking or even handsome).

I feel fresh and well.

I have the idea of falling in love with Audiffret. What can I say about it? That it would be bad. I don't want to fall in love with him, but I'd like to see him in love with me.

I am absolutely alone. My aunt and Mrs. Markevitch went to Monaco at 5:00. I read, I smoke. For a month I have been hoarse, but I think my voice is coming back to me. Today I sang very badly, but I sang, and that's something.

Wednesday, January 6, 1875. I walked with my aunt to the Italien to reserve a box for next Saturday—Belloca will be singing *The Somnambulist*.

Friday, January 8, 1875. Yesterday evening we were all terribly frightened, and today Mama is very ill.

George had again tried to come and make a scandal. When I wanted to throw him out, Mama, wild, jumped out of bed to prevent me, and Dina, watching this, started to scream, sobbing, crying, and falling on her knees . . . her hands clasped, shouting, begging for I don't know what. I pushed her back with my foot, but she didn't stop her crying. She'd make a good hired mourner. In the meantime, George, wailing in an unpleasant monotone, protected by Mama from me in spite of the calumnies he has broadcast against us, was trying to get us to take Anna in as a member of the family and isolate us with her—hoping, being sure that there would be no obstacle for her then to be one of us. Oh, this man, a hundred times a coward! He was the executioner of his mother, the disgrace of his family. He passes his life casting a shadow over ours, trying with all his might to blacken us and drag us into the hole where he stands!

Tuesday, January 12, 1875. After a little scene suited to the occasion, I left for Paris. How I would like to do without these scenes! But the fact is that if I don't make scenes, I have nothing. Really, these people make me have a horrible character. But what to do?

Tomorrow is our New Year's Day. In my family we neglect the holidays, but days like Christmas and New Year's should be spent in family reunion. It is a way to maintain good relations, respect, and everything. We should pay great attention to the little things; it's these that make up life.

Wednesday, January 13, 1875 [January 1st, 1875, by the Russian calendar]. This eternal noise, this smoke! At seven we were in Paris at the Grand Hotel, in room 132 on the third floor.

Thursday, January 14, 1875. We went to Ferry's and to Caroline's, where I entered with some anxiety, but Caroline was tolerable. I ordered three dresses and a coat; at Vertus's, a corset in white satin; and at last, at Reboux's, a grey felt hat with feather, soft and gracious. Then we went to Duval's about the furniture. We'll have a few difficulties with him, I suppose, because when we ordered the furniture he said that my aunt would pay as she pleased, and she thought that the payments would be as Schmidt had proposed—over a period of several years. But she was wrong not to say it to Duval, who also, each time they talked, said that it would be as she wanted, that she should choose the conditions. It was a sneaky way to answer; now Master Duval says that he had understood that he would be paid during this current year!

Thursday, January 14, 1875. We saw *Around the World in 80 Days* at the Porte San Martin. A great success.

Friday, January 15, 1875. A ride to the Bois, and in the evening *Madame Archduchess* by Offenbach at the Light Opera Theater.

Sunday, January 17, 1875. Paris is beautiful, but to live here as we are doing just now is silly. . . .

BOOK TWENTY-NINE

Book 29
Begun Wednesday, January 20, 1875
Finished Thursday, February 18, 1875

Wednesday, January 20, 1875. My dresses arrived, and they are all beautiful. My aunt has taken a box at the new opera, number eighteen on the eighth floor. I wore the new white taffeta dress—long, with a train. My first long dress! The building is superb, and I can see better. It is big, majestic. The house was full, and the women were in low-cut dresses. I was not embarrassed with the train; in fact, it pleased me very much. There is nothing uglier than the evening dresses made for young girls who are not children nor yet grown up.

I was noticed a lot. I'm always noticed. I'm not bragging; it's not because of my worth, but because of the way God made me.

The opera was *The Jewess,* with Miss Strauss. The stage is so big that the actors seem like flies, and fifteen horses could not fill up the stage.

Friday, January 22, 1875. We arrived in Nice at 8:00. At home I went directly to Mama's room, where I found her up and quite well, with Pelikan, Mrs. Sapogenikoff, and her two daughters, Mary, fifteen, and Olga, fourteen. Mary is as little as she was in Geneva, and she's in love with Stephen, the boy from Geneva. He loves her, and they're going to be married soon; but they look so young that it seems ridiculous. No one would guess Mary to be more than twelve or the young man to be more than fifteen . . . I wanted to laugh. Can you imagine that boy married? Olga looks like her father, Mr. Sapogenikoff. Nina met Paris [Yourkoff] only after Olga's birth.

Sunday, January 24, 1875. At 1:00 we left for the Carnival—my aunt, Olga, Mary, and I, with Stephen between Mary and me and Paul on the front seat. We took a place in the third row of carriages just opposite the grandstand, but in spite of that I couldn't recognize the people there.

Tuesday, January 26, 1875. We went into different places to tell them not to give credit to my honorable brother. Tomorrow we have the races and the next day the Tir, and for these two days I consent to being bored for nine months—three at Nice, two in Russia, and four more at Nice, after which we shall go to Rome and I'll be in society! *Botheration*! [written later]

Sunday, January 31, 1875. After supper, during which we had talked about the magnetism of Hume and Cagliostro, I took them all to the pavilion, and there Stephen tried to put Olga to sleep. During that time I was trying to put Mary asleep, but I just ended by giving her a headache. (I'd heard and read about it, but I'd never seen it done.) But Olga was asleep. I was all eyes and was holding my breath. She got up, twisting her arms and sobbing. Stephen told her, "Shut up," and she stopped. But before that she was moaning, blindfolded with a towel so she couldn't see. Then Stephen ordered her, with a gesture, to put her head on her shoulder, and she obeyed. Then Dina told Stephen in a low voice to ask Olga to kiss him, and once more she obeyed. The poor little thing started to tremble so much that Miss Collignon, after entering with a smile on her face, was afraid and asked him to wake her up. When he wakened her, he looked at her with pride and satisfaction. I was stupefied. But as long as the little girl stayed in the same room with him, she continued to tremble.

Oh, I hope it's not all a joke.

Sunday, February 7, 1875. At 9:30 Dina, Paul, and I went to the station to meet Alexander and his family as they arrived from Russia. No matter what he is, he is my uncle, and I went to show him courtesy. But the train arrived without them . . . Alexander and the others arrived at 10:00. It's five years since I'd seen them, when I was eleven. Stepa is the older child, and Julie is six.

Nadianka's smile is more false than ever, and in spite of all my good will I can't find her sympathetic, but that will come! I have a benevolent nature, and if I should change, it will be because of her. My uncle is still the same, and I still do not know what to think of him. Is he a good man? Or is he shrewd?

Monday, February 8, 1875. I was not expecting to go to the Carnival, but Paul came at 2:30 with Mary, and we went together. We had the same confetti battles as yesterday. Two hours later we came back.

I noticed something peculiar. It's that the worse things are, the more we laugh, the more fun there is around us, the more serious I am and the more withdrawn into myself. It's hard for me to get used to Stepa's voice, and Julie speaks and reasons very wisely with the vocal seriousness peculiar to children.

Mardi Gras, Tuesday, February 9, 1875. At 2:00 Mary, Olga, Paul, and Stephen—these last two masked—and I left. With the motley crowd, the gaiety surrounding me, I did not have the time to become sad and indifferent. We had to fight seriously. All of us went crazy, and we were fighting so hard that some asked for peace.

Paul was full of spirit. He and Stephen, not satisfied to bombard the crowd from the carriage, went down into the street. They were running after other carriages, attacking pedestrians, saying thousands of foolish things, and then taking off. We, with our wire masks, were perfectly recognizable; but we seemed to forget it and were acting as if we were covered by the most carefully concealing masks. We were fighting, calling everyone, stopping people, saying silly things to them or kind words, and laughing. Oh, yes, laughing! I stopped laughing only to talk, but as soon as the sentence was finished I started in a wild chorus with everyone else. Did we need good lungs!

I came home all dizzy, my ears buzzing. At 8:00 we returned to see the lighting and the execution of Mr. Carnival, burned on the square of the Prefecture. We had to get out of the carriage and walk, crossing through this masked and costumed crowd. We ran toward the big grandstand, but the entrance was in the rear and we had to go around. We started to run again, crossing the street where the post office is, and entered the street of the Prefecture. We passed under the arch of the building and went up, and at last, out of breath, arrived at the platform, all happy.

I have seen the Carnival only in Nice. Probably that is why it seems so beautiful to me. The amphitheater was full of people, and down below, in the street, the people were dancing to the tunes of Offenbach's operas with little candles [macoletti] in their hands, singing and shouting, while in the middle of it all was Father Carnival on his throne, burning. Above the music was the sound of exploding firecrackers, and over everything was the light of an electric star.

Then we went to the Français, arriving at the end of the second act of *Giroflé-Girofla* to join my aunt. Before going home, we stopped at Mrs. Sapogenikoff's. My only regret is that it is all over. When I was at the theater, I wanted to go into the orchestra and into the boxes; constantly on my lips are the things we were saying in the crowd—snatches from the songs of *Giroflé-Girofla*, et cetera. All this is bad, common, childish, but it is amusing; that kind of mood keeps going in me for many days, because I keep hearing all the time the smutty remarks made by the maskers—and by us without masks! During the day, as well as at night, we were alone, without anybody who would prevent our saying everything passing in our heads. Maybe it was imprudent, but it was so gay; it is so seldom that I feel this gaiety. When we were coming down the stairs of the grandstand, I saw the windows of the Prefecture all lighted and the carriages which were bringing the women with naked shoulders and the men in evening clothes, and my heart sank.

Thursday, February 11, 1875. In the evening I went with Nadianka to hear *Ruy Blas*. The singing was bad, and if it had not been that Gioja sat in front of me, I would have been bored. Oh, that beautiful woman! Within her, everything is perfect, as in the Duke . . . I love her because he loved her, and it is an inexpressible happiness for me to look at her. As I looked at her I told myself, "She has been his wife."

Saturday, February 13, 1875. It is with an unequalled joy I realize that my plan of studying is such that I think I need a year in Nice in order not to interrupt my lessons . . . If I find a good painting teacher here, I'll not go to Rome. I'm pleased with the other teachers. Pleased, or accustomed to them. But in this way I'll lose a year. No: I'll have gained one. A year of study is not lost, and if I begin to go into society at eighteen and a half instead of seventeen and a half, it is all the same.

Besides, things at Nice could change; if they do, I'll pass a very happy winter here. I'll not be going into Nice society, but I'll receive people I like; then, in 1876-1877, I'll go to

Rome, and by the twenty-fifth of January I'll be eighteen years old. [Actually, nineteen. By moving her birthday from November to January, Marie loses a year here.] As one can see, I am not an old lady; but if things don't change, well then, I'll be what I'll . . . That's all. It will be what it will be.

Alexander wants to talk to my dear Aunt Tutcheff and to convince her that she risks a lot when she defames us as she does. Probably she will give up, because this dear Alexander has such irresistible arguments.

Alexander says that Miloradovitch is courting the daughter of our neighbor Zaukovsky in Russia. His information upset Mama and my aunt. While I stayed in Mama's room, the conversation was only about this Prince Charming. Mama becomes excited at the idea that someone might marry me; and as sick and weak as she is, when Miloradovitch was mentioned she raised herself from the bed, her eyes shone, and some color came into her cheeks. Only for the pleasure of seeing her like that I stayed and listened to what was said about this brilliant "pretender." I tried, but in vain, to prove that he is a very ordinary candidate and to think too much about it one must have a very narrow mind. Poor Mama! It is her dream. Maybe it will be realized. I wish it for her, not for me. He is from excellent and old nobility, young—barely twenty—handsome they say, and very rich, with something like 300,000 francs of income. And I would have no disgust in marrying him. I don't love and shall not love anyone.

I am getting used to our visitors, and sometimes I think they are both nice and sincere. In fact, they do nothing wrong except get rich at our expense. But *Deo juvante* [with God's help], I hope to put things in order for when I go to Russia.

I have almost resumed my work; I have eight hours in the week that I must fill with drawing and math. These two subjects will occupy all my time. The more time I have, the less I work. For the time being, I don't know of anything that makes me happier than to study.

And for the time being, the thought of my planned trip to Russia amuses me. I constantly need something to be desired or to be waited for. My uncle pretends that, in spite of the proverb, "no one is a prophet in his own land," I'll be popular in mine. That will be good, if it's true.

Thursday, February 18, 1875. The Sapogenikoffs are having terrible fears in their house. They imagine spirits and ghosts, and Stephen has proved these ideas to them, saying that this house is under attack by spirits—to the point that Mary felt kissed by one of these beings. I wouldn't swear that it was not Stephen who may have taken the shape of the spirit.

Well, as you can see, I am now desperate. For three years I have been pestering Mama and my aunt, and they have always answered that when I'm grown up everything will be as I wish. I'm a teenager, and nothing is changed or done; it's only worse.

Really, I have only hope in you, my God. Have pity on me just as a charity. I have to fight for everything, fight eternally against apathy, imbecility, numbness, unconcern.

BOOK THIRTY

H. G. T. D. O. H.
Book 30
Begun Friday, February 19, 1875
Finished Friday, April 2, 1875
Promenade des Anglais, 55 bis, in my villa [Nice]

Friday, February 19, 1875. To my great surprise I saw the Countess Mirzisky in the Rue de France. As soon as I got to Mama's room, I heard them talking about the Count. He is sick and had sent for Walitsky.

Sacha [Uncle Alexander] was always asking me what I would do if I fell in love with a poor man. I explained my way of thinking to him again.

"Are you really so materialistic?" he asked [in Russian].

"Yes. Listen to me. If I found a man I liked who was rich at the same time I fancied a poor one, of course I'd choose the rich one. We have only one lifetime. I was born. I studied. I'm learning to live well. Because of a caprice, should one try to live poorly?"

My aunt's comment was that I cannot find anyone suitable.

Thursday, February 25, 1875. Mama [who is sick] is leaving for San Remo [to be near her doctor]. It's awful! The doctors understand nothing about her illness and attribute everything to her nerves.

Men are made to live in society. God gave them words to express their thoughts—but to whom? Even dogs don't stay alone. Ferocious and wild wolves don't live alone. Birds fly in flocks, and fishes swim in schools. But why do I tell you these things that everybody knows? I'm not speaking of society life . . . I ask only to live comfortably, reasonably—nothing more; to cry openly—not in shame.

"But Moussia," Sacha said, "You study. You are busy."

"Oh, there you are! Why should I study? Why do I have a beautiful voice? Why do I speak several languages? Definitely it's not to be locked within four walls. Is it to be praised before a few relatives just arrived from Russia?"

"But why despair? You, to whom God gave everything?"

"Oh, yes . . . but I'll answer you like Rosine, 'What good is it to have intelligence, youth, beauty locked in as I am, hidden, isolated, miserable—and that way all the time?'"

At 10:30 I went to work, and at 11:00 to bed, broken and despairing, because now to my permanent anxieties was joined the fear for my mother's life. I feel so lonely, especially sad, since her departure. It's never been like this before.

Friday, February 26, 1875. Mrs. Markevitch has come back. I took her to Rumpelmayer's and walked alone for an hour.

During dinner Alexander recalled some anecdotes of all kinds, referring to the lawsuit. He almost reassured me. He has the management of our properties, and if he doesn't forget himself, there will not be great harm in that; it is better than to have a stranger.

Saturday, March 6, 1875. I went to take my lesson at Laussel's. I don't work with enthusiasm. No matter what I do, I'll never play better than in an average way.

Sunday, March 7, 1875. I went out in a little white dress and black velvet hat. There weren't many people out—that is to say, nobody whom I knew.

By not showing himself, Audiffret makes himself desired, on my word of honor.

Friday, March 12, 1875. Quickly, write, write, write. I want to pour out all my feelings in writing. Oh, my Uncle George, how many curses on your head? If you were able to see what bitterness there is at the bottom of my soul and on my face while I write this, you would surely be frightened. If you could know my anger and my hate for you, as stupid as you are, you would stop yourself. If you could see how badly you have hurt me, see my tears, my heartaches, my humiliation, my rage, and my despair—even as a man without faith or honor that you are, you would have pity for me! That's not all: We are deprived of clothes; we don't build the house. I hoped to see my aunt in my house; I have no room; we have only one servant; we are in debt; and we buy a villa for George! . . . May God forgive him, but I have no pity!

Saturday, March 13, 1875. I ordered my books. In two months they'll be here, and I'll devote myself to reading the classics, the saints, and philosophy. I'm waiting impatiently for that time. After the *Voluptuous Woman*, I'm disgusted with Dumas.

The Count came today, and I was very cold with him—very noble.

But what a pity it is to be sixteen and not to have any lovers! But we don't know anybody. Maybe I've had some unknown admirers—as many as have had me for an unknown admirer. When will God let me live well!

Sunday, March 14, 1875. I slept twelve hours. Since Mama returned, the house has been alive because, as sick as she is, she is the soul of the house.

Monday, March 15, 1875. The spring! The spring! The spring!

The people have gone away. The Promenade is less populous, the sun hotter, the afternoons more beautiful, the nights more perfumed, and the sunset—but oh, here is what I love! The departure of visitors this year does not make me sad. On the contrary, I'd like to be alone more often. Alone, I mean, with Audiffret or someone like him. Otherwise I'll be bored. Spring reminds me of my walks with the Princess, our conversations about the Duke, the Villa Baquis, the song of the frogs, Black Prince on his little horse, the London House, and then Audiffret all in white (whom I did not see, he being too busy to see me). It's true: our sweetest pleasures are in our memories—good or indifferent.

Tuesday, March 16, 1875. We went to the music, and then I came home to study; instead I went to see Mama and then to the pavilion to take I don't know what all from the closet. When I opened it, a lot of perfumes and memories poured from it. Then I found the shells from Ostend, the boxes from Spa, Gericke's fan, etc., and the peasant hat from Spa that I myself lined in pink. I grabbed the hat and started to go out. As I started to close the closet, I saw myself in the mirror in the white wool cashmere dress.

Surprised, I saw the hat on my head, a fresh face as pink as a rose, eyes shining, and an excited face . . . I grew pensive. Why, I thought, am I so beautiful? Is it to see the ugliest and the most common swimming in the amusing events of all kinds? Is it so that I may regret more, if that's possible, what I like and desire? The eternal torment!

Wednesday, March 17, 1875. We were in the garden, and when I raised my eyes I saw Terffidua, who was watching as long as one could see. I am dying to have an intrigue this summer in Nice. I'll be horribly bored without it. Mama believed that all my thoughts are for a trip to Russia. She is sure that I'll bring that Russian man back—as sure as I was of winning Alcibiades [Hamilton]. But I don't want to marry Miloradovitch. Of course, if he had an income of 10,000 rubles, I wouldn't be so sure of that. But then, he is known to be a miser.

Thursday, March 18, 1875. I walked with Nadine and Dina and Sacha and the children. Mrs. Lewin and Lucie Durand were the first to pass us. They were wearing colorful clothes, and Sacha asked in Russian, *"Is that a cocotte?"* Those poor women! When they saw him they took him for a swell—and the impudence and the effrontery of his manners for gallantry! As young as they are, they were all made up.

Friday, March 19, 1875. Family argument—Sacha has beaten Adam, and I am extremely pleased about it. It's a long time since he got what he had coming. This serf deserved to be beaten for the last four years, since the death of my excellent Uncle Romanoff. In all circumstances he feels that he is an important personage and necessary for the lawsuit. Especially, he thought he could keep his hold on us as a witness. But we have the evidence, and if he dares to change his mind in his second disposition (in case a second one will be necessary), it will be of no value since he would have given this one after having been beaten and thrown out. Without speaking of the matter, it is a great happiness for our stomachs, because no one can imagine how badly he was feeding us or how much we suffered because of that. Through the family's indolence and because of this kind of lethargy, we endured him. Well, it is done—provided that we don't take him back! But for the family all is possible, as long as one has no pain.

Saturday, March 20, 1875. I saw Audiffret, but the more I see him, the less I look at him. Poor me! Obliged to look at an Audiffret! I sent many smiles to the villainous Count because I was so bored!

Sunday, March 21, 1875. Audiffret was walking back and forth in the Public Gardens. He wasn't looking at me, but that doesn't prove anything since I no longer look at him. How can anyone be without friends to the extent of being occupied with such a peasant!

We have a cook who is passable and who seems excellent after Adam.

Monday, March 22, 1875. I think I am becoming a fool. I pray to God, but I don't hope and I don't believe any more. I am more than unhappy. Before, I had nothing. Now I have nothing more. Before, I believed in God. Now I don't believe anymore. Horror! I believe in Him, but He doesn't hear me anymore. He has abandoned me. He tests me. I am not Job. I complain. I revolt. I cry. I blaspheme. Those happy pagans who could have recourse to several gods could turn, when abandoned by some, to others. I have only one God, and He abandons me. Will He never hear me again? Will He abandon me forever? I'm crazy! I asked, "Will He abandon me?" *But He has already done so!*

Why wasn't I made like the others, since I'm to rot in the shadows? I am not worthy. But Alcibiades, Alexander, Caesar—were they worthy? They were extravagant, ambitious, eager for popularity—glory—like me.

Wednesday, March 24, 1875. Nadia and I strolled around the garden like two little girls. My aunt joined us below. At 6:00 it was still daylight; we could still see our door and iron gate, which has just been put up.

At the theater, Terffidua was seated by another young man as fresh as he, but more ugly. I am in an impossible mood, sitting straight and mute. I have death in my soul. With each day, each hour, my torment grows. It's that each day and each hour passes without bringing me anything good, and I age. Don't make fun of me. I know very well that I am not and will not be old for a long time, but time passes, flies, unfeelingly.

The minutes become hours, the hours days, the days months, and the months years. It has been a long time since I was eleven and left Russia, but to me it seems a week ago. Well, I'll find myself to be twenty as fast as I became sixteen. Four years. Four days. But what days! Nobody does anything for me. I have only God.

I am in a rage; I lock myself in the bathroom to smoke, read Caesar eagerly, and try all kind of stories to make myself fall asleep. Nothing worked until I was exhausted.

Thursday, March 25, 1875. And I am crying while writing. An outdoor festival is organized for the benefit of the public school of fine arts. Everybody else is helping; only we are left out, avoided like the plague. We are not part of it. But are we ever, anywhere? We go only where we have to pay or where everybody else can go.

What makes me think that our way of living cannot last this way—that somehow there will be a big blowup or a big disaster—or a little change for the better?

Friday, March 26, 1875. My journal, my confidant, my consoler—it is to this that I have recourse when I am too unhappy, and that is each evening.

In writing I find relief when I am very, very miserable. Another winter ends, to which another one will succeed, as humiliating, as terrible for me. I am consumed like a candle; if this condition continues, soon I'll not be here any more.

Oh, truly, I could have been more happy selling violets at two centimes a bunch than to live as I do. I am crushed, overwhelmed, wandering like Dante's suspended shades.

Sunday, March 28, 1875. I was right to say there would be a change. Olga and Mary came, and I was amused as a king. How little it takes to amuse me! . . . a carriage, I was the guest this time . . . Mary drove.

Mary was telling me everything I had been thinking: We must establish a women's club. It's not fair for men to have one and women not.

"Yes, yes!"

Men will not be admitted. We'll wear, like everybody else, some special clothing, white and gold wool, and a smooth ring with a large pearl will be our sign of recognition.

We chattered so much and laughed so much that it is impossible to imagine anything like it. We didn't leave the Promenade. Since Collignon's first year, I've never been on the Promenade so much. We were going very fast, like fools, and making changes about the club without worrying about anybody else, except Girofla—or Terffidua, as one wishes—whom we met at each instant and who watched us, smiling. It would have been hard not to smile, we were laughing so much. Never, never, have I been so amused, or rather, laughed so much.

At 6:00 we went to Rumpelmayer's café . . . my aunt met us there. We sat in the mezzanine, and some minutes afterward Girofla arrived with some others. I turned my back to them. My aunt was talking, and I was listening. We were far from being calmed down. On the contrary, we were laughing like imbeciles.

Girofla pleases me today, really a lot. In a way, he pleases me a lot and still infuriates me. . . . Such a peasant, who does not even have the grace to love me. I say that because if he thought as much about me as I do about him, he would already have found a way to be introduced. But by whom? Well, by Galula—by Satan—it doesn't matter whom.

When one wants to—fie, how miserable I am to be hunting excuses for this lazy bum!

Monday, March 29, 1875. Mary and I have started portraits of Olga. Olga has a well-defined profile, good for study. After lunch we went to Nina's, carrying our easels and everything else. Nina read to us in Russian while we worked.

I sketched in charcoal. Now it is time to think in colors, and then the painting. It will be a cornerstone for me. I am good at drawing, but I have never painted from life.

I didn't go out at all. During my Latin lesson I saw Terffidua from the window. If he is not interested in me, it's not important whether he sees me or not. If, on the contrary, I am interested in him, it is excellent to miss a day.

Tuesday, March 30, 1875. My stupid brother is going to Russia with Sacha. This beast makes money out of everything. He just sold me his Dumas, Hugo, and W. Scott for sixty francs. Take note that he could not take them because, to get these books back from Russia, he would have to pass by the Censor's Committee, which would take two months and cost a lot of trouble.

Wednesday, March 31, 1875. I am tired of all this unhappiness. I feel that I'm dying morally because I am physically. But thank God I'm feeling better and I'm white and fresh again.

I went out to reserve a box at the Français. The Prince of Wales will be there and has insisted upon their playing *Madame the Archduchess.* I also reserved a box at the Opera. The children will go there, and I'm happy to go without them.

Nadine and Dina also came. Toward the end of the first act the Prince entered, and I blushed with pleasure.

The Prince of Wales has charming manners, but one cannot say that he is good-looking. He is below average height, quite fat, and has a rather beautiful oval face with grey eyes, an aquiline nose, a short, thick beard and . . . very little hair. The forehead is high. He has some hair on the top of his head that he manages to part, a bald spot, and in the back some hair that's quite thick. I remember that in Baden-Baden, in 1872, he was far less bald. It was a very agreeable evening—an amusing play and a future king!

Some minutes after he sat down, he picked up the opera glass and directed it at me. At first I thought he was looking next to us, but having fixed my eyes on the binoculars, I was sure he was looking at me.

Thursday, April 1, 1875. Decidedly, I have a strong character. Everybody was crying, even Miss Catherine, the children's governess, but not me. On the contrary, I was calm and gay. What a sad thing, a departure! I would like to build a big house and live with all my relatives and all my friends. [Added later, in August 1875:] Like Epicurus?

Sacha and his wife are leaving for Russia and are taking Paul with them; Mama is going to Cannes with Dina and Walitsky. [Doctor] Botkin will pass a week there and told her to go there, too, so that he can see her more often.

Mama cried, Paul cried, . . . and Nadya, Sacha, Catherine, Dina, Walitsky, Triphon, and even Grandpapa cried!

Ouf! It's enough tears to fill a basin. I'd like to analyze them chemically and learn which moral causes make them fall. I forgot to say that Paris also cried, and at the station, Pelikan too. We all went to the station with them, and were saying goodbye when Nadianka shouted, "Here's the Prince of Wales!" The adorable Prince was preceded by two cocottes. That's practically nothing for him—this playboy, this Lovelace, this Don Juan. To be what he is is only to be better loved, and I am altogether certain that he is in every divorce court. Women play around with all kinds of rascals, and wouldn't it be absurd for them to resist such a prince?

As we were approaching Monte Carlo, Stepa put his little arms around me and begged me in his little voice to go with them to Russia. After five minutes of that, I was exasperated and had to hold myself not to hit him with my elbow in order to make him leave me alone. Finally we arrived, and everybody embraced again and again. Finally the train left.

At night in Nice, on the edge of the sea, the sky spread with stars shining like diamonds, an absolute silence troubled only by the chant of the frogs; from time to time the whistle of the train, a worldly and prosaic invention, made the sublime calm more noticeable. And all that, you see, is not an ordinary spectacle. It is not an enjoyment that one understands at any age, even with all intelligence. And just now, here, it seems to me that it is only I who know how to admire, to love, and to suffer!

Friday, April 2, 1875. My aunt is also in Cannes, so I am altogether alone. I went out with Papa. Olga dined here, my aunt returned, Paris and Mary arrived, and we went to the Français. The first face I saw was Terffidua's. "Girofla is here," I said.

Mary repeated, "Girofla is here."

Olga said, "Girofla is here."

"Well," I said, sitting down, "Fie on Girofla! Can we look at anyone else after the Prince of Wales?"

At that moment, he [Audiffret] took the glasses and stared at me for the first time in an age. For an instant I stared right into them, and then I pretended not to have seen him at all—only because I was blinded by the lights. I kept myself hidden behind a huge Japanese fan, through which I could see Terffidua looking at me from time to time.

Galula left his orchestra seat, and I said to myself, He's coming to see us and is going to introduce Audiffret! In fact, he entered our box and stopped in the middle, like a man who is going to make an announcement.

See the next chapter in my next book.

BOOK THIRTY-ONE

Journal begun May 1872
H. G. T. D. O. H.
Book 31
Begun Friday, April 2, 1875
Ended Thursday, April 22, 1875
Promenade des Anglais, 55 bis, in my villa, Nice

Friday, April 2, 1875. At the theater, Galula came to our box like a man who is about to make an announcement. I am ashamed to admit that my heart began to pound, because I thought we were going to hear that he wanted to introduce Audiffret, even though I felt that after all this time the man should have introduced himself.

"Good evening, Madame and Mademoiselle," he said.

"Please be seated," my aunt said to him. He sat and began to talk about the Durands. I listened. I listened, and finally became impatient. But nothing happened. He stayed a few minutes longer and then went away as he came. What a way to act!

Tuesday, April 6, 1875. Grandpapa went out with me to the music. More people than usual were there, but Nice empties in the wink of an eye. Papa returned, and I went with my aunt to the café.

Wednesday, April 7, 1875. I progress at full speed in Latin, even though I don't study.

Saturday, April 10, 1875. I'm crazy about *The Archduchess of Gerolstein.* I haven't stopped singing it. Upon arriving at 7:00 in Cannes, instead of speaking I sang *The Archduchess* and conducted myself like a fool.

Miss Collignon is coming to stay a month and I am happy; she is very agreeable and extremely useful, even indispensable. And I believe that Mama is going to be a little better.

Sunday, April 11, 1875. I went to church with Collignon and Dina. There is nothing I like better than the English prayers. While waiting to become a declared Protestant, I am already one at heart.

I must not forget that I have not smoked for four or five days. And I have sworn an oath not to be impertinent but keep my mouth shut rather than answer rudely, no matter what anyone says to me. (The relatives, of course!) And if I betray my oath, I'm to be damned!

So I failed, and having read again the book where I made the oath, I became so frightened that, to compensate and not be cursed, I don't allow myself to smoke anymore. It's quite hard for me. But really, if one could know how Grandpapa is so foolishly provoking, and how much Mama irritates and pushes—even an angel . . .

Every night I dream about the stars—how I reach up and take them with my hands. The dream predicts for me great fame and high fortune. Don't you mock this. It's necessary to believe in dreams; all great men have had their own.

Tuesday, April 13, 1875. Oh, what a terrible thing! Brunet brought me a "key" to dreams, and I'm reading it: to see the stars fall means—death. Fie, the horror! I believe in dreams, but not always in the explanation. And then, death—death for me is a close relative. . . . In the fifth dream the star that fell was not a star but a tiny piece of silver paper that I detached with my thumb. . . . Seeing them fall, I wanted them and held out my hand, and without difficulty I touched the sky. That was the time the sky was made of cardboard.

It seems that Collignon has never been absent.

Nadine writes that Paul has been received at his father's house with salvos of cannons, champagne, etc., etc., and that they are preparing a magnificent apartment for him in the big house. The wretch will have his head turned all the way around. All this pomp makes me want to go over there.

But where does this idea that I am going to die come from? To die! Yes, but if I die—horrible thought!—my dream is predicting it and the cards, too! God knows what He is doing. He does not wish to give me everything I want and makes me die in pity. But, in fact, what am I asking? What all the women in the world ask—nothing more—and for that do I have to be killed? My God, it has been a long time that I have not prayed to you. I say some prayers, I repeat my questions, but I don't succeed in reaching You. Direct my mind, deliver me from doubt, protect me and let me live.

Mama has fainted again. I don't know what to think about that.

Thursday, April 22, 1875. Last night at church I saw Mrs. Voiekoff. She greeted me very nicely, so I went up to her. She said, "Do you know that Julie is getting married?"

"No, I did not. To whom?"

"The Baron of Benkendorf, Secretary of the Embassy in Berlin. Come to see us and wish her happiness."

"I'll come with pleasure to wish her well, Madame. But you, too, you'll come to my house, won't you?"

"Yes, certainly," etc., etc.

She begged me very hard to come, but I'll not go first.

This morning, again at the church. How tiresome it is for me—the incense, the priest, the funeral chants, the heat. We met Mrs. Voiekoff again, and after lunch she came to our house with Julie, staying an hour to talk about the fiancé, the parents, and the superb connections of the families, and the dowry (not bigger than mine—300,000 rubles).

We heard that the little bride is going to enter high society with this marriage. She will be allied to all the great families of Belgium, Russia, and France. Do I need to say that I'm envious? And I almost have the right to be because I'm pretty, educated, and well-bred, whereas she is ugly and ignorant. But since she's dressed up like an adult, she looks much better than she did. Monday they will leave for Paris, and next Monday for Brussels, where the next day there will be a big party at the mother-in-law's home—with the King. Wednesday they'll be married, and right away the new Baroness of Benkendorf will return to Paris with her husband. They'll stay there for six weeks.

Julie insists that I come to her house and promises me that I'll not be bored. I believe her. From Paris they'll go to London to the Prince of Wales' ball. Benkendorf presented the Prince to his future mother-in-law when he was in Nice and staying at the same hotel— the Luxembourg.

Unfortunately, I am not rich enough to buy a husband. I'll buy one only when I've lost the hope of being bought myself. A husband is a luxury animal.

Tonight we went to the Passion. (Hair loose, black velvet hat. Very good.) The church was full, and people were suffocating while the priest was reading of the suffering of our Savior Jesus Christ. Impious as I am, I noticed a handsome Russian who also noticed me. Upon our return we had a most animated conversation about marriage and all sorts of things because I'm not at all embarrassed. I say everything. . . .

BOOK THIRTY-TWO

[Notebook 32: there is no cover page.]
[Begun Friday, April 23, 1875
Finished Saturday, May 15, 1875.]

Friday, April 23, 1875. I did not go to Mass. The day after tomorrow is Easter. At 3:00 they carry out the bier of Christ. In the church the heat is suffocating, and upon leaving we went to Mrs. Voiekoff's, where we stayed quite a while. I adore the Hotel Luxembourg for 100,000 reasons. My aunt was in the salon with Mrs. V., and I and Dina were on the balcony with Julie. We could see everyone passing and all the horizon, all the Promenade. I would like to sell my villa and live in Nice in the hotel.

Dina came home, and my aunt took me to Mrs. Angel's. There we found Mrs. Patton, who crossed the entire room to curtsey to me! What's happened to her?

Then we went to dine at the London House, and I ordered what I wanted: bisque of crawfish, beef fillets with artichoke hearts, green peas and truffles, asparagus hollandaise, roast chicken, and strawberries with cream. Also, we had Château Villegeorges wine, of 1865. What a dinner I had! And what extraordinary wine! I drank so much, so much, so much!

Saturday, April 24, 1875. I had a dream in which I saw an enormous bouquet of yellow heads of wheat, as big as my bedroom, hanging from the ceiling. It was hanging above a table all covered with flowers and magnificent fruits. This dream put me in a good mood all day. I was so happy that it was a pity to be that way for nothing. I put on the white silk skirt, and, for a blouse, the top of the white Jewish dress in light wool embroidered in white. I wore not even one plain gold bracelet and no gloves. There was nothing on my head, either, except two long curls tied together. Oh, yes—two diamond earrings.

In the church they gave us some chairs, and we sat in front, on the right, as usual. My aunt went first to confession, then Dina, and afterward I entered. [In Russian]: *"Cross yourself and kiss the crucifix,"* said the priest to me, and then asked, *"Against which commandment do you sin the most?"*

"I really don't know," I answered him from under my fan because I wanted very much to laugh.

"Well, what sins do you admit to having?"

"Different sins."

"For instance, are you rude to your elders? Do you take what belongs to others? Do you hate anyone? Do you speak falsely? Evilly?"

"No."

"Well, what else is there? Do you like to gratify yourself?"

"Yes." This time I hid my face completely behind my fan, the question was so ridiculous.

"This is bad."

"Yes. That's how it is. What can one do?"

"Well, do you love finery?"

"I like it very much."

"This is a big sin. Do you think that because of wearing fine clothes a person is more beautiful?"

"Of course. He is more beautiful," I said behind the fan, laughing. This evening I had the proof of what I said with all assurance.

"No, a person is much better simply attired. What is there in finery? Everyone can look and see that it's all on the surface."

I said nothing, preferring not to discuss it with him.

"Do you also like to flirt?" this ass continued. He was talking with his elbow on the table and looking at the ceiling.

"What do you mean? I do not understand," I said, thinking to myself, explain, Father. Move away from there.

"That is—do you draw attention to yourself?"

Oh, what a dirty thing to say! *"Well, yes. It happens by itself. I do not know how."*

"Well, so there is nothing more?" he asked.

"There is nothing more."

"You have to pray to God. He will forgive you."

Then he pronounced the usual prayer, and I put a louis into his hand and left, biting my lips as I went down the two steps, holding myself in so as not to burst out laughing.

Mrs. Voiekoff entered with her daughter and sat with us.

Nothing this day has bothered me from morning to night. I was gay and happy and content with myself and others.

At midnight on the dot, the priest, my charming confessor, began to sing "Our Resurrection, Lord!"

God, I believe in you; but your priests are imbeciles.

During the midnight Easter service, I stood up almost all the time, exchanging only a few words with Mrs. V. and Julie, who was relating her confession to me. It was a beautiful service—all those women in white carrying huge lighted candles.

I had not fasted, but I was hungry. The mass finished about 4:00 in the morning. The priest went out carrying the Holy Sacrament, saying, "I also believe that this is the very body of You and that this is the very blood shed by You." I raised my eyes to heaven to ask forgiveness of God for having received communion without the faith to believe in it, and also to pray to Him to inspire me with what I must think if I am wrong.

The bread is not the flesh, and the wine is not the blood of Christ. It is not just now that I think this way; I have never thought otherwise, but only two years ago I understood the absurdity uttered by the priest. Stop! Not so silly! I believe that we give the wine and the bread in memory of *la Cena* [the last supper] (I said this in Italian because I don't know it any other way). When Jesus gave the bread and wine to his apostles, he told them it was his flesh and blood, but he said it allegorically. I'm sure that God doesn't want us to believe blindly in what the priest tells us. Christianity is good because one can reason, and the more one reasons, the more we think Him just and true.

But then it's not for me to reform my religion, or rather, I don't want to. The shortest way is to become a Protestant. I think I said something like this last year about this same time. This is the fifth Easter I've been in Nice. When I arrived I was eleven and now I'm sixteen. How old I am!

At 4:15 we went home. I put on a dressing robe, and we ate a lot of good things ordered at the London House and placed on a well-decorated table, as is the custom. For the second time in my life, I went to bed at 5:00 in the morning. . . .

Tuesday, April 27, 1875. I have to say that I beat George. It was a delicate matter, I believe. He was dirty, half-naked, drunk, awful. He came to my room, and I ordered him to go away. He didn't want to and played the idiot. Then I took a brush and scratched him with it, so hard I'm sure he felt it. I was furious, and in the mirror I saw my mouth full of froth. Now, a half hour later, dressed in a pretty, straw-colored dress from Worth, with gloves and shoes to match and a pink-lined umbrella with bamboo handle, I'm no longer recognizable as that girl.

For the first time I walked in the street in a long dress. . . .

Thursday, May 6, 1875. [After a careful delineation of her physical parts, Marie goes on to say this:] I have not flattered nor humiliated myself. . . . I am elegant, gracious, graceful, lively or indolent, according to the moment. As for my spirit, it is seen in this journal. Basically I am good, charitable, and delicate. I never offend a weaker person and never humiliate an inferior. I am loving by spurts, always coquettish, and always and everywhere flirting. I love beauty, greatness, society—the noise, style, and brilliance of society. Also, sometimes I like mysteries. I can't stand to be contradicted, but the dominating flaw of my character is ambition, for which I would sacrifice all. I am proud and imperious— ambitious like—like myself. There is no other to compare me with. This ambition will drive me to great things if God wishes, or will tear me constantly.

Saturday, May 8, 1875. I saw Girofla. He looked at me—stared at me, but I acted as if I had not seen him. After a noisy dinner [with the Sapogenikoffs] we went to the Français to see *Uncle Sam*, a play that gives me the desire to go to America. I'll go next summer to the Philadelphia Exposition.

Sunday, May 9, 1875. Why am I going to Russia? I say it's to buy some horses and a fur coat, but I feel that fate pushes me there. To the devil with such sad ideas! I'd rather tell about the expedition "with the fork" than to be busy with vain fantasies.

From 2:00 to 3:30 Mary and Olga and I went on our side, not the seaside, of the Promenade, without hats. We were admiring the garden of the little purple houses. Rosalie Leon's is a love of a garden. I stopped in front of Gioja's, as she is not here; as it is all locked up, I picked some daisies by passing my arm through the iron gate, and we solemnly pulled the petals off one flower. I thought, "You, who are from her garden, from the garden where he walked, tell me once and for all—shall I ever be at least once for him what she was to him?" I pulled the petals from my side and the two girls from theirs, and my flower told me Yes. I told myself that this would compensate me for everything, and I could spit on everything as long as such a thing was promised to me. We went upstairs into my study and I spoke: "My dears, we are forming a masonic society, you know *for the gathering of young men*. For the moment we are only three, but with time each of us will recruit. Every society has a beginning. We are going to make a philtre which will be divided in three parts, each of us to receive one."

My proposal was received with enthusiasm. We prepared the philtre, or talisman, with seltzer water and the pebbles and leaves we had gathered from two places favorable for what we wished; and furthermore, each of us pricked our fingers with the courage of Spartans and poured three drops of blood into the mixture. The whole thing was boiled and dissolved through a chemical procedure. "And now," I said, "let's swear, and I will tell you our motto and our seal: we'll have three graces supporting a ribbon twisted with roses on which is written 'Andacter and Amanter' which means 'Daringly and Tenderly.'" We swore our oaths, and having carefully hidden the beverage, we went downstairs to arrange our appearance a little and went out. For the lack of better things, we spotted three American playboys who are students at the Nash school. It is unworthy!!

Let's think about the fork! In the evening, wearing large Conspirator coats, we left furtively, like the thieves we are, as you are going to see. Hidden under the coats, I carried a fork, Mary a knife, and Olga nothing at all. So the moon had to be out, shining! It was disturbing, but no matter. We passed Gioja's villa without being noticed. Mary gave several jabs with her knife between two stones of the terrace. Then we passed again, and this time I drove my fork into the ground and pulled out a trophy—a very little cactus the size of a small coin. But how proud we were! We went at once to the garden and I planted the stolen thing, saying, "Thrive and prosper. I'll give you a name worthy of you. In time I'll put a sign beside you, as is done for rare plants, and I'll write *planta furum*."

How happy I am, my God, to busy myself with foolishness! Mary proposed stealing all of Gioja's cactus, and I went so far as to propose taking her, herself [Gioja] and putting her in our pond. It's really a happy thing to be able to have so different a mood! It's happiness in foolishness. . . .

After dinner I went out . . . with Collignon to Delbecchi's to buy an album. I have often wanted to draw or copy certain pictures, but I never have had anything but single sheets to work with. Now, with an album, I am content.

For some unavowable reason, I believe I would like very much to marry. Oh, you—you think you caught me—thinking about what you're thinking. But no, I don't have those ideas. . . . If Miloradovitch asks for me in marriage, I'll not refuse. And in fact, why refuse the positive and run after bubbles? However, it is not such a marriage as I want. . . . But what a crazy girl I am! He'll not want me. . . . That's the point. He'd be difficult for me, and I'd be obstinate. But, as the beautiful Hélène says, "If Olympus wants my fall one day or another, it will happen."

Tuesday, May 11, 1875. From the day of my marriage my freedom will begin, while it should be the other way around.

Friday, May 14, 1875. Again at the theater, I was irritated. I like to look at Audiffret, but if I do he will put his imagination to work. Yet he's the only man here, and *I want him.* If there were others, I would love to have all of them. But seriously, his imperturbable conduct enrages me!

On a Saturday morning in mid-May, when Mama and my aunt and Nina Sapogenikoff had taken the train to Monaco, Mary and Olga brought their landau to our house and proposed that we drive up to Audiffret's castle. The coachman smiled as we started off. He took us up through a steep little street. I had never been so close to the castle before, although it dominated the town and I had always set my watch by its tower clock. Flushed and laughing, we girls chatted in French as we admired the surrounding walls. "If you look out from the top of the tower, you can see the whole city," the coachman told us. "Would you like to go in?"

"Oh, no! No!"

He insisted he had been paid for that, but we still refused.

"Well, do you want to do the tour? Go around?"

Thinking he would take us around by another street, I said yes, but to my surprise he stopped right in front of the doors.

The building has two towers, windows set in the shape of a cross, and a number of terraces. The immense door on the ground floor suggests that the space behind it is large enough to be called a second story. I wondered whether it opens on a kitchen or a dining room. It's all very beautiful, including the terraced garden, although there are no trees. In front are a huge lawn, some alleys, and grass-framed flower beds. The towers flank the entrance, and there are several openings in the walls. In front of everything is an iron gate surmounted by an arch or something I could not identify. As the towers are detached from the main building, I think they probably mark the entrance to the old castle. Everything is big, rich, beautiful, even if not a marvel of taste. The driver began to call, "Mr. Émile! Mr. Émile!"

At first we didn't understand. Then in a chorus said, "Not him! Don't call him!"

Surprised, he told us, "But you've only seen the garden."

"But we don't want to see him!" I was shouting, almost screaming. "We don't want. . . . Who were you calling?"

"The master of the castle, of course. Mr. Émile."

Oh, if he had heard! We were screaming and laughing at once—screaming because we were afraid to go in and laughing because we wanted to. I found it nightmarish.

To Mary's questions, the man said he had been coachman at the castle, driven Émile to his college, and sometimes played billiards with him at the café in Cassini Street.

"How long ago was that?"

"Eight years."

Then I asked, "How old is he?"

"Twenty-three."

"But he hasn't finished his studies . . ."

"No. When he got the fortune, he quit school."

"Who left it to him?"

"His grandfather."

"He lives alone here?"

"Yes. I know him well—Mr. Émile."

With this word the driver returned to his horses, satisfied with himself.

As we descended the narrow little street, I was praying that we would not meet Émile. It was not until we arrived on the Promenade that we saw him walking between Saëtone and Pepino, as we had often seen him before.

BOOK THIRTY-THREE

H. G. T. D. O. H.
Book 33
Begun Sunday, May 16, 1875
Finished Sunday, June 6, 1875
Promenade des Anglais, No. 55 bis, in my villa

Monday, May 24, 1875. Muse! Tell how we walked in front of the window of Girofla, he without his vest, looking at us from one of the windows without suspecting anything.

After preparing myself for bed, I took my pen and wrote an Iliadic invocation to the muse of our coming exploit. Or, rather, it was Dante's lines—early in his *Hell*—that were closer to my mind:

Oh, Muse, oh high intellect, now aid me,
O Mind, that I may write what I saw—
Here will appear your nobility.

(*O Muse, o alto ingegno, or m'aiutate;*
o mente che scrivesti cio ch'io vidi,
qui si parrà la tua nobilitate.

[*Inferno* II, 7-9])

From this morning I have been running around town, and now at 2:00 everything is ready. And Ovid's metaphors have nothing to compare to the one I've made. We know that I have a good posture, that I have broad shoulders, a high chest, hips and derrière well-rounded and prominent, and small feet. Within five minutes, I became a flat monster, emaciated, with sunken chest and one shoulder higher than the other, which pushes everything else out of shape. My feet became flat and long, my eyes sunken and my teeth black. And my greyish-black hair crowned this image. In a black silk dress, very plain, and a brown hat tied under the chin, a veil of the same color, and blue glasses, I was a figure not even Satan would recognize.

Mary and Olga were two little girls in blonde wigs. They wore percale dresses, little English hats, and long, flat-heeled boots of grey linen. They wore thick blue veils.

Nina, whom I adore for her compliance in this masquerade, wore black and covered her face with a triple veil, like the woman in the elegy, in long mourning garb.

Dressed like that, we glided along the pathway that crosses the courtyard and climbed into a carriage. But oh! Surprise! The coachman was Ange, the same Ange who has been our driver for several months. It's certain that at first he did not recognize us. Collignon instructed him to drive these English ladies to the Audiffret Tower. Imagine our state of mind! After all the foolish things we've done along the Promenade, at the theater, and everywhere—to be recognized would produce a frightful scandal; everyone would be talking about it, especially now.

But in spite of my British accent and my changed voice, the cursed Ange suspected and smiled, and it was very easy for him to guess because he has served us so long. I went out every day in his carriage, and today he saw us leave from our house. He especially recognized Nina, and he guessed the rest.

At the door of the castle, I asked for the doorman, and he came. Seeing two old ladies badly dressed and two little girls in even less becoming garb, he looked at us askance and said he had no order to permit anyone to see the castle. But a fifty-centime coin melted his resistance, and we entered. I asked him several naïve and strange questions, all the time limping and looking at the windows. I asked if the Master was the old Baron Audiffret, and the old man told me "Yes," when I suddenly glimpsed the young baron in a shirt, opening the window and looking with sleepy eyes at these strange monkeys. But what was funny was that the doorman was telling us that the Master was in Italy and that only the servants were at present in the castle.

I understood nothing about it; I had hoped to get into the house, expecting that our appearance as petitioners would help us. We had to be satisfied with a walk under the windows, but believe me, even that was really audacious. We were soaked with perspiration, what with the wigs, the veils, the ribbons, which were suffocating us. And it was only 4:00. We drove back down through the streets and greeted all the people by waving to them. All this activity in our carriage produced such gaiety as to make me almost suffocate.

Audiffret was on his way to the baths, and we followed him. The bathers honored us as newcomers. Saëtone put on his monocle and stared at us, and then turned away as from such unattractive objects.

I sat alone with Nina on a bench, and the children sat on the sand, playing with pebbles. At that moment, Collignon came with Dina, who was wearing my white dress and my hat, carrying my umbrella, and wearing my thick white veil and my false curls. She was supposed to represent me, and the deception succeeded. Yourkoff thought her to be me, but I was afraid to look at her; almost immediately Girofla came close, slowly. Everybody took her for me because we are about the same height. But she is a little smaller, yet my clothing is unique here and everywhere. As Girofla approached her, I was very much afraid, not being able to talk to Dina; I said to Nina Sapogenikoff in Russian, loudly enough for Dina to hear, "Lower your umbrella; he's going to recognize you." She understood and did what I told her to. All the usual crowd at the beach saw us, taking Dina for me and me for a Mrs. Samuels. I held myself in to keep from exploding with laughter. To stay longer would become dangerous, so I went away still limping enough to show my pretty feet, more than a foot long. Once in the carriage, we raced home. Dina also hurried home. We recovered our own shapes—for me, happily; for her. . . . And then she rushed back to the baths with the Sapogenikoffs and with me, now veiled as she had been. In a word, it was the operetta *Giroflé-Girofla* that we were playing! Collignon stayed home, and only I went walking alone. I found the family seated near Girofla and Company. All of them turned toward me, saying such things as, "At last you're here!" and "Where were you, Marie?"

I answered, "I was looking for you. I was here with Miss Collignon just a half-hour ago, and I'm in a hurry. Help me take off this veil; I'm as red as a lobster." Girofla was staring at me, but we looked at no one. We were laughing.

Paris was bathing, and encouraged by his example, we ran to the cabin and undressed; one after the other, like Panurge's sheep, we jumped into the sea from the bridge! I've never been so happy, so foolish; never before had we done so many silly things and returned triumphantly.

After supper everybody sang in the garden—even Papa! What a concert!

Tuesday, May 25, 1875. I boiled, I burned, I melted! . . .

But let's not forget to say, first, what I did at the bath. I went there with my helpers, Walitsky and Yourkoff, following. Girofla saw us arriving, and when we were seated, his second, Saëtone, came near us, then himself, as if he were saying, "Oh, ho, here you are!"

As soon as he came close to me, I said, "Well, let's go, Mary, Olga," and we left.

You are really taken in, handsome Niçois! You were not expecting that, were you?

He left right after we did. *Will* alone, my girl. You have character!

I dressed up for the theater—a white dress from Worth. My seconds were also in white—my aunt and Paris, also. When Ravel came on stage, I threw him a bouquet, and I received two of his monkey smiles. He is charming. Galula was with Audiffret. [Felix Galula Dechiar was a notary and clerk to the attorney Desforges, who handled the sale of the villa at No. 55, Promenade des Anglais, to Marie's aunt, Nadya Romanoff.]

Faithful to my promise to despise, I didn't look downstairs; but the door opened and Mary shouted, "Here is Galula!"

After the first sentences, "How is Mr. Desforges?" I asked. "Is it true that he is sick?"

Mary and Olga burst out laughing, and I, after biting my lips until I drew blood, did as they did. Galula looked and followed our example. My aunt and Paris made a chorus. For five minutes, Mr. Desforges amused us.

When we calmed down, Galula leaned toward my aunt, "Madame, I have a permission to ask you," and then in a lower voice, "let me introduce my friend Mr. Émile Audiffret to you."

I didn't listen to any more. I had something twisting like a corkscrew in my heart and I was full of happiness and ease. [Re-reading this passage in 1877, she wrote in the margin:] "It was one of the most beautiful moments of my life." [And below that appears:] "Approved. 1880."

Unexpected triumph! I have often desired many things, and never has what I desired been accomplished or realized. I never before felt such vibrant, agreeable, satisfactory contentment as this. I couldn't believe my ears. I am not the disdaining one who cannot be pleased.

Mary and Olga jumped up and came toward us. "Go away," I told them in Russian. "Get out." I did this without moving because, in Audiffret's box, I saw the Durands behind the fat papa Saëtone and Audiffret, himself, who was watching the effect of the words of his friend on us. And I saw Daouis behind Saëtone's shoulder, also watching us.

Fine! At last it was time. After six months of a desperate coquettishness, I was already meditating revenge. Good people, listen to the end of the story: I *thought* I heard Galula saying, "At the next intermission."

How long the play lasted it is impossible to say. It was as if I were sitting on burning coals, and my heart was beating fast. And for what? For a man I don't even love a little. Why? Because in this world there is not a joy which equals the one that one feels when knowing or believing one is loved.

Women—real women, will understand me. Galula and Girofla embraced each other. Finally they left. I composed my face, and I was shaking all over. I waited one minute, two minutes, three, five, ten minutes. Finally the gong sounded, the curtain rose, and the two men, Almaviva and Figaro, entered their own box.

What happened? Do you know, what he did was very smart! Oh, how disappointed I was! Oh, miserable wretch! Oh, traitor! Oh, scoundrel! I didn't know where I was any more. I wanted to be underground. Such an insult! Can you see that dog's face, that monkey of a man? It was he who made fun of me! A thousand thunders! We were all soaked in warm water.

The last act seemed horrible. However, I laughed and saved face as much as possible.

That miserable so-and-so didn't sit still; sometimes he threw his arm around the neck of his Figaro; then he changed seats; then he moved again. He looked as if he were sitting on pins, and he finally left before the end.

Galula assisted at our departure. Fortunately I told him good night politely. I wanted to strangle him.

I say *fortunately* because they are not so miserable as I thought. I'll tell you why, but first, I saw that awful Audiffret seated in the Maison Dorée as we drove home. What a horror!

I was in such an awful state and didn't know how to calm myself that I repeated Galula's words to my aunt. "But," she said, "he didn't say 'At the next intermission.' He said, 'Permit me to present one of my friends, Mr. Émile Audiffret,' and then he lowered his voice and said, 'He has tormented me for a long time to be introduced, but I had to ask you whether you wished it.'"

Well, now, are they Galula's words? Why is my aunt unworthy of trust? She has the respectable habit of perverting all the words and all the facts. Especially this time I wanted to believe her, and with some effort I succeeded. However, not entirely.

I threw myself into bed to shorten the time. I didn't have the patience to wait for tomorrow to recall it and to comment on it. Either he is a vile person or he is a vulgar, badly brought-up brat! The next day nothing was equal to my anxiety. It was a question of self-esteem, because, if he dared to joke, it was a little too common a joke.

As we were returning from the theater, I made this promise in a loud voice: "I'll make this man fall in love with me; I'll mistreat him; I'll make him walk on his knees, have his hair dyed yellow, have his head shaved; I'll make him roll in the mud. . . . I'll have my revenge!

In the morning we talked in Mama's room about what had happened. After all, we agreed, he is a nice man, and if he was aware that we were those crazy old English women who visited the castle last week, it was a way to pay us back. My aunt and Mama took the thing as it is without the "next intermission" promise. They were amused, saying silly things such as "he is handsome" and "you are sixteen" and "he is a neighbor." They also argued that he has a thousand means of pleasing—saddle horses, electric-lighting decorations at the castle—things like that, as if they were on his side! They even suggested that it might in the end be *I* who would crawl; that *he* would make *me* walk on *my* knees, that it could be dangerous, and that I must be careful. They said all this laughing and completely satisfied and glowing.

None of that changed the fact that I had been insulted. *Where* was he to be introduced? Would it be like last year when he was supposed to be introduced? What an abominable situation! I asked myself, What shall I do for a man I could love? But here my self-respect and pride were at stake, and these two beasts seemed a hundred times stronger than love. I vowed to myself that he must pay; but I forgive easily, and I am not sure of myself. That's the trouble.

Friday, May 28, 1875. It was two or three days later, when I went with my aunt and one of her friends to the beach, that Galula was there to give us his hand and help us out of the carriage. My aunt whispered in Russian, *"Here he comes dressed in white"*; I blushed slightly but continued with Galula. My heart was beating very fast, and I was afraid of a new insult. Audiffret stayed behind us with Saëtone and some others. Finally, after ten or fifteen minutes, Galula looked at him, got up, and brought him. Ah!

"Permit me, Madam, to introduce my friend Mr. Émile Audiffret." He bowed. My aunt, too. He bowed to me, and I made a slight sign to him with a light, cold smile, looking indifferent, I felt sure. Inside I was proudly satisfied.

But Girofla was very much at ease and spoke without timidity. Only he seemed so young! He looked to me like those little sparrows not yet feathered out. The young expression pleases me. (It was his Niçois hat which gave him this expression.) I was afraid before this to look him in the face, believing he might think absurd things. Now, when speaking to him, I saw I had to; I saw his beautiful black eyes—not brown, but black—really black, his beautiful teeth, his beautiful mouth, and a very mediocre moustache. I realized he was much better-looking at a distance. That poor, elegant Niçois, with a suit of yellow-white like my dresses, wore grey pearl gloves so clean that they were ugly. We talked about Desforges's health, and we laughed. He had a tic in his face, but then almost all men have tics. I don't know why.

"I hope, Sir," my aunt told him, getting up, "that you will come to see us, and you, also, Mr. Galula."

My aunt is enchanted and already believes that Audiffret is in love with me. But what makes me believe that he was running after me—was interested, in a word—is that in his smile there is a certain expression that makes me believe what, through an incomprehensible modesty and a certain false shame, I don't dare to believe.

Saturday, May 29, 1875. Today we left St. Peter's Church and went to the music, where Audiffret greeted us with a smile. It seems so extraordinary to know him, since I've seen him for five years and have been talking about him for five months. Now it seems strange to know him. I can't believe it.

I was with my aunt, and we introduced him to the Sapogenikoffs, who blushed and stayed silent.

All the time Girofla stayed near us and then asked if we would go to the café.

"Why, Sir?" my aunt asked.

"To have the pleasure of talking with you ladies longer." Then interrupting himself, he said to me, "You're blushing, Miss. Why?" He turned and looked. "It was Galula passing by," he said.

"But no, Sir. I did not blush. It is you who are blushing. Oh! Look how red you are!"

"Pay no attention to it," he said. "I blush very often, and for nothing."

"Like a young girl," I said.

As we started to drive off he asked, "You will be at the theater tonight?"

"Yes."

Monday, May 31, 1875. I've had one lover, but I despised him; whereas I don't detest this man at all. . . .

Incidentally, he was here yesterday. I found his card on my dressing table. Without doubt it's Audiffret who brings happiness to my face. Mama has noticed it and told me, and my aunt also.

I am today, like every day since the introduction of Audiffret, animated and agitated. . . . I don't touch the earth from joy, and I see myself as beautiful. It seems that the world is mine.

Today I went to bathe with my aunt, and Audiffret, seeing us coming, turned his carriage around and arrived at the baths two minutes later. When I came out of the water, he asked, "Well, how was the water?"

"Excellent, but a little cold," I lied. I was hot.

"Oh, if it's cold, we must walk," my aunt said.

And we walked, I in the middle, with Audiffret on my left and my aunt on the right. It was exactly as I had imagined it the other evening, and ten other times, always the same.

Tomorrow all of Nice will say that he's in love with me, and within a week they'll be prophesying a marriage. Yourkoff and Walitsky came toward us, and Girofla left us at the moment we regained our carriage. As he said goodbye he held my hand so tightly that I thought about it all the rest of the day. And when I think about it, I feel the tightening of my hand again, and it seems to me that it was not altogether innocent.

He asked permission to come to see us this evening, but my aunt told him to come when we'll have music with the family.

All the house talked to me about Audiffret, laughing and whispering; I smiled then, and I can't stop doing it.

Thursday, June 3, 1875. At 8:00 we opened all the doors and lighted the second floor, and I came down, in white as always (my archduchess dress). Nina and Paris arrived with Mary and Olga, but I'm beginning to be tired of these nice girls. Then Galula came, and two minutes after him, Audiffret, very well dressed and looking nice. Then Ricardo Barnola, and that was all.

I presented Girofla to Mama and Dina and, with my sweet dove smile, I exchanged a few words with him.

There's no way to have five minutes' worth of serious talk with Audiffret; he always changes the subject. I've changed my mind about him, though: I find him more agreeable nearby than at a distance. Collignon said he gains enormously close up. He has a beautiful mouth, superb eyes, a long nose (but beautifully made), and an admirable complexion. From afar he looks like a very ordinary boy.

When leaving, Audiffret held my hand tightly again. I think it's simply his way.

I don't dare to say what comes to my mind, but well—it doesn't mean anything to me. It's that in touching his hand I received the same kind of shock that I felt when touching the hand of the awful Pole. I've touched the hands of many men, but only two have had this effect on me. As Mirzisky loved me, I wonder now whether Girofla does, also. I say this with very great care. We can be ridiculous when we make mistakes in such matters.

Saturday, June 5, 1875. It rained. Girofla was supposed to come, but in his place we saw Galula, who came to our house to see him, expecting to find him here. Audiffret is not courting me at all; he hardly distinguishes me from the others. Why did he make our acquaintance? He doesn't come for my brother, nor my aunt, nor our house. Nor for our acquaintance. Why, then?

Mama believes and says that he's in love with me. But he didn't have himself presented for the pleasure of coming here; there is no attraction in our house, nor any pleasure. Here people are often very badly received. If it's for me, I accept the idea willingly, but he hides it very adroitly and, except for some signs that I have noticed in his conversation that he paid attention to us and knew what we were doing, he shows nothing of that.

Sunday, June 6, 1875. We saw Audiffret at the music, dressed in white. He's always badly shaved. What a pity! He came and found us on my terrace, which is a copy of my darling Gioja's terrace. Nina, my aunt, and my graces had been there since 8:00. First we imitated the frogs, which were singing melodiously in the pond, and then we started to bark—everybody, including Nina—at all the pedestrians and all the carriages.

"For these girls of sixteen," Nina asked, "is it well to howl at the moon as the old maïds do?"

I had bought some honey in the comb, and Audiffret, not knowing what it was, started to put it in his pocket. I had the extreme stupidity to warn him, but it would have been very funny if he had.

We talked about his castle, the people who visit his house, and the reception he gave to us; then Collignon said that a few days ago four English ladies came to our house asking what the castle on the hill was and saying that they were going to see it.

"Yes," Audiffret said, and he recalled our exhibition point by point. "I had given the order not to let them come in."

I chided him for treating people who came to his house that way and then complaining that nobody comes to see him!

"Oh, but they were so ugly. And what nerve they had to call for the gardener. He didn't want to let the carriage inside, but then they said, 'We'll walk in.' And they did as if they were at home! I quietly opened my window, and I saw those monkeys. They went straight to the baths after they left my house."

"Yes," I said. "I saw them there. I was with Miss Collignon. They were on the sand and sitting on the bench."

"Oh, yes. They sat everywhere."

It was too much. I was almost bursting with laughter; I started running, as if looking for my fan. We spoke more about the English ladies, and he told how one could not walk. It had been Nina, who was sinking in the pebbles.

BOOK THIRTY-FOUR

H. G. T. D. O. H.
Book 34
Begun Monday, June 7, 1875
Finished Friday, June 25, 1875
Promenade des Anglais, 55 bis, in my villa

[Monday, June 7, 1875.] On Monday at 4:00 everything was ready. Audiffret brought the break drawn by four beautiful horses, and we left—my aunt, Dina, Mary, Olga, de Daillens, Yourkoff, Galula, and Audiffret. Mama, Collignon, and Mrs. de Mouzay followed in a landau. We went to the banks of the Var. The road was fresh and agreeable. I liked seeing that Audiffret was known by all the peasants, especially the peasant girls. They called him "Mr. Émile," and he seems to be the child of the villagers. It isn't enough to be a child of the country; it's important to look like it. Truly Audiffret is well brought up. Yourkoff attempted several questionable jokes, and Girofla ignored them and did not even smile. But the Sapogenikoffs were silly enough to tell Audiffret and Galula that we called them Girofla and Tiouloulou. We were obliged to tell them, as Yourkoff threatened to tell the story of our masquerade as the funny English women if we did not. He learned of it through Nina's inconceivable stupidity of revealing it to him. We had to get out of this delicate position by choosing the less difficult. Audiffret had a hard time accepting his nickname, but he finally did. Tiouloulou laughed and amused us all by saying this name in the most sentimental way possible, looking at the stars as he said, "Tiouloulou."

"Tomorrow at the beach?" Audiffret asked me low enough to make me aware of it.

"I don't know, Sir."

"You never know when I ask you anything," he said in the same low voice, even more softly.

"I have my lessons."

"Send your professors for a walk. Really, Miss . . ."

"What did he say?" someone asked.

"Counsels of a father to his daughter," the man replied.

"Yes," I said, "to send my professors to the devil."

We let the others off first, arriving home alone with the two Niçois. When helping me down from the carriage, he pressed my hand so hard that I blushed. Happily it was dark. The man is young and handsome, and I like him very much.

Mama likes him, too, but when going to bed she said, "How sad he's not a prince." She and my aunt think I'm in love with him. Fools! No, not fools, because if I surprise myself being made as I am, then the more reason that they can't understand me. Is it natural, I wonder, that at sixteen one has only selfish motives in heart and head? I don't complain about it, on the contrary! Madame, my mother, is not satisfied because I didn't shine. Well, I didn't feel like shining!

I forgot one thing: Girofla, when singing all the verses in the world, sang the one about the bandits that starts, "One day a prince, beautiful as the day. . . ." Later the song tells that all the ladies were dying of love for him, especially one, the most beautiful, who loved him so much that she came to the court. In place of singing that, he sang, "Went up to the tower," sending a smile to Galula as he did so. My aunt opened her mouth to shout, but I pinched her so hard she stopped.

Well, no. He doesn't know about the English ladies; he clearly knows about our first escapade without the disguises. The coachman told him.

Tuesday, June 8, 1875. I would like to know if by any chance my Journal will be read. And I would like to know whether anyone will think that I am thinking of the Duke of Hamilton when talking of the handsome Niçois. . . . For a summer in Nice, I like a distraction like Audiffret, but after this summer I want to go into society and be interested in others than these young Niçois, no matter how beautiful they are.

Wednesday, June 9, 1875. The Durands, seeing me with this man who was their escort and who now gives them only mocking smiles, seemed to appear from all sides. They surround me, monopolize me, saying the nicest things in the world.

I have pain in the chest. It seems to me I have tuberculosis. But this chest pain worries me, and for the last five days I have spit blood. It's awful!

Saturday, June 12, 1875. Audiffret came and spent the evening with us.

I feel a lot of pleasure in looking at Audiffret, and he looks at me the same way; we don't speak to each other without smiling. And Mama and my aunt are sure he is in love with me and don't stop talking about it from morning to night. But I have an idea that Girofla thinks about me the way I think about him, and it's not very flattering. I have these thoughts about all this: for the last four years, we have lived in the same city, seeing each other every day. We even entertained a little and never had the idea of being introduced. Then our door was closed, my mother being ill. But I've grown up, and here he is coming often, going where we go, giving parties, providing all sorts of amusements—I have to ask myself, Why? For whom? For me? Well, it is evident, but always because of this false shame and modesty I am not sure.

Monday, June 14, 1875. I got up lazy. However, I took my chemistry lesson with Leclerc. We prepared some sulfuric acid to decolorize the flowers and some dioxide.

How much I would like to have Dina married!

Miss Collignon has lowered all the shades of the second floor. Now Girofla will find everything locked up, as he said. He notices our least move. Before he told us that, everything was open. Then we closed it, except at the last window—my dressing room. I was afraid to be seen from the Rue de France. He told us everything that happened—at what time our carriage comes, when we go out, who comes to see us. In a word, everything! To know these things, he would have to remain at his window all day long. I really believe he does that.

Tuesday, June 15, 1875. We left at 6:00 and Girofla stayed next to me. We stopped at St. Jean, a very pretty place, and went all around the Gulf in a boat. I talked most of the time with Saëtone; Audiffret did not really look after me, so I am really out of temper with him.

We ate badly. He sat next to me on my left at the dinner table, and Saëtone was on my right. I like to hear Audiffret speak in spite of his southern accent, which he pronounces very agreeably.

In the moonlight we went on the terrace across from the inn. I made a wish with Girofla discreetly, and we promised each other the most unreasonable things in the world. Silently I swore to make him crawl on his hands and knees from our house to the beach and once there to jump in all dressed up. Of course I didn't tell him that! What we did say made everyone else laugh. But we did not have as much fun as we had at the other party he gave. Tiouloulou was missing, and Saëtone took his place.

When we returned, I changed my aunt's seating plan and put myself opposite Girofla instead of next to him. It's better that way because I have the idea that he believes I'm in love with him.

He plays with Olga, who is familiar with him, like a child. They don't address each other as Miss and Mister, but simply as Giroflé and Girofla. It was nice to see it. We laughed a lot—I, too, but not whole-heartedly.

He spoke to Olga principally, and to me only when it was necessary, or when I talked to him. "Quick, quick! My journal," I told myself. Yes, my dear, my only confidant is this. It shares my troubles and my anger. Imagine! I'm jealous of Olga. It's silly, but it's true. She's a little girl, and to irritate me the man pays attention only to her.

When we walked to the house, I took her arm and smiled at her, but I wanted to hit her with a stick, slap her face, tear her hair, and send her rolling in the street.

I know he behaves like that to enrage me. I know it, and in spite of that I am enraged. . . . Just to think about vengeance makes me feel better. I'd like to beat someone, break something. . . . If Olga notices, she'll be too proud. . . . She's a pretty brunette with grey eyes. She has a nice complexion and disdainful lips. Her hair is short—and there's not much of it. This stupid man chose her for his purpose, as he would have chosen Dina or Mary. Of the three Olga is the prettiest, the most free. Anyway, I'm horribly disappointed.

Why am I so proud? Why must I be all-powerful? I am humiliated to have been caught by this stupidity. I'm angry with myself. I think I've made a mistake. It's not important. I would like to speak Latin. I want to smoke. I want to drink. I want everything tonight.

O Muse, do not sing the anger of Achilles. Sing mine!

Thursday, June 17, 1875. Now, I just got an idea: possibly Girofla acts the way he does because he's in love and doesn't want to show it. It's a question. . . .

Maybe he thinks like me. . . .

We received a letter from Paul. They had a big dinner and drank to the health of the absent, dear hostess (Mama). They celebrated Paul's return and expressed only one fear: that Mama, if she returned to Russia, would cause everybody to fall in love with her.

My father is waiting for my arrival impatiently. I want to go, but why doesn't this uncle come faster?

[At a dinner party at Marie's house.] Collignon improvised a dance, and Audiffret danced with me. When he put his hands on my waist and I leaned lightly on his shoulder and put my right hand in his, I felt that electric shock I spoke of before. He dances well. His cheek brushed mine; what a happy man! (I hope he felt that way!) We played little games, and he was near me as much as possible.

Everybody was gay, and at one in the morning we thought it was only 11:00 in the evening, which ended with a waltz I was dancing with this man.

How silly we are in this world! To appear in a corset is considered improper, but we show much more in a low-cut ball gown. To touch the hand once more is not permitted, but in dancing we embrace as much as possible. I don't know how the others were doing, but I lean very much on my partner when I am dancing—without insisting, however, but enough to brush his face with my hair if he is tall and with my cheek is he is like Audiffret. I recalled the evening last summer in Ostend, when I excused the Pole, permitting him to talk to me. When waltzing with him many times I touched his face with my hair. I didn't want to with my cheek.

And I flirted—with Saëtone and with Galula—and remembered what the priest asked me at Easter confession.

It was a simple evening—innocent and gay. The time will come, God willing, when I'll give such parties, myself.

I'm dying to go to Russia. . . . When I said that I'll spend the winter in Florence, Audiffret said that he will also be there. And since I've been talking about Russia, he wants to go there, too. . . . I am going to bed at 2:00 (I wrote this Sunday morning) still feeling the touch of A's cheek on my right cheek.

I dreamed all night that I was in a magnificent garden, green and shaded, and the branches were touching so low and the foliage was so lush and the grass was so green. I was in a bower with Audiffret. There was only one opening; to look out from it I was obliged to go so close to him that my face touched his, and it was like that all night. From my side love is impossible; from his side fidelity is difficult.

It is raining, and to pass the time faster I spent the afternoon in sweet idleness.

Tomorrow Audiffret is leaving, he said, for Milan, but I think it is for Marseille to pay court to the rich aunt to obtain money. (It is said he will have the fortune if he will marry the daughter. . . .) He is short of money now. I'd like to see him before this stupid departure.

At dinner I did a silly thing; I drank a whole bottle of Saint Emilion wine. It's the first time I've ever done such a thing, and it's entirely my fault. After dinner I went up to my rooms and undressed, but fearing to let my mother and my aunt think silly things (that I might be drunk), I went downstairs at once and sat with them an hour. I wasn't the least bit tipsy. I understood and heard everything, only I was a little numb.

Thursday, June 24, 1875. Today I learned some Niçois songs.

And today I played the piano like an angel. I played everything upon impulse. . . . Herodotus begins to amuse me seriously. I find in his work some incomparable naïvetés! Yet he understood a multitude of things. It is a delight!

When, for Pete's sake, will my uncle ever come!

Friday, June 25, 1875. I scribble less since Audiffret left.

What annoyances I have!

Nobody knows how to run this house. The money goes; we have debts. We are in a muddle, a terrible mess! No fortune whatever could withstand such a disorderly life!

BOOK THIRTY-FIVE

H. G. T. D. O. H.
Book 35
Started Sunday, June 27, 1875
Finished Thursday, July 8, 1875
Promenade des Anglais, 55 bis, in my villa, Nice

Monday, June 28, 1875. Audiffret will be back in two days, and I was believing him already here! This morning his shutters were open, and because of that I was impatient to go out, and I missed the translation of a chapter of Caesar and the practice of a Chopin tarantella.

This evening they all gathered here—Bihovitz, Saëtone, and Galula.

We danced "Sir Roger de Coverly" and played a lot of innocent games and laughed like happy children. The rascals stayed until 1:00 A.M. and would have stayed longer if Mary and Olga had not given the signal.

Mama was in her room, sick in bed.

Wednesday, June 30, 1875. Paul writes that they are waiting for me in Russia.

Thursday, July 1, 1875. We went to the music with the Sapogenikoffs in two landaus. Audiffret, pale and wearing a straw hat, stayed near us; as it was raining my aunt gave him her umbrella in pity. He said he was going to leave again, but since we were staying, he would stay as long as we would be here, and a lot of other silly things.

Saëtone left first, and before the rain, so that Girofla alone was invited to our house tonight.

I stayed in the room; Audiffret dared to come with his chair next to my armchair, but our talk had no value. We went to have tea, talking about my trip to Russia. He insisted that we'll not be going and that we'll stay in Nice. He said all that with his familiar air, but without impertinence.

After that he proposed that we try tipping tables. The young people went into the salon, and the old ones stayed at the tea table. We laughed and joked, but I am horribly shocked by the attitude of these girls, and even Dina, who do not stay in the background. I have an atrocious fear of being identified with these girls with gesticulating arms, legs spread out, yelling mouths—and I am no longer jealous of Olga. On the contrary, I am amused to see her calling him Émile and him calling her plain Olga. They are funny. Girofla wanted absolutely to touch my finger to make the contact and tip the table. We succeeded in making it tip and jump on its legs. We wrote a lot of silly rhymes.

We got some tickets for the Café Américain, a garden where they offer light plays and singing. Tonight it is for the benefit of the flood victims of Toulouse, and everybody is going.

Friday, July 2, 1875. The others went to Monaco. I detest it. At home alone, I can go nowhere except to Nina's. Nina got dressed and took us to Rumpelmayer's. She's a woman I love. She doesn't show off and is as crazy as we are. In the evening she told us some love stories, her own adventures, which I am obliged to doubt. She has never been beautiful, it's true, but of course there's no need of beauty for that.

I have a new torment: for the relief of the poor people flooded in Toulouse and elsewhere, there are going to be some benefit events—country balls, solicitings of funds. Mrs. de Mouzay came Wednesday to tell us that they want us to be patronesses, that they'd come to our house for that. But nobody came, and I've heard no more about it.

Saturday, July 3, 1875. Because I must confess that I like this man and because I think about him a lot, I try to be able to say that I love him. But no, I don't love him. But I like him, and above all he occupies my thoughts so much that people could think I do. I desire so ardently, so insanely to have him love me that I would give many things for that! But I don't know what is the matter with me tonight; I am silly with joy and happiness. And why?

Audiffret has asked me at different times whether I was going to the country ball tomorrow for the flooded refugees of the South. He gave my aunt an invitation signed by President Daouis.

Sunday, July 4, 1875. It was terribly hot, and I rested when writing or in the garden. Afterwards we went to the music in two carriages, but we stayed side-by-side all the time. Terffidua, Enoteas [Saëtone's name spelled backwards], and Tiouloulou came, and we laughed with Girofla and Giroflé. In the evening these three masculine "graces" arrived at our house, and we all went together to this country ball.

Girofla prowled alone with his "uncle" and grabbed each maple trunk he passed until somebody came to take him away.

He danced with me; instead of taking me back to my seat (we occupied one whole corner), he led me to a long space under the beautiful trees lighted and trimmed with flags, and we danced there. Then, instead of leading me to my seat, he said to me, "Let's go strolling, or you'll hide yourself over there with the others." And he said it in such a voice that I said, "Let's go."

"Is it true that you are leaving?"

"Yes, it's true," I answered. "They've even said that I'll not come back, but that is . . ."

"Yes, that is . . ." he repeated in the same tone.

I need to explain that at the music they talked about what Barnola had said—that he has a premonition that I'll marry in Russia. And then I asked Mama, "What would you say to that if I did?" I could see that what I said made an impression. I talked about Audiffret's hat and suggested that he never appear in it again. I sat out a contra dance . . . and Girofla and Giroflé amused me. But when a polka started, he said, "Miss, I assure you that this is our dance." (The other wasn't very good.)

The Skariatines and those other ladies were in a rage to see me and the others dancing with their escorts.

At 12:30 it started to rain, and I said, "Let's go, Sir. Give me your arm until we reach our carriages." All the others, following his example, offered their arms to the ladies.

Decidedly, it is impossible for me to love Girofla. I only amuse myself. "Take off your hat and put it over mine," I said, and he did. Not a drop touched me. "See how you are," I said. "I have to tell you everything!"

Monday, July 5, 1875.
    Vanity, smoke,
    Vapor, dust.

Why do I have the crazy idea to desire the love of this man? Since I don't love him, he's a pest. If I continue this way, I'll not go to heaven. God won't forgive the wrong I've willingly done. I'm going to make myself ugly, dress myself badly, and renounce all my coquettishness. I've had two carnations, one white and one red, since Saturday night. They give me this gaiety. I went in my very long white dress from Worth to the baths. . . . Dina and Mary were swimming. Giroflé did not talk with Girofla, who stayed quietly near me. Thank God I've started to lose the fear that he can think me in love with him! I behave with him as I do with all the others.

My aunt went to Monaco at 8:00. I think the little one had wanted to come to see us, and when he heard her say she would not be there, he told her, "You will not go," in that tone peculiar to him (a kind of advice). Well, he's a simpleton! But he knows that we have a terrace and that we sit there every evening. Yet he didn't even pass by!

When the girls came, Dina, Mary, Olga, and I all hid. Slipping along the walls of the pavilion, passing by the stables, and climbing into the carriage, we went to Nina's. She was in Monaco with Mama and the others. We dressed ourselves in Mary's percale dresses, like the Niçois girls, and covered our heads with hats and veils and went walking in the town. I wasn't afraid, because if we were attacked, I would have unveiled myself immediately and made myself known.

    Vanity, smoke,
    Vapor, dust.

These all threaten my good resolutions; I have an excuse: Nobody tells me that a man loves me.

It is even strange for me to pose as a conqueror who has pity and who, by excess of pride, repents. Probably Audiffret thinks the way I do.

Tuesday, July 6, 1875. Almost all my gaiety is gone.

Saëtone says that Audiffret is waiting to finish the arrangements for the holiday in the public gardens before he leaves again. Well! The little gaiety I had has changed into discontent. . . . You see, this ignoble creature is my only distraction here!

I dreamed all night about Girofla.

He has paid court to all the pretty girls, and now it's my turn. That's all.

But I think like a fool. He hasn't paid court to me at all. And that's what intrigues me. On the contrary, he is very timid with me. There's never a familiarity as with Giroflé. I am deeply sad, but I don't show it. How can they justify the fact that he doesn't court me at all?

Wednesday, July 7, 1875. I dreamed again about the wretch. I saw him all night. I'm sad and upset.

My mother, Dina, and Walitsky left at 2:00 for Schlangenbad. But that's not what makes me sad. I'm angry because when Audiffret left I was bored. My aunt thinks I love him, and I'm sad because of that.

Even though I want his love, I don't love him; that's a sin. I do not have the courage to forbid myself these feelings. God will punish me. Yes, if he loves me. But if he does not, he will have no reason to punish me. Something tells me he will punish me.

We didn't cry when they left, I sang some departure songs. When will I leave?

The family's departure explained my sad look; if Mama had been obliged to stay, I would have been very embarrassed.

My aunt invited Audiffret to come to the house, "And we'll go riding in the carriage," she said.

"Oh, that will be nice."

We talked about husbands who beat their wives, and as a good son he said that the only way to get rid of a disagreeable wife is to knock her down.

How encouraging!

I think I see his game clearly; he wants *me* to fall in love with him. But of course I want the same thing—the other way around. But "Even a sharp scythe cannot cut a stone," as the Russian proverb says. Another goes, "A fool gets rich by his thinking."

Thursday, July 8, 1875. Triphon, by order of my grandfather, has killed my dog Mops. This unhappy dog was given to Ambroise to be taken care of, and Ambroise kept him tied up. The poor animal broke loose and rushed here, and they killed him without mercy.

Tell me, good people, is your heart not revolted and are you not indignant? I, who had the best disposition toward this frightful old man, find his action so unworthy, so cruel, so atrocious and violent that I cannot express all I feel about it.

I am in frightful spirits [in English].

I told the others what I felt about that miserable old man, calling him what he deserved to be called, and said that I would not go any more to see him in the pavilion and that I would not speak to him any more.

When I called Triphon to reprimand him, he answered with an insolent air, saying that I could have nothing against him. It is true. It was my grandfather's doing. Oh, but I would kiss on both cheeks the person who would whip the villain!

To be like me in the height of fury is like having a fit. . . .

I dined without saying a word under the orange trees and palms of the London House, dejected and miserable. Two minutes after having learned of the assassination of this poor, defenseless creature who loved me, and who was killed as she rushed toward me, I sat down and wrote to Mama: "They are doing frightful things here. Your father just had Mops killed. I am, unfortunately, too good to have Reynard killed; but if I am further aggravated, I will do it. I am furious, and I swear to you that I am not joking." I sent it without a signature.

BOOK THIRTY-SIX

H. G. T. D. O. H.
Book 36
Started Friday, July 9, 1875
Finished Wednesday, July 14, 1875
Promenade des Anglais, 55 bis, in my villa, Nice

Saturday, July 10, 1875. Our big event [for the flood victims] in the public gardens is a pleasure for all except me. Girofla was selling tickets in a cage, and we bought some from him. But I was dying of loneliness—and furious.

The garden was lighted. Those three orchestras, the singers, the crowd, everything irritated me. They drew the raffle numbers from Audiffret at 10:30, and the prizes were very amusing: wine, a live sheep, a peacock, etc., etc. Girofla was a great lord among all those people. Dressed in grey, as at the time when he was imitating the real one [Hamilton], he ran, he hurried, and was everywhere, and all of this with a very smart appearance. He did leave his raffle and come to where we were sitting. I was yawning like a miserable wretch and paid him no attention.

I barely spoke a word to him. Often I pretended I didn't hear what he said to me, as he has done to me. In a word, if Audiffret cares for me only as much as I care for him, I don't owe him anything more. Several times this young man has angered and humiliated me. I believe I have entirely paid him back. I can't stand him nor see him, since it's not my fault. But yes, I think it is mine.

I talked with my aunt about him. I told her that to catch him is difficult because he's not an innocent man, but a rake of the first quality. And I added that I would not find it disagreeable to catch him, that I would be delighted to do so, and then he would see what he does to others.

Sunday, July 11, 1875. Pale and all tired out, I went to the music with my aunt and the two girls. At the music, Audiffret proposed having dinner at the London House and going straight from there to a ball like the one we went to last Sunday.

At last you see a woman happy and satisfied. Let's admire the kindness of God and praise His forgiveness. But truly I am not worthy of it. I danced with all the young men and waltzed with Girofla, but the two of us danced very little. He spoke of a dream he had in which he was with me all the time. I begged him to tell it to me, and he made a face. Then I forbade him to tell it to me, and I said that the dream was too good to speak about anymore. In a word—a lot of monkey-business. Again, when he was holding my waist dancing, I felt the shock. . . . We danced behind the house; light came from little lanterns hidden in the grass. I suggested that they give a party at the tower. I took the responsibility of talking about it with the owner, and they promised to make the preparations. Girofla said that he didn't want to dance anymore and seemed to affect a discouraged air. Then I danced with Saëtone, and after that no one let me sit out a dance. When Émile's waltz arrived, I was tired and said so.

First he and I danced over where everybody was, and then where we were alone. With half words and half enigmas, by barely perceptible pressures on my arm, and by silences, the boy told me he loves me! He even mentioned almost wanting to die. "I'll never die as beautifully as now," he said, in a way to soften anybody but me.

It's nothing serious. I am for him what he is for me. And I'm a little vexed. Do I have the right to ask more than I can give back? Well, we are twenty-four and sixteen years old. We are good-looking and having a good time. What is better? I suspect this creature of having bad thoughts. He wants to lead me to tell him that I love him, and then to withdraw himself. But he'll not have this pleasure. I'll let him see now that I understand his game.

Hurrah for the three graces! The society is prospering. Three girls and nine boys—three for each one. How we are going to talk and love!

Secretly, to my diary only, I can confide that I have a terrible desire for him.

Tuesday, July 13, 1875. I would so much like my uncle to arrive! I have absurd fears that my Niçois will leave. Then all these people will look at me as abandoned. I will be furious!

We saw each other at the music, and Saëtone requested, for him and all his friends, the right to come to our house tonight. Girofla did not leave the carriage.

I like the country balls better than the evenings at home. There we are free and can get lost and be found. Here there is no way to listen to any special conversation meant only for me. The talk is always so general here that there is no opportunity for an intimate word.

Wednesday, July 14, 1875. The house is so empty! And I am so lonely! I feel fine only when I see Audiffret, and when I don't see him I feel a great sadness. Yesterday we talked about Latin, about college, about finals. That has given me a furious desire to study, and when Brunet came I didn't make him wait for a moment. I asked him for information about the examination, and he gave me such information that I believe, after a year of preparation, I'll be able to pass the baccalaureate in science. We talked about it with Brunet. What a pity that I must leave Nice! And what a silly thing not to have thought about it seriously a year ago! I would have been able to pass now. Well, in spite of that, I'll prepare myself. I can do it in Florence, and I'll return to Nice for the exam.

I have studied Latin since February of this year, and in these five months, according to Brunet, I have covered what they do in college in three years. That is phenomenal. Never can I forgive myself for losing this year. It's an enormous sorrow, and I'll never forget it.

No sight of Audiffret today, and I am lonely. This detestable creature did not come to the beach, but we saw him at the Café Victoire. It's a shame. And I doubt everything.

BOOK THIRTY-SEVEN

Book 37
From Thursday, July 15, 1875
To Saturday, July 31, 1875
Promenade des Anglais, 55 bis, in my villa, Nice

Thursday, July 15, 1875. It was raining, and I was sad and silent at the music. When the young men came, I blushed a lot on seeing Audiffret, but he was some distance away and didn't see me. The wretch has plainly succeeded. Then he came up to our carriage and addressed my aunt, "Madame, when may I come to say goodbye? I am leaving tomorrow."

It was like a thunderbolt. I went pale and red and embarrassed and wished I were underground. I hid myself in the back of the carriage. He and Saëtone saw it, and out of pity they did not stare.

It's terrible! I am the most miserable of creatures! I wanted to have him and torment him, and instead it is he who takes me and torments me. It is well done. You are punished by your own sins. It is a lesson. So much the worse for you, the most unlucky of all women! I am punished for my pride and my stupid arrogance. Read that, good people, and learn! This journal is the most useful and the most instructive of all writings. It is a complete life; it will be possible to follow me from childhood to death.

"I am going away for a week, and probably when I return I'll not find you here," he was saying.

"Oh, true. For sure I'll be gone," I said.

"Will you be at home this evening?"

I turned to my aunt.

"Yes," she told him.

"Then I'll come to say goodbye, if that will not be any inconvenience." He continued after a moment, "Miss Marie doesn't seem to wish to be at home."

"What are you saying, Sir?" I asked.

"Because you'll not want to be disturbed for one lone man."

I was sure he wanted to come alone, but my aunt invited the others as well. He seemed sad. He put on this air purposely; I don't know why, but everything with him seems deceitful—lies and bad motives. I even believe that he has a conspiracy with all these men, that he has promised to make me fall in love with him, that all these acts have been planned with them.

At last the three men came. The Sapogenikoff girls were already here. We went to the garden. Audiffret climbed our neighbor's wall and from there made comic gestures, speaking to the passersby the way gypsies and beggars do. "Son of an ex-military man, covered with wounds, but poor; my poor mother, a worthy and excellent woman, et cetera." I would have laughed if I hadn't been so vexed.

At dinner he wrote on a little cake the initials for *I love you*. I don't believe him and regard it as a bad joke. He smiled, traced the letters again with his fork on the tablecloth, and then smoothed them away, smirking, as if to say, "Oh, no, I don't dare," and things like that. He flirted a lot with Olga. I leaned on the piano while Nina was playing, and for fifteen minutes he begged me to give him my picture; I refused, turning a cold shoulder to him.

"Since I am leaving?" he persisted.

"No. Then I would be obliged to give one to each of the other gentlemen." Oh, fool! Oh, stupid girl! I should have said, "If you want to see me, why are you leaving?"

Saëtone suspected my annoyance at Girofla's paying attention to Olga to make me jealous. "Do you mind it?" he asked. I told him that I make no distinction, that I found all the people present very nice. I wonder: did he ask that for himself? Or was he charged by the other to do it? Am I in love with the man? I have no idea.

They were leaving.

"Goodbye, Miss."

"Goodbye, Sir." We shook hands . . . and I barely felt the shock that used to make me tremble so sweetly. I sang and laughed with my graces and we pretended we were fainting very comically because of the departure of the handsome Niçois. I wished I could really do it, because I am most miserable! So he doesn't love me? Would he be going away if he did? He wanted to amuse himself. And I wanted to amuse myself. . . .

Friday, July 16, 1875. I sent a cable to Stepa Babanine: "You are upsetting all my plans by this abominable delay. If I'd known it would be like this, I would never have counted on you. Marie."

In September they are celebrating the centennial of Michelangelo in Florence. I want to go there. But I must go to Russia, too. These thoughts, added to all my pleasures, enrage me. O, you who are furious and unhappy, write! Complain to your paper. . . . *I could barely eat I was in such haste to write, to complain. Take courage, heart!* [in Italian].

But how silly I am to take everything so seriously! I endured the Hamilton affair, and I can endure this.

It was already moonlight when we got home. After supper, when I went to my room with only that divine moonlight lighting it, I sang a song to Phoebe; invaded by a great sadness I went inside and began to write. Oh, Audiffret, I had the absurdity to regret my conduct, to feel guilty, to worry, believing that I had hurt his feelings. Then I scolded myself that I had been stupid and silly: "Your conduct towards him," I told myself, "matters very little. And if it bothered him, then for me it is a joy to have settled it!" I was sure he deserved it, and told myself that the colder one is, the better off one is: "Who follows Love, Love flees from him. Who flies from Love, Love follows him." But why, I keep asking myself, did he say all those things to me? Why that sad air, those soulful eyes, and why all those whispered, tender things at the ball? If he loves me, why has he planned to go away from me? Yet he never looks serious, and during the most sentimental moments he always seems gay and laughing.

Saturday, July 17, 1875. I am annoyed at being without a goal. Writing is my greatest diversion. It seems to me that I could pass my days in scribbling. If at least I could write well!

Why did he ask to be introduced if he doesn't like me? And why, since that introduction, has he not left us for a moment, until now? Even in summer there are many homes where he is received. Then why did he come only to us? To make me hope a lot of sillinesses by all sorts of things he did? Really, he is an unworthy creature! People will think I'm ugly and stupid! Not having been able to catch him . . . To catch? It's easy to say. What can a young girl do? If I were a married woman, it would be a different thing. A woman has all the means, a girl none. A girl must behave quietly; as soon as she shows the least interest, she is thought to be in love, or wanting to be married. I realize that my conduct with Girofla has been absurd. I should have taken a light and joking tone with him instead of the serious, tender tone I used. I should have laughed at him and used a dazzling, flirting style with him, instead of looking for a serious declaration, like a stupid fool. However, nothing is lost, but I've decided to do otherwise in the future.

Sunday, July 18, 1875. Heaven and earth!!!!!!!! Fortuné just came to tell me, "Mr. Stepa is here."

"What? Stepa? What Mr. Stepa? Where?"

"See this man! He deserves to be beaten," I said in Russian. "Why did you make me wait so long? I thought you'd never come. Too bad you didn't arrive before the departure of that Niçois scoundrel!" I would have liked Émile to eat his words after insisting, "You'll stay in Nice. You'll not go to Russia," and "This uncle will never get here."

With Mashenka and Stepa, we went to the beach to swim. Mary and I jumped from the bridge while our young men friends, my aunt, and Olga watched us from the shore. Mashenka stayed near the rope, and the fat Stepa had a good time in the middle of the waves. Saëtone told Olga that Girofla is at Marseille and that he'll be here in ten days. The later, the better. I'll have time to leave.

When pointing out the magnificent castle to Stepa and his wife, my aunt said to them, *"Here is the castle of our suitor"* [in Russian].

Saëtone asked me when I am leaving for sure.

"Next week, Wednesday or Thursday."

"And you'll stay in Paris?"

"About ten days."

"I received a telegram from Audiffret." (I clenched my teeth not to blush.) "He's just arrived in Paris and will be there ten or twelve days at the Hotel Splendide. Perhaps you'll see him . . ."

"Perhaps," I said, clenching my teeth harder. . . . Faithful messenger!

Tuesday, July 27, 1875. It is hot, and we wander back and forth from the house to the garden like the shades of Dante's Hell. The dogs follow me. The sun cooks us. And everything irritates me. I can't do anything. Saëtone said at the music, "I informed one of my friends of your departure for Paris."

"Whom?" I asked without emotion.

"Mr. Girofla," he said, looking into my face.

"What for?" I asked simply.

"Because it is an interesting event. To introduce your name is to interest everybody."

"Oh!"

"And to fill two lines of my letter."

Thursday, July 29, 1875. I have to stand for all the annoyances attendant upon leaving. We hurry, get angry, run, forget, and then remember. We shout. I am all at loose ends. . . . Stepa would like to put the departure off from day to day. That's his character. He can't make up his mind. He should have left Russia at the beginning of April, but he did so only at the beginning of July!

Friday, July 30, 1875. I took Mashenka to see Girofla's castle, and then everybody else went to Monaco. I stayed with Mashenka. We walked past No. 77.

"Would you like to go and see it?" she asked me [in Russian].

"All right," I told her.

I became excited, my heart was beating fast, and when we got to the Rue de France we entered Gioja's garden.

Here I stop before writing any more. I am so troubled, I feel so strange that I must rest my head, my hands for a few minutes. I continue. Isn't it strange? Why am I so moved? We crossed the little garden full of marvelous plants. On the balcony of the main floor there are two statues of negroes holding some cushions on their heads, in bronze I think.

At first an antechamber, elegant and gracious, then a drawing room furnished very amusingly and papered in a cretonne oriental pattern. It has a multitude of different kinds of furniture, bronzes, statues, and a thousand things that give it elegance. Two immense divans invite one to sit, or rather, to do something else. Then there is another drawing room in grey and blue wool rep. The dining room is in old oak wood and displays beautiful old porcelain. A beautiful marble stairway leads to the upper floor. In every corner and everywhere are found some art objects and 1,000 things which appeared not so marvelous as expensive.

The bedroom is ugly, with curtains of Pompadour cretonne, a bed of black mahogany with twisted columns, and a canopy of the same fabric as the draperies. An awful bed. Next to it is her portrait in oils. In her picture she has six rows of magnificent pearls around her neck and on her breast an immense emerald. She has pensive eyes and a beautiful mouth, an exquisite nose, and all her face expresses such sweetness, calm, and honesty that it is marvellous.

The shoulders and the bust are poorly rendered.

Another painting represents a naked woman, and another two naked creatures.

The bedroom is at the extreme left of the house; on the right is a door leading to the bathroom, which has a wall covered with mirrors and washbowls for two people. There was a sponge and many bottles, which I examined and smelled one by one. Further on is her boudoir, a very little room walled with paisley cashmere, and behind that another little bedroom. I am slightly disappointed. The house is certainly beautiful, large, elegant—but for the mother of a family, not for Gioja. It lacks fantasy, grace, luxury. My own apartment will be a hundred times more beautiful. Her first name is Amelia. I didn't walk. I ran. I had a fever in the legs. I leaned against a window and thought that maybe he had leaned at that same place. I touched a piece of furniture, and said to myself that maybe he had touched that. I found a pair of mules in pink satin and, quickly taking off my shoes, I tried them on. Her foot is two and a half inches longer than mine. I looked at everything and tried to engrave in my memory each thing I saw. I said almost nothing and only answered Mashenka because my voice was trembling. I was in *her* home! I was where he had so often been. I touched what he had touched. And I sat where he had sat. . . . I picked a rose in the garden as we left, and it is before me as I write. I look at it all the time.

I have been to this house, which I have seen in dreams six times, and it was exactly as I dreamed it—except that I dreamed about a red satin drawing room and red leather. That is the only difference. I can barely write. My heart still is beating fast and my hand trembles. . . . She had the man I loved . . . I can't calm down. . . . I was up to my neck in banalities and now I am up in the clouds. I feel alive again at the memory of him.

MARIE, SUMMER 1875

BOOK THIRTY-EIGHT

Book 38
From Saturday, July 31, 1875
To Thursday, August 12, 1875
Hotel des Îles Britanniques, Paris

Saturday, July 31, 1875. At last I'm leaving, and I am annoyed thinking how long I'll be bored in the train. We just arrived. The trip has not been so dismal as I thought it would be, because we laughed all the time.

We are staying at the Hotel des Îles Britanniques, Rue de la Paix 22. I am not satisfied; we should have gone to the Grand. But after all, it's a savings for me, as here I'm paying only fifteen francs a day. We have three rooms on the mezzanine floor. I need money, but my aunt gave me only 3,175 francs for everything. That's awfully little, but she didn't have any more.

Monday, August 2, 1875. I woke up at 7:00 and at 10:00 we went out. I've become rusty in the country. It'll take me two days to feel at home here. And besides, my clothes are good, since they came from Paris. But what a torture for me! Mashenka adores strolling, admiring the windows of the stores, and visiting all the shops. I detest all that. And to think that I am obliged to take her everywhere! We'll go to Reboux's, Ferry's, and Laferrière's. We've been three times to the last one, alas! But Caroline will be away for two weeks. . . .

And finally Audiffret! It was enchanting to see him so elegant and so elegantly equipped with a pretty horse and carriage, and he himself so well-dressed and handsome. We passed each other quickly, but we turned back and bowed. I blushed slightly, but not enough to be noticed. Stepa, opposite me, said he looked back for some time. As we drove, we met each other several times, and each time he bowed. His mere smile made me feel good. He got out of the carriage and walked with the rich young people. It pleased me to see him surrounded by nice people, well-dressed, and so on! And inside I was smiling to see both of us here, transported from dirty Nice to my beautiful Paris. Instead of losing, we gain by the change. But I'm unhappy because he did not come to the carriage. If he is indifferent . . . but then, he didn't turn his carriage around; so . . . ?

At dinner I talked with Souvaroff about several different governments. My mind is filled with so many different ideas that it's awful. Besides, I never talk of this subject except in a joking way. . . . Afterwards I read my friend Plutarch.

Tuesday, August 3, 1875. But to have thought all day about that monster and as a reward to have been greeted in this way! I'm in a rage. We met near the hotel.

"Hello, Miss."

"Hello, Sir."

"How long have you been here in Paris?"

"Since the day before yesterday."

"And do you expect to stay long?"

"About a week."

"And how is Nice?"

"In Nice we were bored; it's hot."

"You are not going back?"

"No more."

"Never?"

"Oh, no. In two months we'll be there for a week."

"And the winter?"

"We'll be in Florence."

"Ah, what do you know!" He made a gesture of disbelief.

"So you're going to doubt again?"

He made a movement and I said goodbye.

Mashenka asked, *"Moussia, ask him where we can buy some umbrellas"* [in Russian]. So I called him back and asked him her question. And we separated from that unworthy, capricious, mean animal! Yesterday when he saw me, he made a startled gesture, but today he looked composed and icy. But what can I expect, since he does not love me? We must be reasonable. My face is all convulsed. I can hardly contain myself. I silently prayed, "Dear God, count this moment for me in Heaven, for it is a martyrdom." I would have liked to be alone to write or think, but instead I was obliged to wander in the streets, which even in a good mood I detest!

Laferrière has made marvels of simplicity for me. Reboux makes hats like pictures. Ferry makes shoes like poems. Worth makes dresses as sweet as candy. And besides all these, I've bought a charming umbrella and some gloves. How sweet it is to know that everyone is working to make me look more beautiful! People looked at me in the Bois tonight, and I was still silly enough to wait for my torment. Oh, how much better I felt when I was only thinking about horses and the Duke! That was nice. There is nothing more beautiful in the world than the Champs-Élysées, the Avenue de l'Imperatrice, and the Bois de Boulogne. It is all gay, comfortable, cool.

Thursday, August 5, 1875. At home they had the idea that Audiffret was in love with me. I'm furious, because now they'll think I've been jilted. They think of me as a superior person—a conqueror in the style of Alexander the Great. Why? Up to this time nothing has justified this idea. None of them receives any consideration, so it is not surprising that I receive none either. I can do nothing except to please by my appearance, and that's a pity. That ought to be beyond one's value and not a necessity. So I need to understand that it's not because I love Audiffret that I am unglued, but because I find him grown distant like so many others before him. And my plans are upset.

I'm pale, and the fear of being sick, as I was last summer, makes me tremble. What an ordeal it seems to go to Schlangenbad!

Saturday, August 7, 1875. Today, thinking of Girofla has no importance. It is my eternal desire for grandeur that bothers me.

Sunday, August 8, 1875. I went to church and to the Palace of Industry, where we lunched, not too badly. I came back after leading Stepa and his wife around over there. I am tired; we walked for two hours. They wanted to look and admire, whereas I would have preferred to stay alone at home. How long the days are! I must send a telegram to my aunt as I must have more money. Without it, I'll have to leave.

At dinner Stepa and his wife quarreled. I had to hold my sides to keep from laughing. Marital quarrels are very instructive.

Monday, August 9, 1875. As my aunt is sending me 500 francs and as I do not have any paper with me to prove my identity, tomorrow I'll have to go with the owner of this hotel to the commissioner, who will give me a certificate so that I can go to receive my money.

I don't know why this journey to Germany displeases me so much; I'd prefer to return to Nice. . . . But my mother is expecting me, and the pleasure of seeing her consoles me a little.

Girofla is gone, and so I am at peace. I was most vexed at his indifference. However, I think he was not able to come, as I am here alone; he does not know Stepa and his wife.

Tuesday, August 10, 1875. The landau came, and we went to all these places that work to make me beautiful: a yellow-white dress—cream color, as Laferrière calls it—and an Italian straw hat all covered with white feathers, placed in the most elegant style in the world, and turned up in the back by a bunch of lilies-of-the-valley. This ravishing hat suits me gorgeously. This way we drove to the Bois just in time. There was a crowd, but for the most part we saw only men and their cocottes. Then I saw Gioja . . .

Wednesday, August 11, 1875. I saw Gioja, and now I don't want to leave. Something attracts me to her. . . . She looked like the Duke. Her manner, her bearing, her expression, everything about her is like him. Yesterday she looked like a goddess in her chariot.

BOOK THIRTY-NINE

Book 39
From Friday, August 13, 1875
To Friday, August 27, 1875
Hotel Planz, Schlangenbad

Friday, August 13, 1875. What an awful trip! Maybe it was the bad cards, the dark woman, the departure from Paris—or everything, everything.

Walitsky came in a landau to get us, and we arrived one and a half hours later at Schlangenbad. The town is only a few houses between two mountains. One cannot ever give an idea of the profound quiet that reigns in this place! It seems to me that a tomb would be more lively.

Mama met me at the entrance; she is radiant, and I am enchanted to see her again. But at the end of an hour, I was bored. In the evening I felt sick, but everything calmed down and I read to Dina from my journal.

I put on a hat of black felt in a gorgeous style; a dress of dark blue linen, well-tailored on the hips and with a train that is caught up and held on the side like a riding habit, which lets the white petticoat show, but which, itself, trails; yellow kid shoes with buckles; ecru stockings; and my fresh face, royal carriage, and gracious walk. As I went downstairs, Dina shouted to me, "I didn't recognize you. You look like an antique painting!" Justly enchanted with the effect of my appearance, I begged her to accompany me through the town.

It is not like a town, but more like a castle park or a beautiful little hamlet. At every step you see hillsides lost in the greenery, balconies with railings, rustic bridges, mountains and valleys, all truly charming . . . but the trails are deserted and the picturesque and poetic stairways are empty. I complained aloud while admiring these beautiful things.

Sunday, August 15, 1875. We went to the music, as in Baden, and sat around little tables. All of a sudden—surprise! Whom do I see? *"Uncle,"* I said in Russian. Mr. de Toulouse!

We sat together and stayed that way until 6:00.

Tuesday, August 17, 1875. I dreamed about the Fronde. I had just entered the service of Anne of Austria. She distrusted me; so I led her into the midst of the people in revolt, shouting, "Long live the Queen!" and the people shouted after me, "Long live the Queen!" We returned to the Palace, and by way of a ladder placed at the window, all the people began to climb up. We feared that the Palace would fall, and at that moment I saw a royal coach in gold, pulled by magnificent horses; it was being said that all this was only a play and that the carriages and horses were from the theater.

Then I was on the stage, dancing in a ballet. And at last I saw Girofla's face very clearly, and at the end Tiouloulou passed and bowed and smiled.

Mama's had another spell, provoked by a letter from Russia. Paul is going to volunteer for the army. The Zaukovsky family pushed him into this. He fell in love with their youngest daughter, who behaves badly. The mother is a very corrupt person who gambles and always wins, and the daughter procures for her the young men whom she fleeces. Before Paul came along, they had one of our neighbors, a Mr. Doublansky. This girl's brother is an atrocious scamp. All this gang grabbed the poor Bashkirtseff in order to be in the same regiment with the brother of this beauty when he becomes a military man.

But Alexander wants to prevent all this.

We passed the day admiring me. Mama admired me. The Princess really admired me. She constantly tells me that I look like her or like her son. So! That's the greatest compliment one can give. One doesn't think of anyone else as better than himself. Walitsky admired me. And finally, I admired myself.

It's that I am very pretty. In the big room of the Ducal Palace in Venice, Veronese's ceiling painting represents Venice as a woman who is tall, blond, and fresh. I remind myself of that painting. But my photographs will never be able to represent me, because the color is missing. I am completely in love with myself. They should paint me for *La Belle Hélène*. I am not so beautiful as Juno, but I have the grace and the simplicity of Venus.

But if anyone puts me in a bad humor so that I become angry about something, or if I get tired, then goodbye to my beauty! Nothing is more fragile than I. But when I am calm and happy, then I'm adorable. Unfortunately I lose when I'm too much dressed up. I must be as undressed as possible, in long clothes, like the ancient goddesses. This way suits me the best, and in such clothes I don't know anyone with more grace.

I am speaking of myself from a stranger's point of view and that of posterity, because if I became famous I would not want people to guess wrongly about me, as they do for so many famous women. Of course there will be a lot of my portraits left and some descriptions, at least by me.

Friday, August 20, 1875. Mama wrote to Paul to say that his father is ruined, hoping to make him believe that he will not inherit from him in the hope of getting him to study. My father sent this letter back [in Russian].

I read your letter to my son, and I find it necessary to make certain observations. I am not ruined, etc. etc. I am selling my estate because the hatred you and your daughter have for me forces me to do so.

I took a piece of paper and wrote this to my father [in Russian]: *I have read your letter to my mother, and I also find it necessary to make several observations. I do not have any hatred toward you. On the contrary, I love you as a father, but if not very tenderly; for that blame yourself. In your lifetime you have done nothing to bring your daughter close to you.*
  Marie Bashkirtseff

Sunday, August 22, 1875. Since I have a carriage, I am less bored . . . (Archduchess dress, black hat, dark blue jacket—ravishing).

Monday, August 23, 1875. At dinner I was dizzy and had to go outside. I sat in an armchair almost fainting. But by 4:00 I was already pink and pretty and went again to Schwalbach with Mama. I like to drive, and these little horses are quite nice. At 5:00 we went to the music. There were a lot of people, but no one interesting.

Tuesday, August 24, 1875. Every day, upon returning from Schwalbach, I dine; after supper I become so gay that it is charming. I can't tell where this gaiety comes from. It's not that I read anything. I like to be like that. Today I started out with some worries about our plans for Florence and ended with a burst of joy and with a tranquillity equal to nothing I've ever felt before. It seems that everything will go according to my wishes.

I am starting to live and to have my dreams come true—to become famous, as I am already known by many people.

BOOK FORTY

Book 40
From Friday, August 27, 1875
To Wednesday, September 1, 1875
Grand Hotel, No. 146-147, Paris

Saturday, August 28, 1875. Where do you think I am today?

"In Schlangenbad, at the Hotel Planz," you are going to answer.

Well, not at all. Not in Schlangenbad nor in the Hotel Planz, nor in Germany, either! I am in Paris at the Grand Hotel. . . .

Plevako [a Russian lawyer Mrs. Romanoff wants to consult] is in Paris. My aunt plans [to come to Paris] to see him and called Stepa [to leave Schlangenbad for Paris to join her]. Happy for the chance to leave, I packed my things and left within two hours with my uncle. I'm a mean daughter; I left my mother, telling her I was enchanted to be leaving. She doesn't know how much I love her, but the idea of seeing my poor aunt again was in my mind. It was Friday that I left my darling Schlangenbad—the only place in the world that I do not regret. My aunt will probably arrive this evening.

Alexander writes that the lawsuit is going well. The inquest is finished, and the experts have examined Romanoff's signature. Those Samoyeds *dare* to doubt its identity. Everything will depend upon their decision. (As for the trouble Adam was supposed to cause—he hasn't even been in Russia!) It is for the several witnesses to decide whether Romanoff was sane. But he's been dead for five years. I must go on my knees and pray as I've never prayed before. For me it's a matter of life and death—triumph, riches, and a name without tarnish, or a judgment of shame and ruin. God knows whether we are guilty. He will decide. If they say he was insane, we are guilty of abuse, of cheating, of a lot of horrors. I never said what my uncle was like; I never recalled that story. He was from an excellent family, but died at forty-seven without attachments, without love. Those parasites had the use of his money, and they gave his sister the idea of inheriting his fortune. After heavy drinking and living as a playboy for two weeks, he returned to Akhtirka, where he served as Marshal of the Nobility in a state easy to understand. They spread the news that he was becoming insane. It was not true, but once it was said, his least gestures and the facts of his life became suspect. When he beat his servant for stealing, the man screamed, "Insanity!" Then they restrained the poor man, and he received all kinds of violent treatment. A little before that he had made our acquaintance.

He returned to Kharkoff to complain to the governor or to the prefect about the shameful treatment he had received. The prefect and the police captain both pressed his case. At that time we all came to Kharkoff, wishing very much to marry the rich gentleman to my aunt.

It is important to remember that for an instant he had ceased his duties as Marshal of the Nobility. But he never resigned from that work until after he had been married before leaving Russia. The wedding took place in Odessa. The family had decided that the good man should marry my aunt, with whom he was not in love. But he was attached to all of us and loved her as a sister. While he was in Akhtirka, everybody but us gave him trouble. It was only we who treated him with kindness. The good man never joked, but often made very apt remarks, some even with humor, as they say in English. He was very good-looking, but his immense weight destroyed his beauty. I used to say he was stupid, and sometimes his mind wandered, but he was not insane; he knew perfectly well what he was doing when bequeathing his fortune to his wife. What could have been more natural? Was he supposed to leave it to his sister, whom he detested and never wanted to see? But he was punished after his death for the sin of having filed a suit against his sister-in-law for the same reason; his brother had given everything to *his* wife. So because Romanoff had given everything to his own wife, they tried to prove he was insane.

We all came together to Nice [in 1870] after spending a month in Vienna and a month in Baden-Baden. The rest of the time until October we spent in Geneva, having left Russia on the sixth day of May.

At Nice he began to feel good. He had suffered from rheumatism in his legs and had become so fat that he could not live very long. On February 14 he died of an acute case of something in his lungs. I did know the name of the illness; ten doctors told me what it was. We called all of them we could find. I was twelve [thirteen] then, and I didn't want to stay in a house where there was a corpse. I took Mama and Dina to a hotel on the Promenade des Anglais at No. 17, actually in the house of the famous [Mrs.] Prodgers. My aunt sat up with the corpse of her husband all night and was as depressed as a woman can be—one who had never been in love with her husband. As soon as he was dead, the cabals started in Russia. That is his story.

After that winter, we went to Geneva and from there to Baden-Baden. It was there in Baden that I began to see society, that I had Remy, that I knew Bertha; and it was there that I saw the Duke, Carlo, Paskevitch, etc. And it was like Paris again at Nice.

Then again a winter in Nice. It was very calm for me. I forgot to say that in the winter of 1870-71 I belonged to the society for the war wounded. It was my greatest pleasure to go to the station to receive the wounded, to serve them, even to treat them every Sunday. For that we would go to the hospital in the little college. We were all decorated with the Bronze Cross.

In the winter of 1871-72, I fell in love with Borreel, when I was fifteen. [This last entry in the diary has been over-written so that it now reads "I was thirteen, the twelfth of January 1872"; as noted in Marie's preface, she was actually born in November of 1858 and would have been fourteen.] I was born at the beginning of the year, which means that my age can be counted by Januaries. I was born on January 12, 1859.

The noise of Paris, this huge hotel, big as a city, with people always talking, walking, reading, smoking, looking, makes me dizzy. I love Paris, and my heart beats faster here. I want to live faster, to be someone faster. . . . I fear that this desire to live at full speed is a premonition of a short life. . . . Who knows! Come on! Here I become melancholic! No, I don't want any melancholy. . . .

When Stepa went to the station to see whether my aunt had come, I found myself alone. I would have loved to go downstairs, as there were always a lot of people there, but of course I couldn't go alone.

At last my aunt came! At dinner she recalled the events in Nice. Tiouloulou came, telling her about my interview with his patron ("boss") and of everything that we said, even that I asked him where to buy the most beautiful umbrellas. It seems that these men pay more attention to me than I to them, which is more than a lot.

Sunday, August 29, 1875. Plevako stayed almost until dinner time visiting with us. This famous lawyer seems to me as honest as can be for a man in his position.

And Stepa has gone back to Schlangenbad to get his wife and return to Russia.

Monday, August 30, 1875. On our return from the park, by way of the Champs-Élysées, we saw Émile going like an arrow to the Bois . . . in a top hat. My aunt seems more interested in him than I, God forgive me. I don't worry about anything when I'm with her: if I express a desire, she grants my wish; when she contradicts me, I cry, etc. I put myself in impossible states. I get nervous, and she ends by doing what she should have done in the first place—by doing what I wish. But I am very reasonable; I want only what is necessary.

Tuesday, August 31, 1875. It's such fun to go out through the court of the hotel before lunch, afterwards, and each time to go or come back! How different from the little hotel on the Rue de la Paix where we could see nobody!

The devil knows why I have an ugly face since I've been in Paris! I go to bed late, but that's not a reason. I went to bed late in Nice and still looked fresh. And now, because I've gone to bed late three times, must I be disfigured? It's awful to have to go to bed at ten to conserve a beautiful face and not dare to go to the theater or an evening party!

BOOK FORTY-ONE

Book 41
From Wednesday, September 1, 1875
To Tuesday, September 7, 1875
Grand Hotel, Paris

Wednesday, September 1, 1875. At 3:00 I went out in the carriage, still in my dark costume, but with a relatively fresh face.

Downstairs we met the Remy Gonzaleses, father and son. Today the father started up his lyric praises, the son following from a distance.

I don't like to think about it, but we still have never met Mrs. Gonzales. I know the daughter and Remy, but not the other ladies of the family. I treat the two of them like comrades and am simple and frank with them.

My aunt and I went to Mr. Binder's to look at some carriages. He was asking 3,600 francs for the best. Then we went to the Bois and on to the great avenue, but nothing special was going on.

Friday, September 3, 1875. Like a thunderclap I blushed, got up from the table, and almost ran to meet—don't be afraid—to meet my aunt. I don't know how many times I have spoken of the Michelangelo centenary. Well, the first lines of the newspaper I got mention it. I had thought I'd have time for it, but I don't. I am all upset. I don't know where to go, how to start, what to do!

I ran, I laughed, I cried. I'm afraid I'll be late for Florence; nothing is done, nothing is arranged, and I am unusually tormented. I can hardly write.

Saturday, September 4, 1875. Here is an adventure!

Leaving the dining room after lunch, I was approached by an American—an old man who has been staring at me since the first day we came. At first I didn't know what he wanted and answered him politely, but the fact is, he wanted only to meet me and asked permission to pay us a visit. I told him I cannot give it, not having the pleasure of knowing him. Then he asked me to give him the name of someone who knows us, in order to have that person introduce him. I answered that I don't know anyone. Then he said he is very well known in the hotel, and I answered that I was very sorry but that I could not. As we spoke in English, my aunt did not understand what was being said. He *had* to be an American for such impudence! I went to my room on fire with anger.

The ceremonies in Florence will take place September 13, 14, and 15. I just have time. We drove in the Bois, and for the first time in Paris I did not have circles under my eyes. And I wasn't sleepy. We saw several people we knew. There were four lines of carriages, and we were almost crushed. I saw the beaming smile of the surprising but stupid Émile Audiffret. I blushed only when his carriage had passed, replaced by others which follow endlessly. But from that moment, my aunt and I revived; our eyes came to life, and our faces beamed. We spoke. We even smiled. On the second time around, the surprising but stupid person came up to the carriage and, in the strident voice he inherited from his father, he spoke in his Niçois accent, "Where are you staying?"

"At the Grand Hotel," my aunt said.

"Good!"

As for me, I didn't even turn my head toward him. We continued, and I didn't change from my "Archduchess" attitude. I don't know to what I can attribute this interior revolution, but the fact is that whereas before everything appeared all black, now everything seems pink. Thanks to the Niçois. But he is ugly, and more and more I reassure myself and am happy.

Sunday, September 5, 1875. It goes without saying that my aunt and I are waiting for Girofla, but between you and me, we are expecting him in our minds and hiding the thought from each other.

He didn't come, and without my aunt's making a fuss, I ordered a victoria and we went to the Bois. It being Sunday, there was such a crowd that it was frightening. We had gone at 5:30, and little by little the crowd left.

It is September, and Nice is so beautiful in September. I remember my morning walks on the Promenade last year with my dogs. The sky was pure and the sea silvery. We've been gone only two months, and it seems a year. Here in Paris there is neither morning nor evening. In the morning they sweep the streets, and in the evening the numerous gaslights irritate me. I'm lost here; I can't distinguish between sunrise and sunset. In Nice we feel so good! There we are in a nest surrounded by mountains that are not too high nor too dry. On three sides we are protected, as if by a cape . . . and in front of us is the immense window of the sea, an infinite horizon, always the same and always new.

Oh, I love Nice. There is only Nice. It is my land where I grew up. Nice gave me health, fresh color . . . one gets up with the day and sees the sun rise. The mountains stand boldly against the silvery blue sky, so misty and sweet that one almost suffocates with joy.

Around noon the sun is in front of us. It's hot, but the air is not; there is always an incomparable breeze that always refreshes. Everything seems asleep; there's not a soul on the Promenade except two or three old ones sleeping on the benches. Then I go out alone. I breathe, I admire, and I suffocate. The afternoon is sad if I don't have some kind of Girofla. In the early evening, again it's the sky, the sea, the mountain. But at night, it's all black or midnight blue; when the moon lights its immense silver path on the sea, which seems to be a fish with diamond scales, and when I am at my window with the mirror and two candles, quiet, alone, asking for nothing more, I am happy, and I prostrate myself before God—Oh, no. No one will understand what I want to say now—no one will understand because no

---

one else has felt this way. No, it's not that; it is that I feel desperate each time I rush to make myself understood about what I feel. It's like in a nightmare when I have no strength to cry out. Besides, no text will give the least idea of true life. How can one explain this freshness—the fragrance of memory? One can invent, create—but one cannot copy. Besides, why all this? What does it matter to others? They can never understand, since it is not their life, but mine. Each feels about himself as I do about myself. I would like to succeed in having others feel about me as I feel.

But that is impossible. It would be necessary for them to be me.

It is clear in all this that I am homesick for Nice.

Monday, September 6, 1875. A basin for my tears, if you please. My mother wrote me some consolations, which my aunt read to me. Instead of getting into the tub, I sat on the floor like Venus, crouching, and for an hour cried silently. How can I say enough about my everlasting sorrow? I cry, and cry again. I am discouraged, miserable, beaten. I no longer hope for anything for myself. Yes, I hope for death, or for a change. Day after day, the tears and the despair become more frequent. If I die, which seems to me near and probable, I want somebody to make my statue in marble *thirty-three times larger than I* and put it in the middle of the garden of the villa in Nice after all the houses around its site have been demolished. No, instead, let it be a little hill at the rear of the garden sloping toward the Promenade, where there will be some big trees in a half circle near the wall of the Rue de France. The trees will form a wall against which the statue, on its hill, will be seen. The garden will be planted and then cared for from the day of my death. Each week . . . the municipal music will play in the garden and people will come to hear it, as in the Public Gardens. This will be paid for by my mother or my aunt who will invest enough money to provide interest for the maintenance—that is, half of the interest for the costs and the rest will be distributed to the poor on the same day. This must be considered my supreme will and executed absolutely.

For the summit of disgrace there is no money to pay for the things we've ordered. Not knowing that I had come to Paris, my aunt did not bring money with her. It is in Nice, waiting for her. And I am lacking everything. From year to year I have been dragging my pitiful hopes by false promises. For four years I have howled, for four years I have begged, and for four years they promised. And still nothing! Nothing! Nothing! Ruin, dishonor, misery, shame, and isolation.

Tuesday, September 7, 1875. What a position we're in! We have to leave if we are to stop in Marseille to pawn my diamonds. Waiting for the money here is impossible. We would miss the festivities in Florence. There is nothing more terrible in this world than to lack money. Those who have experienced this understand me. It is the ultimate of degradation . . . A person becomes the equal of a table, a log, a stone. Without money, one is garrotted, miserable, pitiable. I read this passage to my aunt and said, "You see, Madam, what I wrote and how much it concerns Mr. Audiffret," in an indifferent voice and depriving the gentleman of his title. I said that to her because, since the time we saw the famous young man in a café, she hasn't stopped telling me that I am vexed and furious because of Girofla. Please notice that I was not the one who gave him this name. . . .

I adore writing, but I have no more paper; and my candle is almost finished.

BOOK FORTY-TWO

H. G. T. D. O. H.
Book 42
From Wednesday, September 8, 1875
Until Thursday, September 9, 1875
Hotel Noailles, Marseille

Wednesday, September 8, 1875. I am drinking my tea and crying about my future. My aunt is making a face like a hanged man. Never have things happened so badly before. I had to leave without taking my dresses and hats. They'll be sent to me (when they're paid for) I know, but perhaps everything will be ugly. We must go to Florence; but we are two women alone, and I'll suffer. It will be a thousand torments if I can't attend all the events.

I am furious and desolate to leave without the dresses, without anything. I passed my time miserably, and I was ugly most of the time. My God, how I detest these trains!

Thursday, September 9, 1875. We are in Marseille. My aunt went out to pawn those unfortunate diamonds, and I had an hour to clean myself up. (One gets so dirty in the train!)

Oh, the beautiful success! Poor aunt, I prostrate myself before her: into what awful places she went, what dreadful people she saw, and all that for me! . . . The truth is, we cannot pawn anything, not having passports. So we left with nothing for our stop in Marseille. At 1:00 we left this city which smells so bad.

Nothing has been done with my room. My aunt had ordered some work, but my dear Uncle George gave some counter orders; I don't know why. The house is empty, in disorder. Nothing is arranged; everything is in a pitiful state.

Here is the Mediterranean Sea, for which I have been sighing, the black trees, and the moon tracing a path on the water. It is a perfect calm—no rolling carriages, no movement, no perpetual races of those people who seemed like dwarfs from my window in the Grand Hotel. Calm, silence, darkness, badly lighted by the hiding moon and barely disturbed by the few lanterns on the Promenade, running after each other. I entered the bedroom and the bathroom, opened the window to look at the castle, and found it still the same. Some clock began to chime a tune, and my heart was not tight. It seemed to me that I had never left, that tomorrow I will have my professors, for whose lessons I am impatient. At 5:00 we'll go to the beach, and in the evening they'll come to our house—Saëtone, Tiouloulou, and especially the surprising but stupid hero. Again I'll start my conquest, and again the evening will end without any change; I'll return to my room almost disappointed, and I'll go to read in my bathroom, and go to bed hoping for a similar tomorrow.

Fritz and Bagatelle met me at the door. Fritz jumped into my arms and showed himself so happy to see me that I found it marvellous in a dog I've owned only four months. It's strange to be here again, and I'm again beginning to sigh. Goodnight; I'm tired. Oh, I love Nice! I love Nice!

What I can't forgive myself for is talking about a man who doesn't give a hoot about me. It's undignified to lower one's self so. Oh! If he could read this, how proud he would be! He would believe that I'm hiding the truth—that I was foolishly in love and only pretending under the cover of specially made sentences. But he would be wrong. Finally, goodnight, my dear journal, or I'll never stop talking drivel in Nice, like those dotards who recall constantly the events of their youth.

BOOK FORTY-THREE

Book 43
From Friday, September 10, 1875
To Tuesday, September 21, 1875
Promenade des Anglais, 55 bis, Nice, and voyage to Florence.

Friday, September 10, 1875. Ten times last night I was wakened by mosquitoes, but although I got up this morning rather pale, I was strong and comfortable. Oh, the English express themselves well when they say *home!* No matter what it is, home is the best place. It has nothing to do with comfort or riches; look at our house: it has neither comfort nor riches. It barely has the necessary furniture. It's disordered and desolate, and yet I feel good. I am home at last, and it's mine, mine, mine!

I've even forgotten my worries, and my dresses seem all right to me. Oh, Nice! I thought I'd never see it again with such joy. And if anyone had heard me swearing and cursing on our way from Marseille, that person would have said I detested it. It's my habit to speak badly about people and things that I love.

All dressed in white and wrapped in a white tulle veil, I went to the Promenade with my two dogs. I am so disgusted with men that there is nothing but dogs.

It is grey and beautiful. It seems to me that every peasant here recognized me. I was glad to talk with all these people. I met everybody I know as I passed by George's baths. I stopped to talk with his mother, and she asked me to come to bring her customers. I did this same thing last year.

Each house, each tree, each telegraph pole is a memory—good or bad, of love or of common things. Now don't let anyone think that behind each word is the handsome Niçois. Of course, he is there, but the other memories dominate.

On the Quai Masséna, Galula took off his hat and waved it triumphantly. Then I picked up my Graces and took them to our house for dinner . . . and then we went to the Français. One of the great satisfactions in my life is to be myself, as I like, in a beautiful stage box on the main floor of the theater with my two beautiful graces—in Nice, in my theater. (Everything is mine here.) We were barely inside when Tiouloulou rushed into our box and stayed as long as possible.

He said that a few men told him they recognized me in Paris at the Bois; among them was Hector [Audiffret], who said that I asked him where to buy the best umbrellas. He's told that to everybody, and it annoys me. What a poor idea of him it gives me!

I asked, "He didn't find anything more witty to say?" (Get that, Hector.) I enjoyed everything; I breathed, I admired myself in the mirror of the box, I was looked at but I looked at nobody.

At last, like a bomb, Saëtone arrived!

"But I was not expecting you!" he shouted. "It's like a thunderclap!" I scolded him for taking so long, telling him we'd been there an hour.

"But, Miss, tell me—are you going to stay?"

"No."

"Oh!" he said pitifully.

I spoke, chatted, was enchanted about everything and everyone.

Finally, someone asked whether I had seen Girofla.

"Yes."

"And what is he doing?"

"I think he is having a good time."

"But did you see him?"

"Yes, at the Bois."

"You saw him? Saw him a lot?" And when he said this, Mercury looked me straight in the eye.

"No," I replied, holding his gaze with big, innocent eyes. "We saw him in the Bois."

"Good."

"So, you are leaving?" he asked.

"Yes, Sir. Of course. Tomorrow."

"Well, tell me, how long shall you be away?"

"About a week."

"Oh," he said, as if meaning, "Good, I know what to do."

This dear Mercury!

I am so excited to be again in my beautiful city. I am at home, at home, at home! There is nothing to be compared with that; I have enough spirit for everyone tonight!

I'm not afraid as I was in Paris to be looked at by brutal men. Inside I feel like a queen. After Saëtone left I said, "It's a steeplechase, Auntie." I didn't say it because I believed it, but because I was bragging. Besides, tonight I would believe anything. Is it really true? Am I in Nice?

Oh, Nice, ungrateful! I who love you so much—why is it that your society mistreats me? It seems that never before have I felt so good. I left the theater free and happy. I didn't hide as I did in Paris. I have no fear of anything. I am known here.

If I could feel about Paris as I do about Nice, what could I not say? That would be too beautiful!

Saturday, September 11, 1875. I ate today as if I had had no food for a long time.

I hurry, hurry. I want to be in Florence at once and come back quickly, in order to pass the winter in Rome. Goodbye, dear city of my heart.

Arriving in Genoa was like a clap of thunder, as is said in Offenbach. I am in love with Italy—this Italy that I despised. That's the way it is! I am speaking Italian with excitement!

We went to the Hotel de France, and I am enchanted with everything: these ancient palaces with their huge windows and their balconies.

Even in our hotel, our room has a beautiful window higher than one can have any idea of in France, with a poetic balustrade. I stood in that window all dressed in white. I was thinking it would be nice to be serenaded. But no. Instead of that, some English sailors passed by, drinking and singing I can't remember which barbarous song. No matter. I was enchanted anyhow.

Sunday, September 12, 1875. [In the 1887 edition, Mrs. Bashkirtseff placed this part of the diary under the 1874 heading. The diarist went to Florence for the first time in 1875.] At 1:10 we got back on the train with an Italian couple—a marquis and his wife, the marquise, with their baby. . . . I know that most husbands don't love their wives. This Italian woman gave me a good lesson in the art of conjugal love. Their baby is charming, I even admired him; but then a normal catastrophe happened, and the mother, in spite of the presence of the nursemaid, did everything for the baby. Disgusting!

I understand very well the men who go away to their clubs or to some clean, pretty mistress, running away from their wives with untidy skirts—nursing mothers with worried faces who have other children with these catastrophes. I don't blame the men. (God preserve me from that!) I am sorry for the women, but how do they dare to complain? Their love can't be maintained. . . . Love comes by itself and slips through your fingers like a puff of smoke.

In the evening we arrived in Florence! We took a fiacre and went to the New York Hotel, which Winslow had recommended to me. (I forgot to say that I met him in Paris at the Grand Hotel.) If there are to be other festivities . . . I'll die of envy and vexation, because I'll certainly not be attending them. What is bad is that we don't know a soul. Alone! Alone! Alone! What can two women alone do? Especially if they are respectable and elegant? Well, let's be resigned.

Monday, September 13, 1875. What life, what animation—music, songs, and shouting everywhere. I am feeling well, and the people surrounding me are like me. "Some live," as Wilkie Collins says, "seated, others walking, and still others running." I live running. Not going anywhere in particular, we drove in a landau all over town all dressed up. Oh, how I love these sombre houses, these porticos, these columns, this grand, massive architecture . . . the immense stones of the Pitti Palace! The city is dirty, in tatters; most of the houses are almost in ruins, but how beautiful it all is! The home of Galileo, Machiavelli, Michelangelo. Oh, city of Dante, the Medici, Savonarola, how full you are of superb memories for those who think, who feel, who know! What masterpieces. . . .

We are here *as in a dark forest,* as Dante wrote. What is worse for us is that we know no one . . . don't know where to go or what festivities are scheduled. Yet, as a Russian poet has said, *"Our happiness is in our own miserable ignorance."* It's true. I don't know anything here, and yet I'm almost tranquil. I would be very grateful to anyone who could lead me out of my ignorance—tell me about a ball here, a festival there.

I am so excited: tomorrow we'll visit the galleries and the palaces. . . . What a good life it is here!

Tuesday, September 14, 1875. I adore paintings and sculpture—the arts, wherever they are. I could pass entire days in these galleries, but my aunt is suffering, tired. She can hardly follow me, so I sacrifice myself. Besides, my life is before me, and I'll have time to see it again.

It's 1:00 and time to go out, but I don't dare to disturb my aunt. She just got up and is dressing. It's so hot and the last day of the Centenary festival. There are crowds everywhere. Having seen so many beautiful things, I become sad; I'd like to possess all these treasures, or at least some of the ones I saw!

But do I dare to say it? Then in confidence, I don't like Raphael's *Virgin of the Chair.* The Virgin is pale, the color is unnatural, and her expression is rather that of a chambermaid than of the Holy Madonna, Mother of Jesus. Oh, but there's a Magdalen by Titian that I'm crazy about! Except that her wrists and hands are too fat; they are all right for a woman of fifty. There are some ravishing things by Rubens and Van Dyck, and *The Lie* by Salvatore Rosa is very natural, very good. I don't judge like a connoisseur; what is most like Nature pleases me the most. Isn't the imitation of Nature the purpose of art? I like the fat, fresh face Paul Veronese painted of his wife. I adore Titian and Van Dyck, but that poor Raphael. . . . But if people saw what I'm writing, they'd take me for a fool. I don't criticize Raphael; I just don't understand him. With time, doubtless, I'll understand his beauties. However, his portrait of Leo X is admirable.

The *Virgin and Child* by Murillo is fresh and natural.

To my great satisfaction I found the picture gallery much smaller than I had thought. Those unending galleries are more terrible than the Labyrinth of Crete!

The corridor that runs from the Pitti Palace to the Uffizi Gallery has its walls covered with the Gobelins tapestries, and they enchant me. But my aunt, who is very little interested in all these things and is tired of all this walking, seemed so tired that I took pity on her, and we left. Although I passed two hours in the Pitti Palace without sitting down, I am not tired. Things that I love don't tire me. As long as there are paintings, and especially statues, to see, I'm made of iron. But if I had to walk through the shops of the Louvre, the Bon Marché, or even at Worth's, I'd be crying within three quarters of an hour. We ride around the city in a landau and are lucky to have a very good one with good horses.

After dinner, we changed our dresses and again went out, first to the Cascine (where there was not a soul) and then to the hill where there are illuminations. It is the last day of the festival. All the city is lighted, and all the surrounding hills. As we passed through the crowd, it was like moving through a human ocean, magnificent to see. The people shout, walk, gesticulate. We started to climb the hill, but near the Piazzale the carriages were stopped by the police, who were very polite, and we had to walk to the concert, which was given in a huge pavilion. In the lighting, the old towers, the *holy door,* seemed to be burning. All the hill, from top to bottom, was garlanded by fires carried by an immense crowd, and there was music at each step.

We got into that crowd, and I was noticed; but the crowd increased at every step and we decided not to go to the concert, so we returned to the carriage. I admired everything we saw, but we came back with difficulty because of the numerous carriages stationed all along the way. The cathedral, with its tower, seemed to be burning, as well as the Palazzo Vecchio, with its colonnades and statues. In this light they were more beautiful than anything else I have ever seen, as was the Baptistery, with its doors. To see all these things lighted at night is surprising. Add to this the animated, immense crowd, a new, surprising masterpiece! And then one finds a modest garden restaurant beside a palace, or a watermelon stand beside a marble statue. There are statues and paintings everywhere. No other journey has ever given me the satisfaction of this one. At last I have found things worthy of being seen. . . .

Oh, my girl! What will you say to Rome?

Wednesday, September 15, 1875. We went to the Uffizi Gallery, which is connected to the Pitti Palace, where I saw as much as was possible by walking through it. Today I spent twelve hours there. The Greek statues and busts held me for a long time. The head of Alcibiades disappointed me: I had never imagined him with such a full forehead, and his small mouth showed the teeth above the little beard. Cicero (I don't take him for a Greek; be sure of that!) is quite good, but poor Socrates—oh, he was right to be a philosopher and speak with his genius, for he couldn't have done anything else, being so ridiculously ugly! Finally, the *Venus de Medici* is a new disappointment: her ankles stand out, her head is too small, and her features are like all the other Greek statues of the period. This is not the charming goddess, the mother of Love. The mouth is cold and the eyes expressionless. Certainly the proportions are admirably adhered to, but what would be left for her if they were less than perfect? Let them call me an ignorant barbarian, arrogant, stupid. But this is my opinion. The *Venus de Milo* is much more the ideal Venus.

I passed by the paintings and at last found a thing worthy of the name of Raphael; not a flat and blank expression, like that on the faces of his madonnas, not a Christ-child-like papier-mâché, but a beautiful living head, fresh—*La Farnarina*. Maybe it's because I don't understand anything about painting, but I much prefer this head to all his other madonnas put together. Titian's mistress, blonde and fat, is admirable as Flora, but in the Pitti, where she served as his model for *Cleopatra Bitten by an Asp*, she looks absurd—too fat, too blonde, and not at all the Greek-Egyptian. I admired the audacity of a composition by [Giovanni da] San Giovanni of Venus combing her hair. A cherub, leaning on her knees, is killing the "inhabitants" in the hair of the cherub, Eros. (Forgive me for mentioning such a matter!) The effects of light in the paintings of Gherardo de la Notte [Gerrit van Honthorst] please me enormously. The faces are beautiful and lively. The big canvas representing the shepherds around the cradle of Jesus is magnificent. In this painting, the halo of the divine child illumines all of the people around him, and he himself seems to be made of light. The Virgin Mary holds the blanket, revealing the child, and looks at the shepherds with a truly heavenly smile. They have radiant, respectful faces, and those who are closest to him use their hands to shade their eyes, as we do when the sun prevents our seeing. One can see very well that the painter knew how to do what he was doing. In the French room there is a very pretty portrait by Mignard, and in the Flemish room a small portrait by Frans van Mieris which thrilled me with its extraordinarily delicate work. The more you look closely, the more beautiful it is, and the more difficult you find it to understand how the artist achieved the effect of his colors. I spent most of my time on the busts of the Roman emperors and certain Roman women—Poppaea [wife of Nero], and Agrippina [Nero's mother]. Nero is better looking than any of the others. Marcus Aurelius has a good fat head, and Titus looks like someone I know (I can't remember who).

We just received a key for our box at the Pagliano Theater for tonight. . . . I have seen this only in Italy.

Tomorrow we must leave. The more I look, the more I want to look. I can hardly tear myself away from these beautiful things. We visited the Egyptian and Etruscan museums.

Thursday, September 16, 1875. We leave this superb Florence: this light and very fast leopard covered with spotted fur [in Italian]: *una lonza leggiera e presta molto / che di pel macolato era coverta* [Dante, *Inferno* 4, 32–33].

Friday, September 17, 1875. At 3:00 we arrived in Genoa and went to bed at 1:00. We were awakened at 5:30, and soon again on the train. It's too bad that there were no trains in Dante's times; he would certainly have used one of them for the torment of his Hell! The pestilent smoke, the noise, the continuous shaking! Thanks to a book, I was not completely miserable. And then Monte Carlo loomed before my eyes and became pink and made me laugh with joy without stopping until we arrived in Nice. We had telegraphed, and the carriage was waiting there.

There, instead of going to clean up, I rushed to see the workmen who are fixing the rooms. Then I went up to the third floor, where we'll live while waiting for them to finish. I didn't forget to notice the closed window of the castle (with a certain vexation). In my room I undressed, and in my nightgown I threw myself on the classics, put them in order, gave them a special place in the cupboards. Then, having finished this work, I threw myself on the rug, where for an hour I received the caresses of my two dogs, the true friends of man—even though the man might be Socrates!

Then, with Dante still on my mind, "Then when my tired body had rested a little, I took my way again on the deserted hill" [in Italian]: *Poi ch'ei posato un poco il corpo lasso / ripresi via per la piaggia diserta* [Dante, *Inferno*, 1, 28–29]. But I didn't do that before I was perfectly washed from head to toe. I pulled on a white shirt and a thin skirt and then the grey batiste dress (without the blouse), which I replaced with a white silk bolero. I am very pretty dressed like that. When I noticed that the windows at the castle were not open and that it was past 6:00, I thought, Well, let's be resigned. We'll pass these few days quite agreeably with a few books. Let's go to see what my ex-beauty Gioja is doing . . . and I walked slowly toward her place. All at once a chariot pulled by two winged dragons came, churning up the white dust of the Promenade des Anglais. The chariot, mounted by two men—my uncle Saëtone and my cousin Audiffret, all in white. They were completely surprised to see me, had their carriage turned around, and came down from the fiacre.

"Good morning, Miss," cried Girofla, in a loud and piercing voice, and then rushed to shake my hand.

"Well," asked Saëtone, "What are we doing? Mademoiselle is staying here? Or continuing her walk?"

"Yes."

"Well, let's go."

And I had to walk between those two guardian angels. I was trembling a little to be seen alone in such company.

"Mademoiselle is taking a walk here, all alone, so poetically, so sweetly."

"Oh, yes. I didn't even take the time to dress myself, or rather, to undress myself from my traveling clothes."

"But what are you saying? You're charming this way!" [Girofla]

I was dying to ask him on what grass he had walked to have such things to say to me. Never, or almost never, has he talked to me this way. But the poor boy looked rather confused and tender and all. They say his business is not doing well. Poor soul! I'm sorry for him, as much as I am for myself. They went to greet my aunt, who was coming toward us. When he said goodbye, he shook my hand; I returned to the house so happy, so gay, that my aunt scolded me and said I was a girl without shame!

"As much as you like, Madame. I am enchanted, enchanted, enchanted, and I don't hide it." I have difficulty understanding this; I have the fever again as before, and I just want to pass the evening very quickly and reach for tomorrow. In five days he'll be returning to Paris before coming back to Nice. I'll manage to persuade him not to go away. So, well, here is my folly again! Seeing him again, I found in his face an expression that I can't be mistaken in. And then, he seemed very happy. Well, I've already said that when a thought enters my mind it stays, and the less reason there is for it, the more it fastens itself in my brain. But then, I don't know what to think. One day I think he likes me, and the next day that I am despised. And from these thoughts come my two extreme moods—extraordinary joy and vexation and anger.

Monday, September 20, 1875. For two days I've written nothing! I forgot my journal, and it was complaining in the white box. And here it is again! On Saturday I went out with my aunt and saw no signs of Audiffret. I am very much annoyed.

On Sunday I spent my time painting Olga's portrait, which earlier I had only started with charcoal. The big oval tired my hand, but I still wanted to paint. Then I took another oval of the same size and made my dog Frederick pose. And that wasn't easy, you know! We got him up on the armchair and called Bagatelle, and we made him play with a stone on the carpet, while Leonie sang to amuse the sitter. She had to tell him all sorts of things to make him hold up his head. I made him life-size, and painted just the bust, like a man's picture. He is superb in full-face position, with his tongue hanging out.

We went to the theater to see Victor Hugo's *Hernani* with the Sapogenikoffs. Although I wore my new pink dress, I didn't feel proud as I usually do when going out. I was furious to be in an ordinary loge, but the room was almost filled and all the beautiful ladies of Nice did me the honor of staring at me.

They say that people are talking about me, especially since the gossip about d'Audiffret. The play was as badly performed as possible, and I didn't listen to it. We saw the man during two acts and two intermissions, sometimes behind my armchair, sometimes seated; what is the best of all, he accompanied us to the exit. And since our carriage was delayed, all those good Niçois saw my aunt and Galula, me and Émile following them, walking toward the

Place Masséna, where we took a fiacre into which these gentlemen handed us, and Girofla himself put up the top. Actually this last business gave me a certain pleasure, to be in an instant like other women—not miserable and alone as before.

I am very strict about my painting; I cannot deny that I have a talent. This is the first time I have worked from a model. Olga has posed twice for me, and I'm almost finished. What I have just done encourages me enormously. The resemblance is perfect, but I hope to improve it.

BOOK FORTY-FOUR

Book 44
From Wednesday, September 22, 1875
To Saturday, September 25, 1875
Promenade des Anglais, in my villa, Nice

Wednesday, September 22, 1875. I went to the Promenade on foot with my aunt, and we sat on a bench. Soon Tiouloulou came up to us, saying that yesterday he and Audiffret came to our house, but seeing all the windows closed, they didn't dare to come in. A few minutes later the super imbecile came up, dressed just as he had been dressed in Paris.

Among other things, we talked of the caricature I had made of him, and he absolutely wanted to see it. I let them come upstairs to my study and had each of them carry a candle. . . . I pulled up my train, as my feet and the Russian leather slippers were asking for eyes to look at them.

After they examined the things in the room, walking back and forth with the candles, Girofla opened a cupboard and read the title of the first book—*Memoirs of the Duke of Richelieu.* Wow! That was just what I did *not* want!

"Oh, oh!" was his comment in a most expressive tone.

This morning I've erased the tower, the horns, and the tail. I wanted to do his picture in full face, but I didn't succeed. And this evening I asked him to wear his top hat and made him pose every way. "You're losing nothing by waiting. Tomorrow you'll be put back in your place," I told him. "Don't laugh. Close your mouth." And of course he was opening it, laughing, et cetera.

I bent my head from right to left, the better to see his face, which I had such a hard time drawing, or even looking at because he is so handsome. I was furious this morning and am enchanted tonight. What can I do about it? He amuses me, and now I find him adorable.

Thursday, September 23, 1875. What is atrocious is that each time I let myself be caught!

Before yesterday evening, all was going well; I had nothing to reproach myself for. But I did let myself go. I found him adorable; I was ready to sing duets with him. It's infamous! You knew very well, absurd, idiotic girl, that it's better to trust the ocean than that monster! And you forgot everything. You let yourself be caught. You acted like a butterfly, for which you deserve to be beaten with a stick!

Admire the politeness of my subject! He came near the carriage in blue, wearing his little Niçois hat. I was expecting to hear about music, opera, painting. Absurd animal! Brainless woman! He came to say that Nice is dead, boring, that he has nothing to do. No, tell me. And that he is leaving Saturday. He was expecting my face to change as it did on other days, but by unbelievable luck I didn't flick an eyelash.

"And you'll be in Paris for some time?" my aunt asked.

"Not long. Ten to twenty days, perhaps."

This was a new arrow, but no more successful than the first one. I didn't move. Only my mood changed, and I became very confused and ashamed inside.

I was so exasperated and furious with myself that from where we were in front of No. 7—where we saw the bataclan and the man—until we got home, I loved him. And I told myself, very low, that I loved him, certainly I did! But arriving at No. 55 bis I became ashamed and did not love him any more.

You can imagine the mood I was in when I went to the table. I opened my mouth only to say spiteful things about the Saps., when all of sudden Olga and Mary entered. Oh, terror! That was the limit!!! *He* had been showing the photographs he and Saëtone stole the other night, and he was told about the English women!!! That means my reputation is sunk! What is he going to think? Oh! He didn't want to believe—he said he saw us almost at the same time at the baths—that on the right were the English ladies and that I was there on the left at the same time. The fact is that the trick was admirably done. As I look back, I am astonished. Seated on his right we were the English ladies, and all at once, with a prodigious change, we were on his left side.

"What? That tall hunchback was Miss Bashkirtseff?" he shouted.

"Yes."

"And the one who walked like that—was?"

"Me," said Mary.

"And the dark one I took for a Russian spy?"

"That was me," Nina said.

"Oh, but that's unbelievable! And I didn't recognize you!"

All this was followed by a spell of laughing, screaming, and astonishment without end. At least, if they were going to tell him, I should have been there to enjoy his surprise.

"You've killed me," I said, hiding my face in my hands and falling into an armchair.

Fortunately I do not love him any more. I'll always remember with despair that I loved him from No. 7 to No. 55 bis. "One who spits into the wind receives what he spat in his own face." O great and sublime truth!

Friday, September 24, 1875. I went out with Fritz, one of my dogs, at 10:00. Not a soul, a furious sun, a blue sea—that kind of purple blue—disagreeable, and a sky on fire! After an hour I came back, and from the landing on the second floor I saw a fiacre at the castle. I thought it would be funny to meet him after yesterday's story and went out again, but I didn't meet anyone. Besides, the miserable one has the habit of passing by the Rue de France in the mornings.

Again I become sentimental; I look at the heavens, the stars, the sea, and the black trees. Again I am beaten, sad, and want to cry. In the spring, Audiffret and his clan awakened and distracted me. But here is autumn and boredom again. No, we must leave. From the first moment we arrived until today, I've received only insults, sorrows, and deceptions. The ground is cut away from under my feet. Although young, pretty, witty, and educated, I languish here without being occupied with anything. My face becomes drawn; I melt. Soon there will be nothing left of me. Oh, Nice, for so much love you should be ashamed to pay me with such black ingratitude. . . .

My plan is all traced in front of me: I am a creature ambitious beyond reason—good, violent, stubborn, generous. I want to be loved, and I love to love. It was silly to say, "I don't know whether I have loved." I know perfectly that I have loved. . . .

From the first moment I saw him, I looked at Audiffret as if he were my man, but soon I realized that I had been foolishly mistaken. But with my usual tenacity I didn't want to give up, and said that if it weren't now it would be later. I got used to this idea, and now I am very unhappy to have to admit my error. That hurt me to the quick, and now I am doing everything possible to recover myself and to triumph over that man. But he doesn't love me, and that is what makes me so angry. I want him! But I mistook anger and vexation for love, as one might take some chablis with soda water and a little sugar for champagne. Isn't that strange?

Saturday, September 25, 1875. I almost do not regret him, but I fear he is dropping *us*.

In a dark blue dress and black hat I'd worn in Schlangenbad, I walked out with my dog Frederick. The few pedestrians opened their eyes wide to see me in dark colors, as I've been wearing only white. Then my aunt took me in the carriage with Fritz. Girofla has not left!

I'll never forget this detestation, and each time I feel joyful a disgusting voice will tell me with a mocking accent, "Be careful! This could be the same thing as it was with Gericke!" I was sick, and Gericke began to avoid us. Then Mama told me that he believed I was crazy about him and didn't want to encourage this passion. And she added that the public thought that was the cause of my illness.

But my journal is here to protest loudly against these smearing calumnies! If I could only forget that he ever existed!

My Graces invited me to the theater this evening. I was gay and made everyone laugh. Bihovitz and Paris were our cavaliers.

And Galula came, probably from the other one's house.

"So he hasn't gone?" I asked.

When we left the theater, I put the adorable white tulle veil over my head. You can't have an idea of the grace it gave my face. And all this in vain.

BOOK FORTY-FIVE

Book 45
From Sunday, September 26, 1875
To Saturday, October 2, 1875
Promenade des Anglais, 55 bis, in my villa, Nice

Sunday, September 26, 1875. The weather was grey and cool. We stayed near the Sapogenikoffs. Audiffret passed and passed again, finally coming close to Nina's carriage. Galula was with him, the vile show-off!

Then he came to the door of my carriage. I felt free and natural. The imbecile doesn't impress me any more. He said silly things and begged me to go with him to Paris: "Let's go—both of us. We'll go to the Hotel Splendide."

"Around the world," I said, laughing.

"Exactly!" he said.

What an idiot! We walked with Paris, and the Niçois stayed near Nina to excite my jealousy. Triple brute! I am not so silly as you think! Tiouloulou is promoted to the rank of suitor and confidant. Tonight we went to Nina's. They were all excited; they were going to see Girofla. When I arrived with my aunt, he was already there. Paris had brought back a very nice game from Dieppe, "The Races." At first we played, and then everybody did as he liked. Nina went out, but Paris stayed. Girofla was posing, and Tiouloulou helped him and imitated him. And Olga was in heaven. Girofla took a penny from her and said he was going to carry it *in* his watch. *Very funny*! Tiouloulou dared to court me, and I let him do it. I paid no attention to the other one, and about halfway through the evening he came back to me. I did as he has done with me; I didn't listen to what he said, and I was busy with everything else.

We sang all together. Then came the stories of the photographs in his pocket. We threw ourselves on him like a pack of dogs on a deer, but there was no way to unbutton his coat and we were unable to take any of our pictures back. My aunt was angry; I begged him to give my picture back because it is signed. Then, after giving him my word to return it to him, I scratched out the inscription at least. The miserable man is capable of saying anything. My aunt has told me so. Four times she called him an imbecile, which seemed to enchant him. What a monster—to steal my photo!

299

Toward the end, we all acted completely free. When it was time to go I seated myself in an arm chair and Tiouloulou took leave of me on his knee. His master did the same thing. "No, I do not take your hand," I said.

"Oh, why not?"

I wrapped my hand in a handkerchief and gave it to him. He tore the handkerchief away and enclosed my hand in his own two hands. Do you understand? And I abandoned my hand to him nonchalantly. We went out together.

"Come on! Don't be the impetuous squire; give me back my photograph."

"Oh, not that! If you knew where I put it!"

"In the famous wardrobe? Please! I know where it is."

Paris accompanied us to the carriage. When we were already in the carriage, Girofla offered me his hand, but I pretended not to see it. Oh, but to have ever said I loved that man—what an idea!

"How strangely he talked to me!" I said on entering my room.

"What? What did he say?" my aunt asked eagerly. She is more interested than I am in the affair.

"Nothing."

"He said nothing to you?" she asked in a provocative, negative tone.

"Nothing. Absolutely nothing."

She would very much like to know what he told me. Let her relax. When something is said, I'll be the first to report to her.

Monday, September 27, 1875. Dark weather, dark mood, dark clothes.

In the evening Barnola came and the three of us talked quietly until 11:00. The Niçois never does this—never sits down to chat, or even talk, except rarely. With him and his friends, it's usually shouting and jumping around. Of course, that way it's happier.

A man can do all kinds of things and afterward get married, and that is seen as very natural. But if a woman dare, not only to do all kinds of things, but almost nothing out of line, she is stoned!! Why is it like that?

They'll only answer me, "You are only a child, and you understand nothing. For a man it is, whereas, for a woman it is completely different."

I understand this very well; there are the children. But often there are none.

Thursday, September 30, 1875. The orchestra seats on the right were taken; so we had the Durands on the left, and consequently we were facing our winter box, Gioja's ex-loge. It was occupied by her two children and the elderly woman. I was with my aunt and my Graces. . . . The play was *Giroflé-Girofla.*

But let's get to the point: Gioja, who was at first hiding in the salon of her box, finally appeared. And from that moment we knew that Audiffret was in her loge, in the rear of the little salon from which we had so often looked at him last spring, when my Graces were with me.

What a dirty thing! For him to go into the same box as we had, with this woman and her children! She sat there, tranquil and nice, speaking from time to time to whomever was there at the back of the little sitting room. He must have told her everything, because she was laughing and turning around to the door each time she spoke. We heard the name "Girofla." Before, this was excusable: one could say he was a child, and that this was new for him. But he is no longer a child, and it is no longer a new thing for him. That was three years ago. He is no longer a child. How can one explain or excuse such vile conduct? To show himself—or rather, to let people guess his presence, with those children—all the family?

My aunt said, "Let's go," and implied that I was jealous.

"Oh, Madame, how wrong you are if you think I'm jealous! Certainly it's disagreeable to have this face *always* before me—everywhere—but I'm not jealous. A little while ago you were telling me that he acted this way on purpose to attract me. But this does not attract me."

"I think so. You like him, and he acts this way on purpose."

But he doesn't think of me. He is a man who thinks he sows love everywhere. "Let's pay attention to this girl for a few weeks; let's excite her," he said to himself. "Then let's find another one." And he's a fortunate man to believe himself so powerful! I went to my room jealous, not for love but out of pride. Is it possible, I thought, loosening my hair, which fell in golden curls on my shoulders and on my back, that anyone can prefer that woman to me? . . . No, it's not possible. She is not preferred as a woman, but as a "merchant of pleasure."

Friday, October 1, 1875. My aunt said she met him in the Avenue de la Gare and that she talked with him. He is leaving for two weeks. But I don't believe my aunt. For the last week, each morning her first words have been, "Miss, your beau is gone!"

I don't care since I don't see him any more and don't have him any more. One thing bothers me. Let's reduce all this to its simplest terms: I have been counting on my charm, and I've failed. Girofla didn't love me, after all. That's what annoys me. One must believe that I have a false idea of myself—that I'm ugly and stupid, that I haven't been able to win him with all my wiles. That's the true humiliation.

BOOK FORTY-SIX

Gloriae Cupiditate
H. G. T. D. O. H.
Book 46
From Sunday, October 3, 1875
To Tuesday, October 12, 1875
Promenade des Anglais, 55 bis, in my villa.

Sunday, October 3, 1875. I went alone to church and asked the coachman to pass by the street opposite the school. That way I could pass in front of No. 77. Everything was closed. They have left, the scoundrels! I imagine the Niçois in the love seat with her and the dogs, like the Englishman who was brought here. All morning we chatted about it with my aunt.

"Well," she said, "You ran after him all winter, and he ran after you."

"Yes, and he, too. Both of us ran after each other, and when we met we didn't find each other interesting enough. Oh, aunt, it's miserable to have lived to sixteen and a half without success and conquest!"

"But you've had some conquest. And Girofla, also."

Ah, the beautiful conquest. You are adorable!

But my little Giroflé is more naïve than I, and she believed all the sweet things Girofla had said to her. "He told me," she shouted, blushing, and I had to set the record straight.

"He told me he loved *me*. He wrote it," I said.

"How? When? Where?"

"On a biscuit he passed to me at home before twenty people."

"How do you like that!"

"Yes. And also at the country dance. And then—everywhere." Olga blushed and her eyes took on all sort of expressions, and I continued unpityingly to tell everything. . . .

I had not realized that it was at that point with Olga. I should have guessed. With her romantic, childish, charming personality, her disposition will do her harm. She is credulous and naïve.

When we talked with Nina, Mary, and my aunt, Nina told us that Saëtone had been coming to bother Olga. He told her that Girofla was madly in love with her and that his letters talked only of her.

Then my aunt told us how Saëtone had acted that way everywhere; he had also meddled in the affairs of Lewin and Clementine Durand.

"With me," I told them, "he didn't go so far. He limited himself to asking how I felt about his lord and master." They were all talking in Russian, and I in French. Here was Olga, in love and disappointed, and her mother, disappointed and hurt, like my aunt, the guardian of my interests. And I, more than anyone else, had mixed myself in the affair. Mary was neutral.

It finished as an evening of confidences and condemnations of that devil Saëtone. After seeing Olga's excitement over Girofla, Mr. Sapogenikoff, who had been in Nice on business during our absence, had had a very serious talk with her and his wife; he told Nina to keep her daughter at home. And Nina took seriously my aunt's suggestion that Girofla might be living quietly with Gioja and thinking of no one else!

Monday, October 4, 1875. Mercury is undoubtedly a sly old fox. I think he tried to provoke an imbroglio with me, Olga, and Girofla, and then withdrew quietly to watch it all. Oh, this is really mixed up! "I find myself in a dark wood where the straight way has disappeared" [in Italian: alteration of Dante: *"mi ritrovai per una selva oscura / ché la diritta via era smarrita," Inferno* I, 2-3].

I like a beau like—like Witgenstein—but I'm afraid of him, whereas the Niçois and I are more nearly equal in age. He is not grave nor serious. I am crazy. He is crazy. He's a rogue and I am one. That's why he amuses me. I feel free with him, as with a friend. So nothing can be serious between us. He only amuses me.

I know Olga loves him, but I would like her to say so. Outside of Girofla, there is no gaiety nor amusement between us. It is strange!

And presently, since the subject is banished, we keep trying to go back to it.

Our new cook feeds us marvellously, and I am in the best possible humor; I can't write a thing tonight!

Friday, October 8, 1875. Good God! Days, weeks, months pass. Too tired to fight, I fall into a kind of numbness; I let everything go and stay silent. But a moment comes when this tranquillity weighs upon me—and I become hopeless. Already October and nothing done! The disorders of the house are a great sorrow for me; the details of the household sewer, the unfinished rooms, this air of devastation, of misery breaks my heart. God take pity on me! I am alone!

As for my aunt, it's all the same to her that the house crumbles, that the garden dries up. I don't even mention the details, but they irritate me and ruin my character. When everything around me is beautiful, comfortable, rich, and gracious, I am gay, good, and well. But this desolation and emptiness make me desolate and empty of everything.

Without pleasure or hurry, I went out; Nina and the children were walking and we joined them. "Oh, if you could know how I treated the human race this morning!" I told Mary.

"And if you could know how little it cares!" she answered wittily. In fact, it doesn't care at all. Paris drove in the carriage with us. He is on the outs with his lady.

Saturday, October 9, 1875. I am tired of my obscurity. Soon I'll be seventeen, but I wither with inaction; I mildew in the shadows. The sun, the sun, the sun!

Let's go—have courage. This time is only a passage that will lead me to where I'll be all right.

Am I mad? Or fated? Be it one way or the other, I'm bored!

Sunday, October 10, 1875. This is the first day of rain—the first day of autumn. But I don't feel refreshed.

We went to Nina's, where we talked about the quarrel between her and her darling; we laughed about it as we would talk with Mary about Stephen. Nina is really quite strange. As for me, I am tormented and in despair. I am not going to Rome; I have found that only in my beautiful Paris do I want, like Mignon, to live, to love, and to die. No, everything but die!

When I think that at sixteen and a half I'm more alone than if I were an orphan . . . ! Nobody thinks about my future, my life. Nobody takes care of it. There's nobody to help me—nobody, nobody, nobody! All around me are stupid people who love me, who close windows to prevent me from being in a draft, who carry my coat in case the weather may turn cold, who check to see that I go to bed early, who make frightful faces when they hear me coughing or sneezing. Oh, my God, no one in this world can understand my position on this earth! Alone, alone everywhere. Alone in everything.

At the moment I was writing this, my aunt entered and with care closed my curtains.

"Do you know," I said, "that we must leave Nice?"

"Let's go."

"When?"

"When you wish."

"I have been telling you for two years. Don't tell me you are taken by surprise?"

"Told me *when*?"

"You always say this. But when the time arrives you always have thousands of obstacles and excuses. I've been telling you that this winter we must go away from here; that I'll be going into society."

After these words Madame my aunt lifted her eyes to me like a mad man lifting his ears like a donkey. She took her cigarette box in one hand and her handkerchief in the other and walked out calmly.

Monday, October 11, 1875. I am very miserable. All this exhausts me; if this fever continues, I'll be very sick! And they are surprised by my pale face. But it's true; they don't understand that one can suffer for what makes me suffer.

A cable from my mother announces that she is coming home today.

We've just passed all day at home amidst shoutings and screamings, runnings in Mama's room, the Graces on the floor, "Coco" [Yourkoff] serious, Nina triumphant.

Nina did come to dine, although she has been angry with her dear friend for the last ten days. How good we are in our home to lead such a scandalous life and even to encourage it as we have this evening! They restrained and publicly forced Yourkoff to make peace; excited by the general mix-up, I forgot myself to the point of shouting, "On your knees, Coco!" We call him that among ourselves. The lady herself has told me many things in such a way that I am not surprised at anything any more, and I almost think that it is very natural that things between them could not go differently. Also, no one is more extraordinary than Mr. Sapogenikoff in this affair. When it is necessary, he puts them together again and looks upon them as his children. It is said that all this is for the love he has for her. I don't understand anything about it.

When we were at last alone, we brought Mama up to date on everything—about Girofla, the latest about the Sapogenikoffs, their expectations, etc.

BOOK FORTY-SEVEN

Gloriae Cupiditate
H. G. T. D. O. H.
Book 47
From Wednesday, October 13, 1875
To Saturday, October 23, 1875
Promenade des Anglais, 55 bis, in my villa, Nice
"What do the letters H.G.T.D.O.H. mean?" I ask you.
His Grace the Duke of Hamilton.

Wednesday, October 13, 1875. For the time being, Mama is in the pavilion, and because of that I stayed there almost all day.

Sunday, October 17, 1875. I never have described the topographic position of our estate. Our villa has about thirty-one feet on the front on the Promenade and runs back 300 feet to the Rue de France, which is parallel to the Promenade and is where Bibi [Audiffret] lives.

Monday, October 18, 1875. I like to talk about Émile, and I smile when anyone speaks of him to me. He interests me terribly. If he loved me, I would love him. "Well, you love him," one could repeat.

But no; the head is stronger than the heart. And I believe that, in me, the heart is in the head. Never will I love anyone first! It bears repeating here: one who spits in the air spits on himself. What I wanted to do to another, he has done to me: *fooled, mocked, maligned, burned!*

For a cocotte! . . . But I am more sorry than angry. All of them seem to have clubbed together not to come any more to our house. . . . I feel just like a beaten dog.

Tuesday, October 19, 1875. I would like to lie down somewhere and not see anyone. What a pity that I can't set fire to No. 77! I swear to you that I am ready to do it and with the greatest pleasure, and also set fire to the castle. I would watch both of them cook without lifting a finger or being upset. In place of doing it, I think of it and write about it. For him to prefer a cocotte to me—can you imagine my anger! I, the queen, the goddess; I who do not want to move my little finger lest I should bestow too much honor; I with my ideas, ambition, pride!

Saturday, October 23, 1875. For the first time in a week, I haven't had a headache. I feel fine and I am pink. . . . But Mama said to Nadya, "Look how Marie is losing weight. In town they say it is because . . ." I didn't hear the ending. The ground is slipping from under my feet. I fell in an armchair, covering my face with my hands. I don't need anything more than that! And once more this idea is from my own mother. I detest her for that. What have I done? How can I atone for my crime? If I have to cut off a finger from my right hand, I'll cut it off. What can I do? Have I committed so many atrocities that my punishment has no limit? My God! Terrible, inexorable God!

Yes, I now am thinking of making up the lost time when I go to Rome. Why should I be happier there than here? I do not want to make plans. I do not want to have another deception as cruel as this one.

I'll take my example from the men. Oh! How much I hate them for their arrogance, for their iron character! I'll raise myself above them, above him, too. He educated me. I am cured. A few lost illusions, a few fallen hopes, and I'll be finished with it. I was going to say "the down of the heart is stripped off," but that's not true; my heart is intact, though my mind is embittered. Let's surround our hearts with triple bronze . . . but I can't even do that. I am out of the affair with the loss of a few feathers, which will grow again and leave nothing showing. I don't want to love this man anymore. I don't want to think of him anymore. I don't want to look for opportunities to talk about him anymore; I forbid him to myself!

BOOK FORTY-EIGHT

Noto omnia [Latin: I take note of everything.]
Gloriae Cupiditate
H. G. T. D. O. H.
Book 48
From Sunday, October 24, 1875
To Saturday, November 6, 1875
Promenade des Anglais, in my villa, Nice
Know everything; do everything.

Sunday, October 24, 1875. A little before we reached my Graces' house, the Surprising One passed us and lifted his head with affection in front of their house. Since I decided yesterday not to occupy myself with him anymore, I didn't blush, nor did I say a word to him. I was very natural and teased Olga, who was blushing and embarrassed. I called her Bibi, like anyone else, and she was delighted. I am angry with myself. I said a silly charm, which had no success. Well, I don't want to make any bad blood between us. The thing I fear most is the general scorn. In a pinch, I'll content myself with simple politeness. As long as people don't turn away from me, I feel reassured.

Antonoff. You don't know about him? He is a very out-of-the-ordinary man. He told us his story.

A miserable clerk in I don't know what shop in Saint Petersburg, he finally realized that it was stupid to stagnate in a slum; so, having realized that, he found a dowry with an excessively ugly woman and became a merchant of novelties. He made a fortune of 500,000 rubles, they say. He abandoned his wife, paid her an indemnity, sold the business, and came with an actress—a singer—to Nice, this receptacle of all kinds of things from the rose family to the laurel leaf. The actress, Mrs. Kronenberg, was passing as his wife. Her voice allowed her to sing at the opera in a post she obtained *because she was a Russian Lady.* Through this association with the people of the opera, Antonoff met the celebrities of Nice: Saëtone, Audiffret, father and son, etc. One day Mrs. Kronenberg left him, and Antonoff put on a good face in spite of his misfortune. He bought a lot on the road to Villefranche and built a house on it.

He is dressed amusingly, with button-in diamonds. He is short, dark, and round, with fish eyes. He is said to be forty-five, but seems to be shaving more. He speaks only Russian and has no education of the mind, but he is practical, a speculator, and his knowledge of money bespeaks the newly rich. Truly, he is not worth this description, but he came to Nina's and then to our house and will have a party for the opening of his house in about a week.

Everybody has made fun of him, and some are very witty about him. Having now been alone for two years, he is looking for a new wife. He likes Mary, and we have laughed about that, God knows.

Tuesday, October 26, 1875. It is surprising. I no longer look at the castle, and I no longer wish to. Before this I did nothing but that.

At the theater we heard *Alice de Nevers.* It was my second time. I found it charming. It has become my favorite, I think, like *Giroflé-Girofla.*

Having ideas of conquest, we took Giroflé, dressed all in pink. I dressed all in white.

Two minutes after we entered the front of the stage on the second floor at the right, Bibi [here, Audiffret] made his own entrance into the front loge at the first floor at the left. This front-stage loge is reserved for him for the season; tonight it was full—Boissard, Saëtone, and Co.—and all these hearties made a hell of a noise, as if they were at home, without any regard for the public. That is to say, they were doing it to show off.

The first to arrive in our box, as always, was Tiouloulou, and a little while after that all the dark company burst into our loge—Saëtone, Pepino, Barnola, and Bibi. This last one—as usual—entered only after he had performed some foolishness at the door.

"How are you since the dance?" I asked my friend Ricardo.

"Not bad at all," he answered, starting to hop.

"Which dance?" asked Bibi.

"At home, last Sunday," I answered.

"What? You danced without us?"

"Alas! But it is your fault. Why don't you come?"

One by one, Saëtone, Barnola, and Tiouloulou left. I sat behind my aunt, and Pepino behind me.

Pepino was the last one to leave, and I returned to the front of the box, being sure to show a glowing face after my conversation with him. Everyone was looking at us as if we were the Princess Souvaroff's party or something more interesting.

I was troubled and enchanted—enchanted because you know why, and troubled because my aunt thinks I should have been nicer. Her criticism made me doubt the kindness of my conduct, with which I was so satisfied. But I don't want to hear that one can be sweet with him; I want to be as I decided. What the devil! Don't prevent me! Each does as he wants. I am polite, nice. Don't anyone ask anything more of me!

When Mama met him and some of the others the following day and did not invite them, I became furious; I took my gloves off angrily, tearing away all the buttons, and I had quite a time calming myself down. Don't you understand that I'm lonely? To spend an evening with the family does for the mind what a watering pot does for a fire. They talk about the miseries of the household or regale me with observations about Girofla. But of the arts, history, and other such things one hears never a word. I want to go to Rome and start studying again. I feel little by little wrapped in the spider web that covers everything here. But I fight! And read. Nobody will come tonight; the clock has already struck ten.

Thursday, October 28, 1875. All those people who came to our loge will come to our house tomorrow, as before!! My aunt did not fail to poison my evening with some arrows that she came to deliver. But who cares? I'm happy.

Friday, October 29, 1875. I have been painting and smiling since this morning, although I spoiled another dress with paint.

The others all arrived at 9:00, but as for the Impetuous Squire, Tiouloulou made excuses for him to arrive later on. It seems he doesn't dare to present himself in his street clothes. At 10:00 he appeared in a tuxedo. What a strange man! He made his first visit without dressing up, and this evening he comes so formally!

In spite of my lack of interest in Pepino's conversation, I had the patience to keep him nearby in such a way that the Squire found me next to him, very busy to the point that I noticed him only when he came very close to me and said "Good evening!" In this society, one must do what is pleasant as much as possible. The man amuses me, and I want him. Staying with Pepino is useful, but not agreeable—not much fun. Besides, the Squire was nice tonight. He did not take his eyes off me all evening. There is something between us—I don't know what—but we seem to understand each other. I don't know how to explain this feeling, but everything we say to each other seems to be only for us two.

No sooner were we at the table than Olga winked at me in this way we have between us. I understood without a word; taking into my handkerchief a piece of sugar, I went to the second floor. In the darkness, I found the vial with the philtre—the one we got for Girofla. I poured a few drops from it onto the sugar cube and came downstairs, this time putting myself between Pepino and Audiffret. "You'll have another cup of tea, Sir?"

"No, thank you."

"What? Not even a little cup? I'll pour it myself." Seized by a sudden attack of kindness, I went to the other end of the table and poured the tea, into which I let fall the cursed sugar, and then carried it to Bibi, who, very surprised, said, "I'd like to frame this cup of tea and drink it all my life."

He's a sugar—this time more than ever! We danced. I'd been dying to—the word is too hard—to touch the man. After the first dance, he sat near me.

"Do you remember the country dances?" he asked.

"Yes, I remember," I said in the simple tone I used in all our private conversations.

"Which one? It was the second that I preferred," he said.

"They were both very nice," I said.

"No, there was one of them I like better," he insisted. "The one Goddard came to."

"He came to both. There was one with light and one without light," I said.

"I preferred the second," he said, looking straight ahead.

His way of saying it pleased me so much that I can still feel the punch at my heart when I remember. Oh, if you knew how difficult it is to gather what he says!

All the names I've used for him until now seem strange. Audiffer, Girofla, Bibi, the Man, the handsome Niçois, Émile—I told him it's difficult to write what Audiffer has said.

Someone brought the cards and the Tarot deck, and I read good fortune to Audiffer. But soon Pepino stayed at the table. Tiouloulou was flattering everyone all around, and soon Dina and my Graces arrived! Good God!

I told Émile that he will run off with someone; that he'll have an unsuccessful love affair, a near death; and also that someone loves him with a secret passion and he will remain a long time without knowing who it is, but that he'll finally know it because of an illness. Before I got to the end, we mixed up the Tarots; and then I told his fortune with the regular cards, asking him to think of a woman. He said, "Yes, Madame," and then corrected himself, saying "Miss" and, adding under his breath so that no one else could hear, that he was thinking of a young girl. You understand that I am taking pleasure in recalling everything.

I've told Dina about the shock, but asked her not to repeat it as the family would attribute it to the cause they like to believe in—that I'm in love with him. "Whether I am or am not, the shock exists," I said. "There are some days when I am sure he is in love with me, and other days when he spits on me."

"Well, my dear," Dina said, "It's because there are days when he is truly in love with you."

"Well, I'm going to write that," I said. "It explains everything. Thanks." It is sublimely true!

I had arranged another gathering for next Sunday. "Are you coming with the others?" I asked as he was leaving.

"Yes," he answered, pressing my hand for a long time, and for the first time in ever so long I felt the shock. I knew then that it does come from him. I explained it later to Dina this way: "So it comes from him since I feel it only when he is Bibi, as you say, and I don't feel it when he spits on me—when he's Girofla."

"You were pretty yesterday," my aunt told me, "because you were not pale." I had to believe her, because for the least paleness I am scolded as if it were my fault! "You were pink. I don't always say that to you, but yesterday you were very pretty and he was melting for you."

"You've been telling me these silly things since the first day, assuring me that he was in love with me."

"No, yesterday he stared so much that I scolded him—as usual."

"If you were telling me the truth, I would kiss you 448 times, it pleases me so much!" I said, giving her a big hug.

When we dance, he holds me tightly by the waist and by the hand. He is a sugar. We are completely friendly now. No more sad things, no more dark spots. I'm not used to it yet. But Olga: this poor girl in love came ten times to interrupt us and ask us to stop so that he could dance with her. My aunt doesn't leave me alone with him for an instant. As soon as we are left alone by any chance whatsoever, she runs after us.

What I regret is that one cannot be married for a limited time; I'm sure that a marriage of two months with Bibi would give me a lot of pleasure. But, things being what they are, I must wait for Freedom (I mean a regular marriage) so I'll *have* to betray! You don't think I'll abandon my Niçois! If I dared after such silliness to speak of God, I'd say I thank Him, that He heard me. But I don't dare. He'll know I thank Him, anyway.

Our talk when we are with the others is always trivial, and we are never alone. I am asking for a country ball. But that is not really what I want. I desire a good declaration, really serious, very nice, in good form. I *must* leave! The absence will show me the truth—whether I am truly in love or only amused. When my aunt began her little jokes and asked me what the man said to me, I, not being able to admit anything serious, preferred to say,

"Nothing, Madame. I assure you. Only frivolities." I am not satisfied with myself; yesterday I was too childish. For a young lady this air seems bad manners. I had sung "Mignon" and "Dormi pure," with all my strength, so that Émile and his friend could hear me at the castle. And when he told me they heard me, I protested, "It's unbelievable!" Actually I was surprised and delighted. He had told me, "I heard everything as if you were singing at the castle. I couldn't believe it, but I recognized your voice." That in spite of the horrible noise of the carriages over cobblestones—and at such a distance!

Audiffret does not love me. I know. I know him. I am really sorry about it because I love him enough to want a great love on his part. They continue to say that I'll marry him, and all the people of Nice look at me in a special way, as if he were their king. Barnola came this afternoon to pick up his cane that he forgot yesterday and asked Mama, "Has he already asked her in marriage?"

"Who?"

"Audiffret, of course."

"What an idea, Sir! He doesn't even act like a man who is thinking about marriage. We see him as little as we see the others."

"Oh, you're hiding it! Yet everybody says it," and Ricardo started to say something malicious, as he did yesterday when he saw me dancing with Émile.

"He does not love me," I said, "any more than I love him. He pays me a little court, and I am enchanted, of course." (Miserable feminine position! Men have all the privileges, whereas women have only that of waiting their good pleasure. It's really the least we can do to betray them as often as we can!)

Fickle, crazy, reckless, crafty, calculating, mean, capricious, and brutalized by his association with bad women, this man, it seems to me, must have very early lost the feelings of delicacy, true love, and honesty, especially, that flower in the human heart.

But I could be wrong. Yet I would be very proud to make myself loved by this man. It really hurts to realize that he can court me the way he does everyone else and that I am not loved. As for this pitiful courtship, I am not sure of it for an hour, his mood changes so often.

O, woman! Unfortunate creature. Made to wait like a passive animal! She does nothing by herself. If someone comes, she entertains. If no one comes, she is immobilized. What can she do? She cannot kick or turn away when someone deigns to talk to her, as our social etiquette requires politeness. This man behaves in such a way that he gives me no hold on him. At the least complaint he can tell me, "You don't have to reject me; I don't want anything from you. I talk to you as to anyone else, so don't get excited. You are mistaken." This is my position. Agreeable, isn't it?

Friday, November 5, 1875. My family had driven out before me, and when they returned they told me that Émile was out in a two-wheeled carriage with livery. But he has left me so cold and so discouraged that I didn't hurry at all. In fact, when I saw him riding in his little carriage, we were walking. My aunt became excited, but I didn't move. "There's Girofla," she said, "coming to meet us."

Oh, my God, I thought, how terribly I'm going to blush! I did not, however, even when he passed us a second time, bowing but not stopping as the carriage wheels whirled him along and out of our sight.

"Here is a real thunder," I said. No one can imagine my anger, my confusion! And I was so much offended. My aunt made some jokes about the servant's livery, the horse, and the tube hat, to which I answered without affectation.

It is impossible to leave. The money has not arrived. No, really, nothing succeeds for me. But I must become reasonable and raise myself above these miseries. So long as I don't become ill. . . .

BOOK FORTY-NINE

Book 49
From Saturday, November 6, 1875
To Wednesday, November 17, 1875
Promenade des Anglais, 55 bis, in my villa, Nice

Saturday, November 6, 1875. The play they're giving is a big three-act drama. Everybody came to our loge except the Surprising One. I had been afraid of a general defection, but since all the others came, I am content. He never does what other people do. But when he was interested, he came at each moment. Then when another idea got into his head, he brutally dropped us.

He didn't move from his loge early this evening. With his head leaning on the back of his chair, he seemed fairly dead. My aunt said, "He's doing it on purpose. He's dying to come up here; he's bored, but he'll not come." I surprised him looking up to our loge from behind Boissard and discovered that he was watching everything that was going on in our group. My aunt repeated, "He's doing it on purpose. Let's go."

Wednesday, November 10, 1875. After the music, we returned to my Graces' home and strutted on the balcony. Bibi passed and did not even look at us, to my very great satisfaction, because Olga hoped that he would.

I was on the point of leaving at 2:00 for Paris, but the first performance at the opera is announced for next week, so I'll stay for that.

Sunday, November 14, 1875. After lunch I took Giroflé to our house, and after having chatted together at home, we went walking with my aunt, who was wearing a magnificent outfit. I was in white flannel—a new but pretty dress, and some yellow boots embroidered with Greek openwork.

While we were walking, Bibi was in a carriage, all stiff and serious. And I was satisfied and proud. And what about? My God!

I am little and vain. This being said, let's continue!

I took care to express the wish to return to our carriage before any of my escorts expressed the desire to leave. They even begged me to walk another time around. Very well.

They took us back to the landau, and we were barely moving when Bibi appeared. "Miss," he said, looking at my dress, "today you are . . ."

"Isn't this a pretty jacket?" I said.

"Ravishing. Exquisite."

"But where do you keep yourself? We don't see you."

"Oh, I stay at home in the countryside. I'm altogether like that—depressed."

"Are you ill?"

"I don't know. I'm just very much depressed."

"Throw your rose away," my aunt suggested. "It's all withered."

"I picked it, myself, in my garden."

"But it is all faded."

"Oh, my rose is like myself, depressed."

"Everything's depressed," said Olga. "Only, your tube hat is not."

"It, too," Girofla said. "It has had all kinds of misadventures. We sat on it. But after all, that's not my business. It's its business."

That's all I remember of the conversation.

I must be crazy!

Pretty soon they'll put me in an asylum administered by Saëtone.

Really, I must be going crazy.

Here is my craze again; the way the man talked to me, the way he looked at me, by something imperceptible—I don't know how, it seemed to me I could see . . . no, it's too silly! To tell it, well—you understand me. You also understand which mood I'm in, and the curious thing is that I don't love him at all.

Monday, November 15, 1875. Mignon! The big day! I've been anxious all day.

At 8:30 we left. I was in white mousseline—a plain skirt with a big ruffle at the bottom, a Mary Stuart-style blouse, and a hairdo matching the dress. Madame, my mother, did not fail to exasperate me with all kinds of remarks so that I arrived at the theater ready to cry.

It was a beautiful crowd; Audiffret was alone in his box, and as handsome as an angel. The opera was admirably sung.

Really, I started to believe that I have blinded myself—that I am ugly—a fright. But no, far from that. I was sure of the contrary by the way people looked at me. Everybody was admiring me except the Squire, who stared at the stage all the time and then at each intermission went to see actresses and actors, but only for a few minutes. Bihovitz and Antonoff alone came to our box. I was outraged to see my mother and my aunt all upset to have nobody. They had been expecting to see my triumph in front of the Howards.

When Pasqua, the prima donna, started to sing "Do You Know the Land?"—the song I sang for the Surprising One when we were on good terms—I stood up to listen. Mama and Dina were in the first row, and I had to stand up to see. The Surprising One did not even look at me. Actually, I don't know that; I see so badly that I could not see the direction of his eyes.

Mama had predicted that his heart would beat faster when they sang my song, but he didn't look at me. On the contrary, he listened to Pasqua with unbelievable attention.

Around the middle of the performance, I began to feel pretty, like a valentine; toward the end the Surprising One started to notice me. At the exit I passed between two rows of gentlemen who stared at me as if their eyes would pop out, and they did not have a dirty look. One could feel it. My heart is filled with pride and joy, because even though one disdained me, many others gave me justice. I'm writing like a mad woman. I don't know what I'm saying.

Leonie came to help me undress; but I sent her away and locked myself in, because when I came back I suddenly saw myself in the mirror. I looked like a queen, like a picture out of La France. I sang in front of the mirror. It always seems to me that other people do not see me as beautiful as I am. But that's ridiculous; they wouldn't look at me as they do if they didn't see me! It is too bad that, instead of these little black letters, I cannot draw my portrait the way I see myself.

Tuesday, November 16, 1875. I went to bed at 5:00 A.M. this morning; at 2 P.M. today I am leaving Nice [for Paris] with my aunt. Coco, Antonoff, and Walitsky drove us. Antonoff gave us candies and bouquets.

Wednesday, November 17, 1875. A lot of things have changed since Monday. First, I don't want to die, at all, no matter where or how. And then I am ashamed of myself. I wanted to make fun of the man, and it is the man who made fun of me. This insult, added to the anger I feel for my weakness last Monday, has made me detest him. Never has anyone made me so angry as he has. Never has anyone made me tell so much. Never have I changed mood for anyone before. Never have I been so agitated! And he has made fun of me. If the opportunity comes to burn the town, I'll burn it.

So, in front of God, I swear that I'll take revenge, no matter how. "One must forgive?" No, never forgive this miserable man! . . . But I'll never be able to give back half of what he did to me, either.

[Paris]

At 6:00 we found nothing at the Grand Hotel, so we took an apartment at the Hotel Splendide, *his* [Audiffret's] hotel.

BOOK FIFTY

Paris, 1875, Hotel Splendide
H. G. T. D. O. H.
Book 50
From Thursday, November 18, 1875
To Saturday, December 25, 1875
Hotel Splendide, Paris
After November 28
Promenade des Anglais, in my villa, Nice

Thursday, November 18, 1875. [Paris] Exhausted, tired, reduced to nothing! I'll always spend too much on clothes, but that's why I came to Paris!

At the table d'hôte I met Winslow and his mother. We talked of the Surprising One with my aunt. She told me he is courting Miss Leech, who is as pretty as a doll—and rich. I'm already jealous of Leech, and furious because I've seen with what animation she responded to him at the opera the other night.

He's really a fortunate man, my Niçois. Everywhere he goes, he is always liked! The women make eyes at him. Oh, it was so clear when he entered her box. She came to life at once, as I did when he came to us.

We saw *The Creole*, Offenbach's new success. Judi is adorable in it. But I'm suffering from the heat and the impudent looks of several men.

Friday, November 19, 1875. "Come this evening to see us," Mama said to the Surprising One the last time we saw him.

But he answered, "I thank you very much, but tonight I have a number of things to do in town and several people to see on business. Another evening—with pleasure!"

"Oh, another evening—that will never be," said Mama, "because the day after tomorrow my sister and my daughter are leaving."

"No! Truly? But no. You are not going. Tell me you're not!"

"Oh, yes, Sir. We're going away."

"But she'll return in a week," Mama interrupted.

"Oh, then!" exclaimed the Surprising One. "So go. Go quickly. Go right away, right away!"

Why did he talk like that, the damned dog?

Tuesday, November 23, 1875. By the grace of God, the mailman, and the telegraph, at last I've learned about our purchase of the Boismillou Villa. It is a very good investment for capitalists like us. But it will provide a big scandal because the property is not yet paid for; I do not want it to be, as there are other payments due that are much more urgent, the furniture, for instance. So it will be a scandal because Mrs. Romanoff will have to resell the Boismillou property because she has not paid for it. And until everybody knows which property we will sell, we'll scream and howl that it is the villa of the English family. That beautiful speculation has been hidden from me for a long time, but dirty actions always come to light. The family assures me that our new house is not paid for, but I don't believe that. For six months they assured me that they had not bought a villa. Besides, where else would the money be that I've been asking about? (Really, by hiding from me you will do many bad things of which you will repent—but you'll do that too late!) And I, absurd creature, was listening to the reproaches they've dared to make about my purchase of the furniture! They are throwing 30,000 francs out the window, and they *dare* to talk to me about *the furniture,* which is necessary to us all! And I, who was listening to them and thinking maybe I was wrong to order such a large amount of money for myself? People who move by dark ways can often wheedle honest ones!

In Nice we now have three villas—ours, the Boismillou, and the one where *my beloved one* is staying. Well, dear Uncle George, may the plague suffocate you!

Sunday, November 28, 1875. [Nice] At the theater the room is even sadder than usual. Never since I have lived in Nice have I had a pleasant evening at the Opera.

I love him but do not want to say it. I do not love him. However, outside of him, there is nothing for me. I think only of him, of going out to see him somewhere. All he does occupies my mind. I dress only for him. When I was in Paris and bought a new hat, I was thinking what the effect would be on him. Where he is not, there is nothing for me. I follow his life, I remember his least words, I have memories of him. And I hate him with all the strength that I could have had to love him. I will never forget that he has hurt me, that I have been despised. Do you understand the word *despised*—all that is awful in this word?

Tuesday, November 30, 1875. I am very happy to be at home in my own house! I am sleeping in my big bathroom, the ex-bedroom of my aunt. In a month my room will be ready when I return from Rome. I am thinking only of when I return—to have my carriage and spend a month in Nice, to continue the studies started in Rome, to follow the orders of my professors. And then to go to Russia! So many things have suffered, so much money has been lost because of my missed trip. And I am thinking of the Russian man. Lacking the other, I could be satisfied with him. I am insane! Lacking everything, I talk like a winner!

Wednesday, December 1, 1875. I went to the music. And here Audiffret appeared near us as usual. He was very jumpy, ready to leave. He asked whether we were going to be in Nice for a long time.

"For eight days, I believe."

"What? You are leaving again? And for where?"

"For Rome," said my aunt.

"But Miss, you are always travelling. It is terrible. You are a revolver!"
Explain, who can. This man is absurd. I am a revolver!
"And what good are you doing?" my aunt asked.
"But nothing. I am going to dinner, then to the theater, and then to sleep."
Triple stupid.

Thursday, December 2, 1875. When it is raining, I am most miserable!
How great is the vanity of mankind, I thought, looking at the castle. If he did not have these stones, I would not even mention him. Each time I am ready to abandon him, I just look at the castle and say to myself, No, he has a castle that is too beautiful. And what is the use? I like it, but not with Audiffret in it.

Friday, December 3, 1875. Dina told me that Robinson fixed Bibi's tie in front of everybody at Mrs. Prodgers's house. Bibi kneeled in front of her, and everybody was scandalized. A Russian proverb says: "One must not be born rich, not handsome, not intelligent, but one must be born happy." Yes, happy. That is the great word. Why am I unhappy? Why always repeat the same thing? Yes, I am saying it all the time. I think of it constantly.

Saturday, December 4, 1875. Yesterday at the station, Audiffret came near Mama. He was handsome in his yellow overcoat, open.
My aunt and I and the General were walking. He made me laugh with one of his observations. "It's interesting," he said. "The men look at your face, and the women at your gown."
"If I could die! I wish harm to everybody." I cried in Mama's bedroom, and at breakfast I announced that I was going to study singing and become an actress. And I'll do it—if God wants to preserve my voice. It is the only way for me to acquire that freedom for which I thirst, for which I would give ten years of my life without hesitation. I cannot become musty, I need noise, renown, and glory! And I'll have them. *Deo juvante.* [With God's help.]
I have the most comprehensive ideas in the world, and I am desolate because of our lack of society.
I was born to be a remarkable woman; it matters little in what way or how. All my tendencies are toward the great people of this world. I shall be famous or I will die. Is it possible that God has given me this *gloria cupiditas* [desire for glory] . . . for nothing, without goal? My time will come!
I went to the music. There was nobody interesting except Mrs. Vigier. Upon seeing her, I shouted a little cry. Never can one imagine anything more absurd, extravagant, and ridiculous! I hope for something unbelievable, fabulous. I want to reveal myself to the world. I want to be famous. So I'll sing!
At the *Barber of Seville* . . . It is funny, all the troup greeted me. Tonight we were in No. 2, and in front was the old dog [Émile's father].
I was wearing my Empire dress, in which I like myself. I had an Olympic hairdo, my hair falling lower than my waist and the tips curling naturally. As usual, I am very much looked at. The father was looking at me, and I let him do it; but I was not looking at him, being very satisfied with myself tonight.

Tuesday, December 7, 1875. I was dressed all in white, as usual, but pretty as two hearts. We walked in the garden. The sun was magnificent. We met a young man who bowed three times without our recognizing him, when all of a sudden my aunt said, "But it is Miloradovitch!" Imagine my trouble! I ordered the coachman to turn around and follow him. At the Avenue de la Gare I was going to stop and go to talk to the man, but he disappeared, I thought to the Hotel des Îles Britanniques; but the doorman told us that no one with this name was in the Hotel. At home I reasoned: How could he recognize me after almost six years of absence? But this man looks like him. I said to Giro [short for Giroflé, Olga]: "He is a perfect Bibi, but he lacks a certain air of vice. He looks too innocent. . . ."

"Oh," my aunt interrupted, "For that he can borrow some from some of my acquaintances. . . ."

We went to the opera. I was hoping to see the stranger. . . . I listened to *Mignon* with pleasure and emotion. All the scenes seemed new to me.

Wednesday, December 8, 1875. It is very cold, and I have to wear my fur with my white dress, trimmed from top to bottom with braid. It makes me look like a princess of old Poland . . . of old Russia. Nothing looks good on me but white.

They all think that Audiffret is interested in me. . . . I did not see my handsome stranger. . . . I am impatient to go to Rome to work, to study. The sight of my books makes me happy.

Friday, December 10, 1875. When looking for my stranger, we found a rare beauty, a young man of twenty-two to twenty-four years old, very tall, admirably well-built, distinguished and superb in his gait and in his least gesture, with an adorable and beautiful face, a complexion such as I never saw before—magnificent features and "Hamiltonian" clothing. In my whole life I have never seen such a male beauty. I blushed looking at him, and automatically I compared him to Audiffret (and not to the latter's advantage). . . . I managed to walk and meet him a few times. The second time I discovered that his hair is fair and his moustache dark.

At the end of the day, when the cold was coming, I left the carriage and walked back by the garden door just at the moment when the superb young man was passing in front of our villa. Mama thought I had not seen him and called me back to the carriage in such a way that my door almost touched him. He is *so* handsome, *so handsome,* that he must be silly. . . .

Such a perfection cannot exist. I want to see him again tomorrow to examine him better.

Saturday, December 11, 1875. Tonight we are going to the opera.

Far from crying, I spent a very nice evening. They gave the *Cenerentola.* By a bizarre fantasy, I dressed in blue—a big dress in light blue silk, plain, with a big ruching on the bottom of the skirt and a square train. It has a tight blouse and tight sleeves to the elbow. The front is open in a special, original way. But the whole was ravishing, and I was pretty.

Émile was in the box. I blushed. Pepino came to our box. He is a nice young man and very amusing. We were flirting. And then Ricardo arrived. Pepino wanted to run away, but I detained him. At the end, after he had been hiding, Mr. Émile Audiffret honored us with his presence. I was not expecting such a favor from this scoundrel, but I received him anyway, with admirable simplicity.

Bibi is still handsome, and his lips please me.

Pepino said a lot of mean things about the direction of the opera and departed, leaving us with Audiffret.

Audiffret talks very nicely with us.

His eyes are piercing, but there was only one instant when he turned his head away as if he were afraid. The animal comes into our box when there is no one outside to see him. It is absurd; I want to see him only for the others.

Our attitude is different from the past; we do not say anything about his coming, and my aunt does not invite him. She knows very well how to behave, and I would like to go into society with her; she is very proper.

Sunday, December 12, 1875. Gonzales said to my aunt that Audiffret pays court to his daughter. I am very jealous. Why? He is nothing to me. But my handsome stranger—I know who he is: he is Lord Loftus. Now I remember! In Baden he was often with Lady Faulkner. He was only a child . . . I want him. I want to adore him. I have never seen anything more beautiful than that man. I am exalted when I think of him. I want to see him! I want! I want!

Monday, December 13, 1875. I am ready to go to the opera in my Marie Antoinette dress. I am quite pretty. And the carriage does not come!!! *Capite?* [Do you understand?]

I waited until 10:00 and went into Mama's room. I wore my robe, and my hair was loose. Half-laughing and half-crying, I asked, "When will you take me to Rome?" Then, to distract me from my idea, she started to speak of Audiffret. I hid my face in my hands. My aunt said that I would be back in two weeks, because that is all the time I could take without seeing him. Walitsky is to have less time absent from here. Mama called him a crow. . . . But I remained firm, and the comical situation became tragic: Mama cried, calling all her sorrows on her head; my aunt shouted, Walitsky sneered, Dina looked sick, and I, my face hidden in my hands, was the prey of the greatest despair.

Wednesday, December 15, 1875. In the *Figaro* I read "Monsieur the Duke of Hamilton, back from Germany, arrived yesterday in Paris."

Oh! My dear dreams, my childish hopes, my innocent love! All this is crushed, broken, mixed in the mire of humiliation watered by bitter tears! Do I still have a clean thought in the world? NO. And I, who thought myself to be on earth only for happiness!

Yes, it is better to leave. At each party or reception I'll lose a month of my life and gain a wrinkle on my face.

Thursday, December 16, 1875. I drove as I like—with Giro; behind were Dina and Mary, and Mama and my aunt following in the landau. I was gay. Audiffret met us several times. Tonight was the premiere of *The Daughter of the Regiment*. We arrived after the first act.

Audiffret bowed, and so did Count de Tournon. Years ago he was very much in love with the little Natalie Galitzine; he followed her into Russia, where she died in his arms a few months ago. I had never met him before, but since I have seen him on the Promenade he has looked at me often, and it is my white apparel that attracts his attention. . . . He seemed to be asking who I am. When he saw me with Mama, whom he recognized, he bowed.

This evening Audiffret said, "You should always be in this box. It is nice."

"That would please you? I don't believe it."

"Oh! Miss, you do not tell me what you are thinking."

"I always say what I think."

"Oh! no," said de Tournon, "you would not be a woman and a Russian if you did!" And the conversation was engaged. He is not so handsome, but well-mannered and charming and even distinguished.

I started to look at someone with the binoculars, and he asked me, "What do you do, Miss, to have such little ears?"

"But nothing," I said blushing. "Is it the first time that you've seen them?"

"No, but truly, aren't they little, Tournon?" And both were in ecstasy looking at my ears. Is this Bibi talking?

Saturday, December 18, 1875. Thursday I am going to leave for Rome. My mothers will not oppose me. They think that Audiffret is the cause of my sorrow.

Sunday, December 19, 1875. Tomorrow there is to be a concert at the Club Méditerranée for the benefit of the Free School of Fine Arts. I went to the Club to get tickets. I was ushered through well-lighted and well-heated corridors to the secretary, who gave me the book containing the by-laws and the names of members. The Clubhouse gave me a charming impression. Oh, women, don't pity yourselves, but attend to your houses.

I learned that you must have an invitation from a permanent member to go to the meeting. The only one I know is Audiffret. I am going to the opera to ask it of him—to beg him. And if he refuses? But with what reason? At the opera Galula said, "Here is Audiffret going to the Willises'."

"Where are they?"

"Oh, not here. Tonight they receive at their home."

That's it. Everybody receives, except us. It is my nightmare.

When I arrived at the theater, I heard a servant saying to the usher, "To Miss Gonzales, from Mr. Audiffret."

What could it be? But I am not offended. He will do with her as he has done with all others before me.

So he had left, and I did not ask for the invitation. Maybe I have avoided a mortal humiliation?

I have been crying, and my mother asked, "Where do you want to go with such a face? If at least you were pretty, fresh, then . . ."

"Yes, and if I am pretty and dressed up and go out, a charming prince will meet me, fall in love, and that's all. That's what you are waiting for. This is how you think." I was out of breath, crying. "Ask me what I want, and I'll be quiet and pretty."

"But what do you want? We do not know . . ." I almost suffocated with indignation and rage.

"What, you do not know? Since I was eleven I have been telling it everyday."

"One does not go into society at eleven."

"Yes, but at eleven I was thinking as I am thinking now. And I thought that at sixteen I would have what I wanted. I have nothing. You want me to repeat to you what I want? Well, listen, and listen well. I want to go into society. I want to go everywhere and to receive at home. I want to give balls, to have receptions. You have heard? You know?"

"But how can you do it?"

"The way others do it. Engage, sell, ruin me; but make me live! What's the use of my fortune if I have nothing, if I am so miserable?"

"It is envy that is eating you. You envy everybody."

"But since you are leaving!"

"Yes, you make me leave. And last year it was the same."

"Yes, and what end do all these studies serve? If I were silly or stupid, and not able to speak many languages, I could marry a Galula, or an Audiffret with a white tie. And I'd be satisfied. But I am not. And that is not what I want. I want to study another year in Italy. Why do I want to leave? Because after two years of absence they will forget us and stop all these gossipings, and we will be able to come back and live here. In Rome I do not want to live as I do here. I want to live in society. Can't you understand that I can't live any other way? Have pity on me!

"You would like me to die, I know, but you will not have that joy. I do not live for you but for myself; so I will not stay here all my life. A day will come when I'll go out of this horror. You should have left me with my father when he kidnapped me, and when you took me back you should have thought about me and not have lived from day to day, like dogs. My God!, my God!

"Listen! Move, engage, sell, throw money, make a noise, and make me live! I swear to you, Madame, I can't accept this any more, as you can see for yourself!"

I have found a way to make an end of my tortures. I'll tell my mother to return to her husband, and that way I'll have an assured position; nobody will ever dare to talk about me. I'll have my aunt's fortune and not owe anything to my father. It is an immense sacrifice; but I have to be saved, because if I continue as things are now, I'll die. I do not want to die. I am afraid!

MY GOD, HELP ME, SAVE ME, HAVE PITY. [These huge words in script fill half a page.] These big letters represent an hour and a half of tears. . . .

Monday, December 20, 1875. In the afternoon we went to the concert. I looked as if I were dead, in a white dress. In the great loge were Belledujour and Audiffret.

On the way to the concert, I stopped the carriage in front of the secretariat of the Club and asked the attendant to call Audiffret, who came out and on the steps. He looked for whoever it was who called on him; he was so nice, so sweet, I would have loved to hug him.

"It is ourselves," said Mama, "but enter the carriage; it's raining."

"With pleasure, Madame, and where are we going?" he asked, smiling. "Well, what is it?"

On any other day I would have felt like a fool, but this time I was cold and trembling.

"Here it is," I said, "I would like to go to a matinee concert, and I am asking you where to go to get an invitation?"

"You have to go to the Vigiers. Ask them. He is in charge of it."

"But a permanent member, doesn't he have the right?" my mother asked.

"No, Madame, no." And my mother said that having been in the city for a long time, she should have received an invitation.

Audiffret said he will talk about it with Vigier tonight at the Club.

He will not ask. . . . That is absurd and hurting. What is the use of knowing people if they serve you nothing? I must have been desperate to ask Audiffret. For people like us, it is atrocious. We are going to Rome. Everything is changed. I do not know anymore.

Tuesday, December 21, 1875. This evening we made great decisions. We are going to Rome; and if there is *nothing* there we shall go to Russia, to my father's home, because there must be an end . . . I want it. I demand it; I am at the end of my rope.

Thursday, December 23, 1875. I am sorrowful and discouraged. My departure is an exile for me. I want to stay in Nice, and it is impossible to do so. We are always obstinate for the impossible. The dirtiest thing, by our resisting it, acquires some value.

Friday, December 24, 1875. Bihovitz has been at our house, and with a few words in the conversation he awoke in me so much love for Nice, so much regret at leaving, that I became unhappy and went to my room to sing—with such warmth and sadness that I am still crying from it—this eternal air; and these delightful words: "Alas, if I could return to those beloved shores . . ."

The others are not like me; they do not understand what beauty and sadness and truth are written in these words, this piece so common and sung so much in all the salons!

Yes, here only, here in Nice, in my beloved city. Around the world one finds many beauties, great cities, . . . but in no other part does one breathe so freely, so joyously. In no other part of the world can one find this extraordinary mixture of true and false, simplicity and sophistication. Well, how can I say it? Nice is my city—"Leave, but regret . . ." I'll come back!

Saturday, December 25, 1875. Ah! son felice! Ah! son rapita! [Italian: I am happy; I am rapt!] Find me another language which expresses thought with so much enthusiasm! So I use it to define my state of mind. You probably expect something with the Surprising One according to this study. I have barely noticed him. It is the others who . . . well.

The weather is heavenly; everybody is out of doors; in spite of my late night vigil, I am pretty.

BOOK FIFTY-ONE

Book 51
From Sunday, December 26, 1875
To Sunday, January 9, 1876
Promenade des Anglais, 55 bis, Nice
From Monday, January 3, 1876
Hotel de Londres, Piazza di Spagna, Rome

Monday, December 27, 1875. Now that it is 2:00 in the morning and I am locked in my room, dressed in a long white peignoir, barefoot, and with my hair loose like a virgin martyr, I can very well devote myself to better thoughts.

A royal supper, magnificent lighting, an adorable outfit, a charming face, all this for Bihovitz, Ricardo, Pepino, Galula! That was worth the trouble, indeed! Gautier arrived first.

A charming evening! Twenty times I wanted to lie down on the ground and howl, but I thought, have patience my girl, maybe God will reward you one day for this torment. And I was patient from the beginning of the evening to 2:00 A.M.

Around 10:00 in the morning I received the following letter, stamped from the Club Méditerranée: "Madame, in spite of my extreme desire to pass the evening with you, I cannot do it, due to a violent headache which makes me suffer horribly. I am begging you, etc." and signed, "É. Audiffret."

Little Audiffret has a little migraine. Charming! Everything disagreeable that happens to me I owe to my dear mother. And a hundred times since my return from Paris I have said, "Do not invite Audiffret." But she believes doing so pleases me, and she invites him anyway! I begged her not to, because I knew very well that he would not come. I think I am drunk. I drank a lot at supper.

I had a funny dream. I was flying high, very high above the earth, holding a lyre in my hand. The strings were constantly unstrung, and I could not produce a single sound from it. I continued rising, seeing immense horizons, clouds—blue, yellow, red, mixed, golden, and silver—torn, strange. Then everything grew grey and then again dazzlingly bright, and I was still rising until at last I reached a most frightening height, but I was not afraid. The clouds seemed wan, greying and shining—like lead. Then all grew dim. I continued holding my lyre with the loosened strings. And far below, under my feet, hung a reddish ball—the earth.

This Journal contains all my life; my quietest moments are those when I am writing. These are probably the only calm ones I have. To burn everything, to be in exasperation, to cry, to suffer everything and live, and live! Why do they let me live? Oh, I am impatient. My time will come. I certainly want to believe this. But something tells me that it will never come, that I will pass all my life waiting, waiting. I prefer to be completely hopeless, because after these burning moments there always comes a little calm, as after the rain the sun comes.

If I should die young, I shall burn this journal; but if I live to be old, people will read it. I believe, if I may say so, that there is no photograph as yet of a woman's existence, of all her thoughts. Yes, all, all. It will be interesting. If I should die young soon, and if by bad luck this Journal is not burnt, it will be said, "Poor child, she was in love with Audiffret, and all her despair comes from that."

Let them say so; I don't attempt to disprove them, for the more I say, the less they believe me. Is there anything more mean, more stupid than mankind?

Tuesday, December 28, 1875. I played all day doing foolish things, and everybody encouraged my silliness. We were at the good Mrs. de Mouzay's. She is sick in bed.

Wednesday, December 29, 1875. We went to see Mrs. de Mouzay. She gave me several letters of introduction for Rome. May God grant that they will be of service! This excellent woman . . . loves me so much! *Let* her be tranquil. Her kindness is not given to an ingrate. I love her with all my heart. I am so little spoiled that the least attention goes straight to my heart. However much I would like to love everybody, almost everybody spits on me.

I have just read Mrs. de Mouzay's letters. No one could be kinder, no one could be more charming. And, just think, the greatest part of the time, those who would like to do things cannot. It is six years since she left Rome, and I doubt whether her acquaintances remember her. She gave me seven letters, one for Miss Sophie Haigh, the aunt of Sir Haigh who is with the Duke of Edinburgh all the time, one for Monseigneur de Falloux, at the Ruspoli Palace; one for Adde Litz, one for the Countess Antonelli (born Garcia) at the Antonelli Palace; one for His Eminence the Cardinal Antonelli, at the Vatican; one for the Baron Visconti, ex-director of the Empirienne; and one for the Marquis D'Espinay, sculptor. What will be the results of all this? God knows! I am very skeptical and have been for a long time. I have the habit of being afraid of enemies, so I am afraid the name of Mrs. de Mouzay will be unfortunate for us, because I think that all who are friendly to us must be rejected and mistreated like us. I have earned the right to know this.

Sappho was given tonight. I wore a sort of Neapolitan shirt of blue crêpe de chine and old lace, with a white front and wide sleeves. It can't be described; it was as original as possible, with a white skirt and an alms bag of white satin. We arrived at the end of the first act and were near Mrs. Prodgers and Miss Row. I heard the voice of the Surprising One, and I was at first stopped by it the way a bit stops a horse that has lost its momentum. During all the intermissions, I remained motionless, listening to what was being said next to us. It is not a mistake that the skinny girl is known as "the beautiful American Girl." Nothing can be said against her face. It is blooming; whether real or artificial is of little consequence. She has hair—oh, I don't know! At Spa, she was fairer than I; here she is darker. . . . She is young and fresh—who cares? but adorable! One could say that she is too thin, but that is not important with so beautiful a face. She has beautiful eyes, and her hair is beautifully dressed. When looking at her, I right away felt my own eyes too clear, my bangs badly arranged. There is nothing which makes one feel so ugly as feeling inferior to another.

I did not speak in the carriage; I was afraid that with words would come a flood of tears. But a moment or two before arriving, I felt strong enough to say, "I am leaving on Sunday at 3:00."

"You have said that for a month."

"Nobody can say what you want."

"I am leaving on Sunday at 3:00."

"Why boil and tear yourself apart?"

"I am leaving at 3:00 on Sunday!!"

I went to my room and ordered some tea.

"I'll come to drink it with you," said Dina.

I did not answer, and I went to the fireplace and stirred up the coals, looking at the wood and thinking of absolutely nothing, which saved me from a big scene. It was a comparatively happy state I was in.

Dina entered and asked me why the tea was not yet served. I heard and turned toward her. I did not say anything, but I thought I said something.

She tried again a few times to make talk, but I did not answer her questions, as if under the influence of a charm. The bellows started to burn because I was keeping it in the fire. It made me smile, and I showed it to Dina, saying slowly, "I don't know what happened." I think I broke it. Then I took my tea, I ate and wrote.

I would like to possess the talent of all the authors combined to be able to give a true, just idea of my deep despair, of my wounded self-esteem, of all my destroyed illusions, of all my thwarted desires. For me, just to have to desire something is to see it aborted.

Shall I ever find a dog in the street starving and beaten by all the urchins, a horse forced from morning to night to carry an enormous weight, a miller's donkey, a church mouse, a mathematics teacher without pupils, a destitute priest, a whatever devil crushed enough, miserable enough, beaten down enough—to compare to me?

I have some dresses, a house, good food, a carriage, theater boxes, and season tickets to the different theaters. How many are there who have none of these things, and seeing me passing in the carriage with a beautiful dress envy me and think that I am happy?

"MY LAMENTS TIRE THE HEAVENS AND MAKE ME BITTER" [in Italian].

But what can I do? What can I do? Where is my pride? Where is my noble arrogance? Where is my resolution? Crushed. And crushed! What is awful in me? It is that the past humiliations do not slide away from me, from my heart, but leave their hideous traces!

Friday, December 31, 1875. It's 2:00 P.M. I've been up since noon. The tribulations of yesterday have given me a gaiety.

The Sapogenikoffs came, and after dinner we began to tell fortunes and laughed almost as much as we used to. That is, the others did; but I could not.

Audiffret started to become distant during July when I was in Paris with Stepa. You remember that he did not come, but let us think that, at that time, he did not know my uncle. And after Schlangenbad, when I was in Paris, he did not visit us. When we returned to Nice, he said that he had come to the Hotel to see us, but by that time we had already left. Lies. In Nice he did not visit us after my trip to Florence. He came in the evening once. After that evening . . . he no longer got out of the carriage to walk with us the way he used to. In a word, he left us. . . .

So the year is over. It is 3:00 in the morning and already 1876. Oh, my God, make this coming year more favorable for me than the last one!

Saturday, January 1, 1876. Here is the New Year. Greetings and mercy! Well, the first day of 1876 was not so bad as I expected.

I went for a ride in the carriage, but the gilded youth did not show up, nor the English women, either. Those happy rascals were having fun somewhere else.

The General dined with us, and we went afterward to see the Sapogenikoffs with him. The room at the theater was full, but the usual elegant men and ladies were completely absent. I found many amusing things to say that made everybody laugh.

Ricardo came as usual. The Englishwoman's husband was all the time in her loge like the fat imbecile that he is, while his wife amused herself and laughed with Brother Émile, Tiouloulou, and others. Pepino watched from behind his column.

Listen. I am furious with *The Death of SAPPHO.* These fat brutes in white, the pagans, stiff and absurd! Poor woman. I think I am speaking foolishly. Too bad! I am happy—very gay; at the exit, Pepino came to talk to me: "Tomorrow I leave. I shall be far from you!" I sang from *Mignon*—in Italian.

"Truly, Miss, tomorrow?"

Then I told him yes, and he was so much moved by my laughter that he put me in the carriage and asked permission to come tomorrow to the station to see us off. Tomorrow, Yes, I am content to leave. Do you believe that it is agreeable for me to see all the pleasures passing under my nose!

"Goodbye then, everybody!" [in Italian].

I do not cry. I didn't feel sad once. It's a very nice day to start the year. I don't know whether it shows, but *I feel* that I am talking and acting like Audiffret. God, please let nothing hold me here. But it is here where I want to live.

I cannot lie down. I am both sorrowful and excited. Oh! Calm yourself, for Heaven's sake. It has nothing to do with Audiffret, but simply *that I am going!* It is the uncertainty, the vagueness, leaving the known for the unknown.

Didn't I say it was awful to see all the pleasures passing under my nose? Oh, yes. It's awful! God let me leave! Let nothing prevent my leaving, and may I never come back!

Monday, January 3, 1876. "I am leaving Sunday at 3:00," I said, or rather shouted, and Sunday at 1:00 everything was upside down. The trunks were still empty and the floor was covered with dresses and clothes. I put on a grey dress and waited quietly. We were still at lunch. Tiouloulou arrived. This little one did not know that we were leaving today, he said.

At half-past two, Collignon and I got into a little cab and went to hear the band, and I listened once more to the municipal music of Nice. "Come," I said to Collignon, "if this piece is gay, our journey will be too. I am superstitious." And the piece was very lively. So much the better!

I saw Galula, who bid me goodbye once more. I have not seen the Surprising One, but that does not matter. We got into the landau again at the Place Masséna; Galula gestured to us to follow him, and we went to the station. Our friends came there, one after another. Ricardo, the General, Giro and Paris, and also two Russian gentlemen Mama knows from Monte Carlo. I skipped about, I laughed, I chattered like a bird. How kind they were; how hard it is to leave them! I promised to write to Ricardo, to Bihovitz, to Olga, to Collignon, who loves me. And I love her. Mama, Dina, my aunt, Walitsky, the two Russians, and I were in one compartment, and the others formed a group outside, in front of the door.

At Monaco we parted. I was sorry for my poor old grandfather, my aunt, Collignon, everybody. I don't like having to go with Mama. I was with her at Spa. Besides, I am used to my aunt. Oh, torture! Imagine the tediousness of a journey in Italy without servants! Mama and Dina do not know Italian, but I refuse to use Russian.

I can scarcely use my limbs and complained because I am not with my aunt, saying "Who asked you to come with us? I ought to be with my aunt," and other most provoking things to my mother. With this I obtain a passive obedience and eagerness impossible to imagine. I complained, wept softly, and said the most provoking things to my mother. At last we were in the train!

Among the other souls, she was the one to see her own daughter disdain her and prefer the aunt to her. I am terrible!

During the twenty-four hours that this awful trip lasted, I threw myself into a corner, my face covered like Caesar's in the "*tu quoque*" scene *[et tu, Brute?]*, opening my mouth to complain with disdain. I tried to say so much to prove that I do not love my mother, that she annoys me, and all alone let my mean tongue go. At last, toward three on Monday, January third, ruins, columns, and aqueducts began to appear on the dreary plain called the Roman Campagna, and soon we entered the station at Rome. We were taken to the Hotel de Londres, Piazza di Spagna, and we occupied an apartment on the ground floor that was very fresh and neat. I am tired and sad. I know nothing. And I know no one. That is the most disagreeable thing! In my state of mind, what I need is someone to stand by. But Mama is crying. Oh, dear!

And my home. There I was accustomed to hearing, "You wanted it; get yourself out of here . . . ," as in the song I heard in the Café American the other night. I wanted this trip. I don't complain about it, but it's very normal to be a little ill-at-ease at the beginning. Before falling asleep, I read *Orlando Furioso* and then imagined some scenes in Nice after returning from Rome next spring. But what's the use? Isn't it true that all my plans must fall in the water—all of my wishes must be in vain?

For six months I was announcing my departure in such a way that they finished by not believing me, and now that I am gone I can say without fear of making a mistake that they don't give a damn—neither the Surprising One nor the others.

At last I am here, after one year! I cried for Rome, the Eternal City, but I have not yet seen anything. Let's hope that all will go well—provided that we have some acquaintances! My God, shall I never live like others? The first step has been taken; I have left!

Tuesday, January 4, 1876. Yesterday Mama wrote to Botkin, the brother of the Empress's doctor, and today he came to see us. An ugly man, he devotes himself to painting. After this visit we went out.

Oh! the ugly city, the impure air! What a deplorable mixture of ancient magnificence and modern filth!

We went through the Corso, the Via Appia, the Coliseum; we saw the Gates [Arches] of Septimus and Constantine, but everything is still vague. I don't recognize myself. The drive on the Pincio is charming; the band was playing, but not many people were there to hear them when we were there. Statues, statues, everywhere! What would Rome be without them? From the summit of the Pincio, we looked at the Dome of Saint Peter's and also the whole city. I am glad to find that it is not too large; it will be easier to know.

On the drive, we were amused to meet the Saëtones, the Audiffrets, and the Prodgerses of Rome. The sun did not appear, and the weather was dull and dreary . . .

Wednesday, January 5, 1876. It is true that there is not a habitable apartment! Where are we? Can this horrible city be called a capital? We are not in Europe! Not a house fit to rent. I am discouraged, annoyed, and tired. But I will not move before May!

O, Rome! I think that we'll take a larger apartment in the hotel and stay here. One can breathe only in the Piazza di Spagna. It is impossible that this is Rome! What a mixture of beautiful antiquities and modern trash!

It is the day before our Russian Christmas, and we have been at the Church, which is in the Embassy Palace. I prayed to God, but He did not hear. I am so afraid, so discouraged! In Nice, at least, I was at home. But here! Who knows what we may find?

I have seen the front view of Saint Peter's. It is superb; it has enchanted me—especially the colonnade on the left, because no house interferes with it, and those pillars with the sky for background produce the most striking effect! You might fancy yourself in ancient Greece. The bridge of Sant'Angelo and the castle are also to my taste. It's grand—sublime! And the Coliseum—what can I say of it after Byron?

> Arches on arches! as it were that Rome,
> Collecting the chief trophies of her line,
> Would build up all her triumphs in one dome,
> Her Coliseum stands; the moonbeams shine
> As 'twere its natural torches, for divine
> Should be the light which streams here to illume
> This long-explored but still exhaustless mine
> Of contemplation.
>
> *Childe Harold* IV 128.

The first thing to do is to take an apartment and to empty the trunks, and then to use the letters of introduction.

Thursday, January 6, 1876. In Russia it is Christmas. We went to church, and the air was full of incense. I had to go out for ten minutes to keep from fainting. Botkin came again to see us; he brought some addresses of professors. Then we took a landau to go home, and Mama went to the Russian priest, Archimandrite Alexander. He is a monk, something more than a priest. Mama said that he is charming. Our embassy does not have any holy days and did not have any special day for receiving. Having a decent courage, we went to the Pincio, and this ride has reconciled me a little with Rome.

A big crowd of people was there, and many carriages, and I saw the King [Vittorio Emanuele II]. I adore kings! I would love to live in a country where there are both a king and princes. Here everybody loves the King: *He is very ugly, but he's very gracious* [in Italian]. The King and a gentleman were in a victoria pulled by horses. If I were Nina, I would have said that he has fallen in love with me, because he quickly turned around and stared hard at me. But, as I am not Nina, I will not say anything.

I have also seen Doria near the door of a carriage. It was the younger brother, the one I called the "white Doria." He saw me and recognized me. I have seen him more often than not in Rumpelmayer's Café at Nice—"the Club." This society made me like Rome. The Pincio is Rome's Promenade des Anglais. I barely regret Nice, ungrateful and mean city!

Sad and undecided yesterday, today I am joyous, gay, and confident. I have asked my aunt to send me Fortuné; the little one will do very well here.

I have had a good dinner and spent the evening reading the history of Charles the Bold.

I thought that there was no society except in Nice, but there is a great deal here, and it is excellent.

After the drive we went down to the Corso, thronged with carriages between rows of pedestrians of all classes. Doria was among them. Now that my eyes are opened to the beauties and antiquities of Rome, I am curious, eager to visit everything. And I am no longer drowsy. I am in a hurry to be everywhere. I want to live at full speed again . . . Ah! If only I could. . . . *The poorest thing, by resisting, gains worth.* Be thoroughly convinced of this genuine truth. Do not believe that I am stupefied to the point of not seeing beyond the city of Saëtone; on the contrary, I am more ambitious than ever. But meanwhile, to spit upon someone who has spit on us—to give that person a kick—is a pleasure that every well-born soul can permit itself.

Friday, January 7, 1876. Goodness! What prices people ask in Rome! For 1,200 francs one has only the barest necessities; we cannot find *anything.* As for the extra, useless things, one has to think of nothing less than 2,000 or 3,000 francs a month. Misery!

At the Hotel de Rome, I saw an apartment so large and so fine that it made my head ache. In France we have no idea of this grandeur, this ancient, visible majesty. After much searching, we are taking an apartment in the second story of the Hotel de Londres, with a balcony looking out on the Piazza di Spagna—a handsome drawing room, two bedrooms, a study, and two bedrooms for the servants.

At last we moved tonight from the street floor to the second floor, and I emptied the trunks as much as I had time for doing that.

Saturday, January 8, 1876. Mama does not yet have her visiting cards, and here is another day lost. I think I am going to leave for America. All these princes, barons, dukes, and marquises leave me cold.

Dina does not feel well. We went—the two of us—with Mama to the Pincio. It was a beautiful day, and finally I could wear white as in Nice. I am not yet accustomed to Rome, but I feel better than at first. I did not see the King, but several other elegant men; I still don't know anyone. This is sad for a person who is used to knowing everyone by sight. Although I've left Nice, in Rome I am no better off; we are alone everywhere. Here we have no relative, friend, or even simple acquaintance.

God have pity on me! At the Pincio I saw the bust of Pinelli. He looks strikingly like Audiffret, only Audiffret doesn't have a beard and Pinelli has a kind of "Royale." That pleases me. Each time I passed it, it was just to look at this resemblance to the Surprising One. Do not forget to add to the features created by the artist the magnificent eyes and admirable coloring; I did not notice the mouth of the bust, but the mouth of the Surprising One is a little pinched.

Put yourself in my place and judge for yourself. Miserable existence! Oh, let it change! Let it change, for God's sake! Let me live like others, who are happy.

Sunday, January 9, 1876. I had a funny dream about Audiffret, who was coming at a run and hit his forehead against mine; then each time when talking to me he put his cheek against mine.

Let the devil take the rain away. I went out only to hear the students of the singing master Facciotti. This Facciotti was in Russia for twenty years and was director of the Opera of Kharkoff when we went every evening with Romanoff, who was almost engaged to my aunt then. But all this does not add anything to his value as a professor. It rains, it rains, it rains. I am bored, not seeing anyone. If, at least, I were missing Audiffret! But not at all; it is a general boredom. I console myself with one thing, that maybe my absence will bring some change in the mind of Émile, I mean. And then (do not be a hypocrite), and then I will turn away like a snake on whose tail someone has stepped. I could act like a good soul, a forgiving one, a forgetting one; but no, I prefer to say the truth.

I would very much prefer that it had been nothing but a love affair. But no. There has been an insult between us—more than impoliteness. He has spit on us. I continue to look for, and still don't find, anything else to tell.

BOOK FIFTY-TWO

Book 52
From Monday, January 10, 1876
To Sunday, January 23, 1876
Hotel de Londres, Piazza di Spagna, Rome

Monday, January 10, 1876. We paid a visit to Monseigneur de Falloux, but he has not left his bed for twenty days. We were at Monseigneur's home in a magnificent salon of the Ruspoli Palace. It is full of antiques and art. The Monseigneur asked us to leave our address and begged us to come to see him as soon as he recovers.

From there we went to the Countess Antonelli's, but she had left Rome ten days ago.

We visited the Vatican! Just think! It is said that Cardinal Antonelli (not actually the Pope) governs the entire papal organization!

We reached the right colonnade when, in sublime self-confidence, I pushed aside (not without difficulty) the crowd of guides surrounding us, and at the foot of the stairs I accosted the first soldier and asked for His Eminence. After seeing this immensity [that is, the Vatican] I should not like to see the Popes abolished.

In a gallery four flights up, we found some officials and two guards dressed like knaves of cards. The officer politely requested my name. I wrote it down, someone took it, and we waited.

"We are not even dressed elegantly enough," Dina said.

"Well, bah!" I said. "The mean priest will not even notice it."

"You think so?"

"Well, no. He must be like Galula! Can you imagine Galula beside Antonelli?"

I had not guessed that the Vatican was such a palace. I am still waiting, admiring our escapade. The officer tells us that the time is wrong to see His Eminence Cardinal Antonelli. He is dining and will not receive anybody.

Indeed, when the man came back, he told us that His Eminence had just returned to his apartment, not feeling well.

We may be back tomorrow morning. I gave my letter to a Swiss, and when he saw the countess's crown on the envelope, he bowed to me.

Tuesday, January 11, 1876. At last I have a painting teacher. That's something! Katorbinsky will come tomorrow. Cavalier Rossi said that for a singing teacher nobody is better than Rosati, a lady who is excellent.

Wednesday, January 12, 1876. My singing studies have begun. Facciotti came and I took my first lesson. Mentally I made the sign of the cross, and I started, trembling. The teacher was expecting the little voice of a rich girl and was astonished to hear a large, strong, full voice. So I have begun studying to cultivate my voice, one of the means available to me for becoming famous, because there is nothing in the world compared to triumph on the stage. When one holds the attention of thousands of people trembling under one's spell—when with one note of inspiration the singer raises the enthusiasm of the crowd and is applauded, acclaimed, covered with flowers, one knows triumph for one's self. When a singer dominates the whole world that is listening and charmed, she must feel herself to be more than a woman; such a triumph and such power can be compared only to that of emperors.

We visited the temple of the Vestal Virgin, the baptistery of Constantine, with its marvelous fifth-century mosaics and porphyry columns taken from the palace of the Caesars, and the fountain of the Palatine Hill, the height of which dominates all Rome. Then we saw the Peace Temple and a number of different ruins. Decidedly I have a taste for the cracked columns—more than a taste, because after all these visits I was so enthusiastic, so moved that I thought I would like to pass the rest of my life admiring these glorious remains, which prove to us how much we have fallen. We found more treasures, more fragments of columns, of cornices, of walls, of garden ornaments—like precious stones. We looked upon a vile bit of a house as a magnificent piece and asked ourselves what we might really have seen at the time of its grandeur. When I think how that imbecile Caracalla had bronze doors of rare beauty in his baths, I shiver with envy. To remind myself of the sound of these doors, I'll have a machine of bronze hanging in my home on which I'll knock to hear that sound again.

Tomorrow is our New Year's Day, and even though I am entirely detached from the Russian world, I put a comb under my pillow and bet 100 francs with Mama. She was insisting that the "Shaved Magpie" will come to our house as soon as we return, and I maintain the opposite. I would like very much to lose!

Thursday, January 13, 1876. Mama and Dina are at church. It's our New Year's Day, and I have stayed home to sew. That is my whim at present, and I must do what I wish. Botkin called to offer his good wishes. Not until four o'clock did they succeed in dragging me out of the house, and at five Mama went to the Embassy. This is the hour when the Ambassadress, Baroness d'Ixkul, receives. I was waiting, trembling, for Mama in the carriage, but she came back and said that the Ambassadress is very kind. I was a little reassured.

In my moments when I am tiger and hyena, I console myself, closing my eyes, trying to imagine revenge. And I see him so clearly in my mind that I almost feel how, with one hand I hold the head, with the other hand the shoulder; how I twist it like a wet bathtowel and how the head falls! I can pass a whole hour in this way. This sweet thought sustains me and calms me. Oh, if I could do it truly!

Friday, January 14, 1876. At eleven o'clock, Katorbinsky, my Polish drawing teacher, came, bringing a model with him. The poor wretch had only one leg; he sits only for the head. Katorbinsky told me that he sits actually only for the head of Christ, and his head is perfect for such a picture. I felt a little nervous on being told to copy from life without any preparation, but I took the charcoal and sketched in the outline. "Very good," said the teacher. "Now do the same thing with the brush." I took the brush and again did as I was told. "Now begin to paint," he said, and it was done in an hour and a half.

My wretched model had not budged, and as for me, I could hardly believe my eyes. With Bensa it used to take me two or three lessons to draw a pencil outline and to make a copy, whereas now it was all done in a single sitting, and from life—outline, color, background, everything! I am satisfied with myself, and I would not say so if the picture were not good.

At five o'clock we went to see Monseigneur de Falloux, a thin, black, agile old priest in a wig, a Jesuit . . . a hypocrite, and, I am sure of this, a great lover of women in earlier times. He received us very courteously in his remarkable drawing rooms filled with things in the best of taste. Gobelins tapestries, pictures, and all this in the dwelling of a detestable Jesuit. Well! Well!

I do not love the Surprising One; but because I am drawn by his beauty, and really because I must love someone, I think I do. It is a habit, thinking of him. He is one of my fancies. He pleases me, and I imagine a lot of things about him. I have grown used to thinking of him, and it is difficult to get out of the habit!

Saturday, January 15, 1876. All of us went to walk in the Villa Borghese, which is more beautiful than the Doria. There was a crowd of people, and the pretty Princess Margherita was walking like any ordinary mortal, followed by her carriage, with the coachman and two footmen in red livery. The great number of carriages with coats of arms saddened me. We know nobody, God help me! Perhaps I don't even have the consolation of desiring Nice, since in Nice we are worse off than in Rome. At least there is some hope here in Rome. My God, it may be that I am ridiculous with my torment and my eternal prayers, but I am *so* miserable!

Monday, January 17, 1876. The only cause of our torment is the lawsuit.

"Oh, I *would* like to be in Nice," Dina complained. "I truly don't know why I'm in Rome!"

"Exactly!" I exclaimed, happy to put my anger on something else than Émile. "Why *are* you in Rome? You and Mama? I didn't need you. This last year it was understood that I would be going with my aunt. . . ." While talking this way I was hurting Mama terribly, but I needed to hurt someone. I felt I was going to cry, and these wicked words chased the tears away. And to know there is nothing to be done about it!

There is nothing to be done about it except to wait until the trial is over. I am seventeen years old. . . . Always deception and humiliation! This lawsuit—it is they who provoked it, and it is on me that it falls. Why on me, who did nothing to cause it? Until now I believed that it was only in books that such injustices existed. Not only am I deprived of all pleasures, but I am calumniated and my name is blackened.

Wednesday, January 19, 1876. My aunt writes that Count Markoff came to see her. You can't believe how much I appreciate these people who, like de Mouzay and de Daillens and the others, do not spit on us. Their names are written in golden letters on my heart, but the names of the others are written in fire.

Thursday, January 20, 1876. Facciotti made me sing all my notes today. I have three octaves, less two notes. I am beside myself with joy. I am only seventeen and I have not yet studied. At twenty, if no accident has happened, I'll have a voice such as few have often heard. [Later, in the margin the diarist has added, "At twenty I am almost without a voice," and after this, "At twenty-two I am deaf."] Facciotti said it, and he is a severe and just man, in spite of being Italian. I fear to say all I am thinking. A strange modesty closes my mouth. However, I have always talked about myself as I would speak of someone else, which has made people think I was blind and arrogant.

We went to the studio of Monteverde, and then to that of the Marquis d'Éspinay, to whom we had a letter. D'Éspinay makes marvelous statues; he showed me all his studies.

After a visit to the Pantheon, Santa Maria Maggiore, and Santa Croce, we went to see the Scala Santa [Holy Stairs], the twenty-two steps of the marble staircase, which has been covered with wood to protect it. I did not know what to do, but as everybody else knelt, so did I. At the third step, I was laughing no more, but praying with all my strength, stopping at each step, not to rest but because everybody else was doing that. At the top of the stairway, we saw a golden altar by an iron gate, all lighted by little trembling flames. Then we came down lateral stairs, as usual.

I climbed twenty steps on my knees, and I brag about it, miserable nature, whereas Jesus climbed the same steps. How did I dare to touch those stairs? But I was praying so much— even for revenge on the Surprising One!

To go to Santa Croce, we passed a deserted part of the city and saw ancient ruined walls. I love ancient ruins, and these little bricks enchanted me because of the way they are placed. I see the Coliseum every day, and I never have enough of it, even when it is dark. I went into a book store and bought some photographs and Byron's *Childe Harold*.

Monseigneur has left a letter for an audience at the Vatican for tomorrow at 11:45. I am so happy that I could not eat anything. But I have no black dress. Quickly I took a dress of Mama's by Caroline, and in one hour I had re-made the blouse. And to think that Caroline is going to send me one in the next few days! I was not expecting to go tomorrow, but I am happy and satisfied. I'll see Pius IX. God, how much I thank you! I am going to write to Mrs. de Mouzay. . . .

From the Vatican, we went to have our photographs made with the black veils. Mine will be a souvenir, and the veil is very becoming to me.

I am so very bored! If, at least, we were all together! What a silly idea it was to separate ourselves in this way. We should always remain together. We'd feel a thousand times happier if we were together—Grandpapa, my aunt, all of us here, and Walitsky. Do you know who he is? From the beginning I've mentioned him only as "W." He is the son of Mr. Walitsky of Warsaw and the Baroness Rosen. Years ago they were rich, but the father ruined himself from trusting others too much and because of his great generosity. Our "W" has two sisters and two brothers, all of them in Russia and Poland. He is our friend, as his father was. He is the most devoted, the most disinterested, the most honest and best man in the world. He is more than a friend and more than a parent. He is for each of us a second self.

BOOK FIFTY-THREE

GLORIAE CUPIDITAS
Book 53
From Monday, January 24, 1876
To Friday, February 11, 1876
Hotel de Londres, Piazza di Spagna, Rome

Monday, January 24, 1876. But I keep thinking that the *Mignon* opera by Ambroise Thomas is the most adorable of all the operas as to subject, words, and music. I seem not to want to hear anything else than that. Some of the melodies move you to the very bottom of your heart; they make you cry and make you crazy! For each circumstance, one can find some melody, certain chords. It is very good for me, who express my every mood in song. I know all the music of this opera by heart—each chord, each accompaniment. I adore and admire it so much that I want to repeat it all the time and can never get enough of it.

On the fourth of February, the Viscountess Vigier is going to sing an opera for the benefit of the poor. Hellfire and damnation! I cannot be there as I am in Rome.

Tuesday, January 25, 1876. I'm so homesick! I took a singing lesson and then drove out with Mama. We went to Mr. d'Éspinay's studio and then to Monseigneur de Falloux's, who yesterday asked whether we had had our audience with the Pope. He called the Court "rascals," and the new government "thieves." He said some people had noticed me at the opera, as my white dress had attracted attention. He said that, to go to Court, we need only to write to the Ambassador or to the Minister.

He said, "I'd like to be able to open the other door for you, as I have opened the Holy One."

"Oh, Monseigneur," I told him, "the Holy Door is far preferable!"

Then we went to Mrs. Soukovkine's house. The archimandrite had told her about us, and she was expecting us. She is at the same time the ugliest and the most charming woman in the world. She spoke of the Quirinal and took us there with her daughter, whom I had noticed last Sunday in church. I'm happy to have met her. I left feeling light-headed and happy, which proves that the lady received us with friendliness. It is only when I leave a home that I really feel the way I have been received *on my own account.*

341

We took Dina and went to hear the music at the Pincio, but we didn't stay there long, as the music soon ended. We were followed all the time by two men in a carriage drawn by a horse like Soroka [magpie, earlier nickname for Audiffret]. That was fun. And then we went to the Corso. They followed us again, and we stopped near several stores. They did the same, at a respectful distance. As it grew dark, we stopped at a watchmaker's; they passed us and stopped a little farther on, but instead of continuing straight ahead I told Luigi to turn around and take us home. In that way we lost them. In the past, I would not have done this, but from now on I will. I don't want anyone to run after me anymore or to make it easy for them to do so. I am going to avoid such people and not involve myself, one way or the other. Heretofore I was doing just the opposite and showing myself, a silly thing to do. If a person wants to find you, he will do it without your doing anything about it.

Bihovitz wrote me a charming letter and signed it "B. B." He said that right now is the most brilliant time in Nice: the shooting, the balls, the races, the concerts—a real crowd everywhere.

These few words cast me into a profound desolation. Vigier sang; the Promenade is full of people. And I know all these people. The whole town laughs, talks, gesticulates. Nice is like an immense drawing room. They compete in elegance. Everybody knows everybody. They run, they look, they are out of breath because of the scandals—and I have seen Nice at this season. I know it, I love it, and it makes me dizzy. I weep, the brute!

Now what preoccupies me is my singing. If I could only achieve perfection and find myself gloriously on the stage, I'd ask for nothing else. But I'd never face the public before being sure of myself by having obtained some private success and before having asked the advice of all competent people on earth. I don't want to sing, because if I were "booed," I'd kill myself. Oh, no, never that! Instead, I would go somewhere away, in America.

Wednesday, January 26, 1876. Mama and Dina went out, and, thank God, I am alone. I can't sing because I am sick. But I play and look at myself in the mirror. I'll do very well on the stage.

Some news from Nice! The Olive is all dressed up in white and has a white hat like mine! My aunt said it was probably Soroka who had sent the young woman the hat from Reboux, since he knows!

That made me so angry that for a while I stayed silent! This *turpis rana*, abominable frog, dares to imitate me! She waited for my departure to do it! Vesuvius' lava! Tiber's mire! Barrel organ! Nothing else in the world makes me angry like this!

I am annoyed to have to wait until Monday again to start my singing lessons. In *Mignon*, where she is alone when she sings, "I become mad with anger and fury" [*folle divengo di rabbio di furor*, in Italian], instead of an octave and a half, as is indicated, and of two octaves, as the sophisticated divas sing it, I can sing almost three octaves higher, a fact which gives me the greatest opportunity to show off the extent of my instrument in the most brilliant way.

Facciotti said that in two years I'll be able to sing completely on the stage. (As for *Mignon*, I sing it *mezza voce* and alone, for fun.) That is to say, I'll be able to stand all the fatigue of the stage. Yes, some fatigue, but also the triumph! When I think of these, I suffocate with the desire for glory. But as for singing an opera for the poor in February '77 and singing well—I am not strong enough for that.

Thursday, January 27, 1876. I have visited the Capitol; the Capitoline Venus is the one I prefer most. Then we saw the magnificence of the colonnades. So be satisfied with what you have after seeing that! *Alas, O envy!* [in Italian].

Family scene: Domenica and Lola!

Lola is not pretty, but in the evening she creates an effect. Domenica is saddened by the scolding of her dear husband. She found him in an impossible state and crying for Anna, asking her in loud sobs in front of his and her daughter [for his freedom].

Tonight we attended the first performance of a new opera, *Dolores.* (Dress, Marie Stuart. Face and everything very good.) I fixed Lola's and Dina's hair. At 3:00 we arrived at the opera. The house was full and my "Soroka" was at his post. All this side is their side. In many loges the barriers are taken away and the gentlemen strolled from one loge to the other. They are the Plobsters of Rome. Finally, I found him—the young man who stared at me so much last time and whom we called the Magpie of Rome. He reminded me in an ugly way of the Magpie of Nice. He did not stop looking at me during the entire act, and I hid myself. This was tiring me; I was obliged to come back to my seat and be stared at by Italian eyes. Besides, he was not the only one; on the parterre a gentleman completely surprised me as I left him free to look. I was looking for a second at the lower floor, but he never lowered his glasses. And then all the other magpies were looking at me ceaselessly. I ought to be satisfied. Well! It is because I am new here. No, I tell myself, no one would look at an ugly newcomer. I believe I've recognized the man who followed us yesterday—the Magpie. By dint of his noticing me, this one made me look at him, and I noticed his most minute absences from the loge.

Soroka starts to interest me.

Never before have I produced such an effect in the theater as on these five evenings in Rome, so that even Lola and Dina, by the same effect, were also under observation. I am ridiculously vain!

Friday, January 28, 1876. Mr. d'Éspinay came, and after fifteen minutes of casual conversation, we went with him to the Medici Villa, l'Académie de France, and he took us in to Mr. Besnard's studio, formerly the studio of Horace Vernet. When entering, Mama backed up. She saw a naked woman reflected in a mirror. She was going to ask d'Éspinay to explain it to her when she realized that it was only a painting. The painter would surely have been satisfied at Mama's reaction; no one could have paid him a greater compliment. After the studio, we visited the famous Villa il Bosco—so dark, so mysterious—adorable. When we were climbing the steep staircase opening on the rotunda, Mama was suddenly very tired; but I went on up. The city was very beautiful from that height. One sees the old walls, the hills. Mr. Besnard really looks like a society gentleman. He is light brown, has a little round beard, and very neat clothing. In a word, for a Galula he is magnificent and very nice.

I *would* like to know who the Magpie is!

Saturday, January 29, 1876. Yesterday there was a ball at the Quirinal. It was a day comparatively rich in events. *First we had a visit from Mrs. Soukovkine, who brought me a new sorrow* [in Russian]. "Without doubt," she said, "one can ask to be presented, but the Embassy can refuse because we don't have any letter of recommendation and because the Embassy is very cold toward those people it doesn't know." Mrs. Soukovkine is charming, and Mama humiliates herself before everybody. Mrs. Soukovkine looks like a gossiper who knows everything that's going on and everything that's being said in this world. She even advised that we ask (I don't know which) monk in Saint Petersburg to obtain the title of a nobleman of the Chamber for my father.

À propos of my father, this pearl of honesty is in Nice, dissipating the last of his fortune and skinning the two young Prince Eristoffs, his nephews. He had the audacity to write a letter to my aunt, saying that he had to speak with her; to that effect he begged her to come to find him at the London House. My aunt answered that those who want to talk to her can find her at our address on the Promenade des Anglais! I could not have done better.

Sunday, January 30, 1876. I forgot the most important event of yesterday! Leonie and Fortuné came yesterday, and we went out with the little black boy on the seat, very well-groomed in white and dark livery. Thanks to him, the general curiosity spared me. (In Rome, I have been looked at as never before in my life. They just stop and look. I think it is due to their kind of character and the custom of the Romans.)

We took Domenica and Lola to visit Saint Peter's, and for me it was the second time. I was completely overwhelmed. This immensity and its details strike, prostrate, and dazzle me. I am lost in astonishment.

At 3:30 we went to the Villa Borghese, where I found everybody: the ravishing Princess Margherita, who was particularly nice; the white Doria, who turned around to look at me; the young dog who followed us the other day, and who is not at all the Soroka. And finally there was the "magpie," whom I noticed for an instant, of whom I saw only the back but who did not see me. He was with the Deputy of the Chamber, who has such beautiful horses.

After the tour of the villa, we went to the Pincio for a drive twice around.

Monseigneur [Falloux] is asking about us. He has sent to let us know that he wishes to see us and have us make the acquaintance of the Countess of Reculot. Monseigneur is ill, but he will try to come if Mama cannot climb the stairs of the Ruspoli Palace. Rossi told me, "At the theater the other night, you were admired by everyone in the house."

"Oh, you are too nice!" I told him. "You are talking about the *Dolores* performance? It was very beautiful."

"Yes, it was!" he said. "It was a large audience, but you have as yet seen only a few of the members of Roman society."

"Oh, Sir, I know absolutely no one. But what has astonished me is that on our side, from our box to the front stage there was *not one lady*! All those boxes are occupied by men. Whose are those boxes?"

"Oh, yes. The first three are for the King's circle. The others are for the Hunt Club. These gentlemen come here all together."

"But tell me. These gentlemen are all from good families?"

"Oh, yes. Among them are the nephew of Cardinal Antonelli, Prince Ruspoli, and many others."

Well, Magpie is not a barber. That's all I wanted to know.

It seems that the adorable George—*may the evil demons strangle him!* [in Italian]—it seems that this monster has been doing other things. To be forgiven by his mistress, he published an article in which he said that he has no connection with Mrs. Domenica de Babanine, and he is going to publish another article to say that he has never been married to her, and that her daughters are not legitimate. And society can admit this monster? He has not been extradited from the country! God! Domenica was a widow and had two daughters by him. [Uncle] Stepa Babanine married her daughter, Mashenka! And George—may the devil suffocate him!—married Domenica. For ten or fourteen years they let the matter go unnoticed, but three years ago it went to court. It appeared that these two marriages could not both be legal, and one of them—George's—has been annulled. George's marriage was ten years older than Stepa's. Stepa worked with the judges about it. But everybody knew that this execrable, infamous George was married. It's unfortunate for his wife and for his children, who are really Babanines. Now he is going to publish these abominations in the newspapers. It is worse than killing his daughters! But he has no feeling left. He has always been like that. And when Mama, under the impression of W's letter, started to recall his exploits, my hair stood on end! It would be necessary to have a whole book of screams and shivers of disgust to tell how he has beaten his mother, stopping only when black marks appeared. His own mother! He is the one who provoked so much annoyance—so much misfortune.

I don't know by what spell he has always been looked upon as an unfortunate man, honest, good, loyal, and loving, whereas he is the biggest coward, villain—the most awful man on earth. Not only has he beaten his mother, he has insulted the authorities, as well as private people; he has never said one word of truth. He has debts that his sisters have been obliged to pay; he has blackened and slandered his family; he has sworn to false documents; he signed in his father's place his own name to be able to marry his present mistress, Anna. The only crime he has not committed is murder—but for that a man needs a certain amount of "guts."

He has no soul, and now he is asking his father for money so that he *can leave with Anna*!

If his father gives it to him, he'll come to Rome to do more than kill us. He is not happy as long as he has not mixed up his sisters with the vileness. Everywhere he has gone there are scandals. And such a monster can live! And lightning does not strike him. If it were not a sin, I swear before God that I would kill this insupportable and shameless being with my own hands, and I would not even tremble.

Let me add, in order to give a small idea of this man, that when Mama went to San Remo to see Dr. Botkin, Dina went with her, devoted herself to and took care of Mama like an angel from heaven. Her father, Mr. George *de* Babanine, as he titles himself, in our kitchen told Adam and everybody else who wanted to hear him that his daughter Dina had gone to San Remo "to be delivered." I don't add anything; judge this rare bird for yourself. Everywhere enemies, and everywhere dirty dealing because of George. It is awful to have only disillusionment. Everything turns tail on me. How dirty is humanity! I was making fun of Byron, but now I understand him:

But why should I for others groan
When none will sigh for me? [*Childe Harold*, I, 9]

Only I still maintain some hope. I still believe in some things; I want to be mistaken. And often I "groan for others." It is awful to know how much humanity is cowardly and mean. The knowledge makes me unhappy, sullen, and hard toward others.

Monday, January 31, 1876. My new model is a woman named Rosa. She is not pretty, but funny.

I stayed alone at home all day.

In the evening, when fixing my hair to go to the opera, someone brought me a letter, which I opened all trembling. My heart was hammering with fear of some new event or old story. It proved something of another kind altogether, a clipping from the newspaper: "Mr. G. S. de Babanine has made known that Mrs. D. Kandelune, who calls herself Mrs. Babanine, has not the right to use this name, as he has never married her." There it is!

We were in a box opposite the Magpie, the nice Princess, and the King. The King was in the front loge, on the right on the first floor. The Princess was above him. The room was full. After the performance of *Ruy Blas* there was frantic applause.

I was dressed as Olympia. I prefer myself that way. This dress, not even of the lowest cut, is open and bulging in front the way the ancient dresses were, whereas behind it reveals only the beginning of the neck. Now you may or may not know that I have a remarkable throat— too much, maybe, for a box on the main floor. These Italians look at you straight on and examine you like a statue or an animal. We arrived during the first intermission, and I sat in the front row only when the curtain was raised, because this black crowd would have devoured me. Right away Soroka grabbed his binoculars. However, this time he looked at me with less persistence, as the others don't deprive themselves of this pleasure. An old one, probably being too small to see, jumped up when passing in front of our loge. Lola was almost dying with laughter. Rossi came to see us. Unfortunately, Soroka was not in his loge to watch him.

"How sneaky Soroka is!" Dina said. "He is watching less now."

"My dear, that's silliness," I told her.

"No, you yourself told me that it was good manners. One looks intensely at another to make him think something and then does not look any more, and, unwilling, the other one wonders why. Then one looks again, but by stealth."

I was feeling miserable enough, but the theater gave me some life. We were talking after the first part of the ballet; there was a crowd of men at the exit, but no Soroka. He contented himself with following us with the binoculars as we left the loge.

All these machinations annoyed and tormented me. I have prayed to God for a long time to calm me down and console me, but that is impossible as long as things don't change. I am sorry to be observed. The scorn from Nice seems to pursue me. However, in Rome we are not yet talked about.

Tuesday, February 1, 1876. Monseigneur de Falloux sent a note to tell us that he was feeling better. He wants to see Mama. So we went to his house. He is becoming more and more charming. He wanted to have us meet his relative, the Countess Reculot, who sings like Patti and goes very much in society.

"I told her," de Falloux said, "that I was going to give her two charming Russian ladies and that she is to entertain them, take them around, in a word, and at the end she must tell me that she has been delighted with you. She receives at 6:00 P.M. and will be delighted to see you at her house."

Lola and her mother will go to see the Pope, and I'll go again, with them. Now I have a ravishing black dress, and I'm going to show myself a little to the Cardinals, who examine the ladies like true magpies.

At dinner, a letter was brought to us with a strange address: "To His Excellency, the Ambassador of H. M. the Empress of All the Russias," asking that it be delivered to Mrs. Marie de Bashkirtseff. It's from Mr. George de Babanine, who wrote a begging letter to my mother. We had not let him know our address. According to his letter, one can suppose that he is dying to come to Rome to make our stay here more agreeable. This cowardly, horrible, bragging letter reminds me of all the wrongs that this man has done to me. If I were as fat as Ruspoli, I would have had a stroke, but I'm not. So all I had was a violent palpitation; all the blood went to my head.

I returned to my room to hide my nervous trembling and the chattering of my teeth. I cannot avoid detesting this awful phantom who poisons my life. "Don't forget," he wrote, "that our poor mother commissioned you not to let me down." (What a cowardly character!) Each time he needs money, he comes to Dina to talk to her about "poor little Stepan who died." [Stepan—Dina's brother—committed suicide with a dagger.] But one day she told him, "Go away. I see what you want: 'Poor little Stepan is dead; give me twenty francs.'" He asked forgiveness and promised to do better, saying he wants to live honestly away from Nice. Miserable, infamous! Oh, don't accuse me of being cruel! Believe me, it has cost me much to be so hard and to have no pity on him. I know him. One has to see what he wrote to Mama when he wanted us to buy a villa for him. She couldn't sleep at night and was crying about the fate of her poor, unfortunate brother! Now we've bought him two villas that we must sell. I am afraid that Paul may become another George. But he'll not kill my children or me. I'll repudiate him before the whole world. I'll protect myself against his villainies. Now that Paul is far away, he seems better to me, but I know very well that I am mistaken. I know that he is and will be a miserable wretch. I have little love for him.

When I am nervous, I can't control myself. My God!! I answered George in place of my mother:

We have asked the Russian Embassy not to receive any more letters for Mrs. Bashkirtseff. All of the people from whom we wish to receive letters have our address.

According to your letter I can see that you are able to come to Rome. But today everything is packed, and tomorrow we are leaving for another Italian city. We have had enough of your scandals in Nice; they forced me to leave because of your knaveries. It is useless for me to say any more. Mr. George de Babanine has made it known that Domenica Kandelune, who calls herself Mrs. de Babanine, has not the right to call herself that because she has not been married to him!

Without a signature, this is an announcement rather than a letter. I wanted to tell him only how we understood his "humility" (provided that my mother does not write to him, herself, without letting me know!). I wrote an eight-page letter to my aunt and watered it with tears of impotent rage. They are sorry for George. And how about me??! Nobody wants to understand me. They order dresses for me—shoes and hats. And they let me be mixed up with scum. They kill me every day.

Wednesday, February 2, 1876. I am lonely and would like to write endlessly—to read what I've written, to correct it, and to comment on it, because I know there are a thousand mistakes which are not due to my ignorance, but really to my laziness of thought and to my too great haste. I never know what I am going to write, but that is better; there is nothing uglier than a *studied* journal, fastened with forty pins, especially when one is not a great writer. But I prefer my letters to those of Madame de Sévigné. "O, Ignorant!" you exclaim. Sévigné's style is so affected, so worked over, without apparent simplicity, that it makes me sick; whereas I have no style. I make mistakes, but at least I don't adorn what I write!

It is with the intimate conviction that I shall [be?] read, and with the hope, still more intimate, of the contrary, that I write my journal. My life is so monotonous, so sad, that I was bored at the Pincio.

We met the big Doria again on the Corso on foot. He is much more elegant and looks better in Rome. I envy all these people; they seem so happy!

I cough, I have a cold. What can I do if I lose my voice or become a consumptive? There's not a corner on earth where I want to go, where I feel well, desired, or loved. I'm bored in Rome, but in Nice I have no more pleasure than here. I'm going to go to Russia, a true wandering Jew. I am seventeen. That is still almost childhood, but time flows very fast.

Do you know what Domenica said? Miloradovitch has seven million rubles and thirty or forty thousand acres of land. Three million, five hundred thousand rubles at 5 percent a year equals 175,000 rubles of yearly income. And each acre is worth two rubles at a minimum, since there are fields and forests. . . . In France that would be about 750,000 francs a year. All that at the minimum and reduced to half (since one must believe only half of what is said) is still a very good fortune.

God, how sad I am! Yet since Lola and her mother came we have laughed nearly all the time. They are chic; everything amuses them, whereas Mama is dead. Some say that she once had a great deal of wit. The illnesses, the sorrows have taken this away from her. She is not stupid; however, she often lacks tact and makes blunders. Oh, if I had her beauty! For want of something better to do I would become an actress—and all that would follow. And I'd be admired by the whole world. With my face, however, such an outcome is doubtful, and I wouldn't risk anything dangerous. I have never seen a more beautiful face than hers; the eyes, the nose, the forehead, the chin, the cheek—everything. The ears are very ordinary, and to fit with the rest of her face they should have been like mine.

Thursday, February 3, 1876. At 11:00 A.M., in a dark outfit, I went with Lola, Dina, and Domenica to the Capitoline Hill. We passed again in front of the statues, Lola all the while making us laugh with her remarks. I think we scandalized a gentleman standing nearby with our scrupulous examination of the Dying Gladiator. When he came into the room, he found two of us in front of the sculpture and two behind it. . . . Fortuné was with us, and I think he was amused. We left a little ashamed, but really anyone would be wrong to think anything bad; I look at the most naked statues without any wrong ideas, and for a good reason. A naked man is very ugly and even ridiculous, but on the other hand I never tire of admiring Agrippina; she has a well-marked plump chin, an admirably shaped nose, and an expressive little pinched mouth that I adore. Her son, the Emperor Nero, looks exactly like her in profile. This cruel expression pleases me.

From there we went to the Pantheon, where we saw only a few busts displayed for viewing.

Our next visit was to the Etruscan Museum, where we entered making a lot of noise.

We saw some small, broken statues, the hind quarters of a bronze bull, the breast of a bronze horse, and a lot of little earthen pots. We were imagining that these were the pots and pans of the gods, and the guards followed us, surprised at our gaiety. The gallery of the paintings was boring . . . awful daubs of virgins without eyebrows—really masks instead of human faces. Abominable museum.

We returned to the hotel for a moment. I took a glass of wine and some bread, and we left again, this time for the Vatican. We had only an hour and a half, so we merely passed through it, speaking aloud and making our remarks through Raphael's rooms. These rooms disappointed me, except the gallery of paintings. That's good! These are living faces, beautiful. . . . In the Sistine Chapel we made so much noise that the guard shouted, "Silence!!"

I should talk about the *Transfiguration* since everybody talks about that. It is a very beautiful and natural work. But that little rascal of a Raphael painted very little of it. He was the designer, but that was not enough. I have not seen enough to criticize.

Friday, February 4, 1876. I don't feel like going out. I am tired and I feel bad.

We visited the gallery of the Doria Palace. It is beautiful. There is one room with high windows that have red curtains which give the place an enchanting light.

Saturday, February 5, 1876. The weather is bad—grey and cold. I have a slight headache.

I went to church with Mama and Domenica. This woman is so common in her speech that I am upset at every moment. It is truly impossible. Never before have I heard such a common pronunciation of Russian as hers. She is more than fifteen years older than her *husband*. Besides, it is a big story. It is only now that Papa permits her to come here. (It has been five or six years since we saw them last.)

It's hailing and cold, but tonight we'll go to the opera *Ruy Blas*. I read the cards to know whether the Magpie will be there. The cards said "yes." Oh, true prophet! Soroka was not there. I was only with Lola and her mother. The loges of the Royal suite and those of the Hunting Committee were full of lorgnettes, which were often directed on me. But I missed Soroka, and so I was bored. *Ruy Blas* is a beautiful opera.

Lola suddenly told me, "The real Soroka has come!" Then I became very animated, but her announcement was not true.

Monday, February 7, 1876. My bedroom walls are already lined in such a way that when I come back I'll find everything in place. Finally—oh, let me not rejoice in advance, because some mean spirit is watching me to spoil my pleasure.

In spite of the horrible weather, we rode to the Corso, and I saw the little one who follows us in his carriage. Is it possible that this man and Soroka are the same person? This one has a rather yellowish complexion. Soroka doesn't have that. I saw the little—what shall I call him? Let's say the little Soroka—and his *Galula*—watched me going in.

Tuesday, February 8, 1876. We visited the Coliseum completely and in detail. We went to the top. I was suffocating, but not tired. I felt nothing but admiration for all this fallen grandeur. This was the loge of the Caesars, and that of the Vestal Virgins. And I stopped to say that maybe the littlest foot of Rome walked just there. Maybe in that time there was a Soroka . . . maybe the beautiful Claudius. I said these things for the others to continue in this tone.

Then we went to see the palace of the Caesars.

All of the guards are French, and we felt at home among them. They showed us the most recent things found in the diggings, among them a Venus Genitrix—without a head, but quite beautiful. Right away I recognized my Nero, and then Germanicus, Vespasian, and his wife, Livia Augusta, if I am not mistaken . . . but I think I am mistaken. Then we passed the Palace of Caligula . . . Vespasian. I was annoyed to see that the modern pavement of the corridor is ugly compared with the ancient floor.

They showed us some ancient frescos, much worn down, in which one can see admirable and beautiful faces of women, but of small size.

From there we went to the church of San Pietro in Vincoli, where the real chains of Saint Peter are kept. Then, in another much more profane place, we saw two Apollos.

They gave *Ruy Blas* tonight, and there was not a loge available on the floor we like. The main floor is too disagreeable; it was hailing and snowing, but the two Sorokas were in their place. After dinner the sky was lighter, and Domenica and Lola went out. This way it was more serious; no one went looking through the window and laughing. Dina is so silly! She just has to be excited, and she will do the silliest things in the world.

Wednesday, February 9, 1876. Only yesterday morning did Mama learn the address of Mr. Visconti. She sent him the letter Mrs. de Mouzay had written for him, and at 3:00 P.M., during the time I was visiting the Coliseum ruin, he went to see Mama. She finds him completely changed and old.

We have begged Rossi to find us a good balcony seat, and Mama right away talked about Mrs. de Reculot so foolishly that I told her afterwards, "You must not be insistent like that! When you are talking, I feel as if I'm on burning charcoals. I'd prefer knowing nobody." During the whole drive I didn't know what to do, I was so bored and disgusted!

But at the Pincio there was a big promenade: the King [Vittorio Emanuele II], Doria, the white Doria, and many others with carriages and horses such as I've never seen in Paris.

The weather is nice. The moon is full, and we went out to the balcony to hear an awful organ grinder to the accompaniment of castanets. Then the Baron Visconti was announced, and I was called away. I stayed in the salon, listening to the Baron Visconti, who, though very old, still has a very supple mind. He advised us to go to the Ambassadress and not to listen to Mrs. Soukovkine. He says that the Russian Embassy is our natural protector here, but that, for his part, he is going to do everything he can to help us. Only we have to choose between the White Salon, those of the Court, and the Black Salon, those who stayed faithful to the Pope. It goes without saying that I choose the Court. Everybody knows Visconti, he is a very old beau—very powerful in the days of the Pope and very much looked up to and loved at present.

Mama has not returned to the Ixkuls'. They have, however, returned her visit. But she has taken on an absurd shyness, encouraged in that by Soukovkine, who seems to want us to stay on the side. All this bothers me. It is painful to ask for favors and to look for them.

Thursday, February 10, 1876. I got up with a throat so sore that I could not cough or speak. What an awful state!

It's probably the Coliseum, with its antique draft, that made me ill. I've stayed at home all day.

Friday, February 11, 1876. Now you are going to hear something extraordinary: I renounce everything. I refuse to meet people, but I am going to devour my rage silently and wait for the trip to Russia. If I manage to arrange everything, we'll not need anybody anywhere. If we don't go there, let God's will be done, since my own will cannot do it.

Our position will always be doubtful and false as long as this unfortunate business in Russia continues. It ought to be better for me to wait quietly now. It will be time lost and will create immense sorrows. The time passes miserably, I know, but one cannot do the impossible. I am resigned. I am going to avoid society. I am not going to desire anything. I'll wait, looking at this waiting time as a sad and ugly necessity. I'll pray God to ask him to let everything end well. Since I've been in Rome and my mother has played the beggar, I've felt let down. I have never run after anyone. I am used to being treated as an equal. I don't want to beg for invitations. The few people we knew in Nice treated us as equals, but I have fallen so low here! That kind of treatment is not what I ask for. No! A hundred times no! I have been, I am, and I shall be myself. Fie! I want to cry, but I'll not cry any more. I'll not go soliciting anything more. I'll wait for Russia.

BOOK FIFTY-FOUR

GLORIAE CUPIDITATE
H. G. T. D. O. H.
Book 54
From Saturday, February 12, 1876
To Tuesday, February 29, 1876
[Written much later:] I was so fond of Antonelli after fifteen days that I could not bear to encounter him in the street. But I was forced to admire him.

Saturday, February 12, 1876. At 11:30 we were to have an audience with the Pope, but on the Via Condotti, Domenica realized that she had forgotten her rosaries, and we returned for them. But arriving in front of the Apollo, we discovered that we did not have the letter for the audience! So we sent Fortuné in the fiacre, and we continued on foot on our way. It goes without saying that without the letter we were not permitted to enter, and through a glass door we saw his Holiness passing by us. Truly he is a venerable old man. He inspires respect and moved us with his sweet majesty. I attribute that to a long habit of his being looked at as a God.

Sunday, February 13, 1876. Visconti came in the morning to tell us that this evening's party is postponed, and instead he proposed an invitation to a ball at the German Embassy.

The lawsuit is the cause of all our misfortunes. We will go to defend ourselves openly against these infamous calumnies. We should have done this a long time ago, but life was unendurable and we were dragging because of pettiness of soul, shyness, and silliness! We did not see that this could bring a kind of malediction.

Monday, February 14, 1876. When Lola and her mother leave, it will be really sad. They are full of fun, and when we are with them we don't have the time to be funereal.

We have ordered our costumes for the ball—dominos.

I have sketched a third study—another woman in a costume. She has a magnificent thirty-seven-year-old face. Unfortunately, she is already engaged in another studio; so I'll take Rosa again. Her face is not yet finished, and the other one, whose name is Stella, can pose only after the first day of March. I shall have to take another one of them between Rosa and Stella. . . . That's all I ask.

Tuesday, February 15, 1876. I am longing for my country. I have had enough of Rome. Everybody else went to the Promenade, but I didn't want anything. I can't go out or dress myself. I don't want to do anything. I don't want to be seen by anyone. If I could live in a cave, I'd be happy. When I show myself, I like having everyone notice me, but in our position I don't want to be noticed. Before, when I didn't realize what our position was, I was happier. I wanted to return to Nice, but if I had done so then, it would have been the height of ugliness. So you see why I stay in Rome.

It will be there in Russia that my fate will be decided. If we should win the case, I'd be the happiest of women.

Rossi came to see us, and my mother asked who the gentleman [Soroka] is. "I asked you because he reminds me a good deal of my son Paul," she said.

"It's Count Antonelli, the Cardinal's nephew. He's a charming young fellow," Rossi told her. "He's rather *pazzerello* [crazy], very spirited, very handsome, very clever."

Now I remember that I mixed up the handsome Count with Soroka, and Soroka with another man not so good-looking. At last I've found everybody now. I saw Soroka below with Galula. I've seen the young man of the first day upstairs with the Duke Cesaro (who has his brigands in Sicily), the Prince Odescalchi, and two others. Count Antonelli is like Gautier, who, as all the world knows, is exceedingly good-looking.

This evening, as he looked less at me, I was able to examine him much more closely. Let's not forget to say that Visconti was at our place before the theater. But let's return to the young man. No longer are Soroka and Galula objects of my concern. I told the others that I am in love with this one, but that I have no luck and that those I look at don't look at me. Rossi had said to Mama, "He is a charming young fellow, and if you would like, I will introduce him to you."

"I shall be delighted," Mama told him.

"The next time I see him I'll tell him." And to think that our letter to the Cardinal has missed its purpose!

No more White drawing rooms. [The Whites were the King's party; the Blacks were the supporters of the Vatican, the Pope, and the Church.] I'll plunge myself into black, to the neck, and if necessary, I'll become a Catholic.

For one instant I thought he had gone to the ball given tonight by Prince Borghese, and I became very sad. But he returned after a few minutes, and I blushed with pleasure. If we were to go into society, we could meet him—and know him! But, oh, when I thought of all this again, this great and deep despair sank me and my heart in an infinite sadness. Everything is lost for me because of . . .

Well, I'll find a hundred more Antonellis. No, no, no! This one pleases me, and next to him, Audiffret seems red and common. Tomorrow I'll go out; I must see that man. Why doesn't he ever show himself? Oh, he's not one to stay for hours under my window, alas! But how suddenly my homesickness has disappeared! My appetite and energy have come back!

What would I call the man? The Count Antonelli? That's too long and too formal for daily use. Antonelli, on the other hand, could be mistaken for the Cardinal. Mama calls him "Pazzerello." I haven't decided yet. He is adorable, and my head is full of him. Good night.

Wednesday, February 16, 1876. At 11:45 we returned to the Vatican. We were the first ones on the right; the Pope, when entering, pointed at me with his finger, saying, *"This one is American"* [in Italian].

My dress deserved the remark. And all those cardinals and dignitaries looked at me and did nothing at all. I was very pretty, and I looked very different from those shapeless women. Pius IX seemed younger to me this time. When leaving, he looked at me straight in the face. I did the same to him. He probably wanted to tell me that I might have done better to give the price of my train to the Church.

From there we went up to the home of the dear Cardinal, who was at table. (I saw the antechamber of the great man. . . .)

We drove to the Corso looking for the nephew of the Cardinal. We saw a group of people he ought to have been with—men we had seen in the loge of the Hunt Club. The door they had gathered by is that of a Club.

We have seen Besnard. We must tell him to come here; I want my portrait in watercolor, with my white dress with the trim and bows in front all the way to the hem—and my white hat. The whole thing is an adorable costume, a little Watteauish, and this is the way I always look. I insist on maintaining this look, which I have had for a year.

Thursday, February 17, 1846. At last I saw him! But let's start at the beginning. At 1:30 I left with the adults in a carriage, and then went with Lola on foot. I am wondering only how others do walking in Rome. As for me, I was losing my balance constantly on the impossible cobblestones, and just when crossing the Via Condotti to the Corso, my hands stretched out so as not to trip. I saw Doria, who passed me in a fiacre and who looked at me with surprise, since I was in black and on foot. We walked that way through Rome's streets until 3:00 P.M., when we returned.

I had barely put on my hat when Dina came to find me, assuming that the invisible one is at the Pincio. I didn't believe anything she said, because she's always lying, but we jumped into a carriage and left. At the Pincio there was nothing left but the remains of a beautiful ride and the sympathetic Doria in a big carriage in which he was driving himself.

It was on the Corso that I finally saw Antonelli, seriously leaning on someone else's arm and looking straight ahead of himself, like Audiffret years ago. We saw him twice again in the same attitude. He looked as if he hadn't even a suspicion of my presence. He had an excessively serious air, like only the ones of his kind have.

He is a handsome man, not too much so, but there is no one in Rome better-looking than he.

Rossi passed the first part of the evening at our house. "I saw Antonelli at the theater the other night, when we were leaving," he said. "He will be absolutely delighted to be introduced to you. Could I present him at the theater?"

They have spoiled my Antonelli interest; we did not ask to meet him, yet this looks as if we had! I was embarrassed. I would have liked this condition to last longer—as with Audiffret. Never have I had such joy as on that evening when Galula came to our loge at the Français to ask permission to introduce his friend. I had desired it so much! I don't know how to express how much.

I have wanted only two things to that degree: in the past, Hamilton; in the present, to be in society. And now, here is this Antonelli making me forget what my brother Émile has said.

Visconti came an hour after Rossi left.

Friday, February 18, 1876. At the Capitol this evening, there was a grand masked ball. Dina, her mother, and I went at 11:00. I didn't wear a domino, but a black silk dress with a long train and a tight-fitting bodice. It has a tunic of black gauze with silver lace trimmings draped in front and bunched up behind so as to make the most graceful hood imaginable. My black velvet mask is trimmed with black lace. I wore light-colored gloves and a rose with lilies-of-the-valley in the bodice. Our appearance created a sensation.

Very nervous, I didn't speak to anybody at first. But when we were surrounded by a number of men, I took the arm of one of them whom I had never seen before. Right away I started to tell him a story, saying that at 8:00 certain things had happened to him. I didn't know what I was saying; but it appears that what I said was true, because the gentleman became very curious. Then I became very bold, but then realized my position, being for the first time at a masked ball and not knowing anything about the people I would meet.

I changed escorts several times.

The Duke Cesaro arrived. "You're a friend of the one I'm looking for," I said. "Give me your arm." And dropping my escort there, I went away with the magnificent Chief of Bandits.

"For whom are you looking?" he asked.

"Antonelli. Is he coming?"

"Yes. In the meantime, stay here with me—the most elegant woman in the world."

I stayed a little longer with this charmer. And after a while we saw Antonelli, and I went close.

"Oh, there he is!"

"Yes, but . . ."

I scolded him for his pronunciation, and he laughed with delight. They thought they knew me. "We recognized your figure," one said, "but why aren't you all in white?"

"I believe I'm in the way," Cesaro said, seeing me talking with Antonelli.

"I believe you are, too!" I agreed. "Go away."

Taking Antonelli's arm, I passed through the several rooms, taking no notice of anyone else, as if they were no more than dogs.

His face is surprisingly handsome with its pale, clear complexion, its black eyes, its aquiline nose, and its well-shaped ears. He has a beautifully shaped mouth, passable teeth, and the moustache of a twenty-three-year-old.

But he is a little smaller than the Surprising One, less handsome, and he reminds me of Émile only by his gestures at the theater. I treated him as a hypocrite, a fop, a wretch, a madman. He told me with the most candid air in the world that he had run away from home at nineteen, that he had plunged into a debauched life, that he is blasé, that he has never been in love, etc.

"How many times have you been in love?" he asked me.

"Twice."

"Oh, ho!"

"Maybe more."

"How I would like to be that more!"

"Mr. Presumptuous!"

"How old are you?" he asked.

"Twenty. And I've been married for two years."

Then he started to laugh because he had recognized me. What made me believe that is what he said. But listen:

"Please tell me why all these people take me for the lady in white?"

"Well, you are like her. That's why I came to you; I'm madly in love with her."

"That's not a very gallant thing to say to me!"

"But what do you want? That's the way it is."

"You've been staring at her enough, God knows. She seems to be very well pleased— and poses."

"No, never! One can say what one likes, but not that! She never poses."

"It's easy to see that you are in love."

"Yes, with you. You are like her."

"Fie, my dear! I'm better made; I have a better figure."

"Never mind. Give me a flower."

I gave him a flower, and he gave me a spray of ivy in exchange. His accent and his languishing air irritated me.

"You look like a priest," I told him. "Is it true that you are going to be ordained?"

That made him laugh. "I hate priests," he said. "I have been a soldier."

"You? You have only been in a seminary."

"I hate the Jesuits, and that is why I am always quarreling with my family."

"My dear, you are ambitious. You would love to have your slipper kissed."

"What an adorable little hand you have!" he said, kissing it, an operation he performed several times during the evening.

"Why have you begun so badly with me?" I asked.

"Because I took you for a Roman I know, and I detest her."

In fact, when I was with Cesaro, he had invited us to sit with him; and Antonelli had placed himself on my left and had tried to put his arm around my waist, looking like a silly fool all the time.

Antonelli does not altogether please me, but he has managed to destroy the Surprising One. I still stayed talking to a lot of people, but I remember nothing. Everything is mixed up. It's 4:00 and I'm going to bed. But oh, that miserable son of a priest took my glove and kissed my left hand. "You must know," he said, "that I am not promising to carry this glove always next to my heart. That would be silly, but it would be a happy reminder of you." We left without Fortuné to avert suspicion. He will leave alone.

Saturday, February 19, 1876. I dreamed about Audiffret.

Before going to our balcony on the Corso, we recalled our impressions of yesterday evening. As I was telling my opinions about Antonelli, my mother said, "My dear, the love declaration of the entire world would not be enough to please you. But if Audiffret were to come and fall at your feet and tell you he loved you, you would be the happiest of women."

"That's the silliest thing I have ever heard," I said aloud. But to myself I added, It is perfectly true!

"He likes you and you like him."

I let her talk. I perfectly understood the need to boast that every born mother must feel.

It is the first day of Carnival. There was not too much doing on the Corso, but we received a good many bouquets. It was the first time I've seen the famous race of the Barbary horses—very beautiful and original. But oh, I am bored! Everybody goes to eat at Spellman's—the London House of Rome.

Someone brought the magazine *La Vie Mondaine* [The Worldly Life] from the post office. In that I read a breathtaking description of the costumes seen at Mrs. Sabatier's masked ball. Audiffret went as Hamlet, and he must have been magnificent. You don't know what he's like. Is that it? Here is a description of the hero of my romance: "He was of average height, nervous, strong, but slim and elegant. His brown hair, almost black, a forehead of brilliant white, an oval face, fresh cheeks and fuzzy as a peach; a little straight moustache, almost blond compared with his hair, and blood-red lips which, when open, revealed a double row of white, perfect teeth; a long, well-shaped nose, large black eyes, not typically Italian, but shiny and very black, bubbling with life and gaiety, yet often deep and full of mockery—these are his features. All this composes a figure that women cannot gaze on with indifference; and when he fixes his clear and haughty gaze on them, the coldest one must feel moved and her heart must beat faster than usual."

(I beg you all to take this with a grain of salt!) The description finishes: "A man like this must be very handsome indeed in the costume of Hamlet."

Then I read this: "We have been asked to comment on the ridicule presented by the imitations of the outstanding white outfits especially worn by a certain someone. We will think about doing so." This comment, plus several others, put the finishing touch on my desperate humor in such a way that I barely swallowed one bowl of soup. And I am on the point of crying.

Sunday, February 20, 1876. Tonight there was a big illumination of the [Spanish] steps and the church at the Piazza di Spagna. We threw it a glance when passing on our way to hear *Ruy Blas* again. The pretty Princess was in a stage box—at about the same place we had our box in Nice.

I kept myself in the back of the loge, where the binoculars from the Court and the Hunt Club came to reach me—especially the ones from a very blond prince, with a really amusing insistence. But I was bored. The door opened, and in came Rossi.

Behind him was Antonelli in a superb outfit—and very serious. I was not expecting him. Nor were you!

Well, here it is. Barely had we exchanged a few words than the Greek diplomat [Paparigapoulo] arrived and sat between the man and me; but Rossi soon left, and the Greek, too, and the "son of a priest" remained with us alone.

Tonight he seemed to me very tall. At first I felt a little confusion, seeing this man after our masquerade at the Capitol. He was serious and behaved well, looking me straight in the eye, probably to be sure that the hood really covered my head. I was avoiding his oily and furious Italian eyes. His teeth were like Audiffret's, and his mouth opened the same way as that of the beautiful Niçois when he laughed. He has long, bony hands, a little red—rarely covered by gloves. After ten minutes he started to chat as if we had known each other two months. He told how he had lost 60,000 francs in Monaco, how his mother had paid it, and how furious the Cardinal was, raising his eyes to heaven like a Cardinal in a painting, saying that he detested society and loved a quiet life. "I came back from a ball," he said, "but I had stayed there only five minutes. I had been begged to go, but I detest society and adore the theater."

Antonelli presents a mixture of languor and vivacity. Sometimes he behaves like a schoolboy, and sometimes he has the manners of a man.

We spoke of music.

"I was a very good violinist," he said.

"Why the past tense?"

"Because I can't play any longer. Look," and he showed his hand, marked with a scar just in the middle in such a way that the third finger seemed dislocated.

"You got that in a duel," I said, because I could see by his look that that was so.

"Oh, no!" he said. "It was when I was catching flies!"

He said it in such a way that I knew there was no doubt as to the origin of the wound.

He never gave a word or a sign that he recognized me from the masked ball. But he didn't know what to do with his legs and hands. He kept rubbing his knees and taking surprising postures. I thought he would never stop.

It was only at the beginning of the ballet that he left to go to see another lady. And immediately I discovered that I was very much annoyed by that. But he soon returned to his box and turned his back to the ballet, looking at me as much as he could through his glasses.

Monday, February 21, 1876. From the time I got up today, I was upset about everything. First, Mama had a terrible nervous spell, and then Dina howled, and that put me in a rage. But around 3:00 everything calmed down, and we went to the Carnival.

Oh, don't let me forget to say that this miserable Antonelli made me go to see the tomb of Cecilia Metella. He had told me yesterday that there would be a rendezvous of the hunting party at that place.

It was very far, but I saw the Appian Way, some ruins, some columbariums, and the great tomb of Cecilia Metella, whose sarcophagus is to be found at the Farnese Palace.

The Corso was more animated than on Saturday, and we had flower battles with a lot of people. There were about a hundred bouquets thrown to us, not counting the smaller ones. A gentleman who stays at the Hotel de Londres—a Neapolitan banker, all in white—was not stingy with his flowers. In a way it was very nice. But there were only two or three carriages. I looked vainly for Antonelli.

On returning home, I found the visiting cards of Pietro Antonelli, on which were stamped a Count's crown.

Right away I began to act foolishly with these cards, remembering the gestures, the pronunciation of Antonelli; I began to imitate him.

Tuesday, February 22, 1876. In the morning I went with Lola to buy the costumes for the Carnival. We dressed in white dominos with huge indigo stripes and the masks with glasses. The fourth seat in the carriage was occupied by a huge basket of confetti.

Before arriving at the Corso, we met Antonelli at the Via del Babuino. That was so nice that I felt a little extra beating of my heart. The Corso was animated for this last day of the confetti.

Protected by our masks, we battled, we made faces, we threw kisses in gestures of despair. At the street corner, we crushed the unfortunate priests under a hail of confetti. I shouted. I was standing, working with my two arms. It was amusing, and there was Antonelli. He stayed, well surrounded by our furious attack and by the shouts of "Pietro!" "Carino!" "Angelo!" At a special signal given on the Piazza del Popolo, they evacuated the Corso, except for the carriages, because the Barbary horses were going to be raced. Then we appeared on the balcony in white dominos, our faces well-covered by the masks. We had a very nice English lady for a neighbor. She is called de Lorncourt. She had horses, carriages, everything.

Well, this person talked to me, and as it was Carnival, I talked with her. Besides, I believe that she is a lady. Right away the gentlemen who came to see her asked her if she knew me— all this in Italian.

As for me, seeing that Antonelli was not coming any more, I sat down, leaning against the wall because I could see the desperate efforts of a handsome young man on the English woman's balcony trying to talk to me.

We left at once after the races, and Mrs. de Lorncourt told me "good evening" very politely. But we had to wait (I don't know why), and I leaned against the door and looked at the ceiling with a bored expression. Immediately the young man came to sit by me; and seeing that I was not moving, he shyly asked me whether I was watching the Roman Carnival for the first time. After the exchange of a few sentences, I left him because everyone was ready to leave.

On the Corso I saw four Antonellis, but none of them was the real one. As our carriage entered the Via Condotti I felt something fall on my knees. It was a bouquet of magnificent roses. The man who threw them there was running away full speed, but Lola had a chance to catch a glimpse of a blond moustache.

I came home exhausted, not feeling my arms or legs. I fell asleep, involuntarily comparing Antonelli with Audiffret, and Audiffret did not seem so strong, so important. But he had around him something so powerful that I found him superb, even noting this little coarse air that charmed me, and everything about him. At least at the moment when I fell asleep, he pleased me more than anyone else, and I could have loved him altogether if Antonelli had not spoiled him.

Wednesday, February 23, 1876. I was going to start the story of this great day when I was interrupted by the arrival of Visconti, who more and more acts like a gentleman of the Court. I had eaten and talked, and by then was locked in my room, quiet and alone, starting my report:

We went, all dressed up, to our balcony on the Corso. Since they throw me flowers, our neighbors had already arrived. The lady was amiable, and the scene was very animated.

There were two beautiful floats. On each of the branches of a tree stripped of its leaves stood a man dressed as a monkey. We applauded, and then a battle of flowers followed. Several of the gentlemen who had given me flowers came to us today more than ever. Especially, there was one very young, very blond, very fat man to whom I gave a camellia attached to a long string . . . which I held to have the pleasure of watching him jump and blush.

While we were there throwing and catching the flowers, we saw our own landau carrying Walitsky, whom I had wired two days ago asking him to come. He buried us under bouquets of flowers, and the others must have asked themselves who that handsome gentleman was, all alone and so gallant.

At best, half an hour passed before he was able to leave the Corso and come to our balcony. But I didn't even have time to kiss him.

At last they fired the cannon, and the race was about to begin. Antonelli had not yet arrived, but the young man we had seen the day before yesterday turned up; and as our balconies adjoined, we began flirting. He gave me a bouquet, and I gave him a camellia; and he made as many tender and amorous speeches as are permissible for a young man who has not had the honor of being introduced. He swore always to keep the flower I had given him and to wear it, dried, in his watch. He asked me by whom he could be introduced to my mother, and I named Visconti and Antonelli. I think that I even told him my name.

"When shall you return to Nice?" he asked, and I told him that that would be in either April or May. Alas, he promised to show me the dried petals of the camellia which would always remain fresh in his heart.

Is this the Carnival or is it not? I had prepared another white camellia for Antonelli, but he had not come. The Count Bruschetti (that's the name of the handsome stranger) did not make me sad. Then, while looking down on the crowd below, I saw Antonelli bowing to me. I became so confused and so red that I did not know what to do, other than to fall into a chair and hide my blushing. Dina threw him a bouquet and ten arms went up from among the crowd to catch it. One man caught it, but Antonelli, with great coolness, seized him by the throat with his strong hands until the wretch let go of his prize. It was so well done that Antonelli looked almost sublime. Forgetting my blushing, I was so enthusiastic that I threw him a camellia, string and all. He picked it up, put it in his pocket, and disappeared. Still full of all this emotion, I turned toward Bruschetti, who took the opportunity to compliment me on my use of Italian and on Heaven knows what else. . . .

It may sound silly, but as I could still see Antonelli's hands on the knave's throat, I said to myself, By such an act as Antonelli's a man can win a woman's love at a stroke. The Barbary horses passed like the wind as the crowd shouted and whistled. But on the balcony, we spoke only of the way in which the adorable Antonelli had recovered Dina's bouquet. That delicate-looking man had acted with the ferocity of a lion or a tiger!

Later, during the height of my flirtation with my neighbor, I saw some rascal carrying an immense paper-wrapped bouquet on a long gilt-wrapped pole. Not being quite sure where it would go, he put it up to the balcony in my direction. It was from Antonelli, accompanied by my camellia! At first I didn't understand, not having seen Antonelli. I smiled down to that awful son of a priest as I lifted the bouquet into my arms.

The English lady exclaimed, "Oh, how splendid!" and complimented me most enthusiastically, but Bruschetti, apparently somewhat vexed, only said, "It really is quite beautiful." To myself I said, It is charming! I was enchanted to the bottom of my heart. I carried my trophy down to the carriage, looking again at Antonelli. Having seen me with the bouquet, he bowed in his calm way and disappeared.

I feel attracted to—I don't know what or whom. It's the beginning of spring fever, like a year ago.

Thursday, February 24, 1876. This evening, masked in the carriage, we drove to see the fair in the Piazza Navona. Walitsky was with us. I love to go out masked. I adore the Carnival; during its time I completely forget our torments, and I'm happy.

Today there were three times more people than yesterday. Everyone threw bouquets, but I didn't notice anyone in particular. "What did you do with my poor friend? You made him crazy," Mrs. de Lorncourt told me.

"What friend, Madame?"

"Bruschetti. He is ill, and I doubt that he could come today. You drive him crazy."

"Oh, that's too bad! But believe me, I didn't mean to."

Bruschetti was in his carriage with his friend, but busy looking in another direction. I let him pass.

He came to the balcony only for the Barbary race—he and his friend, who looks like Prince Eristoff and whom I call "Eris" for short. We left soon after that, and he had only the time to offer me a charming, red-satin candy box with a swallow printed on white satin on its lid. He also showed me yesterday's camellia, attached to a piece of white cardboard like a cheap jewel, locked in a box. "It will always be like this," he said.

"Good evening," I said to him, because in the candy box I found his card: "Count Vincenzo Bruschetti." I didn't have time to say a single word to Eristoff, and unlike yesterday, there was not the constant exchange of flowers and candies.

Bruschetti has golden horses—thoroughbreds—and a beautiful carriage. I have seen him before this—at the Borghese, and on the Pincio. He was very agreeable, and I would have liked someone to introduce him to us.

The miserable, the scoundrelly Cardinalino did not show his face. I was still thinking of yesterday. Each has abandoned the bouquet to its own destiny. Besides, it was not for the bouquet itself; the matter was not about a bouquet. We received some; we threw some. It was about the way it was done. No one else would have done it quite that way . . . only Antonelli; nobody else. With all this silliness, I think I missed him today, and I came back home a little sad.

I was also thinking about Bruschetti—and Audiffret. It is full of interest, as Galula used to say in Nice.

I said that I would not make a move for anyone, and yet at each instant I want to make advances toward Antonelli. If he wanted to see me, he would come looking for me. Yes, that was because he was a Soroka. But as soon as it becomes the matter of a man for whom I care, I am ready to go to look for him myself. And what is the use of this absurdity! Why pay attention to those who are looking in another direction?

Bruschetti has a complexion like Hamilton's, eyes as light grey as his, beautiful lips, and blond hair and moustache. His thin nose gives him a quite elegant look.

I emptied the candy box he gave me and put his and Antonelli's cards in it.

I am hearing Walitsky telling stories from home about our charming George, whom the devils may suffocate, for all I care. Forgive me, God.

Friday, February 25, 1876. There was a gala promenade. We went to the Villa Doria, to the Pincio, and to the Corso. Bruschetti hailed us twice. On the Corso we saw Antonelli. (I've cut my finger and am writing badly.)

At midnight we went to the Apollo, where we had a downstairs loge—Mama and Walitsky, Dina and I.

At last Bruschetti recognized us, but mistook Dina for me and started his tender protestations. He spoke bad French, and Dina spoke bad (or very little) Italian. He ended by finding me; and I took his arm, and we went deep into the crowd. The theater was lighted in a magnificent way. The lights, up and down, pleased the eyes.

Antonelli was straddling the edge of the box and was talking with an unmasked, painted woman—the Count Larderel's cocotte, probably. With a lot of trouble I succeeded in touching his shoulder, and in a disguised voice I said, "Good evening, Cardinalino" [in Italian].

And in return, he said, "Good evening, Carina" [in Italian], making a face that proved he did not recognize me in this mixed crowd.

Saturday, February 26, 1876. I didn't close my eyes; the cut on my finger was hurting me terribly, and I got up at 3:00. At 4:00 we appeared on the balcony.

[The following conversation is reported in Italian:]

"Did you have a good time yesterday?" Bruschetti asked me.

"Where?" I asked in my turn.

"At the theater," he said, looking me in the eye.

"I wasn't at the theater yesterday," I said, admirably withstanding his stare.

"Not at the Apollo?" he asked.

"But wasn't there a dance at the Apollo yesterday?" I asked with a straight face.

"Yes, that's what I said. The dance."

"I didn't go because my hand hurt. I couldn't go out."

"How! You mean that—that was not your party!"

Miss Bashkirtseff, I compliment you sincerely; you are the greatest scoundrel I know! Besides, everything was planned in advance. Usually things planned ahead don't succeed, but this one did, like a charm. You should have seen the consternation on the man's face and heard the questions I asked him. I had a lot of fun. I didn't drop my eyes or blush. Oh, sublime hypocrisy! Oh, Truth, where art thou? And they want me to believe in other people? I am not so stupid. Why not suppose that others know how to lie, like me!

At last the Italian repeated what he said to me yesterday. A true love declaration, my word of honor, accompanied by a true offer of marriage—word of an honest woman! All this while we were separated by the balcony. I had to stay cold or laugh, and I laughed. I told him that, as it was Carnival time, I permitted many liberties that I would not permit otherwise.

"I was not speaking as a reveler," he said, almost crying because of my laughter. He told me that if I should ever fall in love and have people laugh at my love, I would understand how awful it is. He said, "I have never been in love before now, and I've become a child." (I say fool!)

The man told the truth. He is sincere, and he believes he didn't say too much. He offered me all the proof I might want. I refused, saying that all that is part of the Carnival, and that I could think about it when he might be introduced to me.

Never the one I want! How can I have such little good luck? He is nice and very good-looking. But he's not smart. He has not been taught—I hate these brutes; I prefer a hundred times more a package of nerves like the Cardinalino. As for him, he passed under the balcony and honored me only with tipping his hat. And I barely saw him because my tender neighbor was monopolizing me.

Sunday, February 27, 1876. We drove to the Borghese, to the Pincio, to the Corso, and everywhere. We saw Bruschetti with his magnificent horses and his postillion in his periwig. But nowhere, Antonelli! Look, children: I just looked at the visiting cards of this future Pope and everything pleased me—the letters that spell the name, the crown, the paper on which these are printed—everything is agreeable.

It is too bad, however, that those who interest me do not pay attention to me. I know very well that Antonelli did stare at me a lot. That was the way he revealed himself to me. He was just looking at me because I was there, but he never moved to come to see me. He never came out. In a word, it is very annoying.

What have I been thinking this morning? Is it possible that he doesn't think of me the way I think of him? How is that possible? Isn't there a way to bring him to me? My word of honor, it is disgusting! It seems to me that, through the power of wishing, one can attract by the power of the thought.

I wanted to go to the opera. (My pretty sentences are only craziness.) Not one step! Yes, very well. When shall I be able to persuade myself that all this is useless? If he wanted to see me, he would know where to find me. And I know that very well, as I wanted to go to the opera—not for him, but for me, because it pleased me to do so. Let's establish an axiom: Antonelli doesn't give a damn about me. Amen. What revolts me is that Bruschetti dares to want me to love him and dares to hope in his imagination a lot of things which put me in violent furies. Then, only—a kiss from this man! Tiger and hyena! Above everything, I hate bestiality! I do not separate the body from the heart, but the body alone is an abomination!

We made the acquaintance of the Neapolitan banker, a cavalier of Altamura. This morning he left his calling cards, and tonight, after we ate at the table d'hôte, we invited him to our house. I appeared only for fifteen minutes, and I left the ladies to the great pleasure that a dinner produces at the table d'hôte and a conversation with the banker Altamura.

Monday, February 28, 1876. Back on our balcony on the Corso, I found our neighbors all in their places and the Carnival in full swing. Looking down, I found the Cardinalino and his friend on the opposite side. Seeing him, I became confused, and, blushing, rose from my seat. *"What's the matter with you?"* the lady next to me asked. *"Why are you so red?"* [in English].

"I can't say. It's nonsense," I answered, but standing up again, I found that the naughty son of a priest was not any longer there. Turning around to Mama, I found her giving her hand to someone—to Pietro Antonelli!

"What a good idea! You've come to my balcony," I said.

For the sake of politeness, he stayed with Mama for a while, and impatient, I went into my room to get a candy dish. Then he sat down by me. As always, I was at the extreme right corner of the balcony, next to the English lady's seat. Bruschetti was late, and his place was taken by the son of a banker whom the English woman, his countrywoman, introduced to me. He seemed very impressed.

"But what a life you lead!" said Antonelli, in his calm, sweet way. "You don't go to the theater anymore."

"My sore finger was still hurting," I told him.

"Where?" he asked, trying to take hold of my hand. "I've been at the Apollo every evening, staying only five minutes, you know."

"Why?"

"Why?" he asked, looking straight into my eyes.

"Yes, why?"

"Because I went there for you, and you were not there."

"You are very nice."

He said other things like that, looking into my eyes, rolling his own, and behaving very amusingly.

"Give me a rose," he said.

"Why should I?"

I admit that I did ask a very embarrassing question. I like to do that to get a foolish answer or none at all.

"Here is your little servant," said the Cardinalino, seeing Fortuné enter.

"Yes. Isn't he nice? I adore him!" I said.

"Yes, he is nice. I would like to be in his place."

"He was nice, especially that evening he was lost," I said.

"Where?"

"Oh, I don't know. One evening. I don't remember where. It was probably that evening when we let Mrs. Soukovkine borrow him when we were going to the Capitol. Tell me, was it beautiful at the Capitol?"

"I don't know. I was cold. And then I stayed only five minutes. But the little Negro was charming. He was lost, and I think he cried."

Seriously, I don't pretend to deny it. He recognized me very well, but I deny it for convenience.

Then Mama said to him, "If you don't have anything else to do, come and spend the evening with us."

And the Cardinalino offered her his arm to come downstairs. Bruschetti left at the same time, all red and furious, without looking at the flower I threw him. I ask, why this mean anger? To the devil with him!

At nine o'clock Altamura was at our house. I waited forty-five minutes in my bedroom, but the future Pope did not come. Impatient, I went down to the salon, and ten minutes later he was finally announced.

He is charming, but *pazzerello*, as Rossi said.

We were looking at some of my photographs at the big table. I asked for them, and he started to beg me to give him one of them. "You are like those little beggars who ask for alms," I told him.

"*I am hungry, poor; I'm hungry—hungry! Give me a little piece of money!*" [in Italian].

He started to laugh. "Well," he said, "probably I'm hungry. Woman is nothing more than a desire. I am not hungry for bread, but for a photograph. Give it to me!"

I understood his idea, but he expressed himself badly. He is not French. At midnight Altamura rose to leave, and my creature, too.

Tuesday, February 29, 1876. As it is our last day of the Carnival, we went out early.

All the city was excited. Everybody was expecting to have fun, and people were running and shouting. From our carriage on the Corso, we saw Princess Margherita, pretty as an angel. This Corso is too short for the number of carriages moving on it! I don't know whether the others have received as many bouquets and boxes of candies as I have, but I was inundated with them! The blond Doria threw me a beautiful bouquet from his balcony. Everybody, in a word. I had an enormous amount of fun. I threw two big bouquets to the Princess, and later, when I passed by her balcony, she threw me a candy box in white satin, which I'll keep. I won't try to relate the furious gaiety of the Roman Mardi Gras.

It was so amusing that I didn't notice the absence of Antonelli.

It started to get dark, and the game of *moccoli* [the candles] began. Our balcony and that of the English lady were the only ones with Bengal lights. The whole thing produced a beautiful effect.

Regarding the English lady, the gentlemen all said she is Mrs. Oliver. Antonelli talked about her in a bad way. According to what I have learned about her, she does not move in good society. She does not live with her husband, and she is usually surrounded by men, which, according to me, is not compromising—fat, small, and painted as she is. But let's not go against the current; let's obey the general opinion, and we'll have plenty to do.

All the Corso was illuminated with *moccoli,* which are winking lights, jumping from high to low and from low to high, like devil's eyes pursued by fans, brooms, and handkerchiefs, like big night butterflies [moths]. The crowd was yelling; it doesn't know how to do anything else.

I came home quite annoyed; my dress is spoiled by Dina's candles. When she is excited, she loses control of herself. Around 11:00, they brought me a pink domino and a red one for Dina. I longed for gaiety this evening. It seemed to me that I'd fool the whole world—that I'd even have the courage to accost the great Doria!

We went out, but I was completely discouraged. There were so few people that it was ridiculous.

Pietro bent himself double talking with a domino in a very rich red satin. Walitsky was a black domino. He looked like a pregnant woman! His figure amuses me.

But here was Doria, seated with a black domino. Antonelli was still with the red domino, but now in a loge. A little later he came down alongside me, and I talked with him for a while. I can't say that he recognized me. I disguised my voice, speaking Italian. Then a little, slightly masked lady from a loge made a sign to him to come. I told him to go away, not to leave her alone.

"You know," he said, still in Italian, "we should get married."

"I don't want to."

"Why?"

"Because you are ugly and I detest you."

"Too bad for me. The better for you. Go. Do what you want. Your feet always betray you. And you detest me. Has that always been so?"

"Always."

"Then I am very unhappy."

"No, you are silly. Go away."

We were seated on the edge of the loge. He is so lively that I didn't have time to prevent his seeing my glove.

During this time Mama was going toward Doria.

"God, how bored you must be!" I told him in passing. Without moving or turning around, Doria gave me a hoot which pleased me enormously. Of all the ones I have seen in Rome or elsewhere, Doria is the only one who is a gentleman in any way. Compared to him, the others are nothing. Antonelli is a monkey, and the others are peasants.

Doria is a prince in all the meanings of the word. I have already said that if I were Margherita I'd choose someone else. But no. I'd never choose anyone else. What a manner! What use of language! What nobility in the least action! I was very pleased with the way he treated the unknown dominos.

BOOK FIFTY-FIVE

Book 55
Gloria Cupiditas
H. G. T. D. O. H.
From Wednesday, March 1, 1876
To Monday, March 27, 1876
Hotel de Londres, Rome
From March 14, 1876
Hotel de la Ville, Via del Babuino

Wednesday, March 1, 1876. The weather is grey, the carnival is over, and my torment begins again. We started down the hill as Antonelli was coming up. I would have liked to go back up, but it would have looked silly. Besides, we saw him on the Corso a little later.

At 11:00 we went to accompany Domenica and Lola to the train station. In spite of all our efforts to keep them here, they had to leave.

Thursday, March 2, 1876. Mama has made a mistake; she allowed them to rent our apartment, and we are obliged to move to the second floor.

Although it was raining, we went to the Porta Pia. Then we went to hear the music at the Pincio. The Cardinalino came, staying at Mama's carriage door and then finally coming to mine.

I took all the pains in the world to convince him that I was not the pink domino at the ball. I told him I was there, but in a black domino in a loge on the third floor, and that I saw him with a red domino and later a pink one, "*Parola d'onore,*" I told Antonelli [in Italian: word of honor].

"*Si, parola d'un'ora!*" he answered [in Italian: yes, word of an hour!].

I chewed violets and suffered from the presence of Bruschetti. Ouf! When the others were all gone, Antonelli came back. "Give me two violets," he said, "I'm starving," and proceeded to take two from the bouquet on my blouse. We decided to meet at the opera in the evening. Altamura, who was supposed to leave, stayed to go to the theater. In fact, we all met together there, and Antonelli stayed all the time with us. We saw Cesaro; he is no more Cesaro than I am. He is the Marquis or the Count Zucchini—his name and his face make me laugh.

He said he has nothing to do. (Mama had been preaching to him about idleness.) He said that today he waited for us for hours at the Pincio, "I would very much like to be busy in affairs," he told us, "but Papa doesn't give me anything to do." It is charming.

I believe that Antonelli is playing with me. I'm crazy about him and dying to hear him say he is crazy about me. He is a child. He speaks like one and talks in a naïve and charming way, all the while being a scoundrel. I like him too much for me to have bad intentions about him. But what can you do with a woman who cannot live without love? It's a constant fever! I am already afraid. Never the one I want; in Nice, Galula. Here, Bruschetti!

In *Audiffret* there are nine letters. In *Antonelli* also. Both names begin with an A.

Sunday, March 5, 1876. We stopped at the Villa Borghese to see the race.

As we couldn't see well from the carriage, Dina, Walitsky, and I got down. We went by the more or less flowery lawn located on a kind of hillock surrounded by quite high steps that I wouldn't like to climb. We stopped at the edge. When Antonelli came up, I turned away, blushing.

We arranged for a cavalcade in the country for tomorrow.

"Well, I have to ask if Mama will permit it. I can't decide," I said.

"That's right. I'll come this evening to your house if you'll permit it, and we'll decide," Pietro offered.

"Very well."

The race finished, we went to the carriage, and Antonelli asked Mama's permission to come. We asked the others, also. I was calm and gay when we went to dinner. At Spellman the Elder's, I found the food so bad that I went home.

I was in love with Audiffret, and two months were enough to destroy him; or rather, a few days, because until the last moment before Antonelli, I was still interested in the Surprising One. I had nothing to do as long as there was nothing new and the old one lasted.

The Duke lasted until Audiffret, and Audiffret lasted until Antonelli. It has never happened for me to be in good health at heart or to have my heart in good shape. In this case, besides, health is illness. When nobody occupies your mind, you become numb. I know very well that these two are of no importance, that they cannot equal the Duke of Hamilton or Doria, but they please me and I don't fear them. I don't believe I was in love with the Surprising One. He irritated me; that's all. At last it's over. I cannot judge any more.

Monday, March 6, 1876. At 3:00 we arrived at the Porta del Popolo, where Antonelli and Plowden met us with the horses. Antonelli helped me to jump into the saddle.

"How smart you look on horseback!" he said.

Plowden had been trying to keep up with us as we rode, but I was glad when he dropped back to join Mama and the others, who were following us in a landau. Only the groom remained.

Once left alone with the Cardinalino, I found it natural that our conversation should turn to love. We had started talking about Socrates.

"Eternal love is the tomb of love," said Pietro. "So we love for a day and then change."

"What a charming idea! Was it your uncle, the Cardinal, who taught you that?" I asked.

"Yes, it was," he said, laughing. "When I first saw you, I fell in love with you. And then it passed."

"You are really nice!"

"It's the truth," he said.

"Ugly truth."

"Truth is never ugly," he pointed out.

The wretched son of a priest! He annoyed me with this truth, which he expressed so calmly.

In the open country we began to gallop, leaping ditches and racing like the wind. It was delicious. We were often close together—face to face, as we rode. That pleased me. He rides to perfection.

We found ourselves along the bank of the Tiber in the middle of a flock of sheep. I was nervous. "Let's go and see what your mother is doing," said Antonelli.

"Let's go," I said.

"But no," said Plowden. "Let's go around here."

"Well, let's go around." Antonelli turned his horse back toward the carriage, which had stayed a long way behind us.

I had wanted to avoid Plowden, without showing it. I didn't detest him, but I much preferred the Cardinalino. So I came back as fast as the wind, and we stayed behind. He took pleasure in paying me compliments and dared to take my hand.

"Is it so bad to kiss your hand?" he asked.

"It's probably bad."

"You don't want me to?"

"No."

"But there is nothing wrong in it?"

"No. No."

We reached the others in time to see Dina on foot and Plowden running after her horse. She had had the kindness to fall over the head of that animal, and it had jumped over her head. Fortunately, neither of them was hurt!

"And then it passed" does not leave my mind. It makes me speechless.

The country air, the sun, and the sheep with their dirty shepherds excited me, and I started to sing Verdi's *Requiem*. Antonelli turned around, serious. "Well, is it my song that makes you so sad?" I asked.

"I don't know. I am enchanted," he answered, with the same radiant expression.

"I beg your pardon?"

"Nothing," he said.

"I didn't hear."

I had no riding whip, and the Cardinalino asked a man with a cart to let him have his. The peasant listened indifferently to Pietro's persuasive words. Antonelli, realizing that his eloquence had no effect, finally bought the whip from the carter, and such an elegant person as I found herself with a peasant's whip, which was very original and attracted the attention of everybody. I held the thing high, like a real riding whip, completely forgetting its nature.

Again, Antonelli maneuvered to avoid Plowden, and we were alone.

"You don't want me to court you?" he said, following I don't remember what.

"No."

"I love you."

"That is not true."

"You don't believe me."

"Of course not, after all the beautiful things you told me."

"Then I was joking; I love you."

"Silly, silly."

"Allow me to pay court to you."

"No. I permit only those who love me to court me."

"I love you."

"It is not true."

"Oh, if you don't believe me," he said, and turning around, he pressed his lips to make me believe he was vexed.

I thought to myself, He *dares* to joke!

"You are like a child of fifteen," I told him.

"It's true. But must I let my beard grow?"

"Oh, I wasn't talking about appearance."

"But morally how am I?"

"A child."

"And what must I do to be a man?"

"You must change—live differently."

"I have changed a lot lately."

"Since a year ago?"

"I don't know. Since fifteen or twenty days ago."

"It does not show. Besides, I cannot judge. I didn't know you before this."

"Ask those who know me."

Upon this we arrived at the Porta del Popolo. We got off the horses, and I climbed into the carriage.

I'm not tired; I'm in love and furious because I don't believe that Pietro is.

In the evening he sent me a bouquet of lilies-of-the-valley and roses. . . . I think I am beginning to love flowers.

As I write, I look at the Cardinalino's flowers. It's not a bouquet like those made in the shops, but simply some flowers.

Tuesday, March 7, 1876. Again we were late for the meeting at the hunting place. We saw Pietro passing with a huge woman on his arm—his old aunt, I believe. At the Pincio I was quite sad. We saw Plowden there, and he complained that Antonelli had prevented his talking with me during the ride. As we were leaving the hill, our carriage was suddenly stopped by Antonelli. We stayed a few minutes to talk with him, and he asked if he might call on us this evening.

After having dinner at Spellman's, we returned home, where Visconti came to see us. But he didn't stay long enough to meet the Cardinalino, who didn't arrive until 10:00. Since

I had refused to believe that he had been a soldier, he brought a photograph of himself in uniform, as well as a sheet of paper showing his discharge.

He said that, as a lieutenant, once when he was angry, he rolled on the ground, broke everything, and threw the furniture out the window.

To rehabilitate the older Spellman, whom he had recommended to us and who had served us so badly the other day, Antonelli begged us to go with him tomorrow to lunch at the Kiosk on the Pincio, where Spellman will serve.

Through our talking so much nonsense I have fallen in love with this good-for-nothing. It cannot really be called love, but it is a very strong caprice.

Antonelli gave his photograph to Mama; he had gone, I took it to my room. I went to sleep dreaming about it.

Wednesday, March 8, 1876. This was a day full of events—and new emotions, both agreeable and terrible. First, we had a very good lunch at Spellman's. We talked about our religions—the differences between our Russian Catholicism and the Roman Catholic worship.

Then Pietro proposed, "Why not go horseback riding?"

I went to put on my amazone [riding habit], and at 4:30 I found myself outside the Porta del Popolo, where the Cardinalino was waiting for me with two horses. Putting me in the saddle is a story in itself. Antonelli was not strong enough or skilled enough. He missed twice. Then Walitsky tried, and finally the stable man succeeded. Mama, Dina, and Walitsky followed in the carriage.

"Let's go this way," said my cavalier.

"Let's go!"

We entered a kind of field, green and pretty, called La Farnesina. I was not at ease on my horse, and the horse was bad.

"Why do you make me gallop when you know I can't?" I said impatiently.

Above this field there is a hill. Pietro turned to the right, and we went by a very winding trail, where the carriage could not pass any more. "See my glove," I said. "It's torn!" showing him my hand. "Go and see if we can get down that way, over there," I suggested.

"No, we'll take the same trail, but we'll be careful," he said, taking the reins of my horse and pulling the horse toward him. "How much I love you!" he said, looking me straight in the eye.

"It's not true!"

"You don't believe me! But why?"

"Because it's not true. Don't say it. Don't irritate me!"

"But I am telling you I *do* love you! Then how must I say it?" I was not expecting that. Expecting his "I love you" all the time, I lowered my eyes and became confused, angry.

"Oh, don't say another word to me, or I'll hit you with the whip!" I exclaimed furiously. This spell of anger saved me. Without it, I would have beaten him and broken into tears. I was ashamed. And I was taken by surprise . . . I was silly. He took my hand.

"I recognize the hand. It is that of the Capitoline Venus. Give it to me to kiss."

"No. No. What an idea!"

"But at the Campidoglio . . ."

"It was different there, and it was silly. Leave me. Leave me, or I swear I'll never come riding with you again!"

"What! Do you think it is wrong?"

"Probably. Besides, you wouldn't dare!"

"Oh, yes, I would dare!"

"But you'll not dare."

"And why not?"

"Because a proper man must know how to conduct himself."

"That's true. Shall we go up this hill?"

"There is no path."

"True. But we can go there."

"Well. . . ."

And we started to ride up the hill without the trace of a path.

"How beautiful it is here!" he said, following me. And then I followed him. "You know, I am the least poetic of men, and yet there are moments when I am poetic, like now, for example, here."

"Yes," I said. "The weather is beautiful, and the air is good for me." We had arrived at the summit, straight into a flock of sheep guarded by two shepherds near a hut.

"Let's go this way," he said. "It's so good."

"But look; those shepherds are looking at us. Have you no shame?"

"They don't know us. Come on."

"No matter. Leave me or I'll whip you here." I put my riding whip on his face.

"I'd be very happy to be hit by you," he said, without moving.

"Yes. You know very well that I wouldn't strike you," I said. "Let's go back down."

"I love you so much I was losing my head."

"You don't love me. You are joking."

"I am joking?" he exclaimed. "But I swear I'm not. How could I joke with you on such a matter?"

"Oh, it's true; you wouldn't dare."

"Maybe not. But don't go away! Listen. Wait a minute. Listen to me; I don't know how to declare my love. I speak as I feel," he said quickly.

"Be careful; my horse is going to fall. . . ."

"I'd rather mine fell."

"Oh no!"

"I'm in despair," he told me.

"What is despair?"

"It's what happens to you when you want a thing you can't have."

"You are wishing for the moon."

"No. The sun."

"I think it has set," I said, looking at the horizon.

"No. It's right there shining on me. It's you."

"Pretty words. But just words."

"I've never said this to anyone before because I've never loved before. I've hated women. Oh, I've had intrigues with easy women."

"But when you saw me you loved me. Is that it?"

"At first sight. That first evening—in the theater."

"You have told me, 'And then it passed.'"

"That was a joke."

"How can one tell when you are joking and when you are serious?"

"But that's obvious!"

"It is true that one can tell when a person speaks the truth, but your self-contradiction does not inspire confidence, nor do your fine ideas about love!"

"What are my fine ideas? I love you but you don't believe me," he said, biting his lips and turning away.

"You are playing the hypocrite!" I said, laughing.

"So *that's* what you think of me?"

"That and other things. Listen! If at this moment one of your friends came by, you would look at him and wink and laugh."

"So I am a hypocrite! Well, well!"

"Stop martyrizing your horse. Shall we get down?"

"You don't see that I love you," he said, trying to look into my eyes and leaning toward me with an expression so sincere that my heart beat as never before in the world. All the time he was telling me how to ride and how to manage my horse. "You are beautiful—don't let him stumble—but I think you have no heart."

"On the contrary, I have an excellent heart, I assure you."

"You have an excellent heart, and you don't wish to love?"

"That depends."

"You're a spoiled child, aren't you?"

"Why shouldn't I be spoiled? I'm not deformed. I'm witty. I am not ignorant, and I'm good. Of course I have a bad temper."

We went down step by step because the trail was steep and the horses were picking their way through the irregularities of the soil and the grass.

"I, on the other hand, have a bad character; I am violent, hot-tempered, and easily angered. Shall we jump the ditch?"

"No." I crossed by a little bridge while he jumped the ditch.

"Let's just trot to the carriage, as we're no longer going downhill," he said. I set my monster to a trot; but when I'd almost reached the carriage, he started to gallop. I turned to the right, and Antonelli followed me. My horse was now going very fast; I tried to rein him in, but he was running away. I was carried along, with the whole plain before us. My hair had come down, and my hat was gone. I wanted to jump off, but my horse was going like the wind. I was frightened. I heard Antonelli behind me, and I knew what they must be feeling in the carriage. What is true is this: *I love him.* But how stupid to be killed like this, I thought. Someone must save me!

"Hold him in!" Antonelli was trying to catch up with me.

"I can't!" I said in a low voice. My arms trembled, and I thought I would faint. He caught up with me and hit the horse across the face with his whip. I grabbed his arm to keep from falling—and to touch him.

"What a fright you gave me!"

I have never before seen anyone so deadly pale. "If it hadn't been for you, I would have fallen," I said.

As we rode back to the hotel, he told me how he had first seen me at the opera, and, seeing Rossi leaving our box, went over to Rossi's box to meet him.

"Except for my mother, I've never loved anyone before this. I never looked at anyone in the theater. I never went to the Pincio. I saw all that as foolish—until I found you. Now I go there myself! I am obliged to you."

He made a declaration of love: "I think only of you. I live only for you. Especially, I think of you in the evening."

"At your club?"

"Yes. As the night comes on, I stay on there to smoke and dream of you. I try to think how to tell you, but in the morning I lack the courage."

"Or is it the desire?"

"No. The courage. Have you loved anyone yet?"

"It's not that, but I don't wish to throw my love to a man who does not love me, to be humiliated by him and be spoiled. I would probably love if I knew that I was loved very much."

"I love you."

"You don't know what you're saying. You don't know me."

"You don't need to know a person when it's love at first sight."

"I don't know about that, but I've seen you maybe ten times, at most."

"You ought to know—I'm on bad terms with my family."

"Don't they love you?"

"It's not that. I'm unhappy, annoyed. I'm on bad terms with them. Why not believe me?"

"Your ideas about love are not reassuring."

"How? Why?"

"Evidently *eternal love is the tomb* you mean."

"Yes. It is the tomb of love."

"And I am telling you it is the birth of love."

"You see, we have opposite ideas. We must try together. Love is a tomb. Let's get into it together.

"I understand," he continued, "that love after twelve or thirteen years becomes friendship."

"Friendship. That sounds disagreeable."

"Well, it can't last forever."

It was getting dark, and he was staring in front of him. "Well, here is the door," I said. It was almost night.

He explained that this was a new experience for him. "I assume that it must be love."

"How old are you?"

"I began life at seventeen. I'm not like those eighteen-year-olds who make a stupid fuss over a flower or a portrait."

"Yes," I said, as if to myself, "One has the time in six years."

Then we talked about the Capitoline Hill.

"First I took you for a woman I detest—Casta."

"Who is Casta?"

"I don't know. A woman of the demimonde. That's why I acted badly and left you." He turned to face me, saying, "You don't love me."

"I know you so little. Truly, it's impossible to know," I answered.

"But you'll know me better," he said sweetly, lowering his voice. "You'll love me a little, perhaps."

He went to excuse himself to Mama, who gave him some suggestions regarding the horses for the next time we go.

"I look forward to seeing you again soon, Madame," Antonelli said to Mama. Silently I offered him my hand and he clasped it, but not as before.

I went in, undressed, put on a lounging robe, and stretched out on a sofa.

"All goes well?" asked Dina.

"Completely, my dear."

"Tell us. Tell us."

"I knew it!" Walitsky exclaimed. "He told her something, she pushed him away, he made her horse jump, and there's the accident!"

"My dear, you're a medium!" I laughed. "He told me a lot of things."

"Did he . . . ?" Dina asked.

"You guessed it, my dear," I said. Then I told them with as much coherence as my troubled and scattered thoughts allowed.

I would be at the height of joy if I believed Antonelli. But I doubt, in spite of his apparent truth, honesty, gentlemanliness, even his *naïveté*. Besides, it's ten times better that way. I left my journal ten times to lie down on the bed and think and review everything—to dream and to smile. I'm as if I were in a dream. I write looking at the picture of this miserable man. See, good people! I am all upset while he is probably at the club. Decidedly, the woman is the weaker. I would kiss on both cheeks the person who would tell me that he, too, is troubled, lying somewhere on a bed, or on a floor as I am, and that he is thinking about me and that he, I was going to say, also loves me. I have been in love; I have adored, but it has never happened to me before to be loved by the one I wanted, so it seems unbelievable to me now. There is nothing more agreeable in the world! Truly, I feel all new—different. It's silly, no doubt. How calm I am—but still dazzled by all he said to me. If it were true!

He was almost convincing when he told me he had never courted anyone. . . . But there's something else: an evil spirit whispers in my ear that Antonelli is mocking me, and all I've been thinking and feeling is really of another color. I have to go to sleep.

Thursday, March 9, 1876. Who said I was in love with Antonelli? What an idea! Let's leave him for the moment.

Where was my head when I didn't notice the man I had earlier called "the sympathetic Blond"? He looked at me as much as Pietro. He is the very rich Duke Clement Torlonia. He will inherit from his uncle, Prince Alexander Torlonia, the famous millionaire. And I didn't even pay attention to him! I've been biting my nails since this morning thinking about it.

Dina and I went to the Borghese, the Pincio, and the Corso to try to see him. Because, although Antonelli is charming, nice—everything—he is not the companion I need for entering the "tomb," as he calls it. He is the third son and will inherit at most only around 500,000 francs. Misery! I regret it very much. . . .

Mama is in bed. Dina, I, and Walitsky have received Plowden, another one who wants me. I don't detest him; it's just that I'm perfectly indifferent to him. He's a fine fox. Besides, he's very nice and very attentive around me. He is jealous of Antonelli. But someone knocked at the door; I went to open it to hide my blushing. It was Antonelli. Soon Plowden got up, visibly upset, saying he had a previous engagement. As for the Cardinalino, he had probably eaten some meat cooked with garlic, and because of that he disappeared entirely from my horizon. Yet he is the first man, even being my favorite, who is also the favorite of the household. Mama adores him, W. likes him very much, Dina blushes when seeing him, and I also love him. He does not altogether meet our conditions; if he did, I would love him completely.

Friday, March 10, 1876. We went to the Villa Doria, but too early, because it was only when we left that the others arrived. Here was Antonelli in a very beautiful carriage with someone else. It goes without saying that the carriage was not his. He is nothing but a child, entirely dependent upon his family, alas!

Pietro! Pietro! Pietro! Pietro! Pietro! Pietro! My heart doesn't beat faster, but I suffocate.

Yesterday, Rossi was very pleased to learn that Antonelli had not justified his conduct according to his nickname, Pazzerello.

"I acknowledge, Madame," he said, "when I was in Florence, I was afraid for you after I introduced him to you."

What a ravishing triple outing! Borghese, Pincio, and Corso! A crowd of society people; their crowns and coats of arms have positively astonished me.

Pietro was riding in a fiacre to the Pincio, and he hailed everybody he met. It seems to be the custom in Italy. I very much wanted to get down and watch, or at least to stop the carriage at the music. But Pietro and Bruschetti were hunting for me. I ordered our carriage to pass behind theirs instead of going through the alley. They thought that we were stopping and turning toward their carriage, but we only passed and left by the opposite side. It was very funny, and this joke and the topography of the Pincio helped us to do it. I repeated it twice. But at last I noticed Torlonia. He was coming down the hill as we were. His magnificent horses were running three times faster than ours, and we lost track of him on the Corso.

Oh, son of a dog! How miserable I am not to know anyone! How I would like to receive everyone at home! Eagle and parrot. I'll die of it. We saw Torlonia, standing in the middle of the Corso, turned toward the left and speaking with someone. I turned around and looked at him, when he, himself, turned around. Pretending a little confusion, I turned toward Dina. In an instant he passed us and stared at me in his turn. . . . Well, I saw him and he saw me. Poor Pietro! I don't ask anything better than to throw him to all the winds.

I don't think he loves me. He's too mad for that.

Tonight, at the Valle, they are giving *La Vie Parisienne* for the first time, so we were not expecting anyone. When Leonie came to tell me that we had a visitor, I was angry because

I thought it was Bruschetti wanting to make me come out with him through a ruse. But it was Antonelli, about ready to leave because Mama was still sick.

"There are days when you seem nicer, and there are days when you seem less nice," was his first private remark to me.

"And today am I more or less?"

"More."

I knew it without his telling me. And while we were alone he tried to take my hand in a lover-like way. But I withdrew it, forbidding him to do it. Then Walitsky and Dina arrived, and we spent the evening playing "cards and horses" and some other funny things. He is very amusing, but I would like to have someone more important. He is not handsome; but in spite of that, when I touch his hand, I shiver with pleasure. He has a beautiful mouth. I want Torlonia.

Torlonia was a soldier at the same time as Pietro, and they are friends; but he would not introduce him, and each time I pronounced Torlonia's name he changed the subject.

It is silly for Antonelli to come every day as he does.

He'll be tired of me. "When you know me better, you'll love me a little?" he asked. He wants to make himself better known. That would be unnecessary if he conformed to the program. If he did that, what he wants he would already have. But alas! No, truly, he is not husband material. He doesn't even have a watch.

"They are very rich," Rossi said, and he measures riches like a Roman. Olympia Doria will have one and a half millions for a dowry, but Rossi thinks that is not very much. But no, no. Antonelli, no. Torlonia, yes. And he doesn't give a damn about me. We'll see. . . .

Sunday, March 12, 1876. Pietro tells all his family's affairs. He is a charming child. "Here is Torlonia," he said.

"Oh, yes. He has very beautiful horses."

"I believe he is selling them."

"Oh, really?"

"Do you want me to ask him about it?"

"Yes, yes!"

From the Villa Borghese, we went to the Pincio, the Corso, and then to our house.

"Will you have dinner with us?" Mama asked him. "But I warn you," she added, "it's not very good at the hotel."

That we passed all of this day with Pietro has made him like one of the family.

After dinner all the people in the dining room lighted cigarettes, and I did, too, but making a lot of faces as if I had never smoked before. Later on they served tea. I went to sit on a marble step in front of the window. It was a charming place, barely veiled with curtains. Antonelli came to join me there after a few little hesitations. The lamp, Dina, Mama— all annoyed me. However, we talked loudly enough.

Then Mama began to read the newspaper aloud to please me. This way the conversation became more intimate. He asked me to go riding again in the evening and to go to see the Coliseum by moonlight.

"I have my moments of poetry," he said. "It would be a poetic thing for us who are so materialistic."

"Speak for yourself," I said. "I am not at all poetic."

"You love someone in Rome."

"And you?"

"You don't have to ask me that question."

"Why?"

"As if you didn't know!"

"Probably not."

"Innocence!"

"You cannot believe in innocence because you are too perverted!"

"That's true."

"You'll ask Plowden to come?"

"Oh, you want him? He's courting you, isn't that so?"

"How do I know? Everyone courts me."

"But not I."

"You are an exception."

"It is because I don't know how. I have always thrown myself into the arms of easy women, and they have paid court to me in such a way that I do not know how to do it myself. Why," he continued, "don't you believe me?"

"Believe what? What you told me on the horseback ride?"

"Yes."

"Because it is not true, and it is silly."

"Yes, you are always saying it's not true and that I lie, that I am a hypocrite. Again at the Capitol—how you insulted me!"

"And think that at that time I did not know you. Now I would tell you much more."

"No, listen," and he stared at me to make me lower my eyes. "I must have a long talk with you on this subject. When?"

"When we go riding." His eyes were fixed on me. I was not free in mind or in speech.

"But I beg you," he continued, "without Plowden. All alone."

"Well, we'll see," and turning away my eyes I felt strong again.

I thought he would never leave. If Walitsky had not taken out his watch and said it was time to go to bed. . . . He was reciting all his escapades, all his troubles with his father and mother.

"So don't forget the Torlonia horses," I said for the tenth time.

"I will not forget *the cheveux* of Torlonia," he said.

"No! Not the hair—*the chevaux*—the horses!" I said. "I have an ardent desire to have those horses. Do not make a mistake, please."

"I'll tell him. Besides, he knows you very well by sight."

"I am going to read the cards for Torlonia's horses," I said.

"And for the hair, too!" Pietro said.

"And for the hair, too," I repeated.

It seems that I'll have the one and the other, if I believe in the cards.

"When are we going to ride?" he asked before leaving.

"After tomorrow," Mama answered. "And tell Mr. Plowden."

Monday, March 13, 1876. I dressed all in black, and we went to see some apartments.

"Since I am not in white," I said, "let's go to see the palace of the Pamphili."

"Let's go." And we went.

But barely were we out of the carriage and halfway there than I heard a voice behind me, and it was Antonelli's.

"Why are you here, Sir?" I asked.

"I saw Torlonia. I stayed until two in the morning to see him."

"You stayed so late only for that?"

"I talked with him. You know he does not wish to sell the horses—except for your pleasure."

"Well, well . . ."

"Let me introduce Torlonia to you."

"Good. Where is he?"

"There."

We all arrived at the front gate. Torlonia came out of his carriage toward us, he outside the gate and we inside.

"Permit me, Madame, to introduce the Duke Torlonia."

At last!

And our group, enlarged by the Duke, went back toward the Palace. Torlonia gave his arm to Mama to climb the stairs, and Pietro moved around to me. I think that Pietro has told Petruccio many silly things, because he seems to be up-to-date about everything. He knows how much Prater eats and what Fortuné said. It seems that when we abandoned Chocolat at the Capitol, Count Bruschi (not to be confused with the awful Bruschetti) found him crying with all his strength and not knowing where to go. Bruschi talked to him in French, Italian, and English, but Chocolat understood no language and continued to cry his heart out. That was nice of you, Chocolat; you did not want to betray us. Bruschi made a sign to him to climb up on the high seat of his carriage, and barely had they arrived at the Piazza Venezia than Chocolat jumped out of the seat and ran away without saying anything, too happy to have recognized the Corso. This has probably served for nothing; his devotion has fooled no one, but I am very much flattered by the conduct of the little one. The intention is all.

Torlonia understands Russian. His mother, born Ruspoli, married again—with Count Kisseloff, Minister of Russia in Florence. Again she is a widow. Torlonia has been to Petersburg.

He is a small man—fat, blond, elegant, sympathetic. Proof of this is his nickname. He has a little, fresh mouth, a blond beard, and grey eyes. He is not at all an Italian type, but very French. And he speaks French as if it were his own language.

Tuesday, March 14, 1876. We met Pietro at the Borghese in his colored walking clothes and his billycock hat, like the ones used for horseback riding. The poor child was in a fiacre.

"Why don't you ask your father to give you horses?" I asked.

"I have," he said, "but you can't imagine how close the Antonellis are!" I was so sorry to see him in that wretched fiacre, especially as so many rascals have horses and carriages. I was humiliated and angry for him.

Did I say that we left our apartment on the second floor to return to the one on the first, which we had on our arrival in Rome? I don't think I did, and today we leave the Hotel de Londres for an apartment on the first floor of the Hotel de la Ville, in via del Babuino.

Wednesday, March 15, 1876. They are playing *Faust* tonight.

The boxes of the Club members and the Court at the Opera were emptied at 10:30 because there is a meeting at the Quirinal.

Torlonia was not there, and Pietro arrived very late, almost at 11:00; he waited impatiently for Rossi's departure from our loge and then came to see us. He prevented me from hearing my opera. *Faust* is the equivalent of *Mignon* for me.

It was rather badly sung, but the divine music is always beautiful, exciting, and adorable.

Antonelli loves me. Isn't that agreeable? Only what a shame that that can serve for nothing. I don't love Antonelli.

I am going to tell it to you: I am in love with Torlonia. That happened to me during the ride.

I am delighted by his refined manners, his very clean conversation, his pronunciation, his person, his look—in a way, by everything about him. He restrained himself, but in spite of that he said a few silly things.

"I never before saw oxen with such big horns," I exclaimed, watching a passing cart harnessed with a pair of those animals.

"Yes," Torlonia said, "the condition is very well-developed here." [Horns are the sign of a betrayed husband.]

I did not continue the subject, because I would not have been able to understand (out of modesty). Outside of that remark, he behaved perfectly.

I felt very fresh and cool. I saw Pietro looking at me when he was talking to Mama. He was saying to her, "Madame, why was she blushing so much?"

Mama proposed that we go to Spellman's for lunch. I took the landau again, Pietro climbed in with Torlonia, and we all went to Spellman's.

[Later at home at the piano:]

"Bruschetti loves you?" Pietro asked me more than ten times. I was giving him some answers that, although being negative, said "yes." "Besides, everybody loves you. It could not be otherwise," he said.

I did not do it on purpose. I did not know how it happened; I know only that I put him in an impossible state. He laughed, but he was laughing because he could not cry. I forbade him to speak Italian or to speak a foreign language. It is always embarrassing at a certain point.

"For Heaven's sake, I beg you to tell me that you detest me. Throw me out and let's end this! You are a flirt—made of ice. You have an appetite for victims. I can see it. Throw me out!"

"No!"

"Why not?"

"Because I don't detest you," I said, stopping my accompaniment of the conversation. "No. I don't want to tell you that; I don't detest you."

"I don't want to come to your house again," he exclaimed furiously.

"Too bad for you," I said, starting again my "Song Without Words."

"Why?"

"Because you'll never see me again, and you'll be unhappy."

"Then love me."

"Calm down, Sir. I believe you are losing your mind."

"I beg you not to make fun of me," he said again, stopping my right hand on the piano and passing his burning cheek over it. I let him do that, and his eyes looked at me with love and fear.

"I love you too much. Be good! I think only of you; I have not an instant of peace. You like Chocolat? I'll be your Chocolat, and you'll command me!"

"Well, I'll go to Russia. I'll be married, and you'll be my Chocolat." I said that seriously, and he became so enraged that I was obliged to take his hand.

"Suppose I were to marry you now, and in two years you'd cease to love me?" I asked him. Before I had time to hear his answer, I felt his trembling arm around my waist and his lips on my right cheek. I drew back, blushing in anger and grateful for the protecting piano. (And I had thought of returning it only yesterday!)

Mama was calling me. Pietro asked whether he might still hope, and I smiled without answering.

In order to stay with us longer, Antonelli proposed some feats of strength and skill to Walitsky, and together, the one thin and dark, and the other, blond and fat, rolled on the floor, jumping over chairs and competing very well—to do them justice.

"It's time to go, isn't it?" Pietro asked Walitsky.

"Yes."

I begin to understand myself. It is not that I have no feeling for Antonelli, but I cannot consent to marry him. The riches, the villas, the museums of the Ruspoli, the Doria, the Torlonia, the Borghese, the Chiara would crush me. Above all things, I am vain and ambitious—and to think that anyone should love such a creature because he does not know her! But ambition is a noble passion.

Friday, March 17, 1876. My cheek, kissed by the audacious son of a priest, is still tingling. What audacity! The more I think about it, the angrier I am!

Supposing I should not marry him, which is more than likely. So I am soiled. Probably soiled, since another than my husband has touched me with his lips. Well, each honest soul must understand these subtleties. Besides, I don't boast about it; this is produced by selfishness. I don't deprive myself of things which supposedly give pleasure because of a feeling of duty, but really because they displease me supremely and would leave me with a very disagreeable and dirty impression.

I am reluctant to speak about Pietro. He is mine; so there is no more, or very little to say. He talked about Torlonia; when praising him, he said that Torlonia is not rich and that he has such a character that it is impossible to be with him for twenty-four hours and not quarrel many times. He did not say it out of meanness; he is incapable of that.

He has made peace with his father and has had a conversation with him about a very grave matter. With a look toward me, he assured me that he will inherit from the Cardinal and have something else besides.

Saturday, March 18, 1876. I didn't have an instant of a tête-à-tête with Antonelli. That bothered me. I like to hear him saying that he loves me and to feel my hand in his. I would give I don't know what to find myself alone with him somewhere far away from everyone. He, too, would love it. As he has told me *all*, I dream more than ever. I write two words and stop, elbow on the table, my face in my hands, and I think. Maybe I am in love. It is when it is very late and my fingers and toes are cold—when I am tired and half asleep that I believe I love Pietro, especially when I forget the splendors of the Villas Doria and Borghese. Why am I vain and ambitious?

We sent Pietro home at half past midnight. I went quickly to my room, which opens near the little salon by which he should pass. And at the moment he was in front of my door, I opened it to call Leonie.

"Oh, it is your room!" he said.

"Yes."

He took my hand and asked me ten questions to prolong the time, when Walitsky looked at the stairs like a discreet man. I told everything to Mama as soon as he was gone, EXCEPT the kiss on the cheek. No, not that! I still feel it, this kiss, trembling and fearful. He was afraid of me. His voice was trembling, and I was enjoying the sight of this. It was the most amusing sight in the world, and for an instant at least it made me forget everything. I like to love, and I like to be loved.

Sunday, March 19, 1876. I came back home upset and almost furious. I asked the coachman to stop at the music. I remained there for a half hour. Torlonia was passing in a carriage and did not think of getting out. I will like him very much more because he does not pay any attention to me. If Pietro were playing indifference, perhaps I would love him; but it would be an insult now. His great devotion, so honest, is all mine; and yet instead of loving, I let myself *be* loved. But that is still something.

This damned Cardinalino kept me up again until one in the morning. Every day has too many little pleasures and no profits. With people coming and going, we were permitted many ardent looks, the catching of hands, and even two kisses on the hands—always the right hand.

"What a misfortune!" Pietro said, taking my two hands, "not to be able to say anything to you!" Later he said, "I am so unhappy."

"Really?"

"And my happiness depends on you."

I think he is really a bullfrog. If I, without love, desired him, how much he must desire me. And he did not choose badly, the rascal! This choice speaks in his favor.

The little Antonelli charmed everybody here. Mama adores him and defends him against each and all. Walitsky, also. God, don't let me detest him because of this!

Pietro comes every evening. And all this annoys and tires me. We must leave Rome. We must go to Russia! The truth of all this is that I love none of them, and I have not yet loved in my whole life—except the Duke of Hamilton, but that was so long ago!

I would really like to love for an hour, but to be madly in love—to understand what is said about it—only for an hour; that would be enough. One must be terribly tormented, but also know some stunning moments. I love, you love, he loves; we love, you love, they love. Amen!

Monday, March 20, 1876. How time flies!

We were at the Church of Santa Croce in Jerusalem because this is the only day when women are admitted into the Chapel of Santa Helena, the mother of Emperor Constantine. I looked at the relics with the greatest indifference. I looked, and I prayed like a fool within myself. I was praying and I was afraid, because I had earlier prayed for the Duke, and I did not have him; I prayed to have the Surprising One, and I did not have him. I prayed to go into the society of Rome, and I did not go. And today I prayed to have Torlonia. And I'll not have him. Why does God do this? To discourage me? That is unnecessary. I'll never be discouraged. I'll pray always, and for everything.

I am going to hate Antonelli if Torlonia is his confidant, which he probably is. I shall ask him, and this miserable boy will let me know. I must *leave* Rome. Mama torments me to go to Naples. I told her not to think about it before April 16. It is really something to be able to command in your own home!

I would like to know whether we'll have someone here tonight, because, if not, I'd like to undo my hair and go to bed. It is 10:15. Dina is asleep in her room; Mama is in the drawing room, and W. is out. It's cold. But I don't like Antonelli.

Tuesday, March 21, 1876. I painted for two or three hours, and then we went out, as usual. It is cold, and from time to time it is snowing, but I don't care about the weather. Besides, there is some sun.

[Left marginal note: History of Roman acquaintances—a calendar of Roman dates:]

Antonelli was introduced on February 20th and visited us on the 21st. After that we did not see him until the 28th. On that date he came to the balcony, and we invited him to come the same evening to visit us. We met Torlonia March 13th, and on the 14th he visited us. On the 16th we had lunch at Spellman's and passed half of the day together. But let's continue: Antonelli came for the second time in the evening of the 5th of March. Those two evenings were five days apart. Let's continue; this accounting comforts me.

The next day, March 6th, we rode our horses with Plowden and Antonelli. On the 8th, again, with the horses, but only two together. On the 9th Antonelli passed the evening with us. Since that time, there is nothing to count. What is important is the beginning. See February 20th and 28th, and March 5th.

So there is nothing to despair about . . . let's not cry. It is not yet hopeless. . . .

Oh, God; oh, God—How plaintive it would be if I were to *say* that instead of writing it!

Antonelli has brought Tosti with him, the most fashionable singing teacher in Rome and the most often in demand. He gives lessons to Princess Margherita, and all the noblemen of Rome shake his hand and accept him as almost an equal.

For the first time in a month and a half, I tried to sing. I was able to show only half of my voice, and Tosti found it very beautiful. And there is an avalanche of society people who admire the refinement of my style.

Antonelli left early with Tosti.

"Stay!" I told him.

"I can't," he said.

"Well, I'll be angry," I told him. I was impertinent with him and let him leave, remaining behind to laugh with the others.

We went to my studio, which is near the big salon, but I was bored without Pietro. After half an hour, this gentleman so-much-desired came back. Rossi was watching us to go to report to Monseigneur and to the Antonelli family. They want very much to see this bad boy married; he, himself, has told me a hundred times.

I behaved very foolishly, giving rise to all kinds of suppositions that will never be justified. When others are present, Pietro does not amuse me; when we are alone, he speaks of love and marriage. We found ways to isolate ourselves in the studio. He is fiercely jealous. Of whom? Of everybody. I listen to all his speeches, laughing from the height of my cold indifference, and treat him as I did at the Capitoline ball. I allow him to take my hand, and I take his in my turn with an almost maternal air. If he is not yet driven out of his senses by his *passion* for me, as he assures me he is, he must be aware that while I drive him away with my words, I hold him back with my eyes.

Although I tell him I'll never love him, I do love him all the same—or, at least, I behave as if I do. I tell him all kinds of foolish things.

This animal stayed until everybody else had left. . . .

"How can you expect me to believe you when you say what you just said here in the salon—that to be married before you are thirty-five would be foolish?"

"You know I was joking. Couldn't you see that?"

It seems that I'll not leave Rome because he cannot live without me; he will follow me, or I'll stay. He must see me now; otherwise for him to go on living is impossible!

But Visconti asked Mama some questions about me and Pietro. "Where do you want to marry your daughter? The Pope interferes in all the affairs of the Antonellis and will not consent to a marriage except on the condition that the young people would be Catholics."

This young man is very nice and very rich, and he will inherit some tremendous fortunes. He will have a very good position and so forth and so on. It's almost as if . . .

Mama answered that she thinks of Pietro as a son, but that her daughter is altogether too young, that she has not made any plans and has not been thinking about this, and that she believes that human destiny is written in Heaven.

Wednesday, March 22, 1876. We barely arrived at the music before Antonelli came to the carriage. I am upset because people are already gossiping in town. We don't know anything about it, because who is there to inform us? But I know they talk, as they talked about the presentation at the Quirinal.

He is surprised by my reserve. He will see more of that!!

There were many people there, in spite of the Quirinal. I was as if in a dream.

Antonelli came, but I continued to be reserved and a little sad, not to let anyone believe that this gentleman particularly pleases me. As for Pietro, to him it seemed that I was really watching the stage. "With what attention you are watching tonight!" he said to me twice. I think I hurt Pietro, but this wound will be quickly healed. A good smile and everything will be forgotten. The power of a woman is unbelievable; I no longer regret being a woman, because the good role is without doubt hers. It is a hundred times more agreeable, easier, and proper to be on the defensive than to attack or reject, whereas a man is ceaselessly subjected to rebuffs.

Notice that in Nice I had an opinion absolutely opposed to this idea. I was a few months younger, and at my age, regarding love, that is an important measure of time.

Thursday, March 23, 1876. At the Valle Theater they are playing *Madame Angot's Daughter.* We sat in a loge on the first floor, I behind Mama in a very dark corner. I was sad, or tired, as you prefer. I wanted to sleep or to listen to an Antonelli. . . . Around 10:00 he came to our loge and asked to put his chair behind mine. I did not consent, and he consoled himself, saying to me that last night he had accompanied Muliterno to the City Hall, that he had been thinking about someone and had been singing *Dormi pure.* I answered nothing, or almost nothing, but I was happy to feel him near me. Only he thinks so differently from me. He doesn't understand the pleasure of being silent and motionless near a loved one; he must bend, move, gesticulate, fan me, take my hand—he asked me what was the matter with me because, really, I was not myself; I was silent, or I was always laughing, and these manners added to my coolness.

"Good evening, Miss," he said, giving me his hand.

I did not give him mine. I did not even say "Good night." He went out pale and really furious. What a bad temper! Well, here is something to torment me. But should I have been silent and endured such impertinence?

He left angry, furious with me. In a half hour he'd regret having left and accuse himself; he'd be miserable and dying to see me again. Whereas, if his love does not resist such silliness, it's too bad; let the devil take away such love!

Nevertheless, I was worried and offended by the audacity of this man.

"Do you know what?" I answered my own question: "I am laughing about everything tonight. Maybe it is a nervous reaction. I have been too good." His audacity should have been punished after the kiss at the piano. If he is sincere, he deserves nothing. If not—if he is joking, if he did that only to pass the time, if he is only in love with me as I am with him, then it is awful; I would not be able to punish him, because how could I take vengeance for an injury like that? . . . I began to ask myself whether I want this absurd man, or rather, this child.

Friday, March 24, 1876. For the first time in Rome, I went walking on the Pincio. People were surprised to see me walking. Antonelli was walking with a very ugly lady and an old gentleman. Then we saw him near a landau; then ten times more on foot, in a fiacre, and all ways imaginable. He was as active as ever. I told everything to my family, and Mama thought I was right to do as I did.

I met all our acquaintances and all those that I know, without realizing that the sun was hot. Antonelli was cold. . . . Yes, and it is this coolness that makes me think and ask myself, "Will he come tonight?" It isn't nine yet. I have a long time to wait. Does a man who really loves back up for so little? No, but he can pout for a long time through surprise, through fear, or even through love.

At the beginning I was anxious when Antonelli did not come, but seeing that Mama and Dina and all the others were taking the thing as it should be, I calmed myself.

Saturday, March 25, 1876. It is 9:00, and I don't know whether I'll have the patience to wait until ten. What should I do? Read? I can't. Write? I have nothing to write. Play the piano? I am nervous, miserable.

[Marie finds Antonelli in the antechamber. After a long argument about who is the offender—whether Pietro has been talking about Marie to their friends, or she is guilty of such a breach, they are reconciled.]

"Let's forget it. I made a mistake," I said.

"All the better. Good night. I had sworn never to come to your house again."

"Then why did you come?"

"I thought it would be very improper to treat your mother this way. She has been so nice."

"If it is for that, you can go and never come back."

"No, no. It is for you!"

"Then it is different." After the Theater Valle, the unfortunate one remained in bed from anger for forty-six hours. He gave me his hand and told me his despair.

"I was very wrong," he said.

"I know that. How, wrong?"

"To let you understand, to tell you . . ."

"What?"

"That I love you," he said, controlling his lips like a man who does not want to cry.

"But that is not wrong."

"It is an immense wrong because you take advantage of me and play with me like a ball or a doll."

"What an idea!"

"Oh, I know that you are like that! You like to play. So play. It is my fault."

"Let's play!" I said.

"So tell me, it was not to get rid of me that you said what you did at the theater? It was not to get rid of me?"

"Oh, Sir, I don't need such excuses when I want to get rid of anyone. I do it quite straight-forwardly as I did with Bruschetti."

"Aha! And you were saying it was not true with Bruschetti!"

"Let's talk of something else."

He laid his cheek on my hand. "You don't love me?" he asked.

"No, Sir."

"Not at all?"

"Not the least in the world."

He doesn't believe a word of it.

At that moment Dina, Mama, and W. arrived. At the end of a few minutes Pietro had to leave. I had had enough of all that.

Sunday, March 26, 1876. I have my hair done in a different way than usual; the hair is loose on the back, with golden and transparent curls reaching to the baby bonnet of beaver fur. It was very becoming, but I must have had a bored, mean look—because I felt bored and mean.

But let's leave this and start from the moment I fell on the rug after having locked my three doors. I can't stand the annoyances; I am furious. Visconti had barely left when Plowden came in. He became very amorous and silly. Tonight I took pleasure in tormenting two men—Plowden and Pietro. While I played Beethoven, Plowden came next to me and listened, talking about a number of things. Pietro did not find any place. He threw himself into a conversation with Dina, trying to hear what we were saying, but in vain, because we were speaking English. I was especially nice to both of them, and both were dissatisfied. When I talked to Pietro, Plowden rolled his eyes and was agitated. When I was talking to Plowden, Pietro visibly raged. One was at my left on the floor, and the other at my right in a chair. At the end of each musical phrase, I lowered my eyes, first on one and then on the other. If I were going into society, I would certainly like to be courted, but not at home. That only makes me go to bed late—at one o'clock.

No, I am ungrateful! If I did not have these men, I'd die of boredom. But in all this, Pietro is my favorite because he's so amusing. For example, he asked me tonight, "Do you love Plowden? Is he your lover?"

"Yes," I said. "And who is yours?"

"You know very well. But that cannot be when there is nothing reciprocal." He said that hoping for an answer, but he got none.

Tomorrow I'll not go out. I must have twenty-four hours of solitude, of writing, of falls on the floor to calm me down, to make myself numb, to make me ashamed of my silliness. How I have fallen! No, I did not fall; I still want what I wanted: millions, grandeur, and fame. I'll work myself to death if I can have what I am asking.

I am dying of envy, anger, and despair! Such is my state that I cannot even write!

Monday, March 27, 1876. I shall not go out; I've locked myself in. It is 4:00 P.M. I cannot find words to describe my torment. The pen does not obey my fingers. I am dazed, stupid. Oh, God. I love the Duke of Hamilton. I am astonished at how I have been able to lower myself mentally, enough to let my pretensions drop so far! Ambitious like 400 devils! I was dazed when simply thinking. Be careful not to commit any hopeless folly in these moments of dazedness. I would like to break my head when recovering my thinking. I must go into society! I must go into society! I must go into society!

To succeed in that, let's go to Russia. My Lord, take my soul in pity and don't abandon me.

MARIE, SUMMER 1876

BOOK FIFTY-SIX

Gloriae Cupiditas
Book 56
From Monday, March 27, 1876
To Sunday, April 9, 1876
Hotel de la Ville, Via del Babuino, Rome
To the editor: I would like the repetitions about Torlonia and Antonelli to be cut. They would disgust my readers with the remaining parts of the diary. [Instructions of the diarist; much of her repetition on various matters has been cut.]

Monday, March 27, 1876. Around 5:00, as if in a stupor, I went out, tempted by the magnificent sun. I saw Antonelli walking with a gentleman and a lady, and I became a little jealous of him.

I was happy to see him coming to deliver me, because Bruschetti, with equal courage, was coming to the door of our carriage. Mama had said a few words to Pietro about a party at Albano; Pietro went to discuss it with Clement, who proposed meeting there the next day. Pietro would not be able to come that day, nor Plowden.

First let's finish what was disagreeable. The party at Albano is upset, Pietro not being able to come, or Plowden either. Torlonia did not want to come, saying that to have fun we needed many people. I think that was very impolite and wrong.

So I had to talk with Antonelli—and he with me. We had much to say. . . . We almost quarreled.

He ended by kneeling at my feet and begging my forgiveness. He was more offended by my suppositions than by my blunt words.

"To think that of me is to believe me the last of the scoundrels, without education and without anything! How can you think that I could be capable of any disrespect for you?" he asked. He is really right. I probably was crazy. I am in a hurry to give him an answer.

"I know who will succeed with you: a man who will have much patience, but who will love much less than I," he said.

I don't know what to write; I know that I was happy when playing a sonata and feeling his arm around my waist and his chin against my shoulder.

Is it possible to permit such things? It is impossible, but it pleases me.

"You do not believe that I have a passion for you?"

"I believe, because otherwise I would have thrown you out a long time ago."

"Do you love me?"

"No," I said.

"You do not love me?"

"No," I said again, and our faces were so close to each other's that I am surprised sparks did not fly, because in my physics classes I learned that when two [charged] fluids—one negative and the other positive, come close together, a spark results.

"You see!" he shouted, "What is there to do when only one loves? You are as cold as snow, but I love you! Do you love me?" he asked again, more softly and with such tender eyes that . . .

"No, Sir, but it could happen."

"When?"

"In six months."

"Oh! In six months?"

"You don't want to wait?"

"No, I do not want to wait. I love you. I have a passion for you, and you make fun of me. I understand you very well. You are perfectly sure of my love, but you do not love me; you drag it all out for fun."

"Indeed; you are guessing right."

He came close again, so close . . . too close.

"Even if I loved you," I said, "it would be too difficult. I am too young, and there is the religion."

"But, of course! I know it very well! I also would have difficulties. You think I wouldn't? But you cannot understand me because you don't love me. I would have proposed that we run away. . . ."

"Horror!"

"Wait! I'm not proposing that. It's a horror for one who doesn't love. It would not be if you loved me."

But he is right, the animal!

"Sir, I beg you not to talk to me that way."

"I do not talk about it; I would talk about it if you loved me."

"I do not love you." I do not love him, and I am almost in his arms! Here is an absurdity! The other night he said, "I'll follow you."

"Come to Nice," I told him today. "Will you be permitted to come?"

"I do not know," he said, lowering his head. "If I go to Nice, they will think that I'm going to gamble."

"Tell them you'll not go to Monte Carlo."

He did not answer and stayed with his head bowed, which proves to me that he has talked to his father. I do not understand myself at all. Do I love or do I not?

Tuesday, March 28, 1876. But what a pity! . . . A letter was brought to us addressed to Walitsky. We opened it. It is from Triphon, who wrote these four lines only:

Mr. Walitsky,

Yesterday Yourkoff killed himself in Monaco. Mrs. Romanoff at this moment is at Mrs. Sapogenikoff's.

Triphon.

By Jove! By Jove! By Jove! That gave me a chill in my back, and I started to laugh. When I am very much moved, I always laugh. This scoundrel of a Triphon has not been able to keep the news. He is a funny, amusing, curious, intelligent servant, a thief and still devoted, depraved, and honest in his own way.

But that unfortunate Paris! Nina probably has gone mad. I remember how desperate she was at the death of her favorite dog. And when I think that it is Yourkoff, her adoration, for whom she sacrificed everything, for whom she left Russia, her home, her riches, her position! Unfortunate Paris! Unfortunate Nina!

Mama has been so shocked by the death of the unfortunate Paris that she has had a nerve attack. This terrible news reached us at 8:00; now it is 10:00. Mama is still in bed, still suffering.

I must go home to my blue room, to go faster to Russia and to come back even faster. I have no occupation. I languish. I am bored. The ravishing Antonelli world is used up; Plowden doesn't interest me; Torlonia *could* interest me. . . .

Antonelli did not come. Why? (He was supposed to have an interview with his father.) He did not say. A devil is blowing in my ear that he does not love me seriously. I mean, he dares to speak to me of love but does not want to get married because, until now, he has never said frankly and simply, "Will you be my wife?" It is not believable that he said so many pleasant things only to pass the time!

Yesterday evening I wanted to put my head on his shoulder and tell him I loved him. I would have been lying, but not entirely. I'd like to do it as a joke. No not even as a joke. I cannot humiliate myself that way. I want to be adored. . . . But Pietro is not made that way. He wants to be loved the way he loves. *He wants*. He is right. He grows in my mind. He loves me but he does not obey. That surprises me a little. I believed that he could be ordered, treated like a dog. One can order him . . . but without showing it; otherwise he refuses. I have never seen a man so given to rage. He flares up like a match at the least word. Also, he takes my greatest sillinesses seriously. But that is true of all who are really in love.

I would not want to lose Pietro; he is a nice boy, and after all, it would humiliate me.

"It is not love that I have for you," Antonelli said to me, "it is a passion." I make fun of him. If he were far away, he would look like a golden lion, but because he comes everyday, because he passes his time at our home, because he tells me everything, he seems to me a lamb of wax. After I saw him with ladies of fashion and some gentlemen from the Hunt Club, I love him more; I even am jealous of him. He did not come tonight. Why?

I want him to kneel before all my caprices. I want him to have nothing before me, nothing after me, nothing outside me! Such love does not exist! Oh, yes. When I love, I'll love that way.

Wednesday, March 29, 1876. Around 10:00, Antonelli arrived.

Pietro looked at me a great deal tonight; I was carefully dressed and my hair had been done, too . . . you understand? He'll dream about me tonight. You understand? I'll bet that you do.

"I do not love you," I told him, "but I can put up with you, and that is enough."

"No, it is not enough; I don't want that, I want to be loved!"

Pietro is not *a little young man.* I have made a mistake. He shows himself, more and more, and I start to have a certain respect for him.

Thursday, March 30, 1876. At present I am locked in my room. I am going to reason on the big affair. I have been feeling uncertain about my position. Why? Because it is false. And why? I feel a certain insecurity, because Antonelli asked me to be his wife and I did not refuse him roundly, and because he had talked to his parents about it and they are not easy to manipulate, and because Visconti said to Mama what he said. And what did he say?

"Where do you wish to marry your daughter?" Visconti asked, after he had praised Pietro's fortune and person.

"I have no fixed idea," answered Mama, "and anyway my daughter is so young."

"No, Madame. Do you want to marry her in Russia or abroad?"

"Abroad. I think she will be happier abroad, because that is where she has grown up."

"Well, we must also know if all your family will consent to see her married to a Catholic, and to have the children raised in the Catholic religion."

"Our family would see with pleasure everything which will make my daughter happy."

"And what would be the rapport between the two families?"

"I think it would be excellent, especially as they would see each other rarely, or not at all."

"Pietro Antonelli is a charming young man who will be very rich. It is even unnecessary to talk about that, since it is well-known. But the Pope is always involved in the Antonelli affairs, and he will make difficulties."

"But, Sir, why do you tell me all this? There is no question of marriage. I like this young man very much, but as a child, and not as a future son-in-law."

Here is what I have been able to obtain from Madame, my mother's memory.

The Antonellis are objecting. Very well, I'll become docile. Here is my character. It would be reasonable to leave, especially as nothing will be lost if it is postponed to next winter. I judge my feelings and fear the absence; "Far from the eyes is far from the heart." But no, he really loves me, completely.

"I know," he said, getting up, "that it is a great misfortune to love at twenty-three years and to have at this age one's own life already upset and poisoned. I am not talking about the little loves felt twenty times; but the great, the only, the true one should not start at twenty-three, especially if it must be an unfortunate one."

Dirty incertitude! He must feel that this cannot last. We must leave! Tomorrow I'll start to prepare myself. I have meant to go to visit the Roman marvels that I have not yet seen. Yes, but what annoys me is that the opposition does not come from our side, but from Antonelli's. That is ugly, and my pride is revolting.

Why should *they* be opposed to the marriage? Religion? Bah! Provided that the children are Catholics. I would like Mama to speak again with Visconti.

I would like to know if the old Pope has really talked or if what he said was the end of a conversation with the Antonellis. No doubt Pietro must have talked. I laugh, I have fun, I think of nothing but him. But for them, it is something else; they regard the question seriously, discuss it, take care of it. That seems to me very strange; however, it is very natural. I must make Pietro talk.

In the evening Antonelli came. We receive him quite coldly since the Baron's words and Visconti's speech.

"Tomorrow," said Pietro, "I am leaving."

"Pardon?"

"For where?"

"For Terracina. I think I'll remain eight days."

Here is a real thunderbolt!

"They are sending him away!" Mama said in Russian. "What a shame! I am going to cry with rage."

"Yes, it is disagreeable," I answered.

The conversation was embarrassed, and I explained this coldness by comparing the impression Yourkoff's suicide made on us. Mama was so offended and furious that her headache was worse. We accompanied her to her room. Walitsky went with her, and Dina moved off, I don't know why. Apparently they had agreed to leave me alone with Pietro to know the dirty truth.

We joked. Why were they sending him away? Once alone with him, I attacked bravely—even a little tremblingly.

"Why are you leaving? Where are you going?"

He avoided answering my questions. At last we spoke some mean words, and then he said, "But what? You want everything, and you do nothing yourself." Then some protests started, so true: words of love without beginning and without end, some impetuous ones of anger, and I say—of love? I heard these reproaches with as much dignity as calm.

I was listening, motionless, not letting him touch my hand. I wanted at any price to know; I was too miserable in this incertitude, with millions of suspicions.

"I do not trust you. I love you to death, but I have no trust in you; you always make fun of me, you always laugh, you have always been cold with your judge's questions. You want me to tell you when I see that you do not love me, and you say that you'll never love me!"

"Prove to me that you tell me the truth."

"You want me to give up? Never on my life! I will not live with such humiliation!"

"Eh! Sir, you are very strange; you want me to love a man whom I don't know, who hides everything from me. Tell me and I'll believe you, and I promise to give you an answer. NO! Go away, do not enjoy the spectacle of a woman who is begging you. . . . You do not love me."

"But you'll make fun of me if I tell you. You must understand that it is such a secret that to tell it to you is to disclose myself entirely; there are things so intimate that we never tell them to anyone in the world!"

"To anyone—all right, but one can say it to the woman one loves. Tell me, I beg you," I said, putting my hands in his own and coming closer to him with as much reserved wheedling as possible. "I do not order you, I am begging you."

"I have an awful character. I know it. Yours is like mine. That is why we never agree. Neither wants to give up; no one wants to humiliate himself. You cannot love. You are made of ice!"

Smiling softly in his face and abandoning entirely my hands in his own, I said, "Come on, you must tell me all."

"I'll tell you, but you'll make fun of me."

"I swear no."

After many promises, at last he told me. Last year, when in Vicenza, as a soldier, he got into debt to the sum of 34,000 francs.

Since he came back home ten months ago, his father has been cold toward him, not willing to pay his debts. Finally, a few days ago, he pretended that he was leaving, saying he was too unhappy at home. Then his mother told him that his father would pay his debts on the condition that he would live a wise and discreet life and begin to "reconcile himself with God." He has not gone to confession for a long time. In a word, he is going to put himself in the convent of San Giovanni and Paolo, Monte Celio, near the Coliseum. He has to remain there eight days. I had a hard time keeping myself from laughing, I assure you. For us that seems crazy, but it is natural for a male Catholic. So there is the secret! It had tormented me enough!

"You'd better not lie to me!" I said. And I leaned on the chimney, turning away my head and my eyes, which—the devil knows why—were full of tears. He remained near me, and we stayed silent for a few seconds without looking at each other. The ice was broken; with my hands in his hands and my eyes in his eyes, we were there for an hour, standing, talking about what? Love, of course!

I knew all I wanted to know. I pulled everything from him by letting him kiss my hands. Everything seems permissible with him. He seems to belong with us, his relations.

He did not talk to his father and has had no conversation concerning me. The misfortune brought on by the Pope is the eight days in the convent, and only today has he decided to go. But to his mother he said everything, even mentioning my name.

"Besides," he said, "you can be sure that my parents will have nothing against you. There is only the question of religion; but that . . . !"

"I know very well they can have nothing against me, because if I consented to marry you it is you who would be honored. . . ."

I am careful to show myself strict, even prudish; to expose some principles of morals, of spotless purity; to have him mention all this to his mother, to whom he confides everything.

"I love you, I adore you, I am mad about you," he said very low and fast. "Do you love me a little? Say it." And he put his hands around my waist, pulling me against him, without my noticing. Besides I have all the pain in the world to find that improper. With him everything seems very natural.

"I've told you everything; I have no more secrets; I am all yours. Love me, at least a little."

"And if I love you, what will be the result of it? What will happen?"

"We'll be happy."

"I cannot decide, myself. There are the fathers and the mothers."

"Mine have nothing against you, I can assure you!"

"We will see."

"One kiss," he said so low that I barely heard it. "Give me a kiss." And that with eyes which make you full of devilment.

"What silliness!" I said aloud. "I would not kiss my fiancé!"

"Let's be engaged."

"Not so fast. What did you say to your mother? How did you talk to her?"

"I told her, 'You wanted so much for me to get married. Well, I've found a girl whom I love. I want to get married now, and live seriously.' And my mother answered that I must think a long time before taking such a serious step, and all kinds of other things."

"It's very natural. And did you talk to your father?"

"No."

"I am asking you that because they talked in town about it, and Mama has been very shocked about it."

"Who talked? Rossi? A Monseigneur?"

"Yes, a Monseigneur. But you, did you say nothing to your father?"

"Nothing, I swear, but my mother may have talked to him."

It is after 2:00, I'll never finish writing if I write all night. And then it is silly; one can write only the *hard* things. As for the sweet things, they are the only ones amusing to read.

Next Sunday, I'll be in front of the convent at 3:00 and will receive a signal from the window; he will be wiping his face with a white cloth, to be sure I do not make a mistake.

"But," he said, "to go there you will have to explain to the coachman, and you'll be asked why!"

"No, no, I'll manage. Nobody will guess. I'll look at a guide book to hide. I'll be quiet."

At last he left, after kissing my hand a hundred times. I was good, even tender; his love reflects on me.

He does not promise to love me forever, but I can guarantee at least a year if I don't marry him. It is a long time—a year, when one is twenty-three and not loved. Quickly I ran to calm down Mama's wounded pride. I told her everything, laughing, not to look to be in love. For the time being, that is enough; as work proceeds, I'll tell. I am quiet, happy. Above all, I was happy and proud in front of my family, who had already bowed their heads. It is late and I must go to sleep. Now I regret not having kissed him. After the convent, it will be better; but no—when I really throw him out, I'll give him a kiss as consolation.

He is dear to me, now that I have found him again. He seemed lost to me. One loves much more the thing one finds again, the thing believed lost.

Friday, March 31, 1876. It is a real proof of love to have said what he has told me. I did not laugh and said it was well.

Is it ridiculous enough, these eight days in the convent! Poor Pietro! What his friends from the Hunt Club would say if they knew! Poor child. I will never say it to anyone else, but Mama, Dina, and Walitsky will never talk. Poor Pietro, in the convent! It is too funny. And if he had made up all this? Tiger and hyena! No, why would he invent a thing so ridiculous? It is that, in our century, it seems to me so unbelievable!

I am through with the Vatican, I have seen everything, admired all, approved all. I would like to possess the Vatican. Such a gathering of treasures cannot be imagined; the mind is confused by them.

I missed the appointment. It must have been between two and three at the Pincio when I was to go to see the unfortunate hermit. He must have been very disappointed. I did it on purpose; if he had betrayed me, he would have deserved it. I doubt everything! At the present time it seems that he made fun of me. It is awful, such a character as I have. I trust nobody. All men are scoundrels; a woman must change them as she changes her gloves.

Saturday, April 1, 1876. We visited the ruins of the Baths of Caracalla. Is it possible to see something greater than that? I was very much afraid to pass through the entrance gate, because we had our pockets full of pieces of mosaic and sculptured marble. From there the coachman took us to a church; I think it was Santo Stefano, which is near the convent where Pietro is locked up. In this church, which is round, the walls are covered with frescoes representing the martyrdoms of the first Christians. It is not possible to imagine half the atrocities represented there. I, myself, was irritated.

But the most interesting is the convent of San Giovanni and Paolo. I saw nobody at the windows. Is it possible that he really is locked there? It is not possible! But then why make up such a story? How he must be bored! He has been there since yesterday evening. He still has—let's see—until Saturday, which means, counting today, eight days. Unfortunate monk!

At 1:00 we had lunch at Spellman's, and I came back home. Now it is 5:00. My family is at the Promenade, and I stay in my room, writing and reading, singing, playing, and doing nothing.

Pietro was taking my mind off my sad preoccupations; he is no more here, and I am up to my ears in *torment.*

He has agreed with his parents to stay away from me. He left on purpose for that, starting by coldness, to bring the rupture! It is too much of a humiliation. Why am I unworthy to be his wife? No, it is not true, I am saying silly things. They would be happy to accept me. Tonight I am crazy. No, it is not an Antonelli that I need. I need a Hamilton. I don't want to be among the great, but above them. I would rather be the first in Nice than the second in Rome. By taking Pietro, I'll be in the great society, but I'll not be a star—only one of the little constellations that shape the Milky Way. I am tormented—not only tonight, but all my life—by this crazy ambition.

It will be a long time until Saturday. I am bored without Pietro. I would like to take him along with us to Nice. I would give him some meetings in the evening in the garden. I dislike seeing him among all the people, and I adore remaining alone with him, listening to him, touching him. It is too bad that he is what he is! Maybe I could love him very much.

Sunday, April 2, 1876. The monks, the churches, the convent, all this amuses me greatly; I like Rome because of all the monks who are reigning here—from far away of course, because I would not want to be in a convent myself.

At 2:30 I went out by myself and ordered the coachman to go to Santo Stefano Rotondo. Once, after passing the Coliseum, I asked him all kinds of questions about the convents and told him to pass in front of San Giovanni's, *dead slow*. But it was not yet three o'clock. I told him to go farther away, and Luigi, seeing me so hungry for convents, showed me one for women; again I returned by Piazza San Giovanni and Paolo. It was just 3:00, and hot. I asked him to stop the carriage just in front of the convent, and with my back turned toward the sun, I waited. The few windows that looked on the square have iron bars or are blocked.

"You see," Pietro told me, "one must go to the Villa Mattei."

I saw the Villa Mattei across from there, but I did not dare go alone, dressed in white; and I did not have even a penny with me. All I saw were two women lying in the sun, a beggar, a child, and from time to time some monks of different orders, some priests, and some amusing ruins. Not to look like a mad woman, I visited two churches and came back home. He certainly has not been able to show himself, but when he leaves, I'll make a crime of it. I do not doubt anymore. Unfortunately!

Repose in Peace.

I was surprised that he had not yet talked to his parents. But what would he say to them, since I told him that I did not love him? If I had said the contrary, if I had consented to his proposal, it would be another thing.

Five more days and Pietro will come out of his retirement. In a way, because of these five days, I am going to bed early and I'll be fresher and stronger. And Plowden? Plowden never stays later than 11:30 and only arrives at 9:00.

What a pity we have to leave! It will be necessary soon, on the sixteenth or seventeenth of this month. I love Rome.

All of a sudden I feel a great tenderness for my poor monk, and in a hurry I am saying so in writing. It is midnight. What is he doing at this time? Probably he is asleep. Did they, at least, give him a bed? Or does he sleep on a "cold stone"?

Monday, April 3, 1876. I painted all day, and around 6:00 they came to pick me up. I had put on an Italian straw hat covered with white feathers and raised in the back by two yellow roses. It is a Watteau hat, which also gives me the Watteau look. Besides, it is the same shape as my hat last year . . . Reboux knows me, I had just to write to him about seven or eight days ago.

No more rings for our society! Dina has invented an adorable thing—a heart in silver with the initials: A.T.E. You are going to see that nothing better could have been invented. First, a heart is the most natural rallying sign for a society like ours. Everybody is talking about the rings, and this silver heart will have a magnificent effect. Then the initials are the first letters of our three names: Aglae, Thalie, Euphrosine, and these three letters could also mean, in Italian: *a te* [to you]. Then the A can mean Antonelli, the T Torlonia, and for the E we will soon find a meaning, if we are not satisfied with Émile. Isn't it apropos, very simple, and very original? We must not look any farther. It is adorable.

How long it is since Saturday night! Tuesday, Wednesday, Thursday and Friday; four evenings without Antonelli. Is he lonely without me? Of course you doubt, but I don't; because if I am lonely, he must be lonely, too, since he loves me. I don't love him, and so

I don't feel all those emotions. Poor dear monk! We'll go to see the Coliseum on horseback in the moonlight.

Tuesday, April 4, 1876. Spring is here. In spring all women become more beautiful. That is true, if I may judge by myself. The skin becomes clearer, the eyes more shining, the colors fresher. I am no longer lazy; I want to go out, see everything, and go everywhere.

It is the 4th of April, and I still have twelve days of Rome. What shall I do with Pietro?

How strange it is! As long as I wore a felt hat, it was winter; yesterday I put on a straw hat, and it was spring. Often a dress or a hat gives this impression, just as a word or a gesture may hasten an event which has long been in preparation, but which did not seem to come into existence and needed this little impulse. . . . I express myself badly, but do you understand my idea?

Let's not forget to buy the four hearts. One for me, one for Dina, and two for my Graces. "A. T. E." It is really pretty. And to think that the idea is *not* mine!

The time for the much-desired trip to Russia is approaching.

If Pietro were not coming back, I would be sorry and I would cry. I would be desolated.

I am all softened. If at this moment he were coming, I'd throw myself at him. We all have some impulse like that, but it would be an improper act. He'll not arrive at this moment, but I'd not be so touchy.

I am thinking of Pietro. Far from humiliating him, his love raises him and reflects on me. I am grateful to him. Oh, silly girl, if he loves me it is because he likes to do so. He does not love me through philanthropy or self-abnegation.

Wednesday, April 5, 1876. I am painting Stella's son, a baby five years old, beautiful as an angel, with devil's eyes. I'll be finished soon. Today I am doing it without Katorbinsky; he saw it and is as satisfied as surprised.

"In this," he said, "there is so much good work that I am positively surprised." The pose is difficult; the baby is in front of me, his head lowered and his eyes looking at me. There is a yellow background. His white shirt has an open neck. I am very happy to make such good progress.

Today I started another woman, with brown hair, fuzzy like the negro's, and with light grey eyes and a pink and white complexion. She has strong features and an admirable mouth.

I am painting it on a bright yellow background with patches of indecisive colors to soften the tone. This yellow may seem strange to you, but I assure you that it has made all the soft colors come out and produced a very original effect.

I must attach myself to painting, because it must be an imperishable work, whereas the greatest erudition dies with its author. But I have enough with my journal, and there are so many creatures who are writing that I'll be one too many; it is not these works which will give the celebrity I want. With what do I want to be famous? Everything! I'll never be a poet, or a philosopher! I can only be a singer, a painter. It is already pretty. And then I want to be in vogue; that's the principal thing. Strict minds, do not raise your shoulders, do not criticize me with an affected indifference to look more nearly right! But you are right, just the same. You are careful not to let it show. But that does not prevent your finding in time, deep in yourselves, that I tell the truth.

Vanity! Vanity! Vanity!

The beginning and the end of everything, and the sole and eternal cause of everything. Whatever is not produced from vanity is born from our passions. Passions and vanity are the only masters of the world.

Thursday, April 6, 1876. After tomorrow I'll see Pietro. From my impatience, one could believe that I love him.

This morning a considerable emotion was produced by the letter we received from my father. [His letter is not here.]

Certainly he could not say what he is saying, deadly true, and I am surprised that a man whom I barely know has the same ways and manners to envisage things as I myself do. He has touched so well on all my extra-sensitive strings that I have nothing more to say. I do not wish to quarrel with him; I am going to Russia, and it is important for me to be on good terms with him.

> I thank you very much, dear father, for your letter. I know very well that all you are saying is for my benefit, but I hope to make you take back certain of the false ideas that you have of my position and of my life.
>
> Indeed, my position is not what it should be, but it is not what you think, either.
>
> We are planning to go to Russia. If Mama's health does not permit her to come, I'll come alone.
>
> And since it will please you, I'll come to see you and Paul. Is it true that he has changed? His character, I mean. I had almost damned him for his bad conduct. When does Poltava's social season start? I am bent on seeing this city in all its splendor.
>
> Good-bye. Love me and think of me.
>
> Your, anyway, daughter.

I think I did not say too much. Mama wrote what I could not write, but what we needed to write.

I sang Mignon's Prayer to the Madonna. The music of this opera is consolation for all afflicted souls, no matter what the sorrow.

My deplorable state of mind makes me think that Pietro will never come back, that he does not love me and never has, and that I have been a dupe, like the last silly girl in the world.

He should leave his convent tomorrow or the day after.

Everybody went to see the Coliseum in the moonlight. I stayed alone at home, looking at myself in the mirror. I sang and was comforted, full of confidence in the future. Let's go to Russia, even to the heart of my torments.

Friday, April 7, 1876. During my painting lesson I heard a Russian voice in Walitsky's room, next to the studio—a man's voice. I knocked at the door. "You cannot come in," said Walitsky. "I am undressed, and it is Mr. Yssayevitch who just arrived."

I was not at all surprised, because my aunt wrote to us that he was in Nice and would come to Rome. Who is he? Paul Yssayevitch is Domenica's nephew, the son of her brother. Six years ago, in Kharkoff, he was a student.

Paul Yssayevitch was terribly ugly; he had a large nose, an insignificant complexion, and small size. Now Yssayevitch is at the chancellery of the general governor of the city of Vilna. He is twenty-seven years old.

"Well," I said to Walitsky, "open."

"No, I cannot. I am going to send him to you."

"That is right." I received him like a queen, not getting up, but serene and simple.

"No need to introduce myself," he said. "You recognize me?"

"Oh! yes. It is I who cannot be recognized."

"They told me that you are doing marvellously in painting, singing, everything."

"Thanks to Mr. Katorbinsky, I progress, yes."

"I do not want to trouble you more. . . ."

"It is all right, but you can go now. We'll meet again."

When Mama and Dina came back from church, they came to my room and we talked about Nice, Yourkoff, and Nina.

It is tonight that Pietro must come. Tonight or tomorrow. I prefer tonight. I am going to wait for him in order to be disappointed.

Pietro did not come. It is only this evening that he leaves the convent. I saw his clerical and hypocritical brother, Paolo Antonelli. He is a creature to be stomped on, a little black, yellow, base, hypocritical Jesuit!

If the affair of the convent is true, he must know it; and how he must laugh at it with his mysterious little manner, how he must tell it to his friends! Peter and Paul cannot endure one another. It seems to me that *my* Antonelli is oppressed, that his so religious brothers are doing wrong to him with the old Count. Finally Pietro has still until tomorrow evening. Mama had bet with him that he'd not come back Saturday. We'll see who will win!

Yssayevitch spent the day with us, and we went together to vespers.

The death of the unfortunate Yourkoff provokes only a cold feeling among his friends— "So much the better," and a pious "It's better that way for the young Sapogenikoff ladies." There were "charitable" souls who came to console and speak that way to Nina. My aunt is revolted about it.

I am far from agreeing with Nina, but I would say, like Bihovitz, "Since that position is accepted by the husband, we have nothing to say."

Unfortunate Pietro! What did they do with him? These damned Jesuits have poisoned him or suffocated him or drowned him in the Tiber. I'll be patient until tomorrow evening, and after that I'll abandon myself to despair.

No, listen: Pietro, no matter where you are, in this world or in the other, listen to me. I want to make you feel by the strength of my will that I am thinking of you and that I miss you and that I detest those who persecute you! My dear friend, my best souvenir from Rome.

Saturday, April 8, 1876. It is Saturday evening. Pietro must come. If he does not, I'll cry like an unfortunate! Mama is starting her guessings with an offended air. The time between 9:00 and 10:30 seems to me longer than the eight days. I am out of breath with impatience. God, if he were *not* coming! If they took him away or hid him; if he betrayed me or made fun of me! Ah!, what will my face be in front of the household? God! God! God! He'll come. Say that he'll come. I'll give up Torlonia if he comes. I do not want to believe that he makes fun of me. I am used to looking at him as honesty itself, the lion's heart and the impertinent, by excellence! God! I believe that the clock has stopped. No, it runs. It crawls, it is only 9:00. I am waiting, I am waiting! Ah! the cards! I don't believe them any more, but let's try again; it will help to pass the time. . . . They say—no. My God, make him come!

How silly I am! When the clock rang 10:00, my fingers were of ice. I was hot and cold until 10:30. At 11:00 I turned my back to the lamp and was listening to Walitsky's and Yssayevitch's stories. At 11:30 Mama gave the signal, and we all went to bed.

I stole six cigarettes from Walitsky and dragged myself to my room, locked the doors, and plugged the keyholes with handkerchiefs. I looked at myself in the mirror, put on a robe, and lay on the floor, my head against a little armchair. My eyes, wide open, were fixed on an awful garland on the ceiling.

I made the remark that when one cries one does not know at that instant why one is crying, one feels only the need to cry.

I had to move because on each side of my neck was a lake. I thought about the joy I'd have if my bedroom were isolated.

My love story is always the same; it always ends with a paroxysm of tears on a hotel rug.

That last evening at the piano he told me, "If I can enter military life without my family's consent, you can believe that I'll go everywhere for you and without the permission of any devil. Good Lord, yes!" I am smoking.

Tomorrow I am going to confession and will have communion. I opened a drawer and brutally closed it, because I saw Pietro's portrait. How it hurt me; I am dying of the desire to go to take it and to write, looking at it, as if it could give me words to make me understand, to tell how much I look like a drunk woman, half stupid and completely distressed. I've had some shivers all this time. Now I have a headache, and now I smoke to make myself numb.

I have an awful conviction that I won't see him anymore. What's strange about that? Am I supposed to have anything but sorrow? Maybe I'll finish in a convent; I'll go somewhere to hide myself, to cry and to blaspheme. I am disappointed, tired, tired of the constant disillusions, of the eternal desires never satisfied.

Because he loved me, I was treating him as a scoundrel!

If he were dying, I'd make a god of him. However, I don't believe in anything, I love nothing. I value nothing. All these disillusions have made me a notorious wretch. Incredulity, cynicism, and misanthropy!

Here's what I am, and it is not because I wanted it! God made me such. Let's deny God, and it will be complete.

Sunday, April 9, 1876. With fervent faith, a heart full of emotion, and a well-disposed soul, I have been to confession and taken communion. Mama and Dina went also. Then we attended Mass. I listened to every word, and I prayed. I asked nothing else but to see Pietro again.

Mama, all this time, was telling Pietro's story from the time he was sixteen years old until today, and at each paragraph she ended with these words: "He is dead, or they've forced him to take vows. These Jesuits have walled him in. It is over; he is dead."

You can imagine what the effect of these words was on me!

Oh! yes. It is maddening, humiliating, awful! I am breaking my head to guess where they could have put him. What is impossible for the Cardinal when it is a question of giving orders to the ecclesiastics?

Listen! It would be too much if all of a sudden they kidnapped him forever without letting me know what happened to him!!! He can't come back to Rome. But he said so often that he'd be back here on Saturday at the latest!

And not to be able to do anything! And not to know where to go for him! But *he himself?* Pietro. Isn't he doing *something* to come back! Doesn't he scream? Break everything? Doesn't he *want* to come back?

BOOK FIFTY-SEVEN

Book 57
From Sunday, April 9, 1876
To Thursday, April 13, 1876
Hotel de la Ville, Via del Babuino, Rome
From Thursday, April 13, 1876
Hotel de la Ville, Naples

Sunday, April 9, 1876. No, it is impossible. He loves me and he is not coming back.

I have been to confession; I have received absolution and I swear and rage.

Man needs a certain allowance of sin just as much as he needs a certain allowance of air for living. Why do men remain attached to the earth? Why does the weight of their consciences fasten them to it? If their consciences were pure, they would be too light and would fly up to heaven like red balloons. A strange theory, that. Never mind. And what's the use of all this? He is not coming back.

I am singing *Mignon*, and this infamous music is tearing my heart out. If he would come, I'd meet him in the little dark salon; I'd take his hands, I would lean on his chest, and I'd ask him, "Why are you so late?" I've spent two atrocious days.

Ten o'clock! I don't want to look at the clock any more. Saint Mary, take me in mercy! Perhaps I am punished for what I made Bruschetti endure.

If he came now, I would faint. I would give two years of my life to see him for one hour now. I want to know—Tuesday I am leaving for Naples. They'll let him go, and I'll come back unexpectedly. Besides, I don't have to worry; once freed, he'll come to Nice. He loves me, you hear? He loves me! Once he told me that when he was angry he broke everything and threw the furniture out the window. . . . He must be doing that now! He loves me. There's nothing surprising about that, since I love him, too.

Monday, April 10, 1876. They have shut him up forever. No, they shut him up for the time of my stay in Rome. But we are going to see. Tomorrow I shall go to Naples; they can't foresee this trick. Besides, once he is free, he will go in search of me.

At noon we had Plowden's visit. He brought me a little dog. I rode with Paul. It was a wonderful ride from a physical point of view, but annoying for my morale.

Then I changed my hat and put on a cape, and we went to the Corso. Nothing.

"Well, Wednesday or Thursday we'll leave for Naples. After a few days, we'll be back and we'll learn something."

"We don't have the money."

"Ah, of course, we need it! I'll telegraph to my aunt; I am telling you that I want to clear up this mystery."

I do not know what to think about him. Victim, dupe, or martyrized child? I am excessively calm, but very sad.

Tuesday, April 11, 1876. Yssayevitch is courting me, and today I am very capricious. With an air half buffoon and half sleepy, I said silly things to everybody.

After lunch at Spellman's, we bought four glasses and went to drink at the Trevi fountain, afterwards breaking the glasses and then throwing a penny for each into the fountain to be sure to come back to Rome. During this ceremony, there was a crowd around the fountain. We provoked a real riot. The Roman people are even sillier than the Parisians. I've noticed it many times.

Today I feel as if Pietro had never existed. Cat's nature! Here I am so used to Rome that I'll leave it with pain. You see, I am constant.

Nina is in complete despair, and I am so sorry for her! In the interest of morality, it is said to be fortunate, but I judge differently. All her life was centered on Yourkoff; and if you have a heart that's not too hard, you will understand her mortal pain. It is unfortunate, even, that he'll be replaced some time—God knows by whom. Fifteen years in her home have, in a way, "legalized" Paris, whereas a new *paysan* will be an atrocious thing for the daughters.

She'll not love him, of course, but she'll take him, as a habit, through despair. It is strange, but Nina is a bizarre person.

She saw Yourkoff in Astrakhan, on the stage. She said to her husband, "I want that man!" and her husband gave him to her. And at each quarrel, it was Mr. Sapogenikoff who played the role of mediator or pacifier. More and more strange, isn't it?

But let's talk a little about *my* Paris. What, especially, displeases me in the lie? Why make up the convent? I have threatened him with eternal anger if he lied to me. I do not see why he should hide the truth, if it is what I guess it is.

I permit the lie; I look like a crazy girl, without principles and without heart.

Wednesday, April 12, 1876. All night I dreamed about him. He was assuring me that indeed he has been in the convent. In the apartment, everything is upside down; we are packing; we are leaving tonight for Naples. I detest leaving!

When shall I have the happiness of living in my own home, always in the same town, always seeing the same society, and travelling now and then for change?

Rome is the place where I should choose to live, love, and die!

No, I'll tell you: I should like to live where I was happy, love everywhere, and die nowhere. However, I like the Roman life, the Italian, I mean; it still retains a slight tinge of antique magnificence.

People often have false impressions of Italy and of the Italians. They imagine them poor, designing, in a state of decline. It is quite the contrary. You seldom find such wealthy families and such luxuriously appointed houses in other countries. Of course, I am talking about the aristocracy.

Under the Pope, Rome was a city by itself, and in its way is sovereign of the world. Then every Roman prince was like a little king, with his court and his clients, as in ancient times. From this "regime" springs the grandeur of the Roman families. Truly, in two generations, there will be neither grandeur nor riches, for Rome is subject to royal laws and will become just like Naples, Milan, and the other cities of Italy.

Great fortunes will be split up, museums and galleries will be bought by the Government, and the princes of Rome will be transformed into a number of petty people, covered with a great name, as with an old theatrical cloak, to hide their needs.

Well, I am leaving, as always, a little moved, but not sad. I do not know what gives me that calm feeling. It is possibly the presentiment that he will find me. He loves me. I have nothing to fear. He is interested in the affair, and he'll act in his own interest; so I have nothing to worry about.

Botkin and Katorbinsky had dinner with us. Botkin, with a tone of respectful familiarity, talks to me of my love for Pietro, without saying the word love and without naming Antonelli. We are leaving in a half hour.

Imagine! Torlonia came to the station. When we left the hotel, he was prowling in the Via del Babuino. I was quite strong all the day; it was only at the station that I started to feel something like regrets.

I was barely in the wagon when he came to mind, wearing all the charm he possesses. I closed my eyes and started dreaming and making suppositions.

[Thursday, April 13, 1876.] I was not able to sleep, even in a private compartment, and at 6:00 in the morning we arrived in Naples.

Naples could not look very beautiful at 6:00 for me, half asleep, moody, my cheeks red from sleep.

"To which hotel are we going?" asked Mama.

"To the Hotel Victoria; it must be good since Fanny Lear stayed there."

We went to this hotel, but we learned beforehand that it is horrible, as usual, with the things that I pointed out.

Admire Vesuvius, smoking like a cigarette—a great displeasure, like a triple raincoat! I had forgotten that we should have gone directly to the Hotel du Louvre, since it was there that the Duke of Hamilton, all of whose activities I followed in the newspapers, always stayed. But in this hotel are the Prince and Princess of Prussia, who occupy the best apartments.

We were taken to the Hotel de la Ville, a few steps away; we took five rooms on the second floor.

At 8:00 I washed, and feeling clean, I took my coffee in my room, which is separated from the others by a salon. But instead of writing, I fell asleep thinking of the unworthy son of a priest. I do not know what time it is. I am tired; but instead of enjoying this rest, I am annoyed. I regret having come to Naples; we should have come here only around the 17th to see the horse races, and possibly I would see him then. Brute!!! Again!!!

I am coward enough to desire to see him coming for the races! No, it is only for a moment! One must always be independent in everything and never listen to anybody else. Each time I have listened to my family, whatever it has been about, I've had annoyances and regrets.

Did he go *on his own accord,* or did they make him go? That is *the question* that *worries me.*

I am writing in front of a large looking glass. I look like Beatrice Cenci, without the turban. I used some false hair; it is pretty: a white dress and my hair is let down! I do it now in a Pompeian style, as Pietro has called it.

I did not torment him. But he was complaining a little. He said I was made of ice. He said that I have a craze for victims. "Tell me. I do not court you; I do not make declarations. I come and simply tell you that I love you, as I have never loved anyone else before this. Listen, I do not know if I love you, but I have never felt before what I feel now. I look for you, I desire you everywhere, and when I am alone I close my eyes and dream and become weak and silly. Well, I think that this is love. Before this, I had only intrigues, like all the young men who make fun of everybody and everything. Ah! I swear, you drive me insane with your cold air. You do not even change your complexion; you are not even a woman. Look, you are like this:" and he touched the piano's keys. "I love you," and he leaned near to me, "Do you love me?" And seeing that I did not answer: "A little? Do you love me a little?"

Poor soul! I would rather cut a finger off my right hand than believe his villainy. Ah! what a consolation to think that way. . . .

"You are too young," you would tell me; "you do not know men; they can say much more!"

Ah! let the devil take you to suggest such ideas! All right; men can say much more. But to tell it to me, with which intent? They often say these things to obtain something . . . but this is not my case, and it cannot be a question of that here. I remember his speeches very well, and little by little the least of his words comes back to my mind.

I just read again the scene at the piano. I am almost feeling well enough to go out. That has calmed me and given me the confidence I so much needed.

But I have a cold, a headache, a pain in my right side, in a finger—everywhere—and pain in my soul!

BOOK FIFTY-EIGHT

Gloriae Cupiditas
H.G.T.D.O.H.
Book 58
From Thursday, April 13, 1876
To Wednesday, April 19, 1876
Hotel de la Ville, Naples

Thursday, April 13, 1876. After all, I do not have to complain. Anyway, is it not Holy Thursday, and these next days, are they not those that Our Lord Jesus Christ suffered? Is it not just that I also suffer? More than is fair. I did not want to listen to the Gospel in church; I wanted to have fun when I should have been praying. As for the Church, is it not a sin for one to go there only to show oneself, to criticize, to be criticized? All right, but I had to pray at home. I prayed each evening, but only to demand. That is not what I should do. Now I know it, because I am tormented by my lack of piety. Well, *culpa mea, culpa mea* [sic]. I should have been more religious; to believe is not enough. It is true that when one follows all the church's rules, love of and belief in God are imperceptibly scattered among the priests, the pictures, and the trivial practices.

I opened my window to air my room, which was full of smoke from my cigarettes, my indispensable companions for my sadness. I have a blue, pure sky and the sea through the dark trees, the ocean lighted by the moon. How beautiful, after the dark and narrow streets of Rome! It is one o'clock, there's not a soul on the quay. Such a calm night, so beautiful. Oh! if he were there! (If you take that for love!)

One cannot sleep when it is so beautiful!

Friday, April 14, 1876. I have seen Naples! Indeed it is beautiful! Walitsky met us and told us to go walking on the Via di Roma or Toledo. It is the Corso of Naples, but today no carriages were allowed.

Altamura was all kindness. I, also, was nice.

"What is this house?" I asked him about a corner house with a balcony like the one in Paris of the Jockey Club.

"It is the Academia, the Club."

"Do you belong to it?"

"No, Miss, because here all the members are nobles."

He is not a noble and does not belong to the Club! By Jove! And I have been seen with him!

Suddenly I became very tired, and I needed much self-restraint not to drop the banker's son there.

On the balcony there were only three or four plobsters. One of them was in a rocking chair; he must have been a Pietruccio.

At home we found cards left by Rossi, Visconti, and Falloux. Antonelli is already back; so he is free, too. The sea howls, and I am in a rage, like itself. At Rome we left word at the hotel that we had left, without adding anything. But if the Count Antonelli came, they would tell him that we are in Naples. But it is useless to think about that: he resigned himself, weak creature!

I thought I was loved! I had few reasons to believe it, and see, good people!

I have insulted, wounded Bruschetti. But I do not repent it. And what is the use of this detested love? I need someone to love me, and no one does.

I am really a strong woman. In front of everybody I am gay, coquettish, and extravagant, as usual.

Saturday, April 15, 1876. We only see Altamura. I distrust him, as I distrust all Neapolitans. It seems to me that they do not wear any underwear under their well-made trousers and that they all have debts, or are even scoundrels.

I don't have anything to say if I don't talk about Pietro, but I think it would humiliate me to do that after his strange conduct.

He'll spend the day with his family, and after that he'll be able to leave. (Here is the way I fix things in my mind.)

Unwillingly, I am waiting for the arrival of Pietro. If he is free, he can't fail to come. But now I doubt everything. . . . We visited the palace of Capo di Monte. The park is admirable. I am charmed by it; Altamura was with Mama, and I walked alone, Chocolat carrying my train. It was a charming effect in this paradise of green. I amused the company as much as I could. Naples displeases me. In Rome, the houses are black and dirty, but they are palaces, admirable in architecture and antiquity. In Naples, there is as much dirt, but you see only cardboard houses in the French style.

Hear! How angry all the French people would be! Let them be calm. I admire and love them more than any other nation, but I must confess that their palaces will never attain the massive, splendid, and graceful majesty of the Italian palaces, especially those at Rome and Florence.

The palace of Capo di Monte is big and magnificent, but quite barbaric, if one can express oneself that way—a little like army barracks. Whereas in Rome, look at those porticos, those windows, those vaults and sculptures! I am used to these antique splendors, temples, columns. . . . It is not that I blindly admire the cracked walls and columns without bases, but they are beautiful, grandiose, incomparable.

Monday, April 17, 1876. We could not go to Pompeii because it rained all day long.

Altamura came about 10:00. Not able to cross the salon to go to Walitsky's room to steal some cigarettes before I heard Pietro's name, I stood stock-still. "But Antonelli is in Rome, Madame," said Altamura.

"But which Antonelli?"

"The Count Pietro Antonelli. I just received this cable, look!" And Mama read, "Count Pietro Antonelli is in Rome."

I rushed to my bedroom and cried. Then he has been put away *because of me!* He is in Rome. Since when? He has lied all the time, and I thought I was loved! It is right to say *low class.* Indeed he is so low and vile that, at my age, I am disgusted with him.

For this time, let's be undeceived. For the first time, I thought, I was loved by a man whom I did not hate! Mentally I said, let's go to Rome! No, my girl, you'll stay in Pompeii. You climb Vesuvius, you visit the Blue Grotto. You'll admire the museum and attend the horse races on Thursday and leave on Saturday.

So why do you have to run after a man? If at least you could love him with passion, it would be an excuse, perhaps, but *like that . . . !*

I will not go a step. Why be worried about a man who only courts me when I am with him? Who, when I am gone, could not care less?

He is free; he is in Rome. But it is useless to think that he'll come to Naples.

I profoundly despise Antonelli because he betrayed me through his family, or he acted voluntarily. It is possible that they told him to leave under any pretext and then detained him until my departure.

Let's go to Rome. Oh, no! Here I am at war with the Cardinal. Let God send me the opportunity, and I'll fight with dignity. Let's not decide anything. Let's wait. If what happened is not his fault, then there is no reason to be angry. Let's not be silly; let's have fun in Naples; let's do things naturally as if nothing had happened. Let him act and see what he will do.

Tuesday, April 18, 1876. At noon we set out for Pompeii. We drove there because the road is good, and we have views of Vesuvius and the towns of Castellamare and Sorrento, etc.

Altamura let me drive his horse, and we went in the landau. The excavations are splendidly managed. It is a curious thing to go through the streets of this dead city. We took a sedan chair, and Mama and I rested in it in turn.

These skeletons are awful, these unfortunate people are in the most cruel attitudes. I was looking, whistling, at the remains of the houses and the frescoes, and I tried to fit them into my imagination and re-people those houses and streets.

What a terrible force is one that could swallow up a whole city!

I heard Mama talking marriage and saying, "Woman is made to suffer, even with the best of husbands."

"A wife before marriage," I said to her, "is Pompeii *before* the eruption; a wife after marriage is Pompeii *after* the eruption."

So Antonelli is in Rome, and he knows that I am not there any more. He does not go where I am? This is singular love. He knows that I am in Naples for a few more days, and he is waiting for my return. Yes, if he is expecting it. But if they forbid him to think about me and if he has resigned himself? How I would despise such a man!

Everything that has happened proves that he does not love me seriously. I am not blind to his strange conduct. He loves me, and he does not even worry about my whereabouts.

"You read a lot of novels," he said one evening; "your imagination is high, and you always need some extraordinary things." Maybe he is right.

If I could, I would continue another month in Naples, in spite of all the displeasures it would give me, to see whether he were anxious from his long absence, and whether this cardboard hero, this shouter of sillinesses, would not take a few timid steps to hide from the family.

Wednesday, April 19, 1876. You see the disadvantages of my position. Antonelli without me has the club, society, his friends, everything except me; whereas I without Antonelli—I have nothing.

For him I am only a luxurious occupation; for me he is everything. He made me forget our terrible position; I didn't think of it. I was busy only with him, too happy to escape.

No matter what may happen, I bequeath my Journal to the public. I am offering you what has never been seen by any eyes other than my own. All the memoirs, all the newspapers, all the letters that are published are only false inventions made to deceive the public.

I have no interest to deceive, I have no political ideas to hide, nor criminal relations to dissimulate; nobody cares whether I love or not, whether I cry or laugh. My greatest care is to tell exactly the facts. I am a foreigner, and my French is not perfect; but if I had written in my own language, it could have been worse. It is not for these things that I have opened this Journal; it is to say that it is not yet noon, that I am more than ever left with my torments, that my chest hurts terribly, and that I could scream with pleasure.

The sky is grey; the Chiaia is crossed only by cabs and dirty pedestrians; the stupid trees planted between the promenade and the sea shut out our view of the water. At Nice, the Promenade des Anglais has villas on one side and on the other is the sea, which comes and breaks on the pebbles without any obstruction. Here the promenade has houses on one side and on the other a kind of garden that extends as far as the street, which separates the garden from the sea. The street is itself separated from the sea by a quite large space of arid land, covered with rocks from old constructions and offering a spectacle of sadness, of real desolation.

When you arrive on the square that ends the Chiaia, planted with pretty shrubs, you feel much better; this place is appealing. Farther on you get to the quay; on the left hand are the houses. On the right is the sea; but it is stopped by a wall with balustrades, which are lined with the people selling oysters and shells; then come the railings of the harbor, the various constructions used by the men selling services for the boats, and the port itself. But that is no longer the sea; it is a dirty place full of hideous things.

The grey weather always makes me sad; but here, today, it oppresses me.

A few more days and I'll be in Nice. This moment I desired so much before, is so unimportant to me now! I would not delay it just because of my character, which is contradictory to delays, no matter what they are.

I am satisfied to have been in Florence for a few days last summer and this spring in Naples. If I have to return to those cities, I'll not have that aversion I usually have for new cities.

My poor aunt is dying of boredom! She has never been so long alone, and her letters are pitiful. And Grandpapa! And the dogs, and the Sapogenikoffs, and Collignon, and the monkeys!

I believe that Antonelli has been in Rome since Saturday. In that case he delayed his arrival by only one week.

BOOK FIFTY-NINE

Gloria Cupiditas
H. G. T. D. O. H.
Book 59
From Thursday, April 20, 1876
To Tuesday, May 9, 1876
Naples, Hotel de la Ville
From Sunday, April 23, 1876, Rome
From April 29, 1876, Nice

Thursday, April 20, 1876. The horse races!!! The Count Larderel's horses had interested me in advance. Without having any ideas about this gentleman, I felt capable of being interested. I'd never seen him before, but I was curious in advance.

We left at 1:00 in a great heat. Paris cannot brag of being more brilliant than Naples. Thanks to Altamura, we are seated in the middle of this beautiful place, near the paddock and the tribune. There is a multitude of carriages with four horses, with long reins, with postilions, and with stud grooms wearing wigs in great [period] dress, which cannot be imagined. Seeing this parade and these horses, adorned with plumes, one feels transported to the good old times.

Our host is a part of the racing society and presides at the weighing. He's a member of the Hunt Club, a friend of Torlonia's and Pietro's, and so on. He asked permission to present Baron St. Joseph, whom we had noticed in Rome when he sat with his friends at the theater.

They served us a charming lunch and some good cold wines. St. Joseph asked permission to bring his dear friend, Clement Torlonia (who was not drunk!).

I was getting ready to see Larderel; I've been interested in him for the last two days. He is supposed to race last, with the gentlemen riders. For this event, Altamura came to take us to the stands. I went with him and Dina with Walitsky. Mama stayed in the carriage.

I bet on Larderel and was waiting for his appearance in the arena. At last he came, wearing the white satin with green stripes and green pants. I took Altamura's field glasses and examined him. Well, he is charming! Tall, well built, dark brown hair, long nose, beautiful eyes, red lips, a little blond moustache, and an interesting pale complexion—Alexander.

Torlonia was near us, complaining of fatigue. I do not talk to him because his conduct in Rome obliges me to keep a certain reserve; I only answer when he talks to me.

I bet with Altamura for the green jacket. They gave the signal. The horses started! On my soul, here was a beautiful race! I stood on my feet, not even breathing, and my jockey came in only second.

We had barely time to change to go to the Hotel d'Angleterre, where Altamura offered us a magnificent dinner.

Thanks to the change of hours, we were able to hear *La Traviata*. I left the theater tired and thoughtful. It is the first time I've heard the opera, except when I was five or six years old and did not understand it. I thought there was only *Mignon* and *Faust,* but there is *Traviata*, also music and subject—all alive and natural.

People pay attention to Verdi as they attack Dumas. Why? Because these two men amuse, move, and transport their listeners. Listen: in hearing *La Traviata* I almost cried. This music charms; it makes your heart beat faster. Sometimes it makes you dream, and sometimes the heart bleeds. It is true that it is an immoral play for men. Each young man will see a Violetta Valery in his own cocotte. Larderel will ruin himself in buying bracelets and earrings if his beloved woman has the good idea of coughing and wearing a poetic air.

I returned home dreaming. What a noisy day! So many people.

I am beginning to adore Naples, but I fear Rome . . . Rome and Pietro. Poor friend . . . why be sorry for him? I do not know, because I am sorry for myself. I want to hear him saying he loves me, with his veiled eyes and his cheek in hand.

It is good to be loved. Nothing is as good as this.

It is dangerous to hear *Traviata*; this damned music gives you ideas—I dream of Pietro, I miss him, I close my eyes, I believe him to be there, and then I get up discontented. It's strange. . . .

Friday, April 21, 1876. When I went into the salon this morning, I was stifled by the smell of flowers. The room is literally full of them—the flowers from Doenhoff, Altamura, and even from Torlonia.

We have just enough money to go to Rome—a few hundred francs. Real Bohemians. It is funny and sad.

Next Sunday we should be in Rome. Besides, everybody will be gone from Naples. Rome's horse races will be next Thursday, and all this crowd will be transferred to the Eternal City.

Altamura came around 6:00 and brought the bets he had lost—a pair of gloves for Mama and another for Dina. And guess what? He brought two ravishing glove boxes full! Let me die if I know what that man wants. He paid for the carriage yesterday and almost quarrelled with Walitsky, who wanted to pay. It is he who gave us the tickets for the races. He gives us everything in a word. He is an honorable man who is received in society; he knows all the plobsters, so we cannot have any suspicion; and anyway, why should we? But his conduct seems unnatural. The other day we found a big album of views of Pompeii!

He does not even want us to believe he's in love. He likes everybody; Walitsky is his friend, and he told Walitsky that since the first instant in Rome, he felt a great, irresistible sympathy for all of us.

Saturday, April 22, 1876. The second day of the races! There were as many people as before, and even more action.

Today I have a ravishing outfit made of white cashmere. Its blouse is open in front and trimmed with a frill. The sleeves are gathered near the elbow, and all this is trimmed with white embroidery. At the bottom, the skirt has a ruching lined with muslin and trimmed with Valenciennes lace. This ruffle is very flattering to the feet, which are in boots of yellow leather with openwork embroidery of black and gold chenille. The blouse is tied at the waist with silk ribbon, making a point in the front. It falls naturally behind, without a bow, but only crossing and fastened by a hidden hook. Around the neck is some white net, with two long parts floating behind.

We are not going to the stand except for the gentlemen's races. Altamura gave Mama his arm, and I walked alone, and then a little before I reached the stairs, they were blocked by the many tables around which the lions and lionesses of Naples were eating. I was near Torlonia, who was talking on the right . . . with Larderel. He bowed to me, and Larderel, leaning, asked him who I am.

I was happy to cross the crowd on the arm of Don Clement. He is an elegant escort, chic in all respects. He told me that the races would end early today, and I expressed my regrets, adding that I adore the races.

"But stay for the races in Rome, if you have so much liking for Rome."

"Sir, such decisions do not depend on me," I told him. After a few more words we were in the carriage. Altamura called out, "See you tonight," and Torlonia said, "Bon voyage!"

Everybody is still in town; it is still daylight, and the sunset is barely started. Everything is ready, and I am going to put on my travelling clothes. Dear Naples, goodbye; I hope! These two days of races have been the only happy ones in my whole life. I have to leave, thanking God and asking Him to continue his kindness. Amen.

Sunday, April 23, 1876. Everything was fine. We left the hotel in happy spirits, so I was amiable with Altamura and the bouquet from St. Joseph was our subject of conversation; but I am always like that, talking a lot about a little thing and developing the subject for hours. So everything was fine until 5:00, the time the train would leave.

The train started to move, and I had a last view of Larderel's pale face, but getting redder, and of the indifferent Altamura.

It was like a clap of thunder! I fell back on Dina's knees, laughing, lamenting, and beating myself with St. Joseph's flowers. And to think that I am carried away by this brutal force, by this locomotive!

Now I've been in Rome since 7:00. It is now 10:00, and raining. I detest Rome! The houses are more ugly than in Naples, the Corso is miserable after the Toledo. I hope that Larderel will come for the races here in Rome.

I am about to hear an explanation of Pietro's conduct. It is raining, but tonight we have to go to the Apollo theater, where they are playing *Juliet*.

This evening has been nothing important. I had a new dress, and the bodice fitted me so well that I've never before had a dress that fitted me so tight.

The curtain had barely been lowered when Rossi arrived in our box. It is enough to make you shiver; Rossi has become a liberal. I know the cause, but that is a story in itself.

Monseigneur de Falloux was interested in a hospital; and to finance it, he bought some land belonging to the church without asking the authorization of Monseigneur Freppel, his bishop, who was in such a rage that he excommunicated Monseigneur de Falloux, the Prefect, the Vice-Prefect, and the members of City Hall. In a word, it was such a war of priests that Monseigneur de Falloux is tempted to pass to the side of the liberals. This last guess is from me, following my conversation with Rossi. For the last month there has been a lot about it in the newspapers.

Rossi no longer wears the pin with Christ's face, and he has new clothes. He is about to become a "White"!

"And what happened to Antonelli?" he asked.

"We know nothing, Sir. He left ten days before our departure for Naples; so we did not see him any more."

"He was at the theater yesterday."

"Where was he sent?" Mama asked laughing, "and what follies has he committed?"

"I don't know, but it is always the same thing. I believe, and this is between us, strictly secret—I think that he has got himself into debt. Eh! If it were only a few thousand francs, his mother would have paid; but it is quite a large amount—50,000 francs."

"And the father will not pay?"

"In fact, yes, he will. After all, 50,000 francs is not such a big sum for him, as they are so rich! But with this debt he wants to hold the young man in check. He'll pay, but first he wants to teach him a lesson. And the little one is obliged to leave, to turn himself around everywhere, to get along as he can with all these bills of exchange."

"Ah, ah!"

"And at the present time where is he?"

"He is in Rome. I saw him at the theater. But tonight the *barcaccia* is closed because these gentlemen of the hunting club refused to pay 100 pennies more each."

Rossi has changed like a butterfly! After he stayed a long time and left, I went to sit at the back of the loge.

"Well," said Mama, "and we were already making so many guesses!"

"Well, Mama, do you believe what that Monseigneur's son said?"

"Why not? What he said is very simple. I very well believe that he went into hiding from his creditors, even . . . in a convent."

"Maybe," I said, ready to believe. "But, you see, I always draw the most unflattering conclusions."

"Oh, like me! But I assure you that we are wrong. Actually, there is nothing extraordinary about all this. Poor Pietruccio, whom we accused of all villainies possible! Poor, nice Pietruccio!"

I let myself be easily influenced by this speech, so I am quite tranquil and happy to be in Rome. Naples reminds me of Nice by its flashy and doubtful people, whereas here in Rome things are different.

"But," Dina asked, "how does it happen that you always have to fall for . . ."

"Such profligates? Is that what you mean?"

"Yes, if you like the word. I really don't know how you do it!"

"Why not? I adore them—especially Larderel. Ah! Larderel!"

Monday, April 24, 1876. I had something to tell all day; but I can no longer remember anything. I only know that on the Corso we met Antonelli twice. He was with friends. Mama asked to have the carriage stopped; he ran up to us, quite radiant and joyous, and asked whether we should be home this evening. Alas! Tonight Ristari will play Marie Stuart, and there is not one box available.

Around 10:30 I started to be anxious. At 11:00 I threw myself on the floor, I swore to stay there until he arrived. In my state it was awful; I prayed to God and suffered horribly, asking myself whether it was only a caprice. I was already full of disappointment when I heard him in the salon. I got up, thanking God with all my soul. He had heard me!

Pietro came, and I went into the salon and began to talk quite naturally, like the others.

My impatience was big, and I thought that the time to retire would never come. It comes, as everything comes in this world, sooner or later. At 1:00 Antonelli took leave of us. Mama went into her room with Dina, and Walitsky retired. I went to my room, but immediately went out again and met the man in the hall.

He was in the convent for four days and then in the countryside. At present, he is at peace with all his relations. He is going into society. He promises to be wise and think about his future. As for his love for me—not a word! I was in a rage; and even though I knew it was tactless, I was the first to talk about the matter. But he acted as if he did not understand, and politely said good night! I detained him; I don't remember what I said, but enough to be understood. I had no feeling; I leaned against the wall, closing my eyes. But finally I started to reproach him, to say that I was wrong to take anything seriously, that he is just a child, and that the best thing for him to do would be never to talk about his love. Then he told me that he can't love me because I don't love him, that I have strange theories, that I was playing with him and laughing at him. At last he said that I had a good time in Naples, that I was a coquette there as always, which proved very well that I did not love him.

He told me also that he saw me the other Sunday near the convent San Giovanni e Paolo. And to prove that, he said the truth; he told me exactly how I was dressed, and what I did. I had to tell him that he was right.

What can I say? I don't know, except that his hand avoided mine and that he wanted to leave. I said a lot of stupid things, closing my eyes, detaining him, asking useless questions, and charging that he was avoiding any explanations by saying that I do not love him; that if I did love him, it was in a funny way, with all my questions like an examining magistrate; and finally, that I only wanted to hear him saying that I am loved and then laugh about it.

My God! I've never acted more stupidly. I think that he does not love me any more. Because I was in an almost dark hallway, I abandoned my hands. I was very moved; my head was bowed, and he was laughing, saying goodbye, and telling me how serious he is now. He did not reassure me, and I fell on a chair saying that he has hurt me. I was not lying; I was telling the truth. I was very miserable, but he was not moved and did not try to comfort me. He said it is not proper for him to stay so late. I do not know why I did not crush him!

"You love me?" At last he asked.

"And you?"

"Ah! that is your way, you always make fun of me! Now I am reasonable, I am a new man."

"I can see it."

"But what do you expect when you have always told me that you did not love me?"

"Eh, at the first word should I have thrown myself in your arms?"

"But yes, of course!"

"Even if you do not love me!"

"True love does not reason. Do you love me?"

"Ah, again some conditions. Do I have to tell you that I love you?"

"Probably."

"And what will result from that?"

"What always results in such cases!"

He does not love me, and I am insane to be attracted by what eludes me. I don't feel humiliated, but I do not know what to do. Maybe it is bad to read these novels, because he does not answer like a man in one of these novels. No, he wants to stay as we are.

"Do you want me to tell you what all this means? Listen. You courted me as if I were the beautiful girl that I am. Then, seeing it was going too far, you withdrew."

I don't know what he answered, but it was nothing reassuring. I do not know how to write; I feel strange. I do not understand myself any more. I am not furious, but miserable, surprised that a human being exists who dares to receive me so coldly.

Come on! I was alone with him, my voice was trembling; I was almost saying that I loved him, and he did not take my hand. He did not lean toward me, and he did not pull me toward him!

I would not have resisted. I would have let myself go on his chest, and I would have cried; but he was changing the conversation all the time.

Walitsky was calling me, and that irritated me. This position was so false! I was in a rage, I was holding him, and finally I told him that if I had a brother here I would ask him to slap his face; but being a woman alone, I could only despise him. "I could have loved you, but your cowardly conduct has changed this feeling into my scorn for you."

He asked me what happened to me tonight that I am so different. I don't know whether I am angry, furious, or miserable! Never in my life have I found myself in such a situation.

It is 3:00, but I can't sleep; I am calm, but cold. I don't understand anything. And then I need to know what I want. *Seriously, I do not believe that I love this man.*

"I hope to come to Nice," he said.

"You never loved me," I said. "I am leaving, and you do not even care where I'm going! You knew that I was in Naples, and instead of coming to see me, you went to the country."

"Listen! I could not come and disobey when at the same time, I was making peace with my family. I could not choose to do something foolish again this time."

I told him enough to make him happy. I don't understand a thing about it. It's annoying.

Tuesday, April 25, 1876. When I opened my eyes, my first thought was, is it possible for me to forget my pride enough to conduct myself as I did? As long as I had the young and honest but crazy Pietruccio in front of me, I could act as I did; but when the moment came that it was Count Antonelli, I realized I must back off. Let's not forget that we are not children anymore, and that between a young lady and a gentleman there are many subtleties to observe. Modesty and reserve are necessary. You have no idea how much I feel ill at ease.

I was waiting with great impatience for the moment we could go out when the rain started. I have only to go to get my hearts. They are very well made. Here is one model, this one is mine. The others have no key, but are otherwise the same. The heart must be worn on an ecru ribbon of silk; when some member has done something important, she'll be permitted to wear it on a wide yellow ribbon as a pendant. On the back of the heart there is a glass for a portrait. I have already put my own portrait in mine.

It was still raining when Baron Visconti was announced. That charming man is witty in spite of his age. Suddenly they began to talk about Antonelli in the midst of a conversation about the Odescalchi marriage.

"Oh! Madame, little Antonelli, as you call him, is not a match to be despised. The poor Cardinal is getting worse from day to day, so one of these days his nephews will be millionaires, and in consequence Pietro will be a millionaire.

"But the Cardinal has a daughter?"

"Yes, but the daughter is rich, incredibly rich. She has nothing to do in this. The nephews will inherit."

"You know, Baron, I have been told the little fellow has gone to a convent!" said Mama.

"Oh, no; he has something very different on his mind, I assure you."

This evening, contrary to all expectations, there was a tolerably large gathering. Among others who came were Antonelli, Plowden, and Botkin. I did the honors of the house, and my silver heart attracted their attention and comments. By one o'clock, only Pietro was still there. We were seated at a table, and we discussed love in general and Pietro's love in particular. He has deplorable principles; or rather, he is so mad that he has none at all. He spoke so lightly of his love for me that I did not know what to think. Altogether he is not like me in character, and I find that extraordinary. . . . The debts kept him away from Rome, and as proof he offered to bring me his attorney's letters. . . . Then he said that he cannot really love.

At last we said goodbye, but my medallion has opened and I must fix it. Pietro stayed to fix it, and I don't know how—but we found ourselves in the hall.

And now, please do not read any more. I thought that this journal was moral, but you'll be disappointed in me if you continue to read.

I don't know how it started, but after five minutes we were not quarreling any more.

"Good night!" I said.

I wanted a cigarette and went to Walitsky's room for one. Pietro followed me, and then we had a reconciliation. I don't know how it happened!

After the Visconti visit, Mama told me, "You should tell him that you love him; after all, it doesn't engage you." So I was under the influence of this advice. But there was only an hour, and I don't remember what was said.

He was near me; having reassured me completely, he took my hands and waist. Coming closer to me, he said, "I will never say anything silly since that makes you unhappy. You have to excuse my character. I am crazy and thoughtless, but I swear that I love you and that I have always loved you. Besides, you've guessed it; you know it, don't you?"

I did not answer, but did not push him back either; then he pulled me toward him—do not read it; there is still time!—he kissed me on the right cheek!

Visconti's and Mama's words were still in my ears, so instead of pushing him back, I let myself go and put my arms around his neck. He put his head on my shoulder, kissing my neck on the left side and. . . . What a horror! For the first time in my life I was in the arms of a man!

"I will love you forever," he said.

"No. Leave me. What I am promising you is bad. I am doing wrong . . . go away. . . ."

But instead of letting me go, he pressed me in his arms and was looking at me in such a manner that I told him, "You remember what I told you the other day: that never . . . not even . . . nobody . . ."

"Yes, it is different with me, I love you and . . . and you love me?"

"Do you think if I did not love you I would permit this?"

(How difficult it is to tell all this!)

I don't know how, but we agreed to be married; at least he did. I was quiet most of the time.

"You are leaving Thursday."

"You'll forget me?"

"Oh, no! I'll come to Nice."

"When?"

"As soon as possible. But my father will not let me go now."

"You have to tell him the truth, and then he'll not think that you are going to Monaco."

"Yes, I'll tell him that I'm going there for you, that I love you and want to marry you. But not now; you don't know my father. At the present time, he is very good to me. I've been forgiven, but I don't dare to ask for anything. I can't now; I have no confidence yet. Think! For three years he wouldn't speak to me! In a month, I'll be in Nice."

"In a month, I'll not be there any more."

"And where *will* you be?"

"In Russia. And you'll forget me."

"No, in fifteen days I'll be in Nice and we'll go together!"

"Yes."

He took me against his heart and covered my face with kisses; I was closing my eyes not to see this abomination.

"Ah!" I exclaimed, moving away from him, "You are happy now?"

"Ah! Here you are! Always bad thoughts!"

"You know that Mama thinks I am in bed and you have left."

"Really?" he said laughing.

"Now go; only—no. Come here," and I went away, to lean on the frame of my bedroom door.

"I'll love you always. Do you love me?" he asked. I made a little gesture with my head. He was so pleased that he took me in his arms, and I pressed him against my heart, without a word.

"I love you, I love you!" he said, falling on his knees.

"Get up, Sir, I think I am going to faint." But he held me. "You are happy?" I asked; and taking his head in my hands, I passed my hands through his hair. "Tell me."

"Oh, yes," he murmured.

I gathered all my strength, and as our faces were very, very close to each other's, I took a great resolution and kissed him on the mouth—I, who had not until now even touched him lightly with my lips! And this silent first kiss lasted so long that I fell exhausted on his shoulder, held only by his arms, which, like an iron circle, were around my waist.

Two or three times I made a show of being angry, but he held me fast.

"No," he said. "We cannot leave each other every evening like this. You are not angry?"

"No, I am good, you see," I said smiling. "Enough, Sir. This is enough."

"Another kiss before I leave."

Then I went into my dark corner again; and making him swear again that he loves me, that he will come to Nice, I let him go. But he came back again.

"How thin you are!" he said, taking my waist in his hands, which enchanted me. He may have felt how little tightness there was, because my satin corset was yielding like a large blouse and could be moved.

God! it was four o'clock in the morning! I looked at my lips to see if their color had not changed. But no. See how appearances can betray!

Wednesday, April 26, 1876. I do not feel at all ashamed of what happened yesterday. Besides, it was done with such calm and indifference that I am surprised. However, it was bad, very bad. . . . And why? It shocked me, because it is new. I am deplorably positive, and I went as far as I wanted to—not a step farther.

He is like a priest: he wants, and he does not want. He loves, and he does not love. I am in a false position. He does not ask me anything. I am leaving, and he lets me go; he hopes to forget me and will not come to Nice.

The races are postponed until May 14, a fact which made us stop Pietro to inform him, and to ask him to come earlier, because we must leave at 10:00.

He dined with us, and after we started to play at packing together, which leaves one often alone. I was kneeling near the boxes, and he was near me. We always talk the same way. We argue, we take each other's hands, and we do a thousand other silly things that earlier annoyed me.

But suddenly we discovered that there was no train; and instead of going to Nice, we went to the Coliseum at 10:00. Mama did not come down from the carriage. Dina took the Russian arm, and I the Italian; and we tried to get into the ruins. But all the guards were asleep and the gates were closed. I extended the possibilities of staying longer, leaning on the arm, which supported me so nicely.

We took some tea, and then there were some things left to be packed in my room, which is open to everybody.

"How fine we would be," said Pietro, kneeling and taking my waist in his hands, because I let him do it with indifference, "How happy we should be like this alone!"

I did not answer; I had nothing to answer. I am stupid in this affair, but Pietro is also really strange.

"I see that you don't love me," he said. He is revolted by my coldness, but I can't be different. I answer by a sign of my head; I can't say aloud, "I love you," and I do not know whether I do love him. Naturally all these reasonings and all these suppositions—all these doubts which I had about him—are now also his.

I am leaving tomorrow, and all this will have an end. He wants *me* to write, and he'll write to *me!*

"I can't, Sir, what will my mother say?"

"Oh, that's true!"

But instead of his accepting that, wouldn't it be simpler to say that my mother would find nothing wrong in my writing to my fiancé?

Oh God, you have been so good to me until now; do, for pity's sake, get me out of this!

I love no one, but if I could love anybody, it would be Antonelli; and that undecided state freezes me, annoys me, insults me!

Thursday, April 27, 1876. And God took me out of it!

I went to bed at 4:30, and had only three hours of sleep. I got up fresh and well. We went to the station with Potechine and Pietro. At the point of leaving, I did not make any fuss; instead of staying with all of them, I walked back and forth in the station with the Cardinalino. Without affectation, and helped by him, I told him all I had been thinking yesterday.

With a speech, he answered, simply and neatly, "I love you and perhaps always will, to my misfortune."

"I am leaving and you don't care."

"You cannot talk like that. You do not know how much I've suffered; and anyway, far from being worried about you, I knew where you were and what you were doing. And you knew how much I had been thinking of you since I first saw you. I have changed completely, but you have always treated me like a scamp. I have committed follies in my time, so have others; that is not a reason for thinking me a good-for-nothing, a hair-brained fellow. For your sake, I have made peace with my family."

"Not for me, Sir. I don't see what I have to do with this peace."

"It is because I was thinking of you seriously."

"How so?"

"You always want me to explain myself in detail, with mathematical precision, and yet certain things are nonetheless clear for being merely hinted at; and you always make fun of me."

"That is not true."

"Do you love me?"

"Yes; and let me tell you this. I am not in the habit of repeating the same thing twice. I want to be believed at once. I have never said to any other man what I am saying to you. I am very much offended, for my words, instead of being a favor, are taken lightly and commented on. And you dare doubt what I say? Indeed, Sir, you try my patience."

He grew confused and begged me to excuse him; we scarcely spoke after this.

"You'll write to me?"

"No, Sir. I cannot, but I permit you to write to me."

"Ah!, ah! What a fine love!" he exclaimed.

"Sir," I said gravely, "do not ask too much. It is a very great favor when a lady allows a man to write to her; if you don't know that, I tell you so. But we have to get into the train. Don't let us lose our time in idle discussions. *Will you write to me?*"

"Yes, and say what you like, I feel that I love you as I shall never love again. Do you love me?"

I nodded in the affirmative.

"Will you love me always?"

I nodded again.

"Goodbye till we meet again, Sir."

"When?"

"Next year."

"No!"

"Goodbye, Sir." And without giving him my hand, I got into the railway carriage, where all our people were already settled, except for Walitsky, who was embracing Pietro. I opened the window on the side and stayed there.

"You did not give me your hand," said Antonelli, coming close.

I held out my hand.

"I love you," he said looking very white.

"*Au revoir!*" I said softly.

"Think of me sometimes," he said, getting still paler. "As for me, I do nothing but think of you."

"Yes, Sir, *au revoir!*"

The train began moving, and for some minutes I could still see him looking at me with so much emotion that it appeared like indifference; then he made a few steps toward the door, but as I was still visible, he stopped again like an automaton, pulled his hat over his eyes, made another step forwards . . . and then, and then we were already too far to see.

I did not have the time to become sad because they were talking. I took an active part in the conversation.

At the railroad station I had told him, "A woman never shows it if she loves."

"No," he said, "you are mistaken. A woman doesn't say it and doesn't want to show it, but she lets him know she does love him."

"I leave you with your friends and your club. You'll be happy."

"Oh! no. I can't live this type of life anymore. It is over for me. Maybe if you don't love me, I'll start again to forget."

"That would be bad."

I should have felt wretched at leaving Rome, which I have become thoroughly used to, had not an idea struck me in seeing the new moon toward four o'clock.

"Do you see that crescent?" I asked Dina.

"Yes" she replied.

"Well, this crescent will become a fine moon in eleven or twelve days."

"Of course."

"Have you seen the Coliseum by moonlight?"

"Yes," said Dina.

"I have not. I want to see it, and on account of that I'll go back to Rome in ten or twelve days, partly for the races, and partly for the Coliseum."

"Oh?"

"Yes, I'll go with my aunt; and it will be so nice without you and Mama, but only with Aunt. We shall drive out in a victoria, and it will be very amusing."

"Very well," said Mama, "you may go." And she kissed me on both cheeks. At 1:00 we were in Genoa, and at 2:00 in the morning we were asleep.

Friday, April 28, 1876. The house is furnished most exquisitely. My room is dazzling, all decked out in pale blue satin. In opening the door to the balcony to look out at our very pretty garden, the Promenade, and the sea, I was prompted to say aloud, "They may say what they like, but there is no other place so magnificently simple and exquisitely poetical as Nice."

Saturday, April 29, 1876. Here I am at last in this blue bedroom, for which I have sighed, and where I sigh. The Sapogenikoffs came and asked to see my "victims." Everybody gives preference to Pietro.

The weather is good. We have to go to see people and also go to stores to buy what I need for my room.

I have to fix a studio, an oratory, a library. These will be possible only after our return from Russia, when I'll bring money.

I am going to the Sapogenikoffs', where the others already are. Mr. Sapogenikoff looks as if it is the most natural thing in the world that his wife is in mourning and that she has transformed Yourkoff's room into a chapel, where, in front of the altar, made with images of saints and garnished with flowers constantly renewed, she retires ten times a day to pray and look at the bed of the poor defunct one. His nightgown is spread on the bed as if he were coming home to sleep.

This man was either one of the most vile or else an angel from heaven. Nina is swollen and yellow. She eats nothing except potatoes and tea.

After Yourkoff had killed himself, some people from Monaco locked him in the morgue and did not want to acknowledge that he was there until the Consul demanded the information and found the letter which the unfortunate man had written to Nina, telling her he was killing himself.

They used to look at him as a relative; and Mary, seeing him dead so suddenly and from such a terrible death, was pale and trembling and crying.

So, do you know what has been said? It has been said that Yourkoff, after he had been her mother's lover, was the daughter's lover, and pursued by Nina's jealousy, he decided to kill himself!

Poor little girls, angels of patience and indulgence who are living quietly at home, outside society and never seeing anyone, simple and modest; but people find a way to accuse them with the most atrocious slanders!

My God, I am so horrified at these undeserved calumnies and above all, suffering this scorn, that I pray YOU, Lord, have pity on me! Who knows what can be said of me?! This chills me.

We all dined together after, remembering "the good old times." I went with Olga to my house, and at her request told her about Rome, or rather, read her the Journal. It pleases me to see her interested, as if by a novel, and I was flattered.

Sunday, April 30, 1876. The weather is bad. Giro spent the morning with us after I went to her home, and then we went to the concert, where we saw Galula, very happy to see us and, as always, full of wit. There is nobody here. It is a desolation. We have no desire to do anything.

I hope that Pietro did not take my kiss as a caress from a young girl. I think that a kiss on the lips is the most complete consent, the most solemn oath in the world. I am too proud to speak about my love; I said it all with my kiss. I hope he understood all the seriousness that I attach to it. Maybe he does not. He does not understand the sublimity in love. He is intelligent, but does not understand these things as I do.

The idea that the most sacred moment for me passed unnoticed by him makes me sad. He saw it only as a kiss that pleased him, and the next day he asked me if I loved him. He would not have asked that if he had understood. I do not say that I love him, but I want him to believe that I do; and he did not understand!

He has not yet written to me. Three days of absence! I have had an itch on the nose for a week. Is the Cardinal's death being announced?

Monday, May 1, 1876. As for Antonelli, he has already forgotten me; he told me that he could not love for a long time, and after five days he would have forgotten me. I do not regret him, but my self-esteem and my interest as to whether he is really a millionaire are involved.

Tuesday, May 2, 1976. He told me everything from the time of his captivity at the convent. The Superior had been informed that the man who would be coming was most scoundrelly, and they were surprised to see a very polite gentleman. They were so surprised that they sent somebody to the Count to say that he had made a mistake and had sent the wrong man.

"And I was hitting the shutters to attract your attention, but you were looking the other way. I was on top of the tower, at the big window."

I did not know how to draw out confidences from others; now I do. We bring them out by offering our own confidences. I read part of my journal to Olga, and she became more truthful and was ready to spit in Antonelli's face.

Never in my life have I laughed so much as I have with Olga. She and her mother are my favorites of the family. Nina is charming in her type, honest to exaggeration. She was seen everywhere with Yourkoff. She could have done differently, like other women. Then nobody would have accused her. But her husband has an awful disease, which covers him with sores. In a word, he is *rotten*.

It is too bad they are leaving on Sunday, but nothing holds them here. Nina's position is awful. Think of having to be in the middle of her husband's family—people who will have only reproaches for her offences, and she herself, without a friendly soul near her!

The poor Uncle Antonelli is ill, and I fear that he'll die.

Wednesday, May 3, 1876. For the last three days the wind has been bad, and I like to stay home. I am bored. I took a book of J. J. Rousseau's *La Nouvelle Héloïse,* but after a few pages I was disgusted. As for *Émile* [Rousseau's book on education], I read it in honor of the Surprising One and found a few good ideas, but many useless dissertations.

Yesterday, after lunch, I read *La Dame aux Camelias.* I was expecting something better, after all that's been said about it. I read some comedies by Shakespeare, but I find nothing more amusing than the Dumas novels and the masterpieces of Plutarch. The writers from the XVIII century disgust me, and the antique ones put me to sleep. But if I have the strength to surmount the first impressions, I can't tear myself from the book, and that has happened many times.

How has J. J. Rousseau been classified among the writers of merit? How is it that intelligent people did not hang him and burn his books, which are so bad and full of poison? And to think that these horrible books are bound in red and have my monogram in gold! But I will not tear them.

Thursday, May 4, 1876. I have not been in Nice a week, but it seems a month!

After an unavoidable quarrel with Papa, I went for a stroll in the garden. The moon was still young, the frogs were croaking, the murmur of the waves came softly as they broke on the pebbles, and divine silence ruled with divine harmony.

Naples is considered a marvel, but for my part I prefer Nice. Here the sea bathes the shore without any hindrance; in Naples it is stopped by a wall with a stupid balustrade, and even this wretched bit of seaboard is obstructed by shops, stalls, and other nuisances.

"Think of me sometimes. As for me, I shall do nothing else but think of you!"

Oh! God forgive him, for he knew not what he was saying! I've allowed him to write, but he does not avail himself of this permission! Will he even send the promised telegram to Mama?

Friday, May 5, 1876. The races in Rome have been postponed until the eleventh or the fourteenth; so there is time to receive the telegram. I have been writing to the manager of the hotel to place some orders in Rome.

I went out with Mary, and we were back at 1:30 and did not move afterwards. I am bored. One cannot read all day. There are always a few hours required for the new outfit and the Promenade, and it is during these few hours that I am more bored, because I know there is nobody outside. This city is full of insupportable animals—Galulas and Saëtones.

After dinner we all went walking to the Sapogenikoffs'. I had no hat, but only a Bedouin hood like the Turks from the oriental store.

Ah! scoundrel of an Antonelli! However, I should not accuse him completely . . . if he does not write to me. He is so little sure of my changing mood, and I did nothing to reassure him. I never heard a word coming from my heart, but I was asking his forgiveness at the station, telling him, "Really, Sir, you are talking in such an undecided way, so light—so strange . . ."

"I do not want to speak like Bruschetti, and I never talk 'like everybody,'" he interrupted me . . .

I was saying that Pietro was excusable, being very sure of himself. And then he may not dare; I can't understand, because I, myself, do not love.

In certain novels I have read that men in love seem indifferent and forgetful because of their love.

I am sleepy and annoyed, and when I am in that state I always want to see Pietro, to hear him talking about love. I would like to dream a beautiful dream. Reality is dangerous!

The garden is full of daisies, and I play "he loves me, he loves me not" all the time, asking whether he'll come. They say yes, but can we believe them?

I am bored, and when I am bored I am very tender. Ah, when will this state of dullness, disappointment, envy, and vexation come to an end! Ah, when shall I live as I'd like to—when I am married to a great fortune, to a great name, and to a sympathetic man? For I am not a mercenary as you think. But if I am not, it is because I am an egoist. It would be horrible to live with a man one hated, and neither wealth nor position would avail me anything. May God and the Holy Virgin protect me!

Saturday, May 6, 1876. Today is the opening of the exposition of flowers at the Villa Borghese. The Princess will be there, and everybody else. I prefer to be in Nice because there I could not be as I want, comfortably.

It is a pity to be here, alone in front of my mirror, when I've an angel complexion, pink ears, and golden hair! I am almost in a rage about it. I'll not go out.

Oh! my lips soiled! soiled! I accuse only myself; he would never have dared. And the worst thing is that he did not understand, not anything—that a contact . . . I put in his kiss much love, so much that I fell breathless on his shoulder and hid my face and eyes on the black woolen of his jacket, the one he had worn on the eve of Carnival, and the same he wore when at the opera.

This evening I am giving a party such as has not been seen for years in the Rue de France. You must know there is a custom for celebrating May in Nice; they hang up a garland and a lantern, and dance in a circle and sing. Since Nice has become French, this custom has been more or less neglected, and now you scarcely see three or four lanterns in the whole town.

Well, as for me, I give them a *rossignol;* I call it that because the "Rossignol che Vola" [the flying nightingale] is the most popular song in Nice, and the prettiest.

I have prepared a big chain, consisting of foliage and flowers, and suspended it across the street, decorated with Venetian lamps. Triphon has been entrusted with the preparation of fireworks and charged to light up the scene from time to time with Bengal fire. Triphon is beside himself with joy. All these splendors are accompanied by a flute, a harp, and a violin, and cheered with wine in abundance. Some kind neighbors came to ask us to come to their terrace, for Giro and I were looking over the wall, perched on a wooden ladder.

We went to the neighbor's terrace, and Giro, Marie, Dina, W., and I went into the middle of the street, calling the dancers, trying hard, and succeeding in putting spirit into the thing.

I sang and danced with everybody to the delight of the good Niçois, especially the people of our quarter, who all know me and cannot say enough in praise of "Mademoiselle Marie."

Not knowing what else to do, I made myself popular; and it flatters Mama. She does not consider the expense. What pleased them more than anything was my singing and saying some words in their *patois.*

While I was standing on the ladder with Giro, who was pulling me by my skirt, I felt much inclined to make a speech; but I prudently refrained for this year.

I looked at the dancing and listened to the cries, all dreaming, as has happened so often for me. And when the fireworks ended in a magnificent Catherine wheel, we all returned home, accompanied by a murmur of satisfaction.

It is too bad that Nina and Giro are leaving. I love them and they love me. They left at 11:00 asking me to meet them tomorrow at 8:00 at the station. When Giro and I walked in the garden, we recalled our escapades at night, our disguises.

And here I am in my room, dressed with Beatrice Cenci's dress—without the turban. I am not happy; maybe Pietro has forgotten the cable he promised to send me.

"You know," said Mama this morning, "you could think a little about your other parent. You could go into society [there], whereas with us that is impossible. I am telling you clearly."

And of course! I am going to my father, because I can't take it any more. It will be a mortal sorrow for Mama and my aunt, it will be very disagreeable, but I am dying here ten times a day, and I am at the end of my strength.

My mother must go to live with her husband, because when taking the father, I disown and accuse the mother, which is impossible for me, not for my feelings, but for the world, for society. Ah! I assure you my position is not the easiest. Dog of a dog! Who will pull me out of it? GOD.

Also I did not forget to beg Him every night, on my knees, and all my days standing, seated, or in a carriage. I hope that He hears me, and He must know that I am not satisfied to pray only in the evening and that all my thoughts are supplications!

Sunday, May 7, 1876. At 8:00 we were at the station, and the Sapogenikoffs and Collignon met us. I was a little sleepy, but anyway I posed a little for the fat Borreel, who was leaving with his mother. I was walking with Giro, and my aunt was seated on a bench with poor Nina in mourning.

Must we leave each other? I regret so much these charming ones with whom I performed my first follies and who have so often made me forget my torment, the mortal sorrow that is eating me.

"It has been my most happy time," said Giro. "What do you say, Bibi?"

We called each other by our most "riffraff" names before separating, so as to remember our last year together.

I really regretted only when I saw them all, in the train, passing and shouting all together their goodbyes and regrets, some memories, some hopes to see each other again, and some promises to write.

"Each time you pass in front of our church," said Nina, "sign yourself in memory of me. I've suffered a lot here." I bowed and said nothing.

"Give this rose to Dina," said Giro when the train was already moving.

"Yes," I said picking up the flower and giving it to Dina.

Then I went to the end of the station, opened my white parasol, and waved it in the sun so that it would be more visible to our dear travellers, who were waving their pocket handkerchiefs.

Then all of us, with Collignon and Walitsky, returned to take some tea.

Monday, May 8, 1876. It is raining, and I pass my day playing the piano and reading, and above all, complaining, laughing, and crying so much that we all laughed. In the evening we again talked about the Sapogenikoffs and Yourkoff, and the whole affair.

My principal thought is the telegram.

Pietro loves me, but reason dictates to him to be humble and obedient toward his parents, who are not against his project; but they want to hold their young tormentor, who has given them so many troubles.

This wisdom and obedience of Pietro hurts me. I am a coward to make excuses for him. I *must* receive the telegram tomorrow!

My heart beats faster at the thought that tomorrow my doubts will cease for the best or the worst. Besides, I agree to accept the humiliation, provided that nobody knows about it. It could compromise me, not in front of other men. Fie! But society—the dirty brutes who compose what we call the human race—they would judge me.

Tuesday, May 9, 1876. I must say that no cable has been received. And when I think that at each letter, at each ringing of the bell, I blushed and became confused . . .

I am only seventeen, but I see that it would have been better for my pride to be always alert and never to have said what could prevent an honorable retreat.

"Everything is calculated with you," said Antonelli." (And how *not* to be calculating when you are with a scoundrel?) I thought he loved me.

Well, I was about to forget to tell that I went to the convent of the Bon Pasteur, to bring the Pope's portrait, beautifully framed, and the blessed rosaries. The nuns kissed my hand, and the Mother Superior opened the grill of her parlor and kissed me three times. And I stayed talking with her of such serious and religious things that I went out dazed. Can you believe me capable of discussing such matters? Finally the poor caged woman told me that I was under the Virgin's protection because I was in white. May it please Heaven!

Tomorrow I am going to Rome, as much to divert myself as to despise Antonelli, if I have the opportunity. I need that for my own peace. As for the kiss, I do not cry about it any more. It has pleased me, and such innocent pleasure does not hurt. I was more tranquil, I have nothing to reproach myself for. I am not tormented by my conscience, but only by the fear of gossip. Besides, what is the use of being irreproachable, since people make up stories anyway? Amen.

BOOK SIXTY

Book 60
From Wednesday, May 10, 1876
To Saturday, May 20, 1876
Hotel de la Ville, Rome
Book 59 is lost and I am panic-stricken that someone may have stolen it! But who? I just missed it when reading again (1882). It is a question of my departure from Naples to Rome, and from Rome to Nice. I thank God that during that time I did not see Antonelli. Otherwise something bad could have been said about me. I thought I would suppress the book, but it is so funny! Where could it be lost?
Found again. 1882. Found.

Thursday, May 11, 1876. As I said last Tuesday, we left yesterday at 3:00, without any obstacle and without any scene, in which I see God's kindness and that of the Holy Virgin. I left only with my aunt, gay and satisfied.

It is a terrible proof of love I seem to be giving Pietro. Ah, so much worse, if he thinks I love him! If he thinks anything so monstrous, he is only a brute, as are all those who could believe I would love them.

At two o'clock we were in Rome. I jumped into a fiacre; my aunt followed me; the driver of the omnibus of the Hotel de la Ville took the tickets, etc. . . . and I am in Rome! God, what a joy!

I am in Rome! Ah, what a joy! You cannot understand how much better I feel here than in Nice! It's the first time I've drawn a full breath in fifteen days! No, that's too silly!

Our luggage will arrive tomorrow. In order to see the races, we must be satisfied with our travelling dresses. However, I looked very good in my grey outfit and felt hat. I took my aunt to the Corso. How delightful to see the Corso again, after Nice!

And here was the Caccia Club. There was a thrill of excitement as I passed, and the monk stood, gasping open-mouthed and then taking off his hat, smiling from ear to ear. St. Joseph was next to him and bowed, looking not very surprised. Then, thank God! I saw Larderel alone!!

Larderel alone! Do you understand! Farther on, Simonetti, Rossi, and finally . . . Torlonia, who stopped short, smiling with his angelic smile. On the word of a woman! He has an angelic smile.

Then Bruschetti, alone, on foot. Pietro was in grey and very dirty and pale. I have told you that Cesaro and Antonio would corrupt him. Well, at last I hope it is going to end.

This silly Pietro is going to imagine a lot of things, and that bothers me. It is he who should come to Nice; he must be proud, and that is very natural, but it is also vexing. If he could see deep into my mind, he would not be so proud!

My aunt, or rather her vanity, is waiting for tonight—Antonelli's visit. So am I, but without much anxiety. He did not come, and at 11:00 I went quietly to bed, laughing and thinking of my trip to Rome.

Friday, May 12, 1876. We went to the dear Spellman's, and then to Saint Peter's to show it to my aunt, who is stupefied by it. There is a greater pleasure than seeing things by yourself; it is showing to others what we have already seen. After Saint Peter's, we went to the Borghese Gardens, where the Agricultural Fair is still going on. We walked through the exhibition, admiring the flowers and plants, and there we met Zucchini. There were still a good many people at Spellman's, and they seemed surprised at seeing me appear for the third time. I am well-known in Rome.

We stopped at the Pincio. Simonetti came close, and I introduced him to Mrs. Romanoff and told him that it is owing to a wonderful accident that I am here.

Pietro did not come to the Pincio. We saw him in a fiacre at the knees of two other gentlemen. He left them in front of the Hotel de Rome; I gave him a sign to come, and he quite beamed, looking at me with eyes that showed he has taken everything very seriously and remembers everything, poor ass.

Antonelli came to us, and after he had gone my aunt said he was charming and that she was enchanted by him. That's the effect he has on everybody! He made us laugh a great deal by describing his stay at the convent. He said he had agreed to stay four days, and once he was there they detained him for seventeen!

"Why did you lie? Why did you say you had been at Terracina?"

"Because I was ashamed to tell the truth."

"And your friends at the club know about it?"

"Yes. At first I said I had been at Terracina, and then they talked to me about the convent, and at last I told them everything and I laughed; everybody laughed. Torlonia was enraged."

"Why?"

"Because I didn't tell him everything at first, because I didn't confide in him."

Afterwards he told us that, to please his father, he pretended to let a rosary fall out of his pocket as if by accident, to make him believe that he always carried one about with him. I assailed him with sarcasm and impertinent speeches, which he parried very well.

I was enraged to know that he looks at me as a woman who loves him, and I repented having done and said what I did the other evening.

I continue to talk about Larderel, and Pietro asked if I wanted to meet him.

"A lot, because I like him very much, only I fear being involved in scandal," I said, and my aunt added to this a speech on the conduct of young men and on the impossibility of my meeting such a scoundrel.

Pietro defended my friend Alexander, and I laughed. All this is very funny, but sad. Antonelli thinks that I'll wait for him eternally, because I do not assume that he dared to joke. We must send for Visconti.

What a pity that Pietro is such a smart animal and has such good manners! Besides, he is like that because he feels he is loved. I would like to be able to despise him to see what face he'd have. I say *to be able* not because my heart is weak for him, but because I fear losing his adoration and maybe something else. I am not sure of myself.

Saturday, May 13, 1876. I went with my aunt to the Coliseum, the surrounding ruins, and the church of San Giovanni in Laterano.

There were many people at the Borghese. As for the Pincio, we saw Plowden there, surprised to meet my aunt. He'll come tonight. And there was Antonelli in a fiacre with Larderel, both wearing light coats. Does he really think of introducing him? Not very seriously, because leaving him, he came to us. I told him that it is evidence of bad taste to be seen with Larderel.

"I am going to bring him to you," he said.

"I accept, if you think that he is very proper."

Twice he walked a few steps as if to go to get Larderel, who was near us, but my aunt and I restrained him each time.

"Listen," I said, "introduce my dear Larderel to me, only promise me that he'll never talk to me when anyone else is present."

"But how do you want me to guarantee that! I told you that Larderel does not move in society; that he has been expelled from all the clubs."

"So, you see!"

"But he is a very personable man."

"Your companion!"

During all this talk the "hero" was walking back and forth.

At 7:00 we went to Spellman's, I, hoping to see Larderel, because I am angry at what happened. Antonelli brought me some roses.

He has forgotten? *Forgotten!!!* No doubt, since he carried on an indifferent kind of conversation interspersed with words said in such a low tone that I could not catch them! Besides, he said again that he only loved me when I was near him, that I was made of ice, that he should go to America, that he is in love when he sees me, but forgets when I am away.

I begged him very coldly not to speak of it again! And you see for yourself what my feelings must be and how deeply I am insulted!

Never a clear word! Always fleeting sentences on indifferent subjects, his looks insulting by their ardor, his attempts to press my hand or touch my foot, as if I were a nobody, I don't know *who!*

If I were going into society, he would have more respect for me.

I have never been so miserable. Before, it was only my imagination, as with Émile; but here I am really humiliated! It is impossible to be understood. My straight, frank words have not impressed his foxy, impossible mind. I can't make myself understood. I want to be calm, but my chest is oppressed, crying; and my head is on fire. I can't breathe. I can't find space in these two rooms, and I am crying like a child. Oh, no—like an offended woman in her pride!

Tonight I think he asked me if I loved him. I did not hear or understand. After I said yes and gave him my kiss, he stole away.

I've made a mistake—this journal cannot serve as instruction to anyone, because there is not another creature as weak and as tormented as I.

Now I feel better. Tomorrow the races. And Antonelli has been invited by my aunt for noon. Tomorrow I'll be with him as he is with me, if I have the strength. God will give me that strength; I'll pray for it.

Well, I am calm, able to reason and to write. What an awful habit!

Antonelli has splendid eyes. I am capable of sleep.

I am going to close by saying simply that I am inexperienced, weak, and very young— or what is more probable, very much in love. However, no—because when he was frank, I was very happy and not in love!

Sunday, May 14, 1876. Yesterday, as I was lamenting having missed the opportunity to meet Larderel, Antonelli told me, "It's your fault. You let the moment pass when nobody was at the Pincio."

At noon Antonelli came to see us. He seemed very indecisive and languid. I talked very little, and I was very happy to go to eat at Spellman's.

It was raining. We talked very little, or about the bad weather. The stands were almost empty. Princess Margherita was dressed in white. (Now it is the fashion!) Larderel's jockey fell. He ran to pick him up, followed by a crowd and also by Pietro, who came to give us a report of the accident.

I saw Larderel walking with his jockey. This seemed to me so nice that I am crazy about him. He ran, himself. And in his jockey costume, which is ridiculous and without chic, he is a hundred times better than dressed.

My right foot felt a soft pressure, and my left foot was against his right foot. We said nothing, but from time to time the pressure became stronger, so that when I got out of the carriage at 7:30 in the evening, my feet were cold because this mute caress was missing. There was a crowd at the Corso, and Bruschetti, with insane looks, wanted to seem dignified and severe. I was angry to walk like that with Antonelli, as there is enough gossiping without that. He was telling us all his adventures in the convent and ended by saying that the convent had made him half dazed during the seventeen days, and that if they had kept him longer, he would have stayed forever.

At 9:00 Simonetti came bringing us tickets to a concert by Rome's musical society and the compliments of Cavalier Rossi.

I talked and made tea as well as I could until half-past ten. Then Pietro came; Simonetti left soon afterwards, and we three remained. We spoke of my journal—that is, of the subjects which I treat in it—and Antonelli begged me to read him something on the soul and God. So I went into the antechamber and knelt down by the famous white box, looking for what I wanted, while Pietro held a candle. As I found certain passages of mutual interest while turning over the leaves, I read them out and went on for about half an hour. One moment I felt his breath on my hair because I was reading with my head lowered. And far from running away, I did not move, or he either.

All I heard this evening—the conclusions I am forced to draw and what happened before—seems like a weight for my head to carry. Then there is also the simple regret of seeing him go away this evening; it is so long till tomorrow! I felt a great inclination to weep from uncertainty, and perhaps . . . from love.

Then I began writing, but feeling irresistibly impelled to think, I left off for a moment and wrote all I have just put down.

Going to my bathroom, I discovered some wooden bars which prevent entrance to a little winding staircase. I am rushing to write in my journal: I took a candle and, moving the bars aside, I went down eight steps and found another little door which, when opened, showed me the first landing of our staircase. Here is a free passage; the little staircase is directly behind my bedroom door, a little door hidden in the draperies of poor red damask, left over from a grandiose past.

I did not know how this passage could be useful; but as I was taking up this journal I was saying to myself, "Now Antonelli has just to ask for a secret conversation, and he will have it!" But he'll not ask for it, and he has nothing to tell me. He has been forbidden to think of me.

Anyway, I am not angry to have discovered the way to go out or to have the man come into the room where the little door and winding staircase are, because I cannot think of letting him come secretly to my apartment. Do not fear, dear animals who will never read me; you are afraid? Well, one needs a little fear to maintain the interest. I assure you, you are wrong; but the more I assure you, the more you doubt. That's what I want.

My God, have pity on me this time! After he has pulled out a consent and a kiss, he curtseys and withdraws!!! It is almost 4:00, and I'm afraid I'll be ill from staying up so late.

Monday, May 15, 1876. At the moment I am going to Katorbinsky's studio. [The model] came yesterday and we decided to work today, tomorrow, and after tomorrow to finish the woman on a red background.

I painted until 5:00, telling Luisette some stories about a Saint whom I was surprised she did not know about—San Zucchini. This name must have something magical about it, because the girl started to laugh and repeated the name over and over.

At 6:00 we went to the Corso because now there is no use thinking about the Pincio. It is pouring rain. On the Corso we met Antonelli; and after a few minutes of hesitation, I ordered the carriage to stop, and I asked Pietro if he would like to come for dinner at our house.

"But how can I inform my mother?" he asked, indecisively.

"If you don't know how to do it, don't come," I said, painfully, holding back my scorn, or rather the pity he inspires in me.

"Oh, no!" he said, "I'll write as I did the other time." And we took him with us.

The dinner ended at 8:00, and my aunt went to dress, leaving me to keep company with Antonelli, who was having a cup of coffee.

As soon as we were alone and seated on the sofa, he at the extreme right and I at the extreme left, he started to look at me, not talking.

Then he tried, but in vain, to take my hand and started to complain, saying that I am more beautiful than ever and that he loves me more than ever.

"Besides," he said, "with me it is a question of habit; now I am used to seeing you, and I'll be miserable when you leave."

"Listen, Sir," I said, half smiling, "I cannot prevent your thinking that way, but I can forbid your telling it to me; and I am forbidding it."

"But what is bad about it?" he asked.

"There is a lot wrong. Enough!"

At that moment, the noise of a tray in the next room reminded us to move again to each pole of the sofa, laughing about the maneuver.

"I love you so much," he said, when the servant was gone.

"Let's not talk about this any more, I ask you. I should have told you long before this."

"And why? When I am telling you that I love you . . ."

"What love? I am leaving and you do not care!"

"Oh, no! Only what can I do about it? Do you want me to go against my family, my father, my brothers?"

"What are you saying, Sir? How do you mean, go against your family?"

At that moment my aunt had the stupidity to enter, urging me to go and dress.

"Well," I said, "would you like to stay to see me dressed up?"

"With pleasure."

Half an hour later, I appeared with a train so long that there was a general scream of surprise, and Potechine, who had arrived during my absence, raised his arms.

My summer-white pelisse looks very much like a priest's robe, and before putting it on I gave it to Antonelli to hold and sang him some songs from the funeral mass, which put him in a rage. And at 9:00 my aunt and I had to leave.

The lobby was full, and we were quite embarrassed, all alone; but the commissaries rushed and placed us very well in the second row. That is really too close. The chorus was composed of 150 people, accompanied by a large orchestra.

All the public is "Black" [of the Church party], and their women are dressed so badly with their multicolored chiffons that it is pitiful. As for the chorus, it is placed on a kind of balcony, and there the women's dresses presented an agreeable mixture of white, pink, and blue.

I am leaving next Wednesday. But to leave and have things left in the same state!! My aunt entered just at the moment that I was . . . Ah! damn! God, please arrange this.

Tuesday, May 16, 1876. The weather is beautiful, but I am sad. I want to go into society. I am afraid that this feeling could be interpreted as futile as wanting to go dancing. If you knew how much I suffer, you would pity me. If I talk, if I laugh, if I sing, it is to dazzle myself, to forget.

Wednesday, May 17, 1876. I have a lot to tell, but everything fades before this evening. I am still afraid and trembling.

Pietro said he had to leave.

As if nothing had happened, we soon went to the antechamber, and from there to the landing, which is a very little oval salon. To recall this conversation is impossible. He took me ten times in his arms, by force.

At last I explained to him all my scruples, all my doubts, everything.

As for what I said of the kiss, he didn't give a damn, just continued to tell me that he loves me. Then I assured him that it was useless, because my parents would never consent.

"They would be right," he said dreamily, "I am not good enough to make anyone happy. I told my mother; I talked about you. I said, 'She is so religious and good, and I believe in nothing; I am only a miserable unbeliever.' Look; I stayed seventeen days in the convent; I prayed; I meditated; I do not believe in God. Religion does not exist for me; I do not believe in God!"

I looked at him with big, scared eyes.

"You must believe," I said, passing my hand over his shoulders. "You must change. You must be good."

"It is impossible; and as I am, nobody can love me. Isn't that it?"

"Hmm!"

"I am very miserable. You never will have an idea of my position. As far as appearance goes, I seem to be on good terms with my people. I hate them all; my father, my brothers, my mother herself; I am most unhappy. And if you ask me why, I don't know . . . oh, those priests!" he exclaimed, gnashing his teeth, clenching his fists, and turning his face, disfigured with hatred, to heaven. "The priests! Oh, if you knew what they are like!"

It took him five minutes to calm down.

"Yet I love you, and you only. When I am with you, I am happy. If I could stay with you for many days, I'd love life. . . . But no. I am tired of everything. I want nothing. I'll retire into this convent and spend the rest of my life there."

"It is best for you. But you know, I have never seen so much impertinence!"

"How is that?"

"How! You talk to me about love, you ask if I love you, and then you say you'll never marry! This position is original and exceptional. I wanted to be angry, but I laugh. Maybe afterwards I'll cry from humiliation, but for now I am amused! See, we cannot be in accord; you look upon as nothing what I look at as an important event. It is difficult to tell, but since I am at it . . ."

"Well?"

"It is difficult. . . . I am going to teach you what you do not know. The lips of a young girl are sacred. I kissed you on the mouth!"

"When?"

"I told you that I loved you!"

"When?"

"You very well know."

"Yes. This evening by chance, when passing by, after two hours of discussion."

"No matter."

"It is true, I love you very much!"

"Give me proof!"

"Ask for one."

"Come to Nice."

"You make me feel beside myself when you say that. You know very well that I can't."

"Why?"

"Because my father won't give me any money; because my father does not want me to go to Nice."

"I quite understand, but suppose you tell him why you want to go?"

"He won't hear of it. I have talked to my mother. They are so used to my bad habits that they don't believe me any more."

"You must mend your ways; you must come to Nice."

"But since I shall be refused, as you say?"

"I have not said that I would refuse you."

"Ah! it would be too much," he said, looking closely at me. "It would be a dream. Oh, yes!"

"Then ask your father's leave."

"He doesn't want to give it."

"Does he know me?"

"Yes. He does not want me to get married. He insists affairs of this kind ought to be arranged for us by our father confessors."

"Well, let them do so."

"It is you who say so?"

"Yes. You understand, I do not care for you, but I want to give this little satisfaction to my wounded pride."

"So that is what you are!"

"My God, yes!"

"I am a wretch and accursed on earth. I told you at the Campidoglio what I am. I talked seriously."

"I am sorry for you, really."

"Thanks."

"Don't you have anything that belongs to you?"

"Nothing."

"But one day you will have something?"

"Yes, at my father's death, I'll have something like 12,000 francs a year."

"But that is nothing!"

"Don't I know it!"

"So your father is not rich?"

"He has maybe 70,000 francs a year."

"How sorry I am for you, Sir; do you know that I'll have 50,000 francs a year, and I think of myself as poor? You are right. I'll not take you; you are too poor. That's too bad."

It is impossible to follow these hundreds of phrases in detail. I shall only say that he repeated a hundred times that he loved me, in such a soft voice and with such imploring eyes that I went close to him on my own accord, and that we spoke like excellent friends of a number of things. And I assured him that there is a God in heaven and happiness on earth, and that I want him to believe in God and to see Him with my eyes and pray to Him with my voice.

"Then it is all over," I said, turning away: "*Adieu!* I am sorry to have let things go this far; I should have seen what you are."

"I love you! I do not want to make you unhappy; with me you would not have any happiness or peace."

"I believe you," I said, taking his hands, "and I am sorry."

"It is already a lot for me, and I thank you."

"So, *adieu*. I am leaving, I'll marry in Russia and will come to see you in your convent."

"Yes, and I'll court you."

"See how you are! And far from throwing you out, I'll call you; I have a weakness for you, and to my shame I acknowledge it."

"You love me?"

"Probably."

"You love me?" He pulled me toward him, talking so close to me that his lips touched my cheek!

"And you?"

"Yes!"

"Ah!" I said half laughing, half crying, "I am leaving, and in two days you'll not think of me."

"Well, that is true! When I see you I love you like mad, and when I do not see you, I forget!"

"It is because you do not love."

"I love!"

"It is not true love."

"It is the greatest of my life! Do you love me?"

"But yes!"

A strange thing—I had no fear or shame.

"Will you never love me?"

"When you are free."

"When I'll be dead!"

"I can't love you at present, for I pity and despise you. Why, if they told you not to love me, you would obey them."

"That is true."

"It is awful!"

"I love you," he said for the hundredth time, taking me in his arms. I let him do it, enraptured and beside myself, leaning on his chest, speechless and not breathing during the time his lips were running on my cheek.

I do not know how long this lasted, a long time I believe, but never too much. He was all trembling and did not dare to move nor say a word in order not to break the charm. I was in ecstasy and happy as I have never been before, when this man (Jesus, have pity) pulled me closer to him; and I felt his hand sliding along my dress in such a way that I backed up, as if jolted by lightning. All my blood withdrew from my face. I knew this because he seemed frightened.

"Oh!" I shouted after a moment, covering my face with my hands, full of terror, shame, and rage, backing up toward the window.

"I also need some fresh air," he said. "Well, take your hands from your face. How beautiful you are! No, not now; you are ugly, all red," he was saying in a staccato voice. More and more troubled, he said, "Well, what is it? Why don't you answer? Oh! please, Marie, one word, Marie, Marie, answer me. Have pity on me!"

"My God," I murmured, still bewildered. And as he tried to take my hand, "Back up!" I said, looking at him with disgust, anger, pain, and surprise.

"Forgive me! I am crazy. It is not my fault. There are times when we are not ourselves. I love you. It is love that drives me insane! Forgive me! Forgive me!"

"No," I said softly, again covering my face for a few instants. "I do not know what I am saying," and I returned to the salon with a calm face, saying in Russian that the monk had confided in me some interesting things.

One must not forget that I was dealing with an Italian—a Roman—and that his lips are as ready for kisses as his knife is for striking.

As soon as I could [after everyone left], I rushed to my little secret stairs. After a second, he appeared on the stairs, and I half opened the little door.

"Here it is," I said, leaning against the door. He came close and took my hands.

"I came," I said to him, trembling more, "to tell you *adieu*."

"Not *adieu*!"

"Yes, Sir, *adieu*. I loved you until tonight."

"It is impossible!"

"That's the way it is!" I said, weaker and weaker, "but now I despise you. Ah! too bad I said it. I loved you, I was wrong, I know."

"You do not want me to come again?" he asked.

"Yes," I said quickly, but weakening; I leaned against the wall murmuring: "No! We must not see each other anymore. That is why I am here. What I am saying hurts me a lot," I said, swallowing a torrent of tears and sighing, which hurt me more than a groan. I wanted to draw him to me and take his head in my hands and kiss him on the mouth for the second and last time. I was frantic, but my aunt knew I was there. I had told her—she could open the door—but I did not want her to know anything.

"It is not possible," Antonelli was saying, holding my hands.

"It is possible, I do not know why I did not push you away from the stairs, head first!"

"Somebody!" he said, looking toward the door. In fact we could hear the steps of the doorman.

"Wait a minute; come here," I said, looking at him. He kissed my hands.

"Marie, Marie!" shouted my aunt from upstairs.

I made an impatient gesture, and Antonelli, in anxiety, said, "Goodbye!"

I did not answer, but quickly went upstairs.

"Where were you?" asked my aunt.

"Downstairs with Antonelli."

"Why?"

"To talk."

"Tell me."

I sat and told her a lot of silliness to laugh at; the confidences of the monk. After that, I locked myself in and threw myself on the sofa, shouting: "Jesus, Lord. Have pity on me"; and I sobbed, got up, my eyes all dry with not one tear.

"You asked me to talk to my father," said Antonelli, just before leaving. "I'll do it, and I'll come to Nice at all costs. I promise you," and he left.

Thursday, May 18, 1876. At noon my aunt came to see me and told me that downstairs there was an old man who looked like Visconti, whom I had described to her. I sent him a note yesterday, and she was sure it was he. I had barely time to jump out of bed and dress before the Baron was announced. After two minutes, I entered the salon, introducing my aunt and relating our meeting in Genoa and my unexpected return.

I like Visconti very much. He is a remarkable person, learned and famous, and very powerful in the time of the Pope; he also belongs to society.

"You know," he said to my aunt, talking about me, "we have the idea of acquiring her for Rome."

Then he turned to me.

"Have you seen some of your friends?"

"You know, Baron, we have not many friends in Rome."

"I understand, and that is why you should see them."

"Yes, I saw some." I stopped there.

Two days ago, the Countess Antonelli dined at the Villa Mattei, a dinner for Monseigneurs and priests. There was a Monseigneur who talked about me, who knows my name, knows me by sight; and he said that I was a good, pious person; that I have clerical ideas; that I was visiting the Holy Father and often saw Visconti.

"You understand," Antonelli told me, "my mother was very happy to hear that."

"I would like to know who this Monseigneur is who is so busy about me," I said laughing, and that was all.

Now, listen, I am only starting to realize what happened yesterday. My aunt, who does not know and guesses nothing, talked, laughing, about Petruccio as one of my victims. And at each moment, yesterday's scene throws itself into my heart, in a way, and after each time it takes me two minutes to recover; somehow that's good rather than bad, and yet I would like to know if I am really letting go because I love this man, or if each imbecile can obtain as much from me by talking about love. It is this last one which probably is true.

We went to the music and stopped to talk with Simonetti when Antonelli arrived with St. Joseph. This kind young man went to the Hotel de Ville on his return from Naples, but we were already gone. I am simple and polite with Antonelli. He obstinately searched my eyes, but I avoided his.

"You know we are leaving tomorrow," I said to him, as he was bowing to leave.

"So I'll come this evening?" he asked.

I nodded and told St. Joseph that I'll not forget to give his regards to Nice.

Then it started to rain, and we went to the Corso.

"I am going to invite the monk for dinner," said my aunt. "Let's stop the carriage."

"I'll not do it, Madame, do it yourself."

At that moment we were passing in front of the Club, and the monk was under the portico, but I didn't move. At the second round, in spite of my aunt, it was the same thing. And the third time around, when she wanted to call him, he was not there anymore. Fortunately I bought the music of *Traviata*, and I sang it.

I am not proud; I'm vain. My firmness is insensitiveness. I am weak and cowardly, insane and cruel. I think I am strong when everyone else weeps for a death or an illness; I am only heartless.

All the pages you have read have been given to Antonelli to read; but to prevent his reading everything, I covered what I did not let him see. . . . The part where I said that *I did not* tell anyone, not even my aunt. I made him read twice, underlining the words, *because I do not want any scandal.*

"This is why, Sir, I am talking to you and laughing," I said.

"This is why?" he said confused.

"Yes, read it again, and you'll understand."

"I understand very well."

"Good!"

We were all seated around the same table; my aunt, Potechine, Antonelli, and I. I was laughing, letting him read the lines, but I told him in a low voice, "You must understand, I hope, Sir, why I am polite with you. I want no scandal. My aunt knows nothing, and I cannot act differently. Do you understand?"

"Ah! I understand very well."

"That is all I need."

He was very embarrassed when reading.

"Too bad! Anyway I am leaving."

"At least I hope," he said smiling, "that you did not mention my name, because you talk so badly of me that if this book were lost . . ."

"Hey! Sir, the shame would not be on you, I assure you."

"But how can one write such things! You are wrong to think all this."

"That is my business," I assured him.

I could never have told him all this, and now I think he understood.

I complained about the heat.

"It is cooler in the other room," he said. "Come."

"No, I am better here. Thank you."

At 2:00 he said good night to us. I held out to him a cold, soft hand. He pressed it, but I did not answer to this pressure.

"*Buona sera,*" he said with a wry smile. "*Stia bene.*"

I only bowed, lightly.

"Why did you punish this poor monk so much?" my aunt asked.

"Punish?"

"Yes, you stayed in the salon, talking very little."

"I am bored; he bored me. Madame, I have enough of it! I want to go into society!"

"He, too!"

"He is very lucky. He just has to want it!"

"You'll go together."

"Oh! Aunt, it is bad to joke when you see what pain this gives me," I said seriously and ready to cry.

"Nobody is laughing, I'm not joking," she said, troubled.

I went to my room, and instead of writing I cried. It felt good. Since yesterday I felt oppressed, like the weather before the storm; and, as rain refreshes the air, my tears refreshed my soul, and I smiled when crying.

But I have forgiven and forgotten. Only one thing is tormenting me now—he does not love me!

Friday, May 19, 1876. Before, I cried on hearing Mignon's music; now I cry on hearing Traviata's.

Mignon seems to me bourgeois. I explain with naïveté; it is because there is no death.

What a pity to awake! I would like to be always asleep, as we are happiest asleep. I awoke at 1:00, and I think it is too early! My aunt and Potechine went to the Vatican, and as I can't be with Pietro, I prefer to be alone.

He'll come about 5:00. I *hope* that my aunt will still be out. I should like to be alone with him as if by chance, for I must no longer appear to seek him. . . . My aunt invited him, she who knows nothing. He knows that.

When Count Antonelli was announced, I was still alone, as my aunt had the inspiration to go see the Pantheon as well as Santa Maria Maggiore. My heart was beating so violently that I was afraid it might be heard, as they say in novels.

He sat down near me and started by taking my hand, which I withdrew immediately. Then he said he loves me, and I pushed him away, politely, smiling.

"My aunt will be back soon; have patience," I said.

"I have so much to say to you!"

"Really?"

"But your aunt will be back soon."

"Then be quick about it."

"They are serious matters."

"Let's see."

"To begin, you did wrong to write all those things of me."

"Sir, I warn you that I am very nervous; so you will do well to speak simply or say nothing."

"I love you. Listen. I have spoken to my mother, and my mother has spoken to my father."

"Well, what next?"

"I did right, did I not?"

"That is not my concern; what you have done is for your benefit."

"You do love me?"

"No."

"And I love you like a mad man!"

"Too bad for you," I said, smiling and letting him take my hand.

"No, listen," he said like Torlonia, "let us talk seriously; you are never serious, but we cannot go on like that! I love you," then putting his arms around my waist and putting, like a child, his head on my shoulder:

"Be my wife," he said.

"At last!" I said to myself, but did not answer him.

"Well," he said, encouraged. "You know we must get somebody to take it up."

"How?"

"Yes, I can't do it myself; somebody with poise must take the matter in hand—someone respectable, serious, who will talk to my father and, in a word, will arrange everything. Who?"

Laughing, I said, "Visconti."

"Yes," he said, very seriously, "I thought about Visconti. He is the man. He is so old now he is just good enough to play Mercury. Only I am not rich, not rich at all. Ah! I would like to be a hunchback and ugly and have millions."

"You would have won nothing with me."

"Oh! Oh! Oh!"

"I think this is another insult," I said, getting up.

"But no, I am not talking about you; you are an exception."

"So do not speak to me of money or anything else."

"But what did I say?"

"Nothing."

"Forgive me! God! how difficult you are to please! I never can understand what you want. Consent to be my wife!"

He wanted to kiss my hand, and I offered the cross of my rosary, which he kissed, then raised his head.

"How religious you are!" he said, looking at me.

"And you, you believe in nothing?"

"I love you. Do you love me?"

"I cannot tell," I said, turning around.

"But heaven's sake do make it clear to me."

After a moment of hesitation, my head fell on his shoulder. What a masterpiece!

"You, you consent?"

Softly, I said, getting up from my seat, "You know there are my grandfather and my father, and they are very opposed to a Catholic marriage."

"Ah, there's that again."

"Yes, there is also that."

He took me by the arm and made me sit next to him opposite the mirror, bringing my face very close to his. We were very beautiful like that.

"We will ask Visconti to take charge of everything. He is the man we need, as we are young to be married. Do you think we'll be happy?"

"First you will want my consent."

"No doubt; but *supposing* you consent, shall we be happy?"

"If I consent, I'll say, on my oath, that there will not be a happier man on the face of the earth than you."

"Then we will get married."

I smiled.

"Ah!" he cried, leaping about the room. "It will be fun when we have children!"

"Sir, you are going mad!"

"Yes, with love!"

At that moment, hearing voices on the stairs, I quietly sat and waited for my aunt and Potechine, who entered immediately.

A great weight was taken from my heart. I grew lively, and Antonelli was enchanted. He remembered that I had wanted a green umbrella like a monk's, and went to buy one for me.

During dinner my foot did not leave his own. I was happy and calm, but I had a great many things to hear and say, even yet.

With the exception of our apartment, the second floor of the hotel is empty. We took a candle and went through those immense rooms, in which the perfume of the ancient grandeur of the Italian palaces still seems to linger. But my aunt was with us, and I didn't know what to do.

For more than an hour, we stayed in a large, yellow salon and Pietro mimicked the Cardinal, his father, his brothers, Walitsky, Bruschetti, etc.

At around 11:00, we returned to the apartment, and Potechine arrived. We had supper, and my aunt had fun asking Antonelli to write some nonsense in Russian.

"Copy that," I said, taking a book and writing on the first page.

"What?"

"Read."

I indicated the following eight words: "Leave at midnight. I'll speak to you downstairs."

"Did you understand?" I asked, rubbing it out.

"Yes."

Then I felt easier, and yet strangely agitated. Antonelli kept looking at the clock every minute, and I was afraid that the reason could be guessed! Only bad consciences have these terrors.

At midnight he rose, let Potechine leave first, and bade me goodnight, pressing my hand tightly.

"Goodnight, Sir," I said.

Our eyes met, and I cannot describe what a simultaneous flash it was.

"Well, my aunt," I said, "tomorrow we are leaving very early, so go to your room, and I'll lock you in; in that way you'll not prevent my writing, and I shall go to bed quickly."

"You promise?"

"Certainly."

I locked my aunt's room, and after a glance in the mirror I went downstairs. Pietro slipped through the half-open door like a shadow, and I found myself in his arms . . . not realizing it for a few seconds. I opened my mouth to speak, but he guessed my thought.

"Isn't this talking?" he asked tenderly.

"Yes," I said, like him.

"When in love we say everything by keeping silent; I love you."

It amused me to act a scene in a novel and involuntarily I thought of Dumas.

"We leave tomorrow . . ."

"And we have to talk seriously, and I was forgetting that we forget everything when we are in such a state as this."

"Come," I said, shutting the door so as to leave only a faint glimmering of light. I sat down on the last step of the little staircase at the bottom of the passage.

He knelt down.

Every instant I thought I heard somebody coming. I remained motionless, trembling at every drop of rain that beat against the panes.

"But it is nothing," said my impatient lover.

"You speak very much at your ease, Sir. If anyone were to come, you would feel flattered, and I should be lost."

With my head thrown back, I looked at him through my eyelashes!

"With me?" Misunderstanding the meaning of my words, he said, "I love you too much; you are quite safe."

I gave him my hand, hearing those noble words.

"Have I not always been well-behaved and respectful?"

"Oh!," I shouted, backing up, reliving the awful memory like an atrocious pain. "No, no! Not always!"

"But . . ."

"Do not talk about that, I beg you . . . it is awful!" I was suffocating.

"Don't speak of that, I beg you," he urged. "I have begged your pardon so often! Be good! Forgive me!"

"I have forgiven you," I said gently. "And I have forgotten," I added, looking at his chest as a protection against the insult of the past.

We were both as if in a dream. "Is it," I wondered, "one of these moments when one is happy, when one loves? Is it serious?"

It seemed to me that he was going to laugh, serious and tender though he was.

I lowered my eyes under the extraordinary glitter of his own.

"Your mouth," he said, passionately. "Give me your mouth."

I did not dream of disobeying and stretched my neck to meet his lips. . . .

It is right to say that a kiss on the mouth . . . My head leaning back, my eyes closed, my arms hanging, I could not detach myself from him.

"Oh!" I said at last, "you said it is nothing . . ."

"I do not say it any more. But look! We have forgotten again to talk about our affairs; let's be serious. First, you are leaving tomorrow. What can we do? I beg you, do not leave!"

"That is impossible. My aunt . . ."

"She is so good. Oh, stay!" and he clasped me in his arms like a snake.

"She is good, but she will not consent. So *adieu,* forever."

"No, no! I'll come to Nice."

"When?"

"Around the end of the month, I think . . . if you let me escape, leaving debts, I'll leave tomorrow. . . ."

"No, I don't want that! In that case I'll not see you."

"No, you cannot prevent my going to Nice and doing foolish things."

"Yes I can, and I forbid you to do them."

"Then we must wait for my father to give me the money. Listen! I hope that he'll be reasonable. Besides, he has nothing against Nice. I believe the affair is started; my mother has spoken to him. But . . . if he were not going to give me the money! You know how dependent I am, and unhappy enough about it! You who reason like a book, you who talk about the soul and God, give me some advice!"

"Pray God," I told him, presenting my cross, ready to laugh if he would think the thing ridiculous, or ready to keep my serious look if he should take it seriously. His face was impassive; he put the cross on his forehead, lowering his forehead as he was praying while I was tenderly kissing his hair.

"I prayed," he said. "But let's continue. . . . We have agreed to put the matter into Visconti's hands . . ."

I said, "Well," but I thought, *provisionally.* "But it can't be arranged immediately."

"In two months?"

"You are laughing at me?" I inquired, as if it were the most impossible thing in the world.

"Then in six?"

"No!"

"In a year?"

"Yes, in a year. You will wait?"

"If it must be; with the condition of seeing you every day."

"Well, come to Nice, for in a month I'm going to Russia."

"I'll follow you."

"That's not possible. My mother won't allow it."

"No one can prevent my travelling."

"Don't talk nonsense."

"But I love you!"

I leaned toward him, not to lose one of his words.

"I always loved you," he said.

We were entering the commonplaces of lovemaking—banality, which becomes divine if the two really always love.

"Truly," he said, "it would be beautiful to spend our lives together . . . yes, pass life together, always, together, I at your feet adoring you. . . . We will be old together, old enough to take snuff, and we will love each other always. . . ."

Prudently, I was holding his hands, asking him to be good.

"Yes, my dearest," said he, finding no other word, and this commonplace word became a tender caress in his mouth. He was looking at me with his hands clasped—really!

Then we talked sense; then he was at my feet, crying, in a choked voice, that I could not love him as he loved me, that it was impossible.

"Ah! I am really unhappy; I suffer so much!"

"And of what, Sir?"

"Of love!"

It is the first time for me to hear all that (I do not count the others, whom I detested) but I know that it is an old song, known by heart. One must not believe that I let myself be kissed all the time; when it happened, I wrote it, as it was.

[Marginal note: *Only a fool of seventeen years could listen to that!*]

He said we ought to tell each other our secrets.

"Oh! yours, Sir, don't interest me."

"So tell me, how many times have you been in love?"

"Once," I said, "with a man whom I have seen ten or a dozen times in the street, who didn't even know of my existence. I was twelve years old then, and have never spoken to him."

"It is a fable!"

"It is the truth."

"But it is a romance, a fantasy; it is impossible, it is a shadow."

"Yes, I feel that I am not ashamed of having loved him, and that he has grown a kind of divinity for me. I don't compare him to anyone, for no one is worthy of that."

"Where is he?"

"I don't even know; he is married, far away."

"What folly!"

And my confounded Pietro looked rather incredulous and disdainful.

"But it is true, and you see I love you; and that's another matter."

"I give you all my heart, and you give me the half of yours."

Funny thing, he looked as if he was bored, saying these words.

"Don't ask too much, and be satisfied."

"But that isn't all. There is something else."

"That's all."

"Forgive me and permit me not to believe you this time."

(Do you see this depravity?)

"You must believe the truth."

"I can't."

"So much the worse for you," I cried, vexed. "You don't believe that I never allowed anyone to kiss my hand? That I have never touched a man!!!"

"Pardon me, but I don't believe it."

"Come and sit down by my side," said I. "Let us talk, and you tell me everything."

"Well, then you know my family is well-known. And you are strangers in Rome. Well, my mother wrote to Paris to several people."

"Very naturally, what did they say of me?"

"Nothing as yet, but let them say what they like. I shall always love you. Next," he said, "comes religion. Oh!" he said, "do turn Catholic!"

I stopped him short, *very severely*.

"Then you want me to change my religion?" cried Antonelli.

"No. If you did so I should despise you."

(I'd really have been angry only on account of the Cardinal.)

"How I love you! How beautiful you are! How happy we shall be!"

For an answer I took his head in my hands and kissed him on the forehead, on the eyes, on the hair . . . I did it more for his sake than for mine.

"Marie! Marie!" called my aunt from above.

"What's the matter?" I asked in a calm voice, passing my head through the trap door, so my voice seemed coming from my room.

"It is 2:00. You must go to sleep."

"I am sleeping."

"Are you undressed?"

"Yes, do let me write!"

"Go to bed."

I came down and the place was empty; the poor fellow had hidden himself under the staircase.

"Now," he said, taking his place again, "let us speak of the future. Where shall we live? Do you like Rome? Then we'll live in Rome, but not with my family! Quite alone."

"I should think so! In the first place, Mama wouldn't let me live with my husband's family."

"She is quite right. And then my family has such extraordinary principles! It would make us miserable. We will buy a little house in the new part of town."

"I should prefer a big house."

And I tried to hide an expressive grimace on his shoulder.

"Well, then, a big house."

And we began, at least he did, to plan future arrangements.

He was evidently very eager to change his condition, one way or another.

"We shall go into society. We shall live in grand style. Is that right?"

"Oh, yes. Tell me everything. If you were silly, you would think that it is a silly question for vile calculations, but you are intelligent enough to understand that when two people are going to pass their life together, they ought to do so as well as possible."

"I quite understand. You know all about my family, but there is the Cardinal."

"We must be on good terms with him."

"I should think so, indeed; I shall try to be so. And you know the greater part of his fortune is to go to the one who first has a son; so, we must have a son as soon as possible. Only, I am not rich. You understand?"

"What does it matter?" I said, a little hurt, but sufficiently mistress of myself not to make any gesture of contempt; it might be a snare.

Then, as if tired of these discussions, he encircled my waist with his arms, his eyes shining like two candles in the dark.

"*Occhi neri!*" [Italian: black eyes] I said, covering them with my hands, for his eyes frightened me. He prostrated himself before me, and he said again so much that I redoubled in watchfulness and made him sit down at my side. No, it is not a true love; if it were, there would be nothing petty or vulgarly dirty to say or do. Inside I felt angry.

"Be nice."

"Yes," he said joining his hands, "I am nice, respectful; I love you."

Did I love him really or was it an affair of the imagination? Who can tell exactly? And yet from the moment one doubts . . . doubt is no longer possible.

"Yes, I love you," I said, taking his two hands in mine and pressing them hard. I do not know—his words of love, the obscurity, and maybe something that I don't know . . . I leaned back on his shoulder, making a belt with his two arms, closing my eyes.

"I love you, I love you," I said, out of my mind, pressing his two hands on my heart.

He did not answer, but leaned his head on one step of the stairs next to mine. Maybe he did not understand the importance that I attached to my words; maybe he found them natural.

My heart had ceased beating. It was a delicious moment. My arms fell back along my sides. He was probably also as enraptured as I was because he remained motionless like me and speechless. I only felt his oppressed breathing on his shoulder, where I had my head.

But I grew afraid of myself and told him to go.

"Already? Stay a little more near me. How fine we feel like that . . . if we could spend all night like that."

I was too far from the real meaning of these words to protest, so I kept quiet when he went on his knees, his hands together:

"*Thou* wilt always love me? Tell me, always?"

His "thou" chilled me, it seemed humiliating . . .

"Oh, how can you ask such a question? Oh, my darling, yes, I wish it were impossible to get out of here. . . ."

At that moment I heard my aunt, who, still seeing a light in my room, grew very impatient.

"You hear?" I said, tearing myself from his arms, "Go, goodnight!" and grasping his head in my hands, I gave him a last kiss on his mouth and ran away without looking back. It is like the end of a scene that I read somewhere.

Fie! I lowered myself by making a mockery of everything. Shall I always be my own critic, or is it because I am not altogether in love?

"It is four o'clock," my aunt shouted.

"No, Aunt, in the first place it is only ten minutes to two, and then, do leave me alone!" I began undressing, deep in thought all the time.

"It is dreadful! You'll kill yourself sitting up so late!"

"Don't scold me, or I won't tell you anything."

"Oh, what a girl!"

"Oh, dear Aunt, you'll be sorry."

"What is the matter?"

"Well, I have not been writing; I was with Pietro."

"How dreadful! You have been with Antonelli? Well," she said in a voice that made me tremble, "I knew it when I was calling you a little while ago."

"How could you?"

"I dreamed that Mama had come and said to me: 'Don't leave Marie alone with Antonelli.'"

I felt a chill down my back as I realized that I had run a serious risk.

I expressed my fears, lest any one should write scandalous reports of me in Nice.

"There is nothing to be said," replied my aunt, "People may venture to talk slander, but they dare not write it."

Very badly reassured, I stayed seated on her bed, very anxious.

Saturday, May 20, 1876. At 9:30 we left, escorted by Potechine and Mariner, who serve us like princesses. Entering the station, my aunt found Antonelli smiling, in front of the clock, which showed that there was no more than five minutes left. The poor man was too sorry, looking at it. We exchanged a few words.

"You'll come to Nice?"

"I do not know."

I looked at him.

"No," he said, "do not pay any attention to me. I am good for nothing; I'll come."

"That is nice."

Potechine, Mariner, and Pietro were standing near the door.

"Well, Sir," said my aunt, "when will you come to Nice?"

"As soon as my father will give me the money," he answered.

It was silly to say that aloud. We were leaving, which simplified the ceremonies. He held my hand . . .

What an annoyance to go to Nice!

GLOSSARY

Glossary of names, places, and special words.

We have tried to ascertain the correct spelling of names and places where possible. Difficulties are caused in part by Marie's handwriting and the condition of some manuscript pages and in part by Marie's use of both Latin and Cyrillic alphabets for Slavic names. Further, most people in the diary have no historical interest and their names are therefore unverifiable. Many names are spelled in several ways by Marie; we have chosen one spelling and used that throughout. Numbers after each entry refer to the book in which the reference first appears.

Abramovitch, friend of Paul, 2.

Abrial, lawyer in Nice, 8.

Adam, Russian servant, cooking for family in Nice, 4.

Akhtirka, Ukrainian town where Uncle George Babanine spends part of his exile, Preface.

Albano, place outside Rome proposed for a party, 56.

Alcibiades, nickname for Hamilton, 9.

Alexander, Archimandrite, head of a Russian Orthodox monastery, 51.

Alexander, Uncle Babanine, still living at Tcherniakovka in the Ukraine, Preface.

Alexander, Uncle Alexandrovitch (Sacha), Count de Toulouse-Lautrec, 13.

Allard, hairstylist at the Grande Hotel in Nice, 16.

Altamura, banker in Rome and Naples who takes an interest in Marie's family, 54.

Amazone, riding habit, 4.

Ambroise, family servant, 35.

Ange, nickname for Mrs. Angel, 24.

Angel, Mrs., acquaintance in Nice, 24.

Angelle, acquaintance in Spa, 22.

Anitchkoff, Russian family, living in Nice, friendly with Marie's family, 4.

Anna, Uncle George Babanine's mistress, 5.

Antonelli, Countess (Camilla Folchi), Pietro's mother, 52.

Antonelli, Countess (born Garcia), Pietro's aunt, Marie carries a letter of introduction to her from Mrs. de Mouzay, 51.

Antonelli, Cardinal, Pietro's uncle, one of the key figures in Vatican politics, 51.

Antonelli, Domenico and Paolo, Pietro's brothers, 56.

Antonelli, Count Pietro, Marie's conquest and first interest in Rome, nicknames: Pazzerello, Cardinalino, Pietruccio, 54.

Antonoff, acquaintance in Nice, 48.

Archduchess of Gerolstein, operetta by Jacques Offenbach, 31.

Arçon, friend of Paul, 27.

Ashton, young boy, friend of the
Howards, 13.

Audiffer, nickname for Audiffret, 48.

Audiffret, Émile, young man in Nice
who interests Marie; nicknames:
Audiffer, Bibi, Girofla, Hector,
Impetuous Squire, Soroka (magpie),
the Surprising One, Terffidua, 3.

Auguste, family's coachman, replaces
Dominique, 16.

Azarevitch, Mr. and Mrs., friends of
Uncle Sacha, Count of Toulouse-
Lautrec, 18.

Babanine, see genealogy of Marie's
mother's family, Preface.

Stepan Babanine, Marie's maternal
grandfather (addressed as "Papa"
by entire family); lives with family
in Nice. Marie's father,
Constantine Bashkirtseff (q. v.),
visits briefly in Nice (November
1873), but never lives with them
there.

Uncle George, Uncle Alexander,
Uncle Émile, Uncle Stepa.

Aunt Nadianka or Nadya Babanine
Romanoff, Marie's aunt, whose
money makes their stay abroad
possible.

Marie's mother, Marie Babanine
Bashkirtseff, separated from
husband after birth of second
child, Paul. Never returned to
husband.

Domenica Pavlovna Yssayevitch
Babanine, wife of Uncle George.
Her daughter by her first husband
(Mashenka) marries George's
brother, Stepa. Both marriages
cannot be accepted by the Russian
church; George, no longer living
with Domenica but with his
mistress Anna, declares their
marriage annulled, leaving their
three children, Dina, Lola, and
Stepan, without a last name.
Stepan commits suicide after this.

Dina Babanine, Marie's cousin,
daughter of George and
Domenica.

Lola Babanine, Marie's cousin,
daughter of George and
Domenica.

Stepan Babanine, Marie's cousin, son
of George and Domenica, commits
suicide.

Bagatelle, bulldog Marie acquires in
Paris, 20.

Bagdanovna, Maria, acquaintance in
Nice, 6.

Barber, Mr. and sons, friends of the
Howards, 3.

Barisart (Borisart), gathering place
chosen for a picnic at Spa, 21.

Barnola, Ricardo, family friend
connected with theater in Nice, 2.

Bashkirtseff, Marie's father's family,
Preface. This family will appear more
prominently in the second volume of
the diary.

Paul Grigorievitch Bashkirtseff,
Marie's paternal grandfather.

Constantine Bashkirtseff, Marie's
father.

Marie Bashkirtseff, our diarist.

Paul Bashkirtseff, Marie's brother.

Paternal aunts: Mrs. Helen
Gorpintchenko, Princess Natalie
Eristoff, Mrs. Sophie Tutcheff, and
Mrs. De Meyneck.

Bas, nickname for Mrs. Basilovitch, 20.

Basilovitch, Mr. and Mrs.,
acquaintances in Spa, 21.

Bataclan, paraphernalia, stuff,
entourage, Offenbach's 1855 light
opera *Ba-Ta-Clan*, 4.

Bauche, *see* de Bauche.

Belledejour, new nickname for member
of Audiffret's circle, 50.

Belle Hélène, operetta by Offenbach, 2.

Belloca, singer performing in Nice, 28.

Fedaroff, Mrs., friend of the Filimonoffs, 16.

Ferrara, music shop in Nice, 24.

Ferry's, shoe store in Paris, 8.

Filimonoff, Mr. and Mrs., acquaintances in Nice. Marie's family attends their daughter Masur's wedding, 16.

Finot, Baron, Marie thinks Boreel is Baron Finot, which makes her interested in him initially, 1.

Fortuné, Saïd, also called Chocolat, black page boy, 8.

Foster, Florence, English acquaintance at Spa, Ostende, and Nice, 23.

Frederick, Fritz, another of Marie's dogs, 42.

Freppel, Monseigneur, bishop of Monseigneur de Falloux, 59.

Fronde, literally, *sling*, name given to an anti-court political party early in Louis XIV's reign, 39.

Furstenburg, Prince, man known by name, acquaintance of Lambertye, 18.

Gabrielli, Count, acquaintance in Nice, 2.

Galignani's *Messenger*, newspaper, 11.

Galitzine, Princess Nadine, nicknamed Bête, family friend, 5.

Galula, Dechiar, notary clerk for attorney Desforges, nicknamed Tiouloulou, 27.

Galvi, Countess and Miss (also given as (de) Galve), acquaintances in Nice, 3.

Gaspard, Miss, governess of Howard children, 4.

Gaut(h)ier, member of the Audiffret circle, nicknamed Pepino, 51.

Gavronzi, Bashkirtseff country estate in Ukraine, near Poltava, Preface.

George, Uncle Babanine, Preface.

Geroustère, restaurant in Spa, 21.

Gioja, Amelia (or Gioia), mistress of Duke of Hamilton, nicknamed Centifolia, 1.

Giro, shortened (from Giroflé) nickname for Olga Sapogenikoff, 50.

Girofla, heroine kidnapped by pirates in *Giroflé-Girofla*, Alexander Charles Lecocq's 1874 operetta about a pair of twin sisters, ironic nickname for Audiffret, 29.

Giroflé, the other heroine of the operetta, Marie's nickname for Olga Sapogenikoff, which would make Audiffret her "sister" based on their nicknames, 29.

God(d)ard, son of the Prefect, friend of the Skariatines, 35.

Godefroy, Angela, acquaintance at Spa, 21.

Grigorievna, Émile and Sophie, Marie's *cousins*, on her father's side, staying with the family in Nice. Sophie has been misidentified by most previous editors of the diary as Marie's *Aunt* Sophie, 2.

Grigorievitch (Bashkirtseff), Paul, Marie's paternal grandfather, Preface.

Grisyo or Gritz, nicknames for Miloradovitch, 6.

Gros, acquaintance in Nice, 8.

Gutman, friend of Paul in Vienna, 7.

Haigh, Miss Sophie, acquaintance of Mrs. de Mouzay in Rome, 51.

Hamilton, Lord Carlo (Charles), brother to the Duke, 3.

Hamilton, Duke of (Twelfth Duke), Marie's first and lasting crush, 1.

Hector, nickname for Audiffret, 43.

Hélène, Miss Howard, see entry under Howard.

Hippopotamus(es), objectionable people who trouble Marie, 20.

Hitchcock, Miss, English instructor who replaces Miss Elder, 11.